ELEMENTARY & INTERMEDIATE ALGEBRA

GRAPHS & MODELS

STUDENT'S SOLUTIONS MANUAL

JUDITH A. PENNA

Marvin L. Bittinger

Indiana University—Purdue University at Indianapolis

David J. Ellenbogen

Community College of Vermont

Barbara L. Johnson

Indiana University—Purdue University at Indianapolis

 **ADDISON-WESLEY**

An imprint of Addison Wesley Longman, Inc.

Reading, Massachusetts • Menlo Park, California • New York • Harlow, England
Don Mills, Ontario • Sydney • Mexico City • Madrid • Amsterdam

ISBN   0-201-63682-4

1 2 3 4 5 6 7 8 9 10 PHTH 04 03 02 01 00

Table of Contents

Chapter 1

Introduction to Algebraic Expressions

Exercise Set 1.1

1. Substitute 9 for a and multiply.

$5a = 5 \cdot 9 = 45$

2. 63

3. Substitute 2 for t and add.

$t + 6 = 2 + 6 = 8$

4. 4

5. $\dfrac{m - n}{7} = \dfrac{20 - 6}{7} = \dfrac{14}{7} = 2$

6. 7

7. $\dfrac{9m}{q} = \dfrac{9 \cdot 6}{18} = \dfrac{54}{18} = 3$

8. 3

9. $rt = (55 \text{ mph})(3 \text{ hr}) = 165 \text{ mi}$

10. 24 hr

11. $bh = (6.5 \text{ cm})(15.4 \text{ cm})$

$= (6.5)(15.4)(\text{cm})(\text{cm})$

$= 100.1 \text{ cm}^2$, or 100.1 square centimeters

12. $\dfrac{3}{11}$, or about 0.273

13. $A = \dfrac{1}{2}bh$

$= \dfrac{1}{2}(5 \text{ cm})(6 \text{ cm})$

$= \dfrac{1}{2}(5)(6)(\text{cm})(\text{cm})$

$= \dfrac{5}{2} \cdot 6 \text{ cm}^2$

$= 15 \text{ cm}^2$, or 15 square centimeters

14. 150 sec; 450 sec; 10 min

15. $7x$, or $x7$

16. $4a$

17. $b + 6$, or $6 + b$

18. $t + 8$, or $8 + t$

19. $c - 9$

20. $d - 4$

21. $q + 6$, or $6 + q$

22. $z + 11$, or $11 + z$

23. $x \div w$, or $\dfrac{x}{w}$

24. Let s and t represent the numbers. Then we have $s \div t$, or $\dfrac{s}{t}$, or $t \div s$, or $\dfrac{t}{s}$.

25. $n - m$

26. $q - p$

27. Let a and b represent the numbers. Then we have $a + b$, or $b + a$.

28. $d + f$, or $f + d$

29. $9 \cdot 2m$

30. $t - 2r$

31. Let y represent "some number." Then we have $\dfrac{1}{4}y$, or $\dfrac{y}{4}$.

32. Let m and n represent the numbers. Then we have $\dfrac{1}{3}mn$, or $\dfrac{mn}{3}$.

33. Let x represent "some number." Then we have 64% of x, or $0.64x$.

34. Let y represent "a number." Then we have 38% of y, or $0.38y$.

35. $\$50 - x$

36. $65t$ mi

37. $\underline{x + 17 = 32}$ Writing the equation

$15 + 17 \; ? \; 32$ Substituting 15 for x

$32 \mid 32$ $32 = 32$ is TRUE.

Since the left-hand and right-hand sides are the same, 15 is a solution.

38. No

39.

$$\underline{a - 28 = 75} \qquad \text{Writing the equation}$$

$$93 - 28 \ ? \ 75 \qquad \text{Substituting 93 for } a$$

$$65 \ \big| \ 75 \qquad 65 = 75 \text{ is FALSE.}$$

Since the left-hand and right-hand sides are not the same, 93 is not a solution.

40. Yes

41.

$$\underline{\dfrac{t}{7} = 9}$$

$$\dfrac{63}{7} \ ? \ 9$$

$$9 \ \big| \ 9 \qquad 9 = 9 \text{ is TRUE.}$$

Since the left-hand and right-hand sides are the same, 63 is a solution.

42. No

43.

$$\underline{\dfrac{108}{x} = 36}$$

$$\dfrac{108}{3} \ ? \ 36$$

$$36 \ \big| \ 36 \qquad 36 = 36 \text{ is TRUE.}$$

Since the left-hand and right-hand sides are the same, 3 is a solution.

44. No

45. Let x represent the number.

$$\underbrace{\text{What number}} \ \text{added to } 73 \text{ is } 201?$$

Translating: $x \qquad + \quad 73 = 201$

$$x + 73 = 201$$

46. Let w represent the number.

$$7w = 2303$$

47. Let y represent the number.

Rewording: 42 times $\underbrace{\text{what number}}$ is 2352?

Translating: $42 \quad \cdot \qquad y \qquad = 2352$

$$42y = 2352$$

48. Let x represent the number.

$$x + 345 = 987$$

49. Let s represent the number of squares your opponent gets.

Rewording: $\underbrace{\text{The number of squares your opponent gets}}$ $\underbrace{\text{added to}}$ 35 is 64.

Translating: $s \qquad\qquad + \qquad 35 = 64$

$$s + 35 = 64$$

50. Let y represent the number of hours the carpenter worked.

$$25y = 53,400$$

51. Let m represent the length of the average commute in the West, in minutes.

Rewording: $\underbrace{\text{The length of the average commute in the West}}$ is $\underbrace{24.5 \text{ minutes}}$ less $\underbrace{1.8 \text{ minutes}}$.

Translating: $m \qquad = \quad 24.5 \quad - \quad 1.8$

$$m = 24.5 - 1.8$$

52. Let f represent the amount of fuel used by trucks in the U.S. in 1995, in billions of gallons.

$$f = 2(31.4)$$

53. Look for a pattern in the data. Observe that the price of unleaded premium gas at each station is 20¢ more than the price of unleaded regular gas at that station. We reword and translate.

$\underbrace{\text{Price of premium unleaded gas}}$ is 20¢ $\substack{\text{more} \\ \text{than}}$ $\underbrace{\text{price of regular unleaded gas}}$.

$p \qquad = 20 \quad + \qquad r$

We have $p = 20 + r$. This equation could also be written as $p = r + 20$.

54. $c = 100h$

55. Look for a pattern in the data. Observe that the number of calories burned is 300 times the number of hours spent doing calisthenics. We reword and translate.

Number of   number of hours
calories   is 300 times   spent doing
burned   calisthenics.

$$\underbrace{\hspace{2cm}} \qquad \downarrow \downarrow \quad \downarrow \qquad \underbrace{\hspace{2cm}}$$

$$c \qquad = 300 \quad \cdot \qquad t$$

We have $c = 300t$.

56. $c = \$3.00 + p$, or $c = p + \$3.00$

57. ◈

58. ◈

59. ◈

60. ◈

61. Let n represent "a number." Then we have $3n - 5$.

62. Let a and b represent the numbers. Then we have $\frac{1}{3} \cdot \frac{1}{2}ab$, or $\frac{1}{6}ab$, or $\frac{ab}{6}$.

63. $l + w + l + w$, or $2l + 2w$

64. $s + s + s + s$, or $4s$

65. $a + 2 + 7$, or $a + 9$

66. $337.50

67. The shaded area is the area of a rectangle with dimensions 20 cm by 10 cm less the area of a triangle with base 20 cm $- 4$ cm $- 5$ cm, or 11 cm, and height 7.5 cm. We perform the computation

$$(20 \text{ cm})(10 \text{ cm}) - \frac{1}{2}(11 \text{ cm})(7.5)$$

$$= 200 \text{ cm}^2 - 41.25 \text{ cm}^2$$

$$= 158.75 \text{ cm}^2, \text{ or } 158.75 \text{ square centimeters}$$

68. 6

69. $y = 35$, $x = 2y = 2 \cdot 35 = 70$;

$$\frac{x - y}{7} = \frac{70 - 35}{7} = \frac{35}{7} = 5$$

70. 6

71. $\frac{y + x}{2} + \frac{3 \cdot y}{x} = \frac{4 + 2}{2} + \frac{3 \cdot 4}{2} = \frac{6}{2} + \frac{12}{2} = 3 + 6 = 9$

72. $w + 4$

73. The preceding odd number is 2 less than $d + 2$:

$$d + 2 - 2 = d$$

74. d

Exercise Set 1.2

1. We write two factorizations of 30. There are other factorizations as well.

$2 \cdot 15, 3 \cdot 10$

List all of the factors of 30:

1, 2, 3, 5, 6, 10, 15, 30

2. $2 \cdot 35, 5 \cdot 14$; 1, 2, 5, 7, 10, 14, 35, 70

3. We write two factorizations of 42. There are other factorizations as well.

$2 \cdot 21, 6 \cdot 7$

List all of the factors of 42:

1, 2, 3, 6, 7, 14, 21, 42

4. $2 \cdot 30, 5 \cdot 12$; 1, 2, 3, 4, 5, 6, 10, 12, 15, 20, 30, 60

5. $22 = 2 \cdot 11$

6. $3 \cdot 5$

7. We begin factoring 30 in any way that we can and continue factoring until each factor is prime.

$30 = 2 \cdot 15 = 2 \cdot 3 \cdot 5$

8. $2 \cdot 2 \cdot 3 \cdot 7$

9. We begin by factoring 27 in any way that we can and continue factoring until each factor is prime.

$27 = 3 \cdot 9 = 3 \cdot 3 \cdot 3$

10. $2 \cdot 7 \cdot 7$

11. We begin by factoring 18 in any way that we can and continue factoring until each factor is prime.

$18 = 2 \cdot 9 = 2 \cdot 3 \cdot 3$

12. $2 \cdot 2 \cdot 2 \cdot 5$

13. 43 has exactly two different factors, 43 and 1. Thus, 43 is prime.

14. $2 \cdot 2 \cdot 2 \cdot 3 \cdot 5$

15. $210 = 2 \cdot 105 = 2 \cdot 3 \cdot 35 = 2 \cdot 3 \cdot 5 \cdot 7$

16. Prime

17. $\dfrac{10}{14} = \dfrac{2 \cdot 5}{2 \cdot 7}$ Factoring numerator and denominator

$\phantom{\dfrac{10}{14}} = \dfrac{2}{2} \cdot \dfrac{5}{7}$ Rewriting as a product of two fractions

$\phantom{\dfrac{10}{14}} = 1 \cdot \dfrac{5}{7} \quad \dfrac{2}{2} = 1$

$\phantom{\dfrac{10}{14}} = \dfrac{5}{7}$ Using the identity property of 1

18. $\dfrac{2}{7}$

19. $\dfrac{6}{48} = \dfrac{1 \cdot 6}{8 \cdot 6}$ Factoring and using the identity property of 1 to write 6 as $1 \cdot 6$

$\phantom{\dfrac{6}{48}} = \dfrac{1}{8} \cdot \dfrac{6}{6}$

$\phantom{\dfrac{6}{48}} = \dfrac{1}{8} \cdot 1 = \dfrac{1}{8}$

20. $\dfrac{6}{35}$

21. $\dfrac{56}{7} = \dfrac{8 \cdot 7}{1 \cdot 7} = \dfrac{8}{1} \cdot \dfrac{7}{7} = \dfrac{8}{1} \cdot 1 = 8$

22. 12

23. $\dfrac{19}{76} = \dfrac{1 \cdot 19}{4 \cdot 19}$ Factoring and using the identity property of 1 to write 19 as $1 \cdot 19$

$\phantom{\dfrac{19}{76}} = \dfrac{1 \cdot \cancel{19}}{4 \cdot \cancel{19}}$ Removing a factor equal to 1: $\dfrac{19}{19} = 1$

$\phantom{\dfrac{19}{76}} = \dfrac{1}{4}$

24. $\dfrac{1}{3}$

25. $\dfrac{100}{20} = \dfrac{5 \cdot 20}{1 \cdot 20}$ Factoring and using the identity property of 1 to write 20 as $1 \cdot 20$

$\phantom{\dfrac{100}{20}} = \dfrac{5 \cdot \cancel{20}}{1 \cdot \cancel{20}}$ Removing a factor equal to 1: $\dfrac{20}{20} = 1$

$\phantom{\dfrac{100}{20}} = \dfrac{5}{1}$

$\phantom{\dfrac{100}{20}} = 5$ Simplifying

26. $\dfrac{15}{16}$

27. $\dfrac{210}{98} = \dfrac{2 \cdot 7 \cdot 15}{2 \cdot 7 \cdot 7}$ Factoring

$\phantom{\dfrac{210}{98}} = \dfrac{\cancel{2} \cdot \cancel{7} \cdot 15}{\cancel{2} \cdot \cancel{7} \cdot 7}$ Removing a factor equal to 1: $\dfrac{2 \cdot 7}{2 \cdot 7} = 1$

$\phantom{\dfrac{210}{98}} = \dfrac{15}{7}$

28. $\dfrac{2}{5}$

29. $\dfrac{3}{5} \cdot \dfrac{1}{2} = \dfrac{3 \cdot 1}{5 \cdot 2}$ Multiplying numerators and denominators

$\phantom{\dfrac{3}{5} \cdot \dfrac{1}{2}} = \dfrac{3}{10}$

30. $\dfrac{44}{25}$

31. $\dfrac{17}{2} \cdot \dfrac{3}{4} = \dfrac{17 \cdot 3}{2 \cdot 4} = \dfrac{51}{8}$

32. 1

33. $\dfrac{1}{8} + \dfrac{3}{8} = \dfrac{1 + 3}{8}$ Adding numerators; keeping the common denominator

$\phantom{\dfrac{1}{8} + \dfrac{3}{8}} = \dfrac{4}{8}$

$\phantom{\dfrac{1}{8} + \dfrac{3}{8}} = \dfrac{1 \cdot \cancel{4}}{2 \cdot \cancel{4}} = \dfrac{1}{2}$ Simplifying

34. $\dfrac{5}{8}$

35. $\dfrac{4}{9} + \dfrac{13}{18} = \dfrac{4}{9} \cdot \dfrac{2}{2} + \dfrac{13}{18}$ Using 18 as the common denominator

$\phantom{\dfrac{4}{9} + \dfrac{13}{18}} = \dfrac{8}{18} + \dfrac{13}{18}$

$\phantom{\dfrac{4}{9} + \dfrac{13}{18}} = \dfrac{21}{18}$

$\phantom{\dfrac{4}{9} + \dfrac{13}{18}} = \dfrac{7 \cdot \cancel{3}}{6 \cdot \cancel{3}} = \dfrac{7}{6}$ Simplifying

36. $\dfrac{4}{3}$

37. $\dfrac{3}{a} \cdot \dfrac{b}{7} = \dfrac{3b}{7a}$ Multiplying numerators and denominators

38. $\dfrac{xy}{5z}$

39. $\dfrac{4}{a} + \dfrac{3}{a} = \dfrac{7}{a}$ Adding numerators; keeping the common denominator

40. $\dfrac{2}{a}$

41. $\dfrac{3}{10} + \dfrac{8}{15} = \dfrac{3}{10} \cdot \dfrac{3}{3} + \dfrac{8}{15} \cdot \dfrac{2}{2}$ Using 30 as the common denominator

$= \dfrac{9}{30} + \dfrac{16}{30}$

$= \dfrac{25}{30}$

$= \dfrac{5 \cdot \cancel{5}}{6 \cdot \cancel{5}} = \dfrac{5}{6}$ Simplifying

42. $\dfrac{41}{24}$

43. $\dfrac{9}{7} - \dfrac{2}{7} = \dfrac{7}{7} = 1$

44. 2

45. $\dfrac{13}{18} - \dfrac{4}{9} = \dfrac{13}{18} - \dfrac{4}{9} \cdot \dfrac{2}{2}$ Using 18 as the common denominator

$= \dfrac{13}{18} - \dfrac{8}{18}$

$= \dfrac{5}{18}$

46. $\dfrac{31}{45}$

47. $\dfrac{7}{6} \div \dfrac{3}{5} = \dfrac{7}{6} \cdot \dfrac{5}{3}$ Multiplying by the reciprocal of the divisor

$= \dfrac{35}{18}$

48. $\dfrac{28}{15}$

49. $\dfrac{8}{9} \div \dfrac{4}{15} = \dfrac{8}{9} \cdot \dfrac{15}{4} = \dfrac{2 \cdot \cancel{4} \cdot \cancel{3} \cdot 5}{\cancel{3} \cdot 3 \cdot \cancel{4}} = \dfrac{10}{3}$

50. $\dfrac{1}{4}$

51. $24 \div \dfrac{2}{5} = \dfrac{24}{1} \cdot \dfrac{5}{2} = \dfrac{\cancel{2} \cdot 12 \cdot 5}{1 \cdot \cancel{2}} = 60$

52. 468

53. $\dfrac{3x}{4} \div 6 = \dfrac{3x}{4} \cdot \dfrac{1}{6} = \dfrac{\cancel{3} \cdot x}{4 \cdot 2 \cdot \cancel{3}} = \dfrac{x}{8}$

54. $\dfrac{1}{18a}$

55. $\dfrac{5}{3} \div \dfrac{a}{b} = \dfrac{5}{3} \cdot \dfrac{b}{a} = \dfrac{5b}{3a}$

56. $\dfrac{xy}{28}$

57. $\dfrac{x}{6} - \dfrac{1}{3} = \dfrac{x}{6} - \dfrac{1}{3} \cdot \dfrac{2}{2}$ Using 6 as the common denominator

$= \dfrac{x}{6} - \dfrac{2}{6}$

$= \dfrac{x-2}{6}$

58. $\dfrac{9+5x}{10}$

59. $t - 9$

60. $\dfrac{1}{2}m$, or $\dfrac{m}{2}$

61. ◈

62. ◈

63. ◈

64. ◈

65. $\dfrac{256}{192} = \dfrac{4 \cdot \cancel{64}}{3 \cdot \cancel{64}} = \dfrac{4}{3}$

66. $\dfrac{p}{t}$

67. $\dfrac{9 \cdot 4 \cdot 16}{8 \cdot 15 \cdot 12} = \dfrac{\cancel{3} \cdot 3 \cdot \cancel{2} \cdot 2 \cdot \cancel{4} \cdot \cancel{4}}{\cancel{2} \cdot \cancel{4} \cdot \cancel{3} \cdot 5 \cdot \cancel{3} \cdot \cancel{4}} = \dfrac{2}{5}$

68. 1

69. $\dfrac{15 \cdot 4xy \cdot 9}{6 \cdot 25x \cdot 15y} = \dfrac{\cancel{15} \cdot \cancel{2} \cdot 2 \cdot \cancel{4} \cdot \cancel{y} \cdot \cancel{3} \cdot 3}{\cancel{2} \cdot \cancel{3} \cdot 25 \cdot \cancel{4} \cdot \cancel{15} \cdot \cancel{y}} = \dfrac{6}{25}$

70. $\dfrac{5}{2}$

71. We need to find the smallest number that has both 6 and 8 as factors. Starting with 6 we list some numbers with a factor of 6, and starting with 8 we also list some numbers with a factor of 8. Then we find the first number that is on both lists.

6, 12, 18, 24, 30, 36, ...

8, 16, 24, 32, 40, 48, ...

Since 24 is the smallest number that is on both lists, the carton should be 24 in. long.

72.

Product	56	63	36	72	140	96
Factor	7	7	2	36	14	8
Factor	8	9	18	2	10	12
Sum	15	16	20	38	24	20

Product	48	168	110	90	432	63
Factor	6	21	11	9	24	3
Factor	8	8	10	10	18	21
Sum	14	29	21	19	42	24

73. $A = lw = \left(\frac{4}{5} \text{ m}\right)\left(\frac{7}{9} \text{ m}\right)$

$\qquad = \left(\frac{4}{5}\right)\left(\frac{7}{9}\right)(\text{m})(\text{m})$

$\qquad = \frac{28}{45} \text{ m}^2, \text{ or } \frac{28}{45} \text{ square meters}$

74. $\frac{25}{28} \text{ m}^2$

75. $P = 4s = 4\left(\frac{5}{9}\text{m}\right) = \frac{20}{9} \text{ m}$

76. $\frac{142}{45} \text{ m}$

Exercise Set 1.3

1. The real number -3 corresponds to 3 under par, and the real number 7 corresponds to 7 over par.

2. 18, -2

3. The real number -508 corresponds to a drop of 508 points, and the real number 186.84 corresponds to an increase of 186.84 points.

4. 1200, -560

5. The real number -1286 corresponds to 1286 ft below sea level. The real number 29,029 corresponds to 29,029 ft above sea level.

6. Jets: -34, Strikers: 34

7. The real number 750 corresponds to a $750 deposit, and the real number -125 corresponds to a $125 withdrawal.

8. 27, -9.7

9. The real numbers $20, -150$, and 300 correspond to the interception of the missile, the loss of the starship, and the capture of the base, respectively.

10. -10, 235

11. Since $\frac{10}{3} = 3\frac{1}{3}$, its graph is $\frac{1}{3}$ of a unit to the right of 3.

12.

13. The graph of -4.3 is $\frac{3}{10}$ of a unit to the left of -4.

14.

15.

16.

17. $\frac{7}{8}$ means $7 \div 8$, so we divide.

$$
\begin{array}{r}
0.8\,7\,5 \\
8\,\overline{)\,7.0\,0\,0} \\
\underline{6\,4} \\
6\,0 \\
\underline{5\,6} \\
4\,0 \\
\underline{4\,0} \\
0
\end{array}
$$

We have $\frac{7}{8} = 0.875$.

18. -0.125

19. We first find decimal notation for $\frac{3}{4}$. Since $\frac{3}{4}$ means $3 \div 4$, we divide.

$$
\begin{array}{r}
0.7\,5 \\
4\,\overline{)\,3.0\,0} \\
\underline{2\,8} \\
2\,0 \\
\underline{2\,0} \\
0
\end{array}
$$

Thus, $\frac{3}{4} = 0.75$, so $-\frac{3}{4} = -0.75$.

20. $0.8\overline{3}$

21. $\frac{7}{6}$ means $7 \div 6$, so we divide.

$$
\begin{array}{r}
1.1\,6\,6 \\
6\,\overline{)\,7.0\,0\,0} \\
\underline{6} \\
1\,0 \\
\underline{6} \\
4\,0 \\
\underline{3\,6} \\
4\,0 \\
\underline{3\,6} \\
4
\end{array}
$$

We have $\frac{7}{6} = 1.1\overline{6}$.

22. $0.41\overline{6}$

23. $\frac{2}{3}$ means $2 \div 3$, so we divide.

$$\begin{array}{r} 0.6\;6\;6\;... \\ 3\,\overline{\smash{\big)}\,2.0\;0\;0} \\ \underline{1\;8} \\ 2\;0 \\ \underline{1\;8} \\ 2\;0 \\ \underline{1\;8} \\ 2 \end{array}$$

We have $\frac{2}{3} = 0.\overline{6}$.

24. 0.25

25. We first find decimal notation for $\frac{1}{2}$. Since $\frac{1}{2}$ means $1 \div 2$, we divide.

$$\begin{array}{r} 0.5 \\ 2\,\overline{\smash{\big)}\,1.0} \\ \underline{1\;0} \\ 0 \end{array}$$

Thus, $\frac{1}{2} = 0.5$, so $-\frac{1}{2} = -0.5$.

26. -0.375

27. $\frac{1}{10}$ means $1 \div 10$, so we divide.

$$\begin{array}{r} 0.1 \\ 10\,\overline{\smash{\big)}\,1.0} \\ \underline{1\;0} \\ 0 \end{array}$$

We have $\frac{1}{10} = 0.1$.

28. -0.35

29. Since 5 is to the right of 0, we have $5 > 0$.

30. $9 > 0$

31. Since -9 is to the left of 5, we have $-9 < 5$.

32. $8 > -8$

33. Since -6 is to the left of 6, we have $-6 < 6$.

34. $0 > -7$

35. Since -5 is to the right of -11, we have $-5 > -11$.

36. $-4 < -3$

37. Since -12.5 is to the left of -9.4, we have $-12.5 < -9.4$.

38. $-10.3 > -14.5$

39. We convert to decimal notation.
$\frac{5}{12} = 0.41\overline{6}$ and $\frac{11}{25} = 0.44$. Thus, $\frac{5}{12} < \frac{11}{25}$.

40. $-\frac{14}{17} \approx -0.82353$ and $-\frac{27}{35} \approx -0.77143$.
Thus, $-\frac{14}{17} < -\frac{27}{35}$.

41. $-2 > a$ has the same meaning as $a < -2$.

42. $9 < a$

43. $y \geq -10$ has the same meaning as $-10 \leq y$.

44. $t \leq 12$

45. $-3 \geq -11$ is true, since $-3 > -11$ is true.

46. False

47. $0 \geq 8$ is false, since neither $0 > 8$ nor $0 = 8$ is true.

48. True

49. $-8 \leq -8$ is true because $-8 = -8$ is true.

50. True

51. $|-4| = 4$ since -4 is 4 units from 0.

52. 456

53. $|3.1| = 3.1$ since 3.1 is 3.1 units from 0.

54. 5.6

55. $|0| = 0$ since 0 is 0 units from itself.

56. $\frac{2}{5}$

57. $|x| = |-8| = 8$

58. 5

59. $-23, -4.7, 0, \frac{5}{9}, 8.31, 62$

60. 62

61. $-23, 0, 62$

62. $\pi, \sqrt{17}$

63. All are real numbers.

64. $0, 62$

65. $\dfrac{21}{5} \cdot \dfrac{1}{7} = \dfrac{21 \cdot 1}{5 \cdot 7}$ Multiplying numerators and denominators

$= \dfrac{3 \cdot 7 \cdot 1}{5 \cdot 7}$ Factoring the numerator

$= \dfrac{3}{5}$ Removing a factor of 1

66. 42

67. $\dfrac{1}{5} + \dfrac{1}{6} = \dfrac{1}{5} \cdot \dfrac{6}{6} + \dfrac{1}{6} \cdot \dfrac{5}{5}$

$= \dfrac{6}{30} + \dfrac{5}{30}$

$= \dfrac{11}{30}$

68. $\dfrac{1}{9}$

69.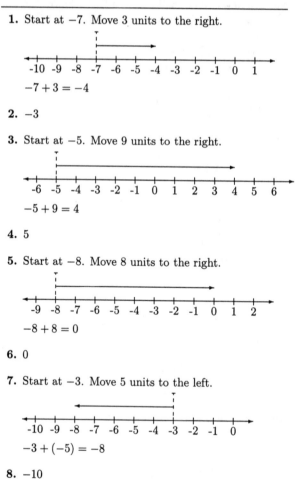

70. ◈

71. ◈

72. ◈

73. List the numbers as they occur on the number line, from left to right: $-17, -12, 5, 13$

74. $-23, -17, 0, 4$

75. Converting to decimal notation, we can write
$$\dfrac{4}{5}, \dfrac{4}{3}, \dfrac{4}{8}, \dfrac{4}{6}, \dfrac{4}{9}, \dfrac{4}{2}, -\dfrac{4}{3} \text{ as}$$
$0.8, 1.3\overline{3}, 0.5, 0.6\overline{6}, 0.4\overline{4}, 2, -1.3\overline{3}$, respectively. List the numbers (in fractional form) as they occur on the number line, from left to right:
$$-\dfrac{4}{3}, \dfrac{4}{9}, \dfrac{4}{8}, \dfrac{4}{6}, \dfrac{4}{5}, \dfrac{4}{3}, \dfrac{4}{2}$$

76. $-\dfrac{5}{6}, -\dfrac{3}{4}, -\dfrac{2}{3}, \dfrac{1}{6}, \dfrac{3}{8}, \dfrac{1}{2}$

77. $|-5| = 5$ and $|-2| = 2$, so $|-5| > |-2|$.

78. $|4| < |-7|$

79. $|-8| = 8$ and $|8| = 8$, so $|-8| = |8|$.

80. $|23| = |-23|$

81. $|-3| = 3$ and $|5| = 5$, so $|-3| < |5|$.

82. $|-19| < |-27|$

83. $|x| = 7$

x represents a number whose distance from 0 is 7. Thus, $x = 7$ or $x = -7$.

84. $-2, -1, 0, 1, 2$

85. $2 < |x| < 5$

x represents an integer whose distance from 0 is greater than 2 and also less than 5. Thus, $x = -4, -3, 3, 4$

86. $\dfrac{1}{9}$

87. $0.9\overline{9} = 3(0.3\overline{3}) = 3 \cdot \dfrac{1}{3} = \dfrac{3}{3}$

88. $\dfrac{50}{9}$

Exercise Set 1.4

1. Start at -7. Move 3 units to the right.

```
        ↱
      ┌────────→
←─┼──┼──┼──┼──┼──┼──┼──┼──┼──┼──┼──→
 -10 -9 -8 -7 -6 -5 -4 -3 -2 -1  0  1
```
$-7 + 3 = -4$

2. -3

3. Start at -5. Move 9 units to the right.

```
     ↱
   ┌──────────────────────→
←─┼──┼──┼──┼──┼──┼──┼──┼──┼──┼──┼──┼──→
  -6 -5 -4 -3 -2 -1  0  1  2  3  4  5  6
```
$-5 + 9 = 4$

4. 5

5. Start at -8. Move 8 units to the right.

```
     ↱
   ┌────────────────────→
←─┼──┼──┼──┼──┼──┼──┼──┼──┼──┼──┼──→
  -9 -8 -7 -6 -5 -4 -3 -2 -1  0  1  2
```
$-8 + 8 = 0$

6. 0

7. Start at -3. Move 5 units to the left.

```
                    ↱
      ←──────────┐
←─┼──┼──┼──┼──┼──┼──┼──┼──┼──┼──→
 -10 -9 -8 -7 -6 -5 -4 -3 -2 -1  0
```
$-3 + (-5) = -8$

8. -10

9. $-15 + 0$ One number is 0. The answer is the other number. $-15 + 0 = -15$

10. -6

11. $0 + (-8)$ One number is 0. The answer is the other number. $0 + (-8) = -8$

12. -2

13. $-15 + 15$ The numbers have the same absolute value. The sum is 0. $-15 + 15 = 0$

14. 0

15. $-24 + (-17)$ Two negatives. Add the absolute values, getting 41. Make the answer negative. $-24 + (-17) = -41$

16. -42

17. $-7 + 8$ The absolute values are 7 and 8. The difference is $8 - 7$, or 1. The positive number has the larger absolute value, so the answer is positive. $-7 + 8 = 1$

18. 3

19. $10 + (-12)$ The absolute values are 10 and 12. The difference is $12 - 10$, or 2. The negative number has the larger absolute value, so the answer is negative. $10 + (-12) = -2$

20. -9

21. $19 + (-19)$ The numbers has the same absolute value. The sum is 0. $19 + (-19) = 0$

22. -26

23. $23 + (-5)$ The absolute values are 23 and 5. The difference is $23 - 5$ or 18. The positive number has the larger absolute value, so the answer is positive. $23 + (-5) = 18$

24. -22

25. $-23 + (-9)$ Two negatives. Add the absolute values, getting 32. Make the answer negative. $-23 + (-9) = -32$

26. 32

27. $40 + (-40)$ The numbers have the same absolute value. The sum is 0. $40 + (-40) = 0$

28. 0

29. $85 + (-65)$ The absolute values are 85 and 65. The difference is $85 - 65$, or 20. The positive number has the larger absolute value, so the answer is positive. $85 + (-65) = 20$

30. 45

31. $-3.6 + 1.9$ The absolute values are 3.6 and 1.9. The difference is $3.6 - 1.9$, or 1.7. The negative number has the larger absolute value, so the answer is negative. $-3.6 + 1.9 = -1.7$

32. -1.8

33. $-5.4 + (-3.7)$ Two negatives. Add the absolute values, getting 9.1. Make the answer negative. $-5.4 + (-3.7) = -9.1$

34. -13.2

35. $-\dfrac{4}{3} + \dfrac{2}{3}$ The absolute values are $\dfrac{4}{3}$ and $\dfrac{2}{3}$. The difference is $\dfrac{4}{3} - \dfrac{2}{3}$, or $\dfrac{2}{3}$. The negative number has the larger absolute value, so the answer is negative.
$$-\frac{4}{3} + \frac{2}{3} = -\frac{2}{3}$$

36. $-\dfrac{1}{5}$

37. $-\dfrac{4}{9} + \left(-\dfrac{6}{9}\right)$ Two negatives. Add the absolute values, getting $\dfrac{10}{9}$. Make the answer negative.
$$-\frac{4}{9} + \left(-\frac{6}{9}\right) = -\frac{10}{9}$$

38. $-\dfrac{8}{7}$

39. $-\dfrac{5}{6} + \dfrac{2}{3}$ The absolute values are $\dfrac{5}{6}$ and $\dfrac{2}{3}$. The difference is $\dfrac{5}{6} - \dfrac{4}{6}$, or $\dfrac{1}{6}$. The negative number has the larger absolute value, so the answer is negative.
$$-\frac{5}{6} + \frac{2}{3} = -\frac{1}{6}$$

40. $-\dfrac{3}{8}$

41. $-\dfrac{5}{8} + \left(-\dfrac{1}{3}\right)$ Two negatives. Add the absolute values, getting $\dfrac{15}{24} + \dfrac{8}{24}$, or $\dfrac{23}{24}$. Make the answer negative.
$$-\frac{5}{8} + \left(-\frac{1}{3}\right) = -\frac{23}{24}$$

42. $-\dfrac{29}{35}$

43. $\quad 35 + (-14) + (-19) + (-5)$
$= 35 + [(-14) + (-19) + (-5)]$ Using the associative law of addition
$= 35 + (-38)$ Adding the negatives
$= -3$ Adding a positive and a negative

44. -62

45. $-44 + \left(-\dfrac{3}{8}\right) + 95 + \left(-\dfrac{5}{8}\right)$

$= \left[-44 + \left(-\dfrac{3}{8}\right) + \left(-\dfrac{5}{8}\right)\right] + 95$

        Using the associative law of addition

$= -45 + 95$ Adding the negatives

$= 50$ Adding a negative and a positive

46. 37.9

47. Rewording:

July bill	plus	payment	plus
↓	↓	↓	↓
-82	$+$	50	$+$

August bill	is	amount owed.
↓	↓	↓
(-37)	$=$	Amount owed

Since $-82 + 50 + (-37) = -32 + (-37)$

$= -69,$

Maya owed $69 at the end of August.

48. 8 yd gain

49. Rewording:

1992 loss	plus	1993 profit	plus
↓	↓	↓	↓
$-28,375$	$+$	$37,425$	$+$

1994 profit	plus	1995 loss	plus	1996 profit	is
↓	↓	↓	↓	↓	↓
$95,485$	$+$	$(-19,365)$	$+$	$98,245$	$=$

total profit or loss.
↓
total profit or loss.

Since $-28,375 + 37,425 + 95,485 + (-19,365) + 98,245$

$= -47,740 + 231,155$

$= 183,415,$

the profit was $183,415.

50. 13 mb drop

51. Rewording:

Elevation of base	plus	total height	is	elevation of peak.
↓	↓	↓	↓	↓

Translating:

$-19,684$	$+$	$33,480$	$=$	elevation of peak.

Since $-19,684 + 33,480 = 13,796$, the elevation of the peak is 13,796 ft above sea level.

52. Owes $85

53. Rewording:

Monday change	plus	Tuesday change	plus
↓	↓	↓	↓

Translating:

$-\dfrac{1}{4}$	$+$	$\dfrac{5}{8}$	$+$

Wednesday change	is	total change.
↓	↓	↓
$\left(-\dfrac{3}{8}\right)$	$=$	total change.

Since $-\dfrac{1}{4} + \dfrac{5}{8} + \left(-\dfrac{3}{8}\right)$

$= \left[-\dfrac{2}{8} + \left(-\dfrac{3}{8}\right)\right] + \dfrac{5}{8}$

$= -\dfrac{5}{8} + \dfrac{5}{8}$

$= 0,$

the change in the value was $0. That is, the value of the stock was the same at the end of the three day period as at the beginning.

54. $85 overdrawn

55. Since -3 is to the left of 0, we have $-3 < 0$.

56. $-\dfrac{1}{3} < \dfrac{1}{4}$

57. Since -2.5 is to the right of -3.8, we have $-2.5 > -3.8$.

58. $1 > -1$

59. ◈

60. ◈

61. ◈

62. ◈

63. Starting with the final value, we "undo" the rise and drop in value by adding their opposites. The result is the original value.

Rewording: $\underbrace{\text{Final value}}$ plus $\underbrace{\text{opposite of rise}}$ plus

$\downarrow \quad\quad \downarrow \quad\quad \downarrow \quad\quad \downarrow$

Translating: $64\frac{3}{8}$ + $\left(-2\frac{3}{8}\right)$ +

$\underbrace{\text{opposite of drop}}$ is original value.

$\downarrow \quad\quad \downarrow \quad\quad \underbrace{\downarrow}$

$3\frac{1}{4}$ = original value.

Since $64\frac{3}{8} + \left(-2\frac{3}{8}\right) + 3\frac{1}{4} = 62 + 3\frac{1}{4}$

$= 65\frac{1}{4},$

the stock's original value was $\$65\frac{1}{4}$.

64. $55.50

65. $P = 2l + 2w = 7x + 10$

We know $2l = 2 \cdot 5 = 10$, so $2w$ is $7x$. Then the width is a number which yields $7x$ when added to itself. Since $3.5x + 3.5x = 7x$, the width is $3.5x$, or $\frac{7}{2}x$.

66. 1 under par

Exercise Set 1.5

---

1. The opposite of 39 is -39 because $39 + (-39) = 0$.

2. 17

3. The opposite of -9 is 9 because $-9 + 9 = 0$.

4. $-\dfrac{7}{2}$

5. The opposite of -3.14 is 3.14 because $-3.14 + 3.14 = 0$.

6. -48.2

7. If $x = 23$, then $-x = -(23) = -23$. (The opposite of 23 is -23.)

8. 26

9. If $x = -\dfrac{14}{3}$, then $-x = -\left(-\dfrac{14}{3}\right) = \dfrac{14}{3}$.
$\left(\text{The opposite of } -\dfrac{14}{3} \text{ is } \dfrac{14}{3}.\right)$

10. $-\dfrac{1}{328}$

11. If $x = 0.101$, then $-x = -(0.101) = -0.101$. (The opposite of 0.101 is -0.101.)

12. 0

13. If $x = -72$, then $-(-x) = -(-72) = 72$ (The opposite of the opposite of 72 is 72.)

14. 29

15. If $x = -\dfrac{2}{5}$, then $-(-x) = -\left[-\left(-\dfrac{2}{5}\right)\right] = -\dfrac{2}{5}$.
$\left(\text{The opposite of the opposite of } -\dfrac{2}{5} \text{ is } -\dfrac{2}{5}.\right)$

16. -9.1

17. When we change the sign of -1 we obtain 1.

18. 7

19. When we change the sign of 7 we obtain -7.

20. -10

21. $4 - 13 = 4 + (-13) = -9$

22. -5

23. $0 - 7 = 0 + (-7) = -7$

24. -10

25. $-7 - (-9) = -7 + 9 = 2$

26. -6

27. $-10 - (-10) = -10 + 10 = 0$

28. 0

29. $20 - 27 = 20 + (-27) = -7$

30. 26

31. $-8 - (-3) = -8 + 3 = -5$

32. 2

33. $-40 - (-40) = -40 + 40 = 0$

34. 0

35. $7 - 7 = 7 + (-7) = 0$

36. 0

37. $6 - (-6) = 6 + 6 = 12$

38. 8

39. $8 - (-3) = 8 + 3 = 11$

40. -11

41. $-6 - 8 = -6 + (-8) = -14$

42. 16

43. $-4 - (-9) = -4 + 9 = 5$

44. -16

45. $-6 - (-5) = -6 + 5 = -1$

46. -1

47. $3 - (-12) = 3 + 12 = 15$

48. 11

49. $-7 - 14 = -7 + (-14) = -21$

50. -25

51. $0 - (-5) = 0 + 5 = 5$

52. 1

53. $-8 - 0 = -8 + 0 = -8$

54. -9

55. $2 - 25 = 2 + (-25) = -23$

56. -45

57. $-71 - 2 = -71 + (-2) = -73$

58. -52

59. $24 - (-92) = 24 + 92 = 116$

60. 121

61. $\dfrac{3}{8} - \dfrac{5}{8} = \dfrac{3}{8} + \left(-\dfrac{5}{8}\right) = -\dfrac{2}{8} = -\dfrac{1}{4}$

62. $-\dfrac{2}{3}$

63. $-\dfrac{3}{4} - \dfrac{2}{3} = -\dfrac{9}{12} - \dfrac{8}{12} = -\dfrac{9}{12} + \left(-\dfrac{8}{12}\right) = -\dfrac{17}{12}$

64. $-\dfrac{11}{8}$

65. $-2.8 - 0 = -2.8 + 0 = -2.8$

66. 4.94

67. $0.09 - 1 = 0.09 + (-1) = -0.91$

68. -0.911

69. $\dfrac{1}{6} - \dfrac{2}{3} = \dfrac{1}{6} - \dfrac{4}{6} = \dfrac{1}{6} + \left(-\dfrac{4}{6}\right) = -\dfrac{3}{6} = -\dfrac{1}{2}$

70. $\dfrac{1}{8}$

71. $-\dfrac{4}{7} - \left(-\dfrac{10}{7}\right) = -\dfrac{4}{7} + \dfrac{10}{7} = \dfrac{6}{7}$

72. 0

73. We subtract the smaller number from the larger.

Translate: $3.8 - (-5.2)$

Simplify: $3.8 - (-5.2) = 3.8 + 5.2 = 9$

74. $-2.1 - (-5.9)$;   3.8

75. We subtract the smaller number from the larger.

Translate: $114 - (-79)$

Simplify: $114 - (-79) = 114 + 79 = 193$

76. $23 - (-17)$;   40

77. $-21 - 37 = -21 + (-37) = -58$

78. -26

79. $9 - (-25) = 9 + 25 = 34$

80. 26

81. $-1.8 - 2.7$ is read "negative one point eight minus two point seven."

$$-1.8 - 2.7 = -1.8 + (-2.7) = -4.5$$

82. Negative two point seven minus five point nine; -8.6

83. $-250 - (-425)$ is read "negative two hundred fifty minus negative four hundred twenty-five."

$$-250 - (-425) = -250 + 425 = 175$$

84. Negative three hundred fifty minus negative one thousand; 650

85. $25 - (-12) - 7 - (-2) + 9 = 25 + 12 + (-7) + 2 + 9 = 41$

86. -22

87. $-31 + (-28) - (-14) - 17 = (-31) + (-28) + 14 + (-17) = -62$

88. 22

89. $-34 - 28 + (-33) - 44 = (-34) + (-28) + (-33) + (-44) = -139$

90. 5

91. We subtract the lower temperature from the higher temperature:
$$44 - (-56) = 44 + 56 = 100$$
The temperature dropped 100°F.

92. $165

93. We add the elevations:
$$14,776 + (-282) = 14,494 \text{ ft}$$
The elevation of Mt. Whitney is 14,494 ft above sea level.

94. 30,340 ft

95. We subtract the smaller number from the larger:
$$-8648 - (-10,415) = -8648 + 10,415 = 1767$$
The difference in elevation is 1767 m.

96. 116 m

97. Area $= lw = (36 \text{ ft})(12 \text{ ft}) = 432 \text{ ft}^2$

98. $2 \cdot 2 \cdot 2 \cdot 2 \cdot 2 \cdot 3 \cdot 3 \cdot 3$

99. ◈

100. ◈

101. ◈

102. ◈

103. False. For example, let $m = -3$ and $n = -5$. Then $-3 > -5$, but $-3 + (-5) = -8 \not> 0$.

104. True. For example, for $m = 5$ and $n = 3$, $5 > 3$ and $5 - 3 > 0$, or $2 > 0$. For $m = -4$ and $n = -9$, $-4 > -9$ and $-4 - (-9) > 0$, or $5 > 0$.

105. False. For example, let $m = 2$ and $n = -2$. Then 2 and -2 are opposites, but $2 - (-2) = 4 \neq 0$.

106. True. For example, for $m = 4$ and $n = -4$, $4 = -(-4)$ and $4 + (-4) = 0$; for $m = -3$ and $n = 3$, $-3 = -3$ and $-3 + 3 = 0$.

107. ◈

Exercise Set 1.6

1. $-9 \cdot 3 = -27$ Think: $9 \cdot 3 = 27$, make the answer negative.

2. -21

3. $-8 \cdot 7 = -56$ Think: $8 \cdot 7 = 56$, make the answer negative.

4. -18

5. $8 \cdot (-3) = -24$

6. -45

7. $-8 \cdot (-2) = 16$ Multiplying absolute values

8. 10

9. $15 \cdot (-8) = -120$

10. 120

11. $-14 \cdot 17 = -238$

12. 195

13. $-3.5 \cdot (-28) = 98$

14. -203.7

15. $-7 \cdot (-3.1) = 21.7$

16. 12.8

17. $\frac{2}{3} \cdot \left(-\frac{3}{5}\right) = -\left(\frac{2 \cdot 3}{3 \cdot 5}\right) = -\left(\frac{2}{5} \cdot \frac{3}{3}\right) = -\frac{2}{5}$

18. $-\dfrac{10}{21}$

19. $-\frac{3}{8} \cdot \left(-\frac{2}{9}\right) = \frac{3 \cdot 2 \cdot 1}{4 \cdot 2 \cdot 3 \cdot 3} = \frac{1}{12}$

20. $\dfrac{1}{4}$

21. $-6.3 \times 2.7 = -17.01$

22. -38.95

23. $-\frac{5}{9} \cdot \frac{3}{4} = -\frac{5 \cdot 3}{3 \cdot 3 \cdot 4} = -\frac{5}{12}$

24. -6

25. $\quad 3 \cdot (-7) \cdot (-2) \cdot 6$
$$= -21 \cdot (-12) \quad \text{Multiplying the first two numbers and the last two numbers}$$
$$= 252$$

26. 756

27. $-\dfrac{1}{3} \cdot \dfrac{1}{4} \cdot \left(-\dfrac{3}{7}\right) = -\dfrac{1}{12} \cdot \left(-\dfrac{3}{7}\right) = \dfrac{3}{12 \cdot 7} =$
$\dfrac{\cancel{3} \cdot 1}{\cancel{3} \cdot 4 \cdot 7} = \dfrac{1}{28}$

28. $\dfrac{3}{35}$

29. $-2 \cdot (-5) \cdot (-3) \cdot 5 = 10 \cdot (-15) = -150$

30. -30

31. $(-8)(-9)(-10) = 72(-10) = -720$

32. 5040

33. $(-6)(-7)(-8)(-9)(-10) = 42 \cdot 72 \cdot (-10) =$
$3024 \cdot (-10) = -30,240$

34. $151,200$

35. 0, The product of 0 and any real number is 0.

36. 0

37. $24 \div (-4) = -6$ Check: $-6 \cdot (-4) = 24$

38. -4

39. $\dfrac{36}{-9} = -4$ $-4 \cdot (-9) = 36$

40. -2

41. $\dfrac{-16}{8} = -2$ Check: $-2 \cdot 8 = -16$

42. 8

43. $\dfrac{-72}{9} = -8$ Check: $-8 \cdot 9 = -72$

44. -2

45. $-100 \div (-50) = 2$ Check: $2(-50) = -100$

46. -25

47. $\dfrac{400}{-50} = -8$ Check: $-8 \cdot (-50) = 400$

48. $\dfrac{300}{13}$

49. Undefined

50. 0

51. $\dfrac{88}{-9} = -\dfrac{88}{9}$ Check: $-\dfrac{88}{9} \cdot (-9) = 88$

52. Indeterminate

53. $\dfrac{0}{-9} = 0$

54. Undefined

55. $0 \div 0$ is indeterminate.

56. 0

57. $\dfrac{-8}{3} = \dfrac{8}{-3}$ and $\dfrac{-8}{3} = -\dfrac{8}{3}$

58. $\dfrac{12}{-7}, \ -\dfrac{12}{7}$

59. $-\dfrac{7}{3} = \dfrac{-7}{3}$ and $-\dfrac{7}{3} = \dfrac{7}{-3}$

60. $\dfrac{-4}{15}, \ \dfrac{4}{-15}$

61. $\dfrac{x}{-2} = \dfrac{-x}{2}$ and $\dfrac{x}{-2} = -\dfrac{x}{2}$

62. $\dfrac{-9}{a}, \ -\dfrac{9}{a}$

63. The reciprocal of $\dfrac{4}{-5}$ is $\dfrac{-5}{4}$ $\left(\text{or equivalently,} -\dfrac{5}{4}\right)$ because $\dfrac{4}{-5} \cdot \dfrac{-5}{4} = 1$.

64. $\dfrac{-9}{2}$, or $-\dfrac{9}{2}$

65. The reciprocal of $-\dfrac{47}{13}$ is $-\dfrac{13}{47}$ because $-\dfrac{47}{13} \cdot \left(-\dfrac{13}{47}\right) = 1$.

66. $-\dfrac{12}{31}$

67. The reciprocal of -10 is $\dfrac{1}{-10}$ $\left(\text{or equivalently,} -\dfrac{1}{10}\right)$ because $-10\left(\dfrac{1}{-10}\right) = 1$.

68. $\dfrac{1}{13}$

69. The reciprocal of 4.3 is $\dfrac{1}{4.3}$ because $4.3\left(\dfrac{1}{4.3}\right) = 1$.

70. $-\dfrac{1}{8.5}$

71. The reciprocal of $\dfrac{-9}{4}$ is $\dfrac{4}{-9}$ $\left(\text{or equivalently,} -\dfrac{4}{9}\right)$ because $\dfrac{-9}{4} \cdot \dfrac{4}{-9} = 1$.

72. $-\dfrac{11}{6}$

73. The reciprocal of -1 is $\dfrac{1}{-1}$, or -1 because $(-1)(-1) = 1$.

74. $\dfrac{1}{2}$

75.
$$\left(\dfrac{-7}{4}\right)\left(-\dfrac{3}{5}\right)$$
$$= \left(-\dfrac{7}{4}\right)\left(-\dfrac{3}{5}\right) \quad \text{Rewriting } \dfrac{-7}{4} \text{ as } -\dfrac{7}{4}$$
$$= \dfrac{21}{20}$$

76. $\dfrac{5}{18}$

77.
$$\left(\dfrac{-6}{5}\right)\left(\dfrac{2}{-11}\right)$$
$$= \left(\dfrac{-6}{5}\right)\left(\dfrac{-2}{11}\right) \quad \text{Rewriting } \dfrac{2}{-11} \text{ as } \dfrac{-2}{11}$$
$$= \dfrac{12}{55}$$

78. $\dfrac{35}{12}$

79. $\left(\dfrac{-9}{5}\right)\left(-\dfrac{10}{7}\right) = \left(-\dfrac{9}{5}\right)\left(-\dfrac{10}{7}\right) = \dfrac{90}{35} = \dfrac{\cancel{5}\cdot 18}{\cancel{5}\cdot 7} = \dfrac{18}{7}$

80. $\dfrac{5}{28}$

81. $\dfrac{7}{8} \div \left(-\dfrac{1}{2}\right) = \dfrac{7}{8}\cdot\left(-\dfrac{2}{1}\right) = -\dfrac{14}{8} = -\dfrac{7\cdot\cancel{2}}{\cancel{2}\cdot 4\cdot 1} = -\dfrac{7}{4}$

82. $-\dfrac{9}{8}$

83. $\dfrac{9}{5}\cdot\dfrac{-20}{3} = \dfrac{9}{5}\left(-\dfrac{20}{3}\right) = -\dfrac{180}{15} = -\dfrac{\cancel{3}\cdot 3\cdot 4\cdot\cancel{5}}{\cancel{5}\cdot\cancel{3}\cdot 1} = -12$

84. $-\dfrac{7}{36}$

85. $\left(-\dfrac{18}{7}\right) + \left(-\dfrac{3}{7}\right) = -\dfrac{21}{7} = -3$

86. -3

87. $-\dfrac{5}{9} \div \left(-\dfrac{5}{6}\right) = -\dfrac{5}{9}\cdot\left(-\dfrac{6}{5}\right) = \dfrac{30}{45} = \dfrac{\cancel{5}\cdot 2\cdot\cancel{3}}{\cancel{3}\cdot 3\cdot\cancel{5}} = \dfrac{2}{3}$

88. $\dfrac{5}{3}$

89. $-44.1 \div (-6.3) = 7$ Do the long division. The answer is positive.

90. -2

91. $\dfrac{-5}{9} - \dfrac{2}{9} = -\dfrac{5}{9} - \dfrac{2}{9} = -\dfrac{5}{9} + \left(-\dfrac{2}{9}\right) = -\dfrac{7}{9}$

92. $-\dfrac{5}{7}$

93.
$$\dfrac{-3}{10} + \dfrac{2}{-5}$$
$$= \dfrac{-3}{10} + \dfrac{-2}{5}$$
$$= \dfrac{-3}{10} + \dfrac{-2}{5}\cdot\dfrac{2}{2} \quad \text{Using a common denominator of 10}$$
$$= \dfrac{-3}{10} + \dfrac{-4}{10}$$
$$= \dfrac{-7}{10}, \text{ or } -\dfrac{7}{10}$$

94. $-\dfrac{11}{9}$

95. $\dfrac{7}{10} \div \left(\dfrac{-3}{5}\right) = \dfrac{7}{10} \div \left(-\dfrac{3}{5}\right) = \dfrac{7}{10}\cdot\left(-\dfrac{5}{3}\right) = -\dfrac{35}{30} = -\dfrac{7\cdot\cancel{5}}{2\cdot\cancel{5}\cdot 3} = -\dfrac{7}{6}$

96. $-\dfrac{3}{2}$

97. $\dfrac{5}{7} - \dfrac{1}{-7} = \dfrac{5}{7} - \left(-\dfrac{1}{7}\right) = \dfrac{5}{7} + \dfrac{1}{7} = \dfrac{6}{7}$

98. $\dfrac{5}{9}$

99. $\dfrac{-4}{15} + \dfrac{2}{-3} = \dfrac{-4}{15} + \dfrac{-2}{3} = \dfrac{-4}{15} + \dfrac{-2}{3}\cdot\dfrac{5}{5} = \dfrac{-4}{15} + \dfrac{-10}{15} = \dfrac{-14}{15}, \text{ or } -\dfrac{14}{15}$

100. $-\dfrac{1}{2}$

101. $\dfrac{264}{468} = \dfrac{\cancel{2}\cdot\cancel{2}\cdot 2\cdot\cancel{3}\cdot 11}{\cancel{2}\cdot\cancel{2}\cdot\cancel{3}\cdot 3\cdot 13} = \dfrac{22}{39}$

102. No

103. ◈

104. ◈

105. ◈

106. ◈

107. Consider the sum $2 + 3$. Its reciprocal is $\dfrac{1}{2+3}$, or $\dfrac{1}{5}$, but $\dfrac{1}{2} + \dfrac{1}{3} = \dfrac{5}{6}$.

108. $-1, 1$

109. When n is negative, $-n$ is positive, so $\dfrac{m}{-n}$ is the quotient of a negative and a positive number and, thus, is negative.

110. Positive

111. When n is negative, $-n$ is positive, so $\dfrac{-n}{m}$ is the quotient of a positive and a negative number and, thus, is negative. When m is negative, $-m$ is positive, so $-m \cdot \left(\dfrac{-n}{m} \right)$ is the product of a positive and a negative number and, thus, is negative.

112. Positive

113. $m + n$ is the sum of two negative numbers, so it is negative; $\dfrac{m}{n}$ is the quotient of two negative numbers, so it is positive. Then $(m + n) \cdot \dfrac{m}{n}$ is the product of a negative and a positive number and, thus, is negative.

114. Positive

115. a) m and n have different signs;
  b) either m or n is zero;
  c) m and n have the same sign

116. Distributive law, law of opposites, multiplicative property of 0, law of opposites

117. ◈

Exercise Set 1.7

1. $x + 3$ Changing the order

2. $2 + a$.

3. $3y + 9x$

4. $7b + 3a$

5. $2(3 + a)$

6. $9(5 + x)$

7. $a \cdot 8$ Changing the order

8. $b7$

9. $5 + ba$

10. $x + y3$

11. $(a + 3)2$

12. $(x + 5)9$

13. $a + (3 + b)$

14. $5 + (m + r)$

15. $(r + t) + 9$

16. $(x + 2) + y$

17. $ab + (c + d)$

18. $m + (np + r)$

19. $3(xy)$

20. $9(ab)$

21. $(4x)y$

22. $(9r)p$

23. $(3 \cdot 2)(a + b)$

24. $(5x)(2 + y)$

25. a) $r + (t + 6) = (t + 6) + r$ Using the commutative law
        $= (6 + t) + r$ Using the commutative law again

  b) $r + (t + 6) = (t + 6) + r$ Using the commutative law
        $= t + (6 + r)$ Using the associative law

Answers may vary.

26. $v + (w + 5)$; $(v + 5) + w$; answers may vary

27. a) $(5a)b = b(5a)$ Using the commutative law
        $= b(a5)$ Using the commutative law again

  b) $(5a)b = (a5)b$ Using the commutative law
        $= a(5b)$ Using the associative law

Answers may vary.

28. $3(yx)$; $(3x)y$; answers may vary

29. $(7 + x) + 2$
        $= (x + 7) + 2$ Commutative law
        $= x + (7 + 2)$ Associative law
        $= x + 9$ Simplifying

30. $(2a)4 = 4(2a)$ Commutative law

      $= (4 \cdot 2)a$ Associative law

      $= 8a$ Simplifying

31. $(m3)7 = m(3 \cdot 7)$ Associative law

      $= (3 \cdot 7)m$ Commutative law

      $= 21m$ Simplifying

32. $4 + (9 + x)$

      $= (4 + 9) + x$ Associative law

      $= x + (4 + 9)$ Commutative law

      $= x + 13$ Simplifying

33. $3(a + 4) = 3 \cdot a + 3 \cdot 4 = 3a + 12$

34. $4x + 12$

35. $6(1 + x) = 6 \cdot 1 + 6 \cdot x = 6 + 6x$

36. $6v + 24$

37. $7(s + 5) = 7 \cdot s + 7 \cdot 5 = 7s + 35$

38. $4 + 4y$

39. $9(2x + 6) = 9 \cdot 2x + 9 \cdot 6 = 18x + 54$

40. $54m + 63$

41. $5(r + 2 + 3t) = 5 \cdot r + 5 \cdot 2 + 5 \cdot 3t = 5r + 10 + 15t$

42. $20x + 32 + 12p$

43. $(a + b)2 = a(2) + b(2) = 2a + 2b$

44. $7x + 14$

45. $(x + y + 2)5 = x(5) + y(5) + 2(5) = 5x + 5y + 10$

46. $12 + 6a + 6b$

47. $7x + 7z = 7(x + z)$ The common factor is 7.

      Check: $7(x + z) = 7 \cdot x + 7 \cdot z = 7x + 7z$

48. $5(y + z)$

49. $5 + 5y = 5 \cdot 1 + 5 \cdot y$ The common factor is 5.

      $= 5(1 + y)$ Using the distributive law

      Check: $5(1 + y) = 5 \cdot 1 + 5 \cdot y = 5 + 5y$

50. $13(1 + x)$

51. $18x + 3y = 3 \cdot 6x + 3 \cdot y = 3(6x + y)$

      Check: $3(6x + y) = 3 \cdot 6x + 3 \cdot y = 18x + 3y$

52. $5(x + 4y)$

53. $5x + 10 + 15y = 5 \cdot x + 5 \cdot 2 + 5 \cdot 3y = 5(x + 2 + 3y)$

      Check: $5(x+2+3y) = 5 \cdot x + 5 \cdot 2 + 5 \cdot 3y = 5x + 10 + 15y$

54. $3(1 + 9b + 2c)$

55. $9x + 3y = 3 \cdot 3x + 3 \cdot y = 3(3x + y)$

      Check: $3(3x + y) = 3 \cdot 3x + 3 \cdot y = 9x + 3y$

56. $5(3x + y)$

57. $2a + 16b + 64 = 2 \cdot a + 2 \cdot 8b + 2 \cdot 32 = 2(a + 8b + 32)$

      Check: $2(a+8b+32) = 2 \cdot a + 2 \cdot 8b + 2 \cdot 32 = 2a + 16b + 64$

58. $5(1 + 4x + 7y)$

59. $11x + 44y + 121 = 11 \cdot x + 11 \cdot 4y + 11 \cdot 11 = 11(x + 4y + 11)$

      Check: $11(x + 4y + 11) = 11 \cdot x + 11 \cdot 4y + 11 \cdot 11 = 11x + 44y + 121$

60. $7(1 + 2b + 8w)$

61. $-7x - 4y = -7x + (-4y)$, so the terms are $-7x$ and $-4y$.

62. $7a, -9b$

63. $-5 + 3m - 6mn = -5 + 3m + (-6mn)$, so the terms are $-5, 3m$, and $-6mn$.

64. $-9, -4t, 10rt$

65. $4x + 7x = (4 + 7)x = 11x$

66. $14a$

67. $7m + (-9m) = [7 + (-9)]m = -2m$

68. $5x$

69. $4x - 7x$

      $= 4x + (-7x)$ Adding the opposite

      $= (4 + (-7))x$ Using the distributive law

      $= -3x$

70. $-11a$

71. $7a - 12a + 4$

      $= 7a + (-12a) + 4$ Adding the opposite

      $= (7 + (-12))a + 4$ Using the distributive law

      $= -5a + 4$

72. $-22x + 7$

73.
$$-8n - 9 + n$$

$= -8n + (-9) + n$ Adding the opposite

$= -8n + n + (-9)$ Using the commutative law of addition

$= -7n - 9$ Adding like terms

74. $9n - 15$

75.
$$2 - 6t - 9 - 2t$$

$= 2 + (-6t) + (-9) + (-2t)$

$= 2 + (-9) + (-6t) + (-2t)$

$= -7 - 8t$

76. $-2b - 12$

77.
$$7 + (-3x) - 9x + 1$$

$= 7 + (-3x) + (-9x) + 1$

$= 7 + 1 + (-3x) + (-9x)$

$= 8 - 12x$

78. $7x + 46$

79. $13x - (-2x) + 45 - (-21) = 13x + 2x + 45 + 21 = 15x + 66$

80. $15x + 39$

81. Perimeter $= 8 + 5x + 9 + 7x$

$= 8 + 9 + 5x + 7x$

$= (8 + 9) + (5 + 7)x$

$= 17 + 12x$

82. $10a + 13$

83. Perimeter $= 9 + 6n + 7 + 8n + 4n$

$= 9 + 7 + 6n + 8n + 4n$

$= (9 + 7) + (6 + 8 + 4)n$

$= 16 + 18n$

84. $19n + 11$

85. $\dfrac{2}{5} + \left(-\dfrac{3}{10}\right)$ The absolute values are $\dfrac{2}{5}$ and $\dfrac{3}{10}$.

The difference is $\dfrac{4}{10} - \dfrac{3}{10}$, or $\dfrac{1}{10}$. The positive number has the larger absolute value, so the answer is positive.

$$\dfrac{2}{5} + \left(-\dfrac{3}{10}\right) = \dfrac{1}{10}$$

86. $\dfrac{7}{10}$

87. $\dfrac{2}{5}\left(-\dfrac{3}{10}\right) = -\dfrac{2 \cdot 3}{5 \cdot 10} = -\dfrac{2 \cdot 3}{5 \cdot 2 \cdot 5} = -\dfrac{\cancel{2} \cdot 3}{5 \cdot \cancel{2} \cdot 5} = -\dfrac{3}{25}$

88. $-\dfrac{4}{3}$

89. ◈

90. ◈

91. ◈

92. ◈

93.
$$4x + \underline{\quad} + (-9x) + (-2y)$$

$= 4x + (-9x) + \underline{\quad} + (-2y)$

$= [4 + (-9)]x + \underline{\quad} + (-2y)$

$= -5x + \underline{\quad} + (-2y)$

This expression is equivalent to $-5x - 7y$, so the missing term is the term which yields $-7y$ when added to $-2y$. Since $-5y + (-2y) = -7y$, the missing term is $-5y$.

94. $-15b$

95.
$$3m + 2n + \underline{\quad} + (-2m)$$

$= 2n + \underline{\quad} + (-2m) + 3m$

$= 2n + \underline{\quad} + (-2 + 3)m$

$= 2n + \underline{\quad} + m$

This expression is equivalent to $2n + (-6m)$, so the missing term is the term which yields $-6m$ when added to m. Since $-7m + m = -6m$, the missing term is $-7m$.

96. $-3y$

97. The expressions are equivalent by the distributive law.

$$8 + 4(a + b) = 8 + 4a + 4b = 4(2 + a + b)$$

98. No; for example, let $m = 1$. Then we have:

$$7 \div 3 \cdot 1 = \dfrac{7}{3} \cdot 1 = \dfrac{7}{3}, \text{ but}$$

$$1 \cdot 3 \div 7 = 3 \div 7 = \dfrac{3}{7}.$$

99. The expressions are equivalent by the distributive law and the commutative law of multiplication.

$$(rt + st)5 = 5(rt + st) = 5 \cdot t(r + s) = 5t(r + s)$$

100. Yes; distributive law, commutative law of addition, and commutative law of multiplication

101. The expressions are not equivalent.

Let $x = 1$ and $y = 0$. Then we have:

$30 \cdot 0 + 1 \cdot 15 = 0 + 15 = 15$, but

$5[2(1 + 3 \cdot 0)] = 5[2(1)] = 5 \cdot 2 = 10$.

102. Yes; commutative law of multiplication, associative law of multiplication, and distributive law

103. ◈

104. ◈

Exercise Set 1.8

1. $\underbrace{17 \times 17 \times 17}_{\text{3 factors}} = 17^3$

2. 5^4

3. $\underbrace{x \cdot x \cdot x \cdot x \cdot x \cdot x \cdot x}_{\text{7 factors}} = x^7$

4. y^6

5. $6y \cdot 6y \cdot 6y \cdot 6y = (6y)^4$

6. $(5m)^5$

7. $3^4 = 3 \cdot 3 \cdot 3 \cdot 3 = 9 \cdot 9 = 81$

8. 125

9. $(-3)^2 = (-3)(-3) = 9$

10. 49

11. $(-1)^5 = (-1)(-1)(-1)(-1)(-1) = 1 \cdot 1 \cdot (-1) = 1 \cdot (-1) = -1$

12. 1

13. $9^1 = 9$ (1 factor)

14. 7

15. $(2x)^4 = (2x)(2x)(2x)(2x) = 2 \cdot 2 \cdot 2 \cdot 2 \cdot x \cdot x \cdot x \cdot x = 16x^4$

16. $9x^2$

17. $(-7x)^3 = (-7x)(-7x)(-7x) = (-7)(-7)(-7)(x)(x)(x) = -343x^3$

18. $625x^4$

19. $5 + 3 \times 7 = 5 + 21$ Multiplying
$ = 26$ Adding

20. 1

21. $8 \times 7 + 6 \times 5 = 56 + 30$ Multiplying
$ = 86$ Adding

22. 51

23. $19 - 5 \times 3 + 3 = 19 - 15 + 3$ Multiplying
$ = 4 + 3$ Subtracting and adding from left to right
$ = 7$

24. 9

25. $9 \div 3 + 16 \div 8 = 3 + 2$ Dividing
$ = 5$ Adding

26. 28

27. $7 + 10 - 10 \div 2 = 7 + 10 - 5$ Dividing
$ = 17 - 5$ Adding and subtracting from left to right
$ = 12$

28. 9

29. $ 2 \cdot 5^3$
$= 2 \cdot 125$ Simplifying the exponential expression
$= 250$ Multiplying

30. 24

31. $8 - 2 \cdot 3 - 9 = 8 - 6 - 9$ Multiplying
$ = 2 - 9$ Adding and subtracting from left to right
$ = -7$

32. 11

33. $(8 - 2 \cdot 3) - 9 = (8 - 6) - 9$ Multiplying inside the parentheses
$ = 2 - 9$ Subtracting inside the parentheses
$ = -7$

34. -36

35. $(-24) \div (-3) \cdot \left(-\dfrac{1}{2}\right) = 8 \cdot \left(-\dfrac{1}{2}\right) = -\dfrac{8}{2} = -4$

36. 32

37. $ 13(-10) + 45$
$= -130 + 45$ Multiplying
$= -85$ Adding

38. 2

39. $2^4 + 2^3 - 10 = 16 + 8 - 10 = 24 - 10 = 14$

40. 23

41. $[2 \cdot (5 - 3)]^2 = [2 \cdot 2]^2 = 4^2 = 16$

42. 76

43. $\dfrac{7 + 2}{5^2 - 4^2} = \dfrac{9}{25 - 16} = \dfrac{9}{9} = 1$

44. 2

45. $8(-7) + |6(-5)| = -56 + |-30| = -56 + 30 = -26$

46. 49

47. $19 - 5(-3) + 3 = 19 + 15 + 3 = 34 + 3 = 37$

48. 33

49. $20 + 4^3 \div (-8) \cdot 2 = 20 + 64 \div (-8) \cdot 2 = 20 + (-8) \cdot 2 =$
$20 + (-16) = 4$

50. -9000

51. $3|7 - (9 - 14)| = 3|7 - (-5)| = 3|7 + 5| = 3|12| =$
$3 \cdot 12 = 36$

52. 65

53. This expression is equivalent to expression (a).

$$\frac{5(3 - 7) + 4^3}{(-2 - 3)^2} = \frac{5(-4) + 4^3}{(-5)^2}$$
$$= \frac{5(-4) + 64}{25}$$
$$= \frac{-20 + 64}{25}$$
$$= \frac{44}{25}$$

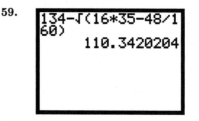

54. (c)

55. This expression is equivalent to expression (d).

$$5(3 - 7) + 4^3 \div (-2 - 3)^2 = 5(-4) + 4^3 \div (-5)^2$$
$$= 5(-4) + 64 \div 25$$
$$= -20 + 2.56$$
$$= -17.44$$

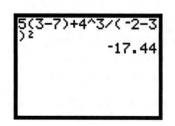

56. (b)

57.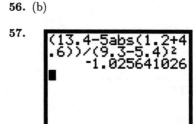

Rounding to the nearest thousandth, we have -1.026.

58. 13,997.521

59.

134−√(16*35−48/160)
        110.3420204

Rounding to the nearest thousandth, we have 110.342.

60. -11.241

61. Since one factor is 0, the product $5.2(-1.7 - 3.8)^2 \cdot 0$ is 0. Thus, we have $-12.86 - 0$, or -12.86.

62. 0

63. $9 - 5x = 9 - 5 \cdot 3$ Substituting 3 for x
          $= 9 - 15$ Multiplying
          $= -6$ Subtracting

64. -1

65. $24 \div t^3$
    $= 24 \div (-2)^3$ Substituting -2 for t
    $= 24 \div (-8)$ Simplifying the exponential expression
    $= -3$ Dividing

66. 16

67. $45 \div 3a = 45 \div 3 \cdot 3$ Substituting 3 for a

       $= 15 \cdot 3$ Dividing

       $= 45$ Multiplying

68. 125

69. $\quad 5x \div 15x^2$

$= 5 \cdot 3 \div 15(3)^2$ Substituting 3 for x

$= 5 \cdot 3 \div 15 \cdot 9$ Simplifying the exponential expression

$= 15 \div 15 \cdot 9$ Multiplying and dividing

$= 1 \cdot 9$ in order from

$= 9$ left to right

70. 8

71. $-x^2 - 5x = -(-3)^2 - 5(-3) = -9 - 5(-3) = -9 + 15 = 6$

72. 24

73. $\dfrac{3a - 4a^2}{a^2 - 20} = \dfrac{3 \cdot 5 - 4(5)^2}{(5)^2 - 20} = \dfrac{3 \cdot 5 - 4 \cdot 25}{25 - 20} = \dfrac{15 - 100}{5} = \dfrac{-85}{5} = -17$

74. 0

75.
```
13-(6-4)^3+10
            15
```

76. 143

77.
```
3(1.6+2*5.9)/1.6
         25.125
```

78. 283.74

79.
```
(1/2)(141+5/.2)²
          13778
```

80. 17.25

81. $-(9x + 1) = -9x - 1$ Removing parentheses and changing the sign of each term

82. $-3x - 5$

83. $-(7 - 2x) = -7 + 2x$ Removing parentheses and changing the sign of each term

84. $-6x + 7$

85. $-(4a - 3b + 7c) = -4a + 3b - 7c$

86. $-5x + 2y + 3z$

87. $-(3x^2 + 5x - 1) = -3x^2 - 5x + 1$

88. $-8x^3 + 6x - 5$

89. $\quad 5x - (2x + 7)$

$= 5x - 2x - 7$ Removing parentheses and changing the sign of each term

$= 3x - 7$ Collecting like terms

90. $5y - 9$

91. $2x + 7x - (4x + 6) = 2x + 7x - 4x - 6 = 5x - 6$

92. $a - 7$

93. $9t - 5r - 2(3r + 6t) = 9t - 5r - 6r - 12t = -3t - 11r$

94. $-2m - 6n$

95. $\quad 15x - y - 5(3x - 2y + 5z)$

$= 15x - y - 15x + 10y - 25z$ Multiplying each term in parentheses by -5

$= 9y - 25z$

96. $-16a + 27b - 32c$

97. $3x^2 + 7 - (2x^2 + 5) = 3x^2 + 7 - 2x^2 - 5$

$\qquad\qquad\qquad\qquad\quad = x^2 + 2$

98. $2x^4 + 6x$

99. $5t^3 + t - 3(t + 2t^3) = 5t^3 + t - 3t - 6t^3$

$\qquad\qquad\qquad\qquad\quad = -t^3 - 2t$

100. $2n^2 - n$

101. $\quad 12a^2 - 3ab + 5b^2 - 5(-5a^2 + 4ab - 6b^2)$

$= 12a^2 - 3ab + 5b^2 + 25a^2 - 20ab + 30b^2$

$= 37a^2 - 23ab + 35b^2$

102. $-20a^2 + 29ab + 48b^2$

103.
$$-7t^3 - t^2 - 3(5t^3 - 3t)$$
$$= -7t^3 - t^2 - 15t^3 + 9t$$
$$= -22t^3 - t^2 + 9t$$

104. $9t^4 - 45t^3 + 17t$

105.
$$7(x + 2) - 5(3x - 4)$$
$$= 7x + 14 - 15x + 20$$
$$= -8x + 34$$

106. $-3x - 11$

107.
$$6(3x - 7) - [4(2x - 5) + 2]$$
$$= 6(3x - 7) - [8x - 20 + 2]$$
$$= 6(3x - 7) - [8x - 18]$$
$$= 18x - 42 - 8x + 18$$
$$= 10x - 24$$

108. $52x - 29$

109. Let x represent "a number." Then we have $2x + 9$.

110. Let x and y represent the numbers; $\frac{1}{2}(x + y)$, or $\frac{x + y}{2}$.

111. ◈

112. ◈

113. ◈

114. ◈

115.
$$5t - \{7t - [4r - 3(t - 7)] + 6r\} - 4r$$
$$= 5t - \{7t - [4r - 3t + 21] + 6r\} - 4r$$
$$= 5t - \{7t - 4r + 3t - 21 + 6r\} - 4r$$
$$= 5t - \{10t + 2r - 21\} - 4r$$
$$= 5t - 10t - 2r + 21 - 4r$$
$$= -5t - 6r + 21$$

116. $-4z$

117.
$$\{x - [f - (f - x)] + [x - f]\} - 3x$$
$$= \{x - [f - f + x] + [x - f]\} - 3x$$
$$= \{x - [x] + [x - f]\} - 3x$$
$$= \{x - x + x - f\} - 3x$$
$$= x - f - 3x$$
$$= -2x - f$$

118. ◈

119. ◈

120. False

121. True; $-n + m = m + (-n) = m - n$

122. True

123. True; $n^2 - mn = n(n - m) = (n - m)n = -(-n + m)n = -(m - n)n$

124. False

125. False; let $m = 2$ and $n = 1$. Then $-2(1 - 2) = -2(-1) = 2$, but $-(2 \cdot 1 + 2^2) = -(2 + 4) = -6$.

126. True

127. True; $-n(-n - m) = n^2 + nm = n(n + m)$

Chapter 2
Equations, Inequalities, and Problem Solving

1.
$$x + 7 = 20$$
$$x + 7 - 7 = 20 - 7 \quad \text{Subtracting 7 on both sides}$$
$$x = 13 \quad \text{Simplifying}$$

Check: $\dfrac{x + 7 = 20}{13 + 7 \ ? \ 20}$
$$20 \ | \ 20 \quad \text{TRUE}$$

The solution is 13.

2. 3

3.
$$x + 15 = -5$$
$$x + 15 - 15 = -5 - 15 \quad \text{Subtracting 15 on both sides}$$
$$x = -20$$

Check: $\dfrac{x + 15 = -5}{-20 + 15 \ ? \ -5}$
$$-5 \ | \ -5 \quad \text{TRUE}$$

The solution is -20.

4. -21

5.
$$-5 = x + 8$$
$$-5 - 8 = x + 8 - 8$$
$$-13 = x$$

Check: $\dfrac{-5 = x + 8}{-5 \ ? \ -13 + 8}$
$$-5 \ | \ -5 \quad \text{TRUE}$$

The solution is -13.

6. -31

7.
$$x - 7 = -21$$
$$x - 7 + 7 = -21 + 7$$
$$x = -14$$

Check: $\dfrac{x - 7 = -21}{-14 - 7 \ ? \ -21}$
$$-21 \ | \ -21 \quad \text{TRUE}$$

The solution is -14.

8. 13

9.
$$9 + t = 3$$
$$-9 + 9 + t = -9 + 3$$
$$t = -6$$

Check: $\dfrac{9 + t = 3}{9 - 6 \ ? \ 3}$
$$3 \ | \ 3 \quad \text{TRUE}$$

The solution is -6.

10. 18

11.
$$13 = -7 + y$$
$$7 + 13 = 7 + (-7) + y$$
$$20 = y$$

Check: $\dfrac{13 = -7 + y}{13 \ ? \ -7 + 20}$
$$13 \ | \ 13 \quad \text{TRUE}$$

The solution is 20.

12. 24

13.
$$-3 + t = -9$$
$$3 + (-3) + t = 3 + (-9)$$
$$t = -6$$

Check: $\dfrac{-3 + t = -9}{-3 + (-6) \ ? \ -9}$
$$-9 \ | \ -9 \quad \text{TRUE}$$

The solution is -6.

14. -15

15.
$$r + \frac{1}{3} = \frac{8}{3}$$
$$r + \frac{1}{3} - \frac{1}{3} = \frac{8}{3} - \frac{1}{3}$$
$$r = \frac{7}{3}$$

Check: $\dfrac{r + \dfrac{1}{3} = \dfrac{8}{3}}{\dfrac{7}{3} + \dfrac{1}{3} \ ? \ \dfrac{8}{3}}$
$$\frac{8}{3} \ \Big| \ \frac{8}{3} \quad \text{TRUE}$$

The solution is $\dfrac{7}{3}$.

16. $-\dfrac{3}{2}$

17.
$$x - \frac{5}{6} = \frac{7}{8}$$
$$x - \frac{5}{6} + \frac{5}{6} = \frac{7}{8} + \frac{5}{6}$$
$$x = \frac{7}{8} \cdot \frac{3}{3} + \frac{5}{6} \cdot \frac{4}{4}$$
$$x = \frac{21}{24} + \frac{20}{24}$$
$$x = \frac{41}{24}$$

Check:
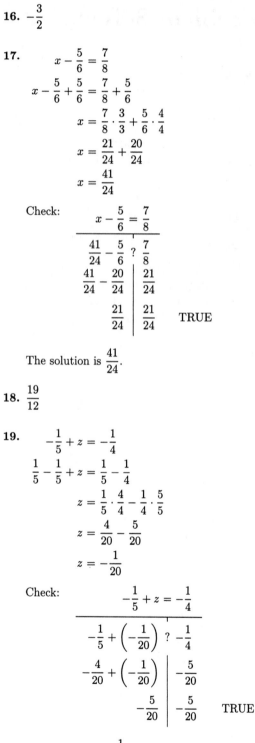

The solution is $\dfrac{41}{24}$.

18. $\dfrac{19}{12}$

19.
$$-\frac{1}{5} + z = -\frac{1}{4}$$
$$\frac{1}{5} - \frac{1}{5} + z = \frac{1}{5} - \frac{1}{4}$$
$$z = \frac{1}{5} \cdot \frac{4}{4} - \frac{1}{4} \cdot \frac{5}{5}$$
$$z = \frac{4}{20} - \frac{5}{20}$$
$$z = -\frac{1}{20}$$

Check:

$$-\frac{1}{5} + z = -\frac{1}{4}$$

$$-\frac{1}{5} + \left(-\frac{1}{20}\right) \;?\; -\frac{1}{4}$$

$$-\frac{4}{20} + \left(-\frac{1}{20}\right) \;\Big|\; -\frac{5}{20}$$

$$-\frac{5}{20} \;\Big|\; -\frac{5}{20} \qquad \text{TRUE}$$

The solution is $-\dfrac{1}{20}$.

20. $-\dfrac{5}{8}$

21.
$$m + 3.9 = 5.4$$
$$m + 3.9 - 3.9 = 5.4 - 3.9$$
$$m = 1.5$$

Check:

$$m + 3.9 = 5.4$$

$$1.5 + 3.9 \;?\; 5.4$$

$$5.4 \;\Big|\; 5.4 \qquad \text{TRUE}$$

The solution is 1.5.

22. 4.7

23.
$$-9.7 = -4.7 + y$$
$$4.7 + (-9.7) = 4.7 + (-4.7) + y$$
$$-5 = y$$

Check:

$$-9.7 = -4.7 + y$$

$$-9.7 \;?\; -4.7 + (-5)$$

$$-9.7 \;\Big|\; -9.7 \qquad \text{TRUE}$$

The solution is -5.

24. -10.6

25.
$$5x = 80$$
$$\frac{5x}{5} = \frac{80}{5} \qquad \text{Dividing by 5 on both sides}$$
$$1 \cdot x = 16 \qquad \text{Simplifying}$$
$$x = 16 \qquad \text{Identity property of 1}$$

Check:

$$5x = 80$$

$$5 \cdot 16 \;?\; 80$$

$$80 \;\Big|\; 80 \qquad \text{TRUE}$$

The solution is 16.

26. 13

27.
$$84 = 7x$$
$$\frac{84}{7} = \frac{7x}{7} \qquad \text{Dividing by 7 on both sides}$$
$$12 = 1 \cdot x$$
$$12 = x$$

Check:

$$84 = 7x$$

$$84 \;?\; 7 \cdot 12$$

$$84 \;\Big|\; 84 \qquad \text{TRUE}$$

The solution is 12.

28. 7

29.
$$-x = 23$$
$$-1 \cdot x = 23$$
$$-1 \cdot (-1 \cdot x) = -1 \cdot 23$$
$$1 \cdot x = -23$$
$$x = -23$$

Check:

$$-x = 23$$

$$-(-23) \;?\; 23$$

$$23 \;\Big|\; 23 \qquad \text{TRUE}$$

The solution is -23.

30. -100

31.
$$-x = -8$$
$$-1 \cdot x = -8$$
$$-1 \cdot (-1 \cdot x) = -1 \cdot (-8)$$
$$1 \cdot x = 8$$
$$x = 8$$

Check:
$$\frac{-x = -8}{}$$
$$-(8) \ ? \ -8$$
$$-8 \ | \ -8 \qquad \text{TRUE}$$

The solution is 8.

32. 68

33.
$$7x = -49$$
$$\frac{7x}{7} = \frac{-49}{7}$$
$$1 \cdot x = -7$$
$$x = -7$$

Check:
$$\frac{7x = -49}{}$$
$$7(-7) \ ? \ -49$$
$$-49 \ | \ -49 \qquad \text{TRUE}$$

The solution is -7.

34. -4

35.
$$-12x = 72$$
$$\frac{-12x}{-12} = \frac{72}{-12}$$
$$1 \cdot x = -6$$
$$x = -6$$

Check:
$$\frac{-12x = 72}{}$$
$$-12(-6) \ ? \ 72$$
$$72 \ | \ 72 \qquad \text{TRUE}$$

The solution is -6.

36. -7

37.
$$-3.4t = -20.4$$
$$\frac{-3.4t}{-3.4} = \frac{-20.4}{-3.4}$$
$$1 \cdot t = 6$$
$$t = 6$$

Check:
$$\frac{-3.4t = -20.4}{}$$
$$-3.4(6) \ ? \ -20.4$$
$$-20.4 \ | \ -20.4 \qquad \text{TRUE}$$

The solution is 6.

38. 8

39.
$$\frac{a}{4} = 12$$
$$\frac{1}{4} \cdot a = 12$$
$$4 \cdot \frac{1}{4} \cdot a = 4 \cdot 12$$
$$a = 48$$

Check:
$$\frac{\frac{a}{4} = 12}{}$$
$$\frac{48}{4} \ ? \ 12$$
$$12 \ | \ 12 \qquad \text{TRUE}$$

The solution is 48.

40. -88

41.
$$\frac{3}{4}x = 27$$
$$\frac{4}{3} \cdot \frac{3}{4}x = \frac{4}{3} \cdot 27$$
$$1 \cdot x = \frac{4 \cdot \cancel{3} \cdot 3 \cdot 3}{\cancel{3} \cdot 1}$$
$$x = 36$$

Check:
$$\frac{\frac{3}{4}x = 27}{}$$
$$\frac{3}{4} \cdot 36 \ ? \ 27$$
$$27 \ | \ 27 \qquad \text{TRUE}$$

The solution is 36.

42. 20

43.
$$\frac{-t}{3} = 7$$
$$3 \cdot \frac{1}{3} \cdot (-t) = 3 \cdot 7$$
$$-t = 21$$
$$-1 \cdot (-1 \cdot t) = -1 \cdot 21$$
$$1 \cdot t = -21$$
$$t = -21$$

Check:
$$\frac{\frac{-t}{3} = 7}{}$$
$$\frac{-(-21)}{3} \ ? \ 7$$
$$\frac{21}{3} \ \Big| $$
$$7 \ | \ 7 \qquad \text{TRUE}$$

The solution is -21.

44. -54

45.

$$\frac{2}{9} = -\frac{t}{4}$$

$$\frac{2}{9} = -\frac{1}{4} \cdot t$$

$$-4\left(\frac{2}{9}\right) = -4\left(-\frac{1}{4} \cdot t\right)$$

$$-\frac{8}{9} = t$$

Check: $\dfrac{2}{9} = -\dfrac{t}{4}$

$$\frac{2}{9} \;?\; \frac{-8/9}{4}$$

$$\left| \; -\left(-\frac{8}{9}\right)\left(\frac{1}{4}\right) \right.$$

$$\frac{8}{36}$$

$$\frac{2}{9} \;\left|\; \frac{2}{9} \right. \qquad \text{TRUE}$$

The solution is $-\dfrac{8}{9}$.

46. $-\dfrac{7}{9}$

47.

$$-\frac{3}{5}r = -\frac{9}{10}$$

$$-\frac{5}{3} \cdot \left(-\frac{3}{5}r\right) = -\frac{5}{3} \cdot \left(-\frac{9}{10}\right)$$

$$r = \frac{\cancel{5} \cdot \cancel{3} \cdot 3}{\cancel{3} \cdot \cancel{5} \cdot 2}$$

$$r = \frac{3}{2}$$

Check: $-\dfrac{3}{5}r = -\dfrac{9}{10}$

$$-\frac{3}{5} \cdot \frac{3}{2} \;?\; -\frac{9}{10}$$

$$-\frac{9}{10} \;\left|\; -\frac{9}{10} \right. \qquad \text{TRUE}$$

The solution is $\dfrac{3}{2}$.

48. $\dfrac{2}{3}$

49.

$$\frac{-3r}{2} = -\frac{27}{4}$$

$$-\frac{3}{2}r = -\frac{27}{4}$$

$$-\frac{2}{3} \cdot \left(-\frac{3}{2}r\right) = -\frac{2}{3} \cdot \left(-\frac{27}{4}\right)$$

$$r = \frac{\cancel{2} \cdot \cancel{3} \cdot 3 \cdot 3}{\cancel{3} \cdot \cancel{2} \cdot 2}$$

$$r = \frac{9}{2}$$

Check: $\dfrac{-3r}{2} = -\dfrac{27}{4}$

$$-\frac{3}{2} \cdot \frac{9}{2} \;?\; -\frac{27}{4}$$

$$-\frac{27}{4} \;\left|\; -\frac{27}{4} \right. \qquad \text{TRUE}$$

The solution is $\dfrac{9}{2}$.

50. -1

51.

$$2.8 + t = -3.1$$

$$2.8 + t - 2.8 = -3.1 - 2.8$$

$$t = -5.9$$

The solution is -5.9.

52. 24

53.

$$-8.2x = 20.5$$

$$\frac{-8.2x}{-8.2} = \frac{20.5}{-8.2}$$

$$x = -2.5$$

The solution is -2.5.

54. -5.5

55.

$$17 = y + 29$$

$$17 - 29 = y + 29 - 29$$

$$-12 = y$$

The solution is -12.

56. -128

57.

$$a - \frac{1}{6} = -\frac{2}{3}$$

$$a - \frac{1}{6} + \frac{1}{6} = -\frac{2}{3} + \frac{1}{6}$$

$$a = -\frac{4}{6} + \frac{1}{6}$$

$$a = -\frac{3}{6}$$

$$a = -\frac{1}{2}$$

The solution is $-\dfrac{1}{2}$.

58. $-\dfrac{14}{9}$

59.
$$-24 = \frac{8x}{5}$$
$$-24 = \frac{8}{5}x$$
$$\frac{5}{8}(-24) = \frac{5}{8} \cdot \frac{8}{5}x$$
$$-\frac{5 \cdot \cancel{8} \cdot 3}{\cancel{8} \cdot 1} = x$$
$$-15 = x$$

The solution is -15.

60. $-\dfrac{1}{2}$

61. $3x + 4x = (3 + 4)x = 7x$

62. $-x + 5$

63. $3x - (4 + 2x) = 3x - 4 - 2x = x - 4$

64. $-5x - 23$

65.

66.

67.

68.

69.
$$-356.788 = -699.034 + t$$
$$699.034 + (-356.788) = 699.034 + (-699.034) + t$$
$$342.246 = t$$

The solution is 342.246.

70. -8655

71.
$$5 + x = 5 + x$$
$$5 + x - 5 = 5 + x - 5$$
$$x = x$$

$x = x$ is true for all real numbers. Thus, all real numbers are solutions.

72. No solution

73.
$$4|x| = 48$$
$$|x| = 12$$

x represents a number whose distance from 0 is 12. Thus, $x = -12$ or $x = 12$.

The solution is -12 or 12.

74. No solution

75. For all x, $0 \cdot x = 0$. Thus, all real numbers are solutions.

76. 0

77.
$$x + 4 = 5 + x$$
$$x + 4 - x = 5 + x - x$$
$$4 = 5$$

Since $4 = 5$ is false, the equation has no solution.

78. -2, 2

79.
$$mx = 9.4m$$
$$\frac{mx}{m} = \frac{9.4m}{m}$$
$$x = 9.4$$

The solution is 9.4.

80. 4

81.
$$\frac{7cx}{2a} = \frac{21}{a} \cdot c$$
$$\frac{7c}{2a} \cdot x = \frac{21}{a} \cdot c$$
$$\frac{2a}{7c} \cdot \frac{7c}{2a} \cdot x = \frac{2a}{7c} \cdot \frac{21}{a} \cdot \frac{c}{1}$$
$$x = \frac{2 \cdot \cancel{a} \cdot 3 \cdot \cancel{7} \cdot \cancel{c}}{\cancel{7} \cdot \cancel{c} \cdot \cancel{a} \cdot 1}$$
$$x = 6$$

The solution is 6.

82. 2

83.
$$5a = ax - 3a$$
$$5a + 3a = ax - 3a + 3a$$
$$8a = ax$$
$$\frac{8a}{a} = \frac{ax}{a}$$
$$8 = x$$

The solution is 8.

84. -13, 13

85.
$$x - 4720 = 1634$$
$$x - 4720 + 4720 = 1634 + 4720$$
$$x = 6354$$
$$x + 4720 = 6354 + 4720$$
$$x + 4720 = 11,074$$

86. 250

87.

Exercise Set 2.2

1.
$$4x + 5 = 41$$
$$4x + 5 - 5 = 41 - 5 \qquad \text{Subtracting 5 on both sides}$$
$$4x = 36 \qquad \text{Simplifying}$$
$$\frac{4x}{4} = \frac{36}{4} \qquad \text{Dividing by 4 on both sides}$$
$$x = 9 \qquad \text{Simplifying}$$

Check: $\quad 4x + 5 = 41$

$$4 \cdot 9 + 5 \ ? \ 41$$
$$36 + 5$$
$$41 \ \big| \ 41 \qquad \text{TRUE}$$

The solution is 9.

2. 9

3.
$$5x - 8 = 27$$
$$5x - 8 + 8 = 27 + 8 \qquad \text{Adding 8 on both sides}$$
$$5x = 35$$
$$\frac{5x}{5} = \frac{35}{5} \qquad \text{Dividing by 5 on both sides}$$
$$x = 7$$

Check: $\quad 5x - 8 = 27$

$$5 \cdot 7 - 8 \ ? \ 27$$
$$35 - 8$$
$$27 \ \big| \ 27 \qquad \text{TRUE}$$

The solution is 7.

4. 3

5.
$$7x + 2 = -54$$
$$7x + 2 - 2 = -54 - 2$$
$$7x = -56$$
$$\frac{7x}{7} = \frac{-56}{7}$$
$$x = -8$$

Check: $\quad 7x + 2 = -54$

$$7(-8) + 2 \ ? \ -54$$
$$-56 + 2$$
$$-54 \ \big| \ -54 \qquad \text{TRUE}$$

The solution is -8.

6. -6

7.
$$-39 = 1 + 8x$$
$$-39 - 1 = 1 + 8x - 1$$
$$-40 = 8x$$
$$\frac{-40}{8} = \frac{8x}{8}$$
$$-5 = x$$

Check: $\quad -39 = 1 + 8x$

$$-39 \ ? \ 1 + 8(-5)$$
$$1 - 40$$
$$-39 \ \big| \ -39 \qquad \text{TRUE}$$

The solution is -5.

8. -11

9.
$$9 - 4x = 37$$
$$9 - 4x - 9 = 37 - 9$$
$$-4x = 28$$
$$\frac{-4x}{-4} = \frac{28}{-4}$$
$$x = -7$$

Check: $\quad 9 - 4x = 37$

$$9 - 4(-7) \ ? \ 37$$
$$9 + 28$$
$$37 \ \big| \ 37 \qquad \text{TRUE}$$

The solution is -7.

10. -24

11.
$$-7x - 24 = -129$$
$$-7x - 24 + 24 = -129 + 24$$
$$-7x = -105$$
$$\frac{-7x}{-7} = \frac{-105}{-7}$$
$$x = 15$$

Check: $\quad -7x - 24 = -129$

$$-7 \cdot 15 - 24 \ ? \ -129$$
$$-105 - 24$$
$$-129 \ \big| \ -129 \qquad \text{TRUE}$$

The solution is 15.

12. 19

13.
$$36 = 5x + 7x$$
$$36 = 12x \qquad \text{Combining like terms}$$
$$\frac{36}{12} = \frac{12x}{12} \qquad \text{Dividing by 12 on both sides}$$
$$3 = x$$

Check: $\quad 36 = 5x + 7x$

$$36 \ ? \ 5 \cdot 3 + 7 \cdot 3$$
$$15 + 21$$
$$36 \ \big| \ 36 \qquad \text{TRUE}$$

The solution is 3.

14. 5

15.
$$27 - 6x = 99$$
$$27 - 6x - 27 = 99 - 27$$
$$-6x = 72$$
$$\frac{-6x}{-6} = \frac{72}{-6}$$
$$x = -12$$

Check:
$$\begin{array}{c|c} \multicolumn{2}{c}{27 - 6x = 99} \\ \hline 27 - 6(-12) \ ? \ 99 & \\ 27 + 72 & \\ 99 & 99 \quad \text{TRUE} \end{array}$$

The solution is -12.

16. 3

17.
$$-2a + 5a = 24$$
$$3a = 24$$
$$\frac{3a}{3} = \frac{24}{3}$$
$$a = 8$$

Check:
$$\begin{array}{c|c} \multicolumn{2}{c}{-2a + 5a = 24} \\ \hline -2 \cdot 8 + 5 \cdot 8 \ ? \ 24 & \\ -16 + 40 & \\ 24 & 24 \quad \text{TRUE} \end{array}$$

The solution is 8.

18. -4

19.
$$10.2y - 7.3y = -58$$
$$2.9y = -58$$
$$\frac{2.9y}{2.9} = \frac{-58}{2.9}$$
$$y = -\frac{58}{2.9}$$
$$y = -20$$

Check:
$$\begin{array}{c|c} \multicolumn{2}{c}{10.2y - 7.3y = -58} \\ \hline 10.2(-20) - 7.3(-20) \ ? \ -58 & \\ -204 + 146 & \\ -58 & -58 \quad \text{TRUE} \end{array}$$

The solution is -20.

20. -20

21.
$$x + \frac{1}{3}x = 8$$
$$\left(1 + \frac{1}{3}\right)x = 8$$
$$\frac{4}{3}x = 8$$
$$\frac{3}{4} \cdot \frac{4}{3}x = \frac{3}{4} \cdot 8$$
$$x = 6$$

Check:
$$\begin{array}{c|c} \multicolumn{2}{c}{x + \frac{1}{3}x = 8} \\ \hline 6 + \frac{1}{3} \cdot 6 \ ? \ 8 & \\ 6 + 2 & \\ 8 & 8 \quad \text{TRUE} \end{array}$$

The solution is 6.

22. 8

23.
$$8y - 35 = 3y$$
$$8y = 3y + 35 \quad \text{Adding 35 and simplifying}$$
$$8y - 3y = 35 \quad \text{Subtracting } 3y \text{ and simplifying}$$
$$5y = 35 \quad \text{Collecting like terms}$$
$$\frac{5y}{5} = \frac{35}{5} \quad \text{Dividing by 5}$$
$$y = 7$$

Check:
$$\begin{array}{c|c} \multicolumn{2}{c}{8y - 35 = 3y} \\ \hline 8 \cdot 7 - 35 \ ? \ 3 \cdot 7 & \\ 56 - 35 & 21 \\ 21 & 21 \quad \text{TRUE} \end{array}$$

The solution is 7.

24. -3

25.
$$6x - 5 = 7 + 2x$$
$$6x - 5 - 2x = 7 + 2x - 2x \quad \text{Subtracting } 2x \text{ on both sides}$$
$$4x - 5 = 7 \quad \text{Simplifying}$$
$$4x - 5 + 5 = 7 + 5 \quad \text{Adding 5 on both sides}$$
$$4x = 12 \quad \text{Simplifying}$$
$$\frac{4x}{4} = \frac{12}{4} \quad \text{Dividing by 4 on both sides}$$
$$x = 3$$

Check:
$$\begin{array}{c|c} \multicolumn{2}{c}{6x - 5 = 7 + 2x} \\ \hline 6 \cdot 3 - 5 \ ? \ 7 + 2 \cdot 3 & \\ 18 - 5 & 7 + 6 \\ 13 & 13 \quad \text{TRUE} \end{array}$$

The solution is 3.

26. 5

27.
$$6x + 3 = 2x + 11$$
$$6x - 2x = 11 - 3$$
$$4x = 8$$
$$\frac{4x}{4} = \frac{8}{4}$$
$$x = 2$$

Check:
$$
\begin{array}{c|c}
\multicolumn{2}{c}{6x + 3 = 2x + 11} \\
\hline
6 \cdot 2 + 3 \ ? \ 2 \cdot 2 + 11 \\
12 + 3 \ \big| \ 4 + 11 \\
15 \ \big| \ 15 \quad \text{TRUE}
\end{array}
$$

The solution is 2.

28. 4

29.
$$
\begin{aligned}
5 - 2x &= 3x - 7x + 25 \\
5 - 2x &= -4x + 25 \\
4x - 2x &= 25 - 5 \\
2x &= 20 \\
\frac{2x}{2} &= \frac{20}{2} \\
x &= 10
\end{aligned}
$$

Check:
$$
\begin{array}{c|c}
\multicolumn{2}{c}{5 - 2x = 3x - 7x + 25} \\
\hline
5 - 2 \cdot 10 \ ? \ 3 \cdot 10 - 7 \cdot 10 + 25 \\
5 - 20 \ \big| \ 30 - 70 + 25 \\
-15 \ \big| \ -40 + 25 \\
-15 \ \big| \ -15 \quad \text{TRUE}
\end{array}
$$

The solution is 10.

30. 10

31.
$$
\begin{aligned}
4 + 3x - 6 &= 3x + 2 - x \\
3x - 2 &= 2x + 2 \qquad \text{Combining like terms} \\
& \qquad\qquad\qquad \text{on each side} \\
3x - 2x &= 2 + 2 \\
x &= 4
\end{aligned}
$$

Check:
$$
\begin{array}{c|c}
\multicolumn{2}{c}{4 + 3x - 6 = 3x + 2 - x} \\
\hline
4 + 3 \cdot 4 - 6 \ ? \ 3 \cdot 4 + 2 - 4 \\
4 + 12 - 6 \ \big| \ 12 + 2 - 4 \\
16 - 6 \ \big| \ 14 - 4 \\
10 \ \big| \ 10 \quad \text{TRUE}
\end{array}
$$

The solution is 4.

32. 0

33.
$$
\begin{aligned}
4y - 4 + y + 24 &= 6y + 20 - 4y \\
5y + 20 &= 2y + 20 \\
5y - 2y &= 20 - 20 \\
3y &= 0 \\
y &= 0
\end{aligned}
$$

Check:
$$
\begin{array}{c|c}
\multicolumn{2}{c}{4y - 4 + y + 24 = 6y + 20 - 4y} \\
\hline
4 \cdot 0 - 4 + 0 + 24 \ ? \ 6 \cdot 0 + 20 - 4 \cdot 0 \\
0 - 4 + 0 + 24 \ \big| \ 0 + 20 - 0 \\
20 \ \big| \ 20 \quad \text{TRUE}
\end{array}
$$

The solution is 0.

34. 7

35. $\dfrac{2}{3} + \dfrac{1}{4}t = 6$

The number 12 is the least common denominator, so we multiply by 12 on both sides.

$$
\begin{aligned}
12\left(\frac{2}{3} + \frac{1}{4}t\right) &= 12 \cdot 6 \\
12 \cdot \frac{2}{3} + 12 \cdot \frac{1}{4}t &= 72 \\
8 + 3t &= 72 \\
3t &= 72 - 8 \\
3t &= 64 \\
t &= \frac{64}{3}
\end{aligned}
$$

Check:
$$
\begin{array}{c|c}
\multicolumn{2}{c}{\dfrac{2}{3} + \dfrac{1}{4}t = 6} \\
\hline
\dfrac{2}{3} + \dfrac{1}{4}\left(\dfrac{64}{3}\right) \ ? \ 6 \\
\dfrac{2}{3} + \dfrac{16}{3} \\
\dfrac{18}{3} \\
6 \ \big| \ 6 \quad \text{TRUE}
\end{array}
$$

The solution is $\dfrac{64}{3}$.

36. $-\dfrac{2}{3}$

37. $\dfrac{2}{3} + 3y = 5y - \dfrac{2}{15}$

The number 15 is the least common denominator, so we multiply by 15 on both sides.

$$
\begin{aligned}
15\left(\frac{2}{3} + 3y\right) &= 15\left(5y - \frac{2}{15}\right) \\
15 \cdot \frac{2}{3} + 15 \cdot 3y &= 15 \cdot 5y - 15 \cdot \frac{2}{15} \\
10 + 45y &= 75y - 2 \\
10 + 2 &= 75y - 45y \\
12 &= 30y \\
\frac{12}{30} &= y \\
\frac{2}{5} &= y
\end{aligned}
$$

Check:
$$
\begin{array}{c|c}
\multicolumn{2}{c}{\dfrac{2}{3} + 3y = 5y - \dfrac{2}{15}} \\
\hline
\dfrac{2}{3} + 3 \cdot \dfrac{2}{5} \ ? \ 5 \cdot \dfrac{2}{5} - \dfrac{2}{15} \\
\dfrac{2}{3} + \dfrac{6}{5} \ \big| \ 2 - \dfrac{2}{15} \\
\dfrac{10}{15} + \dfrac{18}{15} \ \big| \ \dfrac{30}{15} - \dfrac{2}{15} \\
\dfrac{28}{15} \ \big| \ \dfrac{28}{15} \quad \text{TRUE}
\end{array}
$$

The solution is $\dfrac{2}{5}$.

38. -3

39.
$$\frac{1}{3}x + \frac{2}{5} = \frac{4}{15} + \frac{3}{5}x - \frac{2}{3}$$

The number 15 is the least common denominator, so we multiply by 15 on both sides.

$$15\left(\frac{1}{3}x + \frac{2}{5}\right) = 15\left(\frac{4}{15} + \frac{3}{5}x - \frac{2}{3}\right)$$

$$15 \cdot \frac{1}{3}x + 15 \cdot \frac{2}{5} = 15 \cdot \frac{4}{15} + 15 \cdot \frac{3}{5}x - 15 \cdot \frac{2}{3}$$

$$5x + 6 = 4 + 9x - 10$$
$$5x + 6 = -6 + 9x$$
$$5x - 9x = -6 - 6$$
$$-4x = -12$$
$$\frac{-4x}{-4} = \frac{-12}{-4}$$
$$x = 3$$

Check:
$$\frac{1}{3}x + \frac{2}{5} = \frac{4}{15} + \frac{3}{5}x - \frac{2}{3}$$

$$\begin{array}{c|c} \frac{1}{3} \cdot 3 + \frac{2}{5} \;?\; \frac{4}{15} + \frac{3}{5} \cdot 3 - \frac{2}{3} \\[4pt] 1 + \frac{2}{5} & \frac{4}{15} + \frac{9}{5} - \frac{2}{3} \\[4pt] \frac{5}{5} + \frac{2}{5} & \frac{4}{15} + \frac{27}{15} - \frac{10}{15} \\[4pt] \frac{7}{5} & \frac{21}{15} \\[4pt] \frac{7}{5} & \frac{7}{5} \qquad \text{TRUE} \end{array}$$

The solution is 3.

40. -3

41.
$$2.1x + 45.2 = 3.2 - 8.4x$$

Greatest number of decimal places is 1

$$10(2.1x + 45.2) = 10(3.2 - 8.4x)$$

Multiplying by 10 to clear decimals

$$10(2.1x) + 10(45.2) = 10(3.2) - 10(8.4x)$$
$$21x + 452 = 32 - 84x$$
$$21x + 84x = 32 - 452$$
$$105x = -420$$
$$x = \frac{-420}{105}$$
$$x = -4$$

Check:
$$2.1x + 45.2 = 3.2 - 8.4x$$

$$\begin{array}{c|c} 2.1(-4) + 45.2 \;?\; 3.2 - 8.4(-4) \\[4pt] -8.4 + 45.2 & 3.2 + 33.6 \\[4pt] 36.8 & 36.8 \qquad \text{TRUE} \end{array}$$

The solution is -4.

42. $\dfrac{5}{3}$

43.
$$1.03 - 0.6x = 0.71 - 0.2x$$

Greatest number of decimal places is 2

$$100(1.03 - 0.6x) = 100(0.71 - 0.2x)$$

Multiplying by 100 to clear decimals

$$100(1.03) - 100(0.6x) = 100(0.71) - 100(0.2x)$$
$$103 - 60x = 71 - 20x$$
$$32 = 40x$$
$$\frac{32}{40} = x$$
$$\frac{4}{5} = x, \text{ or}$$
$$0.8 = x$$

Check:
$$1.03 - 0.6x = 0.71 - 0.2x$$

$$\begin{array}{c|c} 1.03 - 0.6(0.8) \;?\; 0.71 - 0.2(0.8) \\[4pt] 1.03 - 0.48 & 0.71 - 0.16 \\[4pt] 0.55 & 0.55 \qquad \text{TRUE} \end{array}$$

The solution is $\dfrac{4}{5}$, or 0.8.

44. 1

45.
$$\frac{2}{5}x - \frac{3}{2}x = \frac{3}{4}x + 2$$

The least common denominator is 20.

$$20\left(\frac{2}{5}x - \frac{3}{2}x\right) = 20\left(\frac{3}{4}x + 2\right)$$

$$20 \cdot \frac{2}{5}x - 20 \cdot \frac{3}{2}x = 20 \cdot \frac{3}{4}x + 20 \cdot 2$$

$$8x - 30x = 15x + 40$$
$$-22x = 15x + 40$$
$$-22x - 15x = 40$$
$$-37x = 40$$
$$\frac{-37x}{-37} = \frac{40}{-37}$$
$$x = -\frac{40}{37}$$

Check:
$$\frac{2}{5}x - \frac{3}{2}x = \frac{3}{4}x + 2$$

$$\begin{array}{c|c} \frac{2}{5}\left(-\frac{40}{37}\right) - \frac{3}{2}\left(-\frac{40}{37}\right) \;?\; \frac{3}{4}\left(-\frac{40}{37}\right) + 2 \\[4pt] -\frac{16}{37} + \frac{60}{37} & -\frac{30}{37} + \frac{74}{37} \\[4pt] \frac{44}{37} & \frac{44}{37} \qquad \text{TRUE} \end{array}$$

The solution is $-\dfrac{40}{37}$.

46. $\dfrac{32}{7}$

47. $7(2a - 1) = 21$

$\quad 14a - 7 = 21$ Using the distributive law

$\quad\quad 14a = 21 + 7$ Adding 7

$\quad\quad 14a = 28$

$\quad\quad\quad a = 2$ Dividing by 14

Check: $\dfrac{7(2a - 1) = 21}{}$

$\quad\quad 7(2 \cdot 2 - 1)\ ?\ 21$

$\quad\quad\quad 7(4 - 1)\ \big|$

$\quad\quad\quad\quad 7 \cdot 3\ \big|$

$\quad\quad\quad\quad\quad 21\ \big|\ 21$ TRUE

The solution is 2.

48. 1

49. $2(3 + 4m) - 9 = 45$

$\quad 6 + 8m - 9 = 45$

$\quad\quad 8m - 3 = 45$ Combining like terms

$\quad\quad\quad 8m = 45 + 3$

$\quad\quad\quad 8m = 48$

$\quad\quad\quad\ m = 6$

Check: $\dfrac{2(3 + 4m) - 9 = 45}{}$

$\quad 2(3 + 4 \cdot 6) - 9\ ?\ 45$

$\quad\quad 2(3 + 24) - 9\ \big|$

$\quad\quad\quad 2 \cdot 27 - 9\ \big|$

$\quad\quad\quad\quad 54 - 9\ \big|$

$\quad\quad\quad\quad\quad 45\ \big|\ 45$ TRUE

The solution is 6.

50. 9

51. $5r - (2r + 8) = 16$

$\quad 5r - 2r - 8 = 16$

$\quad\quad 3r - 8 = 16$ Combining like terms

$\quad\quad\quad 3r = 16 + 8$

$\quad\quad\quad 3r = 24$

$\quad\quad\quad\ r = 8$

Check: $\dfrac{5r - (2r + 8) = 16}{}$

$\quad 5 \cdot 8 - (2 \cdot 8 + 8)\ ?\ 16$

$\quad\quad 40 - (16 + 8)\ \big|$

$\quad\quad\quad 40 - 24\ \big|$

$\quad\quad\quad\quad 16\ \big|\ 16$ TRUE

The solution is 8.

52. 8

53. $10 - 3(2x - 1) = 1$

$\quad 10 - 6x + 3 = 1$

$\quad\quad 13 - 6x = 1$

$\quad\quad\quad -6x = 1 - 13$

$\quad\quad\quad -6x = -12$

$\quad\quad\quad\quad x = 2$

Check: $\dfrac{10 - 3(2x - 1) = 1}{}$

$\quad 10 - 3(2 \cdot 2 - 1)\ ?\ 1$

$\quad\quad 10 - 3(4 - 1)\ \big|$

$\quad\quad\quad 10 - 3 \cdot 3\ \big|$

$\quad\quad\quad\quad 10 - 9\ \big|$

$\quad\quad\quad\quad\quad 1\ \big|\ 1$ TRUE

The solution is 2.

54. 17

55. $3(t - 2) = 9(t + 2)$

$\quad 3t - 6 = 9t + 18$

$\quad -6 - 18 = 9t - 3t$

$\quad\quad -24 = 6t$

$\quad\quad\ -4 = t$

Check: $\dfrac{3(t - 2) = 9(t + 2)}{}$

$\quad 3(-4 - 2)\ ?\ 9(-4 + 2)$

$\quad\quad 3(-6)\ \big|\ 9(-2)$

$\quad\quad\ -18\ \big|\ -18$ TRUE

The solution is -4.

56. $-\dfrac{5}{3}$

57. $7(5x - 2) = 6(6x - 1)$

$\quad 35x - 14 = 36x - 6$

$\quad -14 + 6 = 36x - 35x$

$\quad\quad -8 = x$

Check:

$\dfrac{7(5x - 2) = 6(6x - 1)}{}$

$\quad 7(5(-8) - 2)\ ?\ 6(6(-8) - 1)$

$\quad\quad 7(-40 - 2)\ \big|\ 6(-48 - 1)$

$\quad\quad\quad 7(-42)\ \big|\ 6(-49)$

$\quad\quad\quad\ -294\ \big|\ -294$ TRUE

The solution is -8.

58. -12

59. $19 - (2x + 3) = 2(x + 3) + x$

$\quad 19 - 2x - 3 = 2x + 6 + x$

$\quad\quad 16 - 2x = 3x + 6$

$\quad\quad 16 - 6 = 3x + 2x$

$\quad\quad\quad 10 = 5x$

$\quad\quad\quad\ 2 = x$

Check: $\dfrac{19 - (2x + 3) = 2(x + 3) + x}{}$

$\quad 19 - (2 \cdot 2 + 3)\ ?\ 2(2 + 3) + 2$

$\quad\quad 19 - (4 + 3)\ \big|\ 2 \cdot 5 + 2$

$\quad\quad\quad 19 - 7\ \big|\ 10 + 2$

$\quad\quad\quad\quad 12\ \big|\ 12$ TRUE

The solution is 2.

60. 1

61. $\dfrac{1}{3}(6x + 24) - 20 = -\dfrac{1}{4}(12x - 72)$

$\dfrac{1}{3}\cdot 6x + \dfrac{1}{3}\cdot 24 - 20 = -\dfrac{1}{4}\cdot 12x - \dfrac{1}{4}(-72)$

$\qquad 2x + 8 - 20 = -3x + 18$

$\qquad\qquad 2x - 12 = -3x + 18$

$\qquad\qquad\qquad 5x = 30$

$\qquad\qquad\qquad\quad x = 6$

The check is left to the student. The solution is 6.

62. 5

63. $\dfrac{4}{5}(3x + 4) = 10$

The least common denominator is 5.

$5\cdot\dfrac{4}{5}(3x+4) = 5\cdot 10$

$\qquad 4(3x + 4) = 50$

$\qquad 12x + 16 = 50$

$\qquad\qquad 12x = 34$ Subtracting 16 on both sides

$\qquad\qquad x = \dfrac{34}{12}$ Dividing by 12 on both sides

$\qquad\qquad x = \dfrac{17}{6}$ Simplifying

Check: $\qquad \dfrac{4}{5}(3x + 4) = 10$

$$\dfrac{4}{5}\left(3\cdot\dfrac{17}{6} + 4\right) \;?\; 10$$

$$\dfrac{4}{5}\left(\dfrac{17}{2} + 4\right)$$

$$\dfrac{4}{5}\cdot\dfrac{25}{2}$$

$$10 \;\bigg|\; 10 \quad\text{TRUE}$$

The solution is $\dfrac{17}{6}$.

64. $\dfrac{31}{2}$

65. $\dfrac{3}{2}(2x + 5) + \dfrac{1}{4} = -\dfrac{7}{2}$

The least common denominator is 4.

$4\left[\dfrac{3}{2}(2x + 5) + \dfrac{1}{4}\right] = 4\left(-\dfrac{7}{2}\right)$

$4\cdot\dfrac{3}{2}(2x + 5) + 4\cdot\dfrac{1}{4} = -14$

$\qquad 6(2x + 5) + 1 = -14$

$\qquad 12x + 30 + 1 = -14$

$\qquad\qquad 12x + 31 = -14$

$\qquad\qquad\qquad 12x = -45$

$\qquad\qquad\qquad\quad x = \dfrac{-45}{12}$

$\qquad\qquad\qquad\quad x = -\dfrac{15}{4}$

Check: $\qquad \dfrac{3}{2}(2x + 5) + \dfrac{1}{4} = -\dfrac{7}{2}$

$$\dfrac{3}{2}\left(2\left(-\dfrac{15}{4}\right) + 5\right) + \dfrac{1}{4} \;?\; -\dfrac{7}{2}$$

$$\dfrac{3}{2}\left(-\dfrac{15}{2} + 5\right) + \dfrac{1}{4}$$

$$\dfrac{3}{2}\left(-\dfrac{5}{2}\right) + \dfrac{1}{4}$$

$$-\dfrac{15}{4} + \dfrac{1}{4}$$

$$-\dfrac{14}{4}$$

$$-\dfrac{7}{2} \;\bigg|\; -\dfrac{7}{2} \quad\text{TRUE}$$

The solution is $-\dfrac{15}{4}$.

66. $\dfrac{16}{15}$

67. $\quad 0.7(3x + 6) = 1.1 - (x + 2)$

$\qquad 2.1x + 4.2 = 1.1 - x - 2$

$\quad 10(2.1x + 4.2) = 10(1.1 - x - 2)$ Clearing decimals

$\qquad 21x + 42 = 11 - 10x - 20$

$\qquad 21x + 42 = -10x - 9$

$\qquad 21x + 10x = -9 - 42$

$\qquad\qquad 31x = -51$

$\qquad\qquad\quad x = -\dfrac{51}{31}$

The check is left to the student. The solution is $-\dfrac{51}{31}$.

68. $\dfrac{39}{14}$

69. $\quad a + (a - 3) = (a + 2) - (a + 1)$

$\qquad a + a - 3 = a + 2 - a - 1$

$\qquad\quad 2a - 3 = 1$

$\qquad\qquad 2a = 1 + 3$

$\qquad\qquad 2a = 4$

$\qquad\qquad\quad a = 2$

Check: $\dfrac{a + (a - 3) = (a + 2) - (a + 1)}{}$

$$2 + (2 - 3) \ ? \ (2 + 2) - (2 + 1)$$

$$\begin{array}{c|c} 2 - 1 & 4 - 3 \\ 1 & 1 \end{array} \qquad \text{TRUE}$$

The solution is 2.

70. -7.4

71. Do the long division. The answer is negative.

$$\begin{array}{r} 6.5 \\ 3.4_\wedge \overline{\smash{\big)}\ 2\,2\ 2.\,1_\wedge 0} \\ \underline{2\,0\ 4} \\ 1\,7\ 0 \\ \underline{1\,7\ 0} \\ 0 \end{array}$$

$$-22.1 \div 3.4 = -6.5$$

72. $7(x - 3 - 2y)$

73. Since -15 is to the left of -13 on the number line, -15 is less than -13, so $-15 < -13$.

74. -14

75. ◈

76. ◈

77. ◈

78. ◈

79. $8.43x - 2.5(3.2 - 0.7x) = -3.455x + 9.04$

$$8.43x - 8 + 1.75x = -3.455x + 9.04$$

$$10.18x - 8 = -3.455x + 9.04$$

$$10.18x + 3.455x = 9.04 + 8$$

$$13.635x = 17.04$$

$$x = 1.\overline{2497}$$

The solution is $1.\overline{2497}$.

80. 4.4233464

81. $-2[3(x - 2) + 4] = 4(1 - x) + 8$

$$-2[3x - 6 + 4] = 4 - 4x + 8$$

$$-2[3x - 2] = 12 - 4x$$

$$-6x + 4 = 12 - 4x$$

$$4 - 12 = -4x + 6x$$

$$-8 = 2x$$

$$-4 = x$$

The solution is -4.

82. $-\dfrac{7}{2}$

83. $3(x + 4) = 3(4 + x)$

$$3x + 12 = 12 + 3x$$

$$3x + 12 - 12 = 12 + 3x - 12$$

$$3x = 3x$$

Since $3x = 3x$ is true for all real numbers, all real numbers are solutions.

84. $\dfrac{837,353}{1929}$

85. $2x(x + 5) - 3(x^2 + 2x - 1) = 9 - 5x - x^2$

$$2x^2 + 10x - 3x^2 - 6x + 3 = 9 - 5x - x^2$$

$$-x^2 + 4x + 3 = 9 - 5x - x^2$$

$$4x + 3 = 9 - 5x \quad \text{Adding } x^2$$

$$4x + 5x = 9 - 3$$

$$9x = 6$$

$$x = \dfrac{2}{3}$$

The solution is $\dfrac{2}{3}$.

86. -2

87. $9 - 3x = 2(5 - 2x) - (1 - 5x)$

$$9 - 3x = 10 - 4x - 1 + 5x$$

$$9 - 3x = 9 + x$$

$$9 - 9 = x + 3x$$

$$0 = 4x$$

$$0 = x$$

The solution is 0.

88. 0

89. $\dfrac{x}{14} - \dfrac{5x + 2}{49} = \dfrac{3x - 4}{7}$

$$98\left(\dfrac{x}{14} - \dfrac{5x + 2}{49}\right) = 98\left(\dfrac{3x - 4}{7}\right)$$

$$98 \cdot \dfrac{x}{14} - 98\left(\dfrac{5x + 2}{49}\right) = 42x - 56$$

$$7x - 10x - 4 = 42x - 56$$

$$-3x - 4 = 42x - 56$$

$$-4 + 56 = 42x + 3x$$

$$52 = 45x$$

$$\dfrac{52}{45} = x$$

The solution is $\dfrac{52}{45}$.

90. -2

Exercise Set 2.3

1. We substitute 1900 for a and calculate b.
$$b = 30a = 30 \cdot 1900 = 57{,}000$$
The minimum furnace output is 57,000 Btu's.

2. 125,000 Btu's

3. We substitute 3 for s and calculate A.
$$A = 6s^2 = 6 \cdot 3^2 = 6 \cdot 9 = 54$$
The surface area is 54 in^2.

4. 1423

5. Substitute 30 for I and 115 for V and calculate P.
$$P = I \cdot V = 30 \cdot 115 = 3450$$
The wattage is 3450 watts.

6. $\dfrac{43}{3}$ m

7. Enter $y = 0.5x^4 + 3.45x^3 - 96.65x^2 + 347.7x$. Then use a table set in Ask Mode to find the desired values.

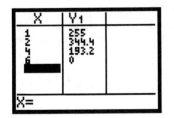

After 1 hr, 255 mg of ibuprofen remain; after 2 hr, 344.4 mg remain; after 4 hr, 193.2 mg remain; and after 6 hr, 0 mg remain.

8. 42, 90, 132, 210

9. $A = bh$
$$\frac{A}{h} = \frac{bh}{h} \qquad \text{Dividing by } h$$
$$\frac{A}{h} = b$$

10. $h = \dfrac{A}{b}$

11. $d = rt$
$$\frac{d}{t} = \frac{rt}{t} \qquad \text{Dividing by } t$$
$$\frac{d}{t} = r$$

12. $t = \dfrac{d}{r}$

13. $I = Prt$
$$\frac{I}{rt} = \frac{Prt}{rt} \qquad \text{Dividing by } rt$$
$$\frac{I}{rt} = P$$

14. $t = \dfrac{I}{Pr}$

15. $H = 65 - m$
$$H + m = 65 \qquad \text{Adding } m$$
$$m = 65 - H \quad \text{Subtracting } H$$

16. $h = d + 64$

17. $P = 2l + 2w$
$$P - 2w = 2l + 2w - 2w \qquad \text{Subtracting } 2w$$
$$P - 2w = 2l$$
$$\frac{P - 2w}{2} = \frac{2l}{2} \qquad \text{Dividing by } 2$$
$$\frac{P - 2w}{2} = l$$

18. $w = \dfrac{P - 2l}{2}$

19. $A = \pi r^2$
$$\frac{A}{r^2} = \frac{\pi r^2}{r^2}$$
$$\frac{A}{r^2} = \pi$$

20. $r^2 = \dfrac{A}{\pi}$

21. $A = \dfrac{1}{2}bh$
$$2A = 2 \cdot \frac{1}{2}bh \qquad \text{Multiplying by } 2$$
$$2A = bh$$
$$\frac{2A}{b} = \frac{bh}{b} \qquad \text{Dividing by } h$$
$$\frac{2A}{b} = h$$

22. $b = \dfrac{2A}{h}$

23. $E = mc^2$
$$\frac{E}{c^2} = \frac{mc^2}{c^2} \qquad \text{Dividing by } c^2$$
$$\frac{E}{c^2} = m$$

24. $c^2 = \dfrac{E}{m}$

25.
$$Q = \frac{c+d}{2}$$

$$2Q = 2 \cdot \frac{c+d}{2} \qquad \text{Multiplying by 2}$$

$$2Q = c+d$$
$$2Q - c = c+d-c \qquad \text{Subtracting } c$$
$$2Q - c = d$$

26. $p = 2Q + q$

27.
$$A = \frac{a+b+c}{3}$$

$$3A = 3 \cdot \frac{a+b+c}{3} \qquad \text{Multiplying by 3}$$

$$3A = a+b+c$$
$$3A - a - c = a+b+c-a-c \qquad \text{Subtracting } a \text{ and } c$$

$$3A - a - c = b$$

28. $c = 3A - a - b$

29.
$$M = \frac{A}{s}$$

$$s \cdot M = s \cdot \frac{A}{s} \qquad \text{Multiplying by } s$$

$$sM = A$$

30. $b = \dfrac{Pc}{a}$

31.
$$Ax + By = C$$

$$Ax + By - Ax = C - Ax \qquad \text{Subtracting } Ax$$
$$By = C - Ax$$

$$\frac{By}{B} = \frac{C - Ax}{B} \qquad \text{Dividing by } B$$

$$y = \frac{C - Ax}{B}$$

32. $x = \dfrac{C - By}{A}$

33.
$$A = \frac{\pi r^2 S}{360}$$

$$\frac{360}{\pi r^2} \cdot A = \frac{360}{\pi r^2} \cdot \frac{\pi r^2 S}{360}$$

$$\frac{360}{\pi r^2} = S$$

34. $P = \dfrac{A}{1 + rt}$

35.
$$A = \frac{1}{2}ah + \frac{1}{2}bh$$

$$2A = 2\left(\frac{1}{2}ah + \frac{1}{2}bh\right)$$

$$2A = ah + bh$$
$$2A = h(a+b)$$
$$\frac{2A}{a+b} = h$$

36. $L = \dfrac{Nr + 400W - NR}{400}$

37. We multiply from left to right:
$$7(-3)2 = (-21)2 = -42$$

38. $-\dfrac{3}{5}$

39.
$$10 \div (-2) \cdot 5 - 4 = -5 \cdot 5 - 4 \qquad \text{Dividing}$$
$$= -25 - 4 \qquad \text{Multiplying}$$
$$= -29 \qquad \text{Subtracting}$$

40. 30

41. ◈

42. ◈

43. ◈

44. ◈

45. First convert w lb to kilograms:
$$w \text{ lb} \cdot \frac{1 \text{ kg}}{2.2046 \text{ lb}} = \frac{w}{2.2046} \text{ kg}$$
Then convert h in. to centimeters:
$$h \text{ in.} \cdot \frac{1 \text{ cm}}{0.3937 \text{ in.}} = \frac{h}{0.3937} \text{ cm}$$
Now rewrite the formula using these converted values:
$$K = 917 + 6\left(\frac{w}{2.2046} + \frac{h}{0.3937} - a\right)$$

46. 35

47.
$$c = \frac{w}{a} \cdot d$$

$$ac = a \cdot \frac{w}{a} \cdot d$$

$$ac = wd$$

$$a = \frac{wd}{c}$$

48. 76.4 in.

49. To find the number of 100 meter rises in h meters we divide: $\dfrac{h}{100}$. Then
$$T = t - \frac{h}{100}.$$

Note that 12 km $= 12 \text{ km} \cdot \dfrac{1000 \text{ m}}{1 \text{ km}} = 12,000$ m.
Thus, we have
$$T = t - \frac{h}{100}, \ 0 \le h \le 12,000.$$

50. $y = \dfrac{z^2}{t}$

51.
$$ac = bc + d$$
$$ac - bc = d$$
$$c(a - b) = d$$
$$c = \frac{d}{a - b}$$

52. $t = \dfrac{rs}{q - r}$

53.
$$3a = c - a(b + d)$$
$$3a = c - ab - ad$$
$$3a + ab + ad = c$$
$$a(3 + b + d) = c$$
$$a = \frac{c}{3 + b + d}$$

54. ◈

Exercise Set 2.4

1. $32\% = 32 \times 0.01$ Replacing % by $\times\ 0.01$
   $= 0.32$

2. 0.49

3. $7\% = 7 \times 0.01$ Replacing % by $\times\ 0.01$
   $= 0.07$

4. 0.913

5. $24.1\% = 24.1 \times 0.01 = 0.241$

6. 0.02

7. $0.46\% = 0.46 \times 0.01 = 0.0046$

8. 0.048

9. 4.54
First move the decimal point	4.54.
two places to the right;	⌐↑
then write a % symbol:	454%

10. 100%

11. 0.998
First move the decimal point	0.99.8
two places to the right;	⌐↑
then write a % symbol:	99.8%

12. 73%

13. 2   (Note: $2 = 2.00$)
First move the decimal point	2.00.
two places to the right;	⌐↑
then write a % symbol:	200%

14. 0.57%

15. 1.34
First move the decimal point	1.34.
two places to the right;	⌐↑
then write a % symbol:	134%

16. 920%

17. 0.0068
First move the decimal point	0.00.68
two places to the right;	⌐↑
then write a % symbol:	0.68%

18. 67.5%

19. $\dfrac{3}{8}$ $\left(\text{Note: } \dfrac{3}{8} = 0.375\right)$
First move the decimal point	0.37.5
two places to the right;	⌐↑
then write a % symbol:	37.5%

20. 75%

21. $\dfrac{7}{25}$ $\left(\text{Note: } \dfrac{7}{25} = 0.28\right)$
First move the decimal point	0.28.
two places to the right;	⌐↑
then write a % symbol:	28%

22. 80%

23. $\dfrac{2}{3}$ $\left(\text{Note: } \dfrac{2}{3} = 0.66\overline{6}\right)$
First move the decimal point	0.66.$\overline{6}$
two places to the right;	⌐↑
then write a % symbol:	66.$\overline{6}$%

   Since $0.\overline{6} = \dfrac{2}{3}$, this can also be expressed as $66\dfrac{2}{3}\%$.

24. $83.\overline{3}\%$, or $83\dfrac{1}{3}\%$

25. *Translate.*
   $\underbrace{\text{What percent}}$ of 75 is 39?
   $\quad\quad\quad\downarrow\quad\quad\quad\downarrow\ \downarrow\ \downarrow\ \downarrow$
   $\quad\quad\quad y\quad\quad\ \cdot\ 75\ =\ 39$

   We solve the equation and then convert to percent notation.
   $$y \cdot 75 = 39$$
   $$y = \frac{39}{75}$$
   $$y = 0.52 = 52\%$$
   The answer is 52%.

26. 12.5%

27. *Translate*.

$$\underbrace{\text{What percent}}_{y} \;\; \overset{\downarrow}{\text{of}} \;\; \overset{\downarrow}{125} \;\; \overset{\downarrow}{\text{is}} \;\; \overset{\downarrow}{30}?$$

$$ y \quad\cdot\quad 125 \;=\; 30$$

We solve the equation and then convert to percent notation.

$$y \cdot 125 = 30$$
$$y = \frac{30}{125}$$
$$y = 0.24 = 24\%$$

The answer is 24%.

28. 19%

29. *Translate*.

$$\underset{18}{\overset{\downarrow}{18}} \;\; \underset{=}{\overset{\downarrow}{\text{is}}} \;\; \underset{30\%}{\overset{\downarrow}{30\%}} \;\; \underset{\cdot}{\overset{\downarrow}{\text{of}}} \;\; \underbrace{\text{what number}}_{y}?$$

We solve the equation.

$$18 = 0.3y \qquad (30\% = 0.3)$$
$$\frac{18}{0.3} = y$$
$$60 = y$$

The answer is 60.

30. 85

31. *Translate*.

$$\underset{0.3}{\overset{\downarrow}{0.3}} \;\; \underset{=}{\overset{\downarrow}{\text{is}}} \;\; \underset{12\%}{\overset{\downarrow}{12\%}} \;\; \underset{\cdot}{\overset{\downarrow}{\text{of}}} \;\; \underbrace{\text{what number}}_{y}?$$

We solve the equation.

$$0.3 = 0.12y \qquad (12\% = 0.12)$$
$$\frac{0.3}{0.12} = y$$
$$2.5 = y$$

The answer is 2.5.

32. 4

33. *Translate*.

$$\underbrace{\text{What number}}_{y} \;\; \underset{=}{\overset{\downarrow}{\text{is}}} \;\; \underset{65\%}{\overset{\downarrow}{65\%}} \;\; \underset{\cdot}{\overset{\downarrow}{\text{of}}} \;\; \underset{420}{\overset{\downarrow}{420}}?$$

We solve the equation.

$$y = 0.65 \cdot 420 \qquad (65\% = 0.65)$$
$$y = 273 \qquad \text{Multiplying}$$

The answer is 273.

34. 10,000

35. *Translate*.

$$\underbrace{\text{What percent}}_{y} \;\; \overset{\downarrow}{\text{of}} \;\; \overset{\downarrow}{60} \;\; \overset{\downarrow}{\text{is}} \;\; \overset{\downarrow}{75}?$$

$$ y \quad\cdot\quad 60 \;=\; 75$$

We solve the equation and then convert to percent notation.

$$y \cdot 60 = 75$$
$$y = \frac{75}{60}$$
$$y = 1.25 = 125\%$$

The answer is 125%.

36. 225%

37. *Translate*.

$$\underset{x}{\overset{\downarrow}{\text{What}}} \;\; \underset{=}{\overset{\downarrow}{\text{is}}} \;\; \underset{2\%}{\overset{\downarrow}{2\%}} \;\; \underset{\cdot}{\overset{\downarrow}{\text{of}}} \;\; \underset{40}{\overset{\downarrow}{40}}?$$

We solve the equation.

$$x = 0.02 \cdot 40 \qquad (2\% = 0.02)$$
$$x = 0.8 \qquad \text{Multiplying}$$

The answer is 0.8.

38. 0.8

39. *Translate*.

$$\underset{2}{\overset{\downarrow}{2}} \;\; \underset{=}{\overset{\downarrow}{\text{is}}} \;\; \underbrace{\text{what percent}}_{y} \;\; \overset{\downarrow}{\text{of}} \;\; \underset{40}{\overset{\downarrow}{40}}?$$

$$ 2 \;\; = y \cdot \;\; 40$$

We solve the equation and convert to percent notation.

$$2 = y \cdot 40$$
$$\frac{2}{40} = y$$
$$0.05 = y, \text{ or } 5\% = y$$

The answer is 5%.

40. 2000

41. If n = the number of women who had babies in good or excellent health, we have:

$$\underset{n}{\overset{\downarrow}{n}} \;\; \underset{=}{\overset{\downarrow}{\text{is}}} \;\; \underset{0.95}{\overset{\downarrow}{95\%}} \;\; \underset{\cdot}{\overset{\downarrow}{\text{of}}} \;\; \underset{300}{\overset{\downarrow}{300}}.$$

$$n = 285$$

285 women had babies in good or excellent health.

42. 16

43. Let p = the number of people who voted in the 1996 presidential election, in millions. Then we have:

45.3 is 49% of p.

$$\downarrow \quad \downarrow \quad \downarrow \quad \downarrow \quad \downarrow$$
$$45.3 = 0.49 \cdot p$$
$$\frac{45.3}{0.49} = p$$
$$92.4 \approx p$$

About 92.4 million people voted in the 1996 presidential election.

44. $88.9 billion

45. Let $p =$ the percentage by which the average annual healthcare bill grew from 1985 to 1993. Then we have:

668 is what percent of 1108?

$$\downarrow \quad \downarrow \qquad \downarrow \qquad \downarrow \quad \downarrow$$
$$668 = \qquad p \qquad \cdot 1108$$
$$\frac{668}{1108} = p$$
$$0.60 \approx p, \text{ or}$$
$$60\% \approx p$$

The average annual healthcare bill grew about 60% from 1985 to 1993.

46. 3.75%

47. Let $b =$ the number of brochures the business can expect to be opened and read. Then we have:

b is 78% of 9500.

$$\downarrow \downarrow \quad \downarrow \quad \downarrow \quad \downarrow$$
$$b = 0.78 \cdot 9500$$
$$b = 7410$$

The business can expect 7410 brochures to be opened and read.

48. 27

49. Let $p =$ the percent of people who will catch the cold. Then we have:

56 is what percent of 800?

$$\downarrow \quad \downarrow \qquad \downarrow \qquad \downarrow \quad \downarrow$$
$$56 = \qquad p \qquad \cdot 800$$
$$\frac{56}{800} = p$$
$$0.07 = p, \text{ or}$$
$$7\% = p$$

7% will catch the cold.

50. 86.4%

51. Let $h =$ the percent that were hits. Then we have:

13 is what percent of 25?

$$\downarrow \downarrow \qquad \downarrow \qquad \downarrow \quad \downarrow$$
$$13 = \qquad h \qquad \cdot 25$$
$$\frac{13}{25} = h$$
$$0.52 = h, \text{ or}$$
$$52\% = h$$

52% were hits.

52. $36

53. When the sales tax is 5%, the total amount paid is 105% of the cost of the merchandise. Let $c =$ the cost of the building materials. Then we have:

$987 is 105% of c.

$$\downarrow \quad \downarrow \quad \downarrow \quad \downarrow \downarrow$$
$$987 = 1.05 \cdot c$$
$$\frac{987}{1.05} = c$$
$$940 = c$$

The price of the building materials was $940.

54. 16%

55. The number of calories in a serving of Light Style Bread is 85% of the number of calories in a serving of regular bread. Let $c =$ the number of calories in a serving of regular bread. Then we have:

140 calories is 85% of c.

$$\downarrow \qquad \downarrow \quad \downarrow \quad \downarrow \downarrow$$
$$140 \qquad = 0.85 \cdot c$$
$$\frac{140}{0.85} = c$$
$$165 \approx c$$

There are about 165 calories in a serving of regular bread.

56. 58 calories

57. a) Self-employment income must be 20% more than non-self-employment income. That is, self-employment income must be 120% of non-self-employment income. Let $x =$ non-self-employment income and $y =$ the corresponding self-employment income. Then we have:

Self-employment income is 120% of non-self-employment income.

$$\downarrow \qquad \qquad \downarrow \quad \downarrow \quad \downarrow \qquad \downarrow$$
$$y \qquad = 1.2 \cdot \qquad x$$

Enter $y = 1.2x$ on a grapher and create a table for values of x between $12 and $18.

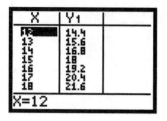

b) From the table we see that $y = 18$ when $x = 15$, so Trey would need to earn $18 per hour.

58. a)

X=157

b) $148.50

59. We divide:

$$
\begin{array}{r}
0.6\,8 \\
2\,5\,\overline{\smash{\big)}\,1\,7.0\,0} \\
\underline{1\,5\,0} \\
2\,0\,0 \\
\underline{2\,0\,0} \\
0
\end{array}
$$

Decimal notation for $\dfrac{17}{25}$ is 0.68.

60. -90

61. $-45.8 - (-32.6) = -45.8 + 32.6 = -13.2$

62. $-21a + 12b$

63. ◈

64. ◈

65. ◈

66. ◈

67.
$$a = 130\% \cdot b$$
$$a = 1.3b$$
$$\frac{a}{1.3} = b$$
$$\frac{1}{1.3}a = b$$
$$0.77a \approx b$$

Thus, b is about 77% of a.

68. 18,500

69. Let $x =$ Claude's pre-tax earnings. Then his taxes are 26% of x, or $0.26x$, and his post-tax earnings are $x - 0.26x$, or $0.74x$. Then the percentage of his post-tax earnings represented by his taxes is given by

$$\frac{0.26x}{0.74x} = \frac{0.26}{0.74} \approx 0.35, \text{ or } 35\%.$$

70. Rollie's Music: $12.83; Sound Warp: $12.97

71. The new price is 125% of the old price. Let $p =$ the new price. Then we have:

p is 125% of $20,800.

$\downarrow\downarrow$ $\downarrow$ $\downarrow$ $\downarrow$

$p = $ 1.25 $\cdot$ $20,800$

$p = 26,000$

Now let $x =$ the percent of the new price represented by the old price. We have:

$20,800 is what percent of $26,000.

$\downarrow$ $\downarrow$ $\downarrow$ $\downarrow$ $\downarrow$

$20,800 = $ x $\cdot$ $26,000$

$$\frac{20,800}{26,000} = x$$
$$0.8 = x, \text{ or}$$
$$80\% = x$$

The old price is $100\% - 80\%$, or 20% lower than the new price.

Exercise Set 2.5

1. *Familiarize.* Let $x =$ the number. Then "three less than twice a number" translates to $2x - 3$.

Translate.

Three less than twice a number is 19.

$\downarrow$

$2x - 3$ $= 19$

Carry out. We solve the equation.

$$2x - 3 = 19$$
$$2x = 22 \quad \text{Adding 3}$$
$$x = 11 \quad \text{Dividing by 2}$$

Check. Twice, or two times, 11 is 22. Three less than 22 is 19. The answer checks.

State. The number is 11.

2. 8

3. *Familiarize.* Let $a =$ the number. Then "five times the sum of 3 and some number" translates to $5(a+3)$.

Translate.

Five times the sum of 3 and some number — is 70.

$$5(a+3) = 70$$

Carry out. We solve the equation.

$$5(a+3) = 70$$
$$5a + 15 = 70 \quad \text{Using the distributive law}$$
$$5a = 55 \quad \text{Subtracting 15}$$
$$a = 11 \quad \text{Dividing by 5}$$

Check. The sum of 3 and 11 is 14, and $5 \cdot 14 = 70$. The answer checks.

State. The number is 11.

4. 13

5. Familiarize. Let $p =$ the regular price of the CD player. At 20% off, Doug paid 80% of the regular price.

Translate.

$72 is 80% of the regular price.

$$72 = 0.8 \cdot p$$

Carry out. We solve the equation.

$$72 = 0.8p$$
$$\frac{72}{0.8} = p \quad \text{Dividing by 0.8}$$
$$90 = p$$

Check. 80% of $90, or 0.8($90), is $72. The answer checks.

State. The regular price was $90.

6. $48

7. Familiarize. Let $x =$ the first integer. Then $x+1 =$ the second integer, and $x + 2 =$ the third integer.

Translate.

The sum of three consecutive integers — is 48.

$$x + (x+1) + (x+2) = 48$$

Carry out. We solve the equation.

$$x + (x+1) + (x+2) = 48$$
$$3x + 3 = 48 \quad \text{Combining like terms}$$
$$3x = 45 \quad \text{Subtracting 3}$$
$$x = 15 \quad \text{Dividing by 3}$$

If x is 15, then $x + 1$ is 16 and $x + 2 = 17$.

Check. 15, 16, and 17 are consecutive integers, and $15 + 16 + 17 = 48$. The result checks.

State. The numbers are 15, 16, and 17.

8. 19, 21

9. Familiarize. Let $x =$ the first even number. Then $x + 2 =$ the next even number.

Translate.

The sum of two consecutive even numbers — is 50.

$$x + (x+2) = 50$$

Carry out. We solve the equation.

$$x + (x+2) = 50$$
$$2x + 2 = 50 \quad \text{Combining like terms}$$
$$2x = 48 \quad \text{Subtracting 2}$$
$$x = 24 \quad \text{Dividing by 2}$$

If x is 24, then $x + 2$ is 26.

Check. 24 and 26 are consecutive even numbers, and $24 + 26 = 50$. The result checks.

State. The numbers are 24 and 26.

10. 52, 54

11. Familiarize. Let $x =$ the smaller odd integer. Then $x + 2 =$ the next odd integer.

Translate. We reword the problem.

Smaller odd integer + next odd integer is 128.

$$x + (x+2) = 128$$

Carry out. We solve the equation.

$$x + (x+2) = 128$$
$$2x + 2 = 128 \quad \text{Combining like terms}$$
$$2x = 126 \quad \text{Subtracting 2}$$
$$x = 63 \quad \text{Dividing by 2}$$

If x is 63, then $x + 2$ is 65.

Check. 63 and 65 are consecutive odd integers, and their sum is 128. The answer checks.

State. The integers are 63 and 65.

12. $\frac{10}{3}$ km

13. Familiarize. Let $d =$ the musher's distance from Nome, in miles. Then $2d =$ the distance from Anchorage, in miles. This is the number of miles the musher has completed. The sum of the two distances is the length of the race, 1049 miles.

Translate.

Distance from Nome plus distance from Anchorage is 1049 mi.

$$d + 2d = 1049$$

Carry out. We solve the equation.

$$d + 2d = 1049$$
$$3d = 1049 \qquad \text{Combining like terms}$$
$$d = \frac{1049}{3}$$

If $d = \frac{1049}{3}$, then $2d = 2 \cdot \frac{1049}{3} = \frac{2098}{3} = 699\frac{1}{3}$.

Check. $\frac{2098}{3}$ is twice $\frac{1049}{3}$, and $\frac{1049}{3} + \frac{2098}{3} = \frac{3147}{3} = 1049$. The result checks.

State. The musher has traveled $699\frac{1}{3}$ miles.

14. 30 m, 90 m, 360 m

15. ***Familiarize***. Let $a =$ the amount spent to remodel bathrooms, in billions of dollars. Then $2a =$ the amount spent to remodel kitchens. The sum of these two amounts is \$35 billion.

Translate.

Amount spent on bathrooms	plus	amount spent on kitchens	is	\$35 billion.
a	$+$	$2a$	$=$	35

Carry out. We solve the equation.

$$a + 2a = 35$$
$$3a = 35 \qquad \text{Combining like terms}$$
$$a = \frac{35}{3}, \text{ or } 11\frac{2}{3}$$

If $a = \frac{35}{3}$, then $2a = 2 \cdot \frac{35}{3} = \frac{70}{3} = 23\frac{1}{3}$.

Check. $\frac{70}{3}$ is twice $\frac{35}{3}$, and $\frac{35}{3} + \frac{70}{3} = \frac{105}{3} = 35$. The answer checks.

State. \$$11\frac{2}{3}$ billion was spent to remodel bathrooms, and \$$23\frac{1}{3}$ billion was spent to remodel kitchens.

16. 30°, 90°, 60°

17. ***Familiarize***. We draw a picture. We let $x =$ the measure of the first angle. Then $4x =$ the measure of the second angle, and $(x + 4x) - 45$, or $5x - 45 =$ the measure of the third angle.

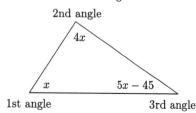

2nd angle
$4x$
x $5x - 45$
1st angle   3rd angle

Recall that the measures of the angles of any triangle add up to 180°.

Translate.

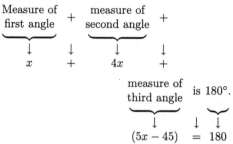

Measure of first angle	$+$	measure of second angle	$+$
x	$+$	$4x$	$+$

measure of third angle	is 180°.
$(5x - 45)$	$= 180$

Carry out. We solve the equation.

$$x + 4x + (5x - 45) = 180$$
$$10x - 45 = 180$$
$$10x = 225$$
$$x = 22.5$$

Possible answers for the angle measures are as follows:

First angle: $x = 22.5°$
Second angle: $4x = 4(22.5) = 90°$
Third angle: $5x - 45 = 5(22.5) - 45$
$$= 112.5 - 45 = 67.5°$$

Check. Consider 22.5°, 90°, and 67.5°. The second is four times the first, and the third is 45° less than five times the first. The sum is 180°. These numbers check.

State. The measure of the first angle is 22.5°, the measure of the second angle is 90°, and the measure of the third angle is 67.5°.

18. 95°

19. ***Familiarize***. Let $x =$ the measure of the first angle. Then $4x =$ the measure of the second angle, and $x + 4x + 5 = 5x + 5 =$ the measure of the third angle. Recall that the sum of the measures of the angles of a triangle is 180°.

Translate.

Measure of first angle	$+$	measure of second angle	$+$
x	$+$	$4x$	$+$

measure of third angle	is 180°.
$(5x + 5)$	$= 180$

Carry out. We solve the equation.

$$x + 4x + (5x + 5) = 180$$
$$10x + 5 = 180$$
$$10x = 175$$
$$x = 17.5$$

If x is 17.5, then $4x$ is 70 and $5x + 5$ is 92.5.

Check. Consider 17.5°, 70°, and 92.5°. The second is four times the first, and the third is 5° more than the sum of the other two. The sum is 180°. These numbers check.

State. The measure of the second angle is 70°.

20. $360,000

21. *Familiarize.* The page numbers are consecutive integers. If we let $p =$ the smaller number, then $p + 1 =$ the larger number.

Translate. We reword the problem.

$$\underbrace{\text{First integer}}_{\downarrow \quad \downarrow} \; + \; \underbrace{\text{Second integer}}_{\downarrow} \; \underbrace{= 285}_{\downarrow \quad \downarrow}$$
$$x \qquad + \qquad (x+1) \qquad = 285$$

Carry out. We solve the equation.

$$x + (x + 1) = 285$$
$$2x + 1 = 285 \qquad \text{Combining like terms}$$
$$2x = 284 \qquad \text{Adding } -1$$
$$x = 142 \qquad \text{Dividing by 2}$$

Check. If $x = 142$, then $x + 1 = 143$. These are consecutive integers, and $142 + 143 = 285$. The answer checks.

State. The page numbers are 142 and 143.

22. 140 and 141

23. *Familiarize.* Let $s =$ the length of the shortest side, in mm. Then $s + 2$ and $s + 4$ represent the lengths of the other two sides. The perimeter is the sum of the lengths of the sides.

Translate.

$$\underbrace{\text{Length of first side}}_{\downarrow} \; \text{plus} \; \underbrace{\text{length of second side}}_{\downarrow} \; \text{plus}$$
$$s \qquad + \qquad (s+2) \qquad +$$

$$\underbrace{\text{length of third side}}_{\downarrow} \; \underbrace{= \underline{195 \text{ mm}}}_{\downarrow}$$
$$(s+4) \qquad = \qquad 195$$

Carry out. We solve the equation.

$$s + (s + 2) + (s + 4) = 195$$
$$3s + 6 = 195$$
$$3s = 189$$
$$s = 63$$

If s is 63, then $s + 2$ is 65 and $s + 4$ is 67.

Check. The numbers 63, 65, and 67 are consecutive odd integers. Their sum is 195. These numbers check.

State. The lengths of the sides of the triangle are 63 mm, 65 mm, and 67 mm.

24. 130 mm, 132 mm, 134 mm

25. *Familiarize.* We draw a picture. Let $w =$ the width of the rectangle in feet. Then $w + 100 =$ the length.

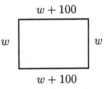

The perimeter of a rectangle is the sum of the lengths of the sides. The area is the product of the length and the width.

Translate. We use the definition of perimeter to write an equation that will allow us to find the width and length.

$$\underbrace{\text{Width}}_{\downarrow} + \underbrace{\text{Width}}_{\downarrow} + \underbrace{\text{Length}}_{\downarrow} + \underbrace{\text{Length}}_{\downarrow} = \underbrace{\text{Perimeter.}}_{\downarrow}$$
$$w + w + (w+100) + (w+100) = 860$$

Carry out. We solve the equation.

$$w + w + (w + 100) + (w + 100) = 860$$
$$4w + 200 = 860$$
$$4w = 660$$
$$w = 165$$

If $w = 165$, then $w + 100 = 165 + 100 = 265$, and the area is $265(165) = 43,725$.

Check. The length is 100 ft more than the width. The perimeter is $165 + 165 + 265 + 265 = 860$ ft. This checks. To check the area we recheck the computation. This also checks.

State. The width of the rectangle is 165 ft, the length is 265 ft, and the area is 43,725 ft^2.

26. Width: 100 ft, length: 160 ft; area: 16,000 ft^2

27. *Familiarize.* We draw a picture. Let $l =$ the length of the state, in miles. Then $l - 90 =$ the width.

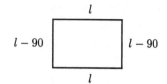

The perimeter is the sum of the lengths of the sides.

Translate. We use the definition of perimeter to write an equation.

Width + Width + Length + Length is 1280.

$$(l - 90) + (l - 90) + l + l = 1280$$

Carry out. We solve the equation.

$$(l - 90) + (l - 90) + l + l = 1280$$
$$4l - 180 = 1280$$
$$4l = 1460$$
$$l = 365$$

Then $l - 90 = 275$.

Check. The width, 275 mi, is 90 mi less than the length, 365 mi. The perimeter is 275 mi + 275 mi + 365 mi + 365 mi, or 1280 mi. This checks.

State. The length is 365 mi, and the width is 275 mi.

28. Length: 27.9 cm, width: 21.6 cm

29. Familiarize. Let $x =$ the original investment. Interest earned in 1 year is found by taking 6% of the original investment. Then 6% of x, or $0.06x =$ the interest. The amount in the account at the end of the year is the sum of the original investment and the interest earned.

Translate.

Original investment plus interest earned is $6996.

$$x + 0.06x = 6996$$

Carry out. We solve the equation.

$$x + 0.06x = 6996$$
$$1 \cdot x + 0.06x = 6996$$
$$1.06x = 6996$$
$$x = \frac{6996}{1.06}$$
$$x = 6600$$

Check. 6% of $6600 is $396. Adding this to $6600 we get $6996. This checks.

State. The original investment was $6600.

30. $6540

31. Familiarize. The total cost is the daily charge plus the mileage charge. The mileage charge is the cost per mile times the number of miles driven. Let $m =$ the number of miles that can be driven for $80.

Translate. We reword the problem.

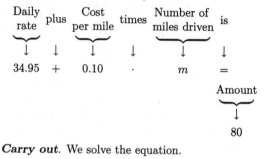

Daily rate	plus	Cost per mile	times	Number of miles driven	is
34.95	+	0.10	$\cdot$	m	=

Amount

80

Carry out. We solve the equation.

$$34.95 + 0.10m = 80$$
$$100(34.95 + 0.10m) = 100(80) \quad \text{Clearing decimals}$$
$$3495 + 10m = 8000$$
$$10m = 4505$$
$$m = 450.5$$

Check. The mileage cost is found by multiplying 450.5 by $0.10 obtaining $45.05. Then we add $45.05 to $34.95, the daily rate, and get $80.

State. The businessperson can drive 450.5 mi on the car-rental allotment.

32. 460.5 mi

33. Familiarize. Let $x =$ the measure of one angle. Then $90 - x =$ the measure of its complement.

Translate.

Measure of one angle	is 15°	more than	twice the measure of its complement.
x	$= 15$	$+$	$2(90 - x)$

Carry out. We solve the equation.

$$x = 15 + 2(90 - x)$$
$$x = 15 + 180 - 2x$$
$$x = 195 - 2x$$
$$3x = 195$$
$$x = 65$$

If x is 65, then $90 - x$ is 25.

Check. The sum of the angle measures is 90°. Also, 65° is 15° more than twice its complement, 25°. The answer checks.

State. The angle measures are 65° and 25°.

34. 105°, 75°

35. Familiarize. We will use the equation $R = -0.028t + 20.8$ where R is in seconds and t is the number of years since 1920. We want to find t when $R = 18.0$ sec.

Translate.

Record $\qquad$ is $\qquad$ 18.0 sec.

$\downarrow \qquad\qquad \downarrow \qquad \downarrow$

$-0.028t + 20.8 \;=\; 18.0$

Carry out.

$$-0.028t + 20.8 = 18.0$$
$$1000(-0.028t + 20.8) = 1000(18.0) \quad \text{Clearing the decimals}$$
$$-28t + 20{,}800 = 18{,}000$$
$$-28t = -2800$$
$$t = 100$$

Check. Substitute 100 for t in the given equation:

$$R = -0.028(100) + 20.8 = -2.8 + 20.8 = 18.0$$

This checks.

State. The record will be 18.0 sec 100 years after 1920, or in 2020.

36. 160

37. $5a + 10b - 45 = 5 \cdot a + 5 \cdot 2b - 5 \cdot 9 = 5(a + 2b - 9)$

38. $3(x - 4y + 20)$

39. $7x - 3(8 - 2x) + 12 = 7x - 24 + 6x + 12 = 13x - 12$

40. $-10x + 30$

41.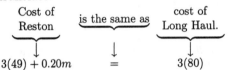

42. ◎

43. ◎

44. ◎

45. Familiarize. Let s = the number of points Stacy would have scored if her three-pointer had been good. Had it been good, the Blazers would have scored $77 + 3$, or 80, points. Since it wasn't good, Stacy actually scored $s - 3$ points.

Translate. We write an equation corresponding to the situation that would have resulted if the shot had been good.

Stacy's point total $\qquad$ is half of $\qquad$ 80 points.

$\downarrow \qquad\quad \downarrow\;\;\downarrow\;\;\downarrow \qquad \downarrow$

$s \qquad\quad =\;\; \dfrac{1}{2}\;\cdot \qquad 80$

Carry out. We carry out the calculation.

$$s = \frac{1}{2} \cdot 80$$
$$s = 40$$

If s is 40, then $s - 3$ is 37.

Check. If the Blazers had scored 80 points and Stacy had scored 40 points, Stacy would have scored half of the Blazer's points. Since the three-pointer wasn't good, Stacy actually scored $40 - 3$, or 37 points. The result checks.

State. Stacy scored 37 points in the loss.

46. $0.19

47. Familiarize. Let m = the number of miles Ed drives. We will find the mileage for which the cost of the two rentals is the same. Then we will examine a mileage less than this and also a mileage greater than this to determine guidelines for the least expensive rental.

Translate.

Cost of Reston $\qquad$ is the same as $\qquad$ cost of Long Haul.

$\downarrow \qquad\qquad\qquad \downarrow \qquad\qquad\qquad \downarrow$

$3(49) + 0.20m \qquad\quad = \qquad\qquad 3(80)$

Carry out. We solve the equation.

$$3(49) + 0.20m = 3(80)$$
$$147 + 0.20m = 240$$
$$0.20m = 93$$
$$m = 465$$

Thus, if Ed drives 465 miles there is no difference in the cost of the rentals.

Note that a three-day rental from Long Haul costs $3(\$80)$, or $240, regardless of the mileage. We find the cost of a Reston rental for a mileage less than 465 mi and also for a mileage greater than 465 mi.

For 460 mi: $3(\$49) + \$0.20(460) = \$239$

For 470 mi: $3(\$49) + \$0.20(470) = \$241$

Thus, the Reston rental is less for mileages less than 465 mi and more expensive for mileages greater than 465 mi.

Check. If Ed drives 465 mi, the Reston rental costs $3(\$49) + \$0.20(465)$, or $240, and the Long Haul rental costs $3(\$80)$, or $240, also, so the cost is the same for 465 mi. Go over the computations for mileages less than and greater than 465 mi. The result checks.

State. If Ed drives less than 465 mi the Reston rental is less expensive. If he drives more than 465 mi the Long Haul rental is less expensive.

48. 19

49. Familiarize. Let s = one score. Then four score $= 4s$ and four score and seven $= 4s + 7$.

Translate. We reword .

| 1776 | plus | four score and seven | is | 1863 |

$$1776 \quad + \quad (4s + 7) \quad = \quad 1863$$

Carry out. We solve the equation.

$$1776 + (4s + 7) = 1863$$
$$4s + 1783 = 1863$$
$$4s = 80$$
$$s = 20$$

Check. If a score is 20 years, then four score and seven represents 87 years. Adding 87 to 1776 we get 1863. This checks.

State. A score is 20.

50. 16, 4

51. *Familiarize.* Let x = the first odd number. Then the next three odd numbers are $x + 2$, $x + 4$, and $x + 6$. The sum of measures of the angles of an n-sided polygon is given by the formula $(n - 2) \cdot 180°$. Thus, the sum of the measures of the angles of a quadrilateral is $(4 - 2) \cdot 180°$, or $2 \cdot 180°$, or $360°$.

Translate.

| The sum of the measures of the angles | is | 360°. |

$$x + (x + 2) + (x + 4) + (x + 6) \quad = \quad 360$$

Carry out. We solve the equation.

$$x + (x + 2) + (x + 4) + (x + 6) = 360$$
$$4x + 12 = 360$$
$$4x = 348$$
$$x = 87$$

If x is 87, then $x + 2$ is 89, $x + 4$ is 91, and $x + 6$ is 93.

Check. The numbers 87, 89, 91, and 93 are consecutive odd numbers. The sum of the numbers is 360. The answer checks.

State. The measures of the angles are 87°, 89°, 91°, and 93°.

52. 104°, 106°, 108°, 110°, 112°

53. *Familiarize.* Let a = the original number of apples in the basket.

Translate.

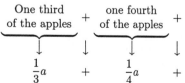

$$\frac{1}{3}a \quad + \quad \frac{1}{4}a \quad +$$

$$\frac{1}{8}a \quad + \quad \frac{1}{5}a \quad + \quad 10 \quad +$$

1 apple is the original number of apples.

$$1 \quad = \quad a$$

Carry out. We solve the equation. Note that the LCD is 120.

$$\frac{1}{3}a + \frac{1}{4}a + \frac{1}{8}a + \frac{1}{5}a + 10 + 1 = a$$

$$\frac{1}{3}a + \frac{1}{4}a + \frac{1}{8}a + \frac{1}{5}a + 11 = a$$

$$120\left(\frac{1}{3}a + \frac{1}{4}a + \frac{1}{8}a + \frac{1}{5}a + 11\right) = 120 \cdot a$$

$$40a + 30a + 15a + 24a + 1320 = 120a$$

$$109a + 1320 = 120a$$

$$1320 = 11a$$

$$120 = a$$

Check. $\frac{1}{3} \cdot 120 = 40$, $\frac{1}{4} \cdot 120 = 30$, $\frac{1}{8} \cdot 120 = 15$, and $\frac{1}{5} \cdot 120 = 24$. Then $40 + 30 + 15 + 24 + 10 + 1 = 120$. The result checks.

State. There were originally 120 apples in the basket.

54. 30

55. *Familiarize.* Let s = Luke's weekly salary. Then Luke spends 12% of s, or $0.12s$ on dining out, and 55% of this amount is given by $0.55(0.12s)$. This is the amount spent on fast-food.

Translate.

| Amount spent on fast-food | is | $39.60. |

$$0.55(0.12s) \quad = \quad 39.60$$

Carry out.

$$0.55(0.12s) = 39.60$$
$$0.066s = 39.60$$
$$s = 600$$

Check. If Luke's weekly salary is $600, then he spends $0.12(\$600)$, or $72, dining out. Then he spends $0.55(\$72)$, or $39.60 on fast-food. The answer checks.

State. Luke's weekly salary is $600.

56. Length: 12 cm, width: 9 cm

57. *Familiarize*. Let h = the height of the triangle. We know that the base is 8 in. Recall that the area of a triangle is given by the formula $A = \frac{1}{2}bh$.

***Translate*.**

$$\underbrace{\text{Area}}_{\downarrow} \quad \underset{\downarrow}{\text{is}} \quad \underbrace{2.9047 \text{ in}^2}_{\downarrow}.$$

$$\frac{1}{2} \cdot 8 \cdot h = 2.9047$$

***Carry out*.** We solve the equation.

$$\frac{1}{2} \cdot 8 \cdot h = 2.9047$$
$$4h = 2.9047$$
$$h = 0.726175$$

***Check*.** The area of a triangle whose base is 8 in. and whose height is 0.726175 in. is $\frac{1}{2}(8)(0.726175)$, or 2.9047. The answer checks.

***State*.** The height of the triangle is 0.726175 in.

58. 76

59. *Familiarize*. Let n = the number of CD's purchased. Assume that two or more CD's were purchased. Then the first CD costs $8.49 and the total cost of the remaining $n-1$ CD's is $3.99(n-1)$. The shipping and handling costs are $2.47 for the first CD, $2.28 for the second, and a total of $1.99(n-2)$ for the remaining $n-2$ CD's. Then the total cost of the shipment is $8.49 + \$3.99(n-1) + \$2.47 + \$2.28 + \$1.99(n-2)$.

***Translate*.**

$$\underbrace{\text{Total cost of shipment}}_{\downarrow} \qquad \underset{\downarrow}{\text{was}} \quad \underset{\downarrow}{\$65.07}.$$

$$8.49 + 3.99(n{-}1) + 2.47 + 2.28 + 1.99(n{-}2) = 65.07$$

***Carry out*.** We solve the equation.

$$8.49 + 3.99(n-1) + 2.47 + 2.28 + 1.99(n-2) = 65.07$$
$$8.49 + 3.99n - 3.99 + 2.47 + 2.28 + 1.99n - 3.98 = 65.07$$
$$5.27 + 5.98n = 65.07$$
$$5.98n = 59.80$$
$$n = 10$$

***Check*.** If 10 CD's are purchased, the total cost of the CD's is $8.49 + \$3.99(9) = \$44.40$. The total shipping and handling costs are $2.47 + \$2.28 + \$1.99(8) = \$20.67$. Then the total cost of the order is $44.40 + \$20.67 = \$65.07$.

***State*.** There were 10 CD's in the shipment.

60. ◈

61. ◈

Exercise Set 2.6

1. $x > -3$

   a) Since $4 > -3$ is true, 4 is a solution.

   b) Since $0 > -3$ is true, 0 is a solution.

   c) Since $-4.1 > -3$ is false, -4.1 is not a solution.

   d) Since $-3.9 > -3$ is false, -3.9 is not a solution.

   e) Since $5.6 > -3$ is true, 5.6 is a solution.

2. a) Yes, b) No, c) Yes, d) Yes, e) No

3. $x \geq 6$

   a) Since $-6 \geq 6$ is false, -6 is not a solution.

   b) Since $0 \geq 6$ is false, 0 is not a solution.

   c) Since $6 \geq 6$ is true, 6 is a solution.

   d) Since $6.01 \geq 6$ is true, 6.01 is a solution.

   e) Since $-3\frac{1}{2} \geq 6$ is false, $-3\frac{1}{2}$ is not a solution.

4. a) Yes, b) Yes, c) Yes, d) No, e) Yes

5. The solutions of $x \geq 6$ are shown by shading the point 6 and all points to the right of 6. The closed circle at 6 indicates that 6 is part of the graph.

6.

7. The solutions of $t < -3$ are those numbers less than -3. They are shown on the graph by shading all points to the left of -3. The open circle at -3 indicates that -3 is not part of the graph.

8.

9. The solutions of $m > -4$ are those numbers greater than -4. They are shown on the graph by shading all points to the right of -4. The open circle at 4 indicates that -4 is not part of the graph.

10.

11. In order to be a solution of the inequality
$-3 < x \le 5$, a number must be a solution of both
$-3 < x$ and $x \le 5$. The solution set is graphed as
follows:

The open circle at -3 means that -3 is not part of
the graph. The closed circle at 5 means that 5 is part
of the graph.

12.

13. In order to be a solution of the inequality $0 < x < 3$,
a number must be a solution of both $0 < x$ and $x < 3$.
The solution set is graphed as follows:

The open circles at 0 and at 3 mean that 0 and 3 are
not part of the graph.

14.

15. All points to the right of -1 are shaded. The open
circle at -1 indicates that -1 is not part of the
graph. We have $(-1, \infty)$, or $\{x | x > -1\}$.

16. $(-\infty, 3)$, or $\{x | x < 3\}$

17. The point 2 and all points to the left of 2 are shaded.
We have $(-\infty, 2]$, or $\{x | x \le 2\}$.

18. $[-2, \infty)$, or $\{x | x \ge -2\}$

19. All points to the left of -2 are shaded. The open circle at -2 indicates that -2 is not part of the graph.
We have $(-\infty, -2)$, or $\{x | x < -2\}$.

20. $(1, \infty)$, or $\{x | x > 1\}$

21. The point 0 and all points to the right of 0 are
shaded. We have $[0, \infty)$, or $\{x | x \ge 0\}$.

22. $(-\infty, 0]$, or $\{x | x \le 0\}$

23.
$$y + 1 > 7$$
$$y + 1 - 1 > 7 - 1 \qquad \text{Adding } -1$$
$$y > 6 \qquad \text{Simplifying}$$

The solution set is $(6, \infty)$, or $\{y | y > 6\}$. The graph
is as follows:

24. $(3, \infty)$, or $\{y | y > 3\}$

25.
$$x + 8 \le -10$$
$$x + 8 - 8 \le -10 - 8 \qquad \text{Subtracting 8}$$
$$x \le -18 \qquad \text{Simplifying}$$

The solution set is $(-\infty, -18]$, or $\{x | x \le -18\}$. The
graph is as follows:

26. $(-\infty, -21]$, or $\{x | x \le -21\}$

27.
$$x - 4 < 6$$
$$x - 4 + 4 < 6 + 4$$
$$x < 10$$

The solution set is $(-\infty, 10)$, or $\{x | x < 10\}$. The
graph is as follows:

28. $(-\infty, 17)$, or $\{x | x < 17\}$

29.
$$x - 6 \ge 2$$
$$x - 6 + 6 \ge 2 + 6$$
$$x \ge 8$$

The solution set is $[8, \infty)$, or $\{x | x \ge 8\}$. The graph
is as follows:

30. $[13, \infty)$, or $\{x | x \ge 13\}$

31.
$$y - 7 > -12$$
$$y - 7 + 7 > -12 + 7$$
$$y > -5$$

The solution set is $(-5, \infty)$, or $\{y | y > -5\}$. The
graph is as follows:

32. $(-6, \infty)$, or $\{y|y > -6\}$

33. $2x + 4 \leq x + 9$

$2x + 4 - 4 \leq x + 9 - 4$ Adding -4

$2x \leq x + 5$ Simplifying

$2x - x \leq x + 5 - x$ Adding $-x$

$x \leq 5$ Simplifying

The solution set is $(-\infty, 5]$, or $\{x|x \leq 5\}$. The graph is as follows:

34. $(-\infty, -3]$, or $\{x|x \leq -3\}$

35. $4x - 6 \geq 3x - 1$

$4x - 6 + 6 \geq 3x - 1 + 6$ Adding 6

$4x \geq 3x + 5$

$4x - 3x \geq 3x + 5 - 3x$ Adding $-3x$

$x \geq 5$

The solution set is $[5, \infty)$, or $\{x|x \geq 5\}$.

36. $[20, \infty)$, or $\{x|x \geq 20\}$

37. $y + \dfrac{1}{3} \leq \dfrac{5}{6}$

$y + \dfrac{1}{3} - \dfrac{1}{3} \leq \dfrac{5}{6} - \dfrac{1}{3}$

$y \leq \dfrac{5}{6} - \dfrac{2}{6}$

$y \leq \dfrac{3}{6}$

$y \leq \dfrac{1}{2}$

The solution set is $\left(-\infty, \dfrac{1}{2}\right]$, or $\left\{y \middle| y \leq \dfrac{1}{2}\right\}$.

38. $\left(-\infty, \dfrac{1}{4}\right]$, or $\left\{x \middle| x \leq \dfrac{1}{4}\right\}$

39. $x - \dfrac{1}{8} > \dfrac{1}{2}$

$x - \dfrac{1}{8} + \dfrac{1}{8} > \dfrac{1}{2} + \dfrac{1}{8}$

$x > \dfrac{4}{8} + \dfrac{1}{8}$

$x > \dfrac{5}{8}$

The solution set is $\left(\dfrac{5}{8}, \infty\right)$, or $\left\{x \middle| x > \dfrac{5}{8}\right\}$.

40. $\left(\dfrac{7}{12}, \infty\right)$, or $\left\{y \middle| y > \dfrac{7}{12}\right\}$

41. $-9x + 17 > 17 - 8x$

$-9x + 17 - 17 > 17 - 8x - 17$ Adding -17

$-9x > -8x$

$-9x + 9x > -8x + 9x$ Adding $9x$

$0 > x$

The solution set is $(-\infty, 0)$, or $\{x|x < 0\}$.

42. $(-\infty, 0)$, or $\{x|x < 0\}$

43. $5x < 35$

$\dfrac{1}{5} \cdot 5x < \dfrac{1}{5} \cdot 35$ Multiplying by $\dfrac{1}{5}$

$x < 7$

The solution set is $(-\infty, 7)$, or $\{x|x < 7\}$. The graph is as follows:

44. $[4, \infty)$, or $\{x|x \geq 4\}$

45. $9y \leq 81$

$\dfrac{1}{9} \cdot 9y \leq \dfrac{1}{9} \cdot 81$ Multiplying by $\dfrac{1}{9}$

$y \leq 9$

The solution set is $(-\infty, 9]$, or $\{y|y \leq 9\}$. The graph is as follows:

46. $(24, \infty)$, or $\{x|x > 24\}$

47. $-7x \leq 13$

$-\dfrac{1}{7} \cdot (-7x) \geq -\dfrac{1}{7} \cdot 13$ Multiplying by $-\dfrac{1}{7}$

The symbol has to be reversed.

$x \geq -\dfrac{13}{7}$ Simplifying

The solution set is $\left[-\dfrac{13}{7}, \infty\right)$, or $\left\{x \middle| x \geq -\dfrac{13}{7}\right\}$.

48. $\left(-\infty, \dfrac{17}{8} \right)$, or $\left\{ y \middle| y < \dfrac{17}{8} \right\}$

49.
$$12x > -36$$
$$\frac{1}{12} \cdot 12x > \frac{1}{12} \cdot (-36)$$
$$x > -3$$

The solution set is $(-3, \infty)$, or $\{x | x > -3\}$. The graph is as follows:

50. $(4, \infty)$, or $\{x | x > 4\}$

51.
$$7y \geq -2$$
$$\frac{1}{7} \cdot 7y \geq \frac{1}{7}(-2) \quad \text{Multiplying by } \frac{1}{7}$$
$$y \geq -\frac{2}{7}$$

The solution set is $\left[-\dfrac{2}{7}, \infty \right)$, or $\left\{ y \middle| y \geq -\dfrac{2}{7} \right\}$.

52. $\left(-\dfrac{3}{5}, \infty \right)$, or $\left\{ x \middle| x > -\dfrac{3}{5} \right\}$

53.
$$-5x < -17$$
$$-\frac{1}{5} \cdot (-5x) > -\frac{1}{5} \cdot (-17) \quad \text{Multiplying by } -\frac{1}{5}$$
$$\underline{\quad} \quad \text{The symbol has to be reversed.}$$
$$x > \frac{17}{5} \qquad \text{Simplifying}$$

The solution set is $\left(\dfrac{17}{5}, \infty \right)$, or $\left\{ x \middle| x > \dfrac{17}{5} \right\}$.

54. $\left[\dfrac{14}{3}, \infty \right)$, or $\left\{ y \middle| y \geq \dfrac{14}{3} \right\}$

55.
$$-4y \leq \frac{1}{3}$$
$$-\frac{1}{4} \cdot (-4y) \geq -\frac{1}{4} \cdot \frac{1}{3}$$
$$\underline{\quad} \quad \text{The symbol has to be reversed.}$$
$$y \geq -\frac{1}{12}$$

The solution set is $\left[-\dfrac{1}{12}, \infty \right)$, or $\left\{ y \middle| y \geq -\dfrac{1}{12} \right\}$.

56. $\left(-\infty, -\dfrac{1}{10} \right]$, or $\left\{ x \middle| x \leq -\dfrac{1}{10} \right\}$

57.
$$-\frac{8}{5} > -2x$$
$$-\frac{1}{2} \cdot \left(-\frac{8}{5} \right) < -\frac{1}{2} \cdot (-2x)$$
$$\frac{8}{10} < x$$
$$\frac{4}{5} < x, \text{ or } x > \frac{4}{5}$$

The solution set is $\left(\dfrac{4}{5}, \infty \right)$, or $\left\{ x \middle| x > \dfrac{4}{5} \right\}$.

58. $\left(-\infty, \dfrac{1}{16} \right)$, or $\left\{ y \middle| y < \dfrac{1}{16} \right\}$

59.
$$5 + 3x < 32$$
$$5 + 3x - 5 < 32 - 5 \quad \text{Adding } -5$$
$$3x < 27 \qquad \text{Simplifying}$$
$$x < 9 \qquad \text{Multiplying by } \frac{1}{3}$$

The solution set is $(-\infty, 9)$.

60. $(-\infty, 8)$

61.
$$6 + 5y \geq 26$$
$$6 + 5y - 6 \geq 26 - 6 \quad \text{Adding } -6$$
$$5y \geq 20$$
$$y \geq 4 \qquad \text{Multiplying by } \frac{1}{5}$$

The solution set is $[4, \infty)$.

62. $[8, \infty)$

63.
$$3x - 5 \leq 13$$
$$3x - 5 + 5 \leq 13 + 5 \quad \text{Adding } 5$$
$$3x \leq 18$$
$$\frac{1}{3} \cdot 3x \leq \frac{1}{3} \cdot 18 \quad \text{Multiplying by } \frac{1}{3}$$
$$x \leq 6$$

The solution set is $(-\infty, 6]$.

64. $(-\infty, 6]$

65.
$$13x - 7 < -46$$
$$13x - 7 + 7 < -46 + 7$$
$$13x < -39$$
$$\frac{1}{13} \cdot 13x < \frac{1}{13} \cdot (-39)$$
$$x < -3$$

The solution set is $(-\infty, -3)$.

66. $(-\infty, -6)$

67.
$$16 < 4 - 3y$$
$$16 - 4 < 4 - 3y - 4 \qquad \text{Adding } -4$$
$$12 < -3y$$
$$-\frac{1}{3} \cdot 12 > -\frac{1}{3} \cdot (-3y) \qquad \text{Multiplying by } -\frac{1}{3}$$
↳ The symbol has to be reversed.
$$-4 > y$$
The solution set is $(-\infty, -4)$.

68. $(-\infty, -2)$

69.
$$3 - 6y > 23$$
$$-3 + 3 - 6y > -3 + 23$$
$$-6y > 20$$
$$-\frac{1}{6} \cdot (-6y) < -\frac{1}{6} \cdot 20$$
↳ The symbol has to be reversed.
$$y < -\frac{20}{6}$$
$$y < -\frac{10}{3}$$
The solution set is $\left(-\infty, -\frac{10}{3} \right)$.

70. $(-\infty, -3)$

71.
$$-3 < 8x + 7 - 7x$$
$$-3 < x + 7 \qquad \text{Collecting like terms}$$
$$-3 - 7 < x + 7 - 7$$
$$-10 < x$$
The solution set is $(-10, \infty)$.

72. $(-13, \infty)$

73.
$$5 - 9y \le 2 - 8y$$
$$5 - 9y + 9y \le 2 - 8y + 9y$$
$$5 \le 2 + y$$
$$-2 + 5 \le -2 + 2 + y$$
$$3 \le y, \text{ or } y \ge 3$$
The solution set is $[3, \infty)$.

74. $[2, \infty)$

75.
$$33 - 12x < 4x + 97$$
$$33 - 12x - 97 < 4x + 97 - 97$$
$$-64 - 12x < 4x$$
$$-64 - 12x + 12x < 4x + 12x$$
$$-64 < 16x$$
$$-4 < x$$
The solution set is $(-4, \infty)$.

76. $\left(-\infty, \frac{9}{5} \right)$

77.
$$2.1x + 43.2 > 1.2 - 8.4x$$
$$10(2.1x + 43.2) > 10(1.2 - 8.4x) \quad \text{Multiplying by}$$
$$\text{10 to clear decimals}$$
$$21x + 432 > 12 - 84x$$
$$21x + 84x > 12 - 432 \quad \text{Adding } 84x \text{ and}$$
$$-432$$
$$105x > -420$$
$$x > -4 \qquad \text{Multiplying by } \frac{1}{105}$$
The solution set is $(-4, \infty)$.

78. $\left(-\infty, \frac{5}{3} \right]$

79.
$$\frac{x}{3} - 4 \le 1$$
$$3\left(\frac{x}{3} - 4 \right) \le 3 \cdot 1 \qquad \text{Multiplying by 3 to}$$
$$\text{to clear the fraction}$$
$$x - 12 \le 3 \qquad \text{Simplifying}$$
$$x \le 15 \qquad \text{Adding 12}$$
The solution set is $(-\infty, 15]$.

80. $(2, \infty)$

81.
$$3(2y - 3) < 27$$
$$6y - 9 < 27 \qquad \text{Removing parentheses}$$
$$6y < 36 \qquad \text{Adding 9}$$
$$y < 6 \qquad \text{Multiplying by } \frac{1}{6}$$
The solution set is $(-\infty, 6)$.

82. $(5, \infty)$

83.
$$3(t - 2) \ge 9(t + 2)$$
$$3t - 6 \ge 9t + 18$$
$$3t - 9t \ge 18 + 6$$
$$-6t \ge 24$$
$$t \le -4 \qquad \text{Multiplying by } -\frac{1}{6} \text{ and}$$
$$\text{reversing the symbol}$$
The solution set is $(-\infty, -4]$.

84. $\left(-\infty, -\frac{5}{3} \right)$

85.
$$3(r - 6) + 2 < 4(r + 2) - 21$$
$$3r - 18 + 2 < 4r + 8 - 21$$
$$3r - 16 < 4r - 13$$
$$-16 + 13 < 4r - 3r$$
$$-3 < r, \text{ or } r > -3$$
The solution set is $(-3, \infty)$.

86. $(-12, \infty)$

87. $\dfrac{2}{3}(2x - 1) \geq 10$

$\dfrac{3}{2} \cdot \dfrac{2}{3}(2x - 1) \geq \dfrac{3}{2} \cdot 10$ Multiplying by $\dfrac{3}{2}$

$2x - 1 \geq 15$

$2x \geq 16$

$x \geq 8$

The solution set is $[8, \infty)$.

88. $(-\infty, 7]$

89. $\dfrac{3}{4}\left(3x - \dfrac{1}{2}\right) - \dfrac{2}{3} < \dfrac{1}{3}$

$\dfrac{3}{4}\left(3x - \dfrac{1}{2}\right) < 1$ Adding $\dfrac{2}{3}$

$\dfrac{9}{4}x - \dfrac{3}{8} < 1$ Removing parentheses

$8 \cdot \left(\dfrac{9}{4}x - \dfrac{3}{8}\right) < 8 \cdot 1$ Clearing fractions

$18x - 3 < 8$

$18x < 11$

$x < \dfrac{11}{18}$

The solution set is $\left(-\infty, \dfrac{11}{18}\right)$.

90. $\left(-\dfrac{5}{32}, \infty\right)$

91. $5 - 3^2 + (8 - 2)^2 \cdot 4 = 5 - 3^2 + 6^2 \cdot 4$

$= 5 - 9 + 36 \cdot 4$

$= 5 - 9 + 144$

$= -4 + 144$

$= 140$

92. 41

93. $5(2x - 4) - 3(4x + 1) = 10x - 20 - 12x - 3 =$
$-2x - 23$

94. $-1 + 37x$

95. ◈

96. ◈

97. ◈

98. ◈

99. $6[4 - 2(6 + 3t)] > 5[3(7 - t) - 4(8 + 2t)] - 20$

$6[4 - 12 - 6t] > 5[21 - 3t - 32 - 8t] - 20$

$6[-8 - 6t] > 5[-11 - 11t] - 20$

$-48 - 36t > -55 - 55t - 20$

$-48 - 36t > -75 - 55t$

$-36t + 55t > -75 + 48$

$19t > -27$

$t > -\dfrac{27}{19}$

The solution set is $\left(-\dfrac{27}{19}, \infty\right)$.

100. $\left(-\infty, \dfrac{5}{6}\right]$

101. $-(x + 5) \geq 4a - 5$

$-x - 5 \geq 4a - 5$

$-x \geq 4a - 5 + 5$

$-x \geq 4a$

$-1(-x) \leq -1 \cdot 4a$

$x \leq -4a$

The solution set is $(-\infty, -4a]$.

102. $(7, \infty)$

103. $y < ax + b$ Assume $a > 0$.

$y - b < ax$

$\dfrac{y - b}{a} < x$ Since $a > 0$, the inequality symbol stays the same.

The solution set is $\left(\dfrac{y - b}{a}, \infty\right)$.

104. $\left(-\infty, \dfrac{y - b}{a}\right)$

105. $|x| < 3$

a) Since $|3.2| = 3.2$, and $3.2 < 3$ is false, 3.2 is not a solution.

b) Since $|-2| = 2$ and $2 < 3$ is true, -2 is a solution.

c) Since $|-3| = 3$ and $3 < 3$ is false, -3 is not a solution.

d) Since $|-2.9| = 2.9$ and $2.9 < 3$ is true, -2.9 is a solution.

e) Since $|3| = 3$ and $3 < 3$ is false, 3 is not a solution.

f) Since $|1.7| = 1.7$ and $1.7 < 3$ is true, 1.7 is a solution.

106.

Exercise Set 2.7

1. Let n represent the number. Then we have
$$n < 9.$$

2. Let n represent the number; $n \geq 5$

3. Let b represent the weight of the bag, in pounds. Then we have
$$b \geq 2.$$

4. Let p represent the number of people who attended the concert; $75 < p < 100$

5. Let s represent the average speed, in mph. Then we have
$$90 < s < 110.$$

6. Let n represent the number of people who attended the Million Man March; $n \geq 400,000$

7. Let a represent the number of people who attended the Million Man March. Then we have
$$a \leq 1,200,000.$$

8. Let a represent the amount of acid, in liters; $a \leq 40$

9. Let c represent the cost, per gallon, of gasoline. Then we have
$$c \geq \$1.20.$$

10. Let t represent the temperature; $t \leq -2$

11. **Familiarize.** The average of the four scores is their sum divided by the number of tests, 4. We let s represent Nadia's score on the last test.

    Translate. The average of the four scores is given by
    $$\frac{82 + 76 + 78 + s}{4}.$$
    Since this average must be at least 80, this means that it must be greater than or equal to 80. Thus, we can translate the problem to the inequality
    $$\frac{82 + 76 + 78 + s}{4} \geq 80.$$

    Carry out. We first multiply by 4 to clear the fraction.
    $$4\left(\frac{82 + 76 + 78 + s}{4}\right) \geq 4 \cdot 80$$
    $$82 + 76 + 78 + s \geq 320$$
    $$236 + s \geq 320$$
    $$s \geq 84$$

Check. As a partial check, we show that Nadia can get a score of 84 on the fourth test and have an average of at least 80:
$$\frac{82 + 76 + 78 + 84}{4} = \frac{320}{4} = 80.$$
State. Scores of 84 and higher will earn Nadia at least a B.

12. 97 and higher

13. **Familiarize.** Let m represent the number of miles driven. Then the cost of those miles is $\$0.39m$. The total cost is the daily rate plus the mileage cost. The total cost cannot exceed $250. In other words the total cost must be less or equal to the budgeted amount of $250.

    Translate.

Daily rate	+	Mileage cost	$\leq$	Budget
↓	↓	↓	↓	↓
44.95	+	0.39m	$\leq$	250

    Carry out.
    $$44.95 + 0.39m \leq 250$$
    $$4495 + 39m \leq 25,000 \quad \text{Clearing decimals}$$
    $$39m \leq 20,505$$
    $$m \leq \frac{20,505}{39}$$
    $$m \leq 525.8 \quad \text{Rounding to the nearest tenth}$$

    Check. We can check to see if the solution set seems reasonable.

    When $m = 525$, the total cost is
    $$44.95 + 0.39(525), \text{ or } \$249.70.$$
    When $m = 525.8$, the total cost is
    $$44.95 + 0.39(525.8), \text{ or } \$250.01.$$
    When $m = 526$, the total cost is
    $$44.95 + 0.39(526), \text{ or } \$250.09.$$

    From these calculations it would appear that the solution is correct considering that rounding occurred.

    State. To stay within the budget, the mileage must not exceed 525.8 mi.

14. Mileages less than or equal to 341.4 mi

15. **Familiarize.** Let m represent the length of a telephone call, in minutes.

    Translate.

$0.75 charge	plus	charge for time used	is at least	$3.00.
↓	↓	↓	↓	↓
0.75	+	0.45m	$\geq$	3

Carry out.
$$0.75 + 0.45m \geq 3$$
$$0.45m \geq 2.25$$
$$m \geq 5$$

Check. As a partial check, we show that if a call lasts 5 minutes it costs at least $3.00:
$$\$0.75 + \$0.45(5) = \$0.75 + \$2.25 = \$3.00$$

State. Simon's calls last at least 5 minutes each.

16. At least 3.5 hr

17. *Familiarize*. Let $s =$ the number of servings Dale eats on Saturday.

Translate.

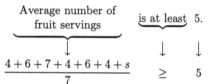

Average number of fruit servings is at least 5.
$$\frac{4+6+7+4+6+4+s}{7} \geq 5$$

Carry out. We first multiply by 7 to clear the fraction.
$$7\left(\frac{4+6+7+4+6+4+s}{7}\right) \geq 7 \cdot 5$$
$$4+6+7+4+6+4+s \geq 35$$
$$31 + s \geq 35$$
$$s \geq 4$$

Check. As a partial check, we show that Dale can eat 4 servings of fruit on Saturday and average at least 5 servings per day for the week:
$$\frac{4+6+7+4+6+4+4}{7} = \frac{35}{7} = 5$$

State. Dale should eat at least 4 servings of fruit on Saturday.

18. At least 8

19. *Familiarize*. Let $d =$ the depth of the well, in feet. Then the cost on the pay-as-you-go plan is $500 + \$8d$. The cost of the guaranteed-water plan is $4000. We want to find the values of d for which the pay-as-you-go plan costs less than the guaranteed-water plan.

Translate.

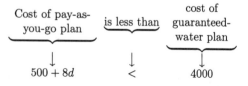

Cost of pay-as-you-go plan is less than cost of guaranteed-water plan
$$500 + 8d \qquad < \qquad 4000$$

Carry out.
$$500 + 8d < 4000$$
$$8d < 3500$$
$$d < 437.5$$

Check. We check to see that the solution is reasonable.

When $d = 437$, $\$500 + \$8 \cdot 437 = \$3996 < \$4000$

When $d = 437.5$, $\$500 + \$8(437.5) = \$4000$

When $d = 438$, $\$500 + \$8(438) = \$4004 > \$4000$

From these calculations, it appears that the solution is correct.

State. It would save a customer money to use the pay-as-you-go plan for a well that is less than 437.5 ft.

20. For calls of less than 4 units of time

21. *Familiarize*. We first make a drawing. We let l represent the length.

$$
\begin{array}{c}
l \\
4 \text{ cm} \boxed{A < 86 \text{ cm}^2} 4 \text{ cm} \\
l
\end{array}
$$

The area is the length times the width, or $4l$.

Translate.

Area is less than 86 cm^2.
$$4l \qquad < \qquad 86$$

Carry out.
$$4l < 86$$
$$l < 21.5$$

Check. We check to see if the solution seems reasonable.

When $l = 22$, the area is $22 \cdot 4$, or 88 cm^2.

When $l = 21.5$, the area is $21.5(4)$, or 86 cm^2.

When $l = 21$, the area is $21 \cdot 4$, or 84 cm^2.

From these calculations, it would appear that the solution is correct.

State. The area will be less than 86 cm^2 for lengths less than 21.5 cm.

22. 16.5 yd or more

23. *Familiarize*. Let $v =$ the blue book value of the car. Since the car was repaired, we know that $8500 does not exceed $0.8v$ or, in other words, $0.8v$ is at least $8500.

Translate.

$$\underbrace{\text{80\% of the}}_{\text{blue book value}} \quad \underbrace{\text{is at least}}_{} \quad \$8500.$$

$$\underset{0.8v}{\downarrow} \qquad \underset{\geq}{\downarrow} \qquad \underset{8500}{\downarrow}$$

Carry out.

$$0.8v \geq 8500$$
$$v \geq \frac{8500}{0.8}$$
$$v \geq 10,625$$

Check. As a partial check, we show that 80% of $10,625 is at least $8500:

$$0.8(\$10,625) = \$8500$$

State. The blue book value of the car was at least $10,625.

24. More than $16,800

25. *Familiarize.* $R = -0.075t + 3.85$

In the formula R represents the world record and t represents the years since 1930. When $t = 0$ (1930), the record was $-0.075 \cdot 0 + 3.85$, or 3.85 minutes. When $t = 2$ (1932), the record was $-0.075(2) + 3.85$, or 3.7 minutes. For what values of t will $-0.075t + 3.85$ be less than 3.5?

Translate. The record is to be less than 3.5. We have the inequality

$$R < 3.5.$$

To find the t values which satisfy this condition we substitute $-0.075t + 3.85$ for R.

$$-0.075t + 3.85 < 3.5$$

Carry out.

$$-0.075t + 3.85 < 3.5$$
$$-0.075t < 3.5 - 3.85$$
$$-0.075t < -0.35$$
$$t > \frac{-0.35}{-0.075}$$
$$t > 4\frac{2}{3}$$

Check. We check to see if the solution set we obtained seems reasonable.

When $t = 4\frac{1}{2}$, $R = -0.075(4.5) + 3.85$, or 3.5125.

When $t = 4\frac{2}{3}$, $R = -0.075\left(\frac{14}{3}\right) + 3.85$, or 3.5.

When $t = 4\frac{3}{4}$, $R = -0.075(4.75) + 3.85$, or 3.49375.

Since $r = 3.5$ when $t = 4\frac{2}{3}$ and R decreases as t increases, R will be less than 3.5 when t is greater than $4\frac{2}{3}$.

State. The world record will be less than 3.5 minutes when t is greater than $4\frac{2}{3}$ years $\left(\text{more than } 4\frac{2}{3}\right.$ years after 1930$\left.\right)$. This occurs in years after 1934.

26. Years after 1984

27. *Familiarize.* Let $w =$ the number of weeks it takes for the puppy's weight to exceed $22\frac{1}{2}$ lb.

Translate.

$$\underbrace{\text{Initial}}_{\text{weight}} \quad \underbrace{\text{plus}}_{} \quad \underbrace{\text{amount gained}}_{\text{in } w \text{ weeks}} \quad \underbrace{\text{exceeds}}_{} \quad \underbrace{22\frac{1}{2} \text{ lb.}}_{}$$

$$\underset{9}{\downarrow} \qquad \underset{+}{\downarrow} \qquad \underset{\frac{3}{4}w}{\downarrow} \qquad \underset{>}{\downarrow} \qquad \underset{22\frac{1}{2}}{\downarrow}$$

Carry out. We solve the inequality.

$$9 + \frac{3}{4}w > 22\frac{1}{2}$$
$$\frac{3}{4}w > 13\frac{1}{2}$$
$$\frac{3}{4}w > \frac{27}{2} \qquad \left(13\frac{1}{2} = \frac{27}{2}\right)$$
$$w > 18 \quad \text{Multiplying by } \frac{4}{3}$$

Check. We check to see if the solution seems reasonable.

When $w = 17$, $9 + \frac{3}{4} \cdot 17 = 21\frac{3}{4}$.

When $w = 18$, $9 + \frac{3}{4} \cdot 18 = 22\frac{1}{2}$.

When $w = 19$, $9 + \frac{3}{4} \cdot 19 = 23\frac{1}{4}$.

It would appear that the solution is correct.

State. The puppy's weight will exceed $22\frac{1}{2}$ lb when the puppy is more than 18 weeks old.

28. Dates at least 6 weeks after July 1

29. *Familiarize.* We will use the formula $F = \frac{9}{5}C + 32$.

Translate.

$$\underbrace{\text{Fahrenheit temperature}}_{} \quad \underbrace{\text{is above}}_{} \quad 98.6°.$$

$$\underset{F}{\downarrow} \qquad \underset{>}{\downarrow} \qquad \underset{98.6}{\downarrow}$$

Substituting $\frac{9}{5}C + 32$ for F, we have

$$\frac{9}{5}C + 32 > 98.6.$$

Carry out. We solve the inequality.

$$\frac{9}{5}C + 32 > 98.6$$

$$\frac{9}{5}C > 66.6$$

$$C > \frac{333}{9}$$

$$C > 37$$

Check. We check to see if the solution seems reasonable.

When $C = 36$, $\frac{9}{5} \cdot 36 + 32 = 96.8$.

When $C = 37$, $\frac{9}{5} \cdot 37 + 32 = 98.6$.

When $C = 38$, $\frac{9}{5} \cdot 38 + 32 = 100.4$.

It would appear that the solution is correct, considering that rounding occurred.

State. The human body is feverish for Celsius temperatures greater than 37°.

30. Temperatures less than $31.\overline{1}°$ C

31. *Familiarize.* The average number of calls per week is the sum of the calls for the three weeks divided by the number of weeks, 3. We let c represent the number of calls made during the third week.

Translate. The average of the three weeks is given by

$$\frac{17 + 22 + c}{3}.$$

Since the average must be at least 20, this means that it must be greater than or equal to 20. Thus, we can translate the problem to the inequality

$$\frac{17 + 22 + c}{3} \geq 20.$$

Carry out. We first multiply by 3 to clear the fraction.

$$3\left(\frac{17 + 22 + c}{3}\right) \geq 3 \cdot 20$$
$$17 + 22 + c \geq 60$$
$$39 + c \geq 60$$
$$c \geq 21$$

Check. Suppose c is a number greater than or equal to 21. Then by adding 17 and 22 on both sides of the inequality we get

$$17 + 22 + c \geq 17 + 22 + 21$$
$$17 + 22 + c \geq 60$$

so

$$\frac{17 + 22 + c}{3} \geq \frac{60}{3}, \text{ or } 20.$$

State. 21 calls or more will maintain an average of at least 20 for the three-week period.

32. Numbers less than or equal to 0

33. *Familiarize.* We first make a drawing. We let w represent the width.

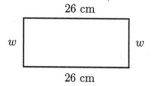

The perimeter is $P = 2l + 2w$, or $2 \cdot 26 + 2w$, or $52 + 2w$.

Translate.

The perimeter   is greater than   80 cm.
$$\downarrow \qquad\qquad \downarrow \qquad\qquad \downarrow$$
$$52 + 2w \qquad\quad > \qquad\quad 80$$

Carry out.

$$52 + 2w > 80$$
$$2w > 28$$
$$w > 14$$

Check. We check to see if the solution seems reasonable.

When $w = 13$, $P = 52 + 2 \cdot 13$, or 78 cm.

When $w = 14$, $P = 52 + 2 \cdot 14$, or 80 cm.

When $w = 15$, $P = 52 + 2 \cdot 15$, or 82 cm.

From these calculations, it appears that the solution is correct.

State. Widths greater than 14 cm will make the perimeter greater than 80 cm.

34. 92 ft or more; 92 ft or less

35. *Familiarize.* We first make a drawing. We let b represent the length of the base. Then the lengths of the other sides are $b - 2$ and $b + 3$.

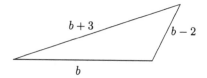

The perimeter is the sum of the lengths of the sides or $b + b - 2 + b + 3$, or $3b + 1$.

Translate.

The perimeter   is greater than   19 cm.
$$\downarrow \qquad\qquad \downarrow \qquad\qquad \downarrow$$
$$3b + 1 \qquad\quad > \qquad\quad 19$$

Carry out.

$$3b + 1 > 19$$
$$3b > 18$$
$$b > 6$$

Check. We check to see if the solution seems reasonable.

When $b = 5$, the perimeter is $3 \cdot 5 + 1$, or 16 cm.

When $b = 6$, the perimeter is $3 \cdot 6 + 1$, or 19 cm.

When $b = 7$, the perimeter is $3 \cdot 7 + 1$, or 22 cm.

From these calculations, it would appear that the solution is correct.

State. For lengths of the base greater than 6 cm the perimeter will be greater than 19 cm.

36. $\dfrac{35}{3}$ ft or less

37. Familiarize. Let $h = $ the number of hours George worked. Then $h + 3 = $ the number of hours Joan worked.

Translate.

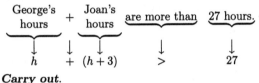

George's hours $+$ Joan's hours | are more than | 27 hours.

$h \quad + \quad (h+3) \qquad > \qquad 27$

Carry out.

$$h + (h + 3) > 27$$
$$2h + 3 > 27$$
$$2h > 24$$
$$h > 12$$

If h is at least 12, then $h + 3$ is at least 15.

Check. We check to see if the solution seems reasonable.

When $h = 11$, together they work

$\quad 11 + (11 + 3)$, or 25 hr.

When $h = 12$, together they work

$\quad 12 + (12 + 3)$, or 27 hr.

When $h = 13$, together they work

$\quad 13 + (13 + 3)$, or 29 hr.

From these calculations, it would appear that the solution is correct.

State. George worked at least 12 hours, and Joan worked 3 hours more than George.

38. $49.02

39. Familiarize. Let $w = $ the weight of the small box, in pounds. Then $w + 1$ and $w + 2$ represent the weights of the medium and large boxes, respectively.

Translate.

Weight of small box $+$ weight of medium box $+$

$w \qquad + \qquad (w+1) \qquad +$

weight of large box | is at most | 30 lb.

$(w+2) \qquad \le \qquad 30$

Carry out.

$$w + (w + 1) + (w + 2) \le 30$$
$$3w + 3 \le 30$$
$$3w \le 27$$
$$w \le 9$$

Check. As a partial check, we show that if the weight of the small box is 9 lb, the total weight of the three boxes is no more than 30 lb:

$$9 + 10 + 11 = 30$$

State. The small box weighs 9 lb or less.

40. 64 km or more

41. Familiarize. Let $r = $ the amount of fat in a serving of the regular cookies, in grams. If a reduced fat cookie has at least 25% less fat than a regular cookie, then it has at most 75% as much fat as the regular cookie.

Translate.

4 g of fat | is at most | 75% | of | the amount of fat in a regular cookie.

$4 \qquad \le \qquad 0.75 \quad \cdot \qquad r$

Carry out.

$$4 \le 0.75r$$
$$5.\overline{3} \le r, \text{ or}$$
$$5\frac{1}{3} \le r$$

Check. As a partial check, we show that 4 g of fat does not exceed 75% of $5\dfrac{1}{3}$ g of fat:

$$0.75\left(5\frac{1}{3}\right) = 0.75\left(\frac{16}{3}\right) = 4$$

State. A regular cookie contains at least $5\dfrac{1}{3}$ g of fat.

42. At least 16 g per serving

43. Familiarize. Let $b = $ the height, in cm. Recall that the area of a triangle with base b and height h is given by $\dfrac{1}{2}bh$. In this case, we have $\dfrac{1}{2} \cdot 16 \cdot h$.

Translate.

Area of triangle | is at least | 72 cm^2.

$\dfrac{1}{2} \cdot 16 \cdot h \qquad \ge \qquad 72$

Carry out.

$$\frac{1}{2} \cdot 16 \cdot h \geq 72$$

$$8h \geq 72$$

$$h \geq 9$$

Check. As a partial check we show that if the height is 9 cm, the area of the triangle is at least 72 cm^2:

$$\frac{1}{2} \cdot 16 \cdot 9 = 72 \text{ cm}^2$$

State. Heights of at least 9 cm will guarantee that the triangle's area is at least 72 cm^2.

44. 4 cm or less

45. ***Familiarize.*** We will use the formula $P = 0.1522Y - 298.592$.

Translate. We have the inequality $P \geq 6$. To find the years that satisfy this condition we substitute $0.1522Y - 298.592$ for P:

$$0.1522Y - 298.592 \geq 6$$

Carry out.

$$0.1522Y - 298.592 \geq 6$$
$$0.1522Y \geq 304.592$$
$$Y \geq 2001 \quad \text{Rounding}$$

Check. We check to see if the solution seems reasonable.

When $Y = 2000$, $P = 0.1522(2000) - 298.592$, or about \$5.81.

When $Y = 2001$, $P = 0.1522(2001) - 298.592$, or about \$5.96.

When $Y = 2002$, $P = 0.1522(2002) - 298.592$, or about \$6.11.

From these calculations, it would appear that the solution is correct considering that rounding occurred.

State. From about 2001 on, the average price of a movie ticket will be at least \$6.

46. $215\frac{5}{27}$ mi or less

47.
$$-3 + 2(-5)^2(-3) - 7$$
$$= -3 + 2(25)(-3) - 7 \quad \text{Evaluating the exponential expression}$$
$$= -3 - 150 - 7 \quad \text{Multiplying}$$
$$= -160 \quad \text{Subtracting}$$

48. $4a^2 - 2$

49.
$$9x - 5 + 4x^2 - 2 - 13x$$
$$= 4x^2 + 9x - 13x - 5 - 2$$
$$= 4x^2 + (9 - 13)x - 5 - 2$$
$$= 4x^2 - 4x - 7$$

50. $-17x + 18$

51.
$$5ab + 9b - 8ab - 12a$$
$$= 5ab - 8ab + 9b - 12a$$
$$= (5 - 8)ab + 9b - 12a$$
$$= -3ab + 9b - 12a$$

52. $-4a^2b - 4ab + 2ab^2$

53. ◈

54. ◈

55. ◈

56. ◈

57. ***Familiarize.*** Let $x =$ the smaller odd integer. Then $x + 2 =$ the larger.

Translate.

The sum of two consecutive odd integers is less than 100.

$$x + (x + 2) \quad\quad < \quad\quad 100$$

Carry out.

$$x + (x + 2) < 100$$
$$2x + 2 < 100$$
$$2x < 98$$
$$x < 49$$

The largest odd integer less than 49 is 47. Thus, a possible solution gives the integers 47 and 49.

Check. We check to see if the solution seems reasonable.

$$47 + 49 = 98 < 100$$

$$49 + 51 = 100 \quad \text{(This sum is not less than 100.)}$$

State. The largest pair of consecutive odd integers whose sum is less than 100 is 47 and 49.

58. 8 cm or less

59. ***Familiarize.*** We use the formula $F = \frac{9}{5}C + 32$.

Translate. We are interested in temperatures such that $5° < F < 15°$. Substituting for F, we have:

$$5 < \frac{9}{5}C + 32 < 15$$

Carry out.

$$5 < \frac{9}{5}C + 32 < 15$$

$$5 \cdot 5 < 5\left(\frac{9}{5}C + 32\right) < 5 \cdot 15$$

$$25 < 9C + 160 < 75$$

$$-135 < 9C < -85$$

$$-15 < C < -9\frac{4}{9}$$

Check. The check is left to the student.

State. Green ski wax works best for temperatures between $-15°$ C and $-9\frac{4}{9}°$ C.

60. More than 6 hr

61. Familiarize. Let $s =$ the gross sales. Then $s - 10,000 =$ the gross sales over \$10,000. Plan A pays $600 + 0.04s$ per month, and Plan B pays $800 + 0.06(s - 10,000)$ per month.

Translate.

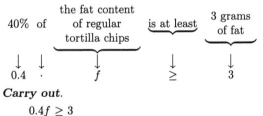

$\underbrace{\text{Plan A pays}}$	$\underbrace{\text{more than}}$	$\underbrace{\text{Plan B pays.}}$
$\downarrow$	$\downarrow$	$\downarrow$
$600 + 0.04s$	$>$	$800 + 0.06(s - 10,000)$

Carry out.

$$600 + 0.04s > 800 + 0.06(s - 10,000)$$
$$600 + 0.04s > 800 + 0.06s - 600$$
$$600 + 0.04s > 200 + 0.06s$$
$$600 - 200 > 0.06s - 0.04s$$
$$400 > 0.02s$$
$$20,000 > s$$

Check. The check is left to the student.

State. For gross sales less than \$20,000, Plan A is better than Plan B.

62. Between 5 and 9 hours

63. Familiarize. Let $f =$ the fat content of a serving of regular tortilla chips, in grams. A product that contains 60% less fat than another product has 40% of the fat content of that product. If Reduced Fat Tortilla Pops cannot be labeled lowfat, then they contain at least 3 g of fat.

Translate.

40%	of	the fat content of regular tortilla chips	is at least	3 grams of fat
$\downarrow$	$\downarrow$	$\downarrow$	$\downarrow$	$\downarrow$
0.4	$\cdot$	f	$\geq$	3

Carry out.

$$0.4f \geq 3$$
$$f \geq 7.5$$

Check. As a partial check, we show that 40% of 7.5 g is not less than 3 g.

$$0.4(7.5) = 3$$

State. A serving of regular tortilla chips contains at least 7.5 g of fat.

64.

65.

Chapter 3

Introduction to Graphing and Functions

1. We go to the top of the bar that is above the body weight 160 lb. Then we move horizontally from the top of the bar to the vertical scale listing numbers of drinks. It appears approximately 5 drinks will give a 160 lb person a blood-alcohol level of 0.10%.

2. 3

3. From $3\frac{1}{2}$ on the vertical scale we move horizontally until we reach a bar whose top is above the horizontal line on which we are moving. The first such bar corresponds to a body weight of 120 lb. Thus, we can conclude an individual weighs at least 120 lb if $3\frac{1}{2}$ drinks are consumed without reaching a blood-alcohol level of 0.10%.

4. The individual weighs more than 160 lb.

5. *Familiarize*. The total amount Leila pays in federal income tax is

    $0.18 \times \$31,200$, or $5616.

    The pie chart indicates that 18% of tax dollars are spent on social programs. We let $y =$ the amount of Leila's taxable income that will be spent on social programs.

    Translate. We reword the problem.

    What is 18% of $5616?
    $\downarrow$ $\downarrow$ $\downarrow$ $\downarrow$ $\downarrow$
    y = 18% · 5616

    Carry out.

    $y = 0.18 \cdot 5616 = 1010.88$

    Check. We go over the calculations again. The result checks.

    State. $1010.88 of Leila's taxable income will be spent on social programs.

6. $374.40

7. *Familiarize*. The total amount the Caseys pay in federal income tax is

    $0.23 \cdot \$101,500$, or $23,345.

    The pie chart indicates that 35% of tax dollars are spent on social security/medicare. We let $y =$ the

amount of the Casey's taxable income that will be spent on social security/medicare.

Translate. We reword the problem.

What is 35% of $23,345?
$\downarrow$ $\downarrow$ $\downarrow$ $\downarrow$ $\downarrow$
y = 35% · 23,345

Carry out.

$y = 0.35 \cdot 23,345 = 8170.75$

Check. We go over the calculations again. The result checks.

State. $8170.75 of the Casey's taxable income will be spent on social security/medicare.

8. $556.80

9. *Familiarize*. From the pie chart we see that 9.3% of solid waste is plastic. We let $x =$ the amount of plastic, in millions of tons, in the waste generated in 1993.

   Translate. We reword the problem.

   What is 9.3% of 206.9?
   $\downarrow$ $\downarrow$ $\downarrow$ $\downarrow$ $\downarrow$
   x = 9.3% · 206.9

   Carry out.

   $x = 0.093 \cdot 206.9 \approx 19.2$

   Check. We can repeat the calculation. The result checks.

   State. In 1993, about 19.2 million tons of waste was plastic.

10. 1.7 lb

11. *Familiarize*. From the pie chart we see that 6.6% of solid waste is glass. From Exercise 10 we know that the average American generates 4.5 lb of solid waste per day. Then the amount of this that is glass is

    $0.066(4.5)$, or 0.297 lb

    We let $x =$ the amount of glass, in pounds, that the average American recycles each day.

    Translate. We reword the problem.

    What is 23% of 0.297?
    $\downarrow$ $\downarrow$ $\downarrow$ $\downarrow$ $\downarrow$
    x = 23% · 0.297

    Carry out.

    $x = 0.23(0.297) \approx 0.07$

Check. We go over the calculations again. The result checks.

State. The average American recycles about 0.07 lb of glass each day.

12. 0.08 lb

13. We locate 1965 on the horizontal scale and then move up to the line representing public education expenditures. At that point we move left to the vertical scale and read the information we are seeking. Approximately 4% of the GNP was spent on public education in 1965.

14. 8%

15. We locate 10% on the vertical scale and then move right until the line representing health care expenditures is reached. At that point we can move down to the horizontal scale and read the information we are seeking. Health care costs represented about 10% of the GNP in 1982.

16. 1990

17. *Familiarize*. From the graph we see that about 4.5% of GNP was spent on public education in 1980. We let p = the amount spent on public education in 1980, in billions of dollars.

Translate. Reword the problem.

What is 4.5% of 2732?
 ↓   ↓   ↓   ↓   ↓
 p = 4.5% · 2732

Carry out.

$$p = 0.045 \cdot 2732 \approx 123$$

Check. We go over the calculations again. The result checks.

State. About $123 billion was spent on public education in 1980.

18. $1012 billion.

19. *Familiarize*. From the graph we see that about 5% of GNP was spent on public education in 1970. We let y = the GNP in 1970, in billions of dollars.

Translate. We reword the problem.

50.8 is 5% of what number?
 ↓   ↓   ↓   ↓   ↓
50.8 = 5% · y

Carry out. We solve the equation.

$$50.8 = 0.05y$$
$$\frac{50.8}{0.05} = y$$
$$1016 = y$$

Check. 5% of 1016 is 50.8. The answer checks.

State. The GNP in 1970 was about $1016 billion.

20. $5344 billion

21. Starting at the origin:

(1,2) is 1 unit right and 2 units up;

(−2,3) is 2 units left and 3 units up;

(4,−1) is 4 units right and 1 unit down;

(−5,−3) is 5 units left and 3 units down;

(4,0) is 4 units right and 0 units up or down;

(0,−2) is 0 units right or left and 2 units down.

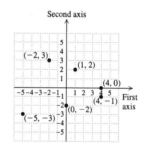

22.

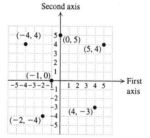

23. Starting at the origin:

(4,4) is 4 units right and 4 units up;

(−2,4) is 2 units left and 4 units up;

(5,−3) is 5 units right and 3 units down;

(−5,−5) is 5 units left and 5 units down;

(0,4) is 0 units right or left and 4 units up;

(0,−4) is 0 units right or left and 4 units down;

(3,0) is 3 units right and 0 units up or down;

(−4,0) is 4 units left and 0 units up or down.

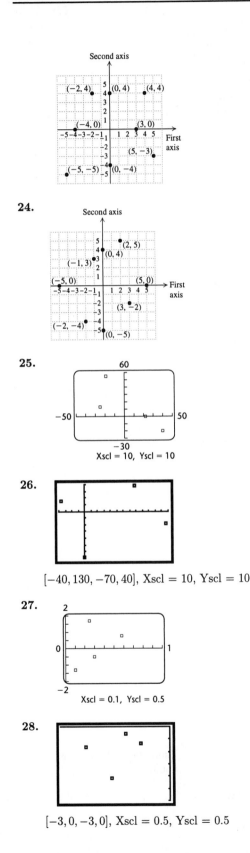

24.

25.

26.

$[-40, 130, -70, 40]$, Xscl $= 10$, Yscl $= 10$

27.

Xscl $= 0.1$, Yscl $= 0.5$

28.

$[-3, 0, -3, 0]$, Xscl $= 0.5$, Yscl $= 0.5$

29.

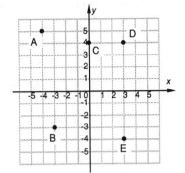

Point A is 4 units left and 5 units up. The coordinates of A are $(-4, 5)$.

Point B is 3 units left and 3 units down. The coordinates of B are $(-3, -3)$.

Point C is 0 units right or left and 4 units up. The coordinates of C are $(0, 4)$.

Point D is 3 units right and 4 units up. The coordinates of D are $(3, 4)$.

Point E is 3 units right and 4 units down. The coordinates of E are $(3, -4)$.

30. $A: (3, 3)$, $B: (0, -4)$, $C: (-5, 0)$, $D: (-1, -1)$, $E: (2, 0)$

31.

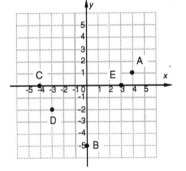

Point A is 4 units right and 1 unit up. The coordinates of A are $(4, 1)$.

Point B is 0 units right or left and 5 units down. The coordinates of B are $(0, -5)$.

Point C is 4 units left and 0 units up or down. The coordinates of C are $(-4, 0)$.

Point D is 3 units left and 2 units down. The coordinates of D are $(-3, -2)$.

Point E is 3 units right and 0 units up or down. The coordinates of E are $(3, 0)$.

32. $A: (-5, 1)$, $B: (0, 5)$, $C: (5, 3)$, $D: (0, -1)$, $E: (2, -4)$

33. Since the first coordinate is negative and the second coordinate positive, the point $(-5, 3)$ is located in quadrant II.

34. II

35. Since the first coordinate is positive and the second coordinate negative, the point $(100, -1)$ is in quadrant IV.

36. IV

37. Since both coordinates are negative, the point $(-6, -29)$ is in quadrant III.

38. III

39. Since both coordinates are positive, the point $(3.8, 9.2)$ is in quadrant I.

40. I

41. In quadrant III, first coordinates are always <u>negative</u> and second coordinates are always <u>negative</u>.

42. Second, first

43. Use the horizontal axis to represent years and the vertical axis to represent percents. Plot the points $(1970, 45\%)$, $(1980, 51\%)$, and $(1990, 54\%)$ and connect adjacent pairs of points with line segments.

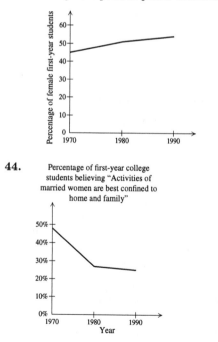

44.

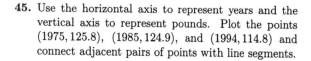

45. Use the horizontal axis to represent years and the vertical axis to represent pounds. Plot the points $(1975, 125.8)$, $(1985, 124.9)$, and $(1994, 114.8)$ and connect adjacent pairs of points with line segments.

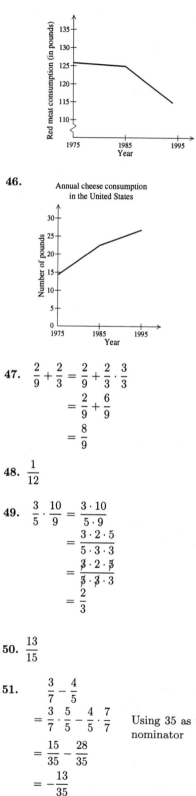

46.

47.
$$\frac{2}{9} + \frac{2}{3} = \frac{2}{9} + \frac{2}{3} \cdot \frac{3}{3}$$
$$= \frac{2}{9} + \frac{6}{9}$$
$$= \frac{8}{9}$$

48. $\dfrac{1}{12}$

49.
$$\frac{3}{5} \cdot \frac{10}{9} = \frac{3 \cdot 10}{5 \cdot 9}$$
$$= \frac{3 \cdot 2 \cdot 5}{5 \cdot 3 \cdot 3}$$
$$= \frac{\cancel{3} \cdot 2 \cdot \cancel{5}}{\cancel{5} \cdot \cancel{3} \cdot 3}$$
$$= \frac{2}{3}$$

50. $\dfrac{13}{15}$

51.
$$\frac{3}{7} - \frac{4}{5}$$
$$= \frac{3}{7} \cdot \frac{5}{5} - \frac{4}{5} \cdot \frac{7}{7} \qquad \text{Using 35 as the common denominator}$$
$$= \frac{15}{35} - \frac{28}{35}$$
$$= -\frac{13}{35}$$

52. $-\dfrac{2}{15}$

53.

54.

55.

56.

57.

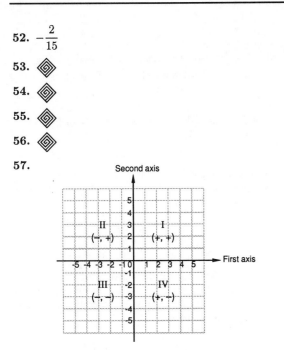

If the first coordinate is negative, then the point must be in either quadrant II or quadrant III.

58. I or II

59. If the first and second coordinates are opposites, then they have different signs. Thus, the point must be in either quadrant II (first coordinate negative, second coordinate positive) or in quadrant IV (first coordinate positive, second coordinate negative.)

60. I or III

61.

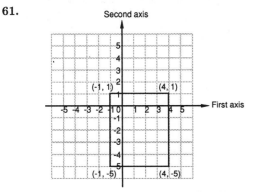

The coordinates of the fourth vertex are $(-1, -5)$.

62. $(5,2)$, $(-7,2)$, or $(3,-8)$

63. Answers may vary.

We select eight points such that the sum of the coordinates for each point is 7.

$$\begin{array}{ll}
(0,7) & 0+7=7 \\
(1,6) & 1+6=7 \\
(2,5) & 2+5=7 \\
(3,4) & 3+4=7 \\
(4,3) & 4+3=7 \\
(5,2) & 5+2=7 \\
(6,1) & 6+1=7 \\
(7,0) & 7+0=7
\end{array}$$

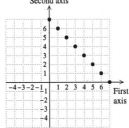

64. Answers may vary.

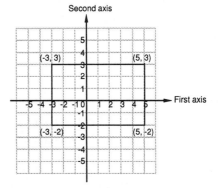

65. Plot the three given points and observe that the coordinates of the fourth vertex are $(5, 3)$

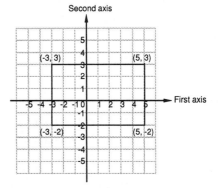

The length of the rectangle is 8 units, and the width is 5 units.

$$P = 2l + 2w$$

$$P = 2 \cdot 8 + 2 \cdot 5 = 16 + 10 = 26 \text{ units}$$

66. $\frac{65}{2}$ sq units

67. Latitude 32.5° North,
Longitude 64.5° West

68. Latitude 27° North,
Longitude 81° West

69. ◈

Exercise Set 3.2

1. We substitute 2 for x and 9 for y (alphabetical order of variables).

$$\frac{y = 4x + 3}{9 \ ? \ 4 \cdot 2 + 3}$$
$$\begin{array}{c|c} & 8 + 3 \\ 9 & 11 \quad \text{FALSE} \end{array}$$

Since $9 = 11$ is false, the pair $(2, 9)$ is not a solution.

2. Yes

3. We substitute 4 for x and 2 for y.

$$\frac{2x + 3y = 12}{2 \cdot 4 + 3 \cdot 2 \ ? \ 12}$$
$$\begin{array}{c|c} 8 + 6 & \\ 14 & 12 \quad \text{FALSE} \end{array}$$

Since $14 = 12$ is false, the pair $(4, 2)$ is not a solution.

4. No

5. We substitute 3 for a and -1 for b.

$$\frac{3a - 4b = 13}{3 \cdot 3 - 4(-1) \ ? \ 13}$$
$$\begin{array}{c|c} 9 + 4 & \\ 13 & 13 \quad \text{TRUE} \end{array}$$

Since $13 = 13$ is true, the pair $(3, -1)$ is a solution.

6. Yes

7.
$$\frac{2a + 5b = 3}{2 \cdot 0 + 5 \cdot \frac{3}{5} \ ? \ 3} \quad \text{Substituting 0 for } a \text{ and } \frac{3}{5} \text{ for } b$$
$$\begin{array}{c|c} 0 + 3 & \text{(alphabetical order of variables)} \\ 3 & \text{TRUE} \end{array}$$

Since $3 = 3$ is true, $\left(0, \frac{3}{5}\right)$ is a solution of $2a + 5b = 3$.

8. Yes

9. $y = 3x^2$

$$\frac{}{3 \ ? \ 3(-1)^2} \quad \text{Substituting } -1 \text{ for } x \text{ and 3 for } y$$
$$\begin{array}{c|c} 3 \cdot 1 & \text{(alphabetical order of variables)} \\ 3 & \text{TRUE} \end{array}$$

Since $3 = 3$ is true, $(-1, 3)$ is a solution of $y = 3x^2$.

10. No

11. To show that a pair is a solution, we substitute, replacing x with the first coordinate and y with the second coordinate in each pair.

$$\frac{y = x - 5}{2 \ ? \ 7 - 5} \qquad \frac{y = x - 5}{-4 \ ? \ -1 - 5}$$
$$\begin{array}{c|c} 2 & 2 \quad \text{TRUE} \end{array} \qquad \begin{array}{c|c} -4 & -4 \quad \text{TRUE} \end{array}$$

In each case the substitution results in a true equation. Thus, $(7, 2)$ and $(1, -4)$ are both solutions of $y = x - 5$. We graph these points and sketch the line passing through them.

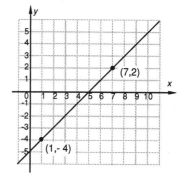

The line appears to pass through $(0, -5)$ also. We check to determine if $(0, -5)$ is a solution of $y = x - 5$.

$$\frac{y = x - 5}{-5 \ ? \ 0 - 5}$$
$$\begin{array}{c|c} -5 & -5 \quad \text{TRUE} \end{array}$$

Thus, $(0, -5)$ is another solution. There are other correct answers, including $(-1, -6)$, $(2, -3)$, $(3, -2)$, $(4, -1)$, $(5, 0)$, and $(6, 1)$.

12.
$$\frac{y = x + 3}{2 \ ? \ -1 + 3} \qquad \frac{y = x + 3}{7 \ ? \ 4 + 3}$$
$$\begin{array}{c|c} 2 & 2 \quad \text{TRUE} \end{array} \qquad \begin{array}{c|c} 7 & 7 \quad \text{TRUE} \end{array}$$

$(0, 3)$; answers may vary

13. To show that a pair is a solution, we substitute, replacing x with the first coordinate and y with the second coordinate in each pair.

$$y = \frac{1}{2}x + 3$$

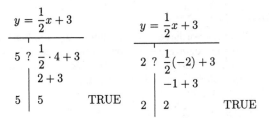

$$5 \ ? \ \frac{1}{2} \cdot 4 + 3$$
$$2 + 3$$

$$5 \ \big| \ 5 \qquad \text{TRUE}$$

$$y = \frac{1}{2}x + 3$$

$$2 \ ? \ \frac{1}{2}(-2) + 3$$
$$-1 + 3$$

$$2 \ \big| \ 2 \qquad \text{TRUE}$$

In each case the substitution results in a true equation. Thus, $(4,5)$ and $(-2,2)$ are both solutions of $y = \frac{1}{2}x + 3$. We graph these points and sketch the line passing through them.

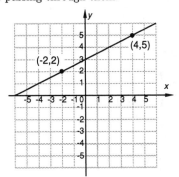

The line appears to pass through $(0,3)$ also. We check to determine if $(0,3)$ is a solution of $y = \frac{1}{2}x + 3$.

$$y = \frac{1}{2}x + 3$$

$$3 \ ? \ \frac{1}{2} \cdot 0 + 3$$

$$3 \ \big| \ 3 \qquad \text{TRUE}$$

Thus, $(0,3)$ is another solution. There are other correct answers, including $(-6,0)$, $(-4,1)$, $(2,4)$, and $(6,6)$.

14. $\quad y = \frac{1}{2}x - 1$

$$2 \ ? \ \frac{1}{2} \cdot 6 - 1$$
$$3 - 1$$

$$2 \ \big| \ 2 \qquad \text{TRUE}$$

$$y = \frac{1}{2}x - 1$$

$$-1 \ ? \ \frac{1}{2} \cdot 0 - 1$$

$$-1 \ \big| \ -1 \qquad \text{TRUE}$$

$(2,0)$; answers may vary

15. To show that a pair is a solution, we substitute, replacing x with the first coordinate and y with the second coordinate in each pair.

$$3x + y = 7$$

$$3 \cdot 2 + 1 \ ? \ 7$$
$$6 + 1$$

$$7 \ \big| \ 7 \quad \text{TRUE}$$

$$3x + y = 7$$

$$3 \cdot 4 - 5 \ ? \ 7$$
$$12 - 5$$

$$7 \ \big| \ 7 \quad \text{TRUE}$$

In each case the substitution results in a true equation. Thus, $(2,1)$ and $(4,-5)$ are both solutions of $3x + y = 7$. We graph these points and sketch the line passing through them.

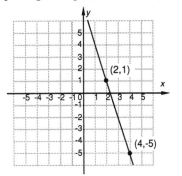

The line appears to pass through $(1,4)$ also. We check to determine if $(1,4)$ is a solution of $3x+y = 7$.

$$3x + y = 7$$

$$3 \cdot 1 + 4 \ ? \ 7$$
$$3 + 4$$

$$7 \ \big| \ 7 \quad \text{TRUE}$$

Thus, $(1,4)$ is another solution. There are other correct answers, including $(3,-2)$.

16. $\quad x + 2y = 5$

$$-1 + 2 \cdot 3 \ ? \ 5$$
$$-1 + 6$$

$$5 \ \big| \ 5 \ \text{TRUE}$$

$$x + 2y = 5$$

$$7 + 2(-1) \ ? \ 5$$
$$7 - 2$$

$$5 \ \big| \ 5 \ \text{TRUE}$$

$(1,2)$; answers may vary

17. $y = -2x$

To find an ordered pair, we choose any number for x and then determine y by substitution.

When $x = 0$, $y = -2 \cdot 0 = 0$.

When $x = 3$, $y = -2 \cdot 3 = -6$.

When $x = -2$, $y = -2 \cdot (-2) = 4$.

x	y	(x,y)
0	0	$(0,0)$
3	-6	$(3,-6)$
-2	4	$(-2,4)$

Plot these points, draw the line they determine, and label the graph $y = -2x$.

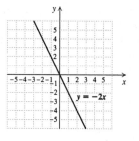

18.

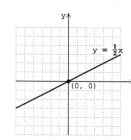

19. $y = x + 3$

To find an ordered pair, we choose any number for x and then determine y. For example, if we choose 1 for x, then $y = 1 + 3$, or 4. We find several ordered pairs, plot them, and draw the line.

x	y	(x, y)
1	4	$(1, 4)$
2	5	$(2, 5)$
-1	2	$(-1, 2)$
-3	0	$(-3, 0)$

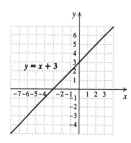

20.

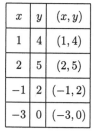

21. $y = 3x - 2$

To find an ordered pair, we choose any number for x and then determine y. For example, if $x = 2$, then $y = 3 \cdot 2 - 2 = 6 - 2 = 4$. We find several ordered pairs, plot them, and draw the line.

x	y	(x, y)
2	4	$(2, 4)$
0	-2	$(0, -2)$
-1	-5	$(-1, -5)$
1	1	$(1, 1)$

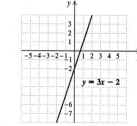

22.

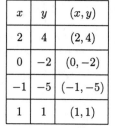

23. $y = -2x + 3$

To find an ordered pair, we choose any number for x and then determine y. For example, if $x = 1$, then $y = -2 \cdot 1 + 3 = -2 + 3 = 1$. We find several ordered pairs, plot them, and draw the line.

x	y
1	1
3	-3
-1	5
0	3

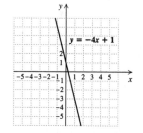

24.

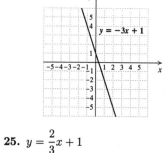

25. $y = \dfrac{2}{3}x + 1$

To find an ordered pair, we choose any number for x and then determine y. For example, if $x = 3$, then

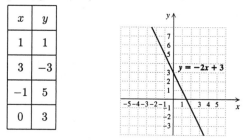

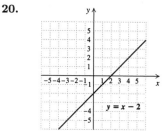

$y = \dfrac{2}{3} \cdot 3 + 1 = 2 + 1 = 3$. We find several ordered pairs, plot them, and draw the line.

x	y
3	3
0	1
-3	-1

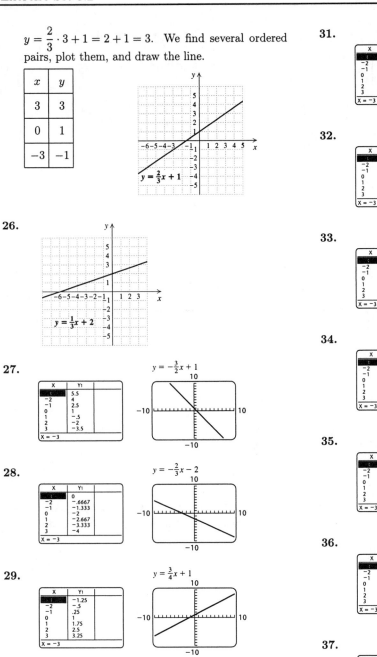

$y = \frac{2}{3}x + 1$

26.

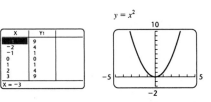

$y = \frac{1}{3}x + 2$

27.

$y = -\frac{3}{2}x + 1$

X	Y₁
-3	5.5
-2	4
-1	2.5
0	1
1	-.5
2	-2
3	-3.5

X = -3

28.

$y = -\frac{2}{3}x - 2$

X	Y₁
-3	0
-2	-.6667
-1	-1.333
0	-2
1	-2.667
2	-3.333
3	-4

X = -3

29.

$y = \frac{3}{4}x + 1$

X	Y₁
-3	-1.25
-2	-.5
-1	.25
0	1
1	1.75
2	2.5
3	3.25

X = -3

30.

$y = x^2$

X	Y₁
-3	9
-2	4
-1	1
0	0
1	1
2	4
3	9

X = -3

31.

$y = -x^2$

X	Y₁
-3	-9
-2	-4
-1	-1
0	0
1	-1
2	-4
3	-9

X = -3

32.

$y = x^2 + 2$

X	Y₁
-3	11
-2	6
-1	3
0	2
1	3
2	6
3	11

X = -3

33.

$y = x^2 - 2$

X	Y₁
-3	7
-2	2
-1	-1
0	-2
1	-1
2	2
3	7

X = -3

34.

$y = 4x^2$

X	Y₁
-3	36
-2	16
-1	4
0	0
1	4
2	16
3	36

X = -3

35.

$y = \text{abs}(x) + 2$

X	Y₁
-3	5
-2	4
-1	3
0	2
1	3
2	4
3	5

X = -3

36.

$y = -\text{abs}(x)$

X	Y₁
-3	-3
-2	-2
-1	-1
0	0
1	-1
2	-2
3	-3

X = -3

37.

$y = 3 - x^2$

X	Y₁
-3	-6
-2	-1
-1	2
0	3
1	2
2	-1
3	-6

X = -3

38.

$y = x^3 - 2$

X	Y₁
-3	-29
-2	-10
-1	-3
0	-2
1	-1
2	6
3	25

X = -3

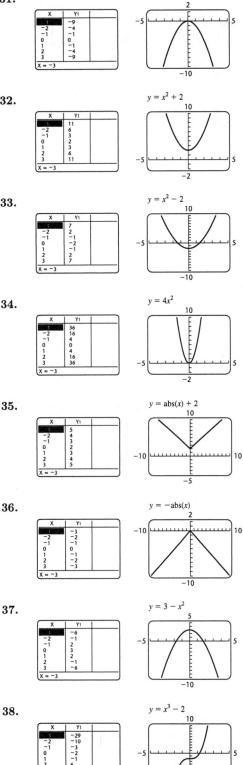

39.

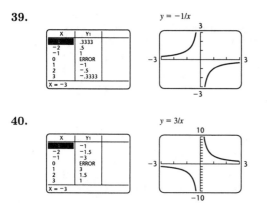

$y = -1/x$

40.

$y = 3/x$

41. Only window (b) shows where the graph crosses the x- and y-axes.

42. (b)

43. Only window (a) shows the shape of the graph and where it crosses the y-axis.

44. (a)

45. Only window (b) shows where the graph crosses the x- and y-axes.

46. (b)

47. The equations in the odd-numbered exercises 17-29 and in Exercise 41 have graphs that are straight lines, so they are linear equations.

48. 18-28 and 42

49. $3x - 7 = -34$
$$3x = -27 \quad \text{Adding } 7$$
$$x = -9 \quad \text{Dividing by } 3$$

Check: $\dfrac{3x - 7 = -34}{}$

$$3(-9) - 7 \ ? \ -34$$
$$-27 - 7 \ \Big| $$
$$-34 \ \Big| \ -34 \quad \text{TRUE}$$

The solution is -9.

50. $-\dfrac{2}{7}$

51. $2(x - 9) + 4 = 2 - 3x$
$$2x - 18 + 4 = 2 - 3x$$
$$2x - 14 = 2 - 3x$$
$$5x - 14 = 2 \qquad \text{Adding } 3x$$
$$5x = 16 \qquad \text{Adding } 14$$
$$x = \dfrac{16}{5}$$

Check: $\dfrac{2(x - 9) + 4 = 2 - 3x}{}$

$$2\left(\dfrac{16}{5} - 9\right) + 4 \ ? \ 2 - 3 \cdot \dfrac{16}{5}$$
$$2\left(-\dfrac{29}{5}\right) + 4 \ \Big| \ 2 - \dfrac{48}{5}$$
$$-\dfrac{58}{5} + 4 \ \Big| \ -\dfrac{38}{5}$$
$$-\dfrac{38}{5} \ \Big| \ -\dfrac{38}{5} \quad \text{TRUE}$$

The solution is $\dfrac{16}{5}$.

52. $p = \dfrac{w}{q + 1}$

53. $Ax + By = C$
$$By = C - Ax \quad \text{Subtracting } Ax$$
$$y = \dfrac{C - Ax}{B} \quad \text{Dividing by } B$$

54. $Q = 2A - T$

55. ◈

56. ◈

57. ◈

58. ◈

59. $x + y = 7$
$$y = -x + 7$$

Beginning with the smallest whole number, 0, substitute whole numbers for x and find the corresponding y-value.

When $x = 0$, $y = -0 + 7 = 7$.
When $x = 1$, $y = -1 + 7 = 6$.
When $x = 2$, $y = -2 + 7 = 5$.
When $x = 3$, $y = -3 + 7 = 4$.
When $x = 4$, $y = -4 + 7 = 3$.
When $x = 5$, $y = -5 + 7 = 2$.
When $x = 6$, $y = -6 + 7 = 1$.
When $x = 7$, $y = -7 + 7 = 0$.

For x-values greater than 7, the corresponding y-values are not whole numbers. Thus, we have all the whole-number solutions. They are $(0, 7)$, $(1, 6)$, $(2, 5)$, $(3, 4)$, $(4, 3)$, $(5, 2)$, $(6, 1)$, and $(7, 0)$. We use the points to graph the equation.

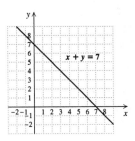

60. $(0,9)$, $(1,8)$, $(2,7)$, $(3,6)$, $(4,5)$, $(5,4)$, $(6,3)$, $(7,2)$, $(8,1)$, $(9,0)$.

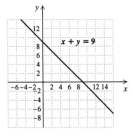

61.

62. $y = -x + 5$, or $x + y = 5$

63. Note that the sum of the coordinates of each point on the graph is 2. Thus, we have $x + y = 2$, or $y = -x + 2$.

64. $y = x + 2$

65. Note that each y-coordinate is 3 times the corresponding x-coordinate. Thus, we have $y = 3x$.

66.

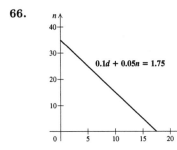

Answers may vary. 5 dimes, 25 nickels; 10 dimes, 15 nickels ; 12 dimes, 11 nickels

67. The equation is $25d + 5l = 225$.

Since the number of dinners cannot be negative, we choose only nonnegative values of d when graphing the equation. The graph stops at the horizontal axis since the number of lunches cannot be negative.

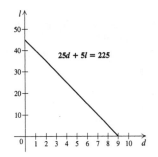

We see that three points on the graph are $(1, 40)$, $(5, 20)$, and $(8, 5)$. Thus, three combinations of dinners and lunches that total \$225 are

  1 dinner, 40 lunches,

  5 dinners, 20 lunches,

  8 dinners, 5 lunches.

68. ◈

69.

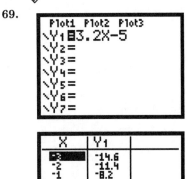

We see that the x-value -2 is paired with the y-value -11.4.

70. (a), (c), and (d)

71. Answers may vary. Trial and error shows that one good choice is $[0, 30, -50, 10]$, Xscl $= 10$, Yscl $= 10$.

Exercise Set 3.3

1. The solution of the equation is the x-coordinate of the point of intersection of the graphs. This coordinate appears to be 11. We check by substituting.

$$3x - 15 = x + 7$$

$3 \cdot 11 - 15$? $11 + 7$	
$33 - 15$	18
18	18 TRUE

The solution is 11.

2. 0.4

3. The solution of the equation is the x-coordinate of the point of intersection of the graphs. This coordinate appears to be -4. We check by substituting.

$$\frac{2x + 5 = x + 1}{}$$

$$
\begin{array}{c|c}
2(-4) + 5 \ ? \ -4 + 1 & \\
-8 + 5 & -3 \\
-3 & -3 \qquad \text{TRUE}
\end{array}
$$

The solution is -4.

4. 0

5. The solution of the equation is the x-coordinate of the point of intersection of the graphs. This coordinate appears to be $-\frac{1}{2}$. We check by substituting.

$$\frac{x + 3 = 2 - x}{}$$

$$
\begin{array}{c|c}
-\frac{1}{2} + 3 \ ? \ 2 - \left(-\frac{1}{2}\right) & \\
2\frac{1}{2} & 2 + \frac{1}{2} \\
2\frac{1}{2} & 2\frac{1}{2} \qquad \text{TRUE}
\end{array}
$$

The solution is $-\frac{1}{2}$, or -0.5.

6. $\frac{1}{2}$, or 0.5

7. $x - 3 = 4$

Graph $f(x) = x - 3$ and $g(x) = 4$ on the same set of axes.

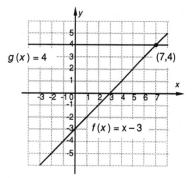

The lines appear to intersect at $(7, 4)$, so the solution is apparently 7.

To check we solve the equation algebraically.

$$x - 3 = 4$$
$$x = 7$$

The solution is 7.

8. 2

9. $2x + 1 = 7$

Graph $f(x) = 2x + 1$ and $g(x) = 7$ on the same grid.

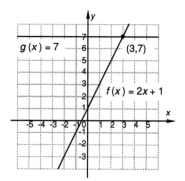

The lines appear to intersect at $(3, 7)$, so the solution is apparently 3.

To check we solve the equation algebraically.

$$2x + 1 = 7$$
$$2x = 6$$
$$x = 3$$

The solution is 3.

10. 2

11. $\frac{1}{3}x - 2 = 1$

Graph $f(x) = \frac{1}{3}x - 2$ and $g(x) = 1$ on the same grid.

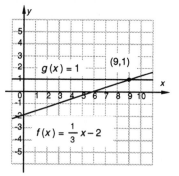

The lines appear to intersect at $(9, 1)$, so the solution is apparently 9.

To check we solve the equation algebraically.

$$\frac{1}{3}x - 2 = 1$$
$$\frac{1}{3}x = 3$$
$$x = 9$$

The solution is 9.

12. -8

13. $x + 3 = 5 - x$

Graph $f(x) = x + 3$ and $g(x) = 5 - x$ on the same grid.

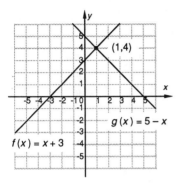

The lines appear to intersect at $(1, 4)$, so the solution is apparently 1.

To check we solve the equation algebraically.

$$x + 3 = 5 - x$$
$$2x + 3 = 5$$
$$2x = 2$$
$$x = 1$$

The solution is 1.

14. -2

15. $5 - \frac{1}{2}x = x - 4$

Graph $f(x) = 5 - \frac{1}{2}x$ and $g(x) = x - 4$ on the same grid.

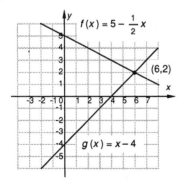

The lines appear to intersect at $(6, 2)$, so the solution is apparently 6.

To check we solve the equation algebraically.

$$5 - \frac{1}{2}x = x - 4$$
$$5 = \frac{3}{2}x - 4$$
$$9 = \frac{3}{2}x$$
$$6 = x$$

The solution is 6.

16. 4

17. $2x - 1 = -x + 3$

Graph $f(x) = 2x - 1$ and $g(x) = -x + 3$ on the same grid.

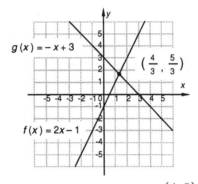

The lines appear to intersect at $\left(\frac{4}{3}, \frac{5}{3}\right)$, so the solution is apparently $\frac{4}{3}$.

To check we solve the equation algebraically.

$$2x - 1 = -x + 3$$
$$3x - 1 = 3$$
$$3x = 4$$
$$x = \frac{4}{3}$$

The solution is $\frac{4}{3}$. If we solve the equation using a grapher, we get 1.33333.

18. $\frac{4}{3}$, or 1.33333

19. $2(x + 6) = 8x$

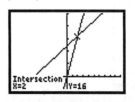

The lines interact at $(2, 16)$, so the solution is 2. To check we solve algebraically.

$$2(x+6) = 8x$$
$$2x + 12 = 8x$$
$$12 = 6x$$
$$2 = x$$

The solution is 2.

20. 3

21. $80 = 10(3t + 2)$

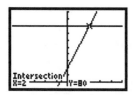

The lines intersect at $(2, 80)$, so the solution is 2. To check we solve algebraically.

$$80 = 10(3t + 2)$$
$$80 = 30t + 20$$
$$60 = 30t$$
$$2 = t$$

22. 1

23. $-6a - 10a = -32$

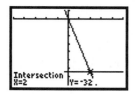

The lines intersect at $(2, -32)$, so the solution is 2. To check we solve algebraically.

$$-6a - 10a = -32$$
$$-16a = -32$$
$$a = 2$$

The solution is 2.

24. -2

25. $0.9x - 0.7 = 4.2$

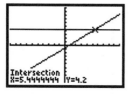

The lines intersect at $(5.4444444, 4.2)$, so the solution is 5.4444444. To check we solve algebraically.

$$0.9y - 0.7 = 4.2$$
$$0.9y - 0.7 + 0.7 = 4.2 + 0.7$$
$$0.9y = 4.9$$
$$\frac{1}{0.9}(0.9y) = \frac{1}{0.9}(4.9)$$
$$y = \frac{4.9}{0.9}$$
$$y = \frac{49}{9}$$

The solution is 5.4444444, or $\frac{49}{9}$.

26. 13

27. $4.23x - 17.898 = -1.65x - 42.454$

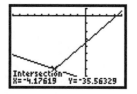

The lines intersect at $(-4.17619, -35.56329)$, so the solution is -4.17619. To check we solve algebraically.

$$4.23x - 17.898 = -1.65x - 42.454$$
$$5.88x - 17.898 = -42.454$$
$$5.88x = -24.556$$
$$x = -\frac{24.556}{5.88}$$
$$x \approx -4.17619$$

The solution is approximately -4.17619.

28. 0.21402

29. $x + 7 = 7 + x$

Since $x + 7$ and $7 + x$ are equivalent by the commutative law of addition, the equation is true regardless of the replacement for x. Thus, all real numbers are solutions and the equation is an identity.

30. All real numbers; identity

31. $x + 2 = x + 1$

Adding 2 to a number produces a different result than adding 1 to that number. Thus, there is no choice for x that is a solution of the equation. The solution set is $\emptyset$, and the equation is a contradiction.

32. $\emptyset$; contradiction

33.
$$4x - 2x - 2 = 2x$$
$$2x - 2 = 2x$$
$$-2x + 2x - 2 = -2x + 2x$$
$$-2 = 0$$

Since the original equation is equivalent to the false equation $-2 = 0$, there is no solution. The solution set is $\emptyset$. The equation is a contradiction.

34. All real numbers; identity

35.
$$2 + 9x = 3(3x + 1) - 1$$
$$2 + 9x = 9x + 3 - 1$$
$$2 + 9x = 9x + 2$$
$$2 + 9x - 9x = 9x + 2 - 9x$$
$$2 = 2$$

The original equation is equivalent to the equation $2 = 2$ which is true for all real numbers. Thus the solution set is the set of all real numbers. The equation is an identity.

36. $\emptyset$; contradiction

37.
$$-8x + 5 = 5 - 10x$$
$$-8x + 5 - 5 = 5 - 10x - 5$$
$$-8x = -10x$$
$$-8x + 10x = -10x + 10x$$
$$2x = 0$$
$$\frac{1}{2} \cdot 2x = \frac{1}{2} \cdot 0$$
$$x = 0$$

There is one solution, 0. The solution set is $\{0\}$. The equation is conditional.

38. All real numbers; identity

39.
$$2\{9 - 3[-2x - 4]\} = 12x + 42$$
$$2\{9 + 6x + 12\} = 12x + 42$$
$$2\{21 + 6x\} = 12x + 42$$
$$42 + 12x = 12x + 42$$
$$42 + 12x - 12x = 12x + 42 - 12x$$
$$42 = 42$$

The original equation is equivalent to the equation $42 = 42$, which is true for all real numbers. Thus the solution set is the set of all real numbers. The equation is an identity.

40. $\{0\}$; conditional

41. The point of intersection of the graphs is $(1, 5)$. At that point and to the right of it, we see that $3x + 2 \geq 2x + 3$. Thus the solution set is $[1, \infty)$, or $\{x | x \geq 1\}$.

42. $(-\infty, 3)$, or $\{x | x < 3\}$

43. The point of intersection is $(-0.6, 3.8)$. To the right of that point we see that $y_1 < y_2$, or $2 - 3x < 2x + 5$. Thus the solution set is $(-0.6, \infty)$, or $\{x | x > -0.6\}$.

44. $[-2.666667, \infty)$, or $\{x | x \geq -2.666667\}$

45. The graph of y_1 lies above the graph of y_2 for x-values to the left of the point of intersection. Thus the solution set is $(-\infty, 4)$, or $\{x | x < 4\}$.

46. $[2, \infty)$, or $\{x | x \geq 2\}$

47. The graph of y_3 lies on or above the graph of y_1 at and to the right of the point of intersection. Thus the solution set is $[3.2, \infty)$, or $\{x | x \geq 3.2\}$.

48. $(-\infty, 6]$, or $\{x | x \leq 6\}$

49. Graph $y_1 = x - 7$ and $y_2 = 3$ and find the point of intersection.

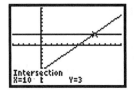

We see that $y_1 < y_2$ to the left of the point of intersection, $(10, 3)$. Thus the solution set is $(-\infty, 10)$, or $\{x | x < 10\}$.

To check we solve algebraically.
$$x - 7 < 3$$
$$x < 10$$

The solution set is $(-\infty, 10)$, or $\{x | x < 10\}$.

50. $(3, \infty)$, or $\{x | x > 3\}$

51. Graph $y_1 = 3x + 2$ and $y_2 = 2 - x$ and find the point of intersection.

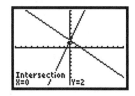

We see that $y_1 \leq y_2$ at the point of intersection, $(0, 2)$, and to the left of that point. Thus the solution set is $(-\infty, 0]$, or $\{x | x \leq 0\}$.

To check we solve algebraically.
$$3x + 2 \leq 2 - x$$
$$4x + 2 \leq 2 \qquad \text{Adding } x \text{ on both sides}$$
$$4x \leq 0 \qquad \text{Subtracting 2 on both sides}$$
$$x \leq 0 \qquad \text{Dividing by 4 on both sides}$$

The solution set is $(-\infty, 0]$, or $\{x | x \leq 0\}$.

52. $\left[\dfrac{8}{3}, \infty\right)$, or $\left\{x \middle| x \geq \dfrac{8}{3}\right\}$

53. Graph $y_1 = 3 - 2(x + 7)$ and $y_2 = 1 - x$ and find the point of intersection of the graphs.

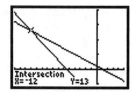

We see that $y_1 \leq y_2$ at the point of intersection, $(-12, 13)$ and to the right of that point. Thus the solution set is $[-12, \infty)$, or $\{x | x \geq -12\}$.

To check we solve algebraically.

$$3 - 2(x + 7) \leq 1 - x$$
$$3 - 2x - 14 \leq 1 - x$$
$$-2x - 11 \leq 1 - x$$
$$-11 \leq 1 + x$$
$$-12 \leq x$$

The solution set is $[-12, \infty)$, or $\{x | x \geq -12\}$.

54. $(-\infty, 1)$, or $\{x | x < 1\}$

55. $3x + 7 = 18$

$\qquad 3x = 11 \qquad$ Subtracting 7 on both sides

$\qquad x = \dfrac{11}{3} \qquad$ Dividing by 3 on both sides

The solution is $\dfrac{11}{3}$.

56. $-\dfrac{43}{2}$

57. $3x + 7 \leq 18$

$\qquad 3x \leq 11 \qquad$ Subtracting 7 on both sides

$\qquad x \leq \dfrac{11}{3} \qquad$ Dividing by 3 on both sides

The solution set is $\left(-\infty, \dfrac{11}{3}\right]$, or $\left\{x \middle| x \leq \dfrac{11}{3}\right\}$.

58. $\left(\infty, -\dfrac{43}{2}\right)$, or $\left\{x \middle| x < -\dfrac{43}{2}\right\}$

59. ◈

60. ◈

61. ◈

62. ◈

63. $2x = |x + 1|$

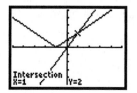

The graphs intersect at $(1, 2)$, so the solution is 1. This value checks.

64. $\dfrac{5}{3}$, 3

65. $\dfrac{1}{2}x = 3 - |x|$

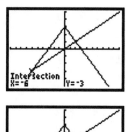

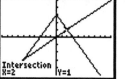

The graphs intersect at $(-6, -3)$ and at $(2, 1)$, so the solutions are -6 and 2. These values check.

66. -0.25, or $-\dfrac{1}{4}$

67. $x^2 = x + 2$

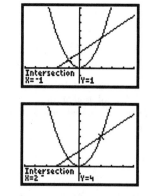

The graphs intersect at $(-1, 1)$ and at $(2, 4)$, so the solutions are -1 and 2. These values check.

68. 0, 1

69. Graph $y_1 = |x|$ and $y_2 = x + 1$.

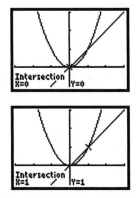

We see that $y_1 \leq y_2$ at the point of intersection, $(-0.5, 0.5)$, and to the right of that point. Thus, the solution set is $[-0.5, \infty)$, or $\{x | x \geq -0.5\}$.

70. $(10, \infty)$

71. Graph $y_1 = x^2$ and $y_2 = x$.

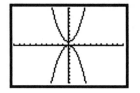

We see that $y_1 < y_2$ between the points of intersection, $(0, 0)$ and $(1, 1)$. Thus the solution set is $(0, 1)$, or $\{x | 0 < x < 1\}$.

72. $\emptyset$

73. Graph $y_1 = x^2 + 1$ and $y_2 = -x^2$.

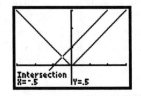

We see that $y_1 > y_2$ for all values of x. Thus the solution set is the set of real numbers.

74. $\emptyset$

Exercise Set 3.4

1. Plot the ordered pairs $(1991, 500)$, $(1992, 501)$, $(1993, 503)$, $(1994, 504)$, $(1995, 506)$, $(1996, 508)$, and $(1997, 511)$ and sketch a line through the points.

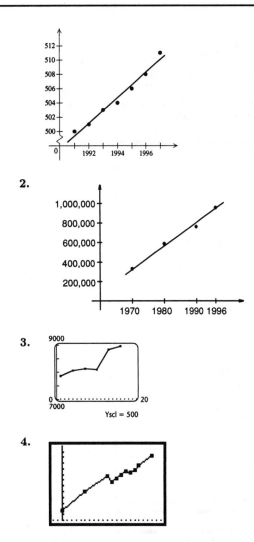

2.

3.

4.

5. Beginning with 1940, enter the years in order as 0, 10, 20, 30, 40, 50, 56, and 60. Then enter the corresponding numbers of households and draw a line graph.

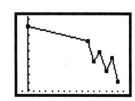

6.

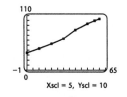

7. Replace f with y and t with x and graph $y = -\frac{1}{50}x + 2.5$ in an appropriate window. One good choice is $[0, 30, 0, 5]$ with Xscl $= 5$. Note that $1985 - 1975 = 10$, so 1985 is 10 years after 1975. Using the Value feature from the CALC menu we see that $y = 2.3$ when $x = 10$.

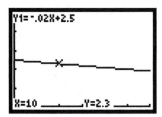

Thus, there were 2.3 million farms in the United States in 1985.

8. 2000

9. Replace n with y and graph $y = 0.2x^2 - 1.3x + 81.3$ in an appropriate window. One good choice is $[0, 10, 70, 100]$ with Yscl $= 5$. Using the TRACE feature we find that there are two points on the graph for which $y \approx 80$. They are $x \approx 1$ and $x \approx 5$.

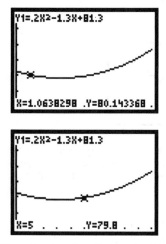

Thus, 1 year after 1990, or in 1991, and 5 years after 1990, or in 1995, there were 80 million refunds.

10. 81 million

11. Replace s with y and t with x and graph $y = -0.04x^2 - 0.9x + 50.2$ in an appropriate window. One good choice is $[-10, 30, -5, 70]$, Xscl $= 5$, Yscl $= 10$. Using the Trace feature, we move the cursor to the smallest x-value. We see that it is approximately 11, so the fewest students were enrolled about 11 years after 1974, or in 1985.

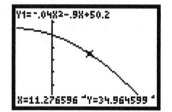

12. 45.1 million

13. We graph $v = -\frac{3}{4}t + 6$. Since time cannot be negative in this application, we select only nonnegative values for t. We also select multiples of 4 to make the computations easier.

If $t = 0$, $v = -\frac{3}{4} \cdot 0 + 6 = 6$.

If $t = 4$, $v = -\frac{3}{4} \cdot 4 + 6 = -3 + 6 = 3$.

If $t = 8$, $v = -\frac{3}{4} \cdot 8 + 6 = -6 + 6 = 0$.

t	v
0	6
4	3
8	0

We plot the points and draw the graph. Since the value of the program cannot be negative, the graph stops at the horizontal axis.

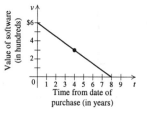

To estimate the program's value after 4 years, we find the second coordinate associated with 4. Actually, we did this when we found ordered pairs to graph. However, if we hadn't, we would locate the point on the line that is above 4 and then find the value on the vertical axis that corresponds to that point. That value is 3, so the program is worth $300 after 4 years.

14.

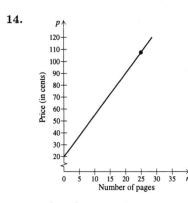

108¢, or $1.08

15. ***Familiarize and Translate.*** We use the given formula, $L = \frac{1}{2}t + 1$.

Carry out. We make a table of values using some convenient choices for t, and then we draw the graph.

When $t = 0$, $L = \frac{1}{2} \cdot 0 + 1 = 1$.

When $t = 4$, $L = \frac{1}{2} \cdot 4 + 1 = 2 + 1 = 3$.

When $t = 6$, $L = \frac{1}{2} \cdot 6 + 1 = 3 + 1 = 4$.

Months	Length
0	1
4	3
6	4

To estimate how long it will take for Tina's hair to be $2\frac{3}{4}$ inches long, locate $2\frac{3}{4}$ on the vertical axis, move horizontally to the graphed line, and then move down to the horizontal axis. It appears that it will take about $3\frac{1}{2}$ months.

Check. After $3\frac{1}{2}$ months, the length of Tina's hair

will be

$$L = \frac{1}{2}\left(3\frac{1}{2}\right) + 1$$
$$= \frac{1}{2} \cdot \frac{7}{2} + 1$$
$$= \frac{7}{4} + 1 = \frac{11}{4} = 2\frac{3}{4}$$

Our estimate was accurate.

State. Tina's hair will be $2\frac{3}{4}$ inches long $3\frac{1}{2}$ months after the haircut.

16.

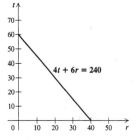

About 25 pounds

17. ***Familiarize.*** Let $V =$ the depreciated value of the house, in dollars, and $t =$ the number of years the house is rented.

Translate. The depreciated value is the original value, $150,000, less $\frac{1}{18}$ of $150,000 for each year the house is rented. We have

$$V = 150,000 - \frac{1}{18} \cdot 150,000 \cdot t, \text{ or}$$
$$V = -\frac{25,000}{3}t + 150,000.$$

Carry out. We make a table of values, using some convenient choices for t, and then we draw the graph.

When $t = 0$, $V = -\frac{25,000}{3} \cdot 0 + 150,000 = 150,000.$

When $t = 6$, $V = -\frac{25,000}{3} \cdot 6 + 150,000 = 100,000.$

When $t = 12$, $V = -\frac{25,000}{3} \cdot 12 + 150,000 = 50,000.$

Years	Value
0	$150,000
6	$100,000
12	$50,000

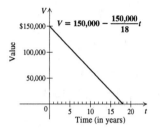

To estimate how long it takes the house to depreci-ate in value from \$125,000 to \$75,000 we first find how long the house has been rented when its value is \$125,000. From the graph we see that this is about 3 years. Then we use the graph to find how long the house has been rented when its value is \$75,000. We see that this is about 9 years. Finally, we find the difference in these times:

$$9 - 3 = 6 \text{ years}$$

Check. When the house is rented for 3 years,

$$V = -\frac{25,000}{3} \cdot 3 + 150,000 = 125,000.$$

When the house is rented for 9 years,

$$v = -\frac{25,000}{3} \cdot 9 + 150,000 = 75,000.$$

Since $9 - 3 = 6$, our estimate is accurate.

State. It takes 6 years for the house to depreciate in value from \$125,000 to \$75,000.

18.

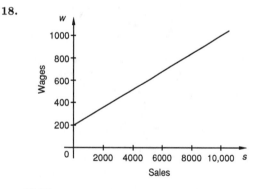

\$7400

19. Familiarize. Let $t =$ the number of 15-min units of time and $c =$ the cost of parking, in dollars.

Translate. The parking fee is \$3 plus 50¢ for each 15-min unit of time, so we have

$$c = 3 + 0.5t.$$

Carry out. We make a table of values, using some convenient choices for t, and then we draw the graph.

When $t = 2$, $c = 3 + 0.5(2) = 4$.

When $t = 6$, $c = 3 + 0.5(6) = 6$.

When $t = 10$, $c = 3 + 0.5(10) = 8$.

Units of time	Fee
2	\$4
6	\$6
10	\$8

To estimate how long someone was parked when the fee was \$7.50, locate \$7.50 on the vertical axis, move horizontally to the graphed line, and then move down to the horizontal axis. It appears that a car can be parked for 9 15-min units of time for \$7.50. This is $9 \cdot 15$, or 135 min, or 2 hr 15 min.

Check. If a vehicle is parked for 9 15-min units of time, the fee will be

$$c = 3 + 0.5(9)$$
$$= 3 + 4.5$$
$$= 7.5$$

Since this is \$7.50, our estimate was accurate.

State. A vehicle was parked for 135 min, or 2 hr, 15 min, when charged \$7.50.

20.

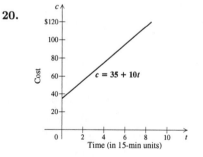

105 min, or 1 hr 45 min

21. Familiarize. Let $p =$ the number of pages and $c =$ the cost of a copy of the report, in dollars.

Translate. The cost of a copy of the report is \$2.25 plus 5¢ per page so we have

$$c = 2.25 + 0.05p.$$

Carry out. We make a table of values, using convenient choices for p, and then draw the graph.

When $p = 25$, $c = 2.25 + 0.05(25) = 3.50$.

When $p = 50$, $c = 2.25 + 0.05(50) = 4.75$.

When $p = 100$, $c = 2.25 + 0.05(100) = 7.25$.

Number of pages	Cost
25	$3.50
50	$4.75
100	$7.25

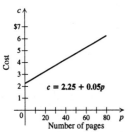

To estimate the length of a report that cost $5.20 per copy, locate $5.20 on the vertical axis, move horizontally to the graphed line, and then move down to the horizontal axis. It appears that a report of about 60 pages costs $5.20 per copy.

Check. If the report has 60 pages, the cost will be

$$c = 2.25 + 0.05(60)$$
$$= 2.25 + 3$$
$$= 5.25$$

Since this is close to $5.20, our estimate of 60 pages is fairly accurate.

State. A report that costs $5.20 per copy is about 60 pages long.

22.

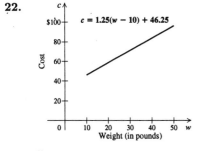

4 lb

23. *Familiarize*. Let $t = $ the time of the descent, in minutes, and $a = $ the altitude, in feet.

   Translate. The altitude is 32,200 ft less 3000 ft for each minute of the descent. We have

$$a = 32,200 - 3000t.$$

Carry out. We make a table of values using some convenient choices for t and then we draw the graph.

When $t = 2$, $a = 32,200 - 3000 \cdot 2 = 26,200$.

When $t = 6$, $a = 32,200 - 3000 \cdot 6 = 14,200$.

When $t = 10$, $a = 32,200 - 3000 \cdot 10 = 2200$.

Time of Descent	Altitude
2	26,200
6	14,200
10	2200

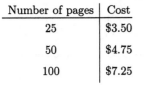

The descent lasts until the plane lands in Denver where the altitude is 5200 ft. Thus, to estimate how long the descent will last, we locate 5200 on the vertical axis, move horizontally to the graphed line, and then move down to the horizontal axis. It appears that the plane is at 5200 ft after about 9 minutes.

Check. If the descent lasts 9 minutes, the altitude is

$$a = 32,200 - 3000 \cdot 9$$
$$= 32,200 - 27,000$$
$$= 5200$$

We see that the estimate of 9 minutes is accurate.

State. The descent will last 9 minutes.

24.

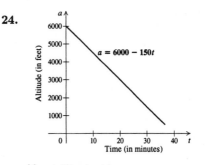

About 37 minutes

25. The ordered pairs in the table created in Exercise 15 can be used to determine the rate at which Tina's hair is growing.

Months	Length
0	1
4	3
6	4

Note that as the time changes from 0 months to 4 months, the length of Tina's hair changes from 1 inch to 3 inches. That is, a change in length of $3 - 1$, or 2 inches corresponds to a time change of $4 - 0$, or 4 months. The length is changing at the rate of

$$\frac{2 \text{ inches}}{4 \text{ months}}, \text{ or } \frac{1}{2} \text{ inch per month.}$$

26. $\frac{7}{2}$ cents per page

27. The rate can be found using the coordinates of any two points on the line. We use $(1991, 11, 400)$ and $(1994, 13, 800)$.

$$\begin{aligned}
\text{Rate} &= \frac{\text{change in cost}}{\text{corresponding change in time}} \\
&= \frac{13,800 - 11,400}{1994 - 1991} \\
&= \frac{2400}{3} \\
&= \$800 \text{ per year}
\end{aligned}$$

28. $100 per year

29. The rate can be found using the coordinates of any two points on the line. We use $(1993, 292)$ and $(1994, 282)$.

$$\begin{aligned}
\text{Rate} &= \frac{\text{change in outlay}}{\text{corresponding change in time}} \\
&= \frac{282 - 292}{1994 - 1993} \\
&= \frac{-10}{1} \\
&= -\$10 \text{ billion per year}
\end{aligned}$$

That is, the outlay is going down at the rate of $10 billion per year.

30. -31 thousand farms per year

31. We can use any two points on the line, such as $(0, 1)$ and $(4, 4)$.

$$\begin{aligned}
m &= \frac{\text{change in } y}{\text{change in } x} \\
&= \frac{4 - 1}{4 - 0} = \frac{3}{4}
\end{aligned}$$

32. $\frac{1}{3}$

33. We can use any two points on the line, such as $(-3, -4)$ and $(0, -3)$.

$$\begin{aligned}
m &= \frac{\text{change in } y}{\text{change in } x} \\
&= \frac{-3 - (-4)}{0 - (-3)} = \frac{1}{3}
\end{aligned}$$

34. 3

35. We can use any two points on the line, such as $(0, 2)$ and $(2, 0)$.

$$\begin{aligned}
m &= \frac{\text{change in } y}{\text{change in } x} \\
&= \frac{2 - 0}{0 - 2} = \frac{2}{-2} = -1
\end{aligned}$$

36. $-\frac{1}{2}$

37. We can use any two points on the line, such as $(-1, 3)$ and $(3, -3)$.

$$\begin{aligned}
m &= \frac{\text{change in } y}{\text{change in } x} \\
&= \frac{-3 - 3}{3 - (-1)} = \frac{-6}{4} = -\frac{3}{2}
\end{aligned}$$

38. $-\frac{1}{3}$

39. $(2, 3)$ and $(5, -1)$

$$m = \frac{-1 - 3}{5 - 2} = \frac{-4}{3} = -\frac{4}{3}$$

40. $\frac{2}{3}$

41. $(-2, 4)$ and $(3, 0)$

$$m = \frac{4 - 0}{-2 - 3} = \frac{4}{-5} = -\frac{4}{5}$$

42. $-\frac{5}{6}$

43. $(4, 0)$ and $(5, 7)$

$$m = \frac{0 - 7}{4 - 5} = \frac{-7}{-1} = 7$$

44. $\frac{2}{3}$

45. $(0, 8)$ and $(-3, 10)$

$$m = \frac{8 - 10}{0 - (-3)} = \frac{8 - 10}{0 + 3} = \frac{-2}{3} = -\frac{2}{3}$$

46. $-\frac{1}{2}$

47. $(-2, 3)$ and $(-6, 5)$

$$m = \frac{5-3}{-6-(-2)} = \frac{2}{-6+2} = \frac{2}{-4} = -\frac{1}{2}$$

48. $-\dfrac{11}{8}$

49. $\left(-2, \dfrac{1}{2}\right)$ and $\left(-5, \dfrac{1}{2}\right)$

$$m = \frac{\frac{1}{2} - \frac{1}{2}}{-2 - (-5)} = \frac{\frac{1}{2} - \frac{1}{2}}{-2 + 5} = \frac{0}{3} = 0$$

50. 0

51. The grade is expressed as a percent.

$$m = \frac{106}{1325} = 0.08 = 8\%$$

52. 0.05

53. The grade is expressed as a percent.

$$m = \frac{1}{12} \approx 0.083 \approx 8.3\%$$

54. 7%

55. $m = \dfrac{2.4}{8.2} = \dfrac{12}{41}$, or about 29%

56. 64%

57. $3^2 - 5^3 = 9 - 125 = -116$

58. 324

59. $(-1)^{17} = -1$

60. $-\dfrac{7}{5}$

61. $3x = 1 - 5x$

$\quad 8x = 1 \qquad$ Adding $5x$

$\quad x = \dfrac{1}{8} \qquad$ Dividing by 8

The solution is $\dfrac{1}{8}$.

62. $[3, \infty)$, or $\{x | x \geq 3\}$

63. ◈

64. ◈

65. ◈

66. ◈

67. Let $t =$ the number of units each tick mark on the vertical axis represents. Note that the graph drops 4 units for every 3 units of horizontal change. Then we have:

$$\frac{-4t}{3} = -\frac{2}{3}$$

$\quad -4t = -2 \quad$ Multiplying by 3

$\quad\quad t = \dfrac{1}{2} \quad$ Dividing by -4

Each tick mark on the vertical axis represents $\dfrac{1}{2}$ unit.

68. $\dfrac{1}{4}$ unit

69. a) Graph IV seems most appropriate for this situation. It reflects driving speeds on local streets for the first 10 and last 5 minutes and freeway cruising speeds from 10 through 30 minutes.

b) Graph III seems most appropriate for this situation. It reflects driving speeds on local streets for the first 10 minutes, an express train speed for the next 20 minutes, and walking speeds for the final 5 minutes.

c) Graph I seems most appropriate for this situation. It reflects walking speeds for the first 10 and last 5 minutes and express bus speeds from 10 through 30 minutes.

d) Graph II seems most appropriate for this situation. It reflects that the speed was 0 mph for the first 10 minutes, the time spent waiting at the bus stop. Then it shows driving speeds that fall to 0 mph several times during the next 20 minutes, indicating that the school bus stops for other students during this period of time. Finally, it shows a walking speed for the last 5 minutes.

70. a) III; b) II; c) I; d) IV

Exercise Set 3.5

1. The correspondence is not a function, because a member of the domain (3) corresponds to more than one member of the range.

2. Yes

3. The correspondence is a function, because each member of the domain corresponds to just one member of the range.

4. Yes

5. The correspondence is a function, because each member of the domain corresponds to just one member of the range.

6. No

7. This correspondence is a function, because each person in the family has only one eye color.

8. A relation but not a function

9. The correspondence is not a function, since it is reasonable to assume that at least one avenue is intersected by more than one road.

The correspondence is a relation, since it is reasonable to assume that each avenue is intersected by at least one road.

10. Function

11. This correspondence is a function, because each number in the domain, when squared and then increased by 4, corresponds to only one number in the range.

12. Function

13. a) Locate 1 on the horizontal axis and then find the point on the graph for which 1 is the first coordinate. From that point, look to the vertical axis to find the corresponding y-coordinate, 3. Thus, $f(1) = 3$.

b) To determine which member(s) of the domain are paired with 2, locate 2 on the vertical axis. From there look left and right to the graph to find any points for which 2 is the second coordinate. Two such points exist, $(-2, 2)$ and $(0, 2)$. Thus, the x-values for which $f(x) = 2$ are -2 and 0.

14. (a) 1; (b) 3

15. a) Locate 1 on the horizontal axis and then find the point on the graph for which 1 is the first coordinate. From that point, look to the vertical axis to find the corresponding y-coordinate, about 2.5 or $\frac{5}{2}$. Thus, $f(1) \approx \frac{5}{2}$.

b) To determine which member(s) of the domain are paired with 2, locate 2 on the vertical axis. From there look left and right to the graph to find any points for which 2 is the second coordinate. One such point exists. Its first coordinate appears to be about $2\frac{1}{3}$ or $\frac{7}{3}$. Thus, the x-value for which $f(x) = 2$ is about $\frac{7}{3}$.

16. (a) About $\frac{5}{2}$; (b) about $\frac{5}{3}$

17. a) Locate 1 on the horizontal axis and the find the point on the graph for which 1 is the first coordinate. From that point, look to the vertical axis to find the corresponding y-coordinate. It appears to be about $2\frac{1}{4}$, or $\frac{9}{4}$. Thus, $f(1) \approx \frac{9}{4}$.

b) To determine which member(s) of the domain are paired with 2, locate 2 on the vertical axis. From there look left and right to the graph to find any points for which 2 is the second coordinate. One such point exists. Its first coordinate is about 0, so the x-value for which $f(x) = 2$ is about 0.

18. (a) About -2; (b) about -2

19. a) Locate 1 on the horizontal axis and then find the point on the graph for which 1 is the first coordinate. From that point, look to the vertical axis to find the corresponding y-coordinate, about 1.5 or $\frac{3}{2}$. Thus, $f(1) \approx \frac{3}{2}$.

b) To determine which member(s) of the domain are paired with 2, locate 2 on the vertical axis. From there look left and right to the graph to find any points for which 2 is the second coordinate. One such point exists. Its first coordinate appears to be about $1\frac{1}{6}$, or $\frac{7}{6}$. Thus, the x-value for which $f(x) = 2$ is about $\frac{7}{6}$.

20. (a) About $\frac{9}{2}$; (b) About $-\frac{1}{2}$ and 3

21. a) Locate 1 on the horizontal axis and then find the point on the graph for which 1 is the first coordinate. From that point, look to the vertical axis to find the corresponding y-coordinate, 2. Thus, $f(1) = 2$.

b) To determine which member(s) of the domain are paired with 2, locate 2 on the vertical axis. From there look left and right to the graph to find any points for which 2 is the second coordinate. All points in the set $\{x | 0 < x \leq 2\}$ satisfy this condition. These are the x-values for which $f(x) = 2$.

22. (a) 1; (b) $\{x | 2 < x \leq 5\}$

23. We can use the vertical line test:

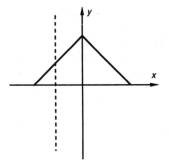

Visualize moving this vertical line across the graph. No vertical line will intersect the graph more than once. Thus, the graph is a graph of a function.

24. No

25. We can use the vertical line test:

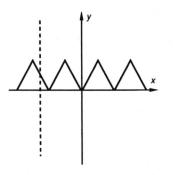

Visualize moving this vertical line across the graph. No vertical line will intersect the graph more than once. Thus, the graph is a graph of a function.

26. No

27. We can use the vertical line test.

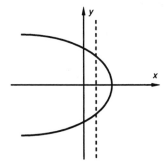

It is possible for a vertical line to intersect the graph more than once. Thus this is not the graph of a function.

28. Yes

29. We can use the vertical line test.

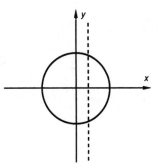

It is possible for a vertical line to intersect the graph more than once. Thus this is not a graph of a function.

30. Yes

31. $g(x) = x + 1$

a) $g(0) = 0 + 1 = 1$

b) $g(-4) = -4 + 1 = -3$

c) $g(-7) = -7 + 1 = -6$

d) $g(8) = 8 + 1 = 9$

e) $g(-0.815) = -0.815 + 1 = 0.185$

f) $g(a + 2) = a + 2 + 1 = a + 3$

32. (a) 0; (b) 4; (c) -7; (d) -8; (e) -1.27; (f) $a - 5$

33. $f(n) = 5n^2 + 4n$

a) $f(0) = 5 \cdot 0^2 + 4 \cdot 0 = 0 + 0 = 0$

b) $f(-1) = 5(-1)^2 + 4(-1) = 5 - 4 = 1$

c) $f(3) = 5 \cdot 3^2 + 4 \cdot 3 = 45 + 12 = 57$

d) $f(1.06) = 5(1.06)^2 + 4(1.06)$
$$= 5(1.1236) + 4(1.06)$$
$$= 5.618 + 4.24$$
$$= 9.858$$

e) $f(t) = 5t^2 + 4t$

f) $f(2a) = 5(2a)^2 + 4 \cdot 2a = 5 \cdot 4a^2 + 8a = 20a^2 + 8a$

34. (a) 0; (b) 5; (c) 21; (d) 48.9552; (e) $3t^2 - 2t$; (f) $12a^2 - 4a$

35. $f(x) = \dfrac{x - 3}{2x - 5}$

a) $f(0) = \dfrac{0 - 3}{2 \cdot 0 - 5} = \dfrac{-3}{0 - 5} = \dfrac{-3}{-5} = \dfrac{3}{5}$

b) $f(4) = \dfrac{4 - 3}{2 \cdot 4 - 5} = \dfrac{1}{8 - 5} = \dfrac{1}{3}$

c) $f(-1) = \dfrac{-1 - 3}{2(-1) - 5} = \dfrac{-4}{-2 - 5} = \dfrac{-4}{-7} = \dfrac{4}{7}$

d) $f(3) = \dfrac{3 - 3}{2 \cdot 3 - 5} = \dfrac{0}{6 - 5} = \dfrac{0}{1} = 0$

e) $f(42.7) = \dfrac{42.7 - 3}{2(42.7) - 5} \approx 0.49378$

f) $f(x + 2) = \dfrac{x + 2 - 3}{2(x + 2) - 5} = \dfrac{x - 1}{2x + 4 - 5} = \dfrac{x - 1}{2x - 1}$

36. (a) $\dfrac{26}{25}$; (b) $\dfrac{2}{9}$; (c) $-\dfrac{5}{12}$; (d) $-\dfrac{7}{3}$; (e) 2.05288;

(f) $\dfrac{3x + 5}{2x + 11}$

37. $A(s) = s^2 \dfrac{\sqrt{3}}{4}$

$A(4) = 4^2 \dfrac{\sqrt{3}}{4} = 4\sqrt{3}$

The area is $4\sqrt{3}$ cm².

38. $9\sqrt{3}$ in²

39. $V(r) = 4\pi r^2$

$V(3) = 4\pi(3)^2 = 36\pi$

The area is 36π in² ≈ 113.097 in².

40. 314.159 cm²

41. $F(C) = \dfrac{9}{5}C + 32$

$F(-10) = \dfrac{9}{5}(-10) + 32 = -18 + 32 = 14$

The equivalent temperature is 14° F.

42. 41° F

43. $H(x) = 2.75x + 71.48$

$H(32) = 2.75(32.15) + 71.48 \approx 159.9$

The predicted height is about 159.9 cm.

44. 168.8 cm

45. Graph $y = 0.084x^2 - 0.851x + 24.142$ in an appropriate window. One good choice is $[0, 60, 0, 250]$, Xscl = 5, Yscl = 25. Then use the Value feature from the CALC menu to find the value of y when $x = 25$.

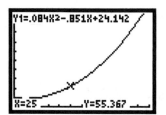

We see that the stopping distance is about 55 ft.

46. About 231 ft

47. Plot and connect the points, using the counter reading as the first coordinate and the time of tape as the second coordinate.

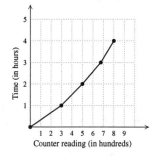

To estimate the time elapsed when the counter has reached 600, first locate the point that is directly above 600. Then estimate its second coordinate by moving horizontally from the point to the vertical axis. Read the approximate function value there. The time elapsed is about 2.5 hr.

48. About $\dfrac{2}{3}$ hr

49. Plot and connect the points, using the year as the first coordinate and the population as the second.

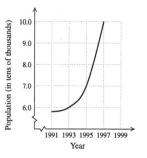

To estimate what the population was in 1994, first locate the point that is directly above 1994. Then estimate its second coordinate by moving horizontally from the point to the vertical axis. Read the approximate function value there. The population was about 64,000.

50. About 85,000

51. Plot and connect the points, using the year as the first coordinate and the sales total as the second coordinate.

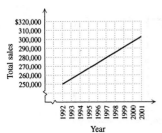

To predict the total sales for 2001, first locate the point directly above 2001. Then estimate its second coordinate by moving horizontally to the vertical axis. Read the approximate function value there. The predicted 2001 sales total is about $300,000.

52. About $270,000

53.
$$3x - 5 - 9x + 15$$
$$= 3x - 9x - 5 + 15$$
$$= (3 - 9)x - 5 + 15$$
$$= -6x + 10$$

54. $-8x - 3$

55. $2x + 4 - 6(5 - 7x) = 2x + 4 - 30 + 42x =$
$44x - 26$

56. $3y - 21$

57.
$$3 - 2[5(x - 7) + 1]$$
$$= 3 - 2[5x - 35 + 1]$$
$$= 3 - 2[5x - 34]$$
$$= 3 - 10x + 68$$
$$= -10x + 71$$

58. $-11x - 6$

59. ◈

60. ◈

61. ◈

62. ◈

63. To find $f(g(-4))$, we first find $g(-4)$:
$g(-4) = 2(-4) + 5 = -8 + 5 = -3$.
Then $f(g(-4)) = f(-3) = 3(-3)^2 - 1 = 3 \cdot 9 - 1 = 27 - 1 = 26$.
To find $g(f(-4))$, we first find $f(-4)$:
$f(-4) = 3(-4)^2 - 1 = 3 \cdot 16 - 1 = 48 - 1 = 47$.
Then $g(f(-4)) = g(47) = 2 \cdot 47 + 5 = 94 + 5 = 99$.

64. 26; 9

65. Graph $y = (4/3)\pi x^3$ in an appropriate window such as $[0, 3, 0, 60]$, Yscl $= 10$. Then use the TRACE feature to find the value of x that corresponds to $y = 50$.

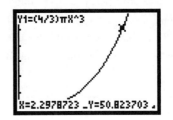

The radius is about 2.3 cm when the volume is 50 cm^3.

66. About 0.7 in.

67. Locate the highest point on the graph. Then move horizontally to the vertical axis and read the corresponding pressure. It is about 22 mm.

68. About $2\frac{3}{4}$ minutes.

69. ◈

70. About 3 minutes

71.

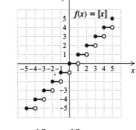

72. $g(x) = \dfrac{15}{4}x - \dfrac{13}{4}$

73. Graph the energy expenditures for walking and for bicycling on the same axes. Using the information given we plot and connect the points $\left(2\frac{1}{2}, 210\right)$ and $\left(3\frac{3}{4}, 300\right)$ for walking. We use the points $\left(5\frac{1}{2}, 210\right)$ and $(13, 660)$ for bicycling.

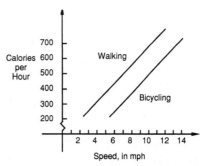

From the graph we see that walking $4\frac{1}{2}$ mph burns about 350 calories per hour and bicycling 14 mph burns about 725 calories per hour. Walking for two hours at $4\frac{1}{2}$ mph, then, would burn about $2 \cdot 350$, or 700 calories. Thus, bicycling 14 mph for one hour burns more calories than walking $4\frac{1}{2}$ mph for two hours.

Exercise Set 3.6

1. The domain is the set of all first coordinates, $\{2, 9, -2, -3\}$. The range is the set of all second coordinates, $\{10, 3\}$.

2. Domain: $\{1, 2, 3, 4\}$; range: $\{2, 3, 4, 5\}$

3. The domain is the set of all first coordinates, $\{0, 1, -1, 3\}$. The range is the set of all second coordinates, $\{0, 2, -2, 6\}$.

4. Domain: $\{-2, 2, -3, 3\}$; range: $\{4, 9\}$

5. a) The domain is the set of all first coordinates, $\{-2, -1, 0, 1, 2, 3\}$.

   b) The range is the set of all second coordinates, $\{2, 1, 0, -1, -2, -3\}$.

6. a) Domain: $\{-2, -1, 0, 1, 2, 3, 4, 5\}$

   b) Range: $\{2, 1, -1, -2\}$

7. a) The domain is the set of all first coordinates, $\{x| -4 \leq x \leq 3\}$ or $[-4, 3]$.

   b) The range is the set of all second coordinates, $\{y| -1 \leq y \leq 3\}$, or $[-1, 3]$.

8. a) Domain: $\{x| -3 \leq x \leq 3\}$, or $[-3, 3]$

   b) Range: $\{y| -2 \leq y \leq 4\}$, or $[-2, 4]$

9. a) The domain is the set of all first coordinates, $\{x| -3 \leq x \leq 5\}$ or $[-3, 5]$.

   b) The range is the set of all second coordinates, $\{y| -3 \leq y \leq 4\}$, or $[-3, 4]$.

10. a) Domain: $\{x| -4 \leq x \leq 4\}$, or $[-4, 4]$

    b) Range: $\{y| -1 \leq y \leq 4\}$, or $[-1, 4]$

11. a) The domain is the set of all first coordinates, $\{x| -4 \leq x \leq 5\}$.

    b) The range is the set of all second coordinates, $\{y|y = -4 \ or \ -2 \leq y < 2 \ or \ y = 4\}$.

12. a) Domain: $\{x| -4 \leq x \leq 5\}$

    b) Range: $\{-3, 1, 3\}$

13.

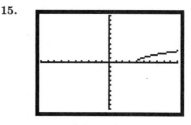

Domain: $\{x|x$ is a real number$\}$;
Range: $\{y|y$ is a real number$\}$

14. Domain: $\{x|x$ is a real number$\}$;
Range: $\{y|y$ is a real number$\}$

15.

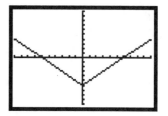

Domain: $\{x|x \geq 4\}$;
Range: $\{y|y \geq 0\}$

16. Domain: $\{x|x \leq 5\}$;
Range: $\{y|y \geq 0\}$

17. The window $[-5, 5, -7, 5]$ is better than $[-5, 5, -5, 5]$ for this function.

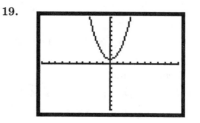

Domain: $\{x|x$ is a real number$\}$;
Range: $\{y|y \geq -6\}$

18. Domain: $\{x|x$ is a real number$\}$;
Range: $\{y|y \geq -3\}$

19.

Domain: $\{x|x$ is a real number$\}$;
Range: $\{y|y \geq 1\}$

20. Domain: $\{x | x$ is a real number$\}$;

Range: $\{y | y \geq 0\}$

21. (a)-(d) Enter $y_1 = (x + 1)/(2x - 3)$. Then enter the given x-values in a table set in ASK mode.

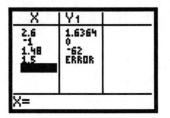

Only $f(1.5)$ is undefined, so 2.6, -1, and 1.48 are in the domain of the function and 1.5 is not.

22. (a) Yes; (b) no; (c) no; (d) yes

23. Enter $y_1 = 1/\text{abs}(4x - 9)$. Then enter the given x-values in a table set in ASK mode.

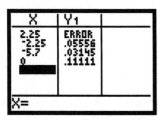

Only $f(2.25)$ is undefined, so -2.25, -57, and 0 are in the domain of the function and 2.25 is not.

24. (a) Yes; (b) no; (c) no; (d) yes

25. $f(x) = 2x + 1$

Since we can compute $2x + 1$ for any real number x, the domain is $\{x | x$ is a real number$\}$.

26. $\{x | x$ is a real number$\}$

27. $f(x) = \dfrac{2}{x - 3}$

Since $\dfrac{2}{x - 3}$ cannot be computed when the denominator is 0, we find the x-value that causes $x - 3$ to be 0:

$$x - 3 = 0$$
$$x = 3 \quad \text{Adding 3 on both sides}$$

Thus, 3 is not in the domain of f, while all other real numbers are. The domain of f is

$\{x | x$ is a real number and $x \neq 3\}$.

28. $\{x | x$ is a real number and $x \neq 5\}$

29. $f(x) = x^2 + 3$

Since we can compute $x^2 + 3$ for any real number x, the domain is $\{x | x$ is a real number$\}$.

30. $\{x | x$ is a real number$\}$

31. $f(x) = \sqrt{x - 2}$

Only numbers for which $x - 2$ is nonnegative are in the domain. We solve an inequality to find these numbers.

$$x - 2 \geq 0$$
$$x \geq 2$$

Thus the domain is $[2, \infty)$, or $\{x | x \geq 2\}$.

32. $\left[-\dfrac{1}{2}, \infty \right)$, or $\left\{ x \,\middle|\, x \geq -\dfrac{1}{2} \right\}$

33. $f(x) = \dfrac{3}{x - 1}$

Since $\dfrac{3}{x - 1}$ cannot be computed when the denominator is 0, we find the x-value that causes $x - 1$ to be 0:

$$x - 1 = 0$$
$$x = 1$$

Thus, 1 is not in the domain of f, while all other real numbers are. The domain is

$\{x | x$ is a real number and $x \neq 1\}$.

34. $\{x | x$ is a real number and $x \neq -3\}$

35. $f(x) = |5 - x|$

Since we can compute $|5 - x|$ for any real number x, the domain is $\{x | x$ is a real number$\}$.

36. $f\{x | x$ is a real number$\}$

37. $f(x) = \sqrt{1 - 3x}$

Only numbers for which $1 - 3x$ is nonnegative are in the domain. We solve an inequality to find these numbers.

$$1 - 3x \geq 0$$
$$-3x \geq -1$$
$$x \leq \dfrac{1}{3}$$

Thus the domain is $\left(-\infty, \dfrac{1}{3} \right]$, or $\left\{ x \,\middle|\, x \leq \dfrac{1}{3} \right\}$.

38. $(-\infty, 10]$, or $\{x | x \leq 10\}$

39. $f(x) = \dfrac{x+1}{2x-3}$

Since $\dfrac{x+1}{2x-3}$ cannot be computed when the denominator is 0, we find the x-value that causes $2x-3$ to be 0.

$$2x - 3 = 0$$
$$2x = 3$$
$$x = \dfrac{3}{2}$$

Thus, $\dfrac{3}{2}$ is not in the domain of f while all other real numbers are. The domain is

$$\left\{ x \middle| x \text{ is a real number } and \ x \neq \dfrac{3}{2} \right\}.$$

40. $\left\{ x \middle| x \text{ is a real number } and \ x \neq -\dfrac{7}{2} \right\}$

41. A student can register for a minimum of 1 credit and a maximum of 25 credits. In addition, the number of credits must be an integer. Thus the domain is $\{c|c \text{ is an integer } and \ 1 \leq c \leq 25\}$.

42. $\{d|d \geq 0\}$

(It could be argued that d must also be an integer.)

43. Both t and w must be nonnegative. We solve an inequality to find the values of t for which $w \geq 0$.

$$15 - t \geq 0$$
$$15 \geq t$$

Thus the domain is $\{t|0 \leq t \leq 15\}$.

44. $\left\{ t \middle| 0 \leq t \leq \dfrac{44}{7} \right\}$

45. a)   Salary is \$200 plus 4% of sales.
$$\downarrow \quad \downarrow \quad \downarrow \quad \downarrow \quad \downarrow \quad \downarrow \quad \downarrow$$
$$w \quad = \quad 200 \quad + \quad 0.04 \quad \cdot \quad s$$
We have $w(t) = 200 + 0.04s$.

b) Sales must be nonnegative, so the domain is $\{s|s \geq 0\}$.

46. a) $c(t) = \dfrac{1}{10}t + 7$

b) $\{t|t \geq 0\}$

47. a) To find the temperature m minutes after 9:00 AM, multiply $2°$ times m and subtract that number from $54°$. We have $t(m) = 54 - 2m$.

b) The number of minutes m must be nonnegative. In addition, t must be no less than -4. We solve an inequality to find the values of m for which $t \geq -4$.

$$54 - 2m \geq -4$$
$$-2m \geq -58$$
$$m \leq 29$$

Thus the domain is $\{m|0 \leq m \leq 29\}$.

48. a) $c(n) = 10 + \dfrac{2}{9}(n - 10)$

b) $\{n|n \geq 10\}$

49.
$$s = vt + d$$
$$s - d = vt \qquad \text{Subtracting } d$$
$$\dfrac{s-d}{v} = t \qquad \text{Dividing by } v$$

50. 25

51. $2(4x + 5y - 3z) = 2 \cdot 4x + 2 \cdot 5y - 2 \cdot 3z = 8x + 10y - 6z$

52. $3(x + 6y - 2z)$

53. ◈

54. ◈

55. ◈

56. ◈

57. $f(x) = \sqrt{x^2}$

Since $x^2 \geq 0$ for any real number x, the domain is $\{x|x \text{ is a real number}\}$.

58. $\left\{ x \middle| x \text{ is a real number } and \ x \neq \dfrac{7}{2} \right\}$

59. $f(x) = \dfrac{2}{\sqrt{x+3}}$

Since $\dfrac{2}{\sqrt{x+3}}$ cannot be computed when the denominator is 0 and since $\sqrt{x+3}$ cannot be computed when $x + 3$ is negative we solve an inequality to find the values of x for which $x + 3$ is positive.

$$x + 3 > 0$$
$$x > -3$$

Thus the domain is $\{x|x > -3\}$.

60. $\{x| - 1 \leq x < 1\}$

61. Domain: $\{x|x \text{ is a real number } and \ x \neq 0\}$; range: $\{y|y \text{ is a real number } and \ y \neq 0\}$

62. Domain: $\{x|x \leq -2 \ or \ x \geq 3\}$; range: $\{y|y \geq 0\}$

63. Domain: $\{x|x \text{ is a real number } and \ x \neq -3\}$; range: $\{y|y \text{ is a real number } and \ y \neq -2\}$

Chapter 4

Linear Equations, Inequalities, and Graphs

1. $y = 4x + 5$

$\uparrow\uparrow$

$y = mx + b$

The slope is 4, and the y-intercept is $(0, 5)$.

2. Slope is 5; y-intercept is $(0, 3)$.

3. $f(x) = -2x - 6$

$\uparrow\uparrow$

$f(x) = mx + b$

The slope is -2, and the y-intercept is $(0, -6)$.

4. Slope is -5; y-intercept is $(0, 7)$.

5. $y = -\dfrac{3}{8}x - 0.2$

$\uparrow\uparrow$

$y = mx + b$

The slope is $-\dfrac{3}{8}$, and the y-intercept is $(0, -0.2)$.

6. Slope is $\dfrac{15}{7}$; y-intercept is $(0, 2.2)$.

7. $g(x) = 0.5x - 9$

$\uparrow\uparrow$

$g(x) = mx + b$

The slope is 0.5, and the y-intercept is $(0, -9)$.

8. Slope is -3.1; y-intercept is $(0, 5)$.

9. $y = 43x + 197$

$\uparrow\uparrow$

$y = mx + b$

The slope is 43, and the y-intercept is $(0, 197)$.

10. Slope is -52; y-intercept is $(0, 700)$.

11. Use the slope-intercept equation, $f(x) = mx + b$, with $m = \dfrac{2}{3}$ and $b = -7$.

$$f(x) = mx + b$$
$$f(x) = \frac{2}{3}x + (-7)$$
$$f(x) = \frac{2}{3}x - 7$$

12. $f(x) = -\dfrac{3}{4}x + 5$

13. Use the slope-intercept equation, $f(x) = mx + b$, with $m = -4$ and $b = 2$.

$$f(x) = mx + b$$
$$f(x) = -4x + 2$$

14. $f(x) = 2x - 1$

15. Use the slope-intercept equation, $f(x) = mx + b$, with $m = -\dfrac{7}{9}$ and $b = 3$.

$$f(x) = mx + b$$
$$f(x) = -\frac{7}{9}x + 3$$

16. $f(x) = -\dfrac{4}{11}x + 9$

17. Use the slope-intercept equation, $f(x) = mx + b$, with $m = 5$ and $b = \dfrac{1}{2}$.

$$f(x) = mx + b$$
$$f(x) = 5x + \frac{1}{2}$$

18. $f(x) = 6x + \dfrac{2}{3}$

19. a) The graph of $y = 3x - 5$ has a positive slope, 3, and the y-intercept is $(0, -5)$. Thus, graph II matches this equation.

b) The graph of $y = 0.7x + 1$ has a positive slope, 0.7, and the y-intercept is $(0, 1)$. Thus graph IV matches this equation.

c) The graph of $y = -0.25x - 3$ has a negative slope, -0.25, and the y-intercept is $(0, -3)$. Thus graph III matches this equation.

d) The graph of $y = -4x + 2$ has a negative slope, -4, and the y-intercept is $(0, 2)$. Thus graph I matches this equation.

20. (a) II; (b) IV; (c) I; (d) III

21. $y = \dfrac{5}{2}x + 1$

Slope is $\dfrac{5}{2}$; y-intercept is $(0, 1)$.

From the y-intercept, we go *up* 5 units and to the *right* 2 units. This gives us the point $(2, 6)$. We can now draw the graph.

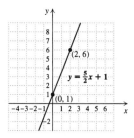

As a check, we can rename the slope and find another point.

$$\frac{5}{2} = \frac{5}{2} \cdot \frac{-1}{-1} = \frac{-5}{-2}$$

From the y-intercept, we go *down* 5 units and to the *left* 2 units. This gives us the point $(-2, -4)$. Since $(-2, -4)$ is on the line, we have a check.

22. Slope is $\frac{2}{5}$; y-intercept is $(0, 4)$.

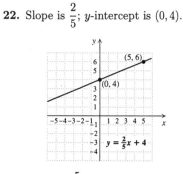

23. $f(x) = -\frac{5}{2}x + 4$

Slope is $-\frac{5}{2}$, or $\frac{-5}{2}$; y-intercept is $(0, 4)$.

From the y-intercept, we go *down* 5 units and to the *right* 2 units. This gives us the point $(2, -1)$. We can now draw the graph.

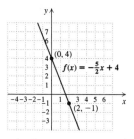

As a check, we can rename the slope and find another point.

$$\frac{-5}{2} = \frac{-5}{2} \cdot \frac{2}{2} = \frac{-10}{4}$$

From the y-intercept, we go *down* 10 units and to the *right* 4 units. This gives us the point $(4, -6)$. Since $(4, -6)$ is on the line, we have a check.

24. Slope is $-\frac{2}{5}$; y-intercept is $(0, 3)$.

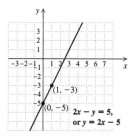

25. Convert to a slope-intercept equation.

$$2x - y = 5$$
$$-y = -2x + 5$$
$$y = 2x - 5$$

Slope is 2, or $\frac{2}{1}$; y-intercept is $(0, -5)$.

From the y-intercept, we go *up* 2 units and to the *right* 1 unit. This gives us the point $(1, -3)$. We can now draw the graph.

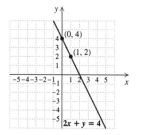

As a check, we can rename the slope and find another point.

$$2 = \frac{2}{1} \cdot \frac{3}{3} = \frac{6}{3}$$

From the y-intercept, we go *up* 6 units and to the *right* 3 units. This gives us the point $(3, 1)$. Since $(3, 1)$ is on the line, we have a check.

26. Slope is -2; y-intercept is $(0, 4)$.

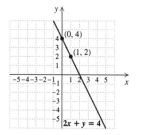

27. Convert to a slope intercept equation:

$$7y + 2x = 7$$
$$7y = -2x + 7$$
$$y = \frac{1}{7}(-2x + 7)$$
$$y = -\frac{2}{7}x + 1$$

Slope is $-\frac{2}{7}$ or $\frac{-2}{7}$; y-intercept is $(0, 1)$.

From the y-intercept we go *down* 2 units and to the *right* 7 units. This gives us the point $(7, -1)$. We can now draw the graph.

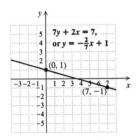

As a check we can rename the slope and find another point.

$$\frac{-2}{7} = \frac{-2}{7} \cdot \frac{-1}{-1} = \frac{2}{-7}$$

From the y-intercept, we go *up* 2 units and to the *left* 7 units. This gives us the point $(-7, 3)$. Since $(-7, 3)$ is on the line, we have a check.

28. Slope is $\frac{1}{4}$; y-intercept is $(0, -5)$.

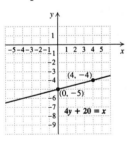

29. $f(x) = -0.25x + 2$

Slope is -0.25, or $\frac{-1}{4}$; y-intercept is $(0, 2)$.

From the y-intercept, we go *down* 1 unit and to the *right* 4 units. This gives us the point $(4, 1)$. We can now draw the graph.

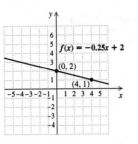

As a check, we can rename the slope and find another point.

$$\frac{-1}{4} = \frac{-1}{4} \cdot \frac{-1}{-1} = \frac{1}{-4}$$

From the y-intercept, we go *up* 1 unit and to the *left* 4 units. This gives us the point $(-4, 3)$. Since $(-4, 3)$ is on the line, we have a check.

30. Slope is 1.5, or $\frac{3}{2}$; y-intercept is $(0, -3)$.

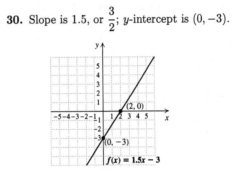

31. Convert to a slope-intercept equation.

$$4x - 5y = 10$$
$$-5y = 4x + 10$$
$$y = \frac{4}{5}x - 2$$

Slope is $\frac{4}{5}$; y-intercept is $(0, -2)$.

From the y-intercept, we go *up* 4 units and to the *right* 5 units. This gives us the point $(5, 2)$. We can now draw the graph.

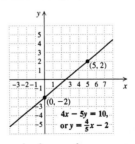

As a check, we choose some other value for x, say -5, and determine y:

$$y = \frac{4}{5}(-5) - 2 = -4 - 2 = -6$$

We plot the point $(-5, -6)$ and see that it *is* on the line.

32. Slope is $-\dfrac{5}{4}$; y-intercept is $(0,1)$.

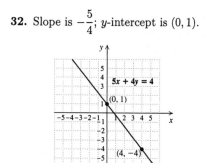

33. $f(x) = \dfrac{5}{4}x - 2$

Slope is $\dfrac{5}{4}$; y-intercept is $(0,-2)$.

From the y-intercept, we go *up* 5 units and to the *right* 4 units. This gives us the point $(4,3)$. We can now draw the graph.

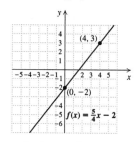

As a check, we choose some other value for x, say -2, and determine $f(x)$:

$$f(x) = \dfrac{5}{4}(-2) - 2 = -\dfrac{5}{2} - 2 = -\dfrac{9}{2}$$

We plot the point $\left(-2, -\dfrac{9}{2}\right)$ and see that it *is* on the line.

34. Slope is $\dfrac{4}{3}$; y-intercept is $(0,2)$.

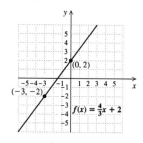

35. Convert to a slope-intercept equation:

$$12 - 4f(x) = 3x$$
$$-4f(x) = 3x - 12$$
$$f(x) = -\dfrac{1}{4}(3x - 12)$$
$$f(x) = -\dfrac{3}{4}x + 3$$

Slope is $-\dfrac{3}{4}$, or $\dfrac{-3}{4}$; y-intercept is $(0,3)$.

From the y-intercept, we go *down* 3 units and to the *right* 4 units. This gives us the point $(4,0)$. We can now draw the graph.

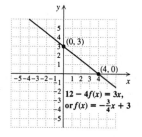

As a check, we choose some other value for x, say -4, and determine $f(x)$:

$$f(-4) = -\dfrac{3}{4}(-4) + 3 = 3 + 3 = 6$$

We plot the point $(-4,6)$ and see that it *is* on the line.

36. Slope is $-\dfrac{2}{5}$; y-intercept is $(0,-3)$.

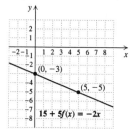

37. a) $N(t) = 7.2t - 32$

Slope is 7.2, or $\dfrac{72}{10}$, or $\dfrac{36}{5}$; vertical intercept is $(0,-32)$.

From the vertical intercept go *up* 36 units and *right* 5 units. This gives us the point $(5,4)$. We can now draw the graph.

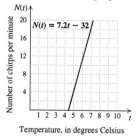

Temperature, in degrees Celsius

b) In graphing the function we found the point $(5,4)$, so we know that there are 4 cricket chirps per minute when the temperature is $5°$ C.

38. a)
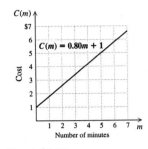

b) About $4.25

c) About 5 min

39. *Familiarize*. A monthly fee is charged after the installation fee is paid. After one month of service, the total cost will be $25+$20 = $45. After two months, the total cost will be $25 + 2 \cdot $20 = $65. We can generalize this with a model, letting $C(t)$ represent the total cost, in dollars, for t months of service.

***Translate*.** The total cost consists of the $25 installation fee plus an additional $20 for each month of service. Thus,

$$C(t) = 25 + 20t,$$

where $t \geq 0$ (since there cannot be a negative number of months).

***Carry out*.** First write the model in slope-intercept form: $C(t) = 20t + 25$. The vertical intercept is $(0, 25)$ and the slope, or rate, is $20 per month. Plot $(0, 25)$ and from there go *up* $20 and to the *right* 1 month. This takes us to $(1, 45)$. Draw a line passing through both points.

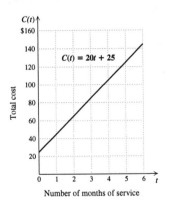

To find the total cost for 6 months, find $C(6)$:

$$C(t) = 20t + 25$$
$$C(6) = 20 \cdot 6 + 25 \quad \text{Substituting 6 for } t$$
$$= 120 + 25$$
$$= 145$$

***Check*.** Note that $(2, 65)$ and $(6, 145)$ are on the graph, as expected from the Familiarize and Carry out steps.

***State*.** The model $C(t) = 20t + 25$ can be used to determine the total cost, in dollars, for t months of basic cable TV service. The total cost for 6 months of service is $145.

40.
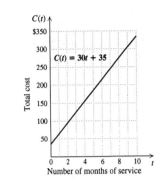

$275

41. *Familiarize*. A monthly fee is charged after the purchase of the phone. After one month of service, the total cost will be $60 + $40 = $100. After two months, the total cost will be $60 + 2 \cdot $40 = $140. We can generalize this with a model, letting $C(t)$ represent the total cost, in dollars, for t months of service.

***Translate*.** The total cost consists of the $60 purchase price of the phone plus an additional $40 for each month of service. Thus,

$$C(t) = 60 + 40t.$$

***Carry out*.** First write the model in slope-intercept form: $C(t) = 40t + 60$. The vertical intercept is $(0, 60)$ and the slope, or rate, is $40 per month. Plot $(0, 60)$ and from there go *up* $40 and to the *right* 1 month. This takes us to $(1, 100)$. Draw a line passing through both points.

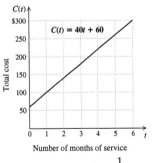

To find the total cost for $5\frac{1}{2}$ months of service, find $C(5.5)$:

$$C(t) = 40t + 60$$
$$C(t) = 40(5.5) + 60$$
$$= 220 + 60$$
$$= 280$$

The domain of C is $\{t|t \geq 0\}$ since there cannot be a negative number of months.

Check. Note that $(2, 140)$ and $(5.5, 280)$ are on the graph, as expected from the Familiarize and Carry out steps.

State. The model $C(t) = 40t + 60$ can be used to determine the total cost, in dollars, for t months of cellular phone service under the economy plan. The total cost for $5\frac{1}{2}$ months of service is $280. The domain of C is $\{t|t \geq 0\}$.

42.

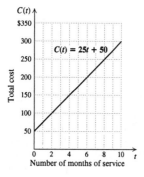

162.50; $\{t|t \geq 0\}$

43. Familiarize. The fax machine's value decreases from its purchase price of $750 by $25 each month. After one month, its value will be $750 - $25 = 725. After two months, its value will be $750 - 2 \cdot $25 = 700. This can be generalized with a model, letting $F(t)$ represent the value of the fax machine, in dollars, t months after its purchase.

Translate. The value of the fax machine consists of the $750 purchase price less $25 for each month after its purchase. Thus,

$$F(t) = 750 - 25t.$$

Carry out. First write the model in slope-intercept form: $F(t) = -25t + 750$. The vertical intercept is $(0, 750)$ and the slope, or rate, is $-$25$ per month. Plot $(0, 750)$ and from there go *down* $25 and to the *right* 1 month. This takes us to $(1, 725)$. Draw a line passing through both points.

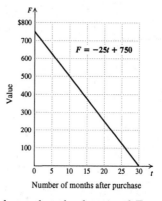

We know that the domain of F cannot contain negative values of t, since there cannot be a negative number of months. In addition, the domain cannot contain values of t that produce negative values of F, since the value of the fax machine cannot be less than $0. We find t when $F(t) = 0$:

$$F(t) = 750 - 25t$$
$$0 = 750 - 25t$$
$$25t = 750$$
$$t = 30$$

Thus, the domain of F is $\{t|0 \leq t \leq 30\}$.

Check. Note that $(2, 700)$ is on the graph, as expected from the Familiarize step.

State. The model $F(t) = -25t + 750$ can be used to determine the value, in dollars, of the fax machine t months after purchase. The domain of F is $\{t|0 \leq t \leq 30\}$.

44.

$\{t|0 \leq t \leq 76\}$

45. $C(d) = 0.75d + 2$ is of the form $y = mx + b$ with $m = 0.75$ and $b = 2$.

0.75 signifies that the cost per mile of a taxi ride is $0.75.

2 signifies that the minimum cost of a taxi ride is $2.

46. 0.1522 signifies that the price increases $0.1522 per year, for years since 1990; 4.29 signifies that the average cost of a movie ticket in 1990 was $4.29.

47. $f(t) = 2.6t + 17.8$ is of the form $y = mx + b$ with $m = 2.6$ and $b = 17.8$.

2.6 signifies that sales increase $2.6 billion per year, for years after 1975.

17.8 signifies that sales in 1975 were $17.8 billion.

48. 0.3 signifies that the cost per mile of renting the truck is $0.30; 20 signifies that the minimum cost is $20.

49. $A(t) = \dfrac{3}{20}t + 72$ is of the form $y = mx + b$ with $m = \dfrac{3}{20}$ and $b = 72$.

$\dfrac{3}{20}$ signifies that the life expectancy of American women increases $\dfrac{3}{20}$ yr per year for years after 1950.

72 signifies that the life expectancy of American women in 1950 was 72 years.

50. $\dfrac{1}{5}$ signifies that the demand increases $\dfrac{1}{5}$ quadrillion joules per year for years after 1960; 20 signifies that the demand was 20 quadrillion joules in 1960.

51. a) Graph II indicated that 200 ml of fluid was dripped in the first 3 hr, a rate of $\dfrac{200}{3}$ ml/hr. It also indicates that 400 ml of fluid was dripped in the next 3 hr, a rate of $\dfrac{400}{3}$ ml/hr, and that this rate continues until the end of the time period shown. Since the rate of $\dfrac{400}{3}$ ml/hr is double the rate of $\dfrac{200}{3}$ ml/hr, this graph is appropriate for the given situation.

b) Graph IV indicates that 300 ml of fluid was dripped in the first 2 hr, a rate of 300/2, or 150 ml/hr. In the next 2 hr, 200 ml was dripped. This is a rate of 200/2, or 100 ml/hr. Then 100 ml was dripped in the next 3 hr, a rate of 100/3, or $33\dfrac{1}{3}$ ml/hr. Finally, in the remaining 2 hr, 0 ml of fluid was dripped, a rate of 0/2, or 0 ml/hr. Since the rate at which the fluid was given decreased as time progressed and eventually became 0, this graph is appropriate for the given situation.

c) Graph I is the only graph that shows a constant rate for 5 hours, in this case from 3 PM to 8 PM. Thus, it is appropriate for the given situation.

d) Graph III indicates that 100 ml of fluid was dripped in the first 4 hr, a rate of 100/4, or 25 ml/hr. In the next 3 hr, 200 ml was dripped. This is a rate of 200/3, or $66\dfrac{2}{3}$ ml/hr. Then 100 ml was dripped in the next hour, a rate of 100 ml/hr. In the last hour 200 ml was dripped, a rate of 200 ml/hr. Since the rate at which the fluid was given gradually increased, this graph is appropriate for the given situation.

52. (a) III; (b) IV; (c) I; (d) II

53.
$$9\{2x - 3[5x + 2(-3x + y^0 - 2)]\}$$
$$= 9\{2x - 3[5x + 2(-3x + 1 - 2)]\} \quad (y^0 = 1)$$
$$= 9\{2x - 3[5x + 2(-3x - 1)]\}$$
$$= 9\{2x - 3[5x - 6x - 2]\}$$
$$= 9\{2x - 3[-x - 2]\}$$
$$= 9\{2x + 3x + 6\}$$
$$= 9\{5x + 6\}$$
$$= 45x + 54$$

54. $1 + 2x + 2y$

55. $2[3(4 - x)] = 2[12 - 3x] = 24 - 6x$

56. $8x - 3y - 12$

57. ◈

58. ◈

59. ◈

60. ◈

61. We first solve for y.
$$rx + py = s$$
$$py = -rx + s$$
$$y = -\frac{r}{p}x + \frac{s}{p}$$

The slope is $-\dfrac{r}{p}$, and the y-intercept is $\left(0, \dfrac{s}{p}\right)$.

62. Slope: $-\dfrac{r}{r+p}$; y-intercept: $\left(0, \dfrac{s}{r+p}\right)$

63. See the answer section in the text.

64. False

65. Let $c = 2$ and $d = 3$. Then $f(cd) = f(2 \cdot 3) = f(6) = m \cdot 6 + b = 6m + b$, but $f(c)f(d) = f(2)f(3) = (m \cdot 2 + b)(m \cdot 3 + b) = 6m^2 + 5mb + b^2$. Thus, the given statement is false.

66. False

67. Let $c = 5$ and $d = 2$. Then $f(c - d) = f(5 - 2) = f(3) = m \cdot 3 + b = 3m + b$, but $f(c) - f(d) = f(5) - f(2) = (m \cdot 5 + b) - (m \cdot 2 + b) = 5m + b - 2m - b = 3m$. Thus, the given statement is false.

68. $-\dfrac{31}{4}$

69. $C(n) = 5n + 17.5$, for $1 \leq n \leq 10$,

$C(n) = 6n + 17.5$, for $11 \leq n \leq 20$,

$C(n) = 7n + 17.5$, for $21 \leq n \leq 30$,

$C(n) = 8n + 17.5$ for $n \geq 31$

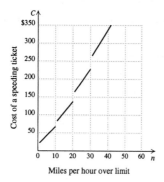

70. (a) $-\dfrac{5c}{4b}$; (b) undefined; (c) $\dfrac{a + d}{f}$

71. a) Graph III indicates that the first 2 mi and the last 3 mi were traveled in approximately the same length of time and at a fairly rapid rate. The mile following the first two miles was traveled at a much slower rate. This could indicate that the first two miles were driven, the next mile was swum and the last three miles were driven, so this graph is most appropriate for the given situation.

b) The slope in Graph IV decreases at 2 mi and again at 3 mi. This could indicate that the first two miles were traveled by bicycle, the next mile was run, and the last 3 miles were walked, so this graph is most appropriate for the given situation.

c) The slope in Graph I decreases at 2 mi and then increases at 3 mi. This could indicate that the first two miles were traveled by bicycle, the next mile was hiked, and the last three miles were traveled by bus, so this graph is most appropriate for the given situation.

d) The slope in Graph II increases at 2 mi and again at 3 mi. This could indicate that the first two miles were hiked, the next mile was run, and the last three miles were traveled by bus, so this graph is most appropriate for the given situation.

72.

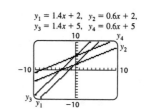

73. The function is in the form $f(x) = mx + b$, so it is linear. The graph of the function also shows that it is linear.

74. Linear

75. The function cannot be written in the form $f(x) = mx + b$, so it is not linear. The graph of the function also shows that it is not linear.

76. Linear

Exercise Set 4.2

1. $5x - 6 = 15$

$5x = 21$

$x = \dfrac{21}{5}$ The graph of $x = \dfrac{21}{5}$ is a vertical line.

Since $5x - 6 = 15$ is equivalent to $x = \dfrac{21}{5}$, the slope of the line $5x - 6 = 15$ is undefined.

2. $\dfrac{3}{5}$

3. $3x = 12 + y$

$3x - 12 = y$

$y = 3x - 12$ $(y = mx + b)$

The slope is 3.

4. Undefined

5. $5y = 6$

$y = \dfrac{6}{5}$ The graph of $y = \dfrac{6}{5}$ is a horizontal line.

Since $5y = 6$ is equivalent to $y = \dfrac{6}{5}$, the slope of the line $5y = 6$ is 0.

6. 0

7. $5x - 7y = 30$

$-7y = -5x + 30$

$y = \dfrac{5}{7}x - \dfrac{30}{7}$ $(y = mx + b)$

The slope is $\dfrac{5}{7}$.

8. $\dfrac{2}{3}$.

9. $12 - 4x = 9 + x$

$\qquad 3 = 5x$

$\qquad \dfrac{3}{5} = x$ The graph of $x = \dfrac{3}{5}$ is a
 vertical line.

Since $12 - 4x = 9 + x$ is equivalent to $x = \dfrac{3}{5}$, the slope of the line $12 - 4x = 9 + x$ is undefined.

10. Undefined

11. $2y - 4 = 35 + x$

$\qquad 2y = x + 39$

$\qquad y = \dfrac{1}{2}x + \dfrac{39}{2}$ $(y = mx + b)$

The slope is $\dfrac{1}{2}$.

12. -2

13. $3y + x = 3y + 2$

$\qquad x = 2$ The graph of $x = 2$ is a
 vertical line.

Since $3y + x = 3y + 2$ is equivalent to $x = 2$, the slope of the line $3y + x = 3y + 2$ is undefined.

14. Undefined

15. $4y + 8x = 6$

$\qquad 4y = -8x + 6$

$\qquad y = -2x + \dfrac{3}{2}$ $(y = mx + b)$

The slope is -2.

16. $-\dfrac{6}{5}$

17. $y - 6 = 14$

$\qquad y = 20$ The graph of $y = 20$ is a
 horizontal line.

Since $y - 6 = 14$ is equivalent to $y = 20$, the slope of the line $y - 6 = 14$ is 0.

18. 0

19. $3y - 2x = 5 + 9y - 2x$

$\qquad 3y = 5 + 9y$

$\qquad -6y = 5$

$\qquad y = -\dfrac{5}{6}$ The graph of $y = -\dfrac{5}{6}$ is a
 horizontal line.

Since $3y - 2x = 5 + 9y - 2x$ is equivalent to $y = -\dfrac{5}{6}$, the slope of the line $3y - 2x = 5 + 9y - 2x$ is 0.

20. 0

21. $7x - 3y = -2x + 1$

$\qquad -3y = -9x + 1$

$\qquad y = 3x - \dfrac{1}{3}$ $(y = mx + b)$

The slope is 3.

22. $\dfrac{3}{2}$

23. Graph $y = 4$.

This is a horizontal line that crosses the y-axis at $(0, 4)$. If we find some ordered pairs, note that, for any x-value chosen, y must be 4.

x	y
-2	4
0	4
3	4

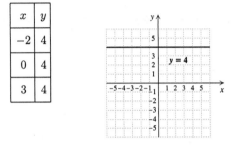

24.

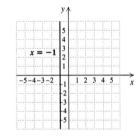

25. Graph $x = 2$.

This is a vertical line that crosses the x-axis at $(2, 0)$. If we find some ordered pairs, note that, for any y-value chosen, x must be -2.

x	y
-2	-1
-2	0
-2	2

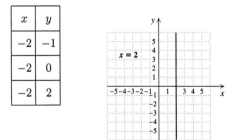

26.

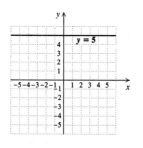

30.

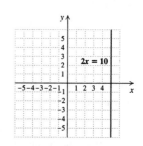

27. Graph $4 \cdot f(x) = 20$.

First solve for $f(x)$.

$$4 \cdot f(x) = 20$$
$$f(x) = 5$$

This is a horizontal line that crosses the vertical axis at $(0, 5)$.

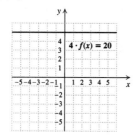

31. Graph $4 \cdot g(x) + 3x = 12 + 3x$.

First solve for $g(x)$.

$$4 \cdot g(x) + 3x = 12 + 3x$$
$$4 \cdot g(x) = 12 \qquad \text{Subtracting } 3x \text{ on both sides}$$
$$g(x) = 3$$

This is a horizontal line that crosses the vertical axis at $(0, 3)$.

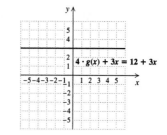

28.

32.

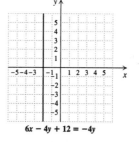

$6x - 4y + 12 = -4y$

29. Graph $3x = -15$.

Since y does not appear, we solve for x.

$$3x = -15$$
$$x = -5$$

This is a vertical line that crosses the x-axis

33. Graph $7 - 3x = 4 + 2x$.

Since y does not appear, we solve for x.

$$7 - 3x = 4 + 2x$$
$$7 - 5x = 4$$
$$-5x = -3$$
$$x = \frac{3}{5}$$

This is a vertical line that crosses the x-axis at $\left(\frac{3}{5}, 0\right)$.

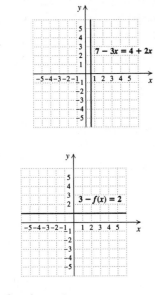

34.

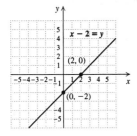

35. Graph $x - 2 = y$.

To find the y-intercept, let $x = 0$.
$$x - 2 = y$$
$$0 - 2 = y, \text{ or } -2 = y$$
The y-intercept is $(0, -2)$.

To find the x-intercept, let $y = 0$.
$$x - 2 = y$$
$$x - 2 = 0, \text{ or } x = 2$$
The x-intercept is $(2,0)$.

Plot these points and draw the line. A third point could be used as a check.

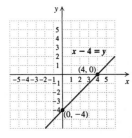

36.

37. Graph $3x - 1 = y$.

To find the y-intercept, let $x = 0$.
$$3x - 1 = y$$
$$3 \cdot 0 - 1 = y, \text{ or } -1 = y$$
The y-intercept is $(0, -1)$.

To find the x-intercept, let $y = 0$.
$$3x - 1 = y$$
$$3x - 1 = 0$$
$$3x = 1$$
$$x = \frac{1}{3}$$
The x-intercept is $\left(\frac{1}{3}, 0\right)$.

Plot these points and draw the line. A third point could be used as a check.

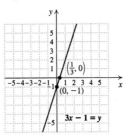

38.

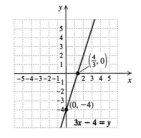

39. Graph $5x - 4y = 20$.

To find the y-intercept, let $x = 0$.
$$5x - 4y = 20$$
$$5 \cdot 0 - 4y = 20$$
$$-4y = 20$$
$$y = -5$$
The y-intercept is $(0, -5)$.

To find the x-intercept, let $y = 0$.
$$5x - 4y = 20$$
$$5x - 4 \cdot 0 = 20$$
$$5x = 20$$
$$x = 4$$
The x-intercept is $(4, 0)$.

Plot these points and draw the line. A third point could be used as a check.

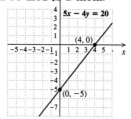

40.

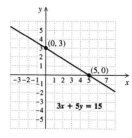

41. Graph $f(x) = -2 - 2x$, or $f(x) = -2x - 2$.

Because the function is in slope-intercept form, we know that the y-intercept is $(0, -2)$. To find the x-intercept, replace $f(x)$ with 0 and solve for x.

$$0 = -2 - 2x$$
$$2x = -2$$
$$x = -1$$

The x-intercept is $(-1, 0)$.

Plot these points and draw the line. As a check, note that the line's slope is -2, as expected.

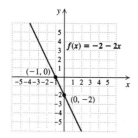

42.

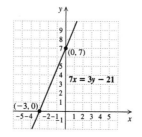

43. Graph $5y = -15 + 3x$.

To find the y-intercept, let $x = 0$.

$$5y = -15 + 3x$$
$$5y = -15 + 3 \cdot 0$$
$$5y = -15$$
$$y = -3$$

$(0, -3)$ is the y-intercept.

To find the x-intercept, let $y = 0$.

$$5y = -15 + 3x$$
$$5 \cdot 0 = = -15 + 3x$$
$$15 = 3x$$
$$5 = x$$

$(5, 0)$ is the x-intercept.

Plot these points and draw the line. A third point could be used as a check.

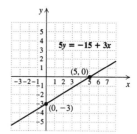

44.

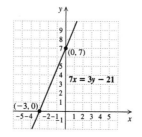

45. Graph $g(x) = 2x - 9$.

Because the function is in slope-intercept form, we know that the y-intercept is $(0, -9)$. To find the x-intercept, replace $f(x)$ with 0 and solve for x.

$$0 = 2x - 9$$
$$9 = 2x$$
$$\frac{9}{2} = x$$

The x-intercept is $\left(\frac{9}{2}, 0\right)$.

Plot these points and draw the line. As a check, note that the line's slope is 2, as expected.

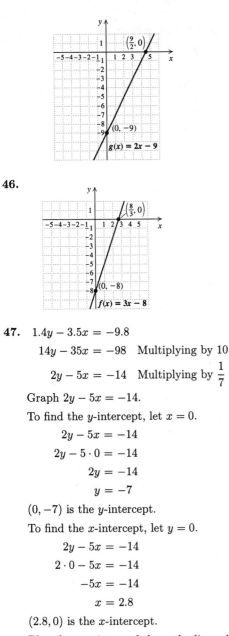

$g(x) = 2x - 9$

46.

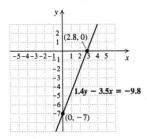

$f(x) = 3x - 8$

47. $1.4y - 3.5x = -9.8$

$14y - 35x = -98$ Multiplying by 10

$2y - 5x = -14$ Multiplying by $\dfrac{1}{7}$

Graph $2y - 5x = -14$.

To find the y-intercept, let $x = 0$.

$$2y - 5x = -14$$
$$2y - 5 \cdot 0 = -14$$
$$2y = -14$$
$$y = -7$$

$(0, -7)$ is the y-intercept.

To find the x-intercept, let $y = 0$.

$$2y - 5x = -14$$
$$2 \cdot 0 - 5x = -14$$
$$-5x = -14$$
$$x = 2.8$$

$(2.8, 0)$ is the x-intercept.

Plot these points and draw the line. A third point could be used as a check.

$1.4y - 3.5x = -9.8$

48.

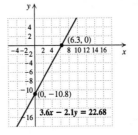

$3.6x - 2.1y = 22.68$

49. Graph $5x + 2y = 7$

To find the y-intercept, let $x = 0$.

$$5x + 2y = 7$$
$$5 \cdot 0 + 2y = 7$$
$$2y = 7$$
$$y = \frac{7}{2}$$

$\left(0, \dfrac{7}{2}\right)$ is the y-intercept.

To find the x-intercept, let $y = 0$.

$$5x + 2y = 7$$
$$5x + 2 \cdot 0 = 7$$
$$5x = 7$$
$$x = \frac{7}{5}$$

$\left(\dfrac{7}{5}, 0\right)$ is the x-intercept.

Plot these points and draw the line. A third point could be used as a check.

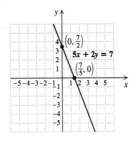

$5x + 2y = 7$

50.

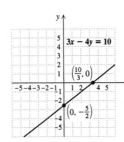

$3x - 4y = 10$

51. $f(x) = 20 - 4x$, or $f(x) = -4x + 20$

From the equation we see that the y-intercept is $(0, 20)$. Next we find the x-intercept.

$$0 = 20 - 4x$$
$$4x = 20$$
$$x = 5$$

The x-intercept is $(5, 0)$. Thus, window (c) will show both intercepts.

52. (a)

53. $p(x) = -35x + 7000$

From the equation we see that the y-intercept is $(0, 7000)$. Next we find the x-intercept.

$$0 = -35x + 7000$$
$$35x = 7000$$
$$x = 200$$

The x-intercept is $(200, 0)$. Thus, window (d) will show both intercepts.

54. (b)

55. We first solve for y and determine the slope of each line.

$$x + 6 = y$$
$$y = x + 6 \quad \text{Reversing the order}$$

The slope of $y = x + 6$ is 1.

$$y - x = -2$$
$$y = x - 2$$

The slope of $y = x - 2$ is 1.

The slopes are the same; the lines are parallel.

56. Yes

57. We first solve for y and determine the slope of each line.

$$y + 3 = 5x$$
$$y = 5x - 3$$

The slope of $y = 5x - 3$ is 5.

$$3x - y = -2$$
$$3x + 2 = y$$
$$y = 3x + 2 \quad \text{Reversing the order}$$

The slope of $y = 3x + 2$ is 3.

The slopes are not the same; the lines are not parallel.

58. No

59. We determine the slope of each line.

The slope of $f(x) = 3x + 9$ is 3.

$$2y = 6x - 2$$
$$y = 3x - 1$$

The slope of $y = 3x - 1$ is 3.

The slopes are the same; the lines are parallel.

60. Yes

61. We determine the slope of each line.

The slope of $f(x) = 4x - 5$ is 4.

$$4y = 8 - x$$
$$4y = -x + 8$$
$$y = -\frac{1}{4}x + 2$$

The slope of $4y = 8 - x$ is $-\frac{1}{4}$.

The product of their slopes is $4\left(-\frac{1}{4}\right)$, or -1; the lines are perpendicular.

62. No

63. We determine the slope of each line.

$$x + 2y = 5$$
$$2y = -x + 5$$
$$y = -\frac{1}{2}x + \frac{5}{2}$$

The slope of $x + 2y = 5$ is $-\frac{1}{2}$.

$$2x + 4y = 8$$
$$4y = -2x + 8$$
$$y = -\frac{1}{2}x + 2.$$

The slope of $2x + 4y = 8$ is $-\frac{1}{2}$.

The product of their slopes is $\left(-\frac{1}{2}\right)\left(-\frac{1}{2}\right)$, or $\frac{1}{4}$; the lines are not perpendicular. For the lines to be perpendicular, the product must be -1.

64. Yes

65. The slope of the given line is 3. Therefore the slope of a line parallel to it is also 3. The y-intercept is $(0, 9)$, so the equation of the desired function is $f(x) = 3x + 9$.

66. $f(x) = -5x - 2$

67. First we find the slope of the given line.

$$2x + y = 3$$
$$y = -2x + 3 \quad \text{Slope-intercept form}$$

The slope of the given line is -2, so the slope of a line parallel to it is also -2. The y-intercept is $(0, -1)$, so the equation of the desired function is $f(x) = -2x - 1$.

68. $f(x) = 3x + 4$

69. First we find the slope of the given line.

$$2x + 5y = 8$$
$$5y = -2x + 8$$
$$\frac{1}{5} \cdot 5y = \frac{1}{5}(-2x + 8)$$
$$y = -\frac{2}{5}x + \frac{8}{5}$$

The slope of the given line is $-\frac{2}{5}$, so the slope of a line parallel to it is also $-\frac{2}{5}$.

The y-intercept is $-\frac{1}{3}$, so the equation of the desired function is $f(x) = -\frac{2}{5}x - \frac{1}{3}$.

70. $f(x) = -5$

71. First we find the slope of the given line.

$$5 = 10y$$
$$\frac{1}{2} = y, \text{ or}$$
$$y = 0 \cdot x + \frac{1}{2}$$

The slope of the given line is 0, so the slope of a line parallel to it is also 0. The y-intercept is $(0, 12)$, so the equation of the desired function is $f(x) = 0 \cdot x + 12$, or $f(x) = 12$.

72. $f(x) = \frac{1}{2}x + \frac{4}{5}$

73. The slope of the given line is 1. The slope of a line perpendicular to it is the opposite of the reciprocal of 1, or -1. The y-intercept is $(0, 4)$, so we have $y = -1 \cdot x + 4$, or $y = -x + 4$.

74. $f(x) = -\frac{1}{2}x - 3$

75. First find the slope of the given line.

$$2x + 3y = 6$$
$$3y = -2x + 6$$
$$\frac{1}{3} \cdot 3y = \frac{1}{3}(-2x + 6)$$
$$y = -\frac{2}{3}x + 2$$

The slope of the given line is $-\frac{2}{3}$. The slope of a line perpendicular to it is the opposite of the reciprocal of $-\frac{2}{3}$, or $\frac{3}{2}$. The y-intercept is $(0, -9)$, so we have $f(x) = \frac{3}{2}x - 9$.

76. $f(x) = \frac{1}{2}x + 1$

77. First find the slope of the given line.

$$5x - y = 13$$
$$-y = -5x + 13$$
$$-1(-y) = -1(-5x + 13)$$
$$y = 5x - 13$$

The slope of the given line is 5. The slope of a line perpendicular to it is the opposite of the reciprocal of 5, or $-\frac{1}{5}$. The y-intercept is $\left(0, \frac{1}{5}\right)$, so we have $f(x) = -\frac{1}{5}x + \frac{1}{5}$.

78. $f(x) = -\frac{5}{2}x - \frac{1}{8}$

79. $5x - 3y = 15$

This equation is in the standard form for a linear equation, $Ax + By = C$, with $A = 5$, $B = -3$, and $C = 15$. Thus, it is a linear equation.

Solve for y to find the slope.

$$5x - 3y = 15$$
$$-3y = -5x + 15$$
$$y = \frac{5}{3}x - 5$$

The slope is $\frac{5}{3}$.

80. Linear; slope is $-\frac{3}{5}$

81. $16 + 4y = 0$
$$4y = -16$$

This equation can be written in the standard form for a linear equation, $Ax + By = C$, with $A = 0$, $B = 4$, and $C = -16$. Thus, it is a linear equation.

Solve for y to find the slope.

$$4y = -16$$
$$y = -4$$

This is a horizontal line, so the slope is 0. (We can think of this as $y = 0 \cdot x - 4$.)

82. Linear; vertical line

83. $3g(x) = 6x^2$

The equation is not linear, because it has an x^2-term.

84. Linear; slope is $-\frac{1}{2}$

85. $3y = 7xy - 5$

The equation is not linear, because it has an xy-term.

86. Not linear

87. $6y - \dfrac{4}{x} = 0$

$6xy - 4 = 0$ Multiplying by x on both sides

The equation is not linear, because it has an xy-term.

88. Not linear

89. $\dfrac{f(x)}{x} = x^2$

Replace $f(x)$ with y and attempt to write the equation in standard form.

$$\frac{y}{x} = x^2$$
$$y = x^3$$
$$-x^3 + y = 0$$

The equation is not linear, because it has an x^3-term.

90. Linear; slope is 2

91. $3(2x - y + 7) = 3 \cdot 2x - 3 \cdot y + 3 \cdot 7 = 6x - 3y + 21$

92. $-2x - 10y + 2$

93. $9x - 15y = 3 \cdot 3x - 3 \cdot 5y = 3(3x - 5y)$

94. $3a(4 + 7b)$

95. $\dfrac{1}{3}x + \dfrac{2}{3}y - \dfrac{4}{3} = \dfrac{1}{3} \cdot x + \dfrac{1}{3} \cdot 2y - \dfrac{1}{3} \cdot 4 =$

$\dfrac{1}{3}(x + 2y - 4)$

96. $-3(x + 2y + 3)$

97. ◈

98. ◈

99. ◈

100. ◈

101. The line contains the points $(5, 0)$ and $(0, -4)$. We use the points to find the slope.

Slope $= \dfrac{-4 - 0}{0 - 5} = \dfrac{-4}{-5} = \dfrac{4}{5}$

Then the slope-intercept equation is $y = \dfrac{4}{5}x - 4$. We rewrite this equation in standard form.

$$y = \frac{4}{5}x - 4$$
$$5y = 4x - 20 \quad \text{Multiplying by 5 on both sides}$$
$$-4x + 5y = -20 \quad \text{Standard form}$$

This equation can also be written as $4x - 5y = 20$.

102. $\left(-\dfrac{b}{m}, 0 \right)$

103. $rx + 3y = p - s$

The equation is in standard form with $A = r$, $B = 3$, and $C = p - s$. It is linear.

104. Linear

105. Try to put the equation in standard form.

$$r^2x = py + 5$$
$$r^2x - py = 5$$

The equation is in standard form with $A = r^2$, $B = -p$, and $C = 5$. It is linear.

106. Linear

107. Let equation A have intercepts $(a, 0)$ and $(0, b)$. Then equation B has intercepts $(2a, 0)$ and $(0, b)$.

Slope of $A = \dfrac{b - 0}{0 - a} = -\dfrac{b}{a}$

Slope of $B = \dfrac{b - 0}{0 - 2a} = -\dfrac{b}{2a} = \dfrac{1}{2}\left(-\dfrac{b}{a}\right)$

The slope of equation B is $\dfrac{1}{2}$ the slope of equation A.

108. $a = 5$, $b = 1$

109. First write the equation in standard form.

$$ax + 3y = 5x - by + 8$$
$$ax - 5x + 3y + by = 8 \qquad \text{Adding } -5x + by \text{ on both sides}$$
$$(a - 5)x + (3 + b)y = 8 \qquad \text{Factoring}$$

If the graph is a vertical line, then the coefficient of y is 0.

$$3 + b = 0$$
$$b = -3$$

Then we have $(a - 5)x = 8$.

If the line passes through $(4, 0)$, we have:

$$(a - 5)4 = 8 \quad \text{Substituting 4 for } x$$
$$a - 5 = 2$$
$$a = 7$$

110. Left to the student.

111. a) Solve each equation for y, enter each on the equation-editor screen, and then examine a table of values for the two functions. Since the difference between the y-values is the same for all x-values, the lines are parallel.

b) Solve each equation for y, enter each on the equation-editor screen, and then examine a table of values for the two functions. Since the difference between the y-values is not the same for all x-values, the lines are not parallel.

Exercise Set 4.3

1. $y - y_1 = m(x - x_1)$ Point-slope equation
$y - 3 = 4(x - 2)$ Substituting 4 for m, 2 for x_1, and 3 for y_1

We graph the equation by plotting $(2, 3)$, counting off a slope of $\frac{4}{1}$, and drawing the line.

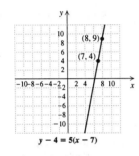

2.

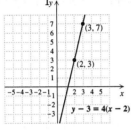

3. $y - y_1 = m(x - x_1)$ Point-slope equation
$y - 7 = -2(x - 4)$ Substituting -2 for m, 4 for x_1, and 7 for y_1

We graph the equation by plotting $(4, 7)$, counting off a slope of $\frac{-2}{1}$, and drawing the line.

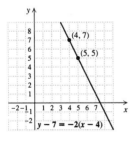

4.

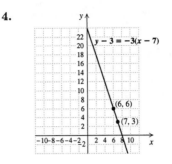

5. $y - y_1 = m(x - x_1)$ Point-slope equation
$y - (-4) = 3[x - (-2)]$ Substituting 3 for m, -2 for x_1, and -4 for y_1

We graph the equation by plotting $(-2, -4)$, counting off a slope of $\frac{3}{1}$, and drawing the line.

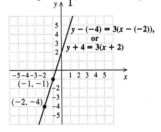

6.

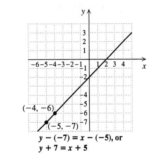

7. $y - y_1 = m(x - x_1)$ Point-slope equation
$y - 8 = \frac{2}{5}[x - (-3)]$ Substituting $\frac{2}{5}$ for m, -3 for x_1, and 8 for y_1

We graph the equation by plotting $(-3, 8)$, counting off a slope of $\frac{2}{5}$, and drawing the line.

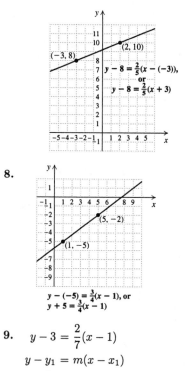

$y - 8 = \frac{2}{5}(x - (-3))$,
or
$y - 8 = \frac{2}{5}(x + 3)$

8.

$y - (-5) = \frac{3}{4}(x - 1)$, or
$y + 5 = \frac{3}{4}(x - 1)$

9. $y - 3 = \frac{2}{7}(x - 1)$

$y - y_1 = m(x - x_1)$

$m = \frac{2}{7}$, $x_1 = 1$, and $y_1 = 3$, so the slope m is $\frac{2}{7}$ and a point (x_1, y_1) on the graph is $(1, 3)$.

10. $9;\ (2, 4)$

11. $y + 2 = -5(x - 7)$

$y - (-2) = -5(x - 7)$

$y - y_1 = m(x - x_1)$

$m = -5$, $x_1 = 7$, and $y_1 = -2$, so the slope m is -5 and a point (x_1, y_1) on the graph is $(7, -2)$.

12. $-\frac{2}{9};\ (-5, 1)$

13. $y - 1 = -\frac{5}{3}(x + 2)$

$y - 1 = -\frac{5}{3}[x - (-2)]$

$y - y_1 = m(x - x_1)$

$m = -\frac{5}{3}$, $x_1 = -2$, and $y_1 = 1$, so the slope m is $-\frac{5}{3}$ and a point (x_1, y_1) on the graph is $(-2, 1)$.

14. $-4;\ (9, -7)$

15. $y - y_1 = m(x - x_1)$ Point-slope equation

$y - (-3) = 5(x - 2)$ Substituting 5 for m, 2 for x_1, and -3 for y_1

$y + 3 = 5x - 10$ Simplifying

$y = 5x - 13$ Subtracting 3 on both sides

$f(x) = 5x - 13$ Using function notation

16. $f(x) = -4x + 1$

17. $y - y_1 = m(x - x_1)$ Point-slope equation

$y - (-7) = -\frac{2}{3}(x - 4)$ Substituting $-\frac{2}{3}$ for m, 4 for x_1, and -7 for y_1

$y + 7 = -\frac{2}{3}x + \frac{8}{3}$ Simplifying

$y = -\frac{2}{3}x - \frac{13}{3}$ Subtracting 7 on both sides

$f(x) = -\frac{2}{3}x - \frac{13}{3}$ Using function notation

18. $f(x) = -\frac{1}{5}x + \frac{3}{5}$

19. $y - y_1 = m(x - x_1)$ Point-slope equation

$y - 0 = -0.6[x - (-3)]$ Substituting -0.6 for m, -3 for x_1, and 0 for y_1

$y = -0.6(x + 3)$

$y = -0.6x - 1.8$

$f(x) = -0.6x - 1.8$ Using function notation

20. $f(x) = 2.3x - 9.2$

21. We are given the slope of the line and the y-intercept, so we can write slope-intercept form directly. We have $f(x) = -6x + 2.4$.

22. $f(x) = 4x + \frac{1}{2}$

23. First find the slope of the line:

$$m = \frac{6 - 4}{5 - 1} = \frac{2}{4} = \frac{1}{2}$$

Use the point-slope equation with $m = \frac{1}{2}$ and $(1, 4) = (x_1, y_1)$. (We could let $(5, 6) = (x_1, y_1)$ instead and obtain an equivalent equation.)

$$y - 4 = \frac{1}{2}(x - 1)$$

$$y - 4 = \frac{1}{2}x - \frac{1}{2}$$

$$y = \frac{1}{2}x + \frac{7}{2}$$

$$f(x) = \frac{1}{2}x + \frac{7}{2} \quad \text{Using function notation}$$

24. $f(x) = -\frac{5}{2}x + 11$

25. First find the slope of the line:

$$m = \frac{3 - (-3)}{6.5 - 2.5} = \frac{3 + 3}{4} = \frac{6}{4} = 1.5$$

Use the point-slope equation with $m = 1.5$ and $(6.5, 3) = (x_1, y_1)$.

$$y - 3 = 1.5(x - 6.5)$$

$$y - 3 = 1.5x - 9.75$$

$$y = 1.5x - 6.75$$

$$f(x) = 1.5x - 6.75 \quad \text{Using function notation}$$

26. $f(x) = 0.6x - 2.5$

27. First find the slope of the line:

$$m = \frac{-2 - 1}{0 - 6} = \frac{-3}{-6} = \frac{1}{2}$$

Use the point-slope equation with $m = \frac{1}{2}$ and $(6, 1) = (x_1, y_1)$.

$$y - 1 = \frac{1}{2}(x - 6)$$

$$y - 1 = \frac{1}{2}x - 3$$

$$y = \frac{1}{2}x - 2$$

$$f(x) = \frac{1}{2}x - 2 \quad \text{Using function notation}$$

28. $f(x) = \frac{5}{2}x + \frac{15}{2}$

29. First find the slope of the line:

$$m = \frac{-6 - (-3)}{-4 - (-2)} = \frac{-6 + 3}{-4 + 2} = \frac{-3}{-2} = \frac{3}{2}$$

Use the point-slope equation with $m = \frac{3}{2}$ and $(-2, -3) = (x_1, y_1)$.

$$y - (-3) = \frac{3}{2}[x - (-2)]$$

$$y + 3 = \frac{3}{2}(x + 2)$$

$$y + 3 = \frac{3}{2}x + 3$$

$$y = \frac{3}{2}x$$

$$f(x) = \frac{3}{2}x \quad \text{Using function notation}$$

30. $f(x) = 3x + 5$

31. a) We form pairs of the type (t, R) where t is the number of years since 1930 and R is the record. We have two pairs, $(0, 46.8)$ and $(40, 43.8)$. These are two points on the graph of the linear function we are seeking. We use the point-slope form to write an equation relating R and t:

$$m = \frac{43.8 - 46.8}{40 - 0} = \frac{-3}{40} = -0.075$$

$$R - 46.8 = -0.075(t - 0)$$

$$R - 46.8 = -0.075t$$

$$R = -0.075t + 46.8$$

$$R(t) = -0.075t + 46.8 \quad \text{Using function notation}$$

b) 1999 is 69 years since 1930, so to predict the record in 1999, we find $R(69)$:

$$R(69) = -0.075(69) + 46.8$$

$$= 41.625$$

The predicted record is 41.625 seconds in 1999.

2002 is 72 years since 1930, so to predict the record in 2002, we find $R(72)$:

$$R(72) = -0.075(72) + 46.8$$

$$= 41.4$$

The predicted record is 41.4 seconds in 2002.

c) Substitute 40 for $R(t)$ and solve for t:

$$40 = -0.075t + 46.8$$

$$-6.8 = -0.075t$$

$$91 \approx t$$

The record will be 40 seconds about **91 years** after 1930, or in **2021**.

32. **(a)** $R(t) = -0.0075t + 3.85$; **(b)** 3.34 minutes, 3.31 minutes; **(c)** 2003

33. a) We form the pairs $(0, 132.7)$ and $(8, 179.6)$.

Use the point-slope form to write an equation relating A and t:
$$m = \frac{179.6 - 132.7}{8 - 0} = \frac{46.9}{8} = 5.8625$$
$$A - 132.7 = 5.8625(t - 0)$$
$$A - 132.7 = 5.8625t$$
$$A = 5.8625t + 132.7$$
$$A(t) = 5.8625t + 132.7 \quad \text{Using function notation}$$

b) 2002 is 16 years since 1986, so we find $A(16)$:
$$A(16) = 5.8625(16) + 132.7$$
$$= 226.5$$
We predict that the amount of PAC contributions in 2002 will be \$226.5 million.

34. (a) $A(p) = -2.5p + 26.5$; (b) 11.5 million lb

35. a) We form the pairs $(0, 33.9)$ and $(5, 56.2)$. Use the point-slope form to write an equation relating N and t:
$$m = \frac{56.2 - 33.9}{5 - 0} = \frac{22.3}{5} = 4.46$$
$$N - 32.9 = 4.46(t - 0)$$
$$N - 32.9 = 4.46t$$
$$N = 4.46t + 32.9$$
$$N(t) = 4.46t + 32.9 \quad \text{Using function notation}$$

b) 2001 is 11 years since 1990, so we find $N(11)$:
$$N(11) = 4.46(11) + 32.9$$
$$\approx 82.96$$
We predict that Americans will recycle about 82.96 million tons of garbage in 2001.

36. (a) $A(p) = 2p - 11$; (b) 1 million lb

37. a) We form the pairs $(0, 76.4)$ and $(4, 74.9)$.

Use the point-slope form to write an equation relating A and t:
$$m = \frac{74.9 - 76.4}{4 - 0} = \frac{-1.5}{4} = -0.375$$
$$A - 76.4 = -0.375(t - 0)$$
$$A - 76.4 = -0.375t$$
$$A = -0.375t + 76.4$$
$$A(t) = -0.375t + 76.4 \quad \text{Using function notation}$$

b) 2002 is 12 years after 1990, so we find $A(12)$:
$$A(12) = -0.375(12) + 76.4$$
$$= 71.9$$
We predict that there will be 71.9 million acres of land in the national park system in 2002.

38. (a) $P(d) = 0.03d + 1$; (b) 21.7 atm

39. a) We form the pairs $(0, 78.8)$ and $(5, 78.9)$.

Use the point-slope form to write an equation relating E and t:
$$m = \frac{78.9 - 78.8}{5 - 0} = \frac{0.1}{5} = 0.02$$
$$E - 78.8 = 0.02(t - 0)$$
$$E - 78.8 = 0.02t$$
$$E = 0.02t + 78.8$$
$$E(t) = 0.02t + 78.8 \quad \text{Using function notation}$$

b) 2004 is 14 years after 1990, so we find $E(14)$:
$$E(14) = 0.02(14) + 78.8$$
$$= 79.08$$
We predict that the life expectancy of females in the United States in 2004 will be 79.08 years.

40. (a) $E(t) = 0.16t + 71.8$; (b) 74.04 years

41. a) Enter the data in a graphing calculator, letting x represent the number of years since 1990. Thus, -70 represents 1920 (since $1920 - 1990 = -70$), -60 represents 1930, and so on, with 0 representing 1990. Then use the linear regression feature to find the desired function. We have $f(x) = 0.3326x + 81.2167$.

b) $2004 - 1990 = 14$, so we use one of the methods discussed earlier in the text to find $f(14)$. We predict that the life expectancy in 2004 will be about 85.87 years.

42. (a) $f(x) = 0.1963x + 71.8905$; (b) 74.64 years

43. a) Enter the data in a graphing calculator, letting the numbers 0 through 9 represent the years 1987 through 1996, respectively. Then use the linear regression feature to find the desired function. We have $f(x) = -6.055x + 99.5336$.

b) $2001 - 1987 = 14$, so we use one of the methods discussed earlier in the text to find $f(14)$. We predict that the average local monthly bill for a cellular phone will be about \$14.76 in 2001.

44. (a) $f(x) = 1.3357x - 31.3214$; (b) $22°$

45. a) Entering the data in a graphing calculator and using the linear regression feature, we have $f(x) = 77.9845x + 7728.5271$.

b) Use one of the methods discussed earlier in the text to find $f(10)$. We estimate that the annual expenditure on a 10-year-old child in 1996 was about \$8508.

46. (a) $f(x) = 0.0445x + 1.7092$; (b) 3.71 lb

47. $-\dfrac{1}{3} + \dfrac{5}{12} = -\dfrac{1}{3} \cdot \dfrac{4}{4} + \dfrac{5}{12}$

$\qquad = -\dfrac{4}{12} + \dfrac{5}{12}$

$\qquad = \dfrac{1}{12}$

48. $-\dfrac{3}{4}$

49. $-\dfrac{1}{3} \cdot \dfrac{5}{12} = -\dfrac{1 \cdot 5}{3 \cdot 12} = -\dfrac{5}{36}$

50. $-\dfrac{4}{5}$

51. ◈

52. ◈

53. ◈

54. ◈

55. *Familiarize*. The value C of the computer, in dollars, after t months can be modeled by a line that contains the points $(0, 2500)$ and $(5, 2150)$.

Translate. We find an equation relating C and t.

$m = \dfrac{2150 - 2500}{5 - 0} = \dfrac{-350}{5} = -70$

$C - 2500 = -70(t - 0)$

$C - 2500 = -70t$

$\qquad C = -70t + 2500$

Carry out. Using function notation we have $C(t) = -70t + 2500$. To find the value after 8 months we find $C(8)$:

$C(8) = -70 \cdot 8 + 2500$

$\qquad = 1940$

Check. We can repeat our calculations. We could also graph the function and determine that $(8, 1940)$ is on the graph.

State. The computer's value after 8 months will be \$1940.

56. \$340

57. *Familiarize*. The total operating costs C, in dollars, for t months can be modeled by a linear equation containing the points $(4, 7500)$ and $(7, 9250)$.

Translate. We find an equation relating C and t.

$m = \dfrac{9250 - 7500}{7 - 4} = \dfrac{1750}{3}$

$C - 7500 = \dfrac{1750}{3}(t - 4)$

$C - 7500 = \dfrac{1750}{3}t - \dfrac{7000}{3}$

$\qquad C = \dfrac{1750}{3}t + \dfrac{15,500}{3}$

Carry out. Using function notation we have $C(t) = \dfrac{1750}{3}t + \dfrac{15,500}{3}$. To predict the total costs after 10 months, we find $C(10)$:

$C(10) = \dfrac{1750}{3} \cdot 10 + \dfrac{15,500}{3}$

$\qquad = 11,000$

Check. We can repeat the calculations. We could also graph the function and determine that $(10, 11,000)$ is on the graph.

State. We predict that the total operating costs after 10 months will be \$11,000.

58. \$1350

59. *Familiarize*. We form the pairs $(32, 0)$ and $(212, 100)$ and plot these data points, choosing suitable scales on the two axes. We will let F represent the Fahrenheit temperature and C represent the Celsius temperature.

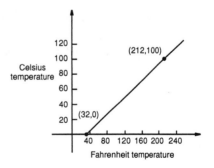

Translate. We seek an equation relating C and F. We find the slope and use the point-slope form:

$m = \dfrac{100 - 0}{212 - 32} = \dfrac{100}{180} = \dfrac{5}{9}$

$C - 0 = \dfrac{5}{9}(F - 32)$

$C = \dfrac{5}{9}(F - 32)$

$C = \dfrac{5}{9}F - \dfrac{160}{9}$

Carry out. Using function notation, we have

$$C(F) = \frac{5}{9}F - \frac{160}{9}.$$

To find the Celsius temperature that corresponds to 70° F, we find

$$C(70) = \frac{5}{9}(70) - \frac{160}{9}$$
$$\approx 21.1$$

Check. We observe that the result seems reasonable since $(70, 21.1)$ appears to lie on the graph. We can also repeat the calculations.

State. A temperature of about 21.1° C corresponds to 70° F.

60. $y = -\frac{1}{2}x + \frac{17}{2}$

61. First solve the equation for y and determine the slope of the given line.

$$3x - y = 7 \qquad \text{Given line}$$
$$y = 3x - 7 \qquad m = 3$$

The slope of the given line is 3.

The slope of every line parallel to the given line must also be 3. We find the equation of the line with slope 3 and containing the point $(-1, 4)$.

$$y - y_1 = m(x - x_1) \qquad \text{Point-slope equation}$$
$$y - 4 = 3(x - (-1))$$
$$y - 4 = 3(x + 1)$$
$$y - 4 = 3x + 3$$
$$y = 3x + 7$$

62. $y = \frac{1}{2}x + 4$

63. First solve the equation for y and determine the slope of the given line.

$$x - 3y = 0 \qquad \text{Given line}$$
$$x = 3y$$
$$\frac{1}{3}x = y \qquad m = \frac{1}{3}$$

The slope of the given line is $\frac{1}{3}$.

The slope of a perpendicular line is given by the opposite of the reciprocal of $\frac{1}{3}$, or -3.

We find the equation of the line with slope -3 containing the point $(4, 0)$.

$$y - y_1 = m(x - x_1) \qquad \text{Point-slope equation}$$
$$y - 0 = -3(x - 4)$$
$$y = -3x + 12$$

64. (a) $f(x) = \frac{1}{3}x + \frac{10}{3}$; **(b)** $\frac{13}{3}$; **(c)** 290

65. a) We have two pairs, $(3, -5)$ and $(7, -1)$. Use the point-slope form:

$$m = \frac{-1 - (-5)}{7 - 3} = \frac{-1 + 5}{4} = \frac{4}{4} = 1$$
$$y - (-5) = 1(x - 3)$$
$$y + 5 = x - 3$$
$$y = x - 8$$
$$g(x) = x - 8 \qquad \text{Using function notation}$$

b) $g(-2) = -2 - 8 = -10$

c) $g(a) = a - 8$

If $g(a) = 75$, we have

$$a - 8 = 75$$
$$a = 83.$$

66. $-\frac{40}{9}$

67. Find the slope of $7y - kx = 9$:

$$7y - kx = 9$$
$$7y = kx + 9$$
$$y = \frac{k}{7}x + \frac{9}{7}$$

The slope is $\frac{k}{7}$.

Find the slope of the line containing $(2, -1)$ and $(-4, 5)$.

$$m = \frac{5 - (-1)}{-4 - 2} = \frac{6}{-6} = -1$$

If the lines are perpendicular, the product of their slopes must be -1:

$$\frac{k}{7}(-1) = -1$$
$$-\frac{k}{7} = -1$$
$$k = 7 \qquad \text{Multiplying by } -7$$

Exercise Set 4.4

---

1. We replace x by -4 and y by 2.

$$\frac{2x + 3y < -1}{2(-4) + 3 \cdot 2 \; ? \; -1}$$
$$-8 + 6$$
$$-2 \;\Big|\; -1 \qquad \text{TRUE}$$

Since $-2 < -1$ is true, $(-4, 2)$ is a solution.

2. No

3. We replace x by 8 and y by 14.

$$\frac{2y - 3x \geq 9}{2 \cdot 14 - 3 \cdot 8 \; ? \; 9}$$
$$28 - 24 \;\big|$$
$$4 \;\big|\; 9 \qquad \text{FALSE}$$

Since $4 > 9$ is false, $(8, 14)$ is not a solution.

4. Yes

5. Graph: $y < \dfrac{1}{2}x$

We first graph the line $y = \dfrac{1}{2}x$. We draw the line dashed since the inequality symbol is $<$. To determine which half-plane to shade, test a point not on the line. We try $(0, 1)$:

$$\frac{y < \dfrac{1}{2}x}{1 \; ? \; \dfrac{1}{2} \cdot 0}$$
$$1 \;\big|\; 0 \qquad \text{FALSE}$$

Since $1 < 0$ is false, (0.1) is not a solution, nor are any points in the half-plane containing $(0, 1)$. The points in the other half-plane are solutions, so we shade that half-plane and obtain the graph.

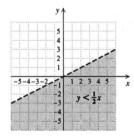

6.

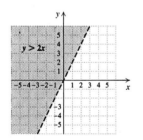

7. Graph: $y \leq x - 4$

First graph the line $y = x - 4$. Draw it solid since the inequality symbol is $\leq$. Test the point $(0, 0)$ to determine if it is a solution.

$$\frac{y \leq x - 4}{0 \; ? \; 0 - 4}$$
$$0 \;\big|\; -4 \qquad \text{FALSE}$$

Since $0 \leq -4$ is false, we shade the half-plane that does not contain $(0, 0)$ and obtain the graph.

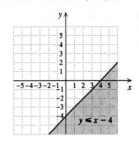

8.

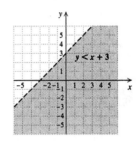

9. Graph: $y \geq x + 4$

First graph the line $y = x + 4$. Draw it solid since the inequality symbol is $\geq$. Test the point $(0, 0)$ to determine if it is a solution.

$$\frac{y \geq x + 4}{0 \; ? \; 0 + 4}$$
$$0 \;\big|\; 4 \qquad \text{FALSE}$$

Since $0 \geq 4$ is false, we shade the half-plane that does not contain $(0, 0)$ and obtain the graph.

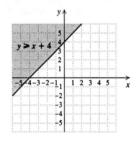

10.

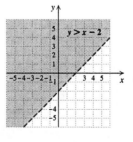

11. Graph: $x - y \geq 5$

First graph the line $x - y = 5$. Draw a solid line since the inequality symbol is $\geq$. Test the point $(0,0)$ to determine if it is a solution.

$$\frac{x - y \geq 5}{0 - 0 \ ? \ 5}$$

$$0 \ \big| \ 5 \quad \text{FALSE}$$

Since $0 \geq 5$ is false, we shade the half-plane that does not contain $(0,0)$ and obtain the graph.

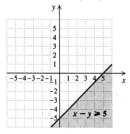

12.

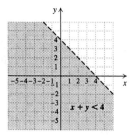

13. Graph: $2x + 3y < 6$

First graph $2x + 3y = 6$. Draw the line dashed since the inequality symbol is $<$. Test the point $(0,0)$ to determine if it is a solution.

$$\frac{2x + 3y < 6}{2 \cdot 0 + 3 \cdot 0 \ ? \ 6}$$

$$0 \ \big| \ 6 \quad \text{TRUE}$$

Since $0 < 6$ is true, we shade the half-plane containing $(0,0)$ and obtain the graph.

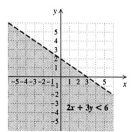

14.

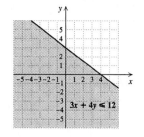

15. Graph: $2x - y \leq 4$

We first graph $2x - y = 4$. Draw the line solid since the inequality symbol is $\leq$. Test the point $(0,0)$ to determine if it is a solution.

$$\frac{2x - y \leq 4}{2 \cdot 0 - 0 \ ? \ 4}$$

$$0 \ \big| \ 4 \quad \text{TRUE}$$

Since $0 \leq 4$ is true, we shade the half-plane containing $(0,0)$ and obtain the graph.

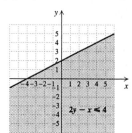

16.

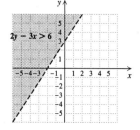

17. Graph: $2x - 2y \geq 8 + 2y$

$$2x - 4y \geq 8$$

First graph $2x - 4y = 8$. Draw the line solid since the inequality symbol is $\geq$. Test the point $(0,0)$ to determine if it is a solution.

$$\frac{2x - 4y \geq 8}{2 \cdot 0 - 4 \cdot 0 \ ? \ 8}$$

$$0 \ \big| \ 8 \quad \text{FALSE}$$

Since $0 \geq 8$ is false, we shade the half-plane that does not contain $(0,0)$ and obtain the graph.

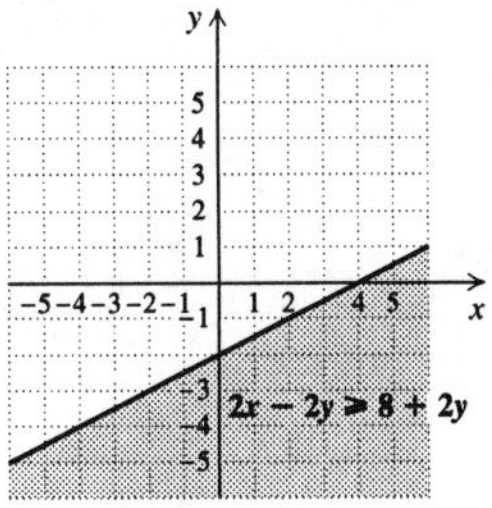
$2x - 2y \geq 8 + 2y$

18.

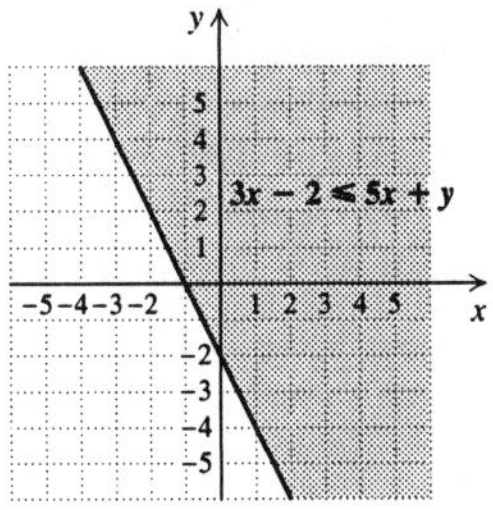
$3x - 2 \leq 5x + y$

19. Graph: $x \leq 6$

We first graph $x = 6$. We draw the line solid since the inequality symbol is $\leq$. Test the point $(0, 0)$ to determine if it is a solution.

$$\begin{array}{c|c} x \leq 6 & \\ \hline 0 \ ? \ 6 & \text{TRUE} \end{array}$$

Since $0 \leq 6$ is true, we shade the half-plane containing $(0, 0)$ and obtain the graph.

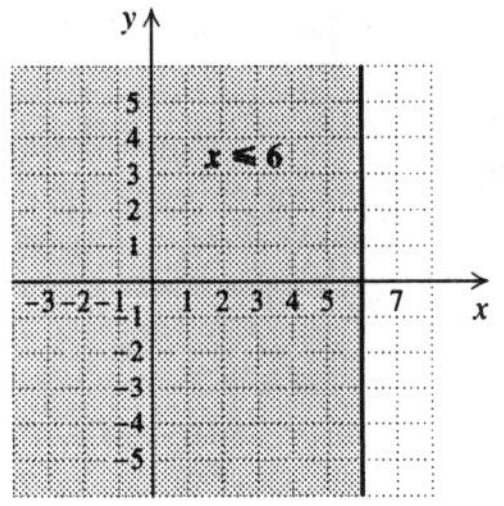
$x \leq 6$

20.

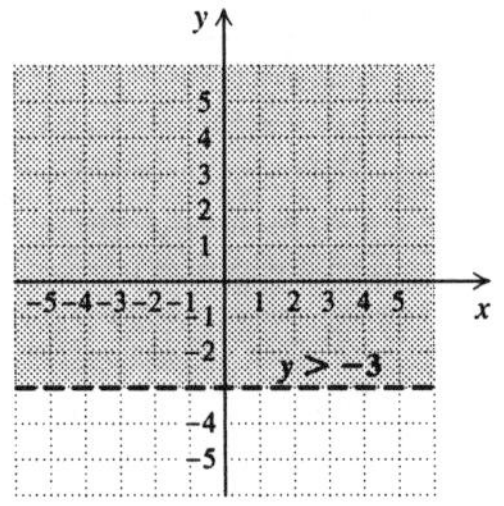
$y > -3$

21. Graph: $-2 < y < 5$

This is a system of inequalities:

$-2 < y,$

$y < 5$

We graph the equation $-2 = y$ and see that the graph of $-2 < y$ is the half-plane above the line $-2 = y$. We also graph $y = 5$ and see that the graph of $y < 5$ is the half-plane below the line $y = 5$.

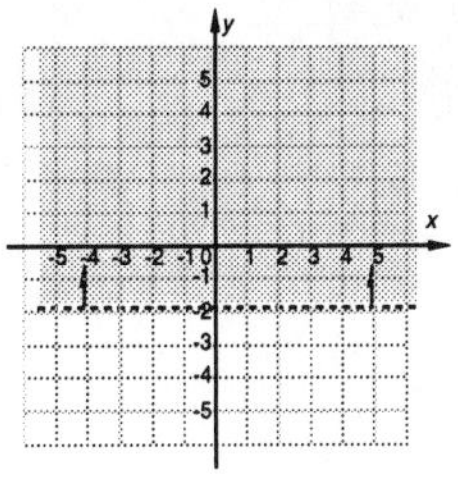

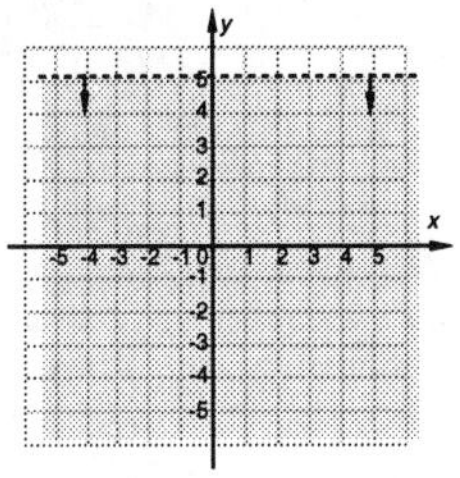

Finally, we shade the intersection of these graphs.

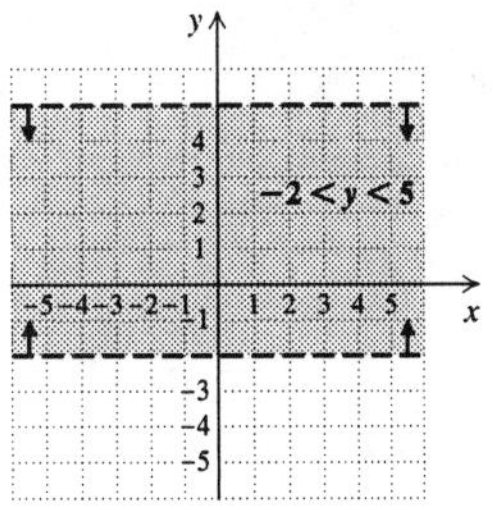
$-2 < y < 5$

22.

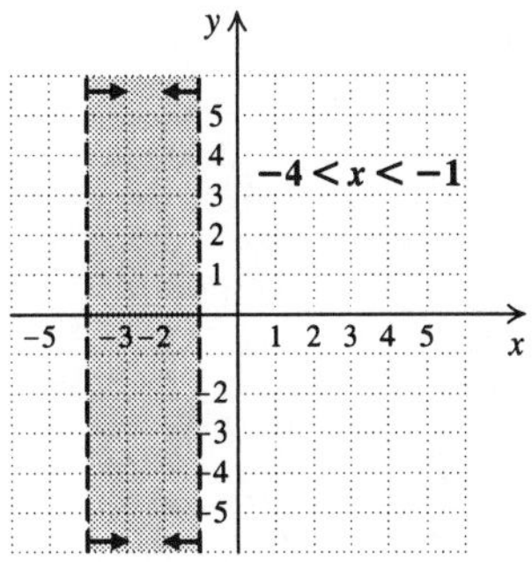
$-4 < x < -1$

23. Graph: $-4 \leq x \leq 4$

This is a system of inequalities:

$-4 \leq x,$

$x \leq 4$

Graph $-4 \leq x$ and $x \leq 4$.

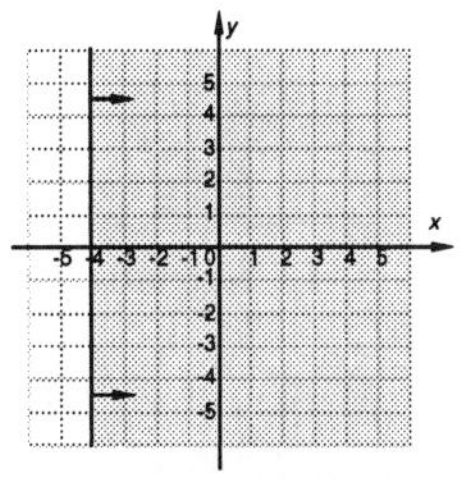

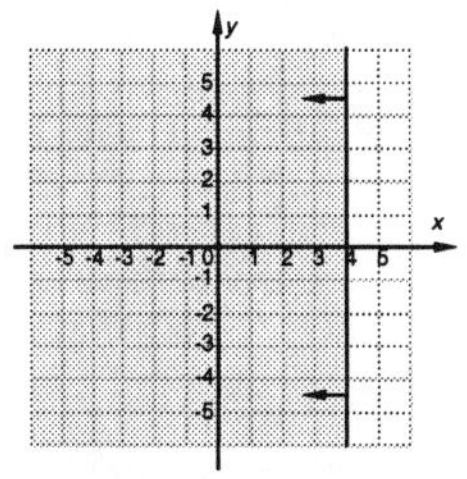

Then we shade the intersection of these graphs.

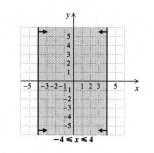

$$-4 \leqslant x \leqslant 4$$

24.

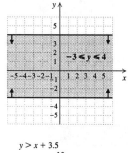

25. $y > x + 3.5$

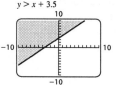

26. $7y \leqslant 2x + 5$

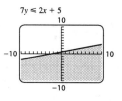

27. First get y alone on one side of the inequality.

$$8x - 2y < 11$$
$$-2y < -8x + 11$$
$$y > \frac{-8x + 11}{-2}$$

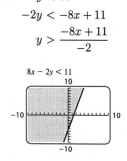

28.

$$11x + 13y + 4 \geqslant 0$$

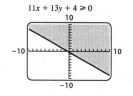

29. Graph: $y < x$,

$$y > -x + 5$$

We graph the lines $y = x$ and $y = -x + 5$, using dashed lines. We indicate the region for each inequality by the arrows at the ends of the lines. Note where the regions overlap and shade the region of solutions.

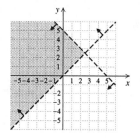

30.

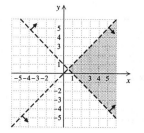

31. Graph: $y \geq x$,

$$y \leq -x + 2$$

Graph $y = x$ and $y = -x + 2$, using solid lines. Indicate the region for each inequality by arrows, and shade the region where they overlap.

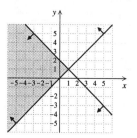

32.

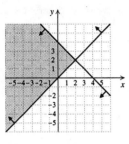

33. Graph: $y \le -2,$

   $x \ge -1$

Graph $y = -2$ and $x = -1$ using solid lines. Indicate the region for each inequality by arrows, and shade the region where they overlap.

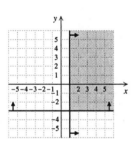

34.

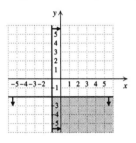

35.   Graph: $x > -2,$

   $y < -2x + 3$

Graph the lines $x = -2$ and $y = -2x + 3$, using dashed lines. Indicate the region for each inequality by arrows, and shade the region where they overlap.

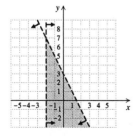

36.

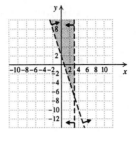

37. Graph: $y \le 4,$

   $y \ge -x + 2$

Graph the lines $y = 4$ and $y = -x + 2$, using solid lines. Indicate the region for each inequality by arrows, and shade the region where they overlap.

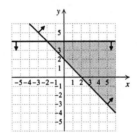

38.

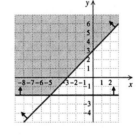

39. Graph: $x + y \le 3,$

   $x - y \le 4$

Graph the lines $x + y = 3$ and $x - y = 4$, using solid lines. Indicate the region for each inequality by arrows, and shade the region where they overlap.

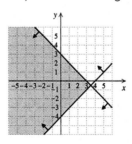

40.

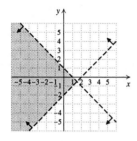

41. Graph: $y + 3x > 0,$

              $y + 3x < 2$

Graph the lines $y + 3x = 0$ and $y + 3x = 2$, using dashed lines. Indicate the region for each inequality by arrows, and shade the region where they overlap.

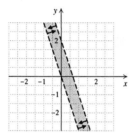

42.

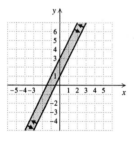

43. Graph: $y \le 2x - 1,$ (1)

              $y \ge -2x + 1,$ (2)

              $x \le 3$ (3)

Graph the lines $y = 2x - 1$, $y = -2x + 1$, and $x = 3$ using solid lines. Indicate the region for each inequality by arrows, and shade the region where they overlap.

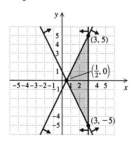

To find the vertex we solve three different systems of related equations.

From (1) and (2) we have $y = 2x - 1,$

                         $y = -2x + 1.$

Solving, we obtain the vertex $\left(\dfrac{1}{2}, 0\right)$.

From (1) and (3) we have $y = 2x - 1,$

                         $x = 3.$

Solving, we obtain the vertex $(3, 5)$.

From (2) and (3) we have $y = -2x + 1,$

                         $x = 3.$

Solving, we obtain the vertex $(3, -5)$.

44.

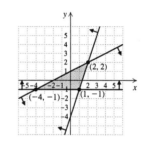

45. Graph: $x + 2y \le 12,$ (1)

              $2x + y \le 12$ (2)

              $x \ge 0,$ (3)

              $y \ge 0$ (4)

Graph the lines $x + 2y = 12$, $2x + y = 12$, $x = 0$, and $y = 0$ using solid lines. Indicate the region for each inequality by arrows, and shade the region where they overlap.

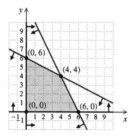

To find the vertices we solve four different systems of equations.

From (1) and (2) we have $x + 2y = 12,$

                         $2x + y = 12.$

Solving, we obtain the vertex $(4, 4)$.

From (1) and (3) we have $x + 2y = 12,$

                         $x = 0.$

Solving, we obtain the vertex $(0, 6)$.

From (2) and (4) we have $2x + y = 12$,

$$y = 0.$$

Solving, we obtain the vertex $(6, 0)$.

From (3) and (4) we have $x = 0$,

$$y = 0.$$

Solving, we obtain the vertex $(0, 0)$.

46.

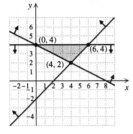

47. Graph: $8x + 5y \leq 40,$ (1)

$$x + 2y \leq 8 \quad (2)$$
$$x \geq 0, \quad (3)$$
$$y \geq 0 \quad (4)$$

Graph the lines $8x+5y = 40$, $x+2y = 8$, $x = 0$, and $y = 0$ using solid lines. Indicate the region for each inequality by arrows, and shade the region where they overlap.

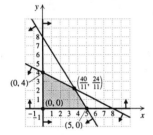

To find the vertices we solve four different systems of equations.

From (1) and (2) we have $8x + 5y = 40$,

$$x + 2y = 8.$$

Solving, we obtain the vertex $\left(\dfrac{40}{11}, \dfrac{24}{11} \right)$.

From (1) and (4) we have $8x + 5y = 40$,

$$y = 0.$$

Solving, we obtain the vertex $(5, 0)$.

From (2) and (3) we have $x + 2y = 8$,

$$x = 0.$$

Solving, we obtain the vertex $(0, 4)$.

From (3) and (4) we have $x = 0$,

$$y = 0.$$

Solving, we obtain the vertex $(0, 0)$.

48.

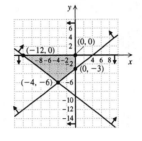

49. Graph: $y - x \geq 1,$ (1)

$$y - x \leq 3, \quad (2)$$
$$2 \leq x \leq 5 \quad (3)$$

Think of (3) as two inequalities:

$$2 \leq x, \quad (4)$$
$$x \leq 5 \quad (5)$$

Graph the lines $y-x = 1$, $y-x = 3$, $x = 2$, and $x = 5$, using solid lines. Indicate the region for each inequality by arrows, and shade the region where they overlap.

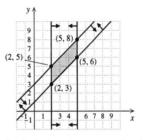

To find the vertices we solve four different systems of equations.

From (1) and (4) we have $y - x = 1$,

$$x = 2.$$

Solving, we obtain the vertex $(2, 3)$.

From (1) and (5) we have $y - x = 1$,

$$x = 5.$$

Solving, we obtain the vertex $(5, 6)$.

From (2) and (4) we have $y - x = 3$,

$$x = 2.$$

Solving, we obtain the vertex $(2, 5)$.

From (2) and (5) we have $y - x = 3$,

$$x = 5.$$

Solving, we obtain the vertex $(5, 8)$.

50.

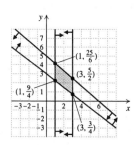

51. *Familiarize*. We first make a drawing. We let x represent the length of a side of the equilateral triangle. Then $x - 5$ represents the length of a side of the square.

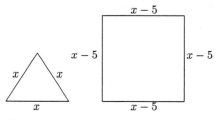

Translate.

Perimeter of triangle = Perimeter of square

$$3x \qquad = \qquad 4(x - 5)$$

Carry out.

$$3x = 4(x - 5)$$
$$3x = 4x - 20$$
$$20 = x$$

Then $x - 5 = 20 - 5 = 15$.

Check. If the length of a side of the triangle is 20 and the length of a side of the square is 15, the perimeter of the triangle is $3 \cdot 20$, or 60 and the perimeter of the square is $4 \cdot 15$, or 60. The values check.

State. The length of a side of the square is 15, and the length of a side of the triangle is 20.

52. All real numbers

53. $5(3x - 4) = -2(x + 5)$

$$15x - 20 = -2x - 10$$
$$17x - 20 = -10$$
$$17x = 10$$
$$x = \frac{10}{17}$$

The solution is $\dfrac{10}{17}$.

54. $-\dfrac{14}{13}$

55.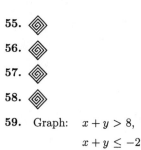

56.

57.

58.

59. Graph: $x + y > 8,$

$\qquad\qquad\quad x + y \le -2$

Graph the line $x + y = 8$ using a dashed line and graph $x + y = -2$, using a solid line. Indicate the region for each inequality by arrows. The regions do not overlap (the solution set is $\emptyset$), so we do not shade any portion of the graph.

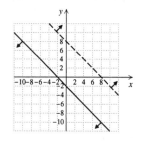

60.

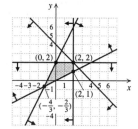

61. Graph: $x + y \ge 1,$

$\qquad\qquad\;\; -x + y \ge 2,$

$\qquad\qquad\qquad\; x \le 4,$

$\qquad\qquad\qquad\; y \ge 0,$

$\qquad\qquad\qquad\; y \le 4,$

$\qquad\qquad\qquad\; x \le 2$

Graph the six inequalities above, and shade the region where they overlap.

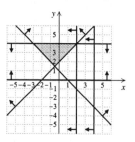

62. $x \geq -2,$
$y \leq 2,$
$x \leq 0,$
$y \geq 0;$ or
$x \geq 0,$
$y \leq 2,$
$x \leq 2,$
$y \geq 0;$ or
$x \geq 0,$
$y \leq 0,$
$x \leq 2,$
$y \geq -2;$ or
$x \geq -2,$
$y \leq 0,$
$x \leq 0,$
$y \geq -2$

63. Both the width and the height must be positive, but they must be less than 62 in. in order to be checked as luggage, so we have:

$$0 < w \leq 62,$$
$$0 < h \leq 62$$

The girth is represented by $2w + 2h$ and the length is 62 in. In order to meet postal regulations the sum of the girth and the length cannot exceed 108 in., so we have:

$$62 + 2w + 2h \leq 108, \text{ or}$$
$$2w + 2h \leq 46, \text{ or}$$
$$w + h \leq 23$$

Thus, have a system of inequalities:

$$0 < w \leq 62,$$
$$0 < h \leq 62,$$
$$w + h \leq 23$$

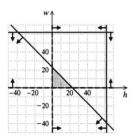

64.

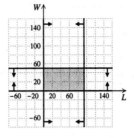

65. We graph the following system of inequalities:

$$2w + t \geq 60,$$
$$w \geq 0,$$
$$t \geq 0$$

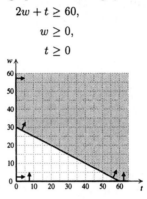

66.

67. The shaded region lies below the graphs of $y = x$ and $y = 2$ and both lines are solid. Thus, we have
$$y \leq x,$$
$$y \leq 2.$$

68. $y \leq x + 1,$
$x \leq 3,$
$y \geq -2.$

69. The shaded region lies below the graphs of $y = x + 2$ and $y = -x + 4$ and above $y = 0$, and all of the lines are solid. Thus, we have
$$y \leq x + 2,$$
$$y \leq -x + 4,$$
$$y \geq 0.$$

70. $y \leq x + 2,$
$y \geq x - 3.$

Exercise Set 4.5

1. $\{9, 10, 11\} \cap \{9, 11, 13\}$

The numbers 9 and 11 are common to both sets, so the intersection is $\{9, 11\}$.

2. $\{2, 4, 8, 9, 10\}$

3. $\{1, 5, 10, 15\} \cup \{5, 15, 20\}$

The numbers in either or both sets are 1, 5, 10, 15, and 20, so the union is $\{1, 5, 10, 15, 20\}$.

4. $\{5\}$

5. $\{a, b, c, d\} \cap \{b, f, g\}$

The only letter common to both sets is b, so the intersection is $\{b\}$.

6. $\{a, b, c\}$

7. $\{r, s, t\} \cup \{r, u, t, s, v\}$

The letters in either or both sets are r, s, t, u, and v, so the union is $\{r, s, t, u, v\}$.

8. $\{m, o, p\}$

9. $\{3, 5, 7\} \cup \emptyset$

The numbers in either or both sets are 3, 5, and 7, so the union is $\{3, 5, 7\}$.

10. $\emptyset$

11. $2 < x < 7$

This inequality is an abbreviation for the conjunction $2 < x$ *and* $x < 7$. The graph is the intersection of two separate solution sets: $\{x | 2 < x\} \cap \{x | x < 7\} = \{x | 2 < x < 7\}$.

Interval notation: $(2, 7)$

12.

$[0, 4]$

13. $-6 \le y \le -2$

This inequality is an abbreviation for the conjunction $-6 \le y$ *and* $y \le -2$.

Interval notation: $[-6, -2]$

14.

$[-9, -5)$

15. $x < -2$ *or* $x > 1$

The graph of this disjunction is the union of the graphs of the individual solution sets $\{x | x < -2\}$ and $\{x | x > 1\}$.

Interval notation: $(-\infty, -2) \cup (1, \infty)$

16.

$(-\infty, -2) \cup (3, \infty)$

17. $x \le -1$ *or* $x > 4$

Interval notation: $(-\infty, -1] \cup (4, \infty)$

18.

$(-\infty, -5] \cup (2, \infty)$

19. $-3 \le -x < 5$

$\quad 3 \ge x > -5$ Multiplying by -1 and reversing
$\qquad\qquad\qquad$ the inequality symbols
$-5 < x \le 3$ Rewriting

Interval notation: $(-5, 3]$

20.

$(-7, -2)$

21. $x > -2$ *and* $x < 4$

This conjunction can be abbreviated as $-2 < x < 4$.

Interval notation: $(-2, 4)$

22.

$(-3, 1]$

23. $5 > a$ *or* $a > 7$

Interval notation: $(-\infty, 5) \cup (7, \infty)$

24.

$(-\infty, -3) \cup [2, \infty)$

25. $x \geq 5 \; or \; -x \geq 4$

Multiplying the second inequality by -1 and reversing the inequality symbols, we get $x \geq 5 \; or \; x \leq -4$.

Interval notation: $(-\infty - 4] \cup [5, \infty)$

26.

$(-\infty, -6) \cup (-3, \infty)$

27. $5 > x \; and \; x \geq -6$

This conjunction can be abbreviated as $-6 \leq x < 5$.

Interval notation: $[-6, 5)$

28.

$(-6, 0]$

29. $x < 7 \; and \; x \geq 3$

This conjunction can be abbreviated as $3 \leq x < 7$.

Interval notation: $[3, 7)$

30.

$[-3, 3)$

31. $t < 2 \; or \; t < 5$

The graph of this disjunction is the union of the graphs of the individual solution sets: $\{t|t < 2\} \cup \{t|t < 5\}$. This is the set $\{t|t < 5\}$.

Interval notation: $(-\infty, 5)$

32.

$(-1, \infty)$

33. $x > -1 \; or \; x \leq 3$

The graph of this disjunction is the union of the graphs of the individual solution sets:

$\{x|x > -1\} \cup \{x|x \leq 3\} =$ the set of all real numbers.

Interval notation: $(-\infty, \infty)$

34.

$(-\infty, \infty)$

35. $x \geq 5 \; and \; x > 7$

The graph of this conjunction is the intersection of two separate solution sets: $\{x|x \geq 5\} \cap \{x|x > 7\} = \{x|x > 7\}$.

Interval notation: $(7, \infty)$

36.

$(-\infty, -4]$

37. $-3 < t + 2 < 7$

$-3 - 2 < t < 7 - 2$

$-5 < t < 5$

The solution set is $\{t| -5 < t < 5\}$, or $(-5, 5)$.

38. $\{t| -3 < t \leq 4\}$, or $(-3, 4]$

39. $-5 \leq 2a - 1 \; and \; 3a + 1 < 7$

$-4 \leq 2a \quad and \quad 3a < 6$

$-2 \leq a \quad and \quad a < 2$

We can abbreviate the answer as $-2 \leq a < 2$. The solution set is $\{a| -2 \leq a < 2\}$, or $[-2, 2)$.

40. $\{n| -2 \leq n \leq 4\}$, or $[-2, 4]$

41. $x + 7 \leq -2 \; or \; x + 7 \geq 5$

$x \leq -9 \quad or \quad x \geq -2$

The solution set is $\{x|x \leq -9 \; or \; x \geq -2\}$, or $(-\infty, -9] \cup [-2, \infty)$.

42. $\{x|x < -8 \; or \; x \geq -1\}$, or $(-\infty, -8) \cup [-1, \infty)$

43. $2 \leq 3x - 1 \leq 8$

$3 \leq 3x \leq 9$

$1 \leq x \leq 3$

The solution set is $\{x|1 \leq x \leq 3\}$, or $[1, 3]$.

44. $\{x|1 \le x \le 5\}$, or $[1, 5]$

45. $-18 \le -2x - 7 < 0$

$-11 \le -2x < 7$

$\dfrac{11}{2} \ge x > -\dfrac{7}{2}$, or

$-\dfrac{7}{2} < x \le \dfrac{11}{2}$

The solution set is $\left\{x \left| -\dfrac{7}{2} < x \le \dfrac{11}{2} \right.\right\}$, or

$\left(-\dfrac{7}{2}, \dfrac{11}{2}\right]$.

46. $\left\{t \left| -4 < t \le -\dfrac{10}{3} \right.\right\}$, or $\left(-4, -\dfrac{10}{3}\right]$

47. $3x - 1 \le 2$ *or* $3x - 1 \ge 8$

$3x \le 3$ *or* $3x \ge 9$

$x \le 1$ *or* $x \ge 3$

The solution set is $\{x|x \le 1 \ or \ x \ge 3\}$, or $(-\infty, 1] \cup [3, \infty)$.

48. $\{x|x \le 1 \ or \ x \ge 5\}$, or $(-\infty, 1] \cup [5, \infty)$

49. $2x - 7 < -1$ *or* $2x - 7 > 1$

$2x < 6$ *or* $2x > 8$

$x < 3$ *or* $x > 4$

The solution set is $\{x|x < 3 \ or \ x > 4\}$, or $(-\infty, 3) \cup (4, \infty)$.

50. $\left\{x \left| x < -4 \ or \ x > \dfrac{2}{3} \right.\right\}$, or

$(-\infty, -4) \cup \left(\dfrac{2}{3}, \infty\right)$.

51. $a + 4 < -1$ *and* $3a - 5 < 7$

$a < -5$ *and* $3a < 12$

$a < -5$ *and* $a < 4$

The solution set is $\{a|a < -5\} \cap \{a|a < 4\} = \{a|a < -5\}$, or $(-\infty, -5)$.

52. $\{a|a > 4\}$, or $(4, \infty)$.

53. $3x + 2 < 2$ *or* $4 - 2x < 14$

$3x < 0$ *or* $-2x < 10$

$x < 0$ *or* $x > -5$

The solution set is $\{x|x < 0\} \cup \{x|x > -5\}$ = the set of all real numbers, or $(-\infty, \infty)$.

54. All real numbers, or $(-\infty, \infty)$

55. $2t - 7 \le 5$ *or* $5 - 2t > 3$

$2t \le 12$ *or* $-2t > -2$

$t \le 6$ *or* $t < 1$

The solution set is $\{t|t \le 6\} \cup \{t|t < 1\} = \{t|t \le 6\}$, or $(-\infty, 6]$.

56. $\{a|a \ge 1\}$, or $[-1, \infty)$

57. Any real number is less than 5 *or* greater than 4, so the solution set is the set of all real numbers, or $(-\infty, \infty)$.

58. $\emptyset$

59. No number is less than 3 *and* greater than 4, so the solution set is $\emptyset$.

60. All real numbers, or $(-\infty, \infty)$

61. From the graph we observe that the values of x for which $2x - 5 > -7$ *and* $2x - 5 < 7$ are $\{x|-1 < x < 6\}$, or $(-1, 6)$.

62. $\{x|x < -3 \ or \ x > 6\}$, or $(-\infty, -3) \cup (6, \infty)$

63. $5x - 4 = 3(2x + 1) - x$

$5x - 4 = 6x + 3 - x$ Removing parentheses

$5x - 4 = 5x + 3$ Collecting like terms

$-4 = 3$ Subtracting $5x$ on both sides

We get a false equation, so there is no solution. The solution set is $\emptyset$.

64. $-\dfrac{8}{3}$

65. $5(2x + 3) = 3(x - 4)$

$10x + 15 = 3x - 12$

$7x + 15 = -12$

$7x = -27$

$x = -\dfrac{27}{7}$

The solution is $-\dfrac{27}{7}$.

66. x-intercept: $(-4, 0)$

y-intercept: $(0, 3)$

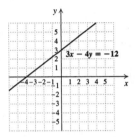

67. Graph: $f(x) = 5$

The graph of any constant function $f(x) = c$ is a horizontal line that crosses the vertical axis at $(0, c)$. Thus, the graph of $f(x) = 5$ is a horizontal line that crosses the vertical axis at $(0, 5)$.

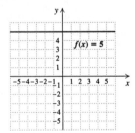

68.

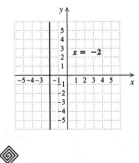

69. ◈

70. ◈

71. ◈

72. ◈

73. **Familiarize.** Let c = the number of crossings per month. Then at the \$3 per crossing rate, the total cost of c crossings is \$3c. A six-month pass costs \$15/6, or \$2.50 per month. The additional 50¢ per crossing toll brings the total cost of c crossings to \$2.50 + \$0.50c. A one-year pass costs \$60/12, or \$5 per month regardless of the number of crossings.

Translate. We write an inequality that states that the cost of c crossings per month using the six-month pass is less than the cost using the \$3 per crossing toll and is less than the cost using the one-year pass.

$$2.50 + 0.50c < 3c \text{ and } 2.50 + 0.50c < 5$$

Carry out. We solve the inequality.

$2.50 + 0.50c < 3c \quad$ and $\quad 2.50 + 0.50c < 5$

$2.50 < 2.5c \quad$ and $\qquad\quad 0.50c < 2.50$

$\quad 1 < c \qquad$ and $\qquad\qquad\quad c < 5$

This result can be written as $1 < c < 5$.

Check. When we substitute values of c less than 1, between 1 and 5, and greater than 5, we find that the result checks. Since we cannot check every possible value of c, we stop here.

State. For more than 1 crossing but less than 5 crossings per month the six-month pass is the most economical choice.

74. Sizes between 6 and 13

75. Solve $1 \le P(d) = 7$, or $1 \le 1 + \dfrac{d}{33} \le 7$.

$1 \le 1 + \dfrac{d}{33} \le 7$

$0 \le \dfrac{d}{33} \le 6$

$0 \le d \le 198$

Thus, $0 \text{ ft} \le d \le 198 \text{ ft}$.

76. **(a)** $1945.4 \le F < 4820$; **(b)** $1761.44 \le F < 3956$

77. Solve $5.0 \le w(t) \le 5.25$, or $5.0 \le 0.05t + 4.3 \le 5.25$

$5.0 \le 0.05t + 4.3 \le 5.25$

$0.7 \le 0.05t \le 0.95$

$14 \le t \le 19$

Thus, from 14 to 19 years after 1991, or from 2005 to 2010, waste production will range from 5.0 to 5.25 pounds per person per day.

78. $1965 \le y \le 1981$

79. $4a - 2 \le a + 1 \le 3a + 4$

$\qquad 4a - 2 \le a + 1 \quad and \quad a + 1 \le 3a + 4$

$\qquad\quad 3a \le 3 \qquad and \qquad -3 \le 2a$

$\qquad\quad\; a \le 1 \qquad and \qquad -\dfrac{3}{2} \le a$

The solution set is $\left\{a \middle| -\dfrac{3}{2} \le a \le 1\right\}$, or $\left[-\dfrac{3}{2}, 1\right]$.

80. $\left\{m \middle| m < \dfrac{6}{5}\right\}$, or $\left(-\infty, \dfrac{6}{5}\right)$

81. $x - 10 < 5x + 6 \le x + 10$

$\qquad -10 < 4x + 6 \le 10$

$\qquad -16 < 4x \le 4$

$\qquad\; -4 < x \le 1$

The solution set is $\{x | -4 < x \le 1\}$, or $(-4, 1]$.

82. $\left\{x \middle| -\dfrac{1}{8} < x < \dfrac{1}{2}\right\}$, or $\left(-\dfrac{1}{8}, \dfrac{1}{2}\right)$

83. If $-b < -a$, then $-1(-b) > -1(-a)$, or $b > a$, or $a < b$. The statement is true.

84. False

85. Let $a = 5$, $c = 12$, and $b = 2$. Then $a < c$ and $b < c$, but $a \not< b$. The given statement is false.

86. True

87. Left to the student.

Exercise Set 4.6

1. The solutions of $|x + 2| = 3$ are the first coordinates of the points of intersection of $y_1 = \text{abs}(x + 2)$ and $y_2 = 3$. They are -5 and 1, so the solution set is $\{-5, 1\}$.

2. $\{x | -5 \le x \le 1\}$, or $[-5, 1]$

3. The graph of $y_1 = \text{abs}(x + 2)$ lies below the graph of $y_2 = 3$ for $\{x | -5 < x < 1\}$, or on $(-5, 1)$.

4. $\{x | x < -5 \ or \ x > 1\}$, or $(-\infty, -5) \cup (1, \infty)$

5. The graph of $y_1 = \text{abs}(x + 2)$ lies on or above the graph of $y_2 = 3$ for $\{x | x \le -5 \ or \ x \ge 1\}$, or on $(\infty, -5] \cup [1, \infty)$.

6. $\emptyset$

7. $|x| = 7$

$\qquad x = -7 \ or \ x = 7$ \quad Using the absolute-value principle

The solution set is $\{-7, 7\}$.

8. $\{-9, 9\}$

9. $|x| = -5$

The absolute value of a number is always nonnegative. Therefore, the solution set is $\emptyset$.

10. $\emptyset$

11. $|y| = 8.6$

$\qquad y = -8.6 \ or \ y = 8.6$ \quad Using the absolute-value principle

The solution set is $\{-8.6, 8.6\}$.

12. $\{0\}$

13. $|m| = 0$

$\qquad m = 0$

$\qquad \{0\}$

The only number whose absolute value is 0 is 0. The solution set is $\{0\}$.

14. $\{-5.5, 5.5\}$

15. $|5x + 2| = 3$

$\qquad 5x + 2 = -3 \ or \ 5x + 2 = 3$ \quad Absolute-value principle

$\qquad\quad 5x = -5 \ or \qquad 5x = 1$

$\qquad\qquad x = -1 \ or \qquad\quad x = \dfrac{1}{5}$

The solution set is $\left\{-1, \dfrac{1}{5}\right\}$.

16. $\left\{-\dfrac{1}{2}, \dfrac{7}{2}\right\}$

17. $|7x - 2| = -9$

Absolute value is always nonnegative, so the equation has no solution. The solution set is $\emptyset$.

18. $\emptyset$

19. $|2y| - 5 = 13$

$\quad\quad |2y| = 18$ Adding 5

$\quad 2y = -18$ *or* $2y = 18$

$\quad\quad y = -9$ *or* $y = 9$

The solution set is $\{-9, 9\}$.

20. $\{-8, 8\}$

21. $7|z| + 2 = 16$ Adding -2

$\quad\quad 7|z| = 14$ Multiplying by $\dfrac{1}{7}$

$\quad\quad\quad |z| = 2$

$\quad z = -2$ *or* $z = 2$

The solution set is $\{-2, 2\}$.

22. $\left\{ -\dfrac{11}{5}, \dfrac{11}{5} \right\}$

23. $|t - 7| + 3 = 4$ Adding -3

$\quad\quad\quad |t - 7| = 1$

$\quad t - 7 = -1$ *or* $t - 7 = 1$

$\quad\quad\quad t = 6$ *or* $t = 8$

The solution set is $\{6, 8\}$.

24. $\{-12, 2\}$

25. $3|2x - 5| - 7 = -1$

$\quad\quad\quad 3|2x - 5| = 6$

$\quad\quad\quad\quad |2x - 5| = 2$

$\quad 2x - 5 = -2$ *or* $2x - 5 = 2$

$\quad\quad\quad 2x = 3$ *or* $2x = 7$

$\quad\quad\quad x = \dfrac{3}{2}$ *or* $x = \dfrac{7}{2}$

The solution set is $\left\{ \dfrac{3}{2}, \dfrac{7}{2} \right\}$.

26. $\left\{ -\dfrac{1}{3}, 3 \right\}$

27. $|3x - 4| = 8$

$\quad 3x - 4 = -8$ *or* $3x - 4 = 8$

$\quad\quad 3x = -4$ *or* $3x = 12$

$\quad\quad\quad x = -\dfrac{4}{3}$ *or* $x = 4$

The solution set is $\left\{ -\dfrac{4}{3}, 4 \right\}$.

28. $\left\{ -\dfrac{3}{2}, \dfrac{17}{2} \right\}$

29. $|x| - 2 = 6.3$

$\quad\quad |x| = 8.3$

$\quad x = -8.3$ *or* $x = 8.3$

The solution set is $\{-8.3, 8.3\}$.

30. $\{-11, 11\}$

31. $\left| \dfrac{3x - 2}{5} \right| = 2$

$\quad \dfrac{3x - 2}{5} = -2$ *or* $\dfrac{3x - 2}{5} = 2$

$\quad 3x - 2 = -10$ *or* $3x - 2 = 10$

$\quad\quad 3x = -8$ *or* $3x = 12$

$\quad\quad\quad x = -\dfrac{8}{3}$ *or* $x = 4$

The solution set is $\left\{ -\dfrac{8}{3}, 4 \right\}$.

32. $\{-1, 2\}$

33. $|x + 4| = |2x - 7|$

$\quad x + 4 = 2x - 7$ *or* $x + 4 = -(2x - 7)$

$\quad\quad 4 = x - 7$ *or* $x + 4 = -2x + 7$

$\quad\quad 11 = x$ *or* $3x + 4 = 7$

$\quad\quad\quad\quad\quad\quad\quad\quad\quad 3x = 3$

$\quad\quad\quad\quad\quad\quad\quad\quad\quad x = 1$

The solution set is $\{1, 11\}$.

34. $\left\{ -\dfrac{11}{2}, \dfrac{1}{4} \right\}$

35. $|x - 9| = |x + 6|$

$\quad x - 9 = x + 6$ *or* $x - 9 = -(x + 6)$

$\quad\quad -9 = 6$ *or* $x - 9 = -x - 6$

$\quad$ False $-$ $2x - 9 = -6$

$\quad$ yields no $2x = 3$

$\quad$ solution $x = \dfrac{3}{2}$

The solution set is $\left\{ \dfrac{3}{2} \right\}$.

36. $\left\{ -\dfrac{1}{2} \right\}$

37. $|5t + 7| = |4t + 3|$

$\quad 5t + 7 = 4t + 3$ *or* $5t + 7 = -(4t + 3)$

$\quad\quad t + 7 = 3$ *or* $5t + 7 = -4t - 3$

$\quad\quad\quad t = -4$ *or* $9t + 7 = -3$

$\quad\quad\quad\quad\quad\quad\quad\quad\quad 9t = -10$

$\quad\quad\quad\quad\quad\quad\quad\quad\quad t = -\dfrac{10}{9}$

The solution set is $\left\{ -4, -\dfrac{10}{9} \right\}$.

38. $\left\{-\dfrac{3}{5}, 5\right\}$

39. $|n - 3| = |3 - n|$

$n - 3 = 3 - n \quad or \quad n - 3 = -(3 - n)$

$2n - 3 = 3 \qquad or \quad n - 3 = -3 + n$

$2n = 6 \qquad or \qquad -3 = -3$

$\quad n = 3 \qquad$ True for all real values of n

The solution set is the set of all real numbers.

40. All real numbers

41. $|7 - a| = |a + 5|$

$7 - a = a + 5 \quad or \quad 7 - a = -(a + 5)$

$7 = 2a + 5 \quad or \quad 7 - a = -a - 5$

$2 = 2a \qquad or \qquad 7 = -5$

$1 = a \qquad\qquad$ False

The solution set is $\{1\}$.

42. $\left\{-\dfrac{1}{2}\right\}$

43. $|a| \leq 6$

$-6 \leq a \leq 6 \qquad$ Part (b)

The solution set is $\{a| -6 \leq a \leq 6\}$, or $[-6, 6]$.

44. $\{x| -2 < x < 2\}$, or $(-2, 2)$

45. $|x| > 7$

$x < -7 \ or \ 7 < x \qquad$ Part (c)

The solution set is $\{x|x < -7 \ or \ x > 7\}$, or $(-\infty, -7) \cup (7, \infty)$.

46. $\{a|a \leq -3 \ or \ a \geq 3\}$, or $(-\infty, -3] \cup [3, \infty)$

47. $|t| > 0$

$t < 0 \ or \ 0 < t \qquad$ Part (c)

The solution set is $\{t|t < 0 \ or \ t > 0\}$, or $\{t|t \neq 0\}$, or $(-\infty, 0) \cup (0, \infty)$.

48. $\{t|t \leq -1.7 \ or \ t \geq 1.7\}$, or $(-\infty, -1.7] \cup [1.7, \infty)$

49. $|x - 3| < 5$

$-5 < x - 3 < 5 \qquad$ Part (b)

$-2 < x < 8$

The solution set is $\{x| -2 < x < 8\}$, or $(-2, 8)$.

50. $\{x| -2 < x < 4\}$, or $(-2, 4)$

51. $|x - 3| + 2 \geq 7$

$|x - 3| \geq 5 \quad$ Adding -2

$x - 3 \leq -5 \ or \ 5 \leq x - 3 \quad$ Part (c)

$x \leq -2 \ or \ 8 \leq x$

The solution set is $\{x|x \leq -2 \ or \ x \geq 8\}$, or $(-\infty, -2] \cup [8, \infty)$.

52. $\{x|x \leq -1 \ or \ x \geq 9\}$, or $(-\infty, -1] \cup [9, \infty)$

53. $|2y - 7| > -1$

Since absolute value is never negative, any value of $2y - 7$, and hence any value of y, will satisfy the inequality. The solution set is the set of all real numbers, or $(-\infty, \infty)$.

54. All real numbers, or $(-\infty, \infty)$

55. $|3a - 4| + 2 \geq 7$

$|3a - 4| \geq 5 \quad$ Adding -2

$3a - 4 \leq -5 \ or \ 5 \leq 3a - 4 \quad$ Part (c)

$3a \leq -1 \ or \ 9 \leq 3a$

$a \leq -\dfrac{1}{3} \ or \ 3 \leq a$

The solution set is $\left\{a\left|a \leq -\dfrac{1}{3} \ or \ a \geq 3\right.\right\}$, or $\left(-\infty, -\dfrac{1}{3}\right] \cup [3, \infty)$.

56. $\{a|a \le -1 \ or \ a \ge 6\}$, or $(-\infty, -1] \cup [6, \infty)$

57. $|y - 3| < 12$

$\qquad -12 < y - 3 < 12 \quad$ Part (b)

$\qquad -9 < y < 15 \qquad$ Adding 3

The solution set is $\{y| -9 < y < 15\}$, or $(-9, 15)$.

58. $\{p| -1 < p < 5\}$ or $(-1, 5)$

59. $9 - |x + 4| \le 5$

$\qquad -|x + 4| \le -4$

$\qquad |x + 4| \ge 4 \qquad$ Multiplying by -1

$x + 4 \le -4 \ or \ 4 \le x + 4 \quad$ Part (c)

$\qquad x \le -8 \ or \ 0 \le x$

The solution set is $\{x|x \le -8 \ or \ x \ge 0\}$, or $(-\infty, -8] \cup [0, \infty)$.

60. $\{x|x \le 2 \ or \ x \ge 8\}$, or $(-\infty, 2] \cup [8, \infty)$

61. $|4 - 3y| > 8$

$4 - 3y < -8 \quad or \quad 8 < 4 - 3y \quad$ Part (c)

$\qquad -3y < -12 \quad or \quad 4 < -3y \qquad$ Adding -4

$\qquad y > 4 \qquad or \quad -\dfrac{4}{3} > y \quad$ Multiplying by $-\dfrac{1}{3}$

The solution set is $\left\{y\middle|y < -\dfrac{4}{3} \ or \ y > 4\right\}$, or $\left(-\infty, -\dfrac{4}{3}\right) \cup (4, \infty)$.

62. $\emptyset$.

63. $|3 - 4x| < -5$

Absolute value is always nonnegative, so the inequality has no solution. The solution set is $\emptyset$.

64. $\left\{a\middle| -\dfrac{7}{2} \le a \le 6\right\}$, or $\left[-\dfrac{7}{2}, 6\right]$

65. $\left|\dfrac{2 - 5x}{4}\right| \ge \dfrac{2}{3}$

$\dfrac{2 - 5x}{4} \le -\dfrac{2}{3} \quad or \quad \dfrac{2}{3} \le \dfrac{2 - 5x}{4} \quad$ Part (c)

$2 - 5x \le -\dfrac{8}{3} \quad or \quad \dfrac{8}{3} \le 2 - 5x \quad$ Multiplying by 4

$-5x \le -\dfrac{14}{3} \ or \quad \dfrac{2}{3} \le -5x \qquad$ Adding -2

$x \ge \dfrac{14}{15} \quad or \ -\dfrac{2}{15} \ge x \quad$ Multiplying by $-\dfrac{1}{5}$

The solution set is $\left\{x\middle|x \le -\dfrac{2}{15} \ or \ x \ge \dfrac{14}{15}\right\}$, or $\left(-\infty, -\dfrac{2}{15}\right] \cup \left[\dfrac{14}{15}, \infty\right)$.

66. $\left\{x\middle|x < -\dfrac{43}{24} \ or \ x > \dfrac{9}{8}\right\}$, or $\left(-\infty, -\dfrac{43}{24}\right) \cup \left(\dfrac{9}{8}, \infty\right)$

67. $|m + 5| + 9 \le 16$

$\qquad |m + 5| \le 7 \quad$ Adding -9

$\qquad -7 \le m + 5 \le 7$

$\qquad -12 \le m \le 2$

The solution set is $\{m| -12 \le m \le 2\}$, or $[-12, 2]$.

68. $\{t|t \le 6 \ or \ t \ge 8\}$, or $(-\infty, 6] \cup [8, \infty)$

69. $25 - 2|a + 3| > 19$

$\qquad -2|a + 3| > -6$

$\qquad |a + 3| < 3 \qquad$ Multiplying by $-\dfrac{1}{2}$

$\qquad -3 < a + 3 < 3 \quad$ Part (b)

$\qquad -6 < a < 0$

The solution set is $\{a| -6 < a < 0\}$, or $(-6, 0)$.

70. $\left\{a\middle| -\dfrac{13}{2} < a < \dfrac{5}{2}\right\}$, or $\left(-\dfrac{13}{2}, \dfrac{5}{2}\right)$

71. $|2x - 3| \le 4$

$\quad -4 \le 2x - 3 \le 4 \quad$ Part (b)

$\quad -1 \le 2x \le 7 \qquad$ Adding 3

$\quad -\dfrac{1}{2} \le x \le \dfrac{7}{2} \qquad$ Multiplying by $\dfrac{1}{2}$

The solution set is $\left\{ x \,\middle|\, -\dfrac{1}{2} \le x \le \dfrac{7}{2} \right\}$, or $\left[-\dfrac{1}{2}, \dfrac{7}{2} \right]$.

72. $\left\{ x \,\middle|\, -1 \le x \le \dfrac{1}{5} \right\}$, or $\left[-1, \dfrac{1}{5} \right]$

73. $2 + |3x - 4| \ge 13$

$\quad |3x - 4| \ge 11$

$\quad 3x - 4 \le -11 \quad or \quad 11 \le 3x - 4 \quad$ Part (c)

$\quad\quad 3x \le -7 \quad or \quad 15 \le 3x$

$\quad\quad\quad x \le -\dfrac{7}{3} \quad or \quad 5 \le x$

The solution set is $\left\{ x \,\middle|\, x \le -\dfrac{7}{3} \ or\ x \ge 5 \right\}$, or

$\left(-\infty, -\dfrac{7}{3} \right] \cup [5, \infty)$.

74. $\left\{ x \,\middle|\, x \le -\dfrac{23}{9} \ or\ x \ge 3 \right\}$, or

$\left(-\infty, -\dfrac{23}{9} \right] \cup [3, \infty)$

75. $7 + |2x - 1| < 16$

$\quad |2x - 1| < 9$

$\quad -9 < 2x - 1 < 9 \quad$ Part (b)

$\quad -8 < 2x < 10$

$\quad -4 < x < 5$

The solution set is $\{ x \,|\, -4 < x < 5 \}$, or $(-4, 5)$.

76. $\left\{ x \,\middle|\, -\dfrac{16}{3} < x < 4 \right\}$, or $\left(-\dfrac{16}{3}, 4 \right)$.

77. *Familiarize.* Let $a =$ the amount originally invested. After 1 yr, the account contains the amount originally invested plus 3.5% of that amount.

Translate.

Amount after 1 yr	is	original amount	plus	3.5%	of	original amount.
↓	↓	↓	↓	↓	↓	↓
2587.50	=	a	+	0.035	·	a

Carry out. We solve the equation.

$\quad 2587.50 = a + 0.035a$

$\quad 2587.50 = 1.035a$

$\quad\quad 2500 = a \qquad$ Dividing by 1.035

Check. 3.5% of $2500 is $87.50 and $2500+$87.50 = $2587.50, so the answer checks.

State. Alyssa originally invested $2500.

78. 24,640 m^2

79. $2x^2 + 3y = 2 \cdot 5^2 + 3 \cdot 6$

$\quad = 2 \cdot 25 + 3 \cdot 6$

$\quad = 50 + 18$

$\quad = 68$

80. 29

81. ◈

82. ◈

83. ◈

84. ◈

85. From the definition of absolute value, $|2x-5| = 2x-5$ only when $2x - 5 \ge 0$. Solve $2x - 5 \ge 0$.

$\quad 2x - 5 \ge 0$

$\quad\quad 2x \ge 5$

$\quad\quad\quad x \ge \dfrac{5}{2}$

The solution set is $\left\{ x \,\middle|\, x \ge \dfrac{5}{2} \right\}$, or $\left[\dfrac{5}{2}, \infty \right)$.

86. $\{x \,|\, x \ge -3\}$, or $[-3, \infty)$

87. $|7x - 2| = x + 4$

From the definition of absolute value, we know $x + 4 \ge 0$, or $x \ge -4$. So we have $x \ge -4$ *and*

$\quad 7x - 2 = x + 4 \quad or \quad 7x - 2 = -(x + 4)$

$\quad\quad 6x = 6 \qquad or \quad 7x - 2 = -x - 4$

$\quad\quad\quad x = 1 \qquad or \quad\quad 8x = -2$

$\quad\quad\quad\quad\quad\quad\quad\quad\quad\quad x = -\dfrac{1}{4}$

The solution set is $\left\{ x \,\middle|\, x \ge -4 \ and\ x=1\ or\ x=-\dfrac{1}{4} \right\}$, or $\left\{1, -\frac{1}{4}\right\}$.

88. All real numbers, or $(-\infty, \infty)$

89. $2 \le |x - 1| \le 5$

  $2 \le |x - 1|$ *and* $|x - 1| \le 5$.

  For $2 \le |x - 1|$:

  $x - 1 \le -2$ *or* $2 \le x - 1$

    $x \le -1$ *or* $3 \le x$

  The solution set of $2 \le |x-1|$ is $\{x | x \le -1 \ or \ x \ge 3\}$.

  For $|x - 1| \le 5$:

  $-5 \le x - 1 \le 5$

  $-4 \le x \le 6$

  The solution set of $|x - 1| \le 5$ is $\{x | -4 \le x \le 6\}$.

  The solution set of $2 \le |x - 1| \le 5$ is

    $\{x | x \le -1 \ or \ x \ge 3\} \cap \{x | -4 \le x \le 6\}$

   $= \{x | -4 \le x \le -1 \ or \ 3 \le x \le 6\}$, *or*

    $[-4, -1] \cup [3, 6]$.

90. $\left\{-6, \frac{4}{3}\right\}$

91. Graph $y_1 = \text{abs}(10x + 7)$ and $y_2 = 5x + 3$. We use the window $[-3, 2, -2, 10]$.

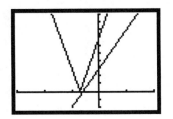

We see that the graphs do not intersect, so the solution set is $\emptyset$.

92. $\{-2\}$

93. Graph $y_1 = \text{abs}(x+7.3)$ and $y_2 = 8.2 - x$. We use the window $[-20, 10, -2, 20]$, Xscl = 5, Yscl = 5. Then find the first coordinate of the point of intersection of the graphs.

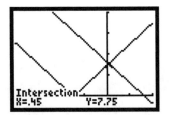

The solution set is $\{0.45\}$.

94. $\{x | x < -9 \ or \ x > -0.3333333\}$, or $(-\infty, -9) \cup (-0.3333333, \infty)$

95. Graph $y_1 = \text{abs}(x+7)$ and $y_2 = \text{abs}((1/2)x-3)$. One good choice for a window is $[-30, 20, -2, 20]$, Xscl = 5, Yscl = 5. Using the INTERSECT feature, we find that the first coordinates of the points of intersection are -20 and about -2.666667. Observe that $y_1 \le y_2$ at the points of intersection and between them. Thus, the solution set is $\{x | -20 \le x \le -2.666667\}$, or $[-20, -2.666667]$.

96. $\{x | x \le -5.4 \ or \ x \ge 0.46666667\}$, or $(-\infty, -5.4] \cup [0.46666667, \infty)$

97. Graph $y_1 = \text{abs}(9.3 - x)$ and $y_2 = \text{abs}(x - 1.5)$. One good choice for a window is $[-15, 25, -2, 15]$, Xscl = 5, Yscl = 5. Using the INTERSECT feature, we find that the first coordinate of the point of intersection is 5.4. Observe that $y_1 < y_2$ for $\{x | x > 5.4\}$, or on $(5.4, \infty)$.

98. $|x| < 3$

99. Using part (b), we find that $-5 \le y \le 5$ is equivalent to $|y| \le 5$.

100. $|x| \ge 6$

101. $x < -4 \ or \ 4 < x$

    $|x| > 4$ Using part (c)

102. $|x + 3| > 5$

103. $-5 < x < 1$

    $-3 < x + 2 < 3$ Adding 2

    $|x + 2| < 3$ Using part (b)

104. $|x - 7| < 2$, or $|7 - x| < 2$

105. The distance from x to 5 is $|x - 5|$ or $|5 - x|$, so we have $|x - 5| > 1$ or $|5 - x| > 1$.

106. $\left\{d \,\middle|\, 5\frac{1}{2} \text{ ft} \le d \le 6\frac{1}{2} \text{ ft}\right\}$, or $\left[5\frac{1}{2} \text{ ft}, 6\frac{1}{2} \text{ ft}\right]$

107. ◈

Chapter 5
Polynomials

1. $m^4 \cdot m^6 = m^{4+6} = m^{10}$

2. 3^7

3. $8^5 \cdot 8^9 = 8^{5+9} = 8^{14}$

4. n^{23}

5. $x^4 \cdot x^3 = x^{4+3} = x^7$

6. y^{16}

7. $5^7 \cdot 5^0 = 5^{7+0} = 5^7$

8. t^{16}

9. $(3y)^4(3y)^8 = (3y)^{4+8} = (3y)^{12}$

10. $(2t)^{25}$

11. $(5t)(5t)^6 = (5t)^1(5t)^6 = (5t)^{1+6} = (5t)^7$

12. $8x$

13. $(a^2b^7)(a^3b^2) = a^2b^7a^3b^2$ Using an associative law
$\qquad = a^2a^3b^7b^2$ Using a commutative law
$\qquad = a^5b^9$ Adding exponents

14. $(m-3)^9$

15. $(x+1)^5(x+1)^7 = (x+1)^{5+7} = (x+1)^{12}$

16. $a^{12}b^4$

17. $r^3 \cdot r^7 \cdot r^2 = r^{3+7+2} = r^{12}$

18. s^{11}

19. $(xy^4)(xy)^3 = (xy^4)(x^3y^3)$
$\qquad = x \cdot x^3 \cdot y^4 \cdot y^3$
$\qquad = x^{1+3}y^{4+3}$
$\qquad = x^4y^7$

20. a^7b^5

21. $\dfrac{7^5}{7^2} = 7^{5-2} = 7^3$ Subtracting exponents

22. 4^4

23. $\dfrac{x^{15}}{x^3} = x^{15-3} = x^{12}$ Subtracting exponents

24. a^8

25. $\dfrac{y^9}{y^5} = y^{9-5} = y^4$

26. x

27. $\dfrac{(5a)^7}{(5a)^6} = (5a)^{7-6} = (5a)^1 = 5a$

28. $3m$

29. $\dfrac{(x+y)^8}{(x+y)^3} = (x+y)^{8-3} = (x+y)^5$

30. $(a-b)^9$

31. $\dfrac{18m^5}{6m^2} = \dfrac{18}{6}m^{5-2} = 3m^3$

32. $5n^4$

33. $\dfrac{a^9b^7}{a^2b} = \dfrac{a^9}{a^2} \cdot \dfrac{b^7}{b^1} = a^{9-2}b^{7-1} = a^7b^6$

34. r^7s^7

35. $\dfrac{m^9n^8}{m^0n^4} = \dfrac{m^9}{m^0} \cdot \dfrac{n^8}{n^4} = m^{9-0}n^{8-4} = m^9n^4$

36. a^8b^9

37. When $x = 13$, $x^0 = 13^0 = 1$. (Any nonzero number raised to the 0 power is 1.)

38. 1

39. When $x = -4$, $5x^0 = 5(-4)^0 = 5 \cdot 1 = 5$.

40. 7

41. For any $n \neq 0$, $n^0 = 1$. (Any nonzero number raised to the 0 power is 1.)

42. 1

43. $9^1 - 9^0 = 9 - 1 = 8$

44. -6

45. $(x^3)^4 = x^{3 \cdot 4} = x^{12}$ Multiplying exponents

46. a^{24}

47. $(5^8)^2 = 5^{8\cdot2} = 5^{16}$ Multiplying exponents

48. 2^{15}

49. $(m^7)^5 = m^{7\cdot5} = m^{35}$

50. n^{18}

51. $(a^{25})^3 = a^{25\cdot3} = a^{75}$

52. a^{75}

53. $(7x)^2 = 7^2 \cdot x^2 = 49x^2$

54. $25a^2$

55. $(-2a)^3 = (-2)^3 a^3 = -8a^3$

56. $-27x^3$

57. $(4m^3)^2 = 4^2(m^3)^2 = 16m^6$

58. $25n^8$

59. $(a^2b)^7 = (a^2)^7(b^7) = a^{14}b^7$

60. x^9y^{36}

61. $(a^3b^2)^5 = (a^3)^5(b^2)^5 = a^{15}b^{10}$

62. $m^{24}n^{30}$

63. $(-5x^4y^5)^2 = (-5)^2(x^4)^2(y^5)^2 = 25x^8y^{10}$

64. $81a^{20}b^{28}$

65. $\left(\dfrac{a}{4}\right)^3 = \dfrac{a^3}{4^3} = \dfrac{a^3}{64}$ Raising the numerator and the denominator to the third power

66. $\dfrac{81}{x^4}$

67. $\left(\dfrac{7}{5a}\right)^2 = \dfrac{7^2}{(5a)^2} = \dfrac{49}{5^2a^2} = \dfrac{49}{25a^2}$

68. $\dfrac{64x^3}{27}$

69. $\left(\dfrac{a^4}{b^3}\right)^5 = \dfrac{(a^4)^5}{(b^3)^5} = \dfrac{a^{20}}{b^{15}}$

70. $\dfrac{x^{35}}{y^{14}}$

71. $\left(\dfrac{y^3}{2}\right)^2 = \dfrac{(y^3)^2}{2^2} = \dfrac{y^6}{4}$

72. $\dfrac{a^{15}}{27}$

73. $\left(\dfrac{x^2y}{z^3}\right)^4 = \dfrac{(x^2y)^4}{(z^3)^4} = \dfrac{(x^2)^4(y^4)}{z^{12}} = \dfrac{x^8y^4}{z^{12}}$

74. $\dfrac{x^{15}}{y^{10}z^5}$

75. $\left(\dfrac{a^3}{-2b^5}\right)^4 = \dfrac{(a^3)^4}{(-2b^5)^4} = \dfrac{a^{12}}{(-2)^4(b^5)^4} = \dfrac{a^{12}}{16b^{20}}$

76. $\dfrac{x^{20}}{81y^{12}}$

77. $\left(\dfrac{2a^2}{3b^4}\right)^3 = \dfrac{(2a^2)^3}{(3b^4)^3} = \dfrac{2^3(a^2)^3}{3^3(b^4)^3} = \dfrac{8a^6}{27b^{12}}$

78. $\dfrac{9x^{10}}{16y^6}$

79. $\left(\dfrac{4x^3y^5}{3z^7}\right)^2 = \dfrac{(4x^3y^5)^2}{(3z^7)^2} = \dfrac{4^2(x^3)^2(y^5)^2}{3^2(z^7)^2} = \dfrac{16x^6y^{10}}{9z^{14}}$

80. $\dfrac{125a^{21}}{8b^{15}c^3}$

81. $3s + 3t + 24 = 3s + 3t + 3\cdot8 = 3(s + t + 8)$

82. $-7(x + 2)$

83. $9x + 2y - 4x - 2y = (9 - 4)x + (2 - 2)y = 5x$

84. 37.5%

85. Graph: $y = x - 5$

We make a table of solutions of the equation. Since the equation is in the form $y = mx + b$, we see that the y-intercept is $(0, -5)$. We find two other pairs.

When $x = 2$, $y = 2 - 5 = -3$.

When $x = 5$, $y = 5 - 5 = 0$.

x	y
0	-5
2	-3
5	0

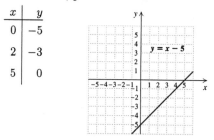

86.

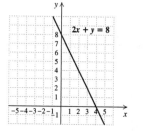

87. ◈

88. ◈

89. ◈

90. ◈

91. $(y^{2x})(y^{3x}) = y^{2x+3x} = y^{5x}$

92. a^{2k}

93. $\dfrac{a^{6t}(a^{7t})}{a^{9t}} = \dfrac{a^{6t+7t}}{a^{9t}} = \dfrac{a^{13t}}{a^{9t}} = a^{13t-9t} = a^{4t}$

94. 2

95. Since the bases are the same, the expression with the larger exponent is larger. Thus, $3^5 > 3^4$.

96. $4^2 < 4^3$

97. Since the exponents are the same, the expression with the larger base is larger. Thus, $4^3 < 5^3$.

98. $4^3 < 3^4$

99. $9^7 = (3^2)^7 = 3^{14}$

When bases are the same, the expression with the larger exponent is larger. Thus, $3^{14} > 3^{13}$, or $9^7 > 3^{13}$.

100. $25^8 > 125^5$

101. Choose any number except 0.

For example, let $a = 1$. Then $(a+5)^2 = (1+5)^2 = 6^2 = 36$, but $a^2 + 5^2 = 1^2 + 5^2 = 1 + 25 = 26$.

102. Choose any number except 0. For example, let $x = 1$.

$$3x^2 = 3 \cdot 1^2 = 3 \cdot 1 = 3, \text{ but}$$
$$(3x)^2 = (3 \cdot 1)^2 = 3^2 = 9.$$

103. Choose any number except $\dfrac{7}{6}$. For example let $a = 0$.

Then $\dfrac{0+7}{7} = \dfrac{7}{7} = 1$, but $a = 0$.

104. Choose any number except 0 or 1. For example, let $t = -1$. Then $\dfrac{t^6}{t^2} = \dfrac{(-1)^6}{(-1)^2} = \dfrac{1}{1} = 1$, but $t^3 = (-1)^3 = -1$.

105. $\dfrac{t^{38}}{t^x} = t^x$

$t^{38-x} = t^x$ Using the quotient rule

$38 - x = x$ The exponents are the same.

$$38 = 2x$$
$$19 = x$$

The solution is 19.

106. $15,638.03

107. We substitute 20,800 for P, 4.5% for r, and 6 for t.

$$A = P(1+r)^t$$
$$A = 20,800(1 + 4.5\%)^6$$
$$A = 20,800(1 + 0.045)^6$$
$$A = 20,800(1.045)^6$$
$$A \approx 27,087.01$$

There is $27,087.01 in the account at the end of 6 years.

108. ◈

Exercise Set 5.2

1. $3x - 7$ can be written as a sum of monomials, so it is a polynomial.

2. Yes

3. $\dfrac{x^2 + x + 1}{x^3 - 7}$ cannot be written as a sum of monomials, so it is not a polynomial.

4. Yes

5. $\dfrac{1}{4}x^{10} - 8.6$ can be written as a sum of monomials, so it is a polynomial.

6. No

7. $3x^4 - 7x^3 + x - 5 = 3x^4 + (-7x^3) + x + (-5)$

The terms are $3x^4$, $-7x^3$, x, and -5.

8. $5a^3$, $4a^2$, $-9a$, -7

9. $-t^4 + 2t^3 - 5t^2 + 3 = (-t^4) + 2t^3 + (-5t^2) + 3$

The terms are $-t^4$, $2t^3$, $-5t^2$, and 3.

10. n^5, $-4n^3$, $2n$, -8

11. $7x^3 - 5x$

Term	Coefficient	Degree
$7x^3$	7	3
$-5x$	-5	1

12. $9a^3 - 4a^2$

Term	Coefficient	Degree
$9a^3$	9	3
$-4a^2$	-4	2

13. $x^4 - x^3 + 4x - 3$

Term	Coefficient	Degree
x^4	1	4
$-x^3$	-1	3
$4x$	4	1
-3	-3	0

14. $3a^4 - a^3 + a - 9$

Term	Coefficient	Degree
$3a^4$	3	4
$-a^3$	-1	3
a	1	1
-9	-9	0

15. $2t + 3 + 4t^2$

a)

Term	$2t$	3	$4t^2$
Degree	1	0	2

b) The term of highest degree is $4t^2$. This is the leading term. Then the leading coefficient is 4.

c) Since the term of highest degree is $4t^2$, the degree of the polynomial is 2.

16. $3a^2 - 7 + 2a^5$

a)

Term	$3a^2$	-7	$2a^5$
Degree	2	0	5

b) Leading term: $2a^5$;

leading coefficient: 2

c) Degree: 5

17. $-5x^4 + x^2 - x + 3$

a)

Term	$-5x^4$	x^2	$-x$	3
Degree	4	2	1	0

b) The term of highest degree is $-5x^4$. This is the leading term. Then the leading coefficient is -5.

c) Since the term of highest degree is $-5x^4$, the degree of the polynomial is 4.

18. $-7x^3 + 6x^2 - 3x - 4$

a)

Term	$-7x^3$	$6x^2$	$-3x$	-4
Degree	3	2	1	0

b) Leading term: $-7x^3$;

leading coefficient: -7

c) Degree: 3

19. $3x^2 + 8x^5 - 4x^3 + 6 - \dfrac{1}{2}x^4$

Term	Coefficient	Degree of Term	Degree of Polynomial
$8x^5$	8	5	
$-\dfrac{1}{2}x^4$	$-\dfrac{1}{2}$	4	
$-4x^3$	-4	3	5
$3x^2$	3	2	
6	6	0	

20. $-7x^4 + 6x^3 - 3x^2 + 8x - 2$

Term	Coefficient	Degree of Term	Degree of Polynomial
$-7x^4$	-7	4	
$6x^3$	6	3	
$-3x^2$	-3	2	4
$8x$	8	1	
-2	-2	0	

21. Three monomials are added, so $x^2 - 10x + 25$ is a trinomial.

22. Monomial

23. The polynomial $x^3 - 7x^2 + 2x - 4$ is none of these because it is composed of four monomials.

24. Binomial

25. Two monomials are added, so $4x^2 - 15$ is a binomial.

26. Trinomial

27. The polynomial $40x$ is a monomial because it is the product of a constant and a variable raised to a whole number power.

28. None of these

29. $3x^2 + 5x + 4x^2 = (3 + 4)x^2 + 5x = 7x^2 + 5x$

30. $7a^2 + 8a$

31. $3a^4 - 2a + 2a + a^4 = (3 + 1)a^4 + (-2 + 2)a = 4a^4 + 0a = 4a^4$

32. $4b^5$

33. $2x^2 - 6x + 3x + 4x^2 = (2 + 4)x^2 + (-6 + 3)x = 6x^2 - 3x$

34. $\frac{3}{4}x^5 - 2x - 42$

35. $\frac{1}{3}x^3 + 2x - \frac{1}{6}x^3 + 4 - 16 =$

$\left(\frac{1}{3} - \frac{1}{6}\right)x^3 + 2x + (4 - 16) =$

$\frac{1}{6}x^3 + 2x - 12$

36. x^4

37. $8x^2 + 2x^3 - 3x^3 - 4x^2 - 4x^2 =$

$(8 - 4 - 4)x^2 + (2 - 3)x^3 =$

$0x^2 - x^3 = -x^3$

38. $13x^3 - 9x + 8$

39. $2x - \frac{5}{6} + 4x^3 + x + \frac{1}{3} - 2x =$

$x - \frac{1}{2} + 4x^3 = 4x^3 + x - \frac{1}{2}$

40. $-\frac{1}{3}a^3 - 4a^2 + \frac{1}{3}$

41. $P(x) = 3x^2 - 2x + 5$

$P(4) = 3 \cdot 4^2 - 2 \cdot 4 + 5$

$= 48 - 8 + 5$

$= 45$

$P(0) = 3 \cdot 0^2 - 2 \cdot 0 + 5$

$= 0 - 0 + 5$

$= 5$

42. $-46; 10$

43. $P(y) = 8y^3 - 12y - 5$

$P(-2) = 8(-2)^3 - 12(-2) - 5$

$= -64 + 24 - 5$

$= -45$

$P\left(\frac{1}{3}\right) = 8\left(\frac{1}{3}\right)^3 - 12 \cdot \frac{1}{3} - 5$

$= 8 \cdot \frac{1}{27} - 4 - 5$

$= \frac{8}{27} - 9$

$= \frac{8}{27} - \frac{243}{27}$

$= -\frac{235}{27}, \text{ or } -8\frac{19}{27}$

44. $-168; -9$

45. $-7x + 5 = -7 \cdot 4 + 5 = -28 + 5 = -23$

46. 3

47. $x^3 - 5x^2 + x = 4^3 - 5 \cdot 4^2 + 4 = 64 - 5 \cdot 16 + 4 =$

$64 - 80 + 4 = -12$

48. 51

49. $f(x) = -5x^3 + 3x^2 - 4x - 3$

$f(-1) = -5(-1)^3 + 3(-1)^2 - 4(-1) - 3$

$= 5 + 3 + 4 - 3$

$= 9$

50. -6

51. $p(n) = n^3 - 3n^2 + 2n$

$p(12) = 12^3 - 3 \cdot 12^2 + 2 \cdot 12$

$= 1728 - 432 + 24$

$= 1320$

A president, vice president, and treasurer can be elected in 1320 ways.

52. 6840

53. $s(t) = 16t^2$

$s(3) = 16 \cdot 3^2 = 16 \cdot 9 = 144$

The scaffold is 144 ft high.

54. 1024 ft

55. $P(a) = 0.4a^2 - 40a + 1039$

$P(20) = 0.4(20)^2 - 40(20) + 1039$

$= 0.4(400) - 40(20) + 1039$

$= 160 - 800 + 1039$

$= 399$

There are approximately 399 accidents daily involving a 20-year-old driver.

56. 289

57. Locate 10 on the horizontal axis. From there move vertically to the graph and then horizontally to the M-axis. This locates an M-value of about 9. Thus, about 9 words were memorized in 10 minutes.

58. About 17

59. Locate 13 on the horizontal axis. From there move vertically to the graph and then horizontally to the M-axis. This locates an M-value of about 15. Thus, $M(13) \approx 15$.

60. About 5

61. We evaluate the polynomial for $h = 6.3$ and $r = 1.2$:

$2\pi rh + 2\pi r^2 = 2\pi(1.2)(6.3) + 2\pi(1.2)^2 \approx 56.5$

The surface area is about 56.5 in^2.

62. About 44.5 in^2

63. We graph $y = x^2 + 2x + 1$ in the standard viewing window.

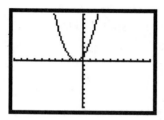

The range appears to be $[0, \infty)$.

64. $[-6.25, \infty)$

65. We graph $y = -2x^2 + 5$ in the standard viewing window.

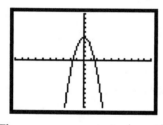

The range appears to be $(-\infty, 5]$.

66. $(-\infty, 1]$

67. We graph $y = -2x^3 + x + 5$ in the standard viewing window.

The range appears to be $(-\infty, \infty)$.

68. $(-\infty, -8.3]$

69. We graph $y = x^4 + 2x^3 - 5$ in the standard viewing window.

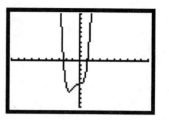

Using TRACE and ZOOM, we estimate that the range is $[-6.7, \infty)$.

70. $(-\infty, \infty)$

71. Since the range is $(-\infty, \infty)$, the degree is odd.

72. Even

73. Since the range is $[m, \infty)$, for some number m, the degree is even.

74. Odd

75. Enter the data and select cubic regression. We have $c(x) = -48.11111x^3 + 691.59524x^2 - 3388.36508x + 10,526.35714$.

76. $w(x) = 0.08601x^2 - 0.56101x + 1.23485$

77. $3(x + 2) = 5x - 9$

$$
\begin{aligned}
3x + 6 &= 5x - 9 && \text{Removing parentheses} \\
6 &= 2x - 9 && \text{Subtracting } 3x \text{ on both} \\
& && \text{sides} \\
15 &= 2x && \text{Adding 9 on both sides} \\
\frac{15}{2} &= x && \text{Dividing by 2 on both sides}
\end{aligned}
$$

The solution is $\dfrac{15}{2}$.

78. 274 and 275

79. Familiarize. Let $x =$ the cost per mile of gasoline in dollars. Then the total cost of the gasoline for the year was $14,800x$.

Translate.

$$
\underbrace{\text{Cost of insurance}} + \underbrace{\substack{\text{cost of} \\ \text{registration} \\ \text{and oil}}} + \underbrace{\substack{\text{cost of} \\ \text{gasoline}}} = \$2011.
$$

$$
\begin{array}{ccccccc}
\downarrow & \downarrow & \downarrow & \downarrow & \downarrow & \downarrow & \downarrow \\
972 & + & 114 & + & 14,800x & = & 2011
\end{array}
$$

Carry out. We solve the equation.

$$
\begin{aligned}
972 + 114 + 14,800x &= 2011 \\
1086 + 14,800x &= 2011 \\
14,800x &= 925 \\
x &= 0.0625
\end{aligned}
$$

Check. If gasoline cost $0.0625 per mile, then the total cost of the gasoline was $14,800(\$0.0625)$, or $925. Then the total auto expense was $972+\$114+\$925$, or $2011. The answer checks.

State. Gasoline cost $0.0625, or 6.25¢ per mile.

80. $b = \dfrac{cx + r}{a}$

81. ◈

82. ◈

83. ◈

84. ◈

85. Using a calculator, evaluate $0.4r^2 - 40r + 1039$ for $r = 10, 20, 30, 40, 50, 60,$ and 70 and list the values in a table.

Age	Average number of accidents per day
r	$0.4r^2 - 40r + 1039$
10	679
20	399
30	199
40	79
50	39
60	79
70	199

The numbers in the chart increase both below and above age 50. We would assume the number of accidents is the smallest near age 50. Now we evaluate for 49 and 51.

49	39.4
50	39
51	39.4

Again the numbers increase below and above 50.

We conclude that the smallest number of daily accidents occurs at age 50.

86. 494.8 cm^3 (Answers may vary depending on when rounding is done.)

Exercise Set 5.3

1. $(5x + 3) + (-7x + 1) = (5 - 7)x + (3 + 1) = -2x + 4$

2. $-5x + 6$

3. $(3x^2 - 5x + 10) + (2x^2 + 8x - 40) =$
$(3 + 2)x^2 + (-5 + 8)x + (10 - 40) = 5x^2 + 3x - 30$

4. $6x^4 + 3x^3 + 4x^2 - 3x + 2$

5. $(1.2x^3 + 4.5x^2 - 3.8x) + (-3.4x^3 - 4.7x^2 + 23) =$
$(1.2 - 3.4)x^3 + (4.5 - 4.7)x^2 - 3.8x + 23 =$
$-2.2x^3 - 0.2x^2 - 3.8x + 23$

6. $2.8x^4 - 0.6x^2 + 1.8x - 3.2$

7. $(3 + 5x + 7x^2 + 8x^3) + (8 - 3x + 9x^2 - 8x^3) =$
$(3 + 8) + (5 - 3)x + (7 + 9)x^2 + (8 - 8)x^3 =$
$11 + 2x + 16x^2 + 0x^3 = 11 + 2x + 16x^2$

8. $2x^4 + 3x + 3x^2 + 4 - 3x^3$, or
$2x^4 - 3x^3 + 3x^2 + 3x + 4$

9. $(9x^8 - 7x^4 + 2x^2 + 5) + (8x^7 + 4x^4 - 2x) =$
$9x^8 + 8x^7 + (-7 + 4)x^4 + 2x^2 - 2x + 5 =$
$9x^8 + 8x^7 - 3x^4 + 2x^2 - 2x + 5$

10. $4x^5 + 9x^2 + 1$

11. $\left(\dfrac{1}{4}x^4 + \dfrac{2}{3}x^3 + \dfrac{5}{8}x^2 + 7\right) + \left(-\dfrac{3}{4}x^4 + \dfrac{3}{8}x^2 - 7\right) =$
$\left(\dfrac{1}{4} - \dfrac{3}{4}\right)x^4 + \dfrac{2}{3}x^3 + \left(\dfrac{5}{8} + \dfrac{3}{8}\right)x^2 + (7 - 7) =$
$-\dfrac{2}{4}x^4 + \dfrac{2}{3}x^3 + \dfrac{8}{8}x^2 + 0 =$
$-\dfrac{1}{2}x^4 + \dfrac{2}{3}x^3 + x^2$

12. $\dfrac{2}{15}x^9 - \dfrac{2}{5}x^5 + \dfrac{1}{4}x^4 - \dfrac{1}{2}x^2 + 7$

13. $\quad -3x^4 + 6x^2 + 2x - 1$
$\quad\quad\quad\quad - 3x^2 + 2x + 1$
$\quad\overline{-3x^4 + 3x^2 + 4x + 0}$
$\quad -3x^4 + 3x^2 + 4x$

14. $-4x^3 + 4x^2 + 6x$

15. Rewrite the problem so the coefficients of like terms have the same number of decimal places.

$$
\begin{array}{l}
0.15x^4 + 0.10x^3 - 0.90x^2 \\
\quad\quad - 0.01x^3 + 0.01x^2 + x \\
1.25x^4 \quad\quad\quad + 0.11x^2 \quad\quad\quad + 0.01 \\
\quad\quad 0.27x^3 \quad\quad\quad\quad\quad + 0.99 \\
-0.35x^4 \quad\quad\quad\quad + 15.00x^2 \quad - 0.03 \\
\hline
1.05x^4 + 0.36x^3 + 14.22x^2 + x + 0.97
\end{array}
$$

16. $1.3x^4 + 0.35x^3 + 9.53x^2 + 2x + 0.96$

17. Two equivalent expressions for the opposite of
$-x^2 + 9x - 4$ are

a) $-(-x^2 + 9x - 4)$ and

b) $x^2 - 9x + 4$. (Changing the sign of every term)

18. $-(-4x^3 - 5x^2 + 2x),\ 4x^3 + 5x^2 - 2x$

19. Two equivalent expressions for the opposite of
$12x^4 - 3x^3 + 3$ are

a) $-(12x^4 - 3x^3 + 3)$ and

b) $-12x^4 + 3x^3 - 3$. (Changing the sign of every
term)

20. $-(4x^3 - 6x^2 - 8x + 1),\ -4x^3 + 6x^2 + 8x - 1$

21. We change the sign of every term inside parentheses.
$-(8x - 9) = -8x + 9$

22. $6x - 5$

23. We change the sign of every term inside parentheses.
$-(4x^2 - 3x + 2) = -4x^2 + 3x - 2$

24. $6a^3 - 2a^2 + 9a - 1$

25. $\quad (7x + 4) - (-2x + 1)$
$= 7x + 4 + 2x - 1$ Changing the sign of every
                         term inside parentheses
$= 9x + 3$

26. $7x + 2$

27. $\quad (6x^4 + 3x^3 - 1) - (4x^2 - 3x + 3)$
$= 6x^4 + 3x^3 - 1 - 4x^2 + 3x - 3$
$= 6x^4 + 3x^3 - 4x^2 + 3x - 4$

28. $-3x^3 + x^2 + 2x - 3$

29. $\quad (1.2x^3 + 4.5x^2 - 3.8x) - (-3.4x^3 - 4.7x^2 + 23)$
$= 1.2x^3 + 4.5x^2 - 3.8x + 3.4x^3 + 4.7x^2 - 23$
$= 4.6x^3 + 9.2x^2 - 3.8x - 23$

30. $-1.8x^4 - 0.6x^2 - 1.8x + 4.6$

31. $\quad (7x^3 - 2x^2 + 6) - (7x^2 + 2x - 4)$
$= 7x^3 - 2x^2 + 6 - 7x^2 - 2x + 4$
$= 7x^3 - 9x^2 - 2x + 10$

32. $-2x^5 - 6x^4 + x + 2$

33. $\quad (6x^2 + 2x) - (-3x^2 - 7x + 8)$
$= 6x^2 + 2x + 3x^2 + 7x - 8$
$= 9x^2 + 9x - 8$

34. $7x^3 + 3x^2 + 2x - 1$

35. $\quad \dfrac{5}{8}x^3 - \dfrac{1}{4}x - \dfrac{1}{3} - \left(-\dfrac{1}{8}x^3 + \dfrac{1}{4}x - \dfrac{1}{3}\right)$
$= \dfrac{5}{8}x^3 - \dfrac{1}{4}x - \dfrac{1}{3} + \dfrac{1}{8}x^3 - \dfrac{1}{4}x + \dfrac{1}{3}$
$= \dfrac{6}{8}x^3 - \dfrac{2}{4}x$
$= \dfrac{3}{4}x^3 - \dfrac{1}{2}x$

36. $\dfrac{3}{5}x^3 - 0.11$

37. $\quad \begin{array}{l} x^2 + 5x + 6 \\ -(x^2 + 2x \quad\quad) \\ \hline \end{array}$

$\begin{array}{ll} x^2 + 5x + 6 & \text{Changing signs and} \\ \underline{-x^2 - 2x} & \text{removing parentheses} \\ 3x + 6 & \text{Adding} \end{array}$

38. $-x^2 + 1$

39. $\quad \begin{array}{l} 5x^4 + 6x^3 - 9x^2 \\ -(-6x^4 - 6x^3 \quad\quad + 8x + 9) \\ \hline \end{array}$

$\begin{array}{ll} 5x^4 + 6x^3 - 9x^2 & \text{Changing signs and} \\ \underline{6x^4 + 6x^3 \quad\quad -8x - 9} & \text{removing parentheses} \\ 11x^4 + 12x^3 - 9x^2 - 8x - 9 & \text{Adding} \end{array}$

40. $5x^4 - 6x^3 - x^2 + 5x + 15$

41. a)

Familiarize. The area of a rectangle is the product
of the length and the width.

Translate. The sum of the areas is found as follows:

$$
\begin{array}{ccccccc}
\text{Area} & & \text{Area} & & \text{Area} & & \text{Area} \\
\text{of } A & + & \text{of } B & + & \text{of } C & + & \text{of } D \\
= 3x \cdot x & + & x \cdot x & + & 4 \cdot x & + & x \cdot x
\end{array}
$$

Carry out. We collect like terms.

$$3x^2 + x^2 + 4x + x^2 = 5x^2 + 4x$$

Check. We can go over our calculations. We can also assign some value to x, say 2, and carry out the computation of the area in two ways.

Sum of areas: $3 \cdot 2 \cdot 2 + 2 \cdot 2 + 4 \cdot 2 + 2 \cdot 2 =$
$$12 + 4 + 8 + 4 = 28$$

Substituting in the polynomial:
$$5(2)^2 + 4 \cdot 2 = 20 + 8 = 28$$

Since the results are the same, our solution is probably correct.

State. A polynomial for the sum of the areas is $5x^2 + 4x$.

b) For $x = 5$: $5x^2 + 4x = 5 \cdot 5^2 + 4 \cdot 5 =$
$$5 \cdot 25 + 4 \cdot 5 = 125 + 20 = 145$$

When $x = 5$, the sum of the areas is 145 square units.

For $x = 7$: $5x^2 + 4x = 5 \cdot 7^2 + 4 \cdot 7 =$
$$5 \cdot 49 + 4 \cdot 7 = 245 + 28 = 273$$

When $x = 7$, the sum of the areas is 273 square units.

42. (a) $r^2\pi + 13\pi$; **(b)** 38π, 140.69π

43.

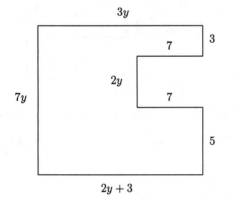

Familiarize. The perimeter is the sum of the lengths of the sides.

Translate. The sum of the lengths is found as follows:

$$3y + 7y + (2y + 3) + 5 + 7 + 2y + 7 + 3$$

Carry out. We collect like terms.

$$(3 + 7 + 2 + 2)y + (3 + 5 + 7 + 7 + 3) = 14y + 25$$

Check. We can go over our calculations. We can also assign some value to y, say 3, and carry out the computation of the perimeter in two ways.

Sum of lengths: $3 \cdot 3 + 7 \cdot 3 + (2 \cdot 3 + 3) + 5 + 7 + 2 \cdot 3 + 7 + 3 =$
$$9 + 21 + 9 + 5 + 7 + 6 + 7 + 3 = 67$$

Substituting in the polynomial:
$$14 \cdot 3 + 25 = 42 + 25 = 67$$

Since the results are the same, our solution is probably correct.

State. A polynomial for the perimeter of the figure is $14y + 25$.

44. $11\frac{1}{2}a + 12$, or $\frac{23}{2}a + 12$

45.

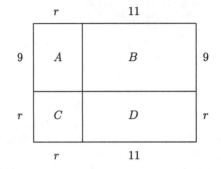

The area of the figure can be found by adding the areas of the four rectangles A, B, C, and D. The area of a rectangle is the product of the length and the width.

$$
\begin{array}{ccccccc}
\text{Area} & + & \text{Area} & + & \text{Area} & + & \text{Area} \\
\text{of } A & & \text{of } B & & \text{of } C & & \text{of } D \\
= \quad 9 \cdot r & + & 11 \cdot 9 & + & r \cdot r & + & 11 \cdot r \\
= \quad 9r & + & 99 & + & r^2 & + & 11r
\end{array}
$$

An algebraic expression for the area of the figure is $9r + 99 + r^2 + 11r$.

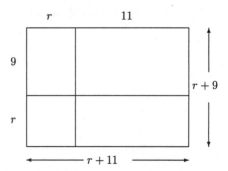

The length and width of the figure can be expressed as $r + 11$ and $r + 9$, respectively. The area of this figure (a rectangle) is the product of the length and width. An algebraic expression for the area is $(r + 11) \cdot (r + 9)$.

The algebraic expressions $9r + 99 + r^2 + 11r$ and $(r + 11) \cdot (r + 9)$ represent the same area.

46. $(x + 3)^2$; $x^2 + 3x + 3x + 9$

47.

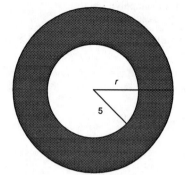

Familiarize. Recall that the area of a circle is the product of π and the square of the radius, r^2.

$$A = \pi r^2$$

Translate.

Area of circle with radius r	$-$	Area of circle with radius 5	$=$	Shaded area
$\pi \cdot r^2$	$-$	$\pi \cdot 5^2$		$=$ Shaded area

Carry out. We simplify the expression.

$$\pi \cdot r^2 - \pi \cdot 5^2 = \pi r^2 - 25\pi$$

Check. We can go over our calculations. We can also assign some value to r, say 7, and carry out the computation in two ways.

Difference of areas: $\pi \cdot 7^2 - \pi \cdot 5^2 = 49\pi - 25\pi = 24\pi$

Substituting in the polynomial: $\pi \cdot 7^2 - 25\pi = 49\pi - 25\pi = 24\pi$

Since the results are the same, our solution is probably correct.

State. A polynomial for the shaded area is $\pi r^2 - 25\pi$.

48. $m^2 - 40$

49. *Familiarize*. We label the figure with additional information.

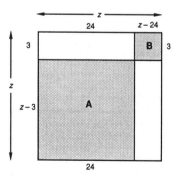

Translate.

Area of shaded sections = Area of A + Area of B

Area of shaded sections = $24(z - 3) + 3(z - 24)$

Carry out. We simplify the expression.

$$24(z-3) + 3(z-24) = 24z - 72 + 3z - 72 = 27z - 144$$

Check. We can go over the calculations. We can also assign some value to z, say 30, and carry out the computation in two ways.

Sum of areas:

$$24 \cdot 27 + 3 \cdot 6 = 648 + 18 = 666$$

Substituting in the polynomial:

$$27 \cdot 30 - 144 = 810 - 144 = 666$$

Since the results are the same, our solution is probably correct.

State. A polynomial for the shaded area is $27z - 144$.

50. $\pi x^2 - 2x^2$

51.

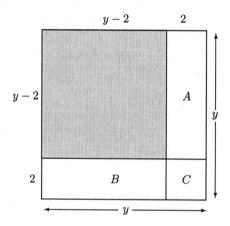

The shaded area is $(y - 2)^2$. We find it as follows:

Shaded area	$=$	Area of square	$-$	Area of A	$-$	Area of B	$-$	Area of C
$(y-2)^2$	$=$	y^2		$-2(y-2)$	$-$	$2(y-2)$	$-$	$2 \cdot 2$

$$(y-2)^2 = y^2 - 2y + 4 - 2y + 4 - 4$$
$$(y-2)^2 = y^2 - 4y + 4$$

52. $100 - 40x + 4x^2$

53.

$$1.5x - 2.7x = 23 - 5.6x$$

$10(1.5x - 2.7x) = 10(23 - 5.6x)$ Clearing decimals

$$15x - 27x = 230 - 56x$$

$\quad\quad -12x = 230 - 56x$ Collecting like terms

$\quad\quad\quad\quad 44x = 230$ Adding $56x$

$\quad\quad\quad\quad\quad x = \dfrac{230}{44}$ Dividing by 44

$\quad\quad\quad\quad\quad x = \dfrac{115}{22}$ Simplifying

The solution is $\dfrac{115}{22}$.

54. 1

55. $8(x-2) = 16$
 $\quad 8x - 16 = 16$ Multiplying to remove
                      parentheses
 $\quad\quad\quad 8x = 32$ Adding 16
 $\quad\quad\quad\quad x = 4$ Dividing by 8

The solution is 4.

56. $-\dfrac{76}{3}$

57. $\quad 3x - 7 \le 5x + 13$
 $\quad -2x - 7 \le 13$ Subtracting $5x$
 $\quad\quad\quad -2x \le 20$ Adding 7
 $\quad\quad\quad\quad x \ge -10$ Dividing by -2 and
                         reversing the inequality
                         symbol

The solution set is $\{x | x \ge -10\}$.

58. $\{x | x < 0\}$

59. ◈

60. ◈

61. ◈

62. ◈

63. $\quad (5a^2 - 8a) + (7a^2 - 9a - 13) - (7a - 5)$
 $= 5a^2 - 8a + 7a^2 - 9a - 13 - 7a + 5$
 $= 12a^2 - 24a - 8$

64. $5x^2 - 9x - 1$

65. $\quad (-8y^2 - 4) - (3y + 6) - (2y^2 - y)$
 $= -8y^2 - 4 - 3y - 6 - 2y^2 + y$
 $= -10y^2 - 2y - 10$

66. $4x^3 - 5x^2 + 6$

67. $\quad (345.099x^3 - 6.178x) - (94.508x^3 - 8.99x)$
 $= 345.099x^3 - 6.178x - 94.508x^3 + 8.99x$
 $= 250.591x^3 + 2.812x$

68. $36x + 2x^2$

69. **Familiarize**. The surface area is $2lw + 2lh + 2wh$, where $l = $ length, $w = $ width, and $h = $ height of the rectangular solid. Here we have $l = 7$, $w = a$, and $h = 4$.

Translate. We substitute in the formula above.

$\quad 2 \cdot 7 \cdot a + 2 \cdot 7 \cdot 4 + 2 \cdot a \cdot 4$

Carry out. We simplify the expression.

$\quad 2 \cdot 7 \cdot a + 2 \cdot 7 \cdot 4 + 2 \cdot a \cdot 4$
$= 14a + 56 + 8a$
$= 22a + 56$

Check. We can go over the calculations. We can also assign some value to a, say 6, and carry out the computation in two ways.

Using the formula: $2 \cdot 7 \cdot 6 + 2 \cdot 7 \cdot 4 + 2 \cdot 6 \cdot 4 = 84 + 56 + 48 = 188$

Substituting in the polynomial: $22 \cdot 6 + 56 = 132 + 56 = 188$

Since the results are the same, our solution is probably correct.

State. A polynomial for the surface area is $22a + 56$.

70. **(a)** $-x^2 + 280x - 5000$; **(b)** \$10,375; **(c)** \$13,000

71. ◈

Exercise Set 5.4

1. $(3x^4)8 = (3 \cdot 8)x^4 = 24x^4$

2. $28x^3$

3. $(-x^2)(-x) = (-1 \cdot x^2)(-1 \cdot x) = (-1)(-1)(x^2 \cdot x) = x^3$

4. $-x^7$

5. $(7t^5)(4t^3) = (7 \cdot 4)(t^5 \cdot t^3) = 28t^8$

6. $30a^4$

7. $(-0.1x^6)(0.2x^4) = (-0.1)(0.2)(x^6 \cdot x^4) = -0.02x^{10}$

8. $-0.12x^9$

9. $\left(-\dfrac{1}{5}x^3\right)\left(-\dfrac{1}{3}x\right) = \left(-\dfrac{1}{5}\right)\left(-\dfrac{1}{3}\right)(x^3 \cdot x) = \dfrac{1}{15}x^4$

10. $-\dfrac{1}{20}x^{12}$

11. $19t^2 \cdot 0 = 0$ Any number multiplied by 0 is 0.

12. $5n^3$

13. $(3x^2)(-4x^3)(2x^6) = (3)(-4)(2)(x^2 \cdot x^3 \cdot x^6) = -24x^{11}$

14. $60y^{12}$

15. $3x(-x + 5) = 3x(-x) + 3x(5)$
 $\quad\quad\quad\quad\quad\quad = -3x^2 + 15x$

16. $8x^2 - 12x$

17. $(x + 7)5x = x \cdot 5x + 7 \cdot 5x$
 $\quad\quad\quad\quad = 5x^2 + 35x$

18. $3x^2 - 18x$

19. $4x^2(3x + 6) = 4x^2(3x) + 4x^2(6)$
$= 12x^3 + 24x^2$

20. $-10x^3 + 5x^2$

21. $-6x^2(x^2 + x) = -6x^2(x^2) - 6x^2(x)$
$= -6x^4 - 6x^3$

22. $-4x^4 + 4x^3$

23. $(x + 6)(x + 3) = (x + 6)x + (x + 6)3$
$= x \cdot x + 6 \cdot x + x \cdot 3 + 6 \cdot 3$
$= x^2 + 6x + 3x + 18$
$= x^2 + 9x + 18$

24. $x^2 + 7x + 10$

25. $(x - 4)(x - 3) = (x - 4)x + (x - 4)(-3)$
$= x \cdot x - 4 \cdot x + x(-3) - 4(-3)$
$= x^2 - 4x - 3x + 12$
$= x^2 - 7x + 12$

26. $x^2 - 10x + 21$

27. $(5 - x)(5 - 2x) = (5 - x)5 + (5 - x)(-2x)$
$= 5 \cdot 5 - x \cdot 5 + 5(-2x) - x(-2x)$
$= 25 - 5x - 10x + 2x^2$
$= 25 - 15x + 2x^2$

28. $18 + 12x + 2x^2$

29. Illustrate $x(x + 5)$ as the area of a rectangle with width x and length $x + 5$.

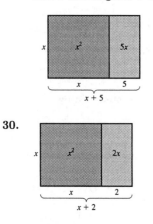

30.

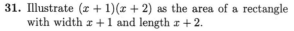

31. Illustrate $(x + 1)(x + 2)$ as the area of a rectangle with width $x + 1$ and length $x + 2$.

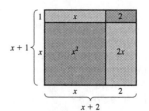

32.

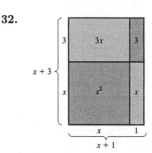

33. Illustrate $(3x + 2)(3x + 2)$ as the area of a square with sides of length $3x + 2$.

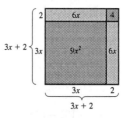

34.

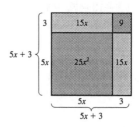

35. $(x^2 - x + 3)(x + 1)$
$= (x^2 - x + 3)x + (x^2 - x + 3)1$
$= x^2 \cdot x - x \cdot x + 3 \cdot x + x^2 \cdot 1 - x \cdot 1 + 3 \cdot 1$
$= x^3 - x^2 + 3x + x^2 - x + 3$
$= x^3 + 2x + 3$

A partial check can be made by selecting a convenient replacement for x, say 1, and comparing the values of the original expression and the result.

$(1^2 - 1 + 3)(1 + 1)$ $1^3 + 2 \cdot 1 + 3$
$= (1 - 1 + 3)(1 + 1)$ $= 1 + 2 + 3$
$= 3 \cdot 2$ $= 6$
$= 6$

Since the value of both expressions is 6, the multiplication is very likely correct.

36. $x^3 - 3x + 2$

37. $(2a + 5)(a^2 - 3a + 2)$
$$= (2a + 5)a^2 - (2a + 5)(3a) + (2a + 5)2$$
$$= 2a \cdot a^2 + 5 \cdot a^2 - 2a \cdot 3a - 5 \cdot 3a + 2a \cdot 2 + 5 \cdot 2$$
$$= 2a^3 + 5a^2 - 6a^2 - 15a + 4a + 10$$
$$= 2a^3 - a^2 - 11a + 10$$
A partial check can be made as in Exercise 55.

38. $3t^3 - 11t^2 - 17t + 4$

39. $(y^2 - 3)(2y^3 + y + 1)$
$$= (y^2 - 3)(2y^3) + (y^2 - 3)y + (y^2 - 3)(1)$$
$$= y^2 \cdot 2y^3 - 3 \cdot 2y^3 + y^2 \cdot y - 3 \cdot y + y^2 \cdot 1 - 3 \cdot 1$$
$$= 2y^5 - 6y^3 + y^3 - 3y + y^2 - 3$$
$$= 2y^5 - 5y^3 + y^2 - 3y - 3$$
A partial check can be made as in Exercise 55.

40. $5a^5 + 7a^3 - a^2 - 6a - 2$

41.

$$\begin{array}{rl} x^2\ -3x+2 & \text{Line up like terms} \\ \underline{x^2 + x\ +1} & \text{in columns} \\ x^2\ -3x+2 & \text{Multiplying by 1} \\ x^3-3x^2+2x & \text{Multiplying by } x \\ \underline{x^4-3x^3+2x^2} & \text{Multiplying by } x^2 \\ x^4-2x^3\quad\ -x+2 & \end{array}$$

A partial check can be made as in Exercise 55.

42. $x^4 + 4x^3 - 3x^2 + 16x - 3$

43. We will multiply horizontally while still aligning like terms.
$$(x + 1)(x^3 + 7x^2 + 5x + 4)$$

$$\begin{array}{ll} = x^4 + 7x^3 + 5x^2 + 4x & \text{Multiplying by } x \\ \underline{\ + x^3 + 7x^2 + 5x + 4} & \text{Multiplying by 1} \\ = x^4 + 8x^3 + 12x^2 + 9x + 4 & \end{array}$$

A partial check can be made as in Exercise 55.

44. $x^4 + 7x^3 + 19x^2 + 21x + 6$

45. $(x + 5)(x^2 + 1)$

$\qquad$ F $\qquad$ O $\qquad$ I $\qquad$ L
$$= x \cdot x^2 + x \cdot 1 + 5 \cdot x^2 + 5 \cdot 1$$
$$= x^3 + x + 5x^2 + 5, \text{ or } x^3 + 5x^2 + x + 5$$

46. $x^3 - x^2 - 3x + 3$

47. $(y + 2)(y - 3)$

$\qquad$ F $\qquad$ O $\qquad$ I $\qquad$ L
$$= y \cdot y + y \cdot (-3) + 2 \cdot y + 2 \cdot (-3)$$
$$= y^2 - 3y + 2y - 6$$
$$= y^2 - y - 6$$

48. $a^2 + 4a + 4$

49. $(3t - 1)(3t + 1)$

$\qquad$ F $\qquad$ O $\qquad$ I $\qquad$ L
$$= 3t \cdot 3t + 3t \cdot 1 + (-1) \cdot 3t + (-1) \cdot 1$$
$$= 9t^2 + 3t - 3t - 1$$
$$= 9t^2 - 1$$

50. $t^2 - 81$

51. $(2x - 7)(x - 1)$

$\qquad$ F $\qquad$ O $\qquad$ I $\qquad$ L
$$= 2x \cdot x + 2x \cdot (-1) + (-7) \cdot x + (-7) \cdot (-1)$$
$$= 2x^2 - 2x - 7x + 7$$
$$= 2x^2 - 9x + 7$$

52. $4m^2 + 12m + 9$

53. $\left(p - \dfrac{1}{4}\right)\left(p + \dfrac{1}{4}\right)$

$\qquad$ F $\qquad$ O $\qquad$ I $\qquad$ L
$$= p \cdot p + p \cdot \frac{1}{4} + \left(-\frac{1}{4}\right) \cdot p + \left(-\frac{1}{4}\right) \cdot \frac{1}{4}$$
$$= p^2 + \frac{1}{4}p - \frac{1}{4}p - \frac{1}{16}$$
$$= p^2 - \frac{1}{16}$$

54. $q^2 + \dfrac{3}{2}q + \dfrac{9}{16}$

55. $(x - 0.1)(x + 0.1)$

$\qquad$ F $\qquad$ O $\qquad$ I $\qquad$ L
$$= x \cdot x + x \cdot (0.1) + (-0.1) \cdot x + (-0.1)(0.1)$$
$$= x^2 + 0.1x - 0.1x - 0.01$$
$$= x^2 - 0.01$$

56. $x^2 - 0.1x - 0.12$

57. $(2x^2 + 6)(x + 1)$

$\qquad$ F $\qquad$ O $\qquad$ I $\qquad$ L
$$= 2x^3 + 2x^2 + 6x + 6$$

58. $4x^3 - 2x^2 + 6x - 3$

59. $(1 + 3t)(1 - 5t)$

$\qquad$ F $\qquad$ O $\qquad$ I $\qquad$ L
$$= 1 - 5t + 3t - 15t^2$$
$$= 1 - 2t - 15t^2$$

60. $-3x^2 - 5x - 2$

61. $(3x^2 - 2)(x^4 - 2)$
     F   O   I   L
$= 3x^6 - 6x^2 - 2x^4 + 4$, or $3x^6 - 2x^4 - 6x^2 + 4$

62. $2x^5 + x^4 - 6x - 3$

63. $(3x^5 + 2)(2x^2 + 6)$
    F   O   I   L
$= 6x^7 + 18x^5 + 4x^2 + 12$

64. $1 + 3x^2 - 2x - 6x^3$, or $1 - 2x + 3x^2 - 6x^3$

65. $(x + 8)(x - 8)$ Product of sum and differ-
                          ence of the same two terms
$= x^2 - 8^2$
$= x^2 - 64$

66. $x^2 - 1$

67. $(5m - 2)(5m + 2)$ Product of sum and diff-
                          erence of the same two terms
$= (5m)^2 - 2^2$
$= 25m^2 - 4$

68. $9x^8 - 4$

69. $(3x^4 - 1)(3x^4 + 1)$
$= (3x^4)^2 - 1^2$
$= 9x^8 - 1$

70. $t^4 - 0.04$

71. $(2y^8 + 3)(2y^8 - 3)$
$= (2y^8)^2 - 3^2$
$= 4y^{16} - 9$

72. $m^2 - \dfrac{4}{9}$

73. $(x + 2)^2$
$= x^2 + 2 \cdot x \cdot 2 + 2^2$ Square of a binomial
$= x^2 + 4x + 4$

74. $4x^2 - 4x + 1$

75. $\left(a - \dfrac{2}{5}\right)^2$ Square of a binomial
$= a^2 - 2 \cdot a \cdot \dfrac{2}{5} + \left(\dfrac{2}{5}\right)^2$
$= a^2 - \dfrac{4}{5}a + \dfrac{4}{25}$

76. $9x^2 + \dfrac{9}{2}x + \dfrac{9}{16}$

77. $(x^2 + 3)^2 = (x^2)^2 + 2 \cdot x^2 \cdot 3 + 3^2$
                $= x^4 + 6x^2 + 9$

78. $64x^2 - 16x^3 + x^4$

79. $(2 - 3x^4)^2 = 2^2 - 2 \cdot 2 \cdot 3x^4 + (3x^4)^2$
                  $= 4 - 12x^4 + 9x^8$

80. $36x^6 - 24x^3 + 4$

81. $5a^3(2a^2 - 1)$
$= 5a^3 \cdot 2a^2 - 5a^3 \cdot 1$ Multiplying each term of
                      the binomial by the monomial
$= 10a^5 - 5a^3$

82. $a^3 - a^2 - 10a + 12$

83. $(x^2 - 5)(x^2 + x - 1)$
$= x^4 + x^3 - x^2$ Multiplying horizontally
$\underline{-5x^2 - 5x + 5}$ and aligning like terms
$= x^4 + x^3 - 6x^2 - 5x + 5$

84. $27x^6 - 9x^5$

85. $(3 - 2x^3)^2$
$= 3^2 - 2 \cdot 3 \cdot 2x^3 + (2x^3)^2$ Squaring a binomial
$= 9 - 12x^3 + 4x^6$

86. $x^2 - 8x^4 + 16x^6$

87. $(-1 + 3p)(1 + 3p)$
$= (3p - 1)(3p + 1)$ Product of the sum and
                  difference of the same two terms
$= (3p)^2 - 1^2$
$= 9p^2 - 1$, or $-1 + 9p^2$

88. $-9q^2 + 4$, or $4 - 9q^2$

89. $3t^2(5t^3 - t^2 + t)$
$= 3t^2 \cdot 5t^3 + 3t^2(-t^2) + 3t^2 \cdot t$ Multiplying each
                            term of the trinomial
                            by the monomial
$= 15t^5 - 3t^4 + 3t^3$

90. $-5x^5 - 40x^4 + 45x^3$

91. $(7x - 0.3)^2$ Squaring a binomial
$= (7x)^2 - 2(7x)(0.3) + (0.3)^2$
$= 49x^2 - 4.2x + 0.09$

92. $16a^2 - 4.8x + 0.36$

93. $(3x + 2)(4x^2 + 5)$ Product of two
                                   binomials; use FOIL

$= 3x \cdot 4x^2 + 3x \cdot 5 + 2 \cdot 4x^2 + 2 \cdot 5$

$= 12x^3 + 15x + 8x^2 + 10,$ or

$\quad 12x^3 + 8x^2 + 15x + 10$

94. $6x^4 - 3x^2 - 63$

95.

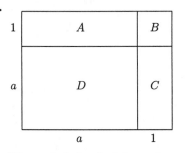

We can find the shaded area in two ways.

Method 1: The figure is a square with side $a + 1$, so
the area is $(a + 1)^2 = a^2 + 2a + 1$.

Method 2: We add the areas of A, B, C, and D.

$1 \cdot a + 1 \cdot 1 + 1 \cdot a + a \cdot a = a + 1 + a + a^2 = a^2 + 2a + 1.$

Either way we find that the total shaded area is
$a^2 + 2a + 1$.

96. $(x + 3)^2 = x^2 + 6x + 9$

97.

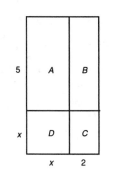

We can find the shaded area in two ways.

Method 1: The figure is a rectangle with dimensions
$x + 5$ by $x + 2$, so the area is

$(x + 5)(x + 2) = x^2 + 2x + 5x + 10 = x^2 + 7x + 10.$

Method 2: We add the areas of A, B, C, and D.

$5 \cdot x + 2 \cdot 5 + 2 \cdot x + x \cdot x = 5x + 10 + 2x + x^2 = x^2 + 7x + 10.$

Either way, we find that the area is $x^2 + 7x + 10$.

98. $t^2 + 7t + 12$

99.

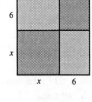

We can find the shaded area in two ways.

Method 1: The figure is a square with side $3x + 4$,
so the area is $(3x + 4)^2 = 9x^2 + 24x + 16$.

Method 2: We add the areas of A, B, C, and D.

$3x \cdot 3x + 3x \cdot 4 + 4 \cdot 4 + 3x \cdot 4 = 9x^2 + 12x + 16 + 12x = 9x^2 + 24x + 16.$

Either way, we find that the total shaded area is
$9x^2 + 24x + 16$.

100. $25t^2 + 20t + 4$

101. We draw a square with side $x + 6$.

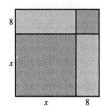

102.

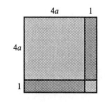

103. We draw a square with side $4a + 1$.

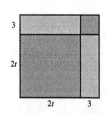

104.

105. Familiarize. Let t = the number of watts used by the television set. Then $10t$ = the number of watts used by the lamps, and $40t$ = the number of watts used by the air conditioner.

Translate.

$$
\underbrace{\begin{array}{c}\text{Lamp}\\\text{watts}\end{array}}_{} + \underbrace{\begin{array}{c}\text{Air}\\\text{conditioner}\\\text{watts}\end{array}}_{} + \underbrace{\begin{array}{c}\text{Television}\\\text{watts}\end{array}}_{} = \underbrace{\begin{array}{c}\text{Total}\\\text{watts}\end{array}}_{}
$$

$$
\begin{array}{ccccccc}
\downarrow & \downarrow & \downarrow & \downarrow & \downarrow & \downarrow & \downarrow \\
10t & + & 40t & + & t & = & 2550
\end{array}
$$

Solve. We solve the equation.

$$10t + 40t + t = 2550$$
$$51t = 2550$$
$$t = 50$$

The possible solution is:

    Television, t: 50 watts

    Lamps, $10t$: $10 \cdot 50$, or 500 watts

    Air conditioner, $40t$: $40 \cdot 50$, or 2000 watts

Check. The number of watts used by the lamps, 500, is 10 times 50, the number used by the television. The number of watts used by the air conditioner, 2000, is 40 times 50, the number used by the television. Also, $50 + 500 + 2000 = 2550$, the total wattage used.

State. The television uses 50 watts, the lamps use 500 watts, and the air conditioner uses 2000 watts.

106. $\dfrac{28}{27}$

107.
$$ab - c = ad$$
$$ab = ad + c$$
$$ab - ad = c$$
$$a(b - d) = c$$
$$a = \frac{c}{b - d}$$

108. IV

109.

110.

111.

112.

113. The shaded area is the area of the large rectangle, $6y(14y - 5)$ less the area of the unshaded rectangle, $3y(3y + 5)$. We have:

$$6y(14y - 5) - 3y(3y + 5)$$
$$= 84y^2 - 30y - 9y^2 - 15y$$
$$= 75y^2 - 45y$$

114. $78t^2 + 40t$

115. Let n = the missing number. Label the figure with the known areas.

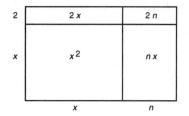

Then the area of the figure is $x^2 + 2x + nx + 2n$. This is equivalent to $x^2 + 7x + 10$, so we have $2x + nx = 7x$ and $2n = 10$. Solving either equation for n, we find that the missing number is 5.

116. 5

117.

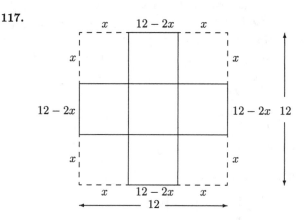

The dimensions of the box are $12 - 2x$ by $12 - 2x$ by x. The volume is the product of the dimensions (volume = length × width × height):

$$\begin{aligned}\text{Volume} &= (12 - 2x)(12 - 2x)x \\ &= (144 - 48x + 4x^2)x \\ &= 144x - 48x^2 + 4x^3, \text{ or} \\ & \quad 4x^3 - 48x^2 + 144x\end{aligned}$$

The outside surface area is the sum of the area of the bottom and the areas of the four sides. The dimensions of the bottom are $12 - 2x$ by $12 - 2x$, and the dimensions of each side are x by $12 - 2x$.

$$\begin{aligned}\begin{array}{c}\text{Surface}\\\text{area}\end{array} &= \begin{array}{l}\text{Area of bottom +}\\ \qquad 4 \cdot \text{Area of each side}\end{array} \\ &= (12 - 2x)(12 - 2x) + 4 \cdot x(12 - 2x) \\ &= 144 - 24x - 24x + 4x^2 + 48x - 8x^2 \\ &= 144 - 48x + 4x^2 + 48x - 8x^2 \\ &= 144 - 4x^2, \text{ or } -4x^2 + 144\end{aligned}$$

118. $x^3 - 5x^2 + 8x - 4$ cm^3

119. $V = (x+2)^3$
$$= (x+2)(x+2)(x+2)$$
$$= (x^2 + 2x + 2x + 4)(x+2)$$
$$= (x^2 + 4x + 4)(x+2)$$
$$= x^3 + 4x^2 + 4x + 2x^2 + 8x + 8$$
$$= x^3 + 6x^2 + 12x + 8$$

The volume of the cube is $x^3 + 6x^2 + 12x + 8$ cm^3.

120. 8 ft by 16 ft

121. $18 \times 22 = (20-2)(20+2) = 20^2 - 2^2 =$
$400 - 4 = 396$

122. $10,000 - 49 = 9951$

123. $(x+2)(x-5) = (x+1)(x-3)$
$x^2 - 5x + 2x - 10 = x^2 - 3x + x - 3$
$x^2 - 3x - 10 = x^2 - 2x - 3$
$-3x - 10 = -2x - 3$ Adding $-x^2$
$-3x + 2x = 10 - 3$ Adding $2x$ and 10
$-x = 7$
$x = -7$

The solution is -7.

124. 0

125. If $l = $ the length, then $l+1 = $ the height, and $l-1 = $ the width. Recall that the volume of a rectangular solid is given by length $\times$ width $\times$ height.
Volume $= l(l-1)(l+1) = l(l^2-1) = l^3 - l$

126. $w^3 + 3w^2 + 2w$

127. Solve: $x^2 + (x+1)^2 + (x+2)^2 = 3x^2 + 65$
$x = 10$

The integers are 10, 11, and 12.

Exercise Set 5.5

---

1. We replace x by 3 and y by -2.
$x^2 - 3y^2 + 2xy = 3^2 - 3(-2)^2 + 2 \cdot 3(-2) =$
$9 - 12 - 12 = -15$

2. 53

3. We replace x by 2, y by -3, and z by -1.
$xyz^2 - z = 2(-3)(-1)^2 - (-1) = -6 + 1 = -5$

4. -1

5. Evaluate the polynomial for $h = 160$ and $A = 50$.
$0.041h - 0.018A - 2.69$
$= 0.041(160) - 0.018(50) - 2.69$
$= 6.56 - 0.9 - 2.69$
$= 2.97$

The woman's lung capacity is 2.97 liters.

6. 3.715 liters

7. Evaluate the polynomial for $h = 50$, $v = 40$, and $t = 2$.
$h + v_0 t - 4.9t^2$
$= 50 + 40 \cdot 2 - 4.9(2)^2$
$= 50 + 80 - 19.6$
$= 110.4$

The rocket will be 110.4 m above the ground 2 seconds after blast off.

8. 205.9 m

9. Evaluate the polynomial for $h = 4$, $r = \dfrac{3}{4}$, and $\pi \approx 3.14$.
$2\pi r h + \pi r^2 \approx 2(3.14)\left(\dfrac{3}{4}\right)(4) + (3.14)\left(\dfrac{3}{4}\right)^2$
$$\approx 2(3.14)\left(\dfrac{3}{4}\right)(4) + (3.14)\left(\dfrac{9}{16}\right)$$
$$\approx 18.84 + 1.76625$$
$$\approx 20.60625$$

The surface area is about 20.60625 in^2.

10. 63.78125 in^2

11. $x^3 y - 2xy + 3x^2 - 5$

Term	Coefficient	Degree	
$x^3 y$	1	4	(Think: $x^3 y = x^3 y^1$)
$-2xy$	-2	2	(Think: $-2xy = -2x^1 y^1$)
$3x^2$	3	2	
-5	-5	0	(Think: $-5 = -5x^0$)

The degree of the polynomial is the degree of the term of highest degree. The term of highest degree is $x^3 y$. Its degree is 4, so the degree of the polynomial is 4.

12. Coefficients: 5, -1, 15, 1
Degrees: 3, 2, 1, 0; 3

13. $17x^2y^3 - 3x^3yz - 7$

Term	Coefficient	Degree	
$17x^2y^3$	17	5	
$-3x^3yz$	-3	5	(Think: $-3x^3yz = -3x^3y^1z^1$)
-7	-7	0	(Think: $-7 = -7x^0$)

The terms of highest degree are $17x^2y^3$ and $-3x^3yz$. Each has degree 5. The degree of the polynomial is 5.

14. Coefficients: 6, -1, 8, -1

Degrees: 0, 2, 4, 5; 5

15. $5a + b - 4a - 3b = (5 - 4)a + (1 - 3)b = a - 2b$

16. $y - 7$

17. $3x^2y - 2xy^2 + x^2$

There are <u>no</u> like terms, so none of the terms can be collected.

18. $m^3 + 2m^2n - 3m^2 + 3mn^2$

19.
$$2u^2v - 3uv^2 + 6u^2v - 2uv^2$$
$$= (2 + 6)u^2v + (-3 - 2)uv^2$$
$$= 8u^2v - 5uv^2$$

20. $-2x^2 - 4xy - 2y^2$

21.
$$8uv + 3av + 14au + 7av$$
$$= 8uv + (3 + 7)av + 14au$$
$$= 8uv + 10av + 14au$$

22. $3x^2y + 3z^2y + 3xy^2$

23.
$$(2x^2 - xy + y^2) + (-x^2 - 3xy + 2y^2)$$
$$= (2 - 1)x^2 + (-1 - 3)xy + (1 + 2)y^2$$
$$= x^2 - 4xy + 3y^2$$

24. $-4r^3 + 2rs - 9s^2$

25.
$$(7a^4 - 5ab + 6ab^2) - (9a^4 + 3ab - ab^2)$$
$$= 7a^4 - 5ab + 6ab^2 - 9a^4 - 3ab + ab^2$$

                               Adding the opposite

$$= (7 - 9)a^4 + (-5 - 3)ab + (6 + 1)ab^2$$
$$= -2a^4 - 8ab + 7ab^2$$

26. $3r + s - 4$

27.
$$(5a^2b + 7ab) + (9a^2b - 5ab) + (a^2b - 6ab)$$
$$= (5 + 9 + 1)a^2b + (7 - 5 - 6)ab$$
$$= 15a^2b - 4ab$$

28. $-x^2 - 8xy - y^2$

29.
$$(x^3 - y^3) - (-2x^3 + x^2y - xy^2 + 2y^3)$$
$$= x^3 - y^3 + 2x^3 - x^2y + xy^2 - 2y^3$$
$$= 3x^3 - 3y^3 - x^2y + xy^2, \text{ or}$$
$$\qquad 3x^3 - x^2y + xy^2 - 3y^3$$

30. $2ab$

31.
$$(4x + 5y) + (-5x + 6y) - (7x + 3y)$$
$$= 4x + 5y - 5x + 6y - 7x - 3y$$
$$= (4 - 5 - 7)x + (5 + 6 - 3)y$$
$$= -8x + 8y$$

32. $-5b$

33. $\quad\quad\quad\quad\quad\quad \text{F}\quad\quad \text{O}\quad\quad \text{I}\quad\quad \text{L}$
$$(3z - u)(2z + 3u) = 6z^2 + 9zu - 2uz - 3u^2$$
$$= 6z^2 + 7zu - 3u^2$$

34. $a^4b^2 - 7a^2b + 10$

35. $\quad\quad\quad\quad\quad\quad \text{F}\quad\quad \text{O}\quad\quad \text{I}\quad\quad\quad \text{L}$
$$(xy + 7)(xy - 4) = x^2y^2 - 4xy + 7xy - 28 - 28$$
$$= x^2y^2 - 3xy - 28$$

36. $a^6 - b^2c^2$

37.
$$
\begin{array}{r}
a^2 + ab + b^2 \\
a - b \\
\hline
-a^2b - ab^2 - b^3 \\
a^3 + a^2b + ab^2 \\
\hline
a^3 \qquad\qquad\quad - b^3
\end{array}
$$

38. $12x^2y^2 + 2xy - 2$

39. $(m^3n + 8)(m^3n - 6)$
$$\quad\quad \text{F}\quad\quad \text{O}\quad\quad\quad \text{I}\quad\quad \text{L}$$
$$= m^6n^2 - 6m^3n + 8m^3n - 48$$
$$= m^6n^2 + 2m^3n - 48$$

40. $12 - c^2d^2 - c^4d^4$

41. $(x + h)^2$
$$= x^2 + 2xh + h^2 \quad [(A + B)^2 = A^2 + 2AB + B^2]$$

42. $9a^2 + 12ab + 4b^2$

43. $(r^3t^2 - 4)^2$
$$= (r^3t^2)^2 - 2 \cdot r^3t^2 \cdot 4 + 4^2$$
$$\qquad\qquad\qquad [(A - B)^2 = A^2 - 2AB + B^2]$$
$$= r^6t^4 - 8r^3t^2 + 16$$

44. $9a^4b^2 - 6a^2b^3 + b^4$

45. $(c^2 - d)(c^2 + d) = (c^2)^2 - d^2$
$$= c^4 - d^2$$

46. $p^6 - 25q^2$

47. $(ab + cd^2)(ab - cd^2) = (ab)^2 - (cd^2)^2$
$$= a^2b^2 - c^2d^4$$

48. $x^2y^2 - p^2q^2$

49. $(x + y - 3)(x + y + 3)$
$$= [(x + y) - 3][(x + y) + 3]$$
$$= (x + y)^2 - 3^2$$
$$= x^2 + 2xy + y^2 - 9$$

50. $x^2 - y^2 - 2yz - z^2$

51. The figure is a rectangle with dimensions $a + b$ by $a + c$. Its area is $(a + b)(a + c) = a^2 + ac + ab + bc$.

52. $x^2 + 2xy + y^2$

53. The figure is a parallelogram with base $x + z$ and height $x - z$. Thus the area is $(x+z)(x-z) = x^2 - z^2$.

54. $\frac{1}{2}a^2b^2 - 2$

55. The figure is a square with side $x + y + z$. Thus the area is
$$(x + y + z)^2$$
$$= [(x + y) + z]^2$$
$$= (x + y)^2 + 2(x + y)(z) + z^2$$
$$= x^2 + 2xy + y^2 + 2xz + 2yz + z^2.$$

56. $a^2 + 2ac + c^2 + ad + cd + ab + bc + bd$

57. The figure is a triangle with base $x + 2y$ and height $x - y$. Thus the area is $\frac{1}{2}(x + 2y)(x - y) = \frac{1}{2}(x^2 + xy - 2y^2) = \frac{1}{2}x^2 + \frac{1}{2}xy - y^2$.

58. $m^2 - n^2$

59. We draw a rectangle with dimensions $r + s$ by $u + v$.

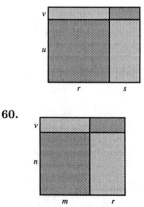

60.

61. We draw a rectangle with dimensions $a + b + c$ by $a + d + f$.

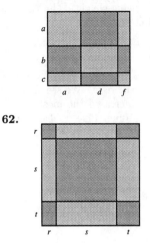

62.

63. $f(x) = 5x + x^2$

a) Replace each occurrence of x by $t - 1$.
$$f(t - 1) = 5(t - 1) + (t - 1)^2$$
$$= 5t - 5 + t^2 - 2t + 1$$
$$= t^2 + 3t - 4$$

b) $f(a + h) - f(a)$
$$= [5(a + h) + (a + h)^2] - [5a + a^2]$$
$$= 5a + 5h + a^2 + 2ah + h^2 - 5a - a^2$$
$$= 5h + 2ah + h^2$$

64. (a) $-p^2 + p + 6$; (b) $3h - 2ah - h^2$

65. $f(x) = 2 - x^2$

a) $f(2t + 1) = 2 - (2t + 1)^2$
$$= 2 - (4t^2 + 4t + 1)$$
$$= 2 - 4t^2 - 4t - 1$$
$$= -4t^2 - 4t + 1$$

b) $f(a + h) - f(a)$
$$= [2 - (a + h)^2] - [2 - a^2]$$
$$= [2 - (a^2 + 2ah + h^2)] - [2 - a^2]$$
$$= 2 - a^2 - 2ah - h^2 - 2 + a^2$$
$$= -2ah - h^2$$

66. (a) $9r^2 - 21r + 10$; (b) $2ah + h^2 - 3h$

67. Locate June, 1994, on the horizontal scale. Then move up to the line representing white office paper and left to the vertical scale to read the information being sought. In June, 1994, the price being paid for white office paper was $50 per ton.

68. December, 1995

69. Locate the highest point on the line representing newsprint. Then move down to the horizontal scale to read the information being sought. The value of newsprint peaked in June, 1995.

70. December, 1991

71. Find the 6-month period for which the line slants up most steeply from left to right. We see that the price paid for newsprint increased the most during the 6-month period from June, 1994, to December, 1994.

72. June, 1995, to December, 1995

73. ◈

74. ◈

75. ◈

76. ◈

77. The unshaded region is a circle with radius $a - b$. Then the shaded area is the area of a circle with radius a less the area of a circle with radius $a - b$. Thus, we have:

$$\begin{aligned}\text{Shaded area} &= \pi a^2 - \pi(a-b)^2 \\ &= \pi a^2 - \pi(a^2 - 2ab + b^2) \\ &= \pi a^2 - \pi a^2 + 2\pi ab - \pi b^2 \\ &= 2\pi ab - \pi b^2\end{aligned}$$

78. $4xy - 4y^2$

79. The shaded area is the area of a square with side a less the areas of 4 squares with side b. Thus, the shaded area is $a^2 - 4 \cdot b^2$, or $a^2 - 4b^2$.

80. $\pi x^2 + 2xy$

81. The lateral surface area of the outer portion of the solid is the lateral surface area of a right circular cylinder with radius n and height h. The lateral surface area of the inner portion is the lateral surface area of a right circular cylinder with radius m and height h. Recall that the formula for the lateral surface area of a right circular cylinder with radius r and height h is $2\pi rh$.

The surface area of the top is the area of a circle with radius n less the area of a circle with radius m. The surface area of the bottom is the same as the surface area of the top.

Thus, the surface area of the solid is

$$2\pi nh + 2\pi mh + 2\pi n^2 - 2\pi m^2.$$

82. $2x^2 + 4xh - 2\pi r^2 + 2\pi rh$

83. Replace t with 2 and multiply.

$$\begin{aligned}&P(1+r)^2 \\ &= P(1 + 2r + r^2) \\ &= P + 2Pr + Pr^2\end{aligned}$$

84. $P - 2Pr + Pr^2$

85. ◈

Exercise Set 5.6

1.
$$\begin{aligned}\frac{32x^5 - 16x}{8} &= \frac{32x^5}{8} - \frac{16x}{8} \\ &= \frac{32}{8}x^5 - \frac{16}{8}x \quad \text{Dividing coefficients} \\ &= 4x^5 - 2x\end{aligned}$$

To check, we multiply the quotient by 8:

$$(4x^5 - 2x)8 = 32x^5 - 16x$$

The answer checks.

2. $2a^4 - \frac{1}{2}a^2$

3.
$$\begin{aligned}&\frac{u - 2u^2 + u^7}{u} \\ &= \frac{u}{u} - \frac{2u^2}{u} + \frac{u^7}{u} \\ &= 1 - 2u + u^6\end{aligned}$$

Check: We multiply.

$$\begin{array}{r}1 - 2u + u^6 \\ u \\ \hline u - 2u^2 + u^7\end{array}$$

4. $50x^4 - 7x^3 + x$

5.
$$\begin{aligned}&(15t^3 - 24t^2 + 6t) \div (3t) \\ &= \frac{15t^3 - 24t^2 + 6t}{3t} \\ &= \frac{15t^3}{3t} - \frac{24t^2}{3t} + \frac{6t}{3t} \\ &= 5t^2 - 8t + 2\end{aligned}$$

Check: We multiply.

$$\begin{array}{r}5t^2 - 8t + 2 \\ 3t \\ \hline 15t^3 - 24t^2 + 6t\end{array}$$

6. $5t^2 - 3t + 6$

7. $(35x^6 - 20x^4 - 5x^2) \div (-5x^2)$

$$= \frac{35x^6 - 20x^4 - 5x^2}{-5x^2}$$

$$= \frac{35x^6}{-5x^2} - \frac{20x^4}{-5x^2} - \frac{5x^2}{-5x^2}$$

$$= -7x^4 - (-4x^2) - (-1)$$

$$= -7x^4 + 4x^2 + 1$$

Check: We multiply.

$$\begin{array}{r} -7x^4 + 4x^2 + 1 \\ -5x^2 \\ \hline 35x^6 - 20x^4 - 5x^2 \end{array}$$

8. $-2x^4 - 4x^3 + 1$

9. $(24x^5 - 40x^4 + 6x^3) \div (4x^3)$

$$= \frac{24x^5 - 40x^4 + 6x^3}{4x^3}$$

$$= \frac{24x^5}{4x^3} - \frac{40x^4}{4x^3} + \frac{6x^3}{4x^3}$$

$$= 6x^2 - 10x + \frac{3}{2}$$

Check: We multiply.

$$\begin{array}{r} 6x^2 - 10x + \dfrac{3}{2} \\ 4x^3 \\ \hline 24x^5 - 40x^4 + 6x^3 \end{array}$$

10. $2x^3 - 3x^2 - \dfrac{1}{3}$

11. $\dfrac{9r^2s^2 + 3r^2s - 6rs^2}{-3rs}$

$$= \frac{9r^2s^2}{-3rs} + \frac{3r^2s}{-3rs} - \frac{6rs^2}{-3rs}$$

$$= -3rs - r + 2s$$

Check: We multiply.

$$\begin{array}{r} -3rs - r + 2s \\ -3rs \\ \hline 9r^2s^2 + 3r^2s - 6rs^2 \end{array}$$

12. $1 - 2x^2y + 3x^4y^5$

13.

$$\begin{array}{r} x + 6 \\ x-2 \overline{\smash{\big)}\, x^2+4x-12} \\ \underline{x^2-2x} \\ 6x-12 \leftarrow (x^2 + 4x) - (x^2 - 2x) = 6x \\ \underline{6x-12} \\ 0 \leftarrow (6x - 12) - (6x - 12) = 0 \end{array}$$

The answer is $x + 6$.

14. $x - 2$

15.

$$\begin{array}{r} x - 5 \\ x-5 \overline{\smash{\big)}\, x^2-10x-25} \\ \underline{x^2-5x} \\ -5x-25 \leftarrow (x^2 - 10x) - (x^2 - 5x) = \\ -5x \\ \underline{-5x+25} \\ -50 \leftarrow (-5x - 25) - (-5x + 25) \end{array}$$

The answer is $x - 5 + \dfrac{-50}{x - 5}$, or $x - 5 - \dfrac{50}{x - 5}$.

16. $x + 4 + \dfrac{-32}{x + 4}$

17.

$$\begin{array}{r} x - 3 \\ x+3 \overline{\smash{\big)}\, x^2+0x-9} \leftarrow \text{Filling in the missing term} \\ \underline{x^2+3x} \\ -3x-9 \leftarrow x^2 - (x^2 + 3x) = -3x \\ \underline{-3x-9} \\ 0 \leftarrow (-3x - 9) - (-3x - 9) \end{array}$$

The answer is $x - 3$.

18. $x - 5$

19.

$$\begin{array}{r} x + 4 \\ 3x-1 \overline{\smash{\big)}\, 3x^2+11x-4} \\ \underline{3x^2- x} \\ 12x-4 \leftarrow (3x^2 + 11x) - (3x^2 - x) = \\ 12x \\ \underline{12x-4} \\ 0 \leftarrow (12x - 4) - (12x - 4) = 0 \end{array}$$

The answer is $x + 4$.

20. $2x + 3$

21.

$$\begin{array}{r} 2x^2- 7x + 4 \\ 4x+3 \overline{\smash{\big)}\, 8x^3-22x^2- 5x +12} \\ \underline{8x^3+6x^2} \\ -28x^2- 5x \leftarrow (8x^3 - 22x^2) - \\ (8x^3 + 6x^2) = -28x^2 \\ \underline{-28x^2-21x} \\ 16x+12 \leftarrow (-28x^2 - 5x) - \\ (-28x^2 - 21x) = 16x \\ \underline{16x+12} \\ 0 \leftarrow (16x + 12) - (16x + 12) \end{array}$$

The answer is $2x^2 - 7x + 4$.

22. $x^2 - 3x + 1$

23.

$$\begin{array}{r} x^2 + 1 \\ x^2-3 \overline{\smash{\big)}\, x^4+0x^3-2x^2+4x-5} \leftarrow \text{Writing in the} \\ \underline{x^4 -3x^2} \text{missing term} \\ x^2+4x-5 \leftarrow (x^4 - 2x^2) - \\ (x^4 - 3x^2) = x^2 \\ \underline{x^2 -3} \\ 4x-2 \leftarrow (x^2 + 4x - 5) - \\ (x^2 - 3) = 4x - 2 \end{array}$$

The answer is $x^2 + 1 + \dfrac{4x - 2}{x^2 - 3}$.

24. $x^2 - 1 + \dfrac{3x - 1}{x^2 + 5}$

25.

$$
\begin{array}{r}
3x^2 \qquad\quad -\ 3 \\
2x^2 + 1\ \overline{\smash{\big)}\ 6x^4 + 0x^3 - 3x^2 + x - 4} \\
\underline{6x^4 \qquad\ + 3x^2} \\
-6x^2 + x - 4 \\
\underline{-6x^2 \qquad\quad -3} \\
x - 1
\end{array}
$$

←Writing in the
missing term

$\leftarrow (6x^4 - 3x^2)-$
$(6x^4 + 3x^2) = -6x^2$

$\leftarrow (-6x^2 + x - 4)-$
$(-6x^2 - 3) = x - 1$

The answer is $3x^2 - 3 + \dfrac{x - 1}{2x^2 + 1}$.

26. $2x^2 + 1 + \dfrac{-x}{2x^2 - 3}$

27. $F(x) = \dfrac{f(x)}{g(x)} = \dfrac{64x^3 - 8}{4x - 2}$

$$
\begin{array}{r}
16x^2 +\ 8x +\ 4 \\
4x - 2\ \overline{\smash{\big)}\ 64x^3 \qquad\qquad\quad - 8} \\
\underline{64x^3 - 32x^2} \\
32x^2 +\ 0x \\
\underline{32x^2 - 16x} \\
16x - 8 \\
\underline{16x - 8} \\
0
\end{array}
$$

Since $g(x)$ is 0 for $x = \dfrac{1}{2}$, we have

$F(x) = 16x^2 + 8x + 4$, provided $x \neq \dfrac{1}{2}$.

28. $4x^2 - 6x + 9$, $x \neq -\dfrac{3}{2}$

29. $F(x) = \dfrac{f(x)}{g(x)} = \dfrac{6x^2 - 11x - 10}{3x + 2}$

$$
\begin{array}{r}
2x -\ 5 \\
3x + 2\ \overline{\smash{\big)}\ 6x^2 - 11x - 10} \\
\underline{6x^2 +\ 4x} \\
-15x - 10 \\
\underline{-15x - 10} \\
0
\end{array}
$$

Since $g(x)$ is 0 for $x = -\dfrac{2}{3}$, we have

$F(x) = 2x - 5$, provided $x \neq -\dfrac{2}{3}$.

30. $4x + 3$, $x \neq \dfrac{7}{2}$

31. $F(x) = \dfrac{f(x)}{g(x)} = \dfrac{x^4 - 3x^2 - 54}{x^2 - 9}$

$$
\begin{array}{r}
x^2 +\ \ 6 \\
x^2 - 9\ \overline{\smash{\big)}\ x^4 - 3x^2 - 54} \\
\underline{x^4 - 9x^2} \\
6x^2 - 54 \\
\underline{6x^2 - 54} \\
0
\end{array}
$$

Since $g(x)$ is 0 for $x = -3$ or $x = 3$, we have

$F(x) = x^2 + 6$, provided $x \neq -3$ and $x \neq 3$.

32. $x^2 + 1$, $x \neq -5$, $x \neq 5$.

33. $(x^3 - 2x^2 + 2x - 5) \div (x - 1)$

$$
\begin{array}{r|rrrr}
1 & 1 & -2 & 2 & -5 \\
  &   & 1 & -1 & 1 \\
\hline
  & 1 & -1 & 1 & -4
\end{array}
$$

The answer is $x^2 - x + 1$, R -4, or $x^2 - x + 1 + \dfrac{-4}{x - 1}$.

34. $x^2 - 3x + 5 + \dfrac{-10}{x + 1}$

35. $(a^2 + 11a - 19) \div (a + 4) =$

$(a^2 + 11a - 19) \div [a - (-4)]$

$$
\begin{array}{r|rrr}
-4 & 1 & 11 & -19 \\
   &   & -4 & -28 \\
\hline
   & 1 & 7 & -47
\end{array}
$$

The answer is $a + 7$, R -47, or $a + 7 + \dfrac{-47}{a + 4}$.

36. $a + 15 + \dfrac{41}{a - 4}$

37. $(x^3 - 7x^2 - 13x + 3) \div (x - 2)$

$$
\begin{array}{r|rrrr}
2 & 1 & -7 & -13 & 3 \\
  &   & 2 & -10 & -46 \\
\hline
  & 1 & -5 & -23 & -43
\end{array}
$$

The answer is $x^2 - 5x - 23$, R -43, or

$x^2 - 5x - 23 + \dfrac{-43}{x - 2}$.

38. $x^2 - 9x + 5 + \dfrac{-7}{x + 2}$

39. $(y^3 - 3y + 10) \div (y - 2) =$

$(y^3 + 0y^2 - 3y + 10) \div (y - 2)$

$$
\begin{array}{r|rrrr}
2 & 1 & 0 & -3 & 10 \\
  &   & 2 & 4 & 2 \\
\hline
  & 1 & 2 & 1 & 12
\end{array}
$$

The answer is $y^2 + 2y + 1$, R 12, or

$y^2 + 2y + 1 + \dfrac{12}{y - 2}$.

40. $x^2 - 4x + 8 + \dfrac{-8}{x + 2}$

41. $(x^5 - 32) \div (x - 2) =$

$(x^5 + 0x^4 + 0x^3 + 0x^2 + 0x - 32) \div (x - 2)$

$$\underline{2|} \begin{array}{rrrrrr} 1 & 0 & 0 & 0 & 0 & -32 \\ & 2 & 4 & 8 & 16 & 32 \\ \hline 1 & 2 & 4 & 8 & 16| & 0 \end{array}$$

The answer is $x^4 + 2x^3 + 4x^2 + 8x + 16$.

42. $y^4 + y^3 + y^2 + y + 1$

43. $(3x^3 + 1 - x + 7x^2) \div \left(x + \dfrac{1}{3}\right) =$

$(3x^3 + 7x^2 - x + 1) \div \left[x - \left(-\dfrac{1}{3}\right)\right]$

$$\underline{-\frac{1}{3}|} \begin{array}{rrrr} 3 & 7 & -1 & 1 \\ & -1 & -2 & 1 \\ \hline 3 & 6 & -3| & 2 \end{array}$$

The answer is $3x^2 + 6x - 3$ R 2, or

$3x^2 + 6x - 3 + \dfrac{2}{x + \dfrac{1}{3}}$.

44. $8x^2 - 2x + 6 + \dfrac{2}{x - \dfrac{1}{2}}$

45. $(2x^4 - x^3 - 5x^2 + x + 7) \div (1 + x) =$
$(2x^4 - x^3 - 5x^2 + x + 7) \div [x - (-1)]$

$$\underline{-1|} \begin{array}{rrrrr} 2 & -1 & -5 & 1 & 7 \\ & -2 & 3 & 2 & -3 \\ \hline 2 & -3 & -2 & 3| & 4 \end{array}$$

The answer is $2x^3 - 3x^2 - 2x + 3$, R4, or

$2x^3 - 3x^2 - 2x + 3 + \dfrac{4}{1 + x}$.

46. $6y^3 - 3y^2 + 9y + 1 + \dfrac{3}{3 + y}$

47. *Familiarize*. Let $w =$ the width. Then $w + 15 =$ the length. We draw a picture.

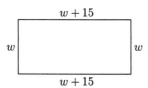

We will use the fact that the perimeter is 640 ft to find w (the width). Then we can find $w + 15$ (the length) and multiply the length and the width to find the area.

Translate.

Width+Width+ Length + Length =Perimeter
$w \;+\; w \;+(w + 15)+(w + 15)= \;\;\;640$

Carry out.

$w + w + (w + 15) + (w + 15) = 640$
$4w + 30 = 640$
$4w = 610$
$w = 152.5$

If the width is 152.5, then the length is $152.5 + 15$, or 167.5. The area is $(167.5)(152.5)$, or $25,543.75 \text{ ft}^2$.

Check. The length, 167.5 ft, is 15 ft greater than the width, 152.5 ft. The perimeter is $152.5 + 152.5 + 167.5 + 167.5$, or 640 ft. We should also recheck the computation we used to find the area. The answer checks.

State. The area is $25,543.75 \text{ ft}^2$.

48. 2

49. $2x > 12 + 7x$
$-5x > 12$ Subtracting $7x$
$x < -\dfrac{12}{5}$ Dividing by -5 and reversing the inequality symbol

The solution set is $\left\{x \middle| x < -\dfrac{12}{5}\right\}$.

50.

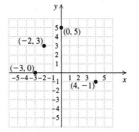

51. To plot a point for which both coordinates are negative, start at the origin and move to the left and then down. Such a point lies in quadrant III.

52.

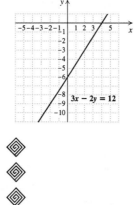

53. ◈

54. ◈

55. ◈

56. ◈

57. $\quad (45x^{8k} + 30x^{6k} - 60x^{4k}) \div (3x^{2k})$

$$= \frac{45x^{8k} + 30x^{6k} - 60x^{4k}}{3x^{2k}}$$

$$= \frac{45x^{8k}}{3x^{2k}} + \frac{30x^{6k}}{3x^{2k}} - \frac{60x^{4k}}{3x^{2k}}$$

$$= 15x^{8k-2k} + 10x^{6k-2k} - 20x^{4k-2k}$$

$$= 15x^{6k} + 10x^{4k} - 20x^{2k}$$

58. $5a^{6k} - 16a^{3k} + 14$

59.

$$
\begin{array}{r}
y^3 - ay^2 + a^2y - a^3 \\
y + a \overline{\smash{\big)}\ y^4 + 0y^3 + 0y^2 + 0y + a^2} \\
\underline{y^4 + ay^3} \\
-ay^3 \\
\underline{-ay^3 - a^2y^2} \\
a^2y^2 \\
\underline{a^2y^2 + a^3y} \\
-a^3y + a^2 \\
\underline{-a^3y \qquad - a^4} \\
a^2 + a^4
\end{array}
$$

The answer is $y^3 - ay^2 + a^2y - a^3 + \dfrac{a^2 + a^4}{y + a}$.

60. $a + 3 + \dfrac{5}{5a^2 - 7a - 2}$

61. $\quad (4x^5 - 14x^3 - x^2 + 3) +$
$$\qquad\qquad (2x^5 + 3x^4 + x^3 - 3x^2 + 5x)$$
$$= 6x^5 + 3x^4 - 13x^3 - 4x^2 + 5x + 3$$

$$
\begin{array}{r}
2x^2 + x - 3 \\
3x^3 - 2x - 1 \overline{\smash{\big)}\ 6x^5 + 3x^4 - 13x^3 - 4x^2 + 5x + 3} \\
\underline{6x^5 \qquad\ - 4x^3 - 2x^2} \\
3x^4 - 9x^3 - 2x^2 + 5x \\
\underline{3x^4 \qquad\qquad - 2x^2 - x} \\
-9x^3 \qquad\quad + 6x + 3 \\
\underline{-9x^3 \qquad\quad + 6x + 3} \\
0
\end{array}
$$

The answer is $2x^2 + x - 3$.

62. $5x^5 + 5x^4 - 8x^2 - 8x + 2$

63.

$$
\begin{array}{r}
3a^{2h} + 2a^h - 5 \\
2a^h + 3 \overline{\smash{\big)}\ 6a^{3h} + 13a^{2h} - 4a^h - 15} \\
\underline{6a^{3h} + 9a^{2h}} \\
4a^{2h} - 4a^h \\
\underline{4a^{2h} + 6a^h} \\
-10a^h - 15 \\
\underline{-10a^h - 15} \\
0
\end{array}
$$

The answer is $3a^{2h} + 2a^h - 5$.

64. 3

65.

$$
\begin{array}{r}
2x + (-3c + 2) \\
x - 1 \overline{\smash{\big)}\ 2x^2 - 3cx - 8} \\
\underline{2x^2 - 2x} \\
(-3c + 2)x - 8 \\
\underline{(-3c + 2)x - (-3c + 2)} \\
-8 + (-3c + 2)
\end{array}
$$

We set the remainder equal to 0:

$$-8 - 3c + 2 = 0$$
$$-3c - 6 = 0$$
$$-3c = 6$$
$$c = -2$$

Thus, c must be -2.

66. -1

Exercise Set 5.7

1. $6^{-2} = \dfrac{1}{6^2} = \dfrac{1}{36}$

2. $\dfrac{1}{2^4} = \dfrac{1}{16}$

3. $(-2)^{-6} = \dfrac{1}{(-2)^6} = \dfrac{1}{64}$

4. $\dfrac{1}{(-3)^4} = \dfrac{1}{81}$

5. $a^{-5} = \dfrac{1}{a^5}$

6. $\dfrac{1}{x^2}$

7. $\dfrac{1}{y^{-4}} = y^4$

8. t^7

9. $7^{-1} = \dfrac{1}{7^1} = \dfrac{1}{7}$

10. $\dfrac{3}{2}$

11. $\left(\dfrac{1}{4}\right)^{-2} = \dfrac{1}{\left(\dfrac{1}{4}\right)^2} = \dfrac{1}{\dfrac{1}{16}} = 1 \cdot \dfrac{16}{1} = 16$

12. $\dfrac{25}{16}$

13. $\dfrac{1}{4^3} = 4^{-3}$

14. 5^{-2}

15. $\dfrac{1}{t^6} = t^{-6}$

16. y^{-2}

17. $\dfrac{1}{5} = \dfrac{1}{5^1} = 5^{-1}$

18. m^{-1}

19. $2^{-5} \cdot 2^8 = 2^{-5+8} = 2^3$, or 8

20. 5

21. $x^{-2} \cdot x = x^{-2+1} = x^{-1}$, or $\dfrac{1}{x}$

22. 1

23. $x^{-7} \cdot x^{-6} = x^{-13}$, or $\dfrac{1}{x^{13}}$

24. y^{-13}, or $\dfrac{1}{y^{13}}$

25. $\dfrac{m^6}{m^{12}} = m^{6-12} = m^{-6}$, or $\dfrac{1}{m^6}$

26. p^{-1}, or $\dfrac{1}{p}$

27. $\dfrac{(8x)^6}{(8x)^{10}} = (8x)^{6-10} = (8x)^{-4}$, or $\dfrac{1}{(8x)^4}$

28. $(9t)^{-7}$, or $\dfrac{1}{(9t)^7}$

29. $\dfrac{18^9}{18^9} = 18^{9-9} = 18^0 = 1$

30. 1

31. $(a^{-5}b^{-7})(a^{-3}b^{-6}) = a^{-5+(-3)}b^{-7+(-6)} =$
$a^{-8}b^{-13}$, or $\dfrac{1}{a^8 b^{13}}$

32. $x^{-5}y^{-9}$, or $\dfrac{1}{x^5 y^9}$

33. $\dfrac{x^7}{x^{-2}} = x^{7-(-2)} = x^9$

34. t^{11}

35. $\dfrac{z^{-6}}{z^{-2}} = z^{-6-(-2)} = z^{-4}$, or $\dfrac{1}{z^4}$

36. y^5

37. $\dfrac{x}{x^{-1}} = x^{1-(-1)} = x^2$

38. x^5

39. $(a^{-3})^5 = a^{-3 \cdot 5} = a^{-15}$, or $\dfrac{1}{a^{15}}$

40. x^{-30}, or $\dfrac{1}{x^{30}}$

41. $(a^{-5})^{-6} = a^{-5(-6)} = a^{30}$

42. x^{12}

43. $(mn)^{-5} = m^{-5}n^{-5}$, or $\dfrac{1}{m^5 n^5}$

44. $a^{-3}b^{-3}$, or $\dfrac{1}{a^3 b^3}$

45. $(4xy)^{-2} = 4^{-2}x^{-2}y^{-2}$, or $\dfrac{1}{16x^2 y^2}$

46. $5^{-2}a^{-2}b^{-2}$, or $\dfrac{1}{25a^2 b^2}$

47. $(3a^{-4})^4 = 3^4(a^{-4})^4 = 81a^{-16}$, or $\dfrac{81}{a^{16}}$

48. $36x^{-10}$, or $\dfrac{36}{x^{10}}$

49. $(t^5 x^3)^{-4} = (t^5)^{-4}(x^3)^{-4} = t^{-20}x^{-12}$, or $\dfrac{1}{t^{20}x^{12}}$

50. $x^{-12}y^{-15}$, or $\dfrac{1}{x^{12}y^{15}}$

51. $(x^{-2}y^{-7})^{-5} = (x^{-2})^{-5}(y^{-7})^{-5} = x^{10}y^{35}$

52. $x^{24}y^8$

53. $(x^3 y^{-4}z^{-5})(x^{-4}y^{-2}z^9) = x^{3+(-4)}y^{-4+(-2)}z^{-5+9} =$
$x^{-1}y^{-6}z^4$, or $\dfrac{z^4}{xy^6}$

54. $a^{-8}b^5 c^4$, or $\dfrac{b^5 c^4}{a^8}$

55. $\left(\dfrac{y^2}{2}\right)^{-2} = \dfrac{(y^2)^{-2}}{2^{-2}} = \dfrac{y^{-4}}{2^{-2}} = \dfrac{2^2}{y^4} = \dfrac{4}{y^4}$

56. $\dfrac{a^{-8}}{3^{-2}}$, or $\dfrac{9}{a^8}$

57. $\left(\dfrac{3}{a^2}\right)^4 = \dfrac{3^4}{(a^2)^4} = \dfrac{81}{a^8}$

58. $\dfrac{49}{x^{14}}$

59. $\left(\dfrac{x^2 y}{z^4}\right)^3 = \dfrac{(x^2)^3 y^3}{(z^4)^3} = \dfrac{x^6 y^3}{z^{12}}$

60. $\dfrac{m^3}{n^{12}p^3}$

61. $\left(\dfrac{a^2 b}{cd^3}\right)^{-5} = \dfrac{(a^2)^{-5}b^{-5}}{c^{-5}(d^3)^{-5}} = \dfrac{a^{-10}b^{-5}}{c^{-5}d^{-15}}$, or $\dfrac{c^5 d^{15}}{a^{10}b^5}$

62. $\dfrac{2^{-3}a^{-6}}{3^{-3}b^{-12}}$, or $\dfrac{27b^{12}}{8a^6}$

63. 9.12×10^4

Since the exponent is positive, the decimal point will move to the right.

9.1200.   The decimal point moves right 4 places.

$9.12 \times 10^4 = 91,200$

64. 892

65. 6.92×10^{-3}

Since the exponent is negative, the decimal point will move to the left.

.006.92   The decimal point moves left 3 places.

$6.92 \times 10^{-3} = 0.00692$

66. 0.000726

67. 8.764×10^{-10}

Since the exponent is negative, the decimal point will move to the left.

0.0000000008.764

10 places

$8.764 \times 10^{-10} = 0.0000000008764$

68. 13,500,000

69. $10^7 = 1 \times 10^7$

Since the exponent is positive, the decimal point will move to the right.

1.0000000.

7 places

$10^7 = 10,000,000$

70. 10,000

71. $10^{-4} = 1 \times 10^{-4}$

Since the exponent is negative, the decimal point will move to the left.

.0001.

4 places

$10^{-4} = 0.0001$

72. 0.0000001

73. $370,000 = 3.7 \times 10^n$

To write 3.7 as 370,000 we move the decimal point 5 places to the right. Thus, n is 5 and

$$370,000 = 3.7 \times 10^5.$$

74. 7.15×10^4

75. $0.00583 = 5.83 \times 10^n$

To write 5.83 as 0.00583 we move the decimal point 3 places to the left. Thus, n is -3 and

$$0.00583 = 5.83 \times 10^{-3}.$$

76. 8.14×10^{-2}

77. $78,000,000,000 = 7.8 \times 10^n$

To write 7.8 as 78,000,000,000 we move the decimal point 10 places to the right. Thus, n is 10 and

$$78,000,000,000 = 7.8 \times 10^{10}.$$

78. 3.7×10^{12}

79. $0.00000486 = 4.86 \times 10^n$

To write 4.86 as 0.00000486 we move the decimal point 6 places to the left. Thus, n is -6 and

$$0.00000486 = 4.86 \times 10^{-6}.$$

80. 2.75×10^{-10}

81. $0.000000018 = 1.8 \times 10^n$

To write 1.8 as 0.000000018 we move the decimal point 8 places to the left. Thus, n is -8 and

$$0.000000018 = 1.8 \times 10^{-8}.$$

82. 2×10^{-11}

83. $10,000,000 = 1 \times 10^n$, or 10^n

To write 1 as 10,000,000 we move the decimal point 7 places to the right. Thus, n is 7 and

$$10,000,000 = 10^7.$$

84. 10^{11}

85. $(4 \times 10^7)(2 \times 10^5) = (4 \cdot 2) \times (10^7 \cdot 10^5)$
$$= 8 \times 10^{7+5} \quad \text{Adding exponents}$$
$$= 8 \times 10^{12}$$

86. 6.46×10^5

87. $(3.8 \times 10^9)(6.5 \times 10^{-2}) = (3.8 \cdot 6.5) \times (10^9 \cdot 10^{-2})$
$$= 24.7 \times 10^7$$

The answer is not yet in scientific notation since 24.7 is not a number between 1 and 10. We convert to scientific notation.

$$24.7 \times 10^7 = (2.47 \times 10) \times 10^7 = 2.47 \times 10^8$$

88. 6.106×10^{-11}

89. $\dfrac{8.5 \times 10^8}{3.4 \times 10^{-5}} = \dfrac{8.5}{3.4} \times \dfrac{10^8}{10^{-5}}$

$\qquad\qquad = 2.5 \times 10^{8-(-5)}$

$\qquad\qquad = 2.5 \times 10^{13}$

90. 2.24×10^{-7}

91. $(3.0 \times 10^6) \div (6.0 \times 10^9) = \dfrac{3.0 \times 10^6}{6.0 \times 10^9}$

$\qquad\qquad\qquad = \dfrac{3.0}{6.0} \times \dfrac{10^6}{10^9}$

$\qquad\qquad\qquad = 0.5 \times 10^{6-9}$

$\qquad\qquad\qquad = 0.5 \times 10^{-3}$

The answer is not yet in scientific notation because 0.5 is not between 1 and 10. We convert to scientific notation.

$\qquad 0.5 \times 10^{-3} = (5.0 \times 10^{-1}) \times 10^{-3} =$

$\qquad 5.0 \times 10^{-4}$

92. 9.375×10^2

93. $\dfrac{(2.5 \times 10^{-8})(6.1 \times 10^{-11})}{1.28 \times 10^{-3}}$

$\quad = \dfrac{(2.5 \cdot 6.1)}{1.28} \times \dfrac{(10^{-8} \cdot 10^{-11})}{10^{-3}}$

$\quad = 11.9140625 \times 10^{-8+(-11)-(-3)}$

$\quad = 11.9140625 \times 10^{-16}$

$\quad = (1.19140625 \times 10) \times 10^{-16}$

$\quad = 1.19140625 \times 10^{-15}$

94. $4.894179894 \times 10^{26}$

95. $\dfrac{5.8 \times 10^{17}}{(4.0 \times 10^{-13})(2.3 \times 10^4)}$

$\quad = \dfrac{5.8}{(4.0 \cdot 2.3)} \times \dfrac{10^{17}}{(10^{-13} \cdot 10^4)}$

$\quad \approx 0.6304347826 \times 10^{17-(-13)-4}$

$\quad \approx (6.304347826 \times 10^{-1}) \times 10^{26}$

$\quad \approx 6.304347826 \times 10^{25}$

96. 3.12×10^{43}

97. *Familiarize*. There are 365 days in one year. Express 3 million and 365 in scientific notation.

$\qquad 3 \text{ million} = 3,000,000 = 3 \times 10$

$\qquad 365 = 3.65 \times 10^2$

Let $a = $ the amount of orange juice Americans consume in one year, in gallons.

Translate. We reword the problem.

What is	daily consumption	times	number of days in a year?
↓ ↓	↓	↓	↓
$a \quad = $	(3×10^6)	$\times$	(3.65×10^2)

Carry out. We do the computation.

$\qquad a = (3 \times 10^6) \times (3.65 \times 10^2)$

$\qquad a = (3 \times 3.65) \times (10^6 \times 10^2)$

$\qquad a = 10.95 \times 10^8$

$\qquad a = (1.095 \times 10) \times 10^8$

$\qquad a = 1.095 \times 10^9$

Check. We review the computation. Also, the answer seems reasonable since it is larger than 3 million.

State. Americans consume 1.095×10^9 gallons of orange juice in one year.

98. 1.512×10^{10} cubic feet; 1.324512×10^{14} cubic feet

99. *Familiarize*. Express 200 million and 1 million in scientific notation:

$\qquad 200 \text{ million} = 200,000,000 = 2 \times 10^8$

$\qquad 1 \text{ million} = 1,000,000 = 10^6$

Let $w = $ the number of gallons of drinking water that can be contaminated by 200 million gal of used motor oil.

Translate. We reword the problem.

What is	contamination caused by 1 gal	times	200 million gal?
↓ ↓	↓	↓	↓
$w \quad = $	10^6	$\times$	2×10^8

Carry out. We do the computation.

$\qquad w = 10^6 \times (2 \times 10^8)$

$\qquad w = 2 \times (10^6 \times 10^8)$

$\qquad w = 2 \times 10^{14}$

Check. We review the computation. Also, the answer is a very large number, as expected.

State. 200 million gal of oil can contaminate 2×10^{14} gal of drinking water.

100. $\$3.2 \times 10^{10}$

101. *Familiarize*. Express 1 billion and 2500 in scientific notation:

$\qquad 1 \text{ billion} = 1,000,000,000 = 10^9$

$\qquad 2500 = 2.5 \times 10^3$

Let $b = $ the number of bytes in the network.

Translate. We reword the problem.

What is   2500   times 1 gigabyte?

$$b \;\; = 2.5 \times 10^3 \;\; \times \;\; 10^9$$

Carry out. We do the computation.

$$b = (2.5 \times 10^3) \times 10^9$$
$$b = 2.5 \times (10^3 \times 10^9)$$
$$b = 2.5 \times 10^{12}$$

Check. We review the computation. Also, the answer seems reasonable since it is larger than 1 billion.

State. There are 2.5×10^{12} bytes in the network.

102. $\$1.32288 \times 10^{12}$

103.

$$\frac{3}{4} - 5\left(-\frac{1}{2}\right)^2 + \frac{1}{3}$$
$$= \frac{3}{4} - 5 \cdot \frac{1}{4} + \frac{1}{3}$$
$$= \frac{3}{4} - \frac{5}{4} + \frac{1}{3}$$
$$= \frac{9}{12} - \frac{15}{12} + \frac{4}{12}$$
$$= -\frac{2}{12} = -\frac{1}{6}$$

104. $8a$

105. $-12x + (-5x) = (-12 - 5)x = -17x$

106.

107. To plot a point with a positive first coordinate, start at the origin and move to the right. Thus, the first coordinate is positive in quadrants I and IV.

108. $t = \dfrac{cx - r}{b}$

109. ◈

110. ◈

111.

$$\frac{4.2 \times 10^8[(2.5 \times 10^{-5}) \div (5.0 \times 10^{-9})]}{3.0 \times 10^{27}}$$
$$= \frac{4.2 \times 10^8[(2.5 \div 5.0) \times (10^{-5} \div 10^{-9})]}{3.0 \times 10^{27}}$$
$$= \frac{4.2 \cdot 10^8(0.5 \times 10^4)}{3.0 \times 10^{27}}$$
$$= \frac{(4.2 \times 0.5)}{3.0} \times \frac{(10^8 \cdot 10^4)}{10^{27}}$$
$$= 0.7 \times 10^{-15}$$
$$= (7 \times 10^{-1}) \times 10^{-15}$$
$$= 7 \times 10^{-16}$$

112. (a) 1.6×10^2; (b) 2.5×10^{-11}

113. $4^{-3} \cdot 8 \cdot 16 = (2^2)^{-3} \cdot 2^3 \cdot 2^4 = 2^{-6} \cdot 2^3 \cdot 2^4 = 2^1$

114. 4^1

115. $(5^{-12})^2 5^{25} = 5^{-24} 5^{25} = 5$

116. 7

117. $9^{23} \cdot 27^{-6} = (3^2)^{23}(3^3)^{-6} = 3^{46} \cdot 3^{-18} = 3^{28}$

118. a^n

119. False; let $x = 2$, $y = 3$, $m = 4$, and $n = 2$:
$$2^4 \cdot 3^2 = 16 \cdot 9 = 144, \text{ but}$$
$$(2 \cdot 3)^{4 \cdot 2} = 6^8 = 1,679,616$$

120. False

121. False; let $x = 5$, $y = 3$, and $m = 2$:
$$(5 - 3)^2 = 2^2 = 4, \text{ but}$$
$$5^2 - 3^2 = 25 - 9 = 16$$

Chapter 6

Polynomials and Factoring

Exercise Set 6.1

---

1. From the graph we see that $f(x) = 0$ when $x = -3$ or $x = 5$. These are the solutions.

2. $-5, -2$

3. From the graph we see that $f(x) = 3$ when $x = -3$ or $x = 1$. These are the solutions.

4. $-2, 2$

5. From the graph we see that $f(x) = 0$ when $x = -4$ or $x = 2$. These are the solutions.

6. 1

7. We can graph $y_1 = x^2$ and $y_2 = 5x$ and use the Intersect feature to find the first coordinates of the points of intersection, or we can begin by rewriting the equation so that one side is 0:

$$x^2 = 5x$$
$$x^2 - 5x = 0 \quad \text{Subtracting } 5x \text{ on both sides}$$

Then graph $y = x^2 - 5x$ and use the Zero feature to find the roots of the equation. In either case, we find that the solutions are 0 and 5.

8. 0, 10

9. We can graph $y_1 = 4x$ and $y_2 = x^2 + 3$ and use the Intersect feature to find the first coordinates of the points of intersection, or we can begin by rewriting the equation so that one side is 0:

$$4x = x^2 + 3$$
$$0 = x^2 + 3 - 4x \quad \text{Subtracting } 4x \text{ on both sides}$$

Then graph $y = x^2 + 3 - 4x$ and use the Zero feature to find the roots of the equation. In either case, we find that the solutions are 1 and 3.

10. $-1, 1$

11. We can graph $y_1 = x^2 + 150$ and $y_2 = 25x$ and use the Intersect feature to find the first coordinates of the points of intersection, or we can begin by rewriting the equation so that one side is 0:

$$x^2 + 150 = 25x$$
$$x^2 + 150 - 25x = 0 \quad \text{Subtracting } 25 \text{ on both sides}$$

Then graph $y = x^2 + 150 - 25x$ and use the Zero feature to find the roots of the equation. In either case, we find that the solutions are 10 and 15.

12. 0.5, 25

13. Graph $y = x^3 - 3x^2 - 2x$ and use the Zero feature to find the roots of the equation. The solutions are 0, 1, and 2.

14. $-2, -1, 1$

15. Graph $y = x^3 - 3x^2 - 198x + 1080$ and use the Zero feature to find the roots of the equation. The solutions are -15, 6, and 12.

16. $-20, 1.5, 6$

17. Graph $y = 21x^2 + 2x - 3$ and use the Zero feature to find the roots of the equation. The solutions are approximately -0.42857 and 0.33333.

18. $-0.09091, 0.83333$

19. Graph $y = x^2 - 4x + 45$ and use the Zero feature to find the zeros of the function. They are -5 and 9.

20. $-5, 4$

21. Graph $y = 2x^2 - 13x - 7$ and use the Zero feature to find the zeros of the function. They are -0.5 and 7.

22. $-2.42013, -0.41320$

23. Graph $y = x^3 - 2x^2 - 3x$ and use the Zero feature to find the zeros of the function. They are -1, 0, and 3.

24. $-2, 0, 2$

25. We see that $2x - 1 = 0$ when $x = 0.5$ and $3x + 1 = 0$ when $x = -0.\overline{3}$, so graph III corresponds to the given function.

26. II

27. We see that $4 - x = 0$ when $x = 4$ and $2x - 11 = 0$ when $x = 5.5$, so graph I corresponds to the given function.

28. IV

29. $x^2 + 6x + 9$ has no equals sign, so it is an expression.

30. Equation

31. $3x^2 = 3x$ has an equals sign, so it is an equation.

32. Expression

33. $2x^3 + x^2 = 0$ has an equals sign, so it is an equation.

34. Expression

35.
$$8t^2 + 2t$$
$$= 2t \cdot 4t + 2t \cdot 1$$
$$= 2t(4t + 1)$$

36. $3y(2y + 1)$

37.
$$y^3 + 9y^2$$
$$= y \cdot y^2 + 9 \cdot y^2$$
$$= y^2(y + 9)$$

38. $x^2(x + 8)$

39.
$$5x^2 - 15x^4$$
$$= 5x^2 \cdot 1 - 5x^2 \cdot 3x^2$$
$$= 5x^2(1 - 3x^2)$$

40. $4y^2(2 + y^2)$

41.
$$4x^2y - 12xy^2$$
$$= 4xy \cdot x - 4xy \cdot 3y$$
$$= 4xy(x - 3y)$$

42. $5x^2y^2(y + 3x)$

43.
$$3y^2 - 3y - 9$$
$$= 3 \cdot y^2 - 3 \cdot y - 3 \cdot 3$$
$$= 3(y^2 - y - 3)$$

44. $5(x^2 - x + 3)$

45.
$$6ab - 4ad + 12ac$$
$$= 2a \cdot 3b - 2a \cdot 2d + 2a \cdot 6c$$
$$= 2a(3b - 2d + 6c)$$

46. $2x(4y + 5z - 7w)$

47.
$$9x^3y^6z^2 - 12x^4y^4z^4 + 15x^2y^5z^3$$
$$= 3x^2y^4z^2 \cdot 3xy^2 - 3x^2y^4z^2 \cdot 4x^2z^2 + 3x^2y^4z^2 \cdot 5yz$$
$$= 3x^2y^4z^2(3xy^2 - 4x^2z^2 + 5yz)$$

48. $7a^3b^3c^3(2ac^2 + 3b^2c - 5ab)$

49. $-5x + 15 = -5(x - 3)$

50. $-5(x + 8)$

51. $-6y - 72 = -6(y + 12)$

52. $-8(t - 9)$

53. $-2x^2 + 4x - 12 = -2(x^2 - 2x + 6)$

54. $-2(x^2 - 6x - 20)$

55. $-3y^3 + 12y^2 - 15y = -3y(y^2 - 4y + 5)$

56. $-4m(m^3 + 8m^2 - 16)$

57. $-x^2 + 5x - 9 = -(x^2 - 5x + 9)$

58. $-(p^3 + 4p^2 - 11)$

59. a) $h(t) = -16t^2 + 96t$
$\qquad h(t) = -16t(t - 6)$ Factoring out $-16t$

   b) Using $h(t) = -16t^2 + 96t$:
$\qquad h(2) = -16 \cdot 2^2 + 96 \cdot 2 = -16 \cdot 4 + 192$
$\qquad\qquad = -64 + 192 = 128$
   Using $h(t) = -16t(t - 6)$:
$\qquad h(2) = -16(2)(2 - 6) = -16(2)(-4) = 128$
   The expressions have the same value for $t = 2$, so the factorization is probably correct.

60. (a) $h(t) = -8t(2t - 9)$; (b) $h(2) = 80$

61. $N(x) = \dfrac{1}{6}x^3 + \dfrac{1}{2}x^2 + \dfrac{1}{3}x$
$\qquad N(x) = \dfrac{1}{6}x(x^2 + 3x + 2)$ Factoring out $\dfrac{1}{6}x$

62. $f(n) = \dfrac{1}{2}n(n - 1)$

63. $2\pi rh + \pi r^2 = \pi r(2h + r)$

64. $P(n) = \dfrac{1}{2}n(n - 3)$

65. $R(x) = 280x - 0.4x^2$
$\qquad R(x) = 0.4x(700 - x)$

66. $C(x) = 0.6x(0.3 + x)$

67.
$$a(b - 2) + c(b - 2)$$
$$= (b - 2)(a + c)$$

68. $(x^2 - 3)(a - 2)$

69.
$$\qquad (x + 7)(x - 1) + (x + 7)(x - 2)$$
$$= (x + 7)(x - 1 + x - 2)$$
$$= (x + 7)(2x - 3)$$

70. $(a + 5)(2a - 1)$

71.
$$\qquad a^2(x - y) + 5(y - x)$$
$$= a^2(x - y) + 5(-1)(x - y) \quad \text{Factoring out } -1$$
$$\qquad\qquad \text{to reverse the second subtraction}$$
$$= a^2(x - y) - 5(x - y) \qquad\quad \text{Simplifying}$$
$$= (x - y)(a^2 - 5)$$

72. $(x - 6)(3x^2 - 2)$

73.
$$\qquad ac + ad + bc + bd$$
$$= a(c + d) + b(c + d)$$
$$= (c + d)(a + b)$$

74. $(y + z)(x + w)$

75.
$$\qquad b^3 - b^2 + 2b - 2$$
$$= b^2(b - 1) + 2(b - 1)$$
$$= (b - 1)(b^2 + 2)$$

76. $(y - 1)(y^2 + 3)$

77.
$$\qquad a^3 - 3a^2 + 6 - 2a$$
$$= a^2(a - 3) + 2(3 - a)$$
$$= a^2(a - 3) + 2(-1)(a - 3) \quad \text{Factoring out } -1$$
$$\qquad\qquad \text{to reverse the second subtraction}$$
$$= a^2(a - 3) - 2(a - 3)$$
$$= (a - 3)(a^2 - 2)$$

78. $(t + 6)(t^2 - 2)$

79.
$$\qquad 24x^3 - 36x^2 + 72x$$
$$= 12x \cdot 2x^2 - 12x \cdot 3x + 12x \cdot 6$$
$$= 12x(2x^2 - 3x + 6)$$

80. $3a^2(4a^2 - 7a - 3)$

81.
$$\qquad x^6 - x^5 - x^3 + x^4$$
$$= x^3(x^3 - x^2 - 1 + x)$$
$$= x^3[x^2(x - 1) + x - 1] \qquad (-1 + x = x - 1)$$
$$= x^3(x - 1)(x^2 + 1)$$

82. $y(y - 1)(y^2 + 1)$

83.
$$\qquad 2y^4 + 6y^2 + 5y^2 + 15$$
$$= 2y^2(y^2 + 3) + 5(y^2 + 3)$$
$$= (y^2 + 3)(2y^2 + 5)$$

84. $(2 - x)(xy - 3)$

85. $x(x + 1) = 0$

We use the principle of zero products.
$$x = 0 \quad or \quad x + 1 = 0$$
$$x = 0 \quad or \qquad x = -1$$
The solutions are 0 and -1.

86. $0, 2$

87. $\quad x^2 - 3x = 0$
$$x(x - 3) = 0 \quad \text{Factoring}$$
$$x = 0 \quad or \quad x - 3 = 0 \quad \text{Using the}$$
$$\qquad\qquad \text{principle of zero products}$$
$$x = 0 \quad or \qquad x = 3$$
The solutions are 0 and 3.

88. $-4, 0$

89. $\quad -5x^2 = 15x$
$$0 = 5x^2 + 15x \quad \text{Adding } 5x^2 \text{ on both sides}$$
$$0 = 5x(x + 3) \quad \text{Factoring}$$
$$5x = 0 \quad or \quad x + 3 = 0 \qquad \text{Using the}$$
$$\qquad\qquad \text{principle of zero products}$$
$$x = 0 \quad or \qquad x = -3$$
The solutions are 0 and -3.

90. $0, \dfrac{1}{2}$

91.
$$\qquad 12x^4 + 4x^3 = 0$$
$$4x^3(3x + 1) = 0 \quad \text{Factoring}$$
$$4x \cdot x \cdot x(3x + 1) = 0$$
$$4x = 0 \; or \; x = 0 \; or \; x = 0 \; or \; 3x + 1 = 0$$
$$x = 0 \; or \; x = 0 \; or \; x = 0 \; or \qquad 3x = -1$$
$$x = 0 \; or \; x = 0 \; or \; x = 0 \; or \qquad x = -\dfrac{1}{3}$$
The solutions are 0 and $-\dfrac{1}{3}$.

92. $0, \dfrac{1}{3}$

93.

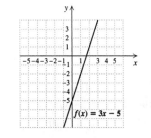

$f(x) = 3x - 5$

94. $6a - 2$

95. We use FOIL.
$$(a+7)(a-3) = a^2 - 3a + 7a - 21$$
$$= a^2 + 4a - 21$$

96. $84°$, $21°$

97. ◈

98. ◈

99. ◈

100. ◈

101. We use the principle of zero products in reverse. Since the solutions of $x^2 - 2x - 15 = 0$ are -3 and 5, we have
$$x = 5 \quad or \quad x = -3$$
$$x - 5 = 0 \quad or \quad x + 3 = 0,$$
so $x^2 - 2x - 15 = (x-5)(x+3)$.

102. $(x+5)(x+2)$

103. We use the principle of zero products in reverse. Since the zeros of $f(x) = x^2 + 2x - 8$ are -4 and 2, we have
$$x = -4 \quad or \quad x = 2$$
$$x + 4 = 0 \quad or \quad x - 2 = 0,$$
so $x^2 + 2x - 8 = (x+4)(x-2)$.

104. $(x-1)(x-1)$

105. $x^5y^4 + \underline{\quad} = x^3y(\underline{\quad} + xy^5)$

The term that goes in the first blank is the product of x^3y and xy^5, or x^4y^6.

The term that goes in the second blank is the expression that is multiplied with x^3y to obtain x^5y^4, or x^2y^3. Thus, we have
$$x^5y^4 + x^4y^6 = x^3y(x^2y^3 + xy^5).$$

106. $a^3b^7 - a^2b^3c^2 = a^2b^3(ab^4 - c^2)$

107.
$$rx^2 - rx + 5r + sx^2 - sx + 5s$$
$$= r(x^2 - x + 5) + s(x^2 - x + 5)$$
$$= (x^2 - x + 5)(r + s)$$

108. $(a^2 + 2a + 10)(3 + 7b)$

109.
$$5x^2 - x^2y + 10x - 2xy + 15xz - 3xyz$$
$$= x(5x - xy + 10 - 2y + 15z - 3yz)$$
$$= x[x(5 - y) + 2(5 - y) + 3z(5 - y)]$$
$$= x(5 - y)(x + 2 + 3z)$$

110. $(x^4 + x^2 + 5)(a^4 + a^2 + 5)$

111.
$$2x^{3a} + 8x^a + 4x^{2a}$$
$$= 2x^a(x^{2a} + 4 + 2x^a)$$

112. $3a^n(a + 2 - 5a^2)$

113.
$$4x^{a+b} + 7x^{a-b}$$
$$= 4 \cdot x^a \cdot x^b + 7 \cdot x^a \cdot x^{-b}$$
$$= x^a(4x^b + 7x^{-b})$$

114. $y^{a+b}(7y^a - 5 + 3y^b)$

Exercise Set 6.2

1. $x^2 + 8x + 12$

We look for two numbers whose product is 12 and whose sum is 8. Since 12 and 8 are both positive, we need only consider positive factors.

Pair of Factors	Sum of Factors
1,12	13
2, 6	8

The numbers we need are 2 and 6. The factorization is $(x+2)(x+6)$.

2. $(x+1)(x+5)$

3. $t^2 - 8t + 15$

Since the constant term is positive and the coefficient of the middle term is negative, we look for a factorization of 15 in which both factors are negative. Their sum must be -8.

Pair of Factors	Sum of Factors
$-1,-15$	-16
$-3, -5$	-8

The numbers we need are -3 and -5. The factorization is $(t-3)(t-5)$.

4. $(y-3)(y-9)$

5. $x^2 - 27 - 6x = x^2 - 6x - 27$

Since the constant term is negative, we look for a factorization of -27 in which one factor is positive and one factor is negative. Their sum must be -6, so the negative factor must have the larger absolute value. Thus we consider only pairs of factors in which the negative factor has the larger absolute value.

Pair of Factors	Sum of Factors
$-27,1$	-26
$-9,3$	-6

The numbers we need are -9 and 3. The factorization is $(x-9)(x+3)$.

6. $(t-5)(t+3)$

7.
$$2n^2 - 20n + 50$$
$$= 2(n^2 - 10n + 25) \quad \text{Removing the common factor}$$

We now factor $n^2 - 10n + 25$. We look for two numbers whose product is 25 and whose sum is -10. Since the constant term is positive and the coefficient of the middle term is negative, we look for factorization of 25 in which both factors are negative.

Pair of Factors	Sum of Factors
$-1, -25$	-26
$-5, -5$	-10

The numbers we need are -5 and -5.
$$n^2 - 10n + 25 = (n-5)(n-5)$$

We must not forget to include the common factor 2.
$$2n^2 - 20n + 50 = 2(n-5)(n-5), \text{ or } 2(n-5)^2$$

8. $2(a-4)(a-4)$, or $2(a-4)^2$

9.
$$a^3 + a^2 - 72a$$
$$= a(a^2 + a - 72) \quad \text{Removing the common factor}$$

We now factor $a^2 + a - 72$. Since the constant term is negative, we look for a factorization of -72 in which one factor is positive and one factor is negative. We consider only pairs of factors in which the positive factor has the larger absolute value, since the sum of the factors, 1, is positive.

Pair of Factors	Sum of Factors
$72, -1$	71
$36, -2$	34
$18, -4$	14
$9, -8$	1

The numbers we need are 9 and -8.
$$a^2 + a - 72 = (a+9)(a-8)$$

We must not forget to include the common factor a.
$$a^3 + a^2 - 72a = a(a+9)(a-8)$$

10. $x(x+9)(x-6)$

11. $14x + x^2 + 45 = x^2 + 14x + 45$

Since the constant term and the middle term are both positive, we look for a factorization of 45 in which both factors are positive. Their sum must be 14.

Pair of Factors	Sum of Factors
$45, 1$	46
$15, 3$	18
$9, 5$	14

The numbers we need are 9 and 5. The factorization is $(x+9)(x+5)$.

12. $(y+8)(y+4)$

13. $3x + x^2 - 10 = x^2 + 3x - 10$

Since the constant term is negative, we look for a factorization of -10 in which one factor is positive and one factor is negative. We consider only pairs of factors in which the positive factor has the larger absolute value, since the sum of the factors, 3, is positive.

Pair of Factors	Sum of Factors
$10, -1$	9
$5, -2$	3

The numbers we need are 5 and -2. The factorization is $(x+5)(x-2)$.

14. $(x+3)(x-2)$

15.
$$3x^2 + 15x + 18$$
$$= 3(x^2 + 5x + 6) \quad \text{Removing the common factor}$$

We now factor $x^2 + 5x + 6$. We look for two numbers whose product is 6 and whose sum is 5. Since 6 and 5 are both positive, we need consider only positive factors.

Pair of Factors	Sum of Factors
$1, 6$	7
$2, 3$	5

The numbers we need are 2 and 3.
$$x^2 + 5x + 6 = (x+2)(x+3)$$

We must not forget to include the common factor 3.
$$3x^2 + 15x + 18 = 3(x+2)(x+3)$$

16. $5(y+1)(y+7)$

17. $56 + x - x^2 = -x^2 + x + 56 = -(x^2 - x - 56)$

We now factor $x^2 - x - 56$. Since the constant term is negative, we look for a factorization of -56 in which one factor is positive and one factor is negative. We consider only pairs of factors in which the negative factor has the larger absolute value, since the sum of the factors, -1, is negative.

Pair of Factors	Sum of Factors
$-56, 1$	-55
$-28, 2$	-26
$-14, 4$	-10
$-8, 7$	-1

The numbers we need are -8 and 7. Thus, $x^2 - x - 56 = (x-8)(x+7)$. We must not forget to include the factor that was factored out earlier:
$$56 + x - x^2 = -(x-8)(x+7), \text{ or}$$
$$(-x+8)(x+7), \text{ or } (8-x)(7+x)$$

18. $(8-y)(4+y)$, or $-(y-8)(y+4)$, or $(-y+8)(y+4)$

19. $32y + 4y^2 - y^3$

There is a common factor, y. We also factor out -1 in order to make the leading coefficient positive.

$$32y + 4y^2 - y^3 = -y(-32 - 4y + y^2)$$
$$= -y(y^2 - 4y - 32)$$

Now we factor $y^2 - 4y - 32$. Since the constant term is negative, we look for a factorization of -32 in which one factor is positive and one factor is negative. We consider only pairs of factors in which the negative factor has the larger absolute value, since the sum of the factors, -4, is negative.

Pair of Factors	Sum of Factors
-32, 1	-31
-16, 2	-14
-8, 4	-4

The numbers we need are -8 and 4. Thus, $y^2 - 4y - 32 = (y - 8)(y + 4)$. We must not forget to include the common factor:

$$32y + 4y^2 - y^3 = -y(y - 8)(y + 4), \text{ or}$$
$$y(-y + 8)(y + 4), \text{ or } y(8 - y)(4 + y)$$

20. $x(8-x)(7+x)$, or $-x(x-8)(x+7)$, or $x(-x+8)(x+7)$

21. $x^4 + 11x^2 - 80$

First make a substitution. We let $u = x^2$, so $u^2 = x^4$. Then we consider $u^2 + 11u - 80$. We look for pairs of factors of -80, one positive and one negative, such that the positive factor has the larger absolute value and the sum of the factors is 11.

Pair of Factors	Sum of Factors
80, -1	79
40, -2	38
20, -4	16
16, -5	11
10, -8	2

The numbers we need are 16 and -5. Then $u^2 + 11u - 80 = (u + 16)(u - 5)$. Replacing u by x^2 we obtain the factorization of the original trinomial: $(x^2 + 16)(x^2 - 5)$

22. $(y^2 + 12)(y^2 - 7)$

23. $x^2 + 12x + 13$

There are no factors of 13 whose sum is 12. This trinomial is not factorable into binomials with integer coefficients. The polynomial is prime.

24. Prime

25. $p^2 - 5pq - 24q^2$

We look for numbers r and s such that $p^2 - 5pq - 24q^2 = (p + rq)(p + sq)$. Our thinking is much the same as if we were factoring $p^2 - 5p - 24$. We look for factors of -24 whose sum is -5, one positive and one negative, such that the negative factor has the larger absolute value.

Pair of Factors	Sum of Factors
-24, 1	-23
-12, 2	-10
-8, 3	-5

The numbers we need are -8 and 3. The factorization is $(p - 8q)(p + 3q)$.

26. $(x + 3y)(x + 9y)$

27. $y^2 + 8yz + 16z^2$

We look for numbers p and q such that $y^2 + 8yz + 16z^2 = (y + pz)(y + qz)$. Our thinking is much the same as if we factor $y^2 + 8y + 16$. Since the constant term is positive and the coefficient of the middle term is negative, we look for a factorization of 16 in which both factors are positive. Their sum must be 8.

Pair of Factors	Sum of Factors
1, 16	17
2, 8	10
4, 4	8

The numbers we need are 4 and 4. The factorization is $(y + 4z)(y + 4z)$, or $(y + 4z)^2$.

28. $(x - 7y)(x - 7y)$, or $(x - 7y)^2$

29. $p^4 + 80p^2 + 79$

Substitute u for p^2 (and hence u^2 for p^4). Consider $u^2 + 80u + 79$. We look for a pair of factors of 79 whose sum is 80. The only positive pair of factors is 1 and 79. These are the numbers we need. Then $u^2 + 80u + 79 = (u + 1)(u + 79)$. Replacing u by p^2 we have $p^4 + 80p^2 + 79 = (p^2 + 1)(p^2 + 79)$.

30. $(x^2 + 1)(x^2 + 49)$

31. $x^2 + 8x + 12 = 0$

$(x + 2)(x + 6) = 0$ From Exercise 1

$x + 2 = 0 \quad or \quad x + 6 = 0$ Using the principle of zero products

$x = -2 \quad or \qquad x = -6$

The solutions are -2 and -6.

32. $-5, -1$

33. $2n^2 + 50 = 20n$

$2n^2 - 20n + 50 = 0$ Subtracting $20n$ on both sides

$2(n - 5)(n - 5) = 0$ From Exercise 7

$n - 5 = 0$ *or* $n - 5 = 0$ Using the
                    principle of zero products
$n = 5$ *or* $n = 5$

The solution is 5.

34. $-4, 8$

35. $a^3 + a^2 = 72a$

$a^3 + a^2 - 72a = 0$ Subtracting $72a$ on both
                                          sides
$a(a + 9)(a - 8) = 0$ From Exercise 9

$a = 0$ *or* $a + 9 = 0$ *or* $a - 8 = 0$
$a = 0$ *or* $a = -9$ *or* $a = 8$

The solutions are 0, -9, and 8.

36. $-7, 0, 8$

37. The x-intercepts are $(-5, 0)$ and $(1, 0)$, so the solutions are -5 and 1.

Check: For -5:

$$\begin{array}{c|c}
x^2 + 4x - 5 = 0 & \\
\hline
(-5)^2 + 4(-5) - 5 \;?\; 0 & \\
25 - 20 - 5 & \\
0 & 0 \quad \text{TRUE}
\end{array}$$

For 1:

$$\begin{array}{c|c}
x^2 + 4x - 5 = 0 & \\
\hline
1^2 + 4 \cdot 1 - 5 \;?\; 0 & \\
1 + 4 - 5 & \\
0 & 0 \quad \text{TRUE}
\end{array}$$

Both numbers check, so they are the solutions.

38. $-2, 3$

39. The x-intercepts are $(-3, 0)$ and $(2, 0)$, so the solutions are -3 and 2.

Check: For -3:

$$\begin{array}{c|c}
x^2 + x - 6 = 0 & \\
\hline
(-3)^2 + (-3) - 6 \;?\; 0 & \\
9 - 3 - 6 & \\
0 & 0 \quad \text{TRUE}
\end{array}$$

For 2:

$$\begin{array}{c|c}
x^2 + x - 6 = 0 & \\
\hline
2^2 + 2 - 6 \;?\; 0 & \\
4 + 2 - 6 & \\
0 & 0 \quad \text{TRUE}
\end{array}$$

Both numbers check, so they are the solutions.

40. $-5, -3$

41. The zeros of $f(x) = x^2 - 4x + 45$ are the solutions of the equation $x^2 - 4x + 45 = 0$. We factor and use the principle of zero products.

$$x^2 - 4x + 45 = 0$$
$$(x - 9)(x + 5) = 0$$

$x - 9 = 0$ *or* $x + 5 = 0$
$x = 9$ *or* $x = -5$

The zeros are 9 and -5.

42. $-5, 4$

43. The zeros of $r(x) = x^3 - 2x^2 - 3x$ are the solutions of the equation $x^3 - 2x^2 - 3x = 0$. We factor and use the principle of zero products.

$$x^3 - 2x^2 - 3x = 0$$
$$x(x^2 - 2x - 3) = 0$$
$$x(x + 1)(x - 3) = 0$$

$x = 0$ *or* $x + 1 = 0$ *or* $x - 3 = 0$
$x = 0$ *or* $x = -1$ *or* $x = 3$

The zeros are 0, -1, and 3.

44. $-5, -2$

45. $x^2 + 4x = 45$

$$x^2 + 4x - 45 = 0$$
$$(x + 9)(x - 5) = 0$$

$x + 9 = 0$ *or* $x - 5 = 0$
$x = -9$ *or* $x = 5$

The solutions are -9 and 5.

46. $-4, 7$

47. $x^2 - 9x = 0$

$$x(x - 9) = 0$$

$x = 0$ *or* $x - 9 = 0$
$x = 0$ *or* $x = 9$

The solutions are 0 and 9.

48. $= 18, 0$

49. $a^3 - 3a^2 = 40a$

$$a^3 - 3a^2 - 40a = 0$$
$$a(a^2 - 3a - 40) = 0$$
$$a(a - 8)(a + 5) = 0$$

$a = 0$ *or* $a - 8 = 0$ *or* $a + 5 = 0$
$a = 0$ *or* $a = 8$ *or* $a = -5$

The solutions are 0, 8, and -5.

50. $-7, 0, 9$

51. $(x-3)(x+2) = 14$
$$x^2 - x - 6 = 14$$
$$x^2 - x - 20 = 0$$
$$(x-5)(x+4) = 0$$
$$x - 5 = 0 \ \ or \ \ x + 4 = 0$$
$$x = 5 \ \ or \ \ \ \ \ x = -4$$
The solutions are 5 and -4.

52. $-3, 1$

53. $$35 - x^2 = 2x$$
$$35 - 2x - x^2 = 0$$
$$(7+x)(5-x) = 0$$
$$7 + x = 0 \ \ \ or \ \ 5 - x = 0$$
$$x = -7 \ \ or \ \ \ \ \ \ 5 = x$$
The solutions are -7 and 5.

54. $-5, 8$

55. From the graph we see that the zeros of $f(x) = x^2 + 10x - 264$ and -22 and 12. We also know that -22 is a zero of $g(x) = x + 22$ and 12 is a zero of $h(x) = x - 12$. Using the principle of zero products in reverse, we have
$$x^2 + 10x - 264 = (x + 22)(x - 12).$$

56. $(x+28)(x-12)$

57. Graph $y = x^2 + 40x + 384$ and find the zeros. They are -24 and -16. We know that -24 is a zero of $g(x) = x + 24$ and -16 is a zero of $h(x) = x + 16$. Using the principle of zero products in reverse, we have
$$x^2 + 40x + 384 = (x + 24)(x + 16).$$

58. $(x+12)(x-25)$

59. Graph $y = x^2 + 26x - 2432$ and find the zeros. They are -64 and 38. We know that -64 is a zero of $g(x) = x + 64$ and 38 is a zero of $h(x) = x - 38$. Using the principle of zero products in reverse, we have
$$x^2 + 26x - 2432 = (x + 64)(x - 38).$$

60. $(x-18)(x-28)$

61. We write a linear function for each zero:
-1 is a zero of $g(x) = x + 1$;
2 is a zero of $h(x) = x - 2$.
Then $f(x) = (x+1)(x-2)$, or $f(x) = x^2 - x - 2$.

62. $f(x) = x^2 - 7x + 10$

63. We write a linear function for each zero:
-7 is a zero of $g(x) = x + 7$;
-10 is a zero of $h(x) = x + 10$.
Then $f(x) = (x+7)(x+10)$, or $f(x) = x^2 + 17x + 70$.

64. $f(x) = x^2 - 5x - 24$

65. We write a linear function for each zero:
0 is a zero of $g(x) = x$;
1 is a zero of $h(x) = x - 1$;
2 is a zero of $k(x) = x - 2$.
Then $f(x) = x(x-1)(x-2)$, or $f(x) = x^3 - 3x^2 + 2x$.

66. $f(x) = x^3 - 2x^2 - 15x$

67.
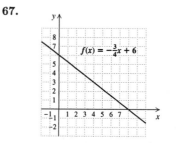

68. $10x^2 + 21x + 8$

69. We use FOIL.
$$(2x - 7)(3x + 2) = 6x^2 + 4x - 21x - 14$$
$$= 6x^2 - 17x - 14$$

70. $\{x | 4 < x < 10\}$, or $(4, 10)$

71. ◈

72. ◈

73. ◈

74. ◈

75. The x-coordinates of the x-intercepts are -1 and 3. These are the solutions of $x^2 - 2x - 3 = 0$.

From the graph we see that the x-values for which $f(x) < 5$ are in the interval $(-2, 4)$. We could also express the solution set as $\{x| -2 < x < 4\}$.

76. $\{-3, 1\}$; $\{x| -4 \le x \le 2\}$, or $[-4, 2]$

77. Answers may vary. A polynomial function of lowest degree that meets the given criteria is of the form $f(x) = ax^3 + bx^2 + cx + d$. Substituting, we have

$$a \cdot 2^3 + b \cdot 2^2 + c \cdot 2 + d = 0,$$
$$a(-1)^3 + b(-1)^2 + c(-1) + d = 0,$$
$$a \cdot 3^3 + b \cdot 3^2 + c \cdot 3 + d = 0,$$
$$a \cdot 0^3 + b \cdot 0^2 + c \cdot 0 + d = 30, \text{ or}$$

$$8a + 4b + 2c + d = 0,$$
$$-a + b - c + d = 0,$$
$$27a + 9b + 3c + d = 0,$$
$$d = 30.$$

Solving the system of equations, we get $(5, -20, 5, 30)$, so the corresponding function is $f(x) = 5x^3 - 20x^2 + 5x + 30$.

78. Answers may vary; $g(x) = 3x^3 - 9x^2 - 39x + 45$

79. Graph $y_1 = -x^2 + 13.80x$ and $y_2 = 47.61$ and use the Intersect feature to find the first coordinate of the point of intersection. The solution is 6.90.

80. $-3.33, 5.15$

81. Graph $y_1 = x^3 - 3.48x^2 + x$ and $y_2 = 3.48$ and use the Intersect feature to find the first coordinates of the points of intersection. The solution is 3.48.

82. $\left(x + \dfrac{4}{5}\right)\left(x - \dfrac{1}{5}\right)$

83. $y^2 - \dfrac{8}{49} + \dfrac{2}{7}y = y^2 + \dfrac{2}{7}y - \dfrac{8}{49}$

We look for factors of $-\dfrac{8}{49}$ whose sum is $\dfrac{2}{7}$. The factors are $\dfrac{4}{7}$ and $-\dfrac{2}{7}$. The factorization is $\left(y + \dfrac{4}{7}\right)\left(y - \dfrac{2}{7}\right).$

84. $(y - 0.1)(y + 0.5)$

85. $x^{2a} + 5x^a - 24$

Substitute u for x^a (and u^2 for x^{2a}). We factor $u^2 + 5u - 24$. We look for factors of -24 whose sum is 5. The factors are 8 and -3. We have $u^2 + 5u - 24 = (u + 8)(u - 3)$. Replace u by x^a: $x^{2a} + 5x^a - 24 = (x^a + 8)(x^a - 3)$.

86. $(x - 4)(x + 8)$

87. $x^2 + mx + 75$

All such m are the sums of the factors of 75.

Pair of Factors	Sum of Factors
75, 1	76
$-75, -1$	-76
25, 3	28
$-25, -3$	-28
15, 5	20
$-15, -5$	-20

m can be 76, -76, 28, -28, 20, or -20.

88. $31, -31, 14, -14, 4, -4$

89. $20(-365) = -7300$ and $20 + (-365) = -345$ so the other factor is $(x - 365)$.

Exercise Set 6.3

1. $6x^2 - 5x - 25$

We will use the FOIL method.

1. There is no common factor (other than 1 or -1.)
2. Factor the first term, $6x^2$. The factors are $6x$, x and $3x$, $2x$. We have these possibilities:

   $(6x+ \quad)(x+ \quad)$ or $(3x+ \quad)(2x+ \quad)$

3. Factor the last term, -25. The possibilities are $25(-1)$, $-25 \cdot 1$, and $-5 \cdot 5$.
4. We need factors for which the sum of the products (the "outer" and "inner" parts of FOIL) is the middle term, $-5x$. Try some possibilities and check by multiplying.

   $$(6x - 5)(x + 5) = 6x^2 + 25x - 25$$

   We try again.

   $$(3x + 5)(2x - 5) = 6x^2 - 5x - 25$$

   The factorization is $(3x + 5)(2x - 5)$.

2. $(3x + 2)(x - 6)$

3. $10y^3 - 12y - 7y^2 = 10y^3 - 7y^2 - 12y$

We will use the grouping method.

1. Look for a common factor. We factor out y:

   $$y(10y^2 - 7y - 12)$$

2. Factor the trinomial $10y^2 - 7y - 12$. Multiply the leading coefficient, 10, and the constant, -12.

$$10(-12) = -120$$

3. Try to factor -120 so the sum of the factors is -7. We need only consider pairs of factors in which the negative factor has the larger absolute value, since their sum is negative.

Pair of Factors	Sum of Factors
$-120, 1$	-119
$-30, 4$	-26
$-15, 8$	-7

4. We split the middle term, $-12y$, using the results of step (3).

$$-7y = -15y + 8y$$

5. Factor by grouping:
$$10y^2 - 7y - 12 = 10y^2 - 15y + 8y - 12$$
$$= 5y(2y - 3) + 4(2y - 3)$$
$$= (2y - 3)(5y + 4)$$

We must include the common factor to get a factorization of the original trinomial:

$$10y^3 - 12y - 7y^2 = y(2y - 3)(5y + 4)$$

4. $x(3x - 5)(2x + 3)$

5. $24a^2 - 14a + 2$

We will use the FOIL method.

1. Factor out the common factor, 2:

$$2(12a^2 - 7a + 1)$$

2. Now we factor the trinomial $12a^2 - 7a + 1$. Factor the first term, $12a^2$. The factors are $12a$, a and $6a$, $2a$ and $4a$, $3a$. We have these possibilities: $(12a+ \ )(a+ \ )$, $(6a+ \ )(2a+ \ )$, $(4a+ \ )(3a+ \ )$.

3. Factor the last term, 1. The possibilities are $1 \cdot 1$ and $-1(-1)$.

4. Look for factors such that the sum of the products is the middle term, $-7a$. Trial and error leads us to the correct factorization:

$$12a^2 - 7a + 1 = (4a - 1)(3a - 1)$$

We must include the common factor to get a factorization of the original trinomial:

$$24a^2 - 14a + 2 = 2(4a - 1)(3a - 1)$$

6. $(3a - 4)(a - 2)$

7. $35y^2 + 34y + 8$

We will use the grouping method.

1. There is no common factor (other than 1 or -1).

2. Multiply the leading coefficient, 35, and the constant, 8: $35(8) = 280$

3. Try to factor 280 so the sum of the factors is 34. We need only consider pairs of positive factors since 280 and 34 are both positive.

Pair of Factors	Sum of Factors
$280, \ 1$	281
$140, \ 2$	142
$70, \ 4$	74
$56, \ 5$	61
$40, \ 7$	47
$28, 10$	38
$20, 14$	34

4. Split $34y$ using the results of step (3):

$$34y = 20y + 14y$$

5. Factor by grouping:
$$35y^2 + 34y + 8 = 35y^2 + 20y + 14y + 8$$
$$= 5y(7y + 4) + 2(7y + 4)$$
$$= (7y + 4)(5y + 2)$$

8. $(3a + 2)(3a + 4)$

9. $4t + 10t^2 - 6 = 10t^2 + 4t - 6$

We will use the FOIL method.

1. Factor out the common factor, 2:

$$2(5t^2 + 2t - 3)$$

2. Now we factor the trinomial $5t^2 + 2t - 3$. Factor the first term, $5t^2$. The factors are $5t$ and t. We have this possibility: $(5t+ \ )(t+ \ )$

3. Factor the last term, -3. The possibilities are $(1)(-3)$ and $(-1)3$ as well as $(-3)(1)$ and $3(-1)$.

4. Look for factors such that the sum of the products is the middle term, $2t$. Trial and error leads us to the correct factorization:

$$5t^2 + 2t - 3 = (5t - 3)(t + 1)$$

We must include the common factor to get a factorization of the original trinomial:

$$4t + 10t^2 - 6 = 2(5t - 3)(t + 1)$$

10. $2(5x + 3)(3x - 1)$

11. $8x^2 - 16 - 28x = 8x^2 - 28x - 16$

We will use the grouping method.

1. Factor out the common factor, 4:

$$4(2x^2 - 7x - 4)$$

2. Now we factor the trinomial $2x^2 - 7x - 4$. Multiply the leading coefficient, 2, and the constant, -4: $2(-4) = -8$

3. Factor -8 so the sum of the factors is -7. We need only consider pairs of factors in which the negative factor has the larger absolute value, since their sum is negative.

Pair of Factors	Sum of Factors
$-4,\ 2$	-2
$-8,\ 1$	-7

4. Split $-7x$ using the results of step (3):
$$-7x = -8x + x$$

5. Factor by grouping:
$$2x^2 - 7x - 4 = 2x^2 - 8x + x - 4$$
$$= 2x(x - 4) + (x - 4)$$
$$= (x - 4)(2x + 1)$$

We must include the common factor to get a factorization of the original trinomial:
$$8x^2 - 16 - 28x = 4(x - 4)(2x + 1)$$

12. $6(3x - 4)(x + 1)$

13. $14x^4 - 19x^3 - 3x^2$

We will use the grouping method.

1. Factor out the common factor, x^2:
$$x^2(14x^2 - 19x - 3)$$

2. Now we factor the trinomial $14x^2 - 19x - 3$. Multiply the leading coefficient, 14, and the constant, -3: $14(-3) = -42$

3. Factor -42 so the sum of the factors is -19. We need only consider pairs of factors in which the negative factor has the larger absolute value, since the sum is negative.

Pair of Factors	Sum of Factors
$-42,\ 1$	-41
$-21,\ 2$	-19
$-14,\ 3$	-11
$-7,\ 6$	-1

4. Split $-19x$ using the results of step (3):
$$-19x = -21x + 2x$$

5. Factor by grouping:
$$14x^2 - 19x - 3 = 14x^2 - 21x + 2x - 3$$
$$= 7x(2x - 3) + 2x - 3$$
$$= (2x - 3)(7x + 1)$$

We must include the common factor to get a factorization of the original trinomial:
$$14x^4 - 19x^3 - 3x^2 = x^2(2x - 3)(7x + 1)$$

14. $2x^2(5x - 2)(7x - 4)$

15. $12a^2 - 4a - 16$

We will use the FOIL method.

1. Factor out the common factor, 4:
$$4(3a^2 - a - 4)$$

2. We now factor the trinomial $3a^2 - a - 4$. Factor the first term, $3a^2$. The possibility is $(3a+\quad)(a+\quad)$.

3. Factor the last term, -4. The possibilities are $-4 \cdot 1$, $4(-1)$, and $-2 \cdot 2$.

4. We need factors for which the sum of the products is the middle term, $-a$. Trial and error leads us to the correct factorization:
$$3a^2 - a - 4 = (3a - 4)(a + 1)$$

We must include the common factor to get a factorization of the original trinomial:
$$12a^2 - 4a - 16 = 4(3a - 4)(a + 1)$$

16. $2(6a + 5)(a - 2)$

17. $9x^2 + 15x + 4$

We will use the grouping method.

1. There is no common factor (other than 1 or -1).

2. Multiply the leading coefficient and constant: $9(4) = 36$

3. Factor 36 so the sum of the factors is 15. We need only consider pairs of positive factors since 36 and 15 are both positive.

Pair of Factors	Sum of Factors
$36,\ \ 1$	37
$18,\ \ 2$	20
$12,\ \ 3$	15
$9,\ \ 4$	13
$6,\ \ 6$	12

4. Split $15x$ using the results of step (3):
$$15x = 12x + 3x$$

5. Factor by grouping:
$$9x^2 + 15x + 4 = 9x^2 + 12x + 3x + 4$$
$$= 3x(3x + 4) + 3x + 4$$
$$= (3x + 4)(3x + 1)$$

18. $(3y - 2)(2y + 1)$

19. $8 - 6z - 9z^2$

We will use the FOIL method.

1. There is no common factor (other than 1 or -1).

2. Factor the first term, 8. The possibilities are $(8+ \quad)(1+ \quad)$ and $(4+ \quad)(2+ \quad)$.

3. Factor the last term, $-9z^2$. The possibilities are $-9 \cdot z$, $-3z \cdot 3z$, and $9z(-z)$.

4. We need factors for which the sum of products is the middle term, $-6z$. Trial and error leads us to the correct factorization:

$$(4 + 3z)(2 - 3z)$$

20. $(3 - a)(1 + 12a)$

21. $18xy^3 + 3xy^2 - 10xy$

We will use the FOIL method.

1. Factor out the common factor, xy.

$$xy(18y^2 + 3y - 10)$$

2. We now factor the trinomial $18y^2 + 3y - 10$. Factor the first term, $18y^2$. The possibilities are $(18y+ \quad)(y+ \quad)$, $(9y+ \quad)(2y+ \quad)$, and $(6y+ \quad)(3y+ \quad)$.

3. Factor the last term, -10. The possibilities are $-10 \cdot 1$, $-5 \cdot 2$, $10(-1)$ and $5(-2)$.

4. We need factors for which the sum of the products is the middle term, $3y$. Trial and error leads us to the correct factorization.

$$18y^2 + 3y - 10 = (6y + 5)(3y - 2)$$

We must include the common factor to get a factorization of the original trinomial:

$$18xy^3 + 3xy^2 - 10xy = xy(6y + 5)(3y - 2)$$

22. $xy^2(3x + 1)(x - 2)$

23. $24x^2 - 2 - 47x = 24x^2 - 47x - 2$

We will use the grouping method.

1. There is no common factor (other than 1 or -1).

2. Multiply the leading coefficient and the constant: $24(-2) = -48$

3. Factor -48 so the sum of the factors is -47. The desired factorization is $-48 \cdot 1$.

4. Split $-47x$ using the results of step (3):

$$-47x = -48x + x$$

5. Factor by grouping:

$$\begin{aligned} 24x^2 - 47x - 2 &= 24x^2 - 48x + x - 2 \\ &= 24x(x - 2) + (x - 2) \\ &= (x - 2)(24x + 1) \end{aligned}$$

24. $(5z + 1)(3z - 10)$

25. $63x^3 + 111x^2 + 36x$

We will use the FOIL method.

1. Factor out the common factor, $3x$.

$$3x(21x^2 + 37x + 12)$$

2. Now we will factor the trinomial $21x^2 + 37x + 12$. Factor the first term, $21x^2$. The factors are $21x$, x and $7x$, $3x$. We have these possibilities: $(21x+ \quad)(x+ \quad)$ and $(7x+ \quad)(3x+ \quad)$.

3. Factor the last term, 12. The possibilities are $12 \cdot 1$, $(-12)(-1)$, $6 \cdot 2$, $(-6)(-2)$, $4 \cdot 3$, and $(-4)(-3)$ as well as $1 \cdot 12$, $(-1)(-12)$, $2 \cdot 6$, $(-2)(-6)$, $3 \cdot 4$, and $(-3)(-4)$.

4. Look for factors such that the sum of the products is the middle term, $37x$. Trial and error leads us to the correct factorization:

$$(7x + 3)(3x + 4)$$

We must include the common factor to get a factorization of the original trinomial:

$$63x^3 + 111x^2 + 36x = 3x(7x + 3)(3x + 4)$$

26. $5t(5t + 4)(2t + 3)$

27. $24x^4 + 2x^2 - 15$

We will use the grouping method. Substitute u for x^2 (and u^2 for x^4), and factor $24u^2 + 2u - 15$.

1. There is no common factor (other than 1 or -1).

2. Multiply the leading coefficient and the constant: $24(-15) = -360$

3. Factor -360 so the sum of the factors is 2. The desired factorization is $-18 \cdot 20$.

4. Split $2u$ using the results of step (3):

$$2u = -18u + 20u$$

5. Factor by grouping:

$$\begin{aligned} 24u^2 + 2u - 15 &= 24u^2 - 18u + 20u - 15 \\ &= 6u(4u - 3) + 5(4u - 3) \\ &= (4u - 3)(6u + 5) \end{aligned}$$

Replace u by x^2 to obtain the factorization of the original trinomial:

$$24x^4 + 2x^2 - 15 = (4x^2 - 3)(6x^2 + 5)$$

28. $4(5y^2 + 3)(2y^2 - 1)$

29.
$$6x^2 - 5x - 25 = 0$$
$$(3x + 5)(2x - 5) = 0 \quad \text{From Exercise 1}$$
$$3x + 5 = 0 \quad or \quad 2x - 5 = 0 \quad \text{Using the}$$
$$\text{principle of zero products}$$
$$3x = -5 \quad or \quad 2x = 5$$
$$x = -\frac{5}{3} \quad or \quad x = \frac{5}{2}$$

The solutions are $-\dfrac{5}{3}$ and $\dfrac{5}{2}$.

30. $-\dfrac{2}{3}, 6$

31. $9z^2 + 6z = 8$

$0 = 8 - 6z - 9z^2$

$0 = (4 + 3z)(2 - 3z)$ From Exercise 19

$4 + 3z = 0$ *or* $2 - 3z = 0$ Using the

principle of zero products

$3z = -4$ *or* $2 = 3z$

$z = -\dfrac{4}{3}$ *or* $\dfrac{2}{3} = z$

The solutions are $-\dfrac{4}{3}$ and $\dfrac{2}{3}$.

32. $-\dfrac{1}{12}, 3$

33. $63x^3 + 111x^2 + 36x = 0$

$3x(7x + 3)(3x + 4) = 0$ From Exercise 25

$3x = 0$ *or* $7x + 3 = 0$ *or* $3x + 4 = 0$

$x = 0$ *or* $7x = -3$ *or* $3x = -4$

$x = 0$ *or* $x = -\dfrac{3}{7}$ *or* $x = -\dfrac{4}{3}$

The solutions are 0, $-\dfrac{3}{7}$, and $-\dfrac{4}{3}$.

34. $-\dfrac{3}{2}, -\dfrac{4}{5}, 0$

35. $3x^2 - 8x + 4 = 0$

$(3x - 2)(x - 2) = 0$ Factoring

$3x - 2 = 0$ *or* $x - 2 = 0$

$3x = 2$ *or* $x = 2$

$x = \dfrac{2}{3}$ *or* $x = 2$

The solutions are $\dfrac{2}{3}$ and 2.

36. $\dfrac{1}{3}, \dfrac{4}{3}$

37. $4t^3 + 11t^2 + 6t = 0$

$t(4t^2 + 11t + 6) = 0$

$t(4t + 3)(t + 2) = 0$

$t = 0$ *or* $4t + 3 = 0$ *or* $t + 2 = 0$

$t = 0$ *or* $4t = -3$ *or* $t = -2$

$t = 0$ *or* $t = -\dfrac{3}{4}$ *or* $t = -2$

The solutions are 0, $-\dfrac{3}{4}$, and -2.

38. $-\dfrac{3}{4}, -\dfrac{1}{2}, 0$

39. $6x^2 = 13x + 5$

$6x^2 - 13x - 5 = 0$

$(2x - 5)(3x + 1) = 0$

$2x - 5 = 0$ *or* $3x + 1 = 0$

$2x = 5$ *or* $3x = -1$

$x = \dfrac{5}{2}$ *or* $x = -\dfrac{1}{3}$

The solutions are $\dfrac{5}{2}$ and $-\dfrac{1}{3}$.

40. $-\dfrac{6}{5}, \dfrac{1}{8}$

41. $x(5 + 12x) = 28$

$5x + 12x^2 = 28$

$5x + 12x^2 - 28 = 0$

$12x^2 + 5x - 28 = 0$ Rearranging

$(4x + 7)(3x - 4) = 0$

$4x + 7 = 0$ *or* $3x - 4 = 0$

$4x = -7$ *or* $3x = 4$

$x = -\dfrac{7}{4}$ *or* $x = \dfrac{4}{3}$

The solutions are $-\dfrac{7}{4}$ and $\dfrac{4}{3}$.

42. $-\dfrac{5}{7}, \dfrac{2}{3}$

43. The zeros of $f(x) = 2x^2 - 13x - 7$ are the roots, or
solutions, of the equation $2x^2 - 13x - 7 = 0$.

$2x^2 - 13x - 7 = 0$

$(2x + 1)(x - 7) = 0$

$2x + 1 = 0$ *or* $x - 7 = 0$

$2x = -1$ *or* $x = 7$

$x = -\dfrac{1}{2}$ *or* $x = 7$

The zeros are $-\dfrac{1}{2}$ and 7.

44. $-\dfrac{3}{2}, -\dfrac{2}{3}$

45. We set $f(a)$ equal to 8.

$a^2 + 12a + 40 = 8$

$a^2 + 12a + 32 = 0$

$(a + 8)(a + 4) = 0$

$a + 8 = 0$ *or* $a + 4 = 0$

$a = -8$ *or* $a = -4$

The values of a for which $f(a) = 8$ are -8 and -4.

46. $-9, -5$

47. We set $g(a)$ equal to 12.
$$2a^2 + 5a = 12$$
$$2a^2 + 5a - 12 = 0$$
$$(2a - 3)(a + 4) = 0$$
$$2a - 3 = 0 \quad or \quad a + 4 = 0$$
$$2a = 3 \quad or \quad a = -4$$
$$a = \frac{3}{2} \quad or \quad a = -4$$

The values of a for which $g(a) = 12$ are $\dfrac{3}{2}$ and -4.

48. $\dfrac{1}{2}, 7$

49. We set $h(a)$ equal to -27.
$$12a + a^2 = -27$$
$$12a + a^2 + 27 = 0$$
$$a^2 + 12a + 27 = 0 \quad \text{Rearranging}$$
$$(a + 3)(a + 9) = 0$$
$$a + 3 = 0 \quad or \quad a + 9 = 0$$
$$a = -3 \quad or \quad a = -9$$

The values of a for which $h(a) = -27$ are -3 and -9.

50. $-4, 8$

51. $f(x) = \dfrac{3}{x^2 - 4x - 5}$

$f(x)$ cannot be calculated for any x-value for which the denominator, $x^2 - 4x - 5$, is 0. To find the excluded values, we solve:
$$x^2 - 4x - 5 = 0$$
$$(x - 5)(x + 1) = 0$$
$$x - 5 = 0 \quad or \quad x + 1 = 0$$
$$x = 5 \quad or \quad x = -1$$

The domain of f is $\{x | x$ is a real number and $x \neq 5$ and $x \neq -1\}$.

52. $\{x | x$ is a real number and $x \neq 6$ and $x \neq 1\}$

53. $f(x) = \dfrac{x - 5}{9x - 18x^2}$

$f(x)$ cannot be calculated for any x-value for which the denominator, $9x - 18x^2$, is 0. To find the excluded values, we solve:
$$9x - 18x^2 = 0$$
$$9x(1 - 2x) = 0$$

$$9x = 0 \quad or \quad 1 - 2x = 0$$
$$x = 0 \quad or \quad -2x = -1$$
$$x = 0 \quad or \quad x = \frac{1}{2}$$

The domain of f is $\{x | x$ is a real number and $x \neq 0$ and $x \neq \dfrac{1}{2}\}$.

54. $\left\{x | x \text{ is a real number and } x \neq 0 \text{ and } x \neq \dfrac{1}{5}\right\}$

55. $f(x) = \dfrac{7}{5x^3 - 35x^2 + 50x}$

$f(x)$ cannot be calculated for any x-value for which the denominator, $5x^3 - 35x^2 + 50x$, is 0. To find the excluded values, we solve:
$$5x^3 - 35x^2 + 50x = 0$$
$$5x(x^2 - 7x + 10) = 0$$
$$5x(x - 2)(x - 5) = 0$$
$$5x = 0 \quad or \quad x - 2 = 0 \quad or \quad x - 5 = 0$$
$$x = 0 \quad or \quad x = 2 \quad or \quad x = 5$$

The domain of f is $\{x | x$ is a real number and $x \neq 0$ and $x \neq 2$ and $x \neq 5\}$.

56. $\{x | x$ is a real number and $x \neq 0$ and $x \neq 3$ and $x \neq -2\}$

57. $(2x + 0.1)(2x - 0.1) = (2x)^2 - (0.1)^2$
$$= 4x^2 - 0.01$$

58. -2

59. Write the equation in slope-intercept form, $y = mx + b$ where m is the slope and b is the y-intercept.
$$4x - 3y = 8$$
$$-3y = -4x + 8$$
$$y = \frac{4}{3}x - \frac{8}{3}$$

The slope is $\dfrac{4}{3}$, and the y-intercept is $\left(0, -\dfrac{8}{3}\right)$.

60. $\{27, -27\}$

61. $|5x - 6| \leq 39$
$$-39 \leq 5x - 6 \leq 39$$
$$-33 \leq 5x \leq 45$$
$$-\frac{33}{5} \leq x \leq 9$$

The solution set is $\left\{x \left| -\dfrac{33}{5} \leq x \leq 9\right.\right\}$, or $\left[-\dfrac{33}{5}, 9\right]$.

62. $\left\{x \middle| x < -\dfrac{33}{5} \text{ or } x > 9\right\}$, or $\left(-\infty, -\dfrac{33}{5}\right) \cup (9, \infty)$

63.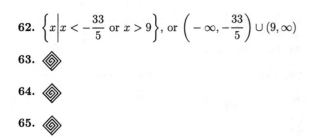

64. ◈

65. ◈

66. ◈

67. Graph $y = 4x^2 + 120x + 675$ and find the zeros. They are -7.5 and -22.5, or $-\dfrac{15}{2}$ and $-\dfrac{45}{2}$. We know that $-\dfrac{15}{2}$ is a zero of $g(x) = 2x + 15$ and $-\dfrac{45}{2}$ is a zero of $h(x) = 2x + 45$. We have $4x^2 + 120x + 675 = (2x + 15)(2x + 45)$.

68. $(2x + 63)(2x + 19)$

69. First factor out the largest common factor.
$$3x^3 + 150x^2 - 3672x = 3x(x^2 + 50x - 1224).$$

Now graph $y = x^2 + 50x - 1224$ and find the zeros. They are -68, and 18. We know that -68 is a zero of $g(x) = x + 68$, and 18 is a zero of $h(x) = x - 18$. We have $x^2 + 50x - 1224 = (x + 68)(x - 18)$, so $3x^3 + 150x^2 - 3672x = 3x(x + 68)(x - 18)$.

70. $5x^2(x + 20)(x - 16)$

71.
$$(8x + 11)(12x^2 - 5x - 2) = 0$$
$$(8x + 11)(3x - 2)(4x + 1) = 0$$
$$8x + 11 = 0 \quad \text{or} \quad 3x - 2 = 0 \quad \text{or} \quad 4x + 1 = 0$$
$$8x = -11 \quad \text{or} \quad 3x = 2 \quad \text{or} \quad 4x = -1$$
$$x = -\dfrac{11}{8} \quad \text{or} \quad x = \dfrac{2}{3} \quad \text{or} \quad x = -\dfrac{1}{4}$$
The solutions are $-\dfrac{11}{8}$, $\dfrac{2}{3}$, and $-\dfrac{1}{4}$.

72. $-2, 2$

73.
$$(x - 2)^3 = x^3 - 2$$
$$x^3 - 6x^2 + 12x - 8 = x^3 - 2$$
$$0 = 6x^2 - 12x + 6$$
$$0 = 6(x^2 - 2x + 1)$$
$$0 = 6(x - 1)(x - 1)$$
$$x - 1 = 0 \quad \text{or} \quad x - 1 = 0$$
$$x = 1 \quad \text{or} \quad x = 1$$
The solution 1.

74. $(2x - 9)(3x - 22)$

75. $2a^4b^6 - 3a^2b^3 - 20$

Let $u = a^2b^3$ (and $u^2 = a^4b^6$). Factor $2u^2 - 3u - 20$. We will use the FOIL method.

1. There is no common factor (other than 1 or -1).
2. Factor the first term, $2u^2$. The factors are $2u$, u. The possibility is $(2u+\quad)(u+\quad)$.
3. Factor the last term, -20. The possibilities are $-20 \cdot 1$, $-10 \cdot 2$, $-5 \cdot 4$, $-4 \cdot 5$, $-2 \cdot 10$, and $-1 \cdot 20$.
4. We need factors for which the sum of the products is the middle term, $-3u$. Trial and error leads us to the factorization: $(2u + 5)(u - 4)$. Replace u by a^2b^3. We have $(2a^2b^3 + 5)(a^2b^3 - 4)$.

76. $5(x^4y^3 + 4)(x^4y^3 + 3)$

77. $4x^{2a} - 4x^a - 3$

Let $u = x^a$ (and $u^2 = x^{2a}$). Factor $4u^2 - 4u - 3$. We will use the grouping method. Multiply the leading coefficient and the constant: $4(-3) = -12$. Factor -12 so the sum of the factors is -4. The desired factorizations is $-6 \cdot 2$.

Split the middle term and factor by grouping.
$$4u^2 - 4u - 3 = 4u^2 - 6u + 2u - 3$$
$$= 2u(2u - 3) + (2u - 3)$$
$$= (2u - 3)(2u + 1)$$

Replace u by x^a. The factorization is $(2x^a - 3)(2x^a + 1)$.

Exercise Set 6.4

1. $x^2 + 8x + 16 = (x + 4)^2$
Find the square terms and write the quantities that were squared with a plus sign between them.

2. $(t + 3)^2$

3. $a^2 - 16a + 64 = (a - 8)^2$
Find the square terms and write the quantities that were squared with a minus sign between them.

4. $(a - 7)^2$

5. $2a^2 + 8a + 8$
$= 2(a^2 + 4a + 4)$ Factoring out the common factor
$= 2(a + 2)^2$ Factoring the perfect-square trinomial

6. $4(a - 2)^2$

7. $y^2 + 36 - 12y$

$= y^2 - 12y + 36$ Changing order

$= (y - 6)^2$ Factoring the perfect-square
           trinomial

8. $(y + 6)^2$

9. $24a^2 + a^3 + 144a$

$= a^3 + 24a^2 + 144a$ Changing order

$= a(a^2 + 24a + 144)$ Factoring out the
                common factor

$= a(a + 12)^2$ Factoring the perfect-square
                trinomial

10. $y(y - 9)^2$

11. $32x^2 + 48x + 18$

$= 2(16x^2 + 24x + 9)$ Factoring out the
                common factor

$= 2(4x + 3)^2$ Factoring the perfect-square
                trinomial

12. $2(x - 10)^2$

13. $64 + 25a^2 - 80a$

$= 25a^2 - 80a + 64$ Changing order

$= (5a - 8)^2$ Factoring the perfect-square
                trinomial

14. $(1 - 4d)^2$

15. $0.25x^2 + 0.30x + 0.09 = (0.5x + 0.3)^2$

Find the square terms and write
the quantities that were squared
with a plus sign between them.

16. $(0.2x - 0.7)^2$

17. $p^2 - 2pq + q^2 = (p - q)^2$

18. $(m + n)^2$

19. $a^4 - 10a^2 + 25 = (a^2)^2 - 10a^2 + 25 = (a^2 - 5)^2$

20. $(n^2 + 4)^2$

21. $25a^2 - 30ab + 9b^2 = (5a - 3b)^2$

22. $(7p - 6q)^2$

23. $t^8 + 2t^4s^4 + s^8 = (t^4 + s^4)^2$

24. $(a^2 + b^2)^2$

25. $x^2 - 16 = x^2 - 4^2 = (x + 4)(x - 4)$

26. $(y + 10)(y - 10)$

27. $p^2 - 49 = p^2 - 7^2 = (p + 7)(p - 7)$

28. $(m + 8)(m - 8)$

29. $a^2b^2 - 81 = (ab)^2 - 9^2 = (ab + 9)(ab - 9)$

30. $(pq + 5)(pq - 5)$

31. $6x^2 - 6y^2$

$= 6(x^2 - y^2)$ Factoring out the common
                factor

$= 6(x + y)(x - y)$ Factoring the difference
                of squares

32. $8(x + y)(x - y)$

33. $7xy^4 - 7xz^4$

$= 7x(y^4 - z^4)$

$= 7x[(y^2)^2 - (z^2)^2]$

$= 7x(y^2 + z^2)(y^2 - z^2)$

$= 7x(y^2 + z^2)(y + z)(y - z)$

34. $25a(b^2 + z^2)(b + z)(b - z)$

35. $4a^3 - 49a = a(4a^2 - 49)$

$= a[(2a)^2 - 7^2]$

$= a(2a + 7)(2a - 7)$

36. $x^2(3x + 5)(3x - 5)$

37. $3x^8 - 3y^8$

$= 3(x^8 - y^8)$

$= 3[(x^4)^2 - (y^4)^2]$

$= 3(x^4 + y^4)(x^4 - y^4)$

$= 3(x^4 + y^4)[(x^2)^2 - (y^2)^2]$

$= 3(x^4 + y^4)(x^2 + y^2)(x^2 - y^2)$

$= 3(x^4 + y^4)(x^2 + y^2)(x + y)(x - y)$

38. $a^2(3a + b)(3a - b)$

39. $9a^4 - 25a^2b^4 = a^2(9a^2 - 25b^4)$

$= a^2[(3a)^2 - (5b^2)^2]$

$= a^2(3a + 5b^2)(3a - 5b^2)$

40. $x^2(4x^2 + 11y^2)(4x^2 - 11y^2)$

41. $\dfrac{1}{25} - x^2 = \left(\dfrac{1}{5}\right)^2 - x^2$

$= \left(\dfrac{1}{5} + x\right)\left(\dfrac{1}{5} - x\right)$

42. $\left(\dfrac{1}{4} + y\right)\left(\dfrac{1}{4} - y\right)$

43. $(a+b)^2 - 9 = (a+b)^2 - 3^2$
$$= [(a+b)+3][(a+b)-3]$$
$$= (a+b+3)(a+b-3)$$

44. $(p+q+5)(p+q-5)$

45. $36 - (x+y)^2 = 6^2 - (x+y)^2$
$$= [6+(x+y)][6-(x+y)]$$
$$= (6+x+y)(6-x-y)$$

46. $(7+a+b)(7-a-b)$

47. $\quad m^3 - 7m^2 - 4m + 28$
$= m^2(m-7) - 4(m-7)$ Factoring by grouping
$= (m-7)(m^2-4)$
$= (m-7)(m+2)(m-2)$ Factoring the difference of squares

48. $(x+8)(x+1)(x-1)$

49. $\quad a^3 - ab^2 - 2a^2 + 2b^2$
$= a(a^2-b^2) - 2(a^2-b^2)$ Factoring by grouping
$= (a^2-b^2)(a-2)$
$= (a+b)(a-b)(a-2)$ Factoring the difference of squares

50. $(p+5)(p-5)(q+3)$

51. $\quad x^2 + 8x + 16 = 0$
$(x+4)^2 = 0$ From Exercise 1
$(x+4)(x+4) = 0$
$x+4 = 0 \quad or \quad x+4 = 0$
$x = -4 \quad or \qquad x = -4$
The solution is -4.

52. 7

53. $\qquad x^2 = 16$
$x^2 - 16 = 0$
$(x+4)(x+4) = 0$ From Exercise 25
$x+4 = 0 \quad or \quad x-4 = 0$
$x = -4 \quad or \qquad x = 4$
The solutions are -4 and 4.

54. $-10, 10$

55. $\qquad a^2 + 1 = 2a$
$a^2 - 2a + 1 = 0$
$(a-1)(a-1) = 0$
$a-1 = 0 \quad or \quad a-1 = 0$
$a = 1 \quad or \qquad a = 1$
The solution is 1.

56. 4

57. $\quad 2x^2 - 24x + 72 = 0$
$2(x^2 - 12x + 36) = 0$
$2(x-6)(x-6) = 0$
$x-6 = 0 \quad or \quad x-6 = 0$
$x = 6 \quad or \qquad x = 6$
The solution is 6.

58. -8

59. $\qquad x^2 - 9 = 0$
$(x+3)(x-3) = 0$
$x+3 = 0 \quad or \quad x-3 = 0$
$x = -3 \quad or \qquad x = 3$
The solutions are -3 and 3.

60. $-8, 8$

61. $\qquad a^2 = \dfrac{1}{25}$
$a^2 - \dfrac{1}{25} = 0$
$\left(a + \dfrac{1}{5}\right)\left(a - \dfrac{1}{5}\right) = 0$
$a + \dfrac{1}{5} = 0 \quad or \quad a - \dfrac{1}{5} = 0$
$a = -\dfrac{1}{5} \quad or \qquad a = \dfrac{1}{5}$
The solutions are $-\dfrac{1}{5}$ and $\dfrac{1}{5}$.

62. $-\dfrac{1}{10}, \dfrac{1}{10}$

63. $\qquad t^4 - 26t^2 + 25 = 0$
$(t^2)^2 - 26t^2 + 25 = 0$
$(t^2-1)(t^2-25) = 0$
$(t+1)(t-1)(t+5)(t-5) = 0$
$t+1 = 0 \quad or \quad t-1 = 0 \ or \ t+5 = 0 \quad or \ t-5 = 0$
$t = -1 \ or \quad t = 1 \ or \quad t = -5 \ or \quad t = 5$
The solutions are -1, 1, -5, and 5.

64. $-3, -2, 2, 3$

65.
$$x^3 + 3 = 3x^2 + x$$
$$x^3 - 3x^2 - x + 3 = 0$$
$$x^2(x - 3) - (x - 3) = 0$$
$$(x - 3)(x^2 - 1) = 0$$
$$(x - 3)(x + 1)(x - 1) = 0$$
$$x - 3 = 0 \ or \ x + 1 = 0 \ \ or \ x - 1 = 0$$
$$x = 3 \ or \ \ \ \ \ x = -1 \ or \ \ \ \ \ x = 1$$
The solutions are 3, -1, and 1.

66. $-4, -1, 4$

67. The polynomial $x^2 - 3x - 7$ is prime. We solve the equation by graphing $y = x^2 - 3x - 7$ and finding the zeros. They are approximately -1.541 and 4.541. These are the solutions.

68. $0.209, 4.791$

69. The polynomial $2x^2 + 8x + 1$ is prime. We solve the equation by graphing $y = 2x^2 + 8x + 1$ and finding the zeros. They are approximately -3.871 and -0.129. These are the solutions.

70. $-0.768, 0.434$

71. The polynomial $x^3 + 3x^2 + x - 1$ is prime. We solve the equation by graphing $y = x^3 + 3x^2 + x - 1$ and finding the zeros. They are approximately -2.414, -1, and approximately 0.414. These are the solutions.

72. 0.544

73. We set $f(a)$ equal to -36.
$$a^2 - 12a = -36$$
$$a^2 - 12a + 36 = 0$$
$$(a - 6)(a - 6) = 0$$
$$a - 6 = 0 \ \ or \ \ a - 6 = 0$$
$$a = 6 \ \ or \ \ \ \ \ \ a = 6$$
The value of a for which $f(a) = -36$ is 6.

74. $-12, 12$

75. $|5 - 7x| = 9$
$$5 - 7x = 9 \ \ \ \ or \ \ 5 - 7x = -9$$
$$-7x = 4 \ \ \ \ or \ \ \ \ \ \ -7x = -14$$
$$x = -\frac{4}{7} \ \ or \ \ \ \ \ \ \ \ \ x = 2$$
The solution set is $\left\{ -\frac{4}{7}, 2 \right\}$.

76. $\left\{ x \middle| x \le -\frac{4}{7} \ or \ x \ge 2 \right\}$, or $\left(-\infty, -\frac{4}{7} \right] \cup [2, \infty)$

77. $|5 - 7x| \le 9$
$$-9 \le 5 - 7x \le 9$$
$$-14 \le -7x \le 4$$
$$2 \ge x \ge -\frac{4}{7}$$
The solution set is $\left\{ x \middle| -\frac{4}{7} \le x \le 2 \right\}$, or $\left[-\frac{4}{7}, 2 \right]$.

78. $\left\{ x \middle| x < \frac{14}{19} \right\}$, or $\left(-\infty, \frac{14}{19} \right)$

79. ◈

80. ◈

81. ◈

82. ◈

83. a) $\pi R^2 h - \pi r^2 h = \pi h(R^2 - r^2)$
$$= \pi h(R + r)(R - r)$$

b) Note that 4 m = 400 cm.
$$\pi R^2 h - \pi r^2 h$$
$$= \pi(50)^2(400) - \pi(10)^2(400)$$
$$= 1,000,000\pi - 40,000\pi$$
$$= 960,000\pi \ cm^3 \ \ \ \ (or \ 0.96\pi \ m^3)$$
$$\approx 3,014,400 \ cm^3 \ \ \ Using \ 3.14 \ for \ \pi$$

$$\pi h(R + r)(R - r)$$
$$= \pi(400)(50 + 10)(50 - 10)$$
$$= \pi(400)(60)(40)$$
$$= 960,000\pi \ cm^3 \ \ \ \ (or \ 0.96\pi \ m^3)$$
$$\approx 3,014,400 \ cm^3 \ \ \ Using \ 3.14 \ for \ \pi$$

If we use the π key on a calculator, the result is approximately 3,015,929 cm³.

84. Enter $y_1 = (x^2 - 3x + 2)^4$ and $y_2 = x^8 + 81x^4 + 16$ and look at a table of values. Observe that $y_1 \ne y_2$.

85. $x^{2a} - y^2 = (x^a)^2 - y^2 = (x^a + y)(x^a - y)$

86. $(x^{2a} + y^b)(x^{2a} - y^b)$

87. $9x^{2n} - 6x^n + 1 = (3x^n)^2 - 6x^n + 1$
$$= (3x^n - 1)^2$$

88. $c(c^w + 1)^2$

89. $5c^{100} - 80d^{100}$

$= 5(c^{100} - 16d^{100})$

$= 5(c^{50} + 4d^{50})(c^{50} - 4d^{50})$

$= 5(c^{50} + 4d^{50})(c^{25} + 2d^{25})(c^{25} - 2d^{25})$

90. $(t-2)(t^2 + 2t + 4)$

91. $x^3 + 64 = x^3 + 4^3$

$= (x+4)(x^2 - 4x + 16)$

$A^3 - B^3 = (A - B)(A^2 + AB + B^2)$

92. $(x+3)(x^2 - 3x + 9)$

93. $z^3 - 1 = z^3 - 1^3$

$= (z-1)(z^2 + z + 1)$

$A^3 - B^3 = (A - B)(A^2 + AB + B^2)$

94. $8(a+5)(a^2 - 5a + 25)$

95. $54x^3 + 2 = 2(27x^3 + 1)$

$= 2((3x)^3 + 1^3)$

$= 2(3x+1)(9x^2 - 3x + 1)$

96. $r(s+4)(s^2 - 4s + 16)$

97. $ab^3 + 125a = a(b^3 + 125)$

$= a(b^3 + 5^3)$

$= a(b+5)(b^2 - 5b + 25)$

98. $2(y-3z)(y^2 + 3yz + 9z^2)$

99. $5x^3 - 40z^3 = 5(x^3 - 8z^3)$

$= 5(x^3 - (2z)^3)$

$= 5(x-2z)(x^2 + 2xz + 4z^2)$

100. $(y+0.5)(y^2 - 0.5y + 0.25)$

101. $x^3 + 0.001$

$= x^3 + (0.1)^3$

$= (x+0.1)(x^2 - 0.1x + 0.01)$

102. $(5c^2 - 2d^2)(25c^4 + 10c^2 d^2 + 4d^4)$

103. $64x^6 - 8t^6 = 8(8x^6 - t^6)$

$= 8((2x^2)^3 - (t^2)^3)$

$= 8(2x^2 - t^2)(4x^4 + 2x^2 t^2 + t^4)$

104. $3z^2(z-1)(z^2 + z + 1)$

105. $2y^4 - 128y = 2y(y^3 - 64)$

$= 2y(y^3 - 4^3)$

$= 2y(y-4)(y^2 + 4y + 16)$

Exercise Set 6.5

1. *Familiarize*. Let x represent the number.

Translate.

$$\underbrace{\text{Square of number}}_{x^2} \quad \underset{+}{\text{plus}} \quad \underset{x}{\underline{\text{number}}} \quad \underset{=}{\text{is}} \quad \underset{156}{156.}$$

Carry out. We solve the equation:

$$x^2 + x = 156$$
$$x^2 + x - 156 = 0$$
$$(x + 13)(x - 12) = 0$$
$$x + 13 = 0 \quad or \ \ x - 12 = 0$$
$$x = -13 \ \ or \qquad x = 12$$

Check. The square of -13, which is 169, plus -13 is 156. The square of 12, which is 144, plus 12 is 156. Both numbers check.

State. The number is -13 or 12.

2. $-12, 11$

3. *Familiarize*. We let w represent the width and $w+5$ represent the length. We make a drawing and label it.

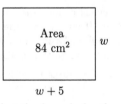

Recall that the formula for the area of a rectangle is $A = \text{length} \times \text{width}$.

Translate.

$$\underbrace{\text{Area}}_{w(w+5)} \quad \underset{=}{\text{is}} \quad \underset{84}{\underline{84 \text{ cm}^2}}.$$

Carry out. We solve the equation:

$$w(w+5) = 84$$
$$w^2 + 5w = 84$$
$$w^2 + 5w - 84 = 0$$
$$(w + 12)(w - 7) = 0$$
$$w + 12 = 0 \quad or \ \ w - 7 = 0$$
$$w = -12 \ \ or \qquad w = 7$$

Check. The number -12 is not a solution, because width cannot be negative. If the width is 7 cm and the length is 5 cm more, or 12 cm, then the area is $12 \cdot 7$, or 84 cm^2. This is a solution.

State. The length is 12 cm, and the width is 7 cm.

4. Length: 12 cm, width: 8 cm

5. *Familiarize*. We make a drawing and label it. We let x represent the length of a side of the original square.

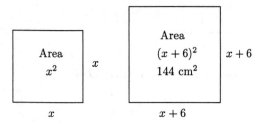

Translate.

Area of new square is 144 cm^2.

$$(x+6)^2 \qquad = \qquad 144$$

Carry out. We solve the equation:

$$(x+6)^2 = 144$$
$$x^2 + 12x + 36 = 144$$
$$x^2 + 12x - 108 = 0$$
$$(x-6)(x+18) = 0$$
$$x - 6 = 0 \quad or \quad x + 18 = 0$$
$$x = 6 \quad or \qquad x = -18$$

Check. We only check 6 since the length of a side cannot be negative. If we increase the length by 6, the new length is $6+6$, or 12 cm. Then the new area is $12 \cdot 12$, or 144 cm^2. We have a solution.

State. The length of a side of the original square is 6 cm.

6. 3 m

7. *Familiarize*. We make a drawing and label it with both known and unknown information. We let x represent the width of the frame.

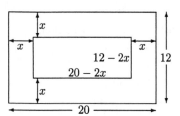

The length and width of the picture that shows are represented by $20 - 2x$ and $12 - 2x$. The area of the picture that shows is 84 cm^2.

Translate. Using the formula for the area of a rectangle, $A = l \cdot w$, we have

$$84 = (20 - 2x)(12 - 2x).$$

Carry out. We solve the equation:

$$84 = 240 - 64x + 4x^2$$
$$84 = 4(60 - 16x + x^2)$$
$$21 = 60 - 16x + x^2 \qquad \text{Dividing by 4}$$
$$0 = x^2 - 16x + 39$$
$$0 = (x-3)(x-13)$$
$$x - 3 = 0 \quad or \quad x - 13 = 0$$
$$x = 3 \quad or \qquad x = 13$$

Check. We see that 13 is not a solution because when $x = 13$, $20 - 2x = -6$ and $12 - 2x = -14$, and the length and width of the frame cannot be negative. We check 3. When $x = 3$, $20 - 2x = 14$ and $12 - 2x = 6$ and $14 \cdot 6 = 84$. The area is 84. The value checks.

State. The width of the frame is 3 cm.

8. 2 cm

9. *Familiarize*. We let x represent the width of the walkway. We make a drawing and label it with both the known and unknown information.

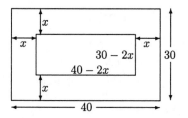

The area of the old garden is $40 \cdot 30$, or 1200 ft^2. The area of the new garden is $\frac{1}{2} \cdot 1200$, or 600 ft^2.

Translate. Rewording, we have

Area of new garden is 600 ft^2.

$$(40 - 2x)(30 - 2x) \quad = \quad 600$$

Carry out. We solve the equation:

$$(40 - 2x)(30 - 2x) = 600$$
$$1200 - 140x + 4x^2 = 600$$
$$4x^2 - 140x + 600 = 0$$
$$x^2 - 35x + 150 = 0 \qquad \text{Dividing by 4}$$
$$(x-5)(x-30) = 0$$
$$x - 5 = 0 \quad or \quad x - 30 = 0$$
$$x = 5 \quad or \qquad x = 30$$

Check. If the walkway is 5 ft wide, the length of the new garden will be $40 - 2 \cdot 5$, or 30 ft, and its width will be $30 - 2 \cdot 5$, or 20 ft. Then the area of the new garden will be $30 \cdot 20$, or 600 ft^2. This is $\frac{1}{2}$ of

1200 ft², the area of the old garden, so this answer checks.

If the walkway is 30 ft wide, the length of the new garden will be $40 - 2 \cdot 30$, or -20 ft. Since the length cannot be negative, 30 is not a solution.

State. The walkway is 5 ft wide.

10. 10 ft

11. *Familiarize*. Using the labels on the drawing in the text, we let x represent the base of the triangle and $x + 2$ represent the height. Recall that the formula for the area of the triangle with base b and height h is $\frac{1}{2}bh$.

Translate.

$$\underbrace{\text{The area}}_{\frac{1}{2}x(x+2)} \; \underbrace{\text{is}}_{=} \; \underbrace{12 \text{ ft}^2}_{12}.$$

Carry out. We solve the equation:

$$\frac{1}{2}x(x+2) = 12$$
$$x(x+2) = 24 \quad \text{Multiplying by 2}$$
$$x^2 + 2x = 24$$
$$x^2 + 2x - 24 = 0$$
$$(x+6)(x-4) = 0$$
$$x + 6 = 0 \quad or \quad x - 4 = 0$$
$$x = -6 \quad or \quad x = 4$$

Check. We check only 4 since the length of the base cannot be negative. If the base is 4 ft, then the height is $4 + 2$, or 6 ft, and the area is $\frac{1}{2} \cdot 4 \cdot 6$, or 12 ft². The answer checks.

State. The height is 6 ft, and the base is 4 ft.

12. -10, -8, and -6 or 6, 8, and 10

13. *Familiarize*. Let x represent the first integer, $x + 2$ the second, and $x + 4$ the third.

Translate.

$$\underbrace{\begin{array}{c}\text{Square of}\\\text{the third}\end{array}}_{(x+4)^2} \; \underbrace{\text{is}}_{=} \; \underbrace{76}_{76} \; \underbrace{\begin{array}{c}\text{more}\\\text{than}\end{array}}_{+} \; \underbrace{\begin{array}{c}\text{square of}\\\text{the second.}\end{array}}_{(x+2)^2}$$

Carry out. We solve the equation:

$$(x+4)^2 = 76 + (x+2)^2$$
$$x^2 + 8x + 16 = 76 + x^2 + 4x + 4$$
$$x^2 + 8x + 16 = x^2 + 4x + 80$$
$$4x = 64$$
$$x = 16$$

Check. We check the integers 16, 18, and 20. The square of 20, or 400, is 76 more than 324, the square of 18. The answer checks.

State. The integers are 16, 18, and 20.

14. Distance d: 12 ft, height of the tower: 16 ft

15. *Familiarize*. We make a drawing. Let w represent the width of the parking lot. Then $w + 50$ represents the length.

Since we have a right triangle, we can use the Pythagorean theorem:

$$a^2 + b^2 = c^2$$

Translate. Substituting, we have

$$w^2 + (w+50)^2 = 250^2$$

Carry out. We solve the equation:

$$w^2 + (w+50)^2 = 250^2$$
$$w^2 + w^2 + 100w + 2500 = 62{,}500$$
$$2w^2 + 100w - 60{,}000 = 0$$
$$w^2 + 50w - 30{,}000 = 0 \quad \text{Dividing by 2}$$
$$(w+200)(w-150) = 0$$
$$w + 200 = 0 \quad or \quad w - 150 = 0$$
$$w = -200 \quad or \quad w = 150$$

Check. We only check 150, since the width cannot be negative. If the width is 150 ft, then the length is $150 + 50$, or 200 ft. The length of a diagonal is $150^2 + 200^2 = 62{,}500 = 250^2$. The answer checks.

State. The parking lot is 150 ft wide and 200 ft long.

16. Height: 16 m, base: 7 m

17. *Familiarize*. We make a drawing. Let $h = $ the height the ladder reaches on the wall. Then the length of the ladder is $h + 1$.

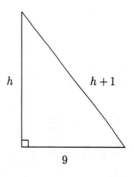

Translate. We use the Pythagorean theorem.

$$9^2 + h^2 = (h+1)^2$$

Carry out. We solve the equation:

$$81 + h^2 = h^2 + 2h + 1$$
$$80 = 2h$$
$$40 = h$$

Check. If $h = 40$, then $h + 1 = 41$; $9^2 + 40^2 = 81 + 1600 = 1681 = 41^2$, so the answer checks.

State. The ladder is 41 ft long.

18. 24 ft

19. *Familiarize*. Let w represent the width and $w + 25$ represent the length. Make a drawing.

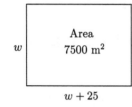

$$w$$

Area
7500 m²

$$w + 25$$

Recall that the formula for the area of a rectangle is $A = $ length $\times$ width.

Translate.

Area   is   7500 m².
$$w(w + 25) = 7500$$

Carry out. We solve the equation:

$$w(w + 25) = 7500$$
$$w^2 + 25w = 7500$$
$$w^2 + 25w - 7500 = 0$$
$$(w + 100)(w - 75) = 0$$
$$w + 100 = 0 \quad or \quad w - 75 = 0$$
$$w = -100 \quad or \quad w = 75$$

Check. The number -100 is not a solution because width cannot be negative. If the width is 75 m and the length is 25 m more, or 100 m, then the area will be $100 \cdot 75$, or 7500 m². This is a solution.

State. The dimensions will be 100 m by 75 m.

20. 9 m by 12 m

21. *Familiarize*. We will use the given function

$$h(t) = -16t^2 + 96t + 880.$$

Translate.

Height   is   0 ft.
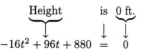
$$-16t^2 + 96t + 880 = 0$$

Carry out. We solve the equation:

$$-16t^2 + 96t + 880 = 0$$
$$t^2 - 6t - 55 = 0 \quad \text{Dividing by } -16$$
$$(t - 11)(t + 5) = 0$$
$$t - 11 = 0 \quad or \quad t + 5 = 0$$
$$t = 11 \quad or \qquad t = -5$$

Check. We check only 11, since time cannot be negative in this application. When $t = 11$, $h(11) = -16 \cdot 11^2 + 96 \cdot 11 + 880 = 0$. The answer checks.

State. The rocket will reach the ground after 11 sec.

22. 7 sec

23. *Familiarize*. The firm breaks even when the cost and the revenue are the same. We use the functions given in the text.

Translate.

Cost   equals   revenue.
$$\frac{1}{9}x^2 + 2x + 1 \quad = \quad \frac{5}{36}x^2 + 2x$$

Carry out. We solve the equation:

$$\frac{1}{9}x^2 + 2x + 1 = \frac{5}{36}x^2 + 2x$$
$$0 = \frac{1}{36}x^2 - 1$$
$$0 = \left(\frac{1}{6}x + 1\right)\left(\frac{1}{6}x - 1\right)$$
$$\frac{1}{6}x + 1 = 0 \quad or \quad \frac{1}{6}x - 1 = 0$$
$$\frac{1}{6}x = -1 \quad or \quad \frac{1}{6}x = 1$$
$$x = -6 \quad or \qquad x = 6$$

Check. We check only 6 since the number of video cameras cannot be negative. If 6 cameras are produced, the cost is $C(6) = \frac{1}{9} \cdot 6^2 + 2 \cdot 6 + 1 = 4 + 12 + 1 = \$17$ thousand. If 6 cameras are sold, the revenue is $R(6) = \frac{5}{36} \cdot 6^2 + 2 \cdot 6 = 5 + 12 = \$17$ thousand. The answer checks.

State. The firm breaks even when 6 video cameras are produced and sold.

24. 2

25. Let $x = $ the number of years since 1850 and $y = $ the number of farms, in millions. A scatterplot shows that the data cannot be modeled by a linear function.

26. Yes

27. Let x = the number of years since 1986 and y = the attendance, in millions. A scatterplot shows that the data cannot be modeled by a linear function.

28. No

29. Let x = the number of years since 1993 and y = the ratio of students to computers. A scatterplot shows that the data can be modeled by a linear function.

30. No

31. a) Enter the data as described in Exercise 25 and use the quartic regression feature. We get $f(x) = 0.00000018x^4 - 0.00005260x^3 + 0.00387914x^2 - 0.00794849x + 2.12144793$.

b) $1980 - 1850 = 130$, so we find $f(130)$; $f(130) \approx 2.686$, so we estimate that there were about 2.686 million farms in 1980.

c) Graph $y_1 = f(x)$ and $y_2 = 4$ and find the first coordinates of the points of intersection. They are about 29 and 116, so we estimate that there were 4 million farms 29 years after 1850 and again 116 years after 1850, or in 1879 and in 1966.

32. (a) $p(x) = x^3 - 10.29761905x^2 + 31.53571429x + 95.97619048$; (b) about 274.69 million; (c) 1995

33. a) Enter the data as described in the example and use the quadratic regression feature. We get $w(x) = 6.125x^2 + 5.36785714x + 9.60714286$.

b) $2010 - 1995 = 15$, so we find $w(15)$; $w(15) \approx 1307$ so we estimate that there will be about 1307 million web sites in 2010.

c) Graph $y_1 = w(x)$ and $y_2 = 200$ and find the first coordinate of the point of intersection. It is about 6, so we estimate that there will be 200 million web sites 6 years after 1995, or in 2001.

34. (a) $l(x) = -0.00012377x^4 + 0.00459090x^3 - 0.00357227x^2 - 1.13695404x + 26.31855116$; (b) about 17.6 hr; (c) 1981, 1993, 1998

35.
$$3x - 7 = 4(x + 3) - x$$
$$3x - 7 = 4x + 12 - x \quad \text{Removing parentheses}$$
$$3x - 7 = 3x + 12 \quad \text{Collecting like terms}$$
$$-7 = 12 \quad \text{Subtracting } 3x \text{ on both sides}$$

We get a false equation, so there is no solution.

36. $|x - 8| \le -1$

Since absolute value must be nonnegative, the inequality has no solution.

36. No solution

37.
$$2x - 14 + 9x > -8x + 16 + 10x$$
$$11x - 14 > 2x + 16 \quad \text{Collecting like terms}$$
$$9x - 14 > 16 \quad \text{Adding } -2x$$
$$9x > 30 \quad \text{Adding } 14$$
$$x > \frac{10}{3} \quad \text{Multiplying by } \frac{1}{9}$$

The solution set is $\left\{ x \middle| x > \frac{10}{3} \right\}$, or $\left(\frac{10}{3}, \infty \right)$.

38. $\frac{10}{3}$

39. ◈

40. ◈

41. ◈

42. ◈

43. *Familiarize*. Using the labels on the drawing in the text, we let x represent the width of the piece of tin and $2x$ represent the length. Then the width and length of the base of the box are represented by $x - 4$ and $2x - 4$, respectively. Recall that the formula for the volume of a rectangular solid with length l, width w, and height h is $l \cdot w \cdot h$.

Translate.

The volume is 480 cm^3.
$$(2x - 4)(x - 4)(2) = 480$$

Carry out. We solve the equation:
$$(2x - 4)(x - 4)(2) = 480$$
$$(2x - 4)(x - 4) = 240 \quad \text{Dividing by 2}$$
$$2x^2 - 12x + 16 = 240$$
$$2x^2 - 12x - 224 = 0$$
$$x^2 - 6x - 112 = 0 \quad \text{Dividing by 2}$$
$$(x + 8)(x - 14) = 0$$
$$x + 8 = 0 \quad \text{or} \quad x - 14 = 0$$
$$x = -8 \quad \text{or} \quad x = 14$$

Check. We check only 14 since the width cannot be negative. If the width of the piece of tin is 14 cm, then its length is $2 \cdot 14$, or 28 cm, and the dimensions of the base of the box are $14 - 4$, or 10 cm by $28 - 4$, or 24 cm. The volume of the box is $24 \cdot 10 \cdot 2$, or 480 cm^3. The answer checks.

State. The dimensions of the piece of tin are 14 cm by 28 cm.

44. Tugboat: 15 km/h, freighter: 8 km/h

45. *Familiarize*. Let t = the length of time it will take the camera to catch up to the skydiver, in seconds. Then $t + 1$ = the length of time the skydiver falls.

Translate.

Length of skydiver's fall	is the same as	length of camera's fall.
$11.12(t+1)^2$	$=$	$15.4t^2$

Carry out. Graph $y_1 = 11.12(x+1)^2$ and $y_2 = 15.4x^2$ in a window that shows the point of intersection of the graphs. The window $[0, 10, 0, 500]$, Xscl = 1, Yscl = 100 is one good choice. Then find the first coordinate of the point of intersection. It is approximately 5.7.

Check. If the camera falls for 5.7 sec, the skydiver falls for 5.7+1, or 6.7, sec. In 6.7 sec the skydiver falls $11.12(6.7)^2$, or about 499 ft; in 5.7 sec the camera falls $15.4(5.7)^2$, or about 500 ft. Since the distances are about the same (remember that the time was rounded), the answer checks.

State. It will take about 5.7 sec for the camera to catch up to the skydiver.

46. 3, 14

Chapter 7

Rational Equations and Functions

1. $r(y) = \dfrac{3y^3 - 2y}{y - 5}$

$r(0) = \dfrac{3 \cdot 0^3 - 2 \cdot 0}{0 - 5} = \dfrac{0 - 0}{0 - 5} = \dfrac{0}{-5} = 0$

$r(4) = \dfrac{3 \cdot 4^3 - 2 \cdot 4}{4 - 5} = \dfrac{192 - 8}{-1} = \dfrac{184}{-1} = -184$

$r(5) = \dfrac{3 \cdot 5^3 - 2 \cdot 5}{5 - 5} = \dfrac{375 - 10}{0}$

Since division by zero is not defined, $r(5)$ does not exist.

2. $-6; 0; -\dfrac{6}{5}$

3. $g(x) = \dfrac{2x^3 - 9}{x^2 - 4x + 4}$

$g(0) = \dfrac{2 \cdot 0^3 - 9}{0^2 - 4 \cdot 0 + 4} = \dfrac{0 - 9}{0 - 0 + 4} = -\dfrac{9}{4}$

$g(2) = \dfrac{2 \cdot 2^3 - 9}{2^2 - 4 \cdot 2 + 4} = \dfrac{16 - 9}{4 - 8 + 4} = \dfrac{7}{0}$

Since division by zero is not defined, $g(2)$ does not exist.

$g(-1) = \dfrac{2(-1)^3 - 9}{(-1)^2 - 4(-1) + 4} = \dfrac{-2 - 9}{1 + 4 + 4} = -\dfrac{11}{9}$

4. $0; \dfrac{2}{5}$; does not exist

5. $\dfrac{5x}{5x} \cdot \dfrac{x - 3}{x + 2} = \dfrac{5x(x - 3)}{5x(x + 2)}$

6. $\dfrac{(3 - a^2)(-1)}{(a - 7)(-1)}$

7. $\dfrac{t - 2}{t + 3} \cdot \dfrac{-1}{-1} = \dfrac{(t - 2)(-1)}{(t + 3)(-1)}$

8. $\dfrac{(x - 4)(x - 5)}{(x + 5)(x - 5)}$

9. $\dfrac{15x}{5x^2}$

$= \dfrac{5x \cdot 3}{5x \cdot x}$ Factoring; the greatest common factor is $5x$.

$= \dfrac{5x}{5x} \cdot \dfrac{3}{x}$ Factoring the rational expression

$= 1 \cdot \dfrac{3}{x}$ $\dfrac{5x}{5x} = 1$

$= \dfrac{3}{x}$ Removing a factor equal to 1

10. $\dfrac{a^2}{3}$

11. $\dfrac{18t^3}{27t^7}$

$= \dfrac{9t^3 \cdot 2}{9t^3 \cdot 3t^4}$ Factoring the numerator and the denominator

$= \dfrac{9t^3}{9t^3} \cdot \dfrac{2}{3t^4}$ Factoring the rational expression

$= \dfrac{2}{3t^4}$ Removing a factor equal to 1

12. $\dfrac{2}{y^4}$

13. $\dfrac{2a - 10}{2} = \dfrac{2(a - 5)}{2 \cdot 1} = \dfrac{2}{2} \cdot \dfrac{a - 5}{1} = a - 5$

14. $a + 4$

15. $\dfrac{15}{25a - 30} = \dfrac{5 \cdot 3}{5(5a - 6)} = \dfrac{5}{5} \cdot \dfrac{3}{5a - 6} = \dfrac{3}{5a - 6}$

16. $\dfrac{7}{2x - 3}$

17. $\dfrac{5x + 20}{x^2 + 4x} = \dfrac{5(x + 4)}{x(x + 4)} = \dfrac{5}{x} \cdot \dfrac{x + 4}{x + 4} = \dfrac{5}{x}$

18. $\dfrac{3}{x}$

19. $\dfrac{3a - 1}{2 - 6a}$

$= \dfrac{3a - 1}{2(1 - 3a)}$

$= \dfrac{-1(1 - 3a)}{2(1 - 3a)}$ Factoring out -1 in the numerator reverses the subtraction.

$= \dfrac{-1}{2} \cdot \dfrac{1 - 3a}{1 - 3a}$

$= -\dfrac{1}{2}$

20. $-\dfrac{1}{2}$

21. $\dfrac{8t-16}{t^2-4}=\dfrac{8(t-2)}{(t+2)(t-2)}=\dfrac{8}{t+2}\cdot\dfrac{t-2}{t-2}=\dfrac{8}{t+2}$

22. $\dfrac{t-3}{5}$

23.
$$\dfrac{2t-1}{1-4t^2}$$
$$=\dfrac{2t-1}{(1+2t)(1-2t)}$$
$$=\dfrac{-1(1-2t)}{(1+2t)(1-2t)}\qquad\text{Factoring out }-1\text{ in the}$$
                                    numerator reverses the
                                    subtraction
$$=\dfrac{-1}{1+2t}\cdot\dfrac{1-2t}{1-2t}$$
$$=-\dfrac{1}{1+2t}$$

24. $-\dfrac{1}{2+3a}$

25. $\dfrac{a^2-25}{a^2+10a+25}=\dfrac{(a+5)(a-5)}{(a+5)(a+5)}=$
$\dfrac{a+5}{a+5}\cdot\dfrac{a-5}{a+5}=\dfrac{a-5}{a+5}$

26. $\dfrac{a+4}{a-4}$

27. $\dfrac{x^2+9x+8}{x^2-3x-4}=\dfrac{(x+1)(x+8)}{(x+1)(x-4)}=\dfrac{x+1}{x+1}\cdot\dfrac{x+8}{x-4}=$
$\dfrac{x+8}{x-4}$

28. $\dfrac{t-9}{t+4}$

29. $\dfrac{16-t^2}{t^2-8t+16}=\dfrac{16-t^2}{16-8t+t^2}=\dfrac{(4+t)(4-t)}{(4-t)(4-t)}=$
$\dfrac{4+t}{4-t}\cdot\dfrac{4-t}{4-t}=\dfrac{4+t}{4-t}$

30. $\dfrac{5-p}{5+p}$

31. First we simplify the rational expression describing
the function.
$$\dfrac{3x-12}{3x+15}=\dfrac{3(x-4)}{3(x+5)}=\dfrac{3}{3}\cdot\dfrac{x-4}{x+5}=\dfrac{x-4}{x+5}$$
$x+5=0$ when $x=-5$. Thus, the vertical asymptote
is $x=-5$.

32. $x=-3$

33. First we simplify the rational expression describing
the function.
$$\dfrac{12-6x}{5x-10}=\dfrac{-6(-2+x)}{5(x-2)}=\dfrac{-6(x-2)}{5(x-2)}=$$
$$\dfrac{-6}{5}\cdot\dfrac{x-2}{x-2}=-\dfrac{6}{5}$$
The denominator of the simplified expression is not
equal to 0 for any value of x, so there are no vertical
asymptotes.

34. None

35. First we simplify the rational expression describing
the function.
$$\dfrac{x^3+3x^2}{x^2+6x+9}=\dfrac{x^2(x+3)}{(x+3)(x+3)}=\dfrac{x^2}{x+3}\cdot\dfrac{x+3}{x+3}=$$
$$\dfrac{x^2}{x+3}$$
$x+3=0$ when $x=-3$. Thus, the vertical asymptote
is $x=-3$.

36. $x=\dfrac{1}{2}$

37. First we simplify the rational expression describing
the function.
$$\dfrac{x^2-x-6}{x^2-6x+8}=\dfrac{(x-3)(x+2)}{(x-4)(x-2)}$$
We cannot remove a factor equal to 1. Observe that
$x-4=0$ when $x=4$ and $x-2=0$ when $x=2$.
Thus, the vertical asymptotes are $x=4$ and $x=2$.

38. $x=1$

39. The vertical asymptote of $h(x)=\dfrac{1}{x}$ is $x=0$. Observe that $h(x)>0$ for $x>0$ and $h(x)<0$ for $x<0$.
Thus, graph (b) corresponds to this function.

40. (e)

41. The vertical asymptote of $f(x)=\dfrac{x}{x-3}$ is $x=3$.
Thus, graph (f) corresponds to this function.

42. (d)

43. $\dfrac{4x-2}{x^2-2x+1}=\dfrac{2(2x-1)}{(x-1)(x-1)}$
The vertical asymptote of $r(x)$ is $x=1$. Thus, graph
(a) corresponds to this function.

44. (c)

45. $\dfrac{5a^3}{3b} \cdot \dfrac{7b^3}{10a^7}$

$= \dfrac{5a^3 \cdot 7b^3}{3b \cdot 10a^7}$ Multiplying the numerators and also the denominators

$= \dfrac{5 \cdot a^3 \cdot 7 \cdot b \cdot b^2}{3 \cdot b \cdot 2 \cdot 5 \cdot a^3 \cdot a^4}$ Factoring the numerator and the denominator

$= \dfrac{\cancel{5} \cdot \cancel{a^3} \cdot 7 \cdot \cancel{b} \cdot b^2}{3 \cdot \cancel{b} \cdot 2 \cdot \cancel{5} \cdot \cancel{a^3} \cdot a^4}$ Removing a factor equal to 1

$= \dfrac{7b^2}{6a^4}$

46. $\dfrac{5}{3ab^3}$

47. $\dfrac{3x-6}{5x} \cdot \dfrac{x^3}{5x-10} = \dfrac{(3x-6)(x^3)}{5x(5x-10)}$

$= \dfrac{3(x-2)(x)(x^2)}{5 \cdot x \cdot 5(x-2)}$

$= \dfrac{3(\cancel{x-2})(\cancel{x})(x^2)}{5 \cdot \cancel{x} \cdot 5(\cancel{x-2})}$

$= \dfrac{3x^2}{25}$

48. $\dfrac{3t^2}{4}$

49. $\dfrac{y^2-16}{2y+6} \cdot \dfrac{y+3}{y-4} = \dfrac{(y^2-16)(y+3)}{(2y+6)(y-4)}$

$= \dfrac{(y+4)(y-4)(y+3)}{2(y+3)(y-4)}$

$= \dfrac{(y+4)(\cancel{y-4})(\cancel{y+3})}{2(\cancel{y+3})(\cancel{y-4})}$

$= \dfrac{y+4}{2}$

50. $\dfrac{m+n}{4}$

51. $\dfrac{x^2-16}{x^2} \cdot \dfrac{x^2-4x}{x^2-x-12} = \dfrac{(x^2-16)(x^2-4x)}{x^2(x^2-x-12)}$

$= \dfrac{(x+4)(x-4)(x)(x-4)}{x \cdot x(x-4)(x+3)}$

$= \dfrac{(x+4)(\cancel{x-4})(\cancel{x})(x-4)}{\cancel{x} \cdot x(\cancel{x-4})(x+3)}$

$= \dfrac{(x+4)(x-4)}{x(x+3)}$

52. $\dfrac{y(y+5)}{y-3}$

53. $\dfrac{7a-14}{4-a^2} \cdot \dfrac{5a^2+6a+1}{35a+7}$

$= \dfrac{(7a-14)(5a^2+6a+1)}{(4-a^2)(35a+7)}$

$= \dfrac{7(a-2)(5a+1)(a+1)}{(2+a)(2-a)(7)(5a+1)}$

$= \dfrac{7(-1)(2-a)(5a+1)(a+1)}{(2+a)(2-a)(7)(5a+1)}$

$= \dfrac{7(-1)(\cancel{2-a})(\cancel{5a+1})(a+1)}{(2+a)(\cancel{2-a})(7)(\cancel{5a+1})}$

$= \dfrac{-1(a+1)}{2+a}$

$= \dfrac{-a-1}{2+a}$, or $-\dfrac{a+1}{2+a}$

54. $-\dfrac{3(a+1)}{a+6}$

55. $\dfrac{6-2t}{t^2+4t+4} \cdot \dfrac{t^3+2t^2}{t^8-9t^6}$

$= \dfrac{(6-2t)(t^3+2t^2)}{(t^2+4t+4)(t^8-9t^6)}$

$= \dfrac{-2(-3+t)(t^2)(t+2)}{(t+2)(t+2)(t^6)(t+3)(t-3)}$

$= \dfrac{-2(\cancel{t-3})(\cancel{t^2})(\cancel{t+2})}{(t+2)(\cancel{t+2})(t^4)(t+3)(\cancel{t-3})}$

$= \dfrac{-2}{t^4(t+2)(t+3)}$

56. $\dfrac{x^2(x+3)(x-3)}{-4}$

57. $\dfrac{x^2-2x-35}{2x^3-3x^2} \cdot \dfrac{4x^3-9x}{7x-49}$

$= \dfrac{(x^2-2x-35)(4x^3-9x)}{(2x^3-3x^2)(7x-49)}$

$= \dfrac{(x-7)(x+5)(x)(2x+3)(2x-3)}{x^2(2x-3)(7)(x-7)}$

$= \dfrac{(\cancel{x-7})(x+5)(\cancel{x})(2x+3)(\cancel{2x-3})}{\cancel{x} \cdot x(\cancel{2x-3})(7)(\cancel{x-7})}$

$= \dfrac{(x+5)(2x+3)}{7x}$

58. $\dfrac{1}{y+1}$

59. $\dfrac{9x^5}{8y^2} \div \dfrac{3x}{16y^9}$

$= \dfrac{9x^5}{8y^2} \cdot \dfrac{16y^9}{3x}$ Multiplying by the reciprocal of the divisor

$= \dfrac{9x^5(16y^9)}{8y^2(3x)}$

$= \dfrac{3 \cdot 3 \cdot x \cdot x^4 \cdot 2 \cdot 8 \cdot y^2 \cdot y^7}{8 \cdot y^2 \cdot 3 \cdot x}$

$= \dfrac{\cancel{3} \cdot 3 \cdot \cancel{x} \cdot x^4 \cdot 2 \cdot \cancel{8} \cdot \cancel{y^2} \cdot y^7}{\cancel{8} \cdot \cancel{y^2} \cdot \cancel{3} \cdot \cancel{x} \cdot 1}$

$= 6x^4 y^7$

60. $\dfrac{4a^4}{b^4}$

61. $\dfrac{6x+12}{x^8} \div \dfrac{x+2}{x^3} = \dfrac{6x+12}{x^8} \cdot \dfrac{x^3}{x+2}$

$= \dfrac{(6x+12)(x^3)}{x^8(x+2)}$

$= \dfrac{6(x+2)(x^3)}{x^3 \cdot x^5(x+2)}$

$= \dfrac{6\cancel{(x+2)}\cancel{(x^3)}}{\cancel{x^3} \cdot x^5\cancel{(x+2)}}$

$= \dfrac{6}{x^5}$

62. $\dfrac{3}{y^5}$

63. $\dfrac{x^2-4}{x^3} \div \dfrac{x^5-2x^4}{x+4} = \dfrac{x^2-4}{x^3} \cdot \dfrac{x+4}{x^5-2x^4}$

$= \dfrac{(x^2-4)(x+4)}{x^3(x^5-2x^4)}$

$= \dfrac{(x+2)(x-2)(x+4)}{x^3(x^4)(x-2)}$

$= \dfrac{(x+2)\cancel{(x-2)}(x+4)}{x^3(x^4)\cancel{(x-2)}}$

$= \dfrac{(x+2)(x+4)}{x^7}$

64. $\dfrac{(y-3)(y+2)}{y^6}$

65. $\dfrac{25x^2-4}{x^2-9} \div \dfrac{5x-2}{x+3} = \dfrac{25x^2-4}{x^2-9} \cdot \dfrac{x+3}{5x-2}$

$= \dfrac{(25x^2-4)(x+3)}{(x^2-9)(5x-2)}$

$= \dfrac{(5x+2)(5x-2)(x+3)}{(x+3)(x-3)(5x-2)}$

$= \dfrac{(5x+2)\cancel{(5x-2)}\cancel{(x+3)}}{\cancel{(x+3)}(x-3)\cancel{(5x-2)}}$

$= \dfrac{5x+2}{x-3}$

66. $\dfrac{-2a-1}{a+2}$

67. $\dfrac{5y-5x}{15y^3} \div \dfrac{x^2-y^2}{3x+3y} = \dfrac{5y-5x}{15y^3} \cdot \dfrac{3x+3y}{x^2-y^2}$

$= \dfrac{(5y-5x)(3x+3y)}{15y^3(x^2-y^2)}$

$= \dfrac{5(y-x)(3)(x+y)}{5 \cdot 3 \cdot y^3(x+y)(x-y)}$

$= \dfrac{5(-1)(x-y)(3)(x+y)}{5 \cdot 3 \cdot y^3(x+y)(x-y)}$

$= \dfrac{\cancel{5}(-1)\cancel{(x-y)}(\cancel{3})\cancel{(x+y)}}{\cancel{5} \cdot \cancel{3} \cdot y^3\cancel{(x+y)}\cancel{(x-y)}}$

$= \dfrac{-1}{y^3}, \text{ or } -\dfrac{1}{y^3}$

68. $-x^2$

69. $\dfrac{x^2-16}{x^2-10x+25} \div \dfrac{3x-12}{x^2-3x-10}$

$= \dfrac{x^2-16}{x^2-10x+25} \cdot \dfrac{x^2-3x-10}{3x-12}$

$= \dfrac{(x^2-16)(x^2-3x-10)}{(x^2-10x+25)(3x-12)}$

$= \dfrac{(x+4)(x-4)(x-5)(x+2)}{(x-5)(x-5)(3)(x-4)}$

$= \dfrac{(x+4)\cancel{(x-4)}\cancel{(x-5)}(x+2)}{\cancel{(x-5)}(x-5)(3)\cancel{(x-4)}}$

$= \dfrac{(x+4)(x+2)}{3(x-5)}$

70. $\dfrac{(y+6)(y+3)}{3(y-4)}$

71. $\dfrac{y^3+3y}{y^2-9} \div \dfrac{y^2+5y-14}{y^2+4y-21}$

$= \dfrac{y^3+3y}{y^2-9} \cdot \dfrac{y^2+4y-21}{y^2+5y-14}$

$= \dfrac{(y^3+3y)(y^2+4y-21)}{(y^2-9)(y^2+5y-14)}$

$= \dfrac{y(y^2+3)(y+7)(y-3)}{(y+3)(y-3)(y+7)(y-2)}$

$= \dfrac{y(y^2+3)\cancel{(y+7)}\cancel{(y-3)}}{(y+3)\cancel{(y-3)}\cancel{(y+7)}(y-2)}$

$= \dfrac{y(y^2+3)}{(y+3)(y-2)}$

72. $\dfrac{a(a^2+4)}{(a+4)(a+3)}$

73. $x^2y^2 - a^2b^2 = (xy)^2 - (ab)^2$

$= (xy+ab)(xy-ab)$

74. $-2, 3$

75. $\quad \frac{2}{3}(3x - 4) = 8$

$\quad \frac{3}{2} \cdot \frac{2}{3}(3x - 4) = \frac{3}{2} \cdot 8 \quad$ Multiplying by $\frac{3}{2}$

$\quad\quad\quad 3x - 4 = 12$

$\quad\quad\quad\quad\; 3x = 16$

$\quad\quad\quad\quad\;\; x = \frac{16}{3}$

76. $-\dfrac{1}{3}$

77. ◈

78. ◈

79. ◈

80. ◈

81. To find the domain of f we set

$\quad\quad x - 3 = 0$

$\quad\quad\quad x = 3.$

The domain of $f = \{x | x$ is a real number and $x \neq 3\}$.

Simplify: $f(x) = \dfrac{x^2 - 9}{x - 3} = \dfrac{(x+3)(x-3)}{(x-3)\cdot 1}$

$\quad\quad\quad = \dfrac{x-3}{x-3} \cdot \dfrac{x+3}{1} = x + 3$

Graph $f(x) = x + 3$ using the domain found above.

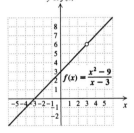

82. (a) $\dfrac{2x + 2h + 3}{4x + 4h - 1}$; (b) $\dfrac{2x + 3}{8x - 9}$; (c) $\dfrac{x + 5}{4x - 1}$

83.

$$\left[\frac{d^2 - d}{d^2 - 6d + 8} \cdot \frac{d - 2}{d^2 + 5d} \right] \div \frac{5d}{d^2 - 9d + 20}$$

$$= \left[\frac{d^2 - d}{d^2 - 6d + 8} \cdot \frac{d - 2}{d^2 + 5d} \right] \cdot \frac{d^2 - 9d + 20}{5d}$$

$$= \frac{(d^2 - d)(d - 2)(d^2 - 9d + 20)}{(d^2 - 6d + 8)(d^2 + 5d)(5d)}$$

$$= \frac{d(d - 1)(d - 2)(d - 5)(d - 4)}{(d - 4)(d - 2)(d)(d + 5)(5d)}$$

$$= \frac{d(d - 1)(d-2)(d - 5)(d-4)}{(d-4)(d-2)(d)(d + 5)(5d)}$$

$$= \frac{(d - 1)(d - 5)}{5d(d + 5)}$$

84. $\dfrac{2s}{r + 2s}$

85.

$$\frac{m^2 - t^2}{m^2 + t^2 + m + t + 2mt}$$

$$= \frac{m^2 - t^2}{(m^2 + 2mt + t^2) + (m + t)}$$

$$= \frac{(m + t)(m - t)}{(m + t)^2 + (m + t)}$$

$$= \frac{(m + t)(m - t)}{(m + t)[(m + t) + 1]}$$

$$= \frac{(m+t)(m - t)}{(m+t)(m + t + 1)}$$

$$= \frac{m - t}{m + t + 1}$$

86. $\dfrac{a^2 + 2}{a^2 - 3}$

87.

$$\frac{x^3 + x^2 - y^3 - y^2}{x^2 - 2xy + y^2}$$

$$= \frac{(x^3 - y^3) + (x^2 - y^2)}{x^2 - 2xy + y^2}$$

$$= \frac{(x - y)(x^2 + xy + y^2) + (x + y)(x - y)}{(x - y)^2}$$

$$= \frac{(x - y)[(x^2 + xy + y^2) + (x + y)]}{(x - y)(x - y)}$$

$$= \frac{(x-y)(x^2 + xy + y^2 + x + y)}{(x-y)(x - y)}$$

$$= \frac{x^2 + xy + y^2 + x + y}{x - y}$$

88. (a) $\dfrac{16(x + 1)}{(x - 1)^2(x^2 + x + 1)}, x \neq -1$; (b) $\dfrac{x^2 + x + 1}{(x + 1)^3}$,

$x \neq -1$; (c) $\dfrac{(x + 1)^3}{x^2 + x + 1}, x \neq -1, x \neq 1$

89. From the graph we see that the domain consists of all real numbers except -2 and 1, so the domain is

$(-\infty, -2) \cup (-2, 1) \cup (1, \infty)$. We also see that the range consists of all real numbers except 2 and 3, so the range is $(-\infty, 2) \cup (2, 3) \cup (3, \infty)$.

90. Domain: $(-\infty, -1) \cup (-1, 0) \cup (0, 1) \cup (1, \infty)$; range: $(-\infty, -3) \cup (-3, -1) \cup (-1, 0) \cup (0, \infty)$

91. From the graph we see that the domain consists of all real numbers except -1 and 1, so the domain is $(-\infty, -1) \cup (-1, 1) \cup (1, \infty)$. We also see that the range consists of all real numbers less than or equal to -1 or greater than 0. Thus, the range is $(-\infty, -1] \cup (0, \infty)$.

Exercise Set 7.2

1. $\dfrac{4}{3a} + \dfrac{8}{3a}$

$= \dfrac{12}{3a}$ Adding the numerators. The denominator is unchanged.

$= \dfrac{3 \cdot 4}{3 \cdot a}$

$= \dfrac{\cancel{3} \cdot 4}{\cancel{3} \cdot a}$

$= \dfrac{4}{a}$

2. $\dfrac{4}{y}$

3. $\dfrac{3}{4a^2 b} - \dfrac{7}{4a^2 b} = \dfrac{-4}{4a^2 b} = \dfrac{-1 \cdot 4}{4a^2 b} = \dfrac{-1 \cdot \cancel{4}}{\cancel{4} a^2 b} = -\dfrac{1}{a^2 b}$

4. $\dfrac{1}{3m^2 n^2}$

5. $\dfrac{a - 5b}{a + b} + \dfrac{a + 7b}{a + b} = \dfrac{2a + 2b}{a + b}$

$= \dfrac{2(a + b)}{a + b}$

$= \dfrac{2(\cancel{a + b})}{1(\cancel{a + b})}$

$= 2$

6. 2

7. $\dfrac{4y + 2}{y - 2} - \dfrac{y - 3}{y - 2} = \dfrac{4y + 2 - (y - 3)}{y - 2}$

$= \dfrac{4y + 2 - y + 3}{y - 2}$

$= \dfrac{3y + 5}{y - 2}$

8. $\dfrac{2t + 4}{t - 4}$

9. $\dfrac{3a - 2}{a^2 - 25} - \dfrac{4a - 7}{a^2 - 25} = \dfrac{3a - 2 - (4a - 7)}{a^2 - 25}$

$= \dfrac{3a - 2 - 4a + 7}{a^2 - 25}$

$= \dfrac{-a + 5}{a^2 - 25}$

$= \dfrac{-1(a - 5)}{(a + 5)(a - 5)}$

$= \dfrac{-1(\cancel{a - 5})}{(a + 5)(\cancel{a - 5})}$

$= \dfrac{-1}{a + 5}, \text{ or } -\dfrac{1}{a + 5}$

10. $-\dfrac{1}{a + 3}$

11. $\dfrac{a^2}{a - b} + \dfrac{b^2}{b - a} = \dfrac{a^2}{a - b} + \dfrac{-1}{-1} \cdot \dfrac{b^2}{b - a}$

$= \dfrac{a^2}{a - b} + \dfrac{-b^2}{a - b}$

$= \dfrac{a^2 - b^2}{a - b} = \dfrac{(a + b)(a - b)}{a - b}$

$= \dfrac{(a + b)(\cancel{a - b})}{1 \cdot (\cancel{a - b})} = a + b$

12. $-(s + r)$

13. $\dfrac{3}{x} - \dfrac{8}{-x} = \dfrac{3}{x} + (-1) \cdot \dfrac{8}{-x} = \dfrac{3}{x} + \dfrac{1}{-1} \cdot \dfrac{8}{-x} =$

$\dfrac{3}{x} + \dfrac{8}{x} = \dfrac{11}{x}$

14. $\dfrac{7}{a}$

15. $\dfrac{x - 7}{x^2 - 16} - \dfrac{x - 1}{16 - x^2} = \dfrac{x - 7}{x^2 - 16} + (-1) \cdot \dfrac{x - 1}{16 - x^2}$

$= \dfrac{x - 7}{x^2 - 16} + \dfrac{1}{-1} \cdot \dfrac{x - 1}{16 - x^2}$

$= \dfrac{x - 7}{x^2 - 16} + \dfrac{x - 1}{x^2 - 16}$

$= \dfrac{2x - 8}{x^2 - 16}$

$= \dfrac{2(x - 4)}{(x + 4)(x - 4)}$

$= \dfrac{2(\cancel{x - 4})}{(x + 4)(\cancel{x - 4})}$

$= \dfrac{2}{x + 4}$

16. $-\dfrac{1}{y + 5}$

17. $\dfrac{t^2+3}{t^4-16}+\dfrac{7}{16-t^4}=\dfrac{t^2+3}{t^4-16}+\dfrac{-1}{-1}\cdot\dfrac{7}{16-t^4}$

$\qquad\qquad\qquad\quad=\dfrac{t^2+3}{t^4-16}+\dfrac{-7}{t^4-16}$

$\qquad\qquad\qquad\quad=\dfrac{t^2-4}{t^4-16}$

$\qquad\qquad\qquad\quad=\dfrac{(t+2)(t-2)}{(t^2+4)(t+2)(t-2)}$

$\qquad\qquad\qquad\quad=\dfrac{1\cdot\cancel{(t+2)}\cancel{(t-2)}}{(t^2+4)\cancel{(t+2)}\cancel{(t-2)}}$

$\qquad\qquad\qquad\quad=\dfrac{1}{t^2+4}$

18. $\dfrac{1}{y^2+9}$

19. $\dfrac{a+2}{a-4}+\dfrac{a-2}{a+3}$

[LCD is $(a-4)(a+3)$.]

$=\dfrac{a+2}{a-4}\cdot\dfrac{a+3}{a+3}+\dfrac{a-2}{a+3}\cdot\dfrac{a-4}{a-4}$

$=\dfrac{(a^2+5a+6)+(a^2-6a+8)}{(a-4)(a+3)}$

$=\dfrac{2a^2-a+14}{(a-4)(a+3)}$

20. $\dfrac{2a^2+22}{(a-5)(a+4)}$

21. $\qquad 2+\dfrac{x-3}{x+1}=\dfrac{2}{1}+\dfrac{x-3}{x+1}$

[LCD is $x+1$.]

$=\dfrac{2}{1}\cdot\dfrac{x+1}{x+1}+\dfrac{x-3}{x+1}$

$=\dfrac{(2x+2)+(x-3)}{x+1}$

$=\dfrac{3x-1}{x+1}$

22. $\dfrac{4y-13}{y-5}$

23. $\qquad\dfrac{4xy}{x^2-y^2}+\dfrac{x-y}{x+y}$

$=\dfrac{4xy}{(x+y)(x-y)}+\dfrac{x-y}{x+y}$

LCD is $(x+y)(x-y)$.]

$=\dfrac{4xy}{(x+y)(x-y)}+\dfrac{x-y}{x+y}\cdot\dfrac{x-y}{x-y}$

$=\dfrac{4xy+x^2-2xy+y^2}{(x+y)(x-y)}$

$=\dfrac{x^2+2xy+y^2}{(x+y)(x-y)}=\dfrac{(x+y)(x+y)}{(x+y)(x-y)}$

$=\dfrac{\cancel{(x+y)}(x+y)}{\cancel{(x+y)}(x-y)}=\dfrac{x+y}{x-y}$

24. $\dfrac{a^2+7ab+b^2}{(a+b)(a-b)}$

25. $\qquad\dfrac{8}{2x^2-7x+5}+\dfrac{3x+2}{2x^2-x-10}$

$=\dfrac{8}{(2x-5)(x-1)}+\dfrac{3x+2}{(2x-5)(x+2)}$

[LCD is $(2x-5)(x-1)(x+2)$.]

$=\dfrac{8}{(2x-5)(x-1)}\cdot\dfrac{x+2}{x+2}+\dfrac{3x+2}{(2x-5)(x+2)}\cdot\dfrac{x-1}{x-1}$

$=\dfrac{8x+16+3x^2-x-2}{(2x-5)(x-1)(x+2)}$

$=\dfrac{3x^2+7x+14}{(2x-5)(x-1)(x+2)}$

26. $\dfrac{3y-4}{(y-1)(y-2)}$

27. $\qquad\dfrac{4}{x+1}+\dfrac{x+2}{x^2-1}+\dfrac{3}{x-1}$

$=\dfrac{4}{x+1}+\dfrac{x+2}{(x+1)(x-1)}+\dfrac{3}{x-1}$

[LCD is $(x+1)(x-1)$.]

$=\dfrac{4}{x+1}\cdot\dfrac{x-1}{x-1}+\dfrac{x+2}{(x+1)(x-1)}+\dfrac{3}{x-1}\cdot\dfrac{x+1}{x+1}$

$=\dfrac{4x-4+x+2+3x+3}{(x+1)(x-1)}$

$=\dfrac{8x+1}{(x+1)(x-1)}$

28. $\dfrac{4y+17}{(y+2)(y-2)}$

29. $\dfrac{x+6}{5x+10} - \dfrac{x-2}{4x+8}$

$= \dfrac{x+6}{5(x+2)} - \dfrac{x-2}{4(x+2)}$

[LCD is $5 \cdot 4(x+2)$.]

$= \dfrac{x+6}{5(x+2)} \cdot \dfrac{4}{4} - \dfrac{x-2}{4(x+2)} \cdot \dfrac{5}{5}$

$= \dfrac{4(x+6) - 5(x-2)}{5 \cdot 4(x+2)}$

$= \dfrac{4x + 24 - 5x + 10}{5 \cdot 4(x+2)}$

$= \dfrac{-x+34}{5 \cdot 4(x+2)}$, or $\dfrac{-x+34}{20(x+2)}$

30. $\dfrac{-2a+14}{15(a+5)}$

31. $\dfrac{x}{x^2+9x+20} - \dfrac{4}{x^2+7x+12}$

$= \dfrac{x}{(x+5)(x+4)} - \dfrac{4}{(x+3)(x+4)}$

[LCD is $(x+5)(x+4)(x+3)$.]

$= \dfrac{x}{(x+5)(x+4)} \cdot \dfrac{x+3}{x+3} - \dfrac{4}{(x+3)(x+4)} \cdot \dfrac{x+5}{x+5}$

$= \dfrac{x^2 + 3x - (4x + 20)}{(x+5)(x+4)(x+3)}$

$= \dfrac{x^2 + 3x - 4x - 20}{(x+5)(x+4)(x+3)}$

$= \dfrac{x^2 - x - 20}{(x+5)(x+4)(x+3)}$

$= \dfrac{(x-5)(x+4)}{(x+5)(x+4)(x+3)}$

$= \dfrac{(x-5)(x+4)}{(x+5)(x+4)(x+3)}$

$= \dfrac{x-5}{(x+5)(x+3)}$

32. $\dfrac{x-6}{(x+6)(x+4)}$

33. $\dfrac{3y}{y^2-7y+10} - \dfrac{2y}{y^2-8y+15}$

$= \dfrac{3y}{(y-5)(y-2)} - \dfrac{2y}{(y-5)(y-3)}$

[LCD is $(y-5)(y-2)(y-3)$.]

$= \dfrac{3y}{(y-5)(y-2)} \cdot \dfrac{y-3}{y-3} - \dfrac{2y}{(y-5)(y-3)} \cdot \dfrac{y-2}{y-2}$

$= \dfrac{3y^2 - 9y - (2y^2 - 4y)}{(y-5)(y-2)(y-3)}$

$= \dfrac{3y^2 - 9y - 2y^2 + 4y}{(y-5)(y-2)(y-3)}$

$= \dfrac{y^2 - 5y}{(y-5)(y-2)(y-3)} = \dfrac{y(y-5)}{(y-5)(y-2)(y-3)}$

$= \dfrac{y(y-5)}{(y-5)(y-2)(y-3)} = \dfrac{y}{(y-2)(y-3)}$

34. $\dfrac{2x^2+21x}{(x-4)(x-2)(x+3)}$

35. $\dfrac{2x+1}{x-y} + \dfrac{5x^2-5xy}{x^2-2xy+y^2}$

$= \dfrac{2x+1}{x-y} + \dfrac{5x(x-y)}{(x-y)(x-y)}$

$= \dfrac{2x+1}{x-y} + \dfrac{5x(x-y)}{(x-y)(x-y)}$

$= \dfrac{2x+1}{x-y} + \dfrac{5x}{x-y}$

$= \dfrac{7x+1}{x-y}$

36. $\dfrac{2}{a-b}$

37. $\dfrac{a-3}{a^2-16} - \dfrac{3a-2}{a^2+2a-24}$

$= \dfrac{a-3}{(a+4)(a-4)} - \dfrac{3a-2}{(a+6)(a-4)}$

[LCD is $(a+4)(a-4)(a+6)$.]

$= \dfrac{a-3}{(a+4)(a-4)} \cdot \dfrac{a+6}{a+6} - \dfrac{3a-2}{(a+6)(a-4)} \cdot \dfrac{a+4}{a+4}$

$= \dfrac{(a-3)(a+6) - (3a-2)(a+4)}{(a+4)(a-4)(a+6)}$

$= \dfrac{a^2 + 3a - 18 - (3a^2 + 10a - 8)}{(a+4)(a-4)(a+6)}$

$= \dfrac{a^2 + 3a - 18 - 3a^2 - 10a + 8}{(a+4)(a-4)(a+6)}$

$= \dfrac{-2a^2 - 7a - 10}{(a+4)(a-4)(a+6)}$

38. $\dfrac{-2t^2+13t-7}{(t+3)(t-3)(t-1)}$

39.

$$3 + \frac{t}{t+2} - \frac{2}{t^2-4} = \frac{3}{1} + \frac{t}{t+2} - \frac{2}{(t+2)(t-2)}$$

[LCD is $(t+2)(t-2)$.]

$$= \frac{3}{1} \cdot \frac{(t+2)(t-2)}{(t+2)(t-2)} + \frac{t}{t+2} \cdot \frac{t-2}{t-2} - \frac{2}{(t+2)(t-2)}$$

$$= \frac{3t^2 - 12 + t^2 - 2t - 2}{(t+2)(t-2)}$$

$$= \frac{4t^2 - 2t - 14}{(t+2)(t-2)}$$

40. $\dfrac{3t^2 + 3t - 21}{(t+3)(t-3)}$

41.

$$\frac{2}{y+3} - \frac{y}{y-1} + \frac{y^2+2}{y^2+2y-3}$$

$$= \frac{2}{y+3} - \frac{y}{y-1} + \frac{y^2+2}{(y+3)(y-1)}$$

[LCD is $(y+3)(y-1)$.]

$$= \frac{2}{y+3} \cdot \frac{y-1}{y-1} - \frac{y}{y-1} \cdot \frac{y+3}{y+3} + \frac{y^2+2}{(y+3)(y-1)}$$

$$= \frac{2(y-1) - y(y+3) + y^2 + 2}{(y+3)(y-1)}$$

$$= \frac{2y - 2 - y^2 - 3y + y^2 + 2}{(y+3)(y-1)}$$

$$= \frac{-y}{(y+3)(y-1)}, \text{ or } -\frac{y}{(y+3)(y-1)}$$

42. 0

43.

$$\frac{5y}{1-2y} - \frac{2y}{2y+1} + \frac{3}{4y^2-1}$$

$$= \frac{-1}{-1} \cdot \frac{5y}{1-2y} - \frac{2y}{2y+1} + \frac{3}{(2y+1)(2y-1)}$$

$$= \frac{-5y}{2y-1} - \frac{2y}{2y+1} + \frac{3}{(2y+1)(2y-1)}$$

[LCD is $(2y-1)(2y+1)$.]

$$= \frac{-5y}{2y-1} \cdot \frac{2y+1}{2y+1} - \frac{2y}{2y+1} \cdot \frac{2y-1}{2y-1} +$$

$$\frac{3}{(2y+1)(2y-1)}$$

$$= \frac{-5y(2y+1) - 2y(2y-1) + 3}{(2y+1)(2y-1)}$$

$$= \frac{-10y^2 - 5y - 4y^2 + 2y + 3}{(2y+1)(2y-1)}$$

$$= \frac{-14y^2 - 3y + 3}{(2y+1)(2y-1)}$$

44. $\dfrac{-3x^2 - 3x - 4}{(x+1)(x-1)}$

45.

$$\frac{2}{x^2-5x+6} - \frac{4}{x^2-2x-3} + \frac{2}{x^2+4x+3}$$

$$= \frac{2}{(x-3)(x-2)} - \frac{4}{(x-3)(x+1)} + \frac{2}{(x+3)(x+1)}$$

[LCD is $(x-3)(x-2)(x+1)(x+3)$.]

$$= \frac{2}{(x-3)(x-2)} \cdot \frac{(x+1)(x+3)}{(x+1)(x+3)} -$$

$$\frac{4}{(x-3)(x+1)} \cdot \frac{(x-2)(x+3)}{(x-2)(x+3)} +$$

$$\frac{2}{(x+3)(x+1)} \cdot \frac{(x-3)(x-2)}{(x-3)(x-2)}$$

$$= \frac{2(x+1)(x+3) - 4(x-2)(x+3) + 2(x-3)(x-2)}{(x-3)(x-2)(x+1)(x+3)}$$

$$= \frac{2x^2 + 8x + 6 - 4x^2 - 4x + 24 + 2x^2 - 10x + 12}{(x-3)(x-2)(x+1)(x+3)}$$

$$= \frac{-6x + 42}{(x-3)(x-2)(x+1)(x+3)}$$

46. $\dfrac{4t+26}{(t+3)(t+2)(t+1)(t-4)}$

47.

$$\frac{15x^{-7}y^{12}z^4}{35x^{-2}y^6z^{-3}} = \frac{15}{35}x^{-7-(-2)}y^{12-6}z^{4-(-3)}$$

$$= \frac{3}{7}x^{-5}y^6z^7 = \frac{3}{7} \cdot \frac{1}{x^5} \cdot y^6z^7$$

$$= \frac{3y^6z^7}{7x^5}$$

48. $y = \dfrac{5}{4}x + \dfrac{11}{2}$

49.

$$x(x+1) = 6$$

$$x^2 + x = 6$$

$$x^2 + x - 6 = 0$$

$$(x+3)(x-2) = 0$$

$$x+3 = 0 \quad or \quad x-2 = 0$$

$$x = -3 \quad or \qquad x = 2$$

The solutions are -3 and 2.

50. $-\dfrac{2}{3}, \dfrac{1}{4}$

51. ◈

52. ◈

53. ◈

54. ◈

55. The smallest number of beats possible is the least common multiple of 6 and 4.

$$6 = 2 \cdot 3$$
$$4 = 2 \cdot 2$$
$$\text{LCM} = 2 \cdot 3 \cdot 2, \text{ or } 12$$

A measure should be divided into 12 beats.

56. Every 420 years

57. $x^8 - x^4 = x^4(x^2 + 1)(x + 1)(x - 1)$

$x^5 - x^2 = x^2(x - 1)(x^2 + x + 1)$

$x^5 - x^3 = x^3(x + 1)(x - 1)$

$x^5 + x^2 = x^2(x + 1)(x^2 - x + 1)$

The LCM is

$x^4(x^2 + 1)(x + 1)(x - 1)(x^2 + x + 1)(x^2 - x + 1)$.

58. $2ab(a^2 + ab + b^2)(a + b)^2(a^2 - ab + b^2)(a - b)(2b + 3a)$

59. The LCM is $8a^4b^7$.

One expression is $2a^3b^7$.

Then the other expression must contain 8, a^4, and one of the following:

no factor of b, b, b^2, b^3, b^4, b^5, b^6, or b^7.

Thus, all the possibilities for the other expression are $8a^4$, $8a^4b$, $8a^4b^2$, $8a^4b^3$, $8a^4b^4$, $8a^4b^5$, $8a^4b^6$, $8a^4b^7$.

60. $\dfrac{x^4 + 6x^3 + 2x^2}{(x + 2)(x - 2)(x + 5)}$

61. $(f - g)(x) = \dfrac{x^3}{x^2 - 4} - \dfrac{x^2}{x^2 + 3x - 10}$

$= \dfrac{x^3}{(x + 2)(x - 2)} - \dfrac{x^2}{(x + 5)(x - 2)}$

$= \dfrac{x^3(x + 5) - x^2(x + 2)}{(x + 2)(x - 2)(x + 5)}$

$= \dfrac{x^4 + 5x^3 - x^3 - 2x^2}{(x + 2)(x - 2)(x + 5)}$

$= \dfrac{x^4 + 4x^3 - 2x^2}{(x + 2)(x - 2)(x + 5)}$

62. $\dfrac{x^5}{(x^2 - 4)(x^2 + 3x - 10)}$

63. $(f/g)(x) = \dfrac{x^3}{x^2 - 4} \div \dfrac{x^2}{x^2 + 3x - 10}$

$= \dfrac{x^2 \cdot x}{(x + 2)(x - 2)} \cdot \dfrac{(x + 5)(x - 2)}{x^2}$

$= \dfrac{x^2(x - 2)}{x^2(x - 2)} \cdot \dfrac{x(x + 5)}{x + 2}$

$= \dfrac{x(x + 5)}{x + 2}$

Note that $x \neq 0$, $x \neq -5$, and $x \neq 2$ are additional restrictions, since $g(0) = 0$, -5 is not in the domain of g, and 2 is not in the domain of either f or g.

64. $\{x | x$ is a real number and $x \neq -2$ and $x \neq 2$ and $x \neq -5\}$, or $(-\infty, -5) \cup (-5, -2) \cup (-2, 2) \cup (2, \infty)$

65. $x + 2 = 0$ when $x = -2$, so -2 is not in the domain of f/g. We also see, from the explanation at the end of Exercise 63, that 0, -5, and 2 are not in the domain. Thus, the domain of f/g is $\{x | x$ is a real number and $x \neq -2$ and $x \neq 0$ and $x \neq -5$ and $x \neq 2\}$, or $(-\infty, -5) \cup (-5, -2) \cup (-2, 0) \cup (0, 2) \cup (2, \infty)$.

66. $\dfrac{9x^2 + 28x + 15}{(x - 3)(x + 3)^2}$

67. $\quad 4(y - 1)(2y - 5)^{-1} + 5(2y + 3)(5 - 2y)^{-1} +$
$$(y - 4)(2y - 5)^{-1}$$

$= \dfrac{4(y - 1)}{2y - 5} + \dfrac{-1}{-1} \cdot \dfrac{5(2y + 3)}{5 - 2y} + \dfrac{y - 4}{2y - 5}$

$= \dfrac{4(y - 1)}{2y - 5} + \dfrac{-5(2y + 3)}{2y - 5} + \dfrac{y - 4}{2y - 5}$

$= \dfrac{4y - 4 - 10y - 15 + y - 4}{2y - 5}$

$= \dfrac{-5y - 23}{2y - 5}, \text{ or } \dfrac{5y + 23}{5 - 2y}$

68. $\dfrac{1}{2x(x - 5)}$

69. $\quad \dfrac{8t^5}{2t^2 - 10t + 12} \div \left(\dfrac{2t}{t^2 - 8t + 15} - \dfrac{3t}{t^2 - 7t + 10} \right)$

$= \dfrac{8t^5}{2t^2 - 10t + 12} \div \left(\dfrac{2t}{(t - 5)(t - 3)} - \dfrac{3t}{(t - 5)(t - 2)} \right)$

$= \dfrac{8t^5}{2t^2 - 10t + 12} \div \left(\dfrac{2t(t - 2) - 3t(t - 3)}{(t - 5)(t - 3)(t - 2)} \right)$

$= \dfrac{8t^5}{2t^2 - 10t + 12} \div \left(\dfrac{2t^2 - 4t - 3t^2 + 9t}{(t - 5)(t - 3)(t - 2)} \right)$

$= \dfrac{8t^5}{2t^2 - 10t + 12} \div \dfrac{-t^2 + 5t}{(t - 5)(t - 3)(t - 2)}$

$= \dfrac{8t^5}{2(t - 3)(t - 2)} \cdot \dfrac{(t - 5)(t - 3)(t - 2)}{-t(t - 5)}$

$= \dfrac{2 \cdot 4 \cdot t \cdot t^4 (t - 5)(t - 3)(t - 2)}{2(t - 3)(t - 2)(-1)(t)(t - 5)}$

$= -4t^4$

70. Domain: $\{x | x$ is a real number and $x \neq -1\}$, or $(-\infty, -1) \cup (-1, \infty)$;
range: $\{y | y$ is a real number and $y \neq 3\}$, or $(-\infty, 3) \cup (3, \infty)$

71.

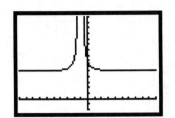

From the graph (shown in the window $[-10, 10, -2, 15]$) we see that the domain of the function consists of all real numbers except -1, so the domain of g is $\{x | x$ is a real number and $x \neq -1\}$, or $(-\infty, -1) \cup (-1, \infty)$. We also see that the range consists of all real numbers greater than 5, so the range of g is $\{x | x > 5\}$, or $(5, \infty)$.

72. Domain: $\{x | x$ is a real number and $x \neq 0$ and $x \neq 1\}$, or $(-\infty, 0) \cup (0, 1) \cup (1, \infty)$; range: $\{x | x > 0\}$, or $(0, \infty)$

Exercise Set 7.3

1. $\dfrac{5 + \dfrac{1}{a}}{\dfrac{1}{a} - 2} = \dfrac{5 + \dfrac{1}{a}}{\dfrac{1}{a} - 2} \cdot \dfrac{a}{a}$ Multiplying by 1, using the LCD

$= \dfrac{\left(5 + \dfrac{1}{a}\right)a}{\left(\dfrac{1}{a} - 2\right)a}$ Multiplying the numerators and the denominator

$= \dfrac{5 \cdot a + \dfrac{1}{a} \cdot a}{\dfrac{1}{a} \cdot a - 2 \cdot a}$

$= \dfrac{5a + \dfrac{\cancel{a}}{\cancel{a}} \cdot 1}{\dfrac{\cancel{a}}{\cancel{a}} \cdot 1 - 2a}$ Removing factors equal to 1

$= \dfrac{5a + 1}{1 - 2a}$ Simplifying

2. $\dfrac{1 + 7y}{1 - 5y}$

3. $\dfrac{x - x^{-1}}{x + x^{-1}} = \dfrac{x - \dfrac{1}{x}}{x + \dfrac{1}{x}}$ Rewriting with positive exponents

$= \dfrac{x - \dfrac{1}{x}}{x + \dfrac{1}{x}} \cdot \dfrac{x}{x}$ Multiplying by 1, using the LCD

$= \dfrac{x \cdot x - \dfrac{1}{x} \cdot x}{x \cdot x + \dfrac{1}{x} \cdot x}$

$= \dfrac{x^2 - 1}{x^2 + 1}$

(Although the numerator can be factored, doing so does not lead to further simplification.)

4. $\dfrac{y^2 + 1}{y^2 - 1}$

5. $\dfrac{\dfrac{3}{x} + \dfrac{4}{y}}{\dfrac{4}{x} - \dfrac{3}{y}} = \dfrac{\dfrac{3}{x} + \dfrac{4}{y}}{\dfrac{4}{x} - \dfrac{3}{y}} \cdot \dfrac{xy}{xy}$ Multiplying by 1, using the LCD

$= \dfrac{\dfrac{3}{x} \cdot xy + \dfrac{4}{y} \cdot xy}{\dfrac{4}{x} \cdot xy - \dfrac{3}{y} \cdot xy}$

$= \dfrac{3y + 4x}{4y - 3x}$

6. $\dfrac{2z + 5y}{4y - z}$

7. $\dfrac{\dfrac{x^2 - y^2}{xy}}{\dfrac{x - y}{y}} = \dfrac{x^2 - y^2}{xy} \cdot \dfrac{y}{x - y}$ Multiplying by the reciprocal of the divisor

$= \dfrac{(x + y)(x - y) \cdot y}{xy(x - y)}$

$= \dfrac{(x + y)(x \cancel{- y}) \cdot y}{xy(x \cancel{- y})}$

$= \dfrac{x + y}{x}$

8. $\dfrac{a + b}{a}$

9. $\dfrac{\dfrac{3x}{y} - x}{2y - \dfrac{y}{x}} = \dfrac{\dfrac{3x}{y} - x}{2y - \dfrac{y}{x}} \cdot \dfrac{xy}{xy}$ Multiplying by 1,
using the LCD

$$= \dfrac{\dfrac{3x}{y} \cdot xy - x \cdot xy}{2y \cdot xy - \dfrac{y}{x} \cdot xy}$$

$$= \dfrac{3x^2 - x^2 y}{2xy^2 - y^2}$$

(Although both the numerator and the denominator can be factored, doing so does not lead to further simplification.)

10. $\dfrac{3}{3x + 2}$

11. $\dfrac{a^{-1} + b^{-1}}{\dfrac{a^2 - b^2}{ab}} = \dfrac{\dfrac{1}{a} + \dfrac{1}{b}}{\dfrac{a^2 - b^2}{ab}}$

$$= \dfrac{\dfrac{1}{a} + \dfrac{1}{b}}{\dfrac{a^2 - b^2}{ab}} \cdot \dfrac{ab}{ab}$$ Multiplying by 1, using the LCD

$$= \dfrac{\dfrac{1}{a} \cdot ab + \dfrac{1}{b} \cdot ab}{\dfrac{a^2 - b^2}{ab} \cdot ab}$$

$$= \dfrac{b + a}{a^2 - b^2} = \dfrac{b + a}{(a + b)(a - b)}$$

$$= \dfrac{(a + b) \cdot (1)}{(a + b)(a - b)} \qquad (b + a = a + b)$$

$$= \dfrac{1}{a - b}$$

12. $\dfrac{1}{x - y}$

13. $\dfrac{\dfrac{1}{x + h} - \dfrac{1}{x}}{h} = \dfrac{\dfrac{1}{x + h} \cdot \dfrac{x}{x} - \dfrac{1}{x} \cdot \dfrac{x + h}{x + h}}{h}$ Adding in the numerator

$$= \dfrac{\dfrac{x - x - h}{x(x + h)}}{h} = \dfrac{\dfrac{-h}{x(x + h)}}{h}$$

$$= \dfrac{-h}{x(x + h)} \cdot \dfrac{1}{h}$$ Multiplying by the reciprocal of the divisor

$$= \dfrac{-1 \cdot h \cdot 1}{x(x + h)(h)} \qquad (-h = -1 \cdot h)$$

$$= -\dfrac{1}{x(x + h)}$$

14. $\dfrac{1}{a(a - h)}$

15. $\dfrac{\dfrac{a^2 - 4}{a^2 + 3a + 2}}{\dfrac{a^2 - 5a - 6}{a^2 - 6a - 7}}$

$$= \dfrac{a^2 - 4}{a^2 + 3a + 2} \cdot \dfrac{a^2 - 6a - 7}{a^2 - 5a - 6}$$ Multiplying by the reciprocal of the divisor

$$= \dfrac{(a + 2)(a - 2)}{(a + 2)(a + 1)} \cdot \dfrac{(a + 1)(a - 7)}{(a + 1)(a - 6)}$$

$$= \dfrac{(a + 2)(a - 2)(a + 1)(a - 7)}{(a + 2)(a + 1)(a + 1)(a - 6)}$$

$$= \dfrac{(a + 2)(a - 2)(a + 1)(a - 7)}{(a + 2)(a + 1)(a + 1)(a - 6)}$$

$$= \dfrac{(a - 2)(a - 7)}{(a + 1)(a - 6)}$$

16. $\dfrac{(x - 4)(x - 7)}{(x - 5)(x + 6)}$

17. $\dfrac{\dfrac{2}{y - 3} + \dfrac{1}{y + 1}}{\dfrac{3}{y + 1} + \dfrac{4}{y - 3}}$

$$= \dfrac{\dfrac{2}{y - 3} + \dfrac{1}{y + 1}}{\dfrac{3}{y + 1} + \dfrac{4}{y - 3}} \cdot \dfrac{(y - 3)(y + 1)}{(y - 3)(y + 1)}$$

$$= \dfrac{\dfrac{2}{y - 3} \cdot (y - 3)(y + 1) + \dfrac{1}{y + 1} \cdot (y - 3)(y + 1)}{\dfrac{3}{y + 1} \cdot (y - 3)(y + 1) + \dfrac{4}{y - 3} \cdot (y - 3)(y + 1)}$$

Multiplying by 1, using the LCD

$$= \dfrac{2(y + 1) + (y - 3)}{3(y - 3) + 4(y + 1)}$$

$$= \dfrac{2y + 2 + y - 3}{3y - 9 + 4y + 4}$$

$$= \dfrac{3y - 1}{7y - 5}$$

18. $\dfrac{4x - 7}{7x - 9}$

19. $\dfrac{a(a+3)^{-1} - 2(a-1)^{-1}}{a(a+3)^{-1} - (a-1)^{-1}}$

$= \dfrac{\dfrac{a}{a+3} - \dfrac{2}{a-1}}{\dfrac{a}{a+3} - \dfrac{1}{a-1}}$

$= \dfrac{\dfrac{a}{a+3} - \dfrac{2}{a-1}}{\dfrac{a}{a+3} - \dfrac{1}{a-1}} \cdot \dfrac{(a+3)(a-1)}{(a+3)(a-1)}$

Multiplying by 1, using the LCD

$= \dfrac{\dfrac{a}{a+3}\cdot(a+3)(a-1) - \dfrac{2}{a-1}\cdot(a+3)(a-1)}{\dfrac{a}{a+3}\cdot(a+3)(a-1) - \dfrac{1}{a-1}\cdot(a+3)(a-1)}$

$= \dfrac{a(a-1) - 2(a+3)}{a(a-1) - (a+3)}$

$= \dfrac{a^2 - a - 2a - 6}{a^2 - a - a - 3} = \dfrac{a^2 - 3a - 6}{a^2 - 2a - 3}$

(Although the denominator can be factored, doing so does not lead to further simplification.)

20. $\dfrac{a^2 - 6a - 6}{a^2 - 4a - 2}$

21. $\dfrac{\dfrac{x}{x^2+3x-4} - \dfrac{1}{x^2+3x-4}}{\dfrac{x}{x^2+6x+8} + \dfrac{3}{x^2+6x+8}}$

$= \dfrac{\dfrac{x-1}{x^2+3x-4}}{\dfrac{x+3}{x^2+6x+8}}$ 　Adding in the numerator and the denominator

$= \dfrac{x-1}{x^2+3x-4} \cdot \dfrac{x^2+6x+8}{x+3}$

$= \dfrac{(x-1)(x+4)(x+2)}{(x+4)(x-1)(x+3)}$

$= \dfrac{\cancel{(x-1)}\cancel{(x+4)}(x+2)}{\cancel{(x+4)}\cancel{(x-1)}(x+3)} = \dfrac{x+2}{x+3}$

22. $\dfrac{x-4}{x-2}$

23. $\dfrac{\dfrac{3}{a^2-9} + \dfrac{2}{a+3}}{\dfrac{4}{a^2-9} + \dfrac{1}{a+3}}$

$= \dfrac{\dfrac{3}{(a+3)(a-3)} + \dfrac{2}{a+3}}{\dfrac{4}{(a+3)(a-3)} + \dfrac{1}{a+3}}$

$= \dfrac{\dfrac{3}{(a+3)(a-3)} + \dfrac{2}{a+3}}{\dfrac{4}{(a+3)(a-3)} + \dfrac{1}{a+3}} \cdot \dfrac{(a+3)(a-3)}{(a+3)(a-3)}$

Multiplying by 1, using the LCD

$= \dfrac{\dfrac{3}{(a+3)(a-3)}\cdot(a+3)(a-3) + \dfrac{2}{a+3}\cdot(a+3)(a-3)}{\dfrac{4}{(a+3)(a-3)}\cdot(a+3)(a-3) + \dfrac{1}{a+3}\cdot(a+3)(a-3)}$

$= \dfrac{3 + 2(a-3)}{4 + a - 3}$

$= \dfrac{3 + 2a - 6}{a+1} = \dfrac{2a-3}{a+1}$

24. $\dfrac{a+1}{2a+5}$

25. $\dfrac{\dfrac{4}{x^2-1} - \dfrac{3}{x+1}}{\dfrac{5}{x^2-1} - \dfrac{2}{x-1}}$

$= \dfrac{\dfrac{4}{(x+1)(x-1)} - \dfrac{3}{x+1}}{\dfrac{5}{(x+1)(x-1)} - \dfrac{2}{x-1}}$

$= \dfrac{\dfrac{4}{(x+1)(x-1)} - \dfrac{3}{x+1}}{\dfrac{5}{(x+1)(x-1)} - \dfrac{2}{x-1}} \cdot \dfrac{(x+1)(x-1)}{(x+1)(x-1)}$

Multiplying by 1, using the LCD

$= \dfrac{\dfrac{4}{(x+1)(x-1)}\cdot(x+1)(x-1) - \dfrac{3}{x+1}\cdot(x+1)(x-1)}{\dfrac{5}{(x+1)(x-1)}\cdot(x+1)(x-1) - \dfrac{2}{x-1}\cdot(x+1)(x-1)}$

$= \dfrac{4 - 3(x-1)}{5 - 2(x+1)}$

$= \dfrac{4 - 3x + 3}{5 - 2x - 2} = \dfrac{7 - 3x}{3 - 2x}$

26. $\dfrac{-1 - 3x}{8 - 2x}$

27.
$$\dfrac{\dfrac{y}{y^2-1}+\dfrac{3}{1-y^2}}{\dfrac{y^2}{y^2-1}+\dfrac{9}{1-y^2}}$$

$$=\dfrac{\dfrac{y}{y^2-1}+\dfrac{-1}{-1}\cdot\dfrac{3}{1-y^2}}{\dfrac{y^2}{y^2-1}+\dfrac{-1}{-1}\cdot\dfrac{9}{1-y^2}}$$

$$=\dfrac{\dfrac{y}{y^2-1}-\dfrac{3}{y^2-1}}{\dfrac{y^2}{y^2-1}-\dfrac{9}{y^2-1}}$$

$$=\dfrac{\dfrac{y-3}{y^2-1}}{\dfrac{y^2-9}{y^2-1}} \qquad \text{Adding in the numerator and the denominator}$$

$$=\dfrac{y-3}{y^2-1}\cdot\dfrac{y^2-1}{y^2-9} \qquad \text{Multiplying by the reciprocal of the divisor}$$

$$=\dfrac{(y-3)(y^2-1)}{(y^2-1)(y+3)(y-3)}$$

$$=\dfrac{\cancel{(y-3)}\cancel{(y^2-1)}(1)}{\cancel{(y^2-1)}(y+3)\cancel{(y-3)}}$$

$$=\dfrac{1}{y+3}$$

28. $\dfrac{1}{y+5}$

29.
$$\dfrac{\dfrac{y^2}{y^2-9}-\dfrac{y}{y+3}}{\dfrac{y}{y^2-9}-\dfrac{1}{y-3}}$$

$$=\dfrac{\dfrac{y^2}{(y+3)(y-3)}-\dfrac{y}{y+3}}{\dfrac{y}{(y+3)(y-3)}-\dfrac{1}{y-3}}$$

$$=\dfrac{\dfrac{y^2}{(y+3)(y-3)}-\dfrac{y}{y+3}}{\dfrac{y}{(y+3)(y-3)}-\dfrac{1}{y-3}}\cdot\dfrac{(y+3)(y-3)}{(y+3)(y-3)}$$

Multiplying by 1, using the LCD

$$=\dfrac{\dfrac{y^2}{(y+3)(y-3)}\cdot(y+3)(y-3)-\dfrac{y}{y+3}\cdot(y+3)(y-3)}{\dfrac{y}{(y+3)(y-3)}\cdot(y+3)(y-3)-\dfrac{1}{y-3}\cdot(y+3)(y-3)}$$

$$=\dfrac{y^2-y(y-3)}{y-(y+3)}=\dfrac{y^2-y^2+3y}{y-y-3}=\dfrac{3y}{-3}$$

$$=\dfrac{\cancel{3}y}{-1\cdot\cancel{3}}=-y$$

30. $-y$

31.
$$\dfrac{\dfrac{a}{a+3}+\dfrac{4}{5a}}{\dfrac{a}{2a+6}+\dfrac{3}{a}}$$

$$=\dfrac{\dfrac{a}{a+3}+\dfrac{4}{5a}}{\dfrac{a}{2(a+3)}+\dfrac{3}{a}}$$

$$=\dfrac{\dfrac{a}{a+3}+\dfrac{4}{5a}}{\dfrac{a}{2(a+3)}+\dfrac{3}{a}}\cdot\dfrac{10a(a+3)}{10a(a+3)}$$

Multiplying by 1, using the LCD

$$=\dfrac{\dfrac{a}{a+3}\cdot10a(a+3)+\dfrac{4}{5a}\cdot10a(a+3)}{\dfrac{a}{2(a+3)}\cdot10a(a+3)+\dfrac{3}{a}\cdot10a(a+3)}$$

$$=\dfrac{10a^2+8(a+3)}{5a^2+30(a+3)}=\dfrac{10a^2+8a+24}{5a^2+30a+90}$$

$$=\dfrac{2(5a^2+4a+12)}{5(a^2+6a+18)}$$

32. $\dfrac{6a^2+30a+60}{3a^2+2a+4}$

33.
$$\dfrac{\dfrac{1}{x^2-3x+2}+\dfrac{1}{x^2-4}}{\dfrac{1}{x^2+4x+4}+\dfrac{1}{x^2-4}}$$

$$=\dfrac{\dfrac{1}{(x-1)(x-2)}+\dfrac{1}{(x+2)(x-2)}}{\dfrac{1}{(x+2)(x+2)}+\dfrac{1}{(x+2)(x-2)}}$$

$$=\dfrac{\dfrac{1}{(x-1)(x-2)}+\dfrac{1}{(x+2)(x-2)}}{\dfrac{1}{(x+2)(x+2)}+\dfrac{1}{(x+2)(x-2)}}\cdot$$

$$\dfrac{(x-1)(x-2)(x+2)(x+2)}{(x-1)(x-2)(x+2)(x+2)}$$

Multiplying by 1, using the LCD

$$=\dfrac{(x+2)(x+2)+(x-1)(x+2)}{(x-1)(x-2)+(x-1)(x+2)}$$

$$=\dfrac{x^2+4x+4+x^2+x-2}{x^2-3x+2+x^2+x-2}$$

$$=\dfrac{2x^2+5x+2}{2x^2-2x}$$

(Although both the numerator and the denominator can be factored, doing so will not lead to further simplification.)

34. $\dfrac{2x^2-5x-3}{2x^2+2x-4}$

35.

$$\cfrac{\cfrac{3}{x^2+2x-3}-\cfrac{1}{x^2-3x-10}}{\cfrac{3}{x^2-6x+5}-\cfrac{1}{x^2+5x+6}}$$

$$=\cfrac{\cfrac{3}{(x+3)(x-1)}-\cfrac{1}{(x-5)(x+2)}}{\cfrac{3}{(x-5)(x-1)}-\cfrac{1}{(x+3)(x+2)}}$$

$$=\cfrac{\cfrac{3}{(x+3)(x-1)}-\cfrac{1}{(x-5)(x+2)}}{\cfrac{3}{(x-5)(x-1)}-\cfrac{1}{(x+3)(x+2)}}\cdot$$

$$\cfrac{(x+3)(x-1)(x-5)(x+2)}{(x+3)(x-1)(x-5)(x+2)}$$

Multiplying by 1, using the LCD

$$=\cfrac{3(x-5)(x+2)-(x+3)(x-1)}{3(x+3)(x+2)-(x-1)(x-5)}$$

$$=\cfrac{3(x^2-3x-10)-(x^2+2x-3)}{3(x^2+5x+6)-(x^2-6x+5)}$$

$$=\cfrac{3x^2-9x-30-x^2-2x+3}{3x^2+15x+18-x^2+6x-5}$$

$$=\cfrac{2x^2-11x-27}{2x^2+21x+13}$$

36. $\cfrac{2a^2+4a+2}{2a^2+5a-3}$

37. $f(x)=x^2-3$

$f(-5)=(-5)^2-3=25-3=22$

38. $y=\cfrac{a-bx}{b}$

39.

(graph showing $f(x)=-3x+7$)

40. $\{6,-1\}$

41. *Familiarize.* Let $t=$ the amount Antonio received in tips on Thursday, in dollars. Then the average tip for the four days is given by $\cfrac{\$28+\$22+\$36+t}{4}$.

Translate.

The average tip is \$30.

$$\cfrac{28+22+36+t}{4}=30$$

Carry out. We solve the equation.

$$\cfrac{28+22+36+t}{4}=30$$

$$28+22+36+t=120 \quad \text{Multiplying by 4}$$

$$86+t=120$$

$$t=34$$

Check. If Antonio receives \$34 in tips on Thursday, then the average tip for the four days is $\cfrac{\$28+\$22+\$36+\$34}{4}=\cfrac{\$120}{4}=\$30$. The answer checks.

State. Antonio needs to earn \$34 in tips on Thursday in order for the average tip to be \$30.

42. 14 yd

43. ◈

44. ◈

45. ◈

46. $\cfrac{5(y+x)}{3(y-x)}$

47.

$$(a^2-ab+b^2)^{-1}(a^2b^{-1}+b^2a^{-1})\cdot$$
$$(a^{-2}-b^{-2})(a^{-2}+2a^{-1}b^{-1}+b^{-2})^{-1}$$

$$=\cfrac{(a^2b^{-1}+b^2a^{-1})(a^{-2}-b^{-2})}{(a^2-ab+b^2)(a^{-2}+2a^{-1}b^{-1}+b^{-2})}$$

$$=\cfrac{\left(\cfrac{a^2}{b}+\cfrac{b^2}{a}\right)\left(\cfrac{1}{a^2}-\cfrac{1}{b^2}\right)}{(a^2-ab+b^2)\left(\cfrac{1}{a^2}+\cfrac{2}{ab}+\cfrac{1}{b^2}\right)}$$

$$=\cfrac{\left(\cfrac{a^3+b^3}{ab}\right)\left(\cfrac{b^2-a^2}{a^2b^2}\right)}{(a^2-ab+b^2)\left(\cfrac{b^2+2ab+a^2}{a^2b^2}\right)}$$

$$=\cfrac{(a+b)(a^2-ab+b^2)(b+a)(b-a)}{a^3b^3}\cdot$$

$$\cfrac{a^2b^2}{(a^2-ab+b^2)(b+a)^2}$$

$$=\cfrac{b-a}{ab}$$

48. $\cfrac{8c}{17}$,

49. The reciprocal is $\cfrac{1}{1+\cfrac{1}{1+\cfrac{1}{1+\cfrac{1}{x}}}}$

We simplify.

$$\cfrac{1}{1+\cfrac{1}{1+\cfrac{1}{1+\cfrac{1}{x}}}} = \cfrac{1}{1+\cfrac{1}{1+\cfrac{1}{\frac{x+1}{x}}}}$$

$$= \cfrac{1}{1+\cfrac{1}{1+\cfrac{x}{x+1}}}$$

$$= \cfrac{1}{1+\cfrac{1}{\frac{x+1+x}{x+1}}}$$

$$= \cfrac{1}{1+\cfrac{1}{\frac{2x+1}{x+1}}}$$

$$= \cfrac{1}{1+\cfrac{x+1}{2x+1}}$$

$$= \cfrac{1}{\frac{2x+1+x+1}{2x+1}}$$

$$= \cfrac{1}{\frac{3x+2}{2x+1}}$$

$$= \frac{2x+1}{3x+2}$$

50. $\dfrac{x^2}{x^4+x^3+x^2+x+1}$

51. $f(x) = \dfrac{1}{1+x}$

$$f(a) = \dfrac{1}{1+a}$$

$$f(f(a)) = \cfrac{1}{1+\cfrac{1}{1+a}}$$

$$= \cfrac{1}{\frac{1+a+1}{1+a}}$$

$$= \cfrac{1}{\frac{2+a}{1+a}}$$

$$= \frac{1+a}{2+a}$$

52. $\dfrac{2a-1}{-a+5}$

53. $\dfrac{f(x+h)-f(x)}{h} = \cfrac{\dfrac{3}{(x+h)^2} - \dfrac{3}{x^2}}{h}$

$$= \frac{3x^2-3(x+h)^2}{x^2(x+h)^2} \cdot \frac{1}{h}$$

$$= \frac{3x^2-3x^2-6xh-3h^2}{x^2(x+h)^2} \cdot \frac{1}{h}$$

$$= \frac{-6xh-3h^2}{x^2(x+h)^2h}$$

$$= \frac{-3h(2x+h)}{x^2(x+h)^2h}$$

$$= \frac{-3\cancel{h}(2x+h)}{x^2(x+h)^2\cancel{h}}$$

$$= \frac{-3(2x+h)}{x^2(x+h)^2}$$

54. $\dfrac{-5}{x(x+h)}$

55. $\dfrac{f(x+h)-f(x)}{h}$

$$= \cfrac{\dfrac{1}{1-x-h} - \dfrac{1}{1-x}}{h}$$

$$= \frac{1-x-(1-x-h)}{(1-x-h)(1-x)} \cdot \frac{1}{h}$$

$$= \frac{1-x-1+x+h}{(1-x-h)(1-x)} \cdot \frac{1}{h}$$

$$= \frac{h}{(1-x-h)(1-x)h}$$

$$= \frac{\cancel{h}\cdot 1}{(1-x-h)(1-x)\cancel{h}}$$

$$= \frac{1}{(1-x-h)(1-x)}$$

56. $\dfrac{1}{(1+x+h)(1+x)}$

57. To avoid division by zero in $\dfrac{1}{x}$ and $\dfrac{8}{x^2}$ we must exclude 0 from the domain of F. To avoid division by zero in the complex fraction we solve:

$$2 - \frac{8}{x^2} = 0$$

$$2x^2 - 8 = 0$$

$$2(x^2 - 4) = 0$$

$$2(x+2)(x-2) = 0$$

$$x + 2 = 0 \quad or \quad x - 2 = 0$$

$$x = -2 \quad or \qquad x = 2.$$

The domain of $F = \{x | x$ is a real number and $x \neq 0$ and $x \neq -2$ and $x \neq 2\}$.

58. $\{x | x$ is a real number and $x \neq 1$ and $x \neq -1$ and $x \neq 4$ and $x \neq -4$ and $x \neq 5$ and $x \neq -5\}$

59.
$$\left[\frac{\frac{x+3}{x-3}+1}{\frac{x+3}{x-3}-1}\right]^4 = \left[\frac{x+3+x-3}{x+3-x+3}\right]^4$$

$$= \left(\frac{2x}{6}\right)^4 = \left(\frac{x}{3}\right)^4 = \frac{x^4}{81}$$

Division by zero occurs in both the numerator and the denominator of the original fraction when $x = 3$. To avoid division by zero in the complex fraction we solve:

$$\frac{x+3}{x-3} - 1 = 0$$

$$\frac{x+3}{x-3} = 1$$

$$x+3 = x-3$$

$$3 = -3$$

The equation has no solution, so the denominator of the complex fraction cannot be zero. Thus, the domain of $f = \{x | x$ is a real number and $x \neq 3\}$.

Exercise Set 7.4

1.
$$\frac{1}{3} + \frac{4}{5} = \frac{x}{9}, \text{ LCD is } 45$$

$$45\left(\frac{1}{3} + \frac{4}{5}\right) = 45 \cdot \frac{x}{9}$$

$$45 \cdot \frac{1}{3} + 45 \cdot \frac{4}{5} = 45 \cdot \frac{x}{9}$$

$$15 + 36 = 5x$$

$$51 = 5x$$

$$\frac{51}{5} = x$$

Check: $\quad \dfrac{1}{3} + \dfrac{4}{5} = \dfrac{x}{9}$

$$\frac{1}{3} + \frac{4}{5} \; ? \; \frac{51/5}{9}$$

$$\frac{5}{15} + \frac{12}{15} \; \bigg| \; \frac{51}{5} \cdot \frac{1}{9}$$

$$\frac{17}{15} \; \bigg| \; \frac{17}{15} \quad \text{TRUE}$$

The solution is $\dfrac{51}{5}$.

2. $\dfrac{51}{2}$

3.
$$\frac{x}{3} - \frac{x}{4} = 12, \text{ LCD is } 12$$

$$12\left(\frac{x}{3} - \frac{x}{4}\right) = 12 \cdot 12$$

$$12 \cdot \frac{x}{3} - 12 \cdot \frac{x}{4} = 12 \cdot 12$$

$$4x - 3x = 144$$

$$x = 144$$

Check: $\quad \dfrac{x}{3} - \dfrac{x}{4} = 12$

$$\frac{144}{3} - \frac{144}{4} \; ? \; 12$$

$$48 - 36 \; \bigg|$$

$$12 \; \bigg| \; 12 \quad \text{TRUE}$$

The solution is 144.

4. $-\dfrac{225}{2}$

5.
$$\frac{5}{8} - \frac{1}{a} = \frac{2}{5}$$

Because $\dfrac{1}{a}$ is undefined when a is 0, we note at the outset that $a \neq 0$. Then we multiply both sides by the LCD, $8 \cdot a \cdot 5$, or $40a$.

$$40a\left(\frac{5}{8} - \frac{1}{a}\right) = 40a \cdot \frac{2}{5}$$

$$40a \cdot \frac{5}{8} - 40a \cdot \frac{1}{a} = 40a \cdot \frac{2}{5}$$

$$25a - 40 = 16a$$

$$-40 = -9a$$

$$\frac{40}{9} = a$$

Check: $\quad \dfrac{5}{8} - \dfrac{1}{a} = \dfrac{2}{5}$

$$\frac{5}{8} - \frac{1}{40/9} \; ? \; \frac{2}{5}$$

$$\frac{5}{8} - 1 \cdot \frac{9}{40} \; \bigg|$$

$$\frac{5}{8} - \frac{9}{40} \; \bigg|$$

$$\frac{25}{40} - \frac{9}{40} \; \bigg|$$

$$\frac{16}{40} \; \bigg|$$

$$\frac{2}{5} \; \bigg| \; \frac{2}{5} \quad \text{TRUE}$$

The solution is $\dfrac{40}{9}$.

6. -2

7. $\dfrac{2}{3} - \dfrac{1}{5} = \dfrac{7}{3x}$

Because $\dfrac{7}{3x}$ is undefined when x is 0, we note at the outset that $x \neq 0$. Then we multiply both sides by the LCD $3 \cdot 5 \cdot x$.

$$3 \cdot 5 \cdot x \left(\dfrac{2}{3} - \dfrac{1}{5} \right) = 3 \cdot 5 \cdot x \cdot \dfrac{7}{3x}$$

$$3 \cdot 5 \cdot x \cdot \dfrac{2}{3} - 3 \cdot 5 \cdot x \cdot \dfrac{1}{5} = 3 \cdot 5 \cdot x \cdot \dfrac{7}{3x}$$

$$10x - 3x = 35$$
$$7x = 35$$
$$x = 5$$

Check: $\dfrac{\dfrac{2}{3} - \dfrac{1}{5} = \dfrac{7}{3x}}{}$

$$\dfrac{2}{3} - \dfrac{1}{5} \mathrel{\overset{?}{=}} \dfrac{7}{3 \cdot 5}$$

$$\dfrac{10}{15} - \dfrac{3}{15} \quad \Big| \quad \dfrac{7}{15}$$

$$\dfrac{7}{15} \quad \Big| \quad \dfrac{7}{15} \qquad \text{TRUE}$$

The solution is 5.

8. 7

9. $\dfrac{2}{6} + \dfrac{1}{2x} = \dfrac{1}{3}$

Because $2x$ is undefined when x is 0, we note at the outset that $x \neq 0$. Then we multiply by the LCD, $2 \cdot 3 \cdot x$.

$$2 \cdot 3 \cdot x \left(\dfrac{2}{6} + \dfrac{1}{2x} \right) = 2 \cdot 3 \cdot x \cdot \dfrac{1}{3}$$

$$2 \cdot 3 \cdot x \cdot \dfrac{2}{6} + 2 \cdot 3 \cdot x \cdot \dfrac{1}{2x} = 2 \cdot 3 \cdot x \cdot \dfrac{1}{3}$$

$$2x + 3 = 2x$$
$$3 = 0$$

We get a false equation. The given equation has no solution.

10. No solution

11. $a + \dfrac{4}{a} = -5$

Because $\dfrac{4}{a}$ is undefined when a is 0, we note at the outset that $a \neq 0$. Then we multiply both sides by the LCD, a.

$$a \left(a + \dfrac{4}{a} \right) = a(-5)$$

$$a \cdot a + a \cdot \dfrac{4}{a} = -5a$$

$$a^2 + 4 = -5a$$

$$a^2 + 5a + 4 = 0$$

$$(a + 1)(a + 4) = 0$$

$$a + 1 = 0 \quad or \quad a + 4 = 0$$

$$a = -1 \quad or \qquad a = -4$$

Both values check. The solutions are -1 and -4.

12. $-\dfrac{1}{2}$

13. $\dfrac{p-1}{p-3} = \dfrac{2}{p-3}$

To ensure that neither denominator is 0, we note at the outset that $p \neq 3$. Then we multiply on both sides by the LCD, $p - 3$.

$$(p - 3) \cdot \dfrac{p-1}{p-3} = (p - 3) \cdot \dfrac{2}{p-3}$$

$$p - 1 = 2$$

$$p = 3$$

Recall that, because of the restriction above, 3 cannot be a solution. A check confirms this.

Check: $\dfrac{\dfrac{p-1}{p-3} = \dfrac{2}{p-3}}{}$

$$\dfrac{3-1}{3-3} \mathrel{\overset{?}{=}} \dfrac{2}{3-3}$$

$$\dfrac{2}{0} \quad \Big| \quad \dfrac{2}{0} \qquad \text{UNDEFINED}$$

The equation has no solution.

14. No solution

15. $\dfrac{3}{x-2} = \dfrac{5}{x+4}$

To assure that neither denominator is 0, we note at the outset that $x \neq 2$ and $x \neq -4$. Then we multiply on both sides by the LCD, $(x - 2)(x + 4)$.

$$(x - 2)(x + 4) \cdot \dfrac{3}{x-2} = (x - 2)(x + 4) \cdot \dfrac{5}{x+4}$$

$$3(x + 4) = 5(x - 2)$$

$$3x + 12 = 5x - 10$$

$$22 = 2x$$

$$11 = x$$

This value checks. The solution is 11.

16. $-\dfrac{10}{3}$

17. $\dfrac{x^2 - 1}{x + 2} = \dfrac{3}{x + 2}$

To assure that neither denominator is 0. we note at the outset that $x \neq -2$. Then we multiply on both sides by the LCD, $x + 2$.

$$(x + 2) \cdot \dfrac{x^2 - 1}{x + 2} = (x + 2) \cdot \dfrac{3}{x + 2}$$
$$x^2 - 1 = 3$$
$$x^2 - 4 = 0$$
$$(x + 2)(x - 2) = 0$$
$$x + 2 = 0 \quad or \quad x - 2 = 0$$
$$x = -2 \quad or \qquad x = 2$$

Recall that, because of the restriction above, -2 cannot be a solution. The number 2 checks, so the solution is 2.

18. -1

19. $\dfrac{4}{a - 7} = \dfrac{-2a}{a + 3}$

To assure that neither denominator is 0, we note at the outset that $a \neq 7$ and $a \neq -3$. Then we multiply on both sides by the LCD, $(a - 7)(a + 3)$.

$$(a - 7)(a + 3) \cdot \dfrac{4}{a - 7} = (a - 7)(a + 3) \cdot \dfrac{-2a}{a + 3}$$
$$4(a + 3) = -2a(a - 7)$$
$$4a + 12 = -2a^2 + 14a$$
$$2a^2 - 10a + 12 = 0$$
$$2(a^2 - 5a + 6) = 0$$
$$2(a - 2)(a - 3) = 0$$
$$a - 2 = 0 \quad or \quad a - 3 = 0$$
$$a = 2 \quad or \qquad a = 3$$

Both values check. The solutions are 2 and 3.

20. $2, 3$

21. $\dfrac{50}{t - 2} - \dfrac{16}{t} = \dfrac{30}{t}$

To assure that none of the denominators is 0, we note at the outset that $t \neq 2$ and $t \neq 0$. Then we multiply on both sides by the LCD, $t(t - 2)$.

$$t(t - 2)\left(\dfrac{50}{t - 2} - \dfrac{16}{t}\right) = t(t - 2) \cdot \dfrac{30}{t}$$
$$50t - 16(t - 2) = 30(t - 2)$$
$$50t - 16t + 32 = 30t - 60$$
$$34t + 32 = 30t - 60$$
$$4t = -92$$
$$t = -23$$

This value checks. The solution is -23.

22. -145

23. $\dfrac{3}{x} + \dfrac{x}{x + 2} = \dfrac{4}{x^2 + 2x}$

$$\dfrac{3}{x} + \dfrac{x}{x + 2} = \dfrac{4}{x(x + 2)}$$

To assure that none of the denominators is 0, we note at the outset that $x \neq 0$ and $x \neq -2$. Then we multiply on both sides by the LCD, $x(x + 2)$.

$$x(x + 2)\left(\dfrac{3}{x} + \dfrac{x}{x + 2}\right) = x(x + 2) \cdot \dfrac{4}{x(x + 2)}$$
$$3(x + 2) + x \cdot x = 4$$
$$3x + 6 + x^2 = 4$$
$$x^2 + 3x + 2 = 0$$
$$(x + 1)(x + 2) = 0$$
$$x + 1 = 0 \quad or \quad x + 2 = 0$$
$$x = -1 \quad or \qquad x = -2$$

Recall that, because of the restrictions above, -2 cannot be a solution. The number -1 checks. The solution is -1.

24. -4

25. We find all values of a for which $2a - \dfrac{15}{a} = 1$. First note that $a \neq 0$. Then multiply on both sides by the LCD, a.

$$a\left(2a - \dfrac{15}{a}\right) = a \cdot 1$$
$$a \cdot 2a - a \cdot \dfrac{15}{a} = a$$
$$2a^2 - 15 = a$$
$$2a^2 - a - 15 = 0$$
$$(2a + 5)(a - 3) = 0$$
$$a = -\dfrac{5}{2} \quad or \quad a = 3$$

Both values check. The solutions are $-\dfrac{5}{2}$ and 3.

26. $-\dfrac{3}{2}, 2$

27. We find all values of a for which $\dfrac{a - 5}{a + 1} = \dfrac{3}{5}$. First note that $a \neq -1$. Then multiply on both sides by the LCD, $5(a + 1)$.

$$5(a + 1) \cdot \dfrac{a - 5}{a + 1} = 5(a + 1) \cdot \dfrac{3}{5}$$
$$5(a - 5) = 3(a + 1)$$
$$5a - 25 = 3a + 3$$
$$2a = 28$$
$$a = 14$$

This value checks. The solution is 14.

28. $\dfrac{17}{4}$

29. We find all values of a for which $\dfrac{12}{a} - \dfrac{12}{2a} = 8$. First note that $a \neq 0$. Then multiply on both sides by the LCD, $2a$.

$$2a\left(\frac{12}{a} - \frac{12}{2a}\right) = 2a \cdot 8$$

$$2a \cdot \frac{12}{a} - 2a \cdot \frac{12}{2a} = 16a$$

$$24 - 12 = 16a$$

$$12 = 16a$$

$$\frac{3}{4} = a$$

This value checks. The solution is $\dfrac{3}{4}$.

30. $\dfrac{3}{5}$

31. $\dfrac{5}{x+2} - \dfrac{3}{x-2} = \dfrac{2x}{4-x^2}$

$$\frac{5}{x+2} - \frac{3}{x-2} = \frac{2x}{(2+x)(2-x)}$$

$$\frac{5}{x+2} + \frac{3}{2-x} = \frac{2x}{(2+x)(2-x)} \quad \left(-\frac{3}{x-2} = \frac{3}{2-x}\right)$$

First note that $x \neq -2$ and $x \neq 2$. Then multiply on both sides by the LCD, $(2+x)(2-x)$.

$$(2+x)(2-x)\left(\frac{5}{x+2} + \frac{3}{2-x}\right) =$$

$$(2+x)(2-x) \cdot \frac{2x}{(2+x)(2-x)}$$

$$5(2-x) + 3(2+x) = 2x$$

$$10 - 5x + 6 + 3x = 2x$$

$$16 - 2x = 2x$$

$$16 = 4x$$

$$4 = x$$

This value checks. The solution is 4.

32. -3

33. $\dfrac{2}{a+4} + \dfrac{2a-1}{a^2+2a-8} = \dfrac{1}{a-2}$

$$\frac{2}{a+4} + \frac{2a-1}{(a+4)(a-2)} = \frac{1}{a-2}$$

First note that $a \neq -4$ and $a \neq 2$. Then multiply on both sides by the LCD, $(a+4)(a-2)$.

$$(a+4)(a-2)\left(\frac{2}{a+4} + \frac{2a-1}{(a+4)(a-2)}\right) =$$

$$(a+4)(a-2) \cdot \frac{1}{a-2}$$

$$2(a-2) + 2a - 1 = a+4$$

$$2a - 4 + 2a - 1 = a+4$$

$$4a - 5 = a+4$$

$$3a = 9$$

$$a = 3$$

This value checks. The solution is 3.

34. $-6, 5$

35. $\dfrac{2}{x+3} - \dfrac{3x+5}{x^2+4x+3} = \dfrac{5}{x+1}$

$$\frac{2}{x+3} - \frac{3x+5}{(x+3)(x+1)} = \frac{5}{x+1}$$

Note that $x \neq -3$ and $x \neq -1$. Then multiply on both sides by the LCD, $(x+3)(x+1)$.

$$(x+3)(x+1)\left(\frac{2}{x+3} - \frac{3x+5}{(x+3)(x+1)}\right) =$$

$$(x+3)(x+1) \cdot \frac{5}{x+1}$$

$$2(x+1) - (3x+5) = 5(x+3)$$

$$2x + 2 - 3x - 5 = 5x + 15$$

$$-x - 3 = 5x + 15$$

$$-18 = 6x$$

$$-3 = x$$

Recall that, because of the restriction above, -3 is not a solution. Thus, the equation has no solution.

36. No solution

37. $\dfrac{x-1}{x^2-2x-3} + \dfrac{x+2}{x^2-9} = \dfrac{2x+5}{x^2+4x+3}$

$$\frac{x-1}{(x-3)(x+1)} + \frac{x+2}{(x+3)(x-3)} = \frac{2x+5}{(x+3)(x+1)}$$

Note that $x \neq 3$ and $x \neq -1$ and $x \neq -3$. Then multiply on both sides by the LCD, $(x-3)(x+1)(x+3)$.

$$(x-3)(x+1)(x+3)\left(\frac{x-1}{(x-3)(x+1)} + \frac{x+2}{(x+3)(x-3)}\right) =$$

$$(x-3)(x+1)(x+3) \cdot \frac{2x+5}{(x+3)(x+1)}$$

$$(x+3)(x-1) + (x+1)(x+2) = (x-3)(2x+5)$$

$$x^2 + 2x - 3 + x^2 + 3x + 2 = 2x^2 - x - 15$$

$$2x^2 + 5x - 1 = 2x^2 - x - 15$$

$$5x - 1 = -x - 15$$

$$6x = -14$$

$$x = -\frac{7}{3}$$

This value checks. The solution is $-\dfrac{7}{3}$.

38. $\dfrac{5}{14}$

39.
$$\dfrac{3}{x^2 - x - 12} + \dfrac{1}{x^2 + x - 6} = \dfrac{4}{x^2 + 3x - 10}$$

$$\dfrac{3}{(x-4)(x+3)} + \dfrac{1}{(x+3)(x-2)} = \dfrac{4}{(x+5)(x-2)}$$

Note that $x \neq 4$ and $x \neq -3$ and $x \neq 2$ and $x \neq -5$.
Then multiply on both sides by the LCD,
$(x-4)(x+3)(x-2)(x+5)$.

$$(x-4)(x+3)(x-2)(x+5)\left(\dfrac{3}{(x-4)(x+3)} + \dfrac{1}{(x+3)(x-2)}\right) =$$

$$(x-4)(x+3)(x-2)(x+5) \cdot \dfrac{4}{(x+5)(x-2)}$$

$$3(x-2)(x+5) + (x-4)(x+5) = 4(x-4)(x+3)$$
$$3(x^2 + 3x - 10) + x^2 + x - 20 = 4(x^2 - x - 12)$$
$$3x^2 + 9x - 30 + x^2 + x - 20 = 4x^2 - 4x - 48$$
$$4x^2 + 10x - 50 = 4x^2 - 4x - 48$$
$$10x - 50 = -4x - 48$$
$$14x = 2$$
$$x = \dfrac{1}{7}$$

This value checks. The solution is $\dfrac{1}{7}$.

40. $\dfrac{3}{5}$

41. $81x^4 - y^4 = (9x^2 + y^2)(9x^2 - y^2)$
$$= (9x^2 + y^2)(3x + y)(3x - y)$$

42. $(x - 36)(x + 35)$

43. $|x - 2| > 3$
$$x - 2 < -3 \quad or \quad x - 2 > 3$$
$$x < -1 \quad or \quad x > 5$$

The solution set is $\{x | x < -1 \ or \ x > 5\}$, or
$(-\infty, -1) \cup (5, \infty)$.

44. $\{x | -1 \leq x \leq 5\}$, or $[-1, 5]$

45. *Familiarize*. Let $x =$ the first number. Then $x+2 =$ the second number.

***Translate*.**

$$\underbrace{\text{The product of two consecutive even integers}}_{x(x+2)} \quad \underset{=}{\text{is}} \quad \underset{288}{288}$$

***Carry out*.** We solve the equation.

$$x(x + 2) = 288$$
$$x^2 + 2x = 288$$
$$x^2 + 2x - 288 = 0$$
$$(x - 16)(x + 18) = 0$$
$$x - 16 = 0 \quad or \quad x + 18 = 0$$
$$x = 16 \quad or \qquad x = -18$$

***Check*.** If the first number is 16, then the next number is $16+2$, or 18, and their product is $16 \cdot 18$, or 288. If the first number is -18, then the next number is $-18 + 2$, or -16, and their product is $-18(-16)$, or 288. Both solutions check.

***State*.** The numbers are 16 and 18 or -18 and -16.

46. $a^{22}b^9$

47.

48.

49.

50.

51. Set $f(a)$ equal to $g(a)$ and solve for a.

$$\dfrac{2 + \dfrac{a}{2}}{2 - \dfrac{a}{4}} = \dfrac{2}{\dfrac{a}{4} - 2}$$

$$\dfrac{2 + \dfrac{a}{2}}{2 - \dfrac{a}{4}} = \dfrac{-1}{-1} \cdot \dfrac{2}{\dfrac{a}{4} - 2}$$

$$\dfrac{2 + \dfrac{a}{2}}{2 - \dfrac{a}{4}} = \dfrac{-2}{2 - \dfrac{a}{4}}$$

$$\left(2 - \dfrac{a}{4}\right)\left[\dfrac{2 + \dfrac{a}{2}}{2 - \dfrac{a}{4}}\right] = \left(2 - \dfrac{a}{4}\right)\left[\dfrac{-2}{2 - \dfrac{a}{4}}\right]$$

$$2 + \dfrac{a}{2} = -2$$

$$2\left(2 + \dfrac{a}{2}\right) = 2(-2)$$

$$4 + a = -4$$

$$a = -8$$

This value checks. Thus, when $a = -8$, $f(a) = g(a)$.

52. $\dfrac{1}{5}$

53. Set $f(a)$ equal to $g(a)$ and solve for a.

$$\frac{1}{1+a} + \frac{a}{1-a} = \frac{1}{1-a} - \frac{a}{1+a}$$

Note that $a \neq -1$ and $a \neq 1$. Then multiply by the LCD, $(1+a)(1-a)$.

$$(1+a)(1-a)\left(\frac{1}{1+a} + \frac{a}{1-a}\right) =$$
$$(1+a)(1-a)\left(\frac{1}{1-a} - \frac{a}{1+a}\right)$$
$$1 - a + a(1+a) = 1 + a - a(1-a)$$
$$1 - a + a + a^2 = 1 + a - a + a^2$$
$$1 + a^2 = 1 + a^2$$
$$1 = 1$$

We get an equation that is true for all real numbers. Recall that, because of the restrictions above, -1 and 1 are not solutions. Thus, for all values of a except -1 and 1, $f(a) = g(a)$.

54. $-\dfrac{7}{2}$

55. Set $f(a)$ equal to $g(a)$ and solve for a.

$$\frac{0.793}{a} + 18.15 = \frac{6.034}{a} - .43.17$$

Note that $a \neq 0$. Then multiply on both sides by the LCD, a.

$$a\left(\frac{0.793}{a} + 18.15\right) = a\left(\frac{6.034}{a} - 43.17\right)$$
$$0.793 + 18.15a = 6.034 - 43.17a$$
$$61.32a = 5.241$$
$$a \approx 0.0854697$$

This value checks. When $a \approx 0.0854697$, $f(a) = g(a)$.

56. -2.955341202

57. $\dfrac{x^2 + 6x - 16}{x - 2} = x + 8, x \neq 2$

$$\frac{(x+8)(x-2)}{x-2} = x + 8$$
$$\frac{(x+8)\cancel{(x-2)}}{\cancel{x-2}} = x + 8$$
$$x + 8 = x + 8$$
$$8 = 8$$

Since $8 = 8$ is true for all values of x, the original equation is true for any possible replacements of the variable. It is an identity.

58. Yes

---

1. ***Familiarize.*** Let $x =$ the number.

Translate.

The reciprocal of 3	plus	the reciprocal of 6	is	the reciprocal of the number.
↓	↓	↓	↓	↓
$\dfrac{1}{3}$	$+$	$\dfrac{1}{6}$	$=$	$\dfrac{1}{x}$

Carry out. We solve the equation.

$$\frac{1}{3} + \frac{1}{6} = \frac{1}{x}, \text{ LCD is } 6x$$
$$6x\left(\frac{1}{3} + \frac{1}{6}\right) = 6x \cdot \frac{1}{x}$$
$$2x + x = 6$$
$$3x = 6$$
$$x = 2$$

Check. $\dfrac{1}{3} + \dfrac{1}{6} = \dfrac{2}{6} + \dfrac{1}{6} = \dfrac{3}{6} = \dfrac{1}{2}$. This is the reciprocal of 2, so the result checks.

State. The number is 2.

2. $\dfrac{35}{12}$

3. ***Familiarize.*** We let $x =$ the number.

Translate.

A number	plus	6	times	its reciprocal	is	-5.
↓	↓	↓	↓	↓	↓	↓
x	$+$	6	$\cdot$	$\dfrac{1}{x}$	$=$	-5

Carry out. We solve the equation.

$$x + \frac{6}{x} = -5, \text{ LCD is } x$$
$$x\left(x + \frac{6}{x}\right) = x(-5)$$
$$x^2 + 6 = -5x$$
$$x^2 + 5x + 6 = 0$$
$$(x+3)(x+2) = 0$$
$$x = -3 \text{ or } x = -2$$

Check. The possible solutions are -3 and -2. We check -3 in the conditions of the problem.

Number:	-3
6 times the reciprocal of the number:	$6\left(-\dfrac{1}{3}\right) = -2$
Sum of the number and 6 times its reciprocal:	$-3 + (-2) = -5$

The number -3 checks.

Now we check -2:

Number:	-2
6 times the reciprocal of the number:	$6\left(-\dfrac{1}{2}\right) = -3$
Sum of the number and 6 times its reciprocal:	$-2 + (-3) = -5$

The number -2 also checks.

State. The number is -3 or -2.

4. $-3, -7$

5. Familiarize. We let $x =$ the first integer. Then $x + 1 =$ the second, and their product $= x(x + 1)$.

Translate.

$$\underbrace{\text{Reciprocal of the product}}_{\displaystyle \frac{1}{x(x+1)}} \ \ \underset{\displaystyle =}{\text{is}} \ \ \frac{\frac{1}{42}}{\frac{1}{42}}.$$

Carry out. We solve the equation.

$$\frac{1}{x(x+1)} = \frac{1}{42}, \text{ LCD is } 42x(x+1)$$

$$42x(x+1) \cdot \frac{1}{x(x+1)} = 42x(x+1) \cdot \frac{1}{42}$$

$$42 = x(x+1)$$

$$42 = x^2 + x$$

$$0 = x^2 + x - 42$$

$$0 = (x+7)(x-6)$$

$$x = -7 \ or \ x = 6$$

Check. When $x = -7$, then $x + 1 = -6$ and $-7(-6) = 42$. The reciprocal of this product is $\dfrac{1}{42}$. When $x = 6$, then $x + 1 = 7$ and $6 \cdot 7 = 42$. The reciprocal of this product is also $\dfrac{1}{42}$. Both possible solutions check.

State. The integers are -7 and -6 or 6 and 7.

6. -9 and -8, 8 and 9

7. Familiarize. The job takes Otto 4 hours working alone and Sally 3 hours working alone. Then in 1 hour, Otto does $\dfrac{1}{4}$ of the job and Sally does $\dfrac{1}{3}$ of the job. Working together, they can do $\dfrac{1}{4} + \dfrac{1}{3}$ of the job in 1 hour. Let t represent the number of hours required for Otto and Sally, working together, to do the job.

Translate. We want to find t such that

$$t\left(\frac{1}{4}\right) + t\left(\frac{1}{3}\right) = 1, \text{ or } \frac{t}{4} + \frac{t}{3} = 1,$$

where 1 represents one entire job.

Carry out. We solve the equation.

$$\frac{t}{4} + \frac{t}{3} = 1, \text{ LCD is } 12$$

$$12\left(\frac{t}{4} + \frac{t}{3}\right) = 12 \cdot 1$$

$$3t + 4t = 12$$

$$7t = 12$$

$$t = \frac{12}{7}$$

Check. In $\dfrac{12}{7}$ hours, Otto will do $\dfrac{1}{4} \cdot \dfrac{12}{7}$, or $\dfrac{3}{7}$ of the job and Sally will do $\dfrac{1}{3} \cdot \dfrac{12}{7}$, or $\dfrac{4}{7}$ of the job. Together, they do $\dfrac{3}{7} + \dfrac{4}{7}$, or 1 entire job. The answer checks.

State. It will take $\dfrac{12}{7}$ hr, or $1\dfrac{5}{7}$ hr, for Otto and Sally, together, to paint the room.

8. $3\dfrac{3}{14}$ hr

9. Familiarize. The pool can be filled in 12 hours with only the pipe and in 30 hours with only the hose. Then in 1 hour, the pipe fills $\dfrac{1}{12}$ of the pool, and the hose fills $\dfrac{1}{30}$ of the pool. Using both the pipe and the hose, $\dfrac{1}{12} + \dfrac{1}{30}$ of the pool can be filled in 1 hour. Suppose that it takes t hours to fill the pool using both the pipe and hose.

Translate. We want to find t such that

$$t\left(\frac{1}{12}\right) + t\left(\frac{1}{30}\right) = 1, \text{ or } \frac{t}{12} + \frac{t}{30} = 1,$$

where 1 represents one entire job.

Carry out. We solve the equation. We multiply on both sides by the LCD, $60t$.

$$60\left(\frac{t}{12} + \frac{t}{30}\right) = 60 \cdot 1$$

$$5t + 2t = 60$$

$$7t = 60$$

$$t = \frac{60}{7}$$

Check. The possible solution is $\dfrac{60}{7}$ hours. If the pipe is used $\dfrac{60}{7}$ hours, it fills $\dfrac{1}{12} \cdot \dfrac{60}{7}$, or $\dfrac{5}{7}$ of the pool. If the hose is used $\dfrac{60}{7}$ hours, it fills $\dfrac{1}{30} \cdot \dfrac{60}{7}$, or $\dfrac{2}{7}$ of the pool. Using both, $\dfrac{5}{7} + \dfrac{2}{7}$ of the pool, or all of it, will be filled in $\dfrac{60}{7}$ hours.

State. Using both the pipe and the hose, it will take $\frac{60}{7}$, or $8\frac{4}{7}$ hours, to fill the pool.

10. 9.9 hr

11. *Familiarize*. In 1 hour Pronto Press does $\frac{1}{4.5}$ of the job and Red Dot Printers does $\frac{1}{5.5}$ of the job. Working together, they can do $\frac{1}{4.5} + \frac{1}{5.5}$ of the job in 1 hour. Suppose it takes them t hours working together.

Translate. We want to find t such that
$$t\left(\frac{1}{4.5}\right) + t\left(\frac{1}{5.5}\right) = 1, \text{ or } \frac{t}{4.5} + \frac{t}{5.5} = 1.$$

Carry out. We solve the equation.
$$4.5(5.5)\left(\frac{t}{4.5} + \frac{t}{5.5}\right) = 4.5(5.5)(1)$$
$$5.5t + 4.5t = 24.75$$
$$10t = 24.75$$
$$t = 2.475$$

Check. In 2.475 hr Pronto Press will do $\frac{2.475}{4.5}$, or 0.55 of the job and Red Dot will do $\frac{2.475}{5.5}$, or 0.45 of the job. Together they will do $0.55 + 0.45$, or 1 entire job.

State. Working together, it will take them 2.475 hours.

12. $3\frac{9}{52}$ hr

13. *Familiarize*. Let t represent the number of hours it takes Henri, working alone, to sand the floor. Then in 1 hr, Mavis does $\frac{1}{3}$ of the job, and Henri does $\frac{1}{t}$ of the job.

Translate. Working together, they can do the entire job in 2 hr, so we want to find t such that
$$2\left(\frac{1}{3}\right) + 2\left(\frac{1}{t}\right) = 1, \text{ or } \frac{2}{3} + \frac{2}{t} = 1.$$

Carry out. We solve the equation.
$$\frac{2}{3} + \frac{2}{t} = 1, \text{ LCD is } 3t$$
$$3t\left(\frac{2}{3} + \frac{2}{t}\right) = 3t \cdot 1$$
$$2t + 6 = 3t$$
$$6 = t$$

Check. In 2 hr, Mavis will do $2 \cdot \frac{1}{3}$, or $\frac{2}{3}$ of the job, and Henri will do $2 \cdot \frac{1}{6}$, or $\frac{1}{3}$ of the job. Together

they will do $\frac{2}{3} + \frac{1}{3}$, or 1 entire job. The answer checks.

State. It would take Henri 6 hours, working by himself, to sand the floor.

14. Skyler: 12 hours, Jake: 6 hours

15. *Familiarize*. Let t represent the number of hours it takes Kate to paint the floor. Then $t + 3$ represents the time it takes Sara to paint the floor. In 1 hour, Kate does $\frac{1}{t}$ of the job and Sara does $\frac{1}{t+3}$.

Translate. Working together, it takes them 2 hr to do the job, so we want to find t such that
$$2\left(\frac{1}{t}\right) + 2\left(\frac{1}{t+3}\right) = 1, \text{ or } \frac{2}{t} + \frac{2}{t+3} = 1.$$

Carry out. We solve the equation. We multiply by the LCD, $t(t+3)$.
$$t(t+3)\left(\frac{2}{t} + \frac{2}{t+3}\right) = t(t+3)(1)$$
$$2(t+3) + 2t = t^2 + 3t$$
$$2t + 6 + 2t = t^2 + 3t$$
$$4t + 6 = t^2 + 3t$$
$$0 = t^2 - t - 6$$
$$0 = (t-3)(t+2)$$
$$t = 3 \text{ or } t = -2$$

Check. We check only 3, since the time cannot be negative. If Kate does the job in 3 hr, then in 2 hr she does $2\left(\frac{1}{3}\right)$, or $\frac{2}{3}$ of the job. If Sara does the job in $3 + 3$ or 6 hr, then in 2 hr she does $2\left(\frac{1}{6}\right)$, or $\frac{1}{3}$ of the job. Together they do $\frac{2}{3} + \frac{1}{3}$, or 1 entire job in 2 hr. The result checks.

State. It would take Kate 3 hours to do the job and it would take Sara 6 hours to do the job working alone.

16. Claudia: 10 days, Jan: 40 days

17. *Familiarize*. Let t represent the number of hours it takes Zsuzanna to deliver the papers alone. Then $3t$ represents the number of hours it takes Stan to deliver the papers alone.

Translate. In 1 hr Zsuzanna and Stan will do one entire job, so we have
$$1\left(\frac{1}{t}\right) + 1\left(\frac{1}{3t}\right) = 1, \text{ or } \frac{1}{t} + \frac{1}{3t} = 1.$$

Carry out. We solve the equation. Multiply on both sides by the LCD, $3t$.

$$3t\left(\frac{1}{t} + \frac{1}{3t}\right) = 3t \cdot 1$$
$$3 + 1 = 3t$$
$$4 = 3t$$
$$\frac{4}{3} = t$$

Check. If Zsuzanna does the job alone in $\frac{4}{3}$ hr, then in 1 hr she does $\frac{1}{4/3}$, or $\frac{3}{4}$ of the job. If Stan does the job alone in $3 \cdot \frac{4}{3}$, or 4 hr, then in 1 hr he does $\frac{1}{4}$ of the job. Together, they do $\frac{3}{4} + \frac{1}{4}$, or 1 entire job, in 1 hr. The result checks.

State. It would take Zsuzanna $\frac{4}{3}$ hours and it would take Stan 4 hours to deliver the papers alone.

18. $1\frac{1}{5}$ hour, or 72 minutes

19. **Familiarize.** We will convert hours to minutes:

$$2 \text{ hr} = 2 \cdot 60 \text{ min} = 120 \text{ min}$$
$$2 \text{ hr } 55 \text{ min} = 120 \text{ min} + 55 \text{ min} = 175 \text{ min}$$

Let $t =$ the number of minutes it takes Deb to do the job alone. Then $t + 120 =$ the number of minutes it takes John alone. In 1 hour (60 minutes) Deb does $\frac{1}{t}$ and John does $\frac{1}{t+120}$ of the job.

Translate. In 175 min John and Deb will complete one entire job, so we have

$$175\left(\frac{1}{t}\right) + 175\left(\frac{1}{t+120}\right) = 1, \text{ or}$$
$$\frac{175}{t} + \frac{175}{t+120} = 1.$$

Carry out. We solve the equation. Multiply on both sides by the LCD, $t(t+120)$.

$$t(t+120)\left(\frac{175}{t} + \frac{175}{t+120}\right) = t(t+120)(1)$$
$$175(t+120) + 175t = t^2 + 120t$$
$$175t + 21,000 + 175t = t^2 + 120t$$
$$0 = t^2 - 230t - 21,000$$
$$0 = (t - 300)(t + 70)$$
$$t = 300 \text{ or } t = -70$$

Check. Since negative time has no meaning in this problem, -70 is not a solution of the original problem. If the job takes Deb 300 min and it takes John $300 + 120 = 420$ min, then in 175 min they would complete

$$175\left(\frac{1}{300}\right) + 175\left(\frac{1}{420}\right) = \frac{7}{12} + \frac{5}{12} = 1 \text{ job.}$$

The result checks.

State. It would take Deb 300 min, or 5 hr, to do the job alone.

20. 8 hr

21. **Familiarize.** Let $t =$ the number of hours it takes the new machine to do the job alone. Then $2t =$ the number of hours it takes the old machine to do the job alone. In 1 hr the new machine does $\frac{1}{t}$ of the job and the old machine does $\frac{1}{2t}$ of the job.

Translate. In 15 hr the two machines will complete one entire job, so we have

$$15\left(\frac{1}{t}\right) + 15\left(\frac{1}{2t}\right) = 1, \text{ or } \frac{15}{t} + \frac{15}{2t} = 1.$$

Carry out. We solve the equation. Multiply on both sides by the LCD, $2t$.

$$2t\left(\frac{15}{t} + \frac{15}{2t}\right) = 2t \cdot 1$$
$$30 + 15 = 2t$$
$$45 = 2t$$
$$\frac{45}{2} = t$$

Check. In 1 hr, the new machine will do $\frac{1}{45}$, or $\frac{2}{45}$ of the job and the old machine will do $\frac{1}{2 \cdot \frac{45}{2}}$, or $\frac{1}{45}$ of the job. Together they will do $\frac{2}{45} + \frac{1}{45} = \frac{3}{45} = \frac{1}{15}$ of the job. Then in 15 hr they will do $15 \cdot \frac{1}{15} = 1$ job. The answer checks.

State. Working alone the job would take the new machine $\frac{45}{2}$, or $22\frac{1}{2}$ hr, and it would take the old machine $2 \cdot \frac{45}{2}$, or 45 hr.

22. 2 hr

23. **Familiarize.** We first make a drawing. Let $r =$ the boat's speed in still water in mph. Then $r - 4 =$ the speed upstream and $r + 4 =$ the speed downstream.

Upstream   6 miles $r - 4$ mph

12 miles $r + 4$ mph   Downstream

We organize the information in a table. The one is the same both upstream and downstream so we use t for each time.

	Distance	Speed	Time
Upstream	6	$r - 4$	t
Downstream	12	$r + 4$	t

Translate. Using the formula Time = Distance/Rate in each row of the table and the fact that the times are the same, we can write an equation.

$$\frac{6}{r-4} = \frac{12}{r+4}$$

Carry out. We solve the equation.

$$\frac{6}{r-4} = \frac{12}{r+4},$$

LCD is $(r-4)(r+4)$

$$(r-4)(r+4) \cdot \frac{6}{r-4} = (r-4)(r+4) \cdot \frac{12}{r+4}$$
$$6(r+4) = 12(r-4)$$
$$6r + 24 = 12r - 48$$
$$72 = 6r$$
$$12 = r$$

Check. If the boat's speed in still water is 12 mph, then its speed upstream is $12 - 4$, or 8 mph, and its speed downstream is $12 + 4$, or 16 mph. Traveling 6 mi at 8 mph takes the boat $\frac{6}{8} = \frac{3}{4}$ hr. Traveling 12 mi at 16 mph takes the boat $\frac{12}{16} = \frac{3}{4}$ hr. Since the times are the same, the answer checks.

State. The boat's speed in still water is 12 mph.

24. 7 mph

25. Familiarize. We first make a drawing. Let $r =$ Camille's speed on a nonmoving sidewalk in ft/sec. Then her speed moving forward on the moving sidewalk is $r+1.8$, and her speed in the opposite direction is $r-1.8$.

Forward $r + 1.8$ 105 ft

                              51 ft $r - 1.8$ Opposite direction

We organize the information in a table. The time is the same both forward and in the opposite direction so we use t for each time.

	Distance	Speed	Time
Forward	105	$r + 1.8$	t
Opposite direction	51	$r - 1.8$	t

Translate. Using the formula Time = Distance/Rate in each row of the table and the fact that the times are the same, we can write an equation.

$$\frac{105}{r+1.8} = \frac{51}{r-1.8}$$

Carry out. We solve the equation.

$$\frac{105}{r+1.8} = \frac{51}{r-1.8},$$

LCD is $(r+1.8)(r-1.8)$

$$(r+1.8)(r-1.8) \cdot \frac{105}{r+1.8} = (r+1.8)(r-1.8) \cdot \frac{51}{r-1.8}$$
$$105(r-1.8) = 51(r+1.8)$$
$$105r - 189 = 51r + 91.8$$
$$54r = 280.8$$
$$r = 5.2$$

Check. If Camille's speed on a nonmoving sidewalk is 5.2 ft/sec, then her speed moving forward on the moving sidewalk is $5.2+1.8$, or 7 ft/sec, and her speed moving in the opposite direction on the sidewalk is $5.2 - 1.8$, or 3.4 ft/sec. Moving 105 ft at 7 ft/sec takes $\frac{105}{7} = 15$ sec. Moving 51 ft at 3.4 ft/sec takes 15 sec. Since the times are the same, the answer checks.

State. Camille would be walking 5.2 ft/sec on a nonmoving sidewalk.

26. 4.3 ft/sec

27. Familiarize. Let $r =$ the speed of the passenger train in mph. Then $r - 14 =$ the speed of the freight train in mph. We organize the information in a table. The time is the same for both trains so we use t for each time.

	Distance	Speed	Time
Passenger train	400	r	t
Freight train	330	$r - 14$	t

Translate. Using the formula Time = Distance/Rate in each row of the table and the fact that the times are the same, we can write an equation.

$$\frac{400}{r} = \frac{330}{r-14}$$

Carry out. We solve the equation.

$$\frac{400}{r} = \frac{330}{r-14}, \text{ LCD is } r(r-14)$$

$$r(r-14) \cdot \frac{400}{r} = r(r-14) \cdot \frac{330}{r-14}$$
$$400(r-14) = 330r$$
$$400r - 5600 = 330r$$
$$-5600 = -70r$$
$$80 = r$$

Check. If the passenger train's speed is 80 mph, then the freight train's speed is $80 - 14$, or 66 mph.

Traveling 400 mi at 80 mph takes $\frac{400}{80} = 5$ hr. Traveling 330 mi at 66 mph takes $\frac{330}{66} = 5$ hr. Since the times are the same, the answer checks.

State. The speed of the passenger train is 80 mph; the speed of the freight train is 66 mph.

28. Rosanna: $3\frac{1}{3}$ mph; Simone: $5\frac{1}{3}$ mph

29. Familiarize. Let $r =$ the speed of the express bus in mph. Then $r - 7 =$ the speed of the local bus in mph. We organize the information in a table. The time is the same for both buses so we use t for each time.

	Distance	Speed	Time
Express	90	r	t
Local	75	$r - 7$	t

Translate. Using the formula Time = Distance/Rate in each row of the table and the fact that the times are the same, we can write an equation.
$$\frac{90}{r} = \frac{75}{r - 7}$$

Carry out. We solve the equation.
$$\frac{90}{r} = \frac{75}{r - 7}, \text{ LCD is } r(r - 7)$$
$$r(r - 7) \cdot \frac{90}{r} = r(r - 7) \cdot \frac{75}{r - 7}$$
$$90(r - 7) = 75r$$
$$90r - 630 = 75r$$
$$-630 = -15r$$
$$42 = r$$

Check. If the speed of the express bus is 42 mph, then the speed of the local bus is $42 - 7$, or 35 mph. Traveling 90 mi at 42 mph takes $\frac{90}{42} = \frac{15}{7}$ hr. Traveling 75 mi at 35 mph takes $\frac{75}{35} = \frac{15}{7}$ hr. Since the times are the same, the answer checks.

State. The speed of the express bus is 42 mph; the speed of the local bus is 35 mph.

30. A: 46 mph; B: 58 mph

31. Familiarize. We let $r =$ the speed of the river. Then $15 + r =$ Suzie's speed downstream in km/h and $15 - r =$ her speed upstream in km/h. The times are the same. Let t represent the time. We organize the information in a table.

	Distance	Speed	Time
Downstream	140	$15 + r$	t
Upstream	35	$15 - r$	t

Translate. Using the formula Time = Distance/Rate in each row of the table and the fact that the times are the same, we can write an equation.
$$\frac{140}{15 + r} = \frac{35}{15 - r}$$

Carry out. We solve the equation.
$$\frac{140}{15 + r} = \frac{35}{15 - r},$$
$$\text{LCD is } (15 + r)(15 - r)$$
$$(15 + r)(15 - r) \cdot \frac{140}{15 + r} = (15 + r)(15 - r) \cdot \frac{35}{15 - r}$$
$$140(15 - r) = 35(15 + r)$$
$$2100 - 140r = 525 + 35r$$
$$1575 = 175r$$
$$9 = r$$

Check. If $r = 9$, then the speed downstream is $15 + 9$, or 24 km/h and the speed upstream is $15 - 9$, or 6 km/h. The time for the trip is downstream is $\frac{140}{24}$, or $5\frac{5}{6}$ hours. The time for the trip upstream is $\frac{35}{6}$, or $5\frac{5}{6}$ hours. The times are the same. The values check.

State. The speed of the river is 9 km/h.

32. $1\frac{1}{5}$ km/h

33. Familiarize. Let $r =$ the speed of Mara's moped in km/h. Then $r + 8 =$ the speed of Jaime's moped in km/h. We organize the information in a table. The time is the same for both mopeds so we use t for each time.

	Distance	Speed	Time
Mara	45	r	t
Jaime	69	$r + 8$	t

Translate. Using the formula Time = Distance/Rate in each row of the table and the fact that the times are the same, we can write an equation.
$$\frac{45}{r} = \frac{69}{r + 8}$$

Carry out. We solve the equation.

$$\frac{45}{r} = \frac{69}{r+8}, \text{ LCD is } r(r+8)$$

$$r(r+8) \cdot \frac{45}{r} = r(r+8) \cdot \frac{69}{r+8}$$

$$45(r+8) = 69r$$

$$45r + 360 = 69r$$

$$360 = 24r$$

$$15 = r$$

Check. If the speed of Mara's moped is 15 km/h, then the speed of Jaime's moped is $15+8$, or 23 mph. Traveling 45 km at 15 km/h takes $\frac{45}{15} = 3$ hr. Traveling 69 km at 23 km/h takes $\frac{69}{23} = 3$ hr. Since the times are the same, the answer checks.

State. The speed of Mara's moped is 15 km/h; the speed of Jaime's moped is 23 mph.

34. 2 km/h

35. Familiarize. Let $r =$ the speed of the current in m per minute. Then Al's speed upstream is $55 - r$, and his speed downstream is $55 + r$. We organize the information in a table.

	Distance	Speed	Time
Upstream	150	$55 - r$	t_1
Downstream	150	$55 + r$	t_2

Translate. Using the formula Time = Distance/Rate we see that $t_1 = \frac{150}{55 - r}$ and $t_2 = \frac{150}{55 + r}$. The total time upstream and back is 5.5 min, so $t_1 + t_2 = 5.5$, or

$$\frac{150}{55 - r} + \frac{150}{55 + r} = 5.5.$$

Carry out. We solve the equation. Multiply on both sides by the LCD, $(55 - r)(55 + r)$.

$$(55 - r)(55 + r)\left(\frac{150}{55 - r} + \frac{150}{55 + r}\right) =$$
$$(55 - r)(55 + r)(5.5)$$
$$150(55 + r) + 150(55 - r) =$$
$$5.5(3025 - r^2)$$
$$8250 + 150r + 8250 - 150r =$$
$$16{,}637.5 - 5.5r^2$$
$$16{,}500 =$$
$$16{,}637.5 - 5.5r^2$$
$$5.5r^2 - 137.5 = 0$$
$$5.5(r^2 - 25) = 0$$
$$5.5(r + 5)(r - 5) = 0$$
$$r = -5 \text{ or } r = 5$$

Check. We check only 5 since the speed cannot be negative. If the speed of the current is 5 m per minute, then Al's speed upstream is $55 - 5$, or 50 m per minute, and his speed downstream is $55 + 5$, or 60 m per minute. Swimming 150 m at 50 m per minute takes $\frac{150}{50}$ or 3 min. Swimming 150 m at 60 m per minute takes $\frac{150}{60}$, or 2.5 min. The total time is $3 + 2.5$, or 5.5 min. The answer checks.

State. The speed of the current is 5 m per minute.

36. 20 mph

37. Familiarize. Let $r =$ the speed at which the van actually traveled in mph, and let $t =$ the actual travel time in hours. We organize the information in a table.

	Distance	Speed	Time
Actual speed	120	r	t
Faster speed	120	$r + 10$	$t - 2$

Translate. From the first row of the table we have $120 = rt$, and from the second row we have $120 = (r+10)(t-2)$. Solving the first equation for t, we have $t = \frac{120}{r}$. Substituting for t in the second equation, we have

$$120 = (r + 10)\left(\frac{120}{r} - 2\right).$$

Carry out. We solve the equation.

$$120 = (r + 10)\left(\frac{120}{r} - 2\right)$$
$$120 = 120 - 2r + \frac{1200}{r} - 20$$
$$20 = -2r + \frac{1200}{r}$$
$$r \cdot 20 = r\left(-2r + \frac{1200}{r}\right)$$
$$20r = -2r^2 + 1200$$
$$2r^2 + 20r - 1200 = 0$$
$$2(r^2 + 10r - 600) = 0$$
$$2(r + 30)(r - 20) = 0$$
$$r = -30 \text{ or } r = 20$$

Check. Since speed cannot be negative in this problem, -30 cannot be a solution of the original problem. If the speed is 20 mph, it takes $\frac{120}{20}$, or 6 hr, to travel 120 mi. If the speed is 10 mph faster, or 30 mph, it takes $\frac{120}{30}$, or 4 hr, to travel 120 mi. Since 4 hr is 2 hr less time than 6 hr, the answer checks.

State. The speed was 20 mph.

38. 12 mph

39. We find the values of x for which the denominator is 0.

$$x^2 - 4x - 5 = 0$$
$$(x - 5)(x + 1) = 0$$
$$x - 5 = 0 \ \ or \ \ x + 1 = 0$$
$$x = 5 \ \ or \ \ \ \ \ \ x = -1.$$

The domain of $f = \{x | x$ is a real number and $x \neq 5$ and $x \neq -1\}$.

40. $\{11, -7\}$

41. a) Enter the data in a graphing calculator and use the linear regression feature. We get $c(x) = 4.8533333x + 46.26$.

   b) Graph $y_1 = c(x)$ and $y_2 = 110$ and use the Intersect feature to find the first coordinate of the point of intersection. It is about 13, so we predict that catalog sales will be \$110 billion about 13 years after 1990, or in 2003.

42. 1500

43.

44.

45.

46.

47. *Familiarize.* Let $t =$ the time, in minutes, it will take to empty a full tub if the water is left on. In 1 minute, $\frac{1}{8}$ of the tub is drained and $\frac{1}{10}$ of the tub is filled for a total change of $\frac{1}{8} - \frac{1}{10}$ of the tub.

Translate. We want to find t such that

$$t\left(\frac{1}{8} - \frac{1}{10}\right) = 1, \text{ or } \frac{t}{8} - \frac{t}{10} = 1.$$

Carry out. We solve the equation.

$$\frac{t}{8} - \frac{t}{10} = 1, \text{ LCD is } 40$$

$$40\left(\frac{t}{8} - \frac{t}{10}\right) = 40 \cdot 1$$

$$5t - 4t = 40$$

$$t = 40$$

Check. In 40 min, $40 \cdot \frac{1}{8}$ or 5 tubs of water are drained and $40 \cdot \frac{1}{10}$ or 4 tubs of water are added. Since the tub was full to begin with, 5 tubs of water

needed to be drained in order to empty the tub. The answer checks.

State. It will take 40 min to empty a full tub if the water is left on.

48. $49\frac{1}{2}$ hr

49. *Familiarize.* Let $p =$ the number of people per hour moved by the 60 cm-wide escalator. Then $2p =$ the number of people per hour moved by the 100 cm-wide escalator. We convert 1575 people per 14 minutes to people per hour:

$$\frac{1575 \text{ people}}{14 \text{ min}} \cdot \frac{60 \text{ min}}{1 \text{ hr}} = 6750 \text{ people/hr}$$

Translate. We use the information that together the escalators move 6750 people per hour to write an equation.

$$p + 2p = 6750$$

Carry out. We solve the equation.

$$p + 2p = 6750$$
$$3p = 6750$$
$$p = 2250$$

Check. If the 60 cm-wide escalator moves 2250 people per hour, then the 100 cm-wide escalator moves $2 \cdot 2250$, or 4500 people per hour. Together, they move $2250 + 4500$, or 6750 people per hour. The answer checks.

State. The 60 cm-wide escalator moves 2250 people per hour.

50. 700 mi from the airport

51. *Familiarize.* Let $d =$ the distance, in miles, the paddleboat can cruise upriver before it is time to turn around. The boat's speed upriver is $12 - 5$, or 7 mph, and its speed downriver is $12 + 5$, or 17 mph. We organize the information in a table.

	Distance	Speed	Time
Upriver	d	7	t_1
Downriver	d	17	t_2

Translate. Using the formula Time = Distance/Rate we see that $t_1 = \frac{d}{7}$ and $t_2 = \frac{d}{17}$. The time upriver and back is 3 hr, so $t_1 + t_2 = 3$, or

$$\frac{d}{7} + \frac{d}{17} = 3.$$

Carry out. We solve the equation.

$$7 \cdot 17 \left(\frac{d}{7} + \frac{d}{17} \right) = 7 \cdot 17 \cdot 3$$
$$17d + 7d = 357$$
$$24d = 357$$
$$d = \frac{119}{8}$$

Check. Traveling $\frac{119}{8}$ mi upriver at a speed of 7 mph takes $\frac{119/8}{7} = \frac{17}{8}$ hr. Traveling $\frac{119}{8}$ mi downriver at a speed of 17 mph takes $\frac{119/8}{17} = \frac{7}{8}$ hr. The total time is $\frac{17}{8} + \frac{7}{8} = \frac{24}{8} = 3$ hr. The answer checks.

State. The pilot can go $\frac{119}{8}$, or $14\frac{7}{8}$ mi upriver before it is time to turn around.

52. $3\frac{3}{4}$ km/h

53. **Familiarize**. Let $d =$ the distance, in miles, Melissa lives from work. Also let $t =$ the travel time in hours, when Melissa arrives on time. Note that 1 min $= \frac{1}{60}$ hr and 5 min $= \frac{5}{60}$, or $\frac{1}{12}$ hr.

Translate. Melissa's travel time at 50 mph is $\frac{d}{50}$. This is $\frac{1}{60}$ hr more than t, so we write an equation using this information:
$$\frac{d}{50} = t + \frac{1}{60}$$

Her travel time at 60 mph, $\frac{d}{60}$, is $\frac{1}{12}$ hr less than t, so we write a second equation:
$$\frac{d}{60} = t - \frac{1}{12}$$

We have a system of equations:
$$\frac{d}{50} = t + \frac{1}{60},$$
$$\frac{d}{60} = t - \frac{1}{12}$$

Carry out. Solving the system of equations, we get $\left(30, \frac{7}{12} \right)$.

Check. Traveling 30 mi at 50 mph takes $\frac{30}{50}$, or $\frac{3}{5}$ hr. Since $\frac{7}{12} + \frac{1}{60} = \frac{36}{60} = \frac{3}{5}$, this time makes Melissa $\frac{1}{60}$ hr, or 1 min late. Traveling 30 mi at 60 mph takes $\frac{30}{60}$, or $\frac{1}{2}$ hr. Since $\frac{7}{12} - \frac{1}{12} = \frac{6}{12} = \frac{1}{2}$, this time makes Melissa $\frac{1}{12}$ hr, or 5 min early. The answer checks.

State. Melissa lives 30 mi from work.

54. $21\frac{9}{11}$ min after 4:00

55. **Familiarize** Express the position of the hands in terms of minute units on the face of the clock. At 10:30 the hour hand is at $\frac{10.5}{12}$ hr $\times \frac{60 \text{ min}}{1 \text{ hr}}$, or 52.5 minutes, and the minute hand is at 30 minutes. The rate of the minute hand is 12 times the rate of the hour hand. (When the minute hand moves 60 minutes, the hour hand moves 5 minutes.) Let $t =$ the number of minutes after 10:30 that the hands will first be perpendicular. After t minutes the minute hand has moved t units, and the hour hand has moved $\frac{t}{12}$ units. The position of the hour hand will be 15 units "ahead" of the position of the minute hand when they are first perpendicular.

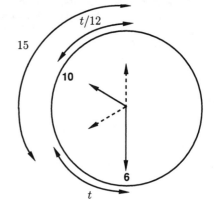

Translate.

Position of hour hand after t min	is	position of minute hand after t min	plus	15 min.
$\downarrow$	$\downarrow$	$\downarrow$	$\downarrow$	$\downarrow$
$52.5 + \frac{t}{12}$	$=$	$30 + t$	$+$	15

Solve. We solve the equation.
$$52.5 + \frac{t}{12} = 30 + t + 15$$
$$52.5 + \frac{t}{12} = 45 + t, \text{ LCM is } 12$$
$$12 \left(52.5 + \frac{t}{12} \right) = 12(45 + t)$$
$$630 + t = 540 + 12t$$
$$90 = 11t$$
$$\frac{90}{11} = t, \text{ or}$$
$$8\frac{2}{11} = t$$

Check. At $\frac{90}{11}$ min after 10:30, the position of the hour hand is at $52.5 + \frac{90/11}{12}$, or $53\frac{2}{11}$ min. The minute hand is at $30 + \frac{90}{11}$, or $38\frac{2}{11}$ min. The hour hand is 15 minutes ahead of the minute hand so the hands are perpendicular. The answer checks.

State. After 10:30 the hands of a clock will first be perpendicular in $8\frac{2}{11}$ min. The time is $10:38\frac{2}{11}$, or $21\frac{9}{11}$ min before 11:00.

56. 48 km/h

57. *Familiarize*. Let r = the speed in mph Chip would have to travel for the last half of the trip in order to average a speed of 45 mph for the entire trip. We organize the information in a table.

	Distance	Speed	Time
First half	50	40	t_1
Last half	50	r	t_2

The total distance is $50 + 50$, or 100 mi.

The total time is $t_1 + t_2$, or $\frac{50}{40} + \frac{50}{r}$, or $\frac{5}{4} + \frac{50}{r}$. The average speed is 45 mph.

Translate.

$$\text{Average speed} = \frac{\text{Total distance}}{\text{Total time}}$$

$$45 = \frac{100}{\frac{5}{4} + \frac{50}{r}}$$

Carry out. We solve the equation.

$$45 = \frac{100}{\frac{5}{4} + \frac{50}{r}}$$

$$45 = \frac{100}{\frac{5r + 200}{4r}}$$

$$45 = 100 \cdot \frac{4r}{5r + 200}$$

$$45 = \frac{400r}{5r + 200}$$

$$(5r + 200)(45) = (5r + 200) \cdot \frac{400r}{5r + 200}$$

$$225r + 9000 = 400r$$

$$9000 = 175r$$

$$\frac{360}{7} = r$$

Check. Traveling 50 mi at 40 mph takes $\frac{50}{40}$, or

$\frac{5}{4}$ hr. Traveling 50 mi at $\frac{360}{7}$ mph takes $\frac{50}{360/7}$, or $\frac{35}{36}$ hr. Then the total time is $\frac{5}{4} + \frac{35}{36} = \frac{80}{36} = \frac{20}{9}$ hr.

The average speed when traveling 100 mi for $\frac{20}{9}$ hr is $\frac{100}{20/9} = 45$ mph. The answer checks.

State. Chip would have to travel at a speed of $\frac{360}{7}$, or $51\frac{3}{7}$ mph for the last half of the trip so that the average speed for the entire trip would be 45 mph.

Exercise Set 7.6

1. $\frac{W_1}{W_2} = \frac{d_1}{d_2}$

$W_1 = \frac{d_1 W_2}{d_2}$ Multiplying by W_2

2. $d = \frac{d_2 W_1}{W_2}$

3. $s = \frac{(v_1 + v_2)t}{2}$

$2s = (v_1 + v_2)t$ Multiplying by 2

$\frac{2s}{t} = v_1 + v_2$ Dividing by t

$\frac{2s}{t} - v_2 = v_1$

This result can also be expressed as $v_1 = \frac{2s - tv_2}{t}$.

4. $t = \frac{2s}{v_1 + v_2}$

5. $\frac{1}{R} = \frac{1}{r_1} + \frac{1}{r_2}$

$Rr_1r_2 \cdot \frac{1}{R} = Rr_1r_2\left(\frac{1}{r_1} + \frac{1}{r_2}\right)$ Multiplying by the LCD

$Rr_1r_2 \cdot \frac{1}{R} = Rr_1r_2 \cdot \frac{1}{r_1} + Rr_1r_2 \cdot \frac{1}{r_2}$

$r_1r_2 = Rr_2 + Rr_1$

$r_1r_2 = R(r_2 + r_1)$ Factoring out R

$\frac{r_1r_2}{r_2 + r_1} = R$ Multiplying by $\frac{1}{r_2 + r_1}$

6. $r_1 = \frac{Rr_2}{r_2 - R}$

7.
$$R = \frac{gs}{g+s}$$

$$(g+s) \cdot R = (g+s) \cdot \frac{gs}{g+s} \quad \text{Multiplying by the LCD}$$

$$Rg + Rs = gs$$

$$Rs = gs - Rg$$

$$Rs = g(s - R) \qquad \text{Factoring out } g$$

$$\frac{Rs}{s-R} = g \qquad \text{Multiplying by } \frac{1}{s-R}$$

8. $t = \dfrac{Kr}{r+K}$

9.
$$I = \frac{2V}{R+2r}$$

$$I(R+2r) = \frac{2V}{R+2r} \cdot (R+2r) \quad \begin{array}{l}\text{Multiplying}\\\text{by the LCD}\end{array}$$

$$I(R+2r) = 2V$$

$$R + 2r = \frac{2V}{I}$$

$$R = \frac{2V}{I} - 2r, \text{ or } \frac{2V - 2Ir}{I}$$

10. $r = \dfrac{2V - IR}{2I}$, or $\dfrac{V}{I} - \dfrac{R}{2}$

11.
$$\frac{1}{p} + \frac{1}{q} = \frac{1}{f}$$

$$pqf\left(\frac{1}{p} + \frac{1}{q}\right) = pqf \cdot \frac{1}{f} \quad \begin{array}{l}\text{Multiplying by}\\\text{the LCD}\end{array}$$

$$qf + pf = pq$$

$$qf = pq - pf$$

$$qf = p(q - f)$$

$$\frac{qf}{q-f} = p$$

12. $q = \dfrac{pf}{p-f}$

13.
$$I = \frac{nE}{R+nr}$$

$$I(R+nr) = \frac{nE}{R+nr} \cdot (R+nr) \quad \begin{array}{l}\text{Multiplying}\\\text{by the LCD}\end{array}$$

$$IR + Inr = nE$$

$$IR = nE - Inr$$

$$IR = n(E - Ir)$$

$$\frac{IR}{E - Ir} = n$$

14. $r = \dfrac{nE - IR}{In}$

15.
$$S = \frac{H}{m(t_1 - t_2)}$$

$$(t_1 - t_2)S = \frac{H}{m} \qquad \text{Multiplying by } t_1 - t_2$$

$$t_1 - t_2 = \frac{H}{Sm} \qquad \text{Dividing by } S$$

$$t_1 = \frac{H}{Sm} + t_2, \text{ or } \frac{H + Smt_2}{Sm}$$

16. $H = m(t_1 - t_2)S$

17.
$$\frac{E}{e} = \frac{R+r}{r}$$

$$er \cdot \frac{E}{e} = er \cdot \frac{R+r}{r} \quad \text{Multiplying by the LCD}$$

$$Er = e(R + r)$$

$$Er = eR + er$$

$$Er - er = eR$$

$$r(E - e) = eR$$

$$r = \frac{eR}{E - e}$$

18. $e = \dfrac{rE}{R+r}$

19.
$$S = \frac{a}{1-r}$$

$$(1 - r)S = a \qquad \text{Multiplying by the LCD, } 1 - r$$

$$1 - r = \frac{a}{S} \qquad \text{Dividing by } S$$

$$1 - \frac{a}{S} = r \qquad \text{Adding } r \text{ and } -\frac{a}{S}$$

This result can also be expressed as $r = \dfrac{S-a}{S}$.

20. $a = \dfrac{S - Sr}{1 - r^n}$

21.
$$P = \frac{A}{1+r}$$

$$P(1+r) = \frac{A}{1+r} \cdot (1+r) \quad \begin{array}{l}\text{Multiplying by}\\\text{the LCD}\end{array}$$

$$P(1+r) = A$$

$$1 + r = \frac{A}{P} \qquad \text{Dividing by } P$$

$$r = \frac{A}{P} - 1, \text{ or } \frac{A-P}{P}$$

22. $t_2 = \dfrac{d_2 - d_1}{v} + t_1$, or $\dfrac{d_2 - d_1 + t_1 v}{v}$

23. From Exercise 22 we know that

$$t_2 = \frac{d_2 - d_1}{v} + t_1.$$

We use this result, replacing v with 60, d_1 with 0, d_2 with 105, and t_1 with 0.

$$t_2 = \frac{105 - 0}{60} + 0$$

$$t_2 = 1.75 \text{ hr, or } 1 \text{ hr } 45 \text{ min}$$

The arrival time is 1 hr 45 min after 2:00 A.M., or 3:45 A.M.

24. 7%

25. First we solve the formula for R.

$$A = \frac{9R}{I}$$

$$\frac{I}{9} \cdot A = \frac{I}{9} \cdot \frac{9R}{I}$$

$$\frac{AI}{9} = R$$

Then substitute 2.4 for A and 45 for I.

$$\frac{2.4(45)}{9} = R$$

$$12 = R$$

Thus, 12 earned runs were given up.

26. $5\frac{5}{23}$ ohms

27. Use the result of Example 4, replacing R with 5 and r_1 with 50.

$$r_2 = \frac{Rr_1}{r_1 - R}$$

$$r_2 = \frac{5 \cdot 50}{50 - 5}$$

$$= \frac{250}{45}$$

$$= \frac{50}{9}, \text{ or } 5\frac{5}{9}$$

A resistor with a resistance of $5\frac{5}{9}$ ohms should be used.

28. $t = \dfrac{ab}{b + a}$

29. First solve the formula for the area of the trapezoid for one of the bases, say b_2.

$$A = \frac{1}{2}h(b_1 + b_2)$$

$$\frac{2A}{h} = b_1 + b_2 \qquad \text{Multiplying by } \frac{2}{h}$$

$$\frac{2A}{h} - b_1 = b_2$$

Then substitute 25 for A, 5 for h, and 4 for b_1.

$$\frac{2 \cdot 25}{5} - 4 = b_2$$

$$10 - 4 = b_2$$

$$6 = b_2$$

The length of the other base is 6 cm.

30. $T = -\dfrac{I_f}{I_t} + 1$, or $1 - \dfrac{I_f}{I_t}$, or $\dfrac{I_t - I_f}{I_t}$

31.
$$\frac{V^2}{R^2} = \frac{2g}{R + h}$$

$$(R + h) \cdot \frac{V^2}{R^2} = (R + h) \cdot \frac{2g}{R + h} \quad \begin{array}{l}\text{Multiplying} \\ \text{by } (R + h)\end{array}$$

$$\frac{(R + h)V^2}{R^2} = 2g$$

$$R + h = \frac{2gR^2}{V^2} \qquad \text{Multiplying by } \frac{R^2}{V^2}$$

$$h = \frac{2gR^2}{V^2} - R \quad \text{Adding } -R$$

The result can also be expressed as

$$h = \frac{2gR^2 - RV^2}{V^2}.$$

32. $d = \dfrac{LD}{R + L}$

33.
$$A = \frac{2Tt + Qq}{2T + Q}$$

$$(2T + Q) \cdot A = (2T + Q) \cdot \frac{2Tt + Qq}{2T + Q}$$

$$2AT + AQ = 2Tt + Qq$$

$$AQ - Qq = 2Tt - 2AT \quad \begin{array}{l}\text{Adding } -2AT \\ \text{and } -Qq\end{array}$$

$$Q(A - q) = 2Tt - 2AT$$

$$Q = \frac{2Tt - 2AT}{A - q}, \text{ or}$$

$$Q = \frac{2AT - 2Tt}{q - A}$$

34. $t_1 = t_2 - \dfrac{v_2 - v_1}{a}$, or $t_2 + \dfrac{v_1 - v_2}{a}$

35. We use the formula for slope:

$$m = \frac{y_1 - y_2}{x_1 - x_2}$$

Substitute $-\dfrac{2}{5}$ for m, 2 for y_1, 8 for y_2, x_1 for x_1 and $2x_1$ for x_2 and solve for x_1.

$$-\frac{2}{5} = \frac{2 - 8}{x_1 - 2x_1}$$

$$-\frac{2}{5} = \frac{-6}{-x_1}$$

$$-\frac{2}{5} = \frac{6}{x_1}$$

$$-2x_1 = 30 \qquad \text{Multiplying by } 5x_1$$

$$x_1 = -15$$

If $x_1 = -15$, then $2x_1 = 2(-15) = -30$. Thus, the coordinates of the points are $(-15, 2)$ and $(-30, 8)$.

36. 3

37. A scatterplot of the data shows that it can be modeled by a function of the form $f(x) = \dfrac{k}{x}$.

38. No

39. A scatterplot of the data shows that it cannot be modeled well by a function of the form $f(x) = \dfrac{k}{x}$.

40. Yes

41. Graph: $6x - y < 6$

First graph the line $6x - y = 6$. The intercepts are $(0, -6)$ and $(1, 0)$. We draw the line dashed since the inequality is $<$. Since the ordered pair $(0, 0)$ is a solution of the inequality ($6 \cdot 0 - 0 < 6$ is true), we shade the half-plane containing $(0, 0)$.

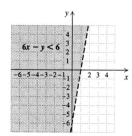

42. $8a^3 - 2a$

43. Graph $y = x^2 - 77x - 2940$ and find the zeros. They are -28 and 105. We know that -28 is a zero of $g(x) = x + 28$ and 105 is a zero of $h(x) = x - 105$. Then $x^2 - 77x - 2940 = (x + 28)(x - 105)$.

44. $-\dfrac{5}{3}, \dfrac{7}{2}$

45. ◈

46. About 567 mi

47.

$$\frac{1}{M} = \frac{\frac{1}{a} + \frac{1}{b}}{2}$$

$$2M \cdot \frac{1}{M} = 2M \cdot \frac{\frac{1}{a} + \frac{1}{b}}{2}$$

$$2 = M\left(\frac{1}{a} + \frac{1}{b}\right)$$

$$2 = \frac{M}{a} + \frac{M}{b}$$

$$ab \cdot 2 = ab\left(\frac{M}{a} + \frac{M}{b}\right)$$

$$2ab = bM + aM$$

$$2ab = M(b + a)$$

$$\frac{2ab}{b + a} = M$$

48. pq, $2pq$

49.

$$a = \frac{\dfrac{d_4 - d_3}{t_4 - t_3} - \dfrac{d_2 - d_1}{t_2 - t_1}}{t_4 - t_2}$$

$$a(t_4 - t_2) = \frac{d_4 - d_3}{t_4 - t_3} - \frac{d_2 - d_1}{t_2 - t_1} \quad \begin{array}{l}\text{Multiplying}\\\text{by } t_4 - t_2\end{array}$$

$$a(t_4{-}t_2)(t_4{-}t_3)(t_2{-}t_1) = (d_4{-}d_3)(t_2{-}t_1){-}(d_2{-}d_1)(t_4{-}t_3)$$

$$\text{Multiplying by } (t_4 - t_3)(t_2 - t_1)$$

$$a(t_4 - t_2)(t_4 - t_3)(t_2 - t_1) - (d_4 - d_3)(t_2 - t_1) =$$
$$-(d_2 - d_1)(t_4 - t_3)$$

$$(t_2 - t_1)[a(t_4 - t_2)(t_4 - t_3) - (d_4 - d_3)] =$$
$$-(d_2 - d_1)(t_4 - t_3)$$

$$t_2 - t_1 = \frac{-(d_2 - d_1)(t_4 - t_3)}{a(t_4 - t_2)(t_4 - t_3) - (d_4 - d_3)}$$

$$t_2 + \frac{(d_2 - d_1)(t_4 - t_3)}{a(t_4 - t_2)(t_4 - t_3) + d_3 - d_4} = t_1$$

Chapter 8

Systems of Equations and Problem Solving

Exercise Set 8.1

1. Familiarize. Let x = the larger number and y = the smaller number.

Translate.

The difference between two numbers is 11.

Rewording:

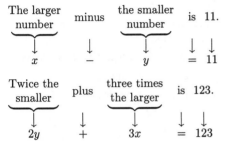

We have a system of equations:

$$x - y = 11,$$
$$3x + 2y = 123$$

2. Let x = the first number and y = the second number.

$$x + y = -42,$$
$$x - y = 52$$

3. Familiarize. Let x = the number of less expensive brushes sold and y = the number of more expensive brushes sold.

Translate. We organize the information in a table.

Kind of brush	Less expensive	More expensive	Total
Number sold	x	y	45
Price	\$8.50	\$9.75	
Amount taken in	$8.50x$	$9.75y$	398.75

The "Number sold" row of the table gives us one equation:

$$x + y = 45$$

The "Amount taken in" row gives us a second equation:

$$8.50x + 9.75y = 398.75$$

We have a system of equations:

$$x + y = 45,$$
$$8.50x + 9.75y = 398.75$$

We can multiply the second equation on both sides by 100 to clear the decimals:

$$x + y = 45,$$
$$850x + 975y = 39,875$$

4. Let x = the number of solid color neckwarmers sold and y = the number of print ones sold.

$$x + y = 40,$$
$$9.9x + 12.75y = 421.65$$

5. Familiarize. Let x = the measure of one angle and y = the measure of the other angle.

Translate.

Two angles are supplementary.

Rewording: The sum of the measures is 180°.

$$x + y \qquad = \qquad 180$$

One angle is 3° less than twice the other.

Rewording: One angle is   twice the other angle   minus 3°.

$$x \quad = \quad 2y \quad - \quad 3$$

We have a system of equations:

$$x + y = 180,$$
$$x = 2y - 3$$

(The second equation could also be written as $y = 2x - 3$.)

6. Let x = the measure of the first angle and y = the measure of the second angle.

$$x + y = 90,$$
$$x + \frac{1}{2}y = 64$$

7. Familiarize. Let g = the number of field goals and t = the number of free throws Amma made.

Translate. We organize the information in a table.

Kind of shot	Field goal	Free throw	Total
Number scored	g	t	18
Points per score	2	1	
Points scored	$2g$	t	30

From the "Number scored" row of the table we get one equation:

$$g + t = 18$$

The "Points scored" row gives us another equation:

$$2g + t = 30$$

We have a system of equations:

$$g + t = 18,$$
$$2g + t = 30$$

8. Let x = the number of children's plates and y = the number of adult's plates served.

$$x + y = 250,$$
$$3.5x + 7y = 1347.5$$

9. *Familiarize*. Let h = the number of vials of Humulin Insulin sold and n = the number of vials of Novolin Insulin sold.

Translate. We organize the information in a table.

Brand	Humulin	Novolin	Total
Number sold	h	n	65
Price	\$15.75	\$12.95	
Amount taken in	$15.75h$	$12.95n$	959.35

The "Number sold" row of the table gives us one equation:

$$h + n = 65$$

The "Amount taken in" row gives us a second equation:

$$15.75h + 12.95n = 959.35$$

We have a system of equations:

$$h + n = 65$$
$$15.75h + 12.95n = 959.35$$

We can multiply the second equation on both sides by 100 to clear the decimals:

$$h + n = 65$$
$$1575h + 1295n = 95{,}935$$

10. Let l = the length, in feet, and w = the width, in feet.

$$2l + 2w = 288,$$
$$l = w + 44$$

11. *Familiarize*. The tennis court is a rectangle with perimeter 228 ft. Let l = the length, in feet, and w = width, in feet. Recall that for a rectangle with length l and width w, the perimeter P is given by $P = 2l + 2w$.

Translate. The formula for perimeter gives us one equation:

$$2l + 2w = 228$$

The statement relating width and length gives us another equation:

The width is 42 ft less than the length.

$$w \qquad = l - 42$$

We have a system of equations:

$$2l + 2w = 228,$$
$$w = l - 42$$

12. Let x = the number of 2-pointers scored and y = the number of 3-pointers scored.

$$x + y = 40,$$
$$2x + 3y = 89$$

13. *Familiarize*. Let l = the number of units of lumber produced and p = the number of units of plywood produced. Then the total profit from the lumber is $25l$ and the total profit from the plywood is $40p$.

Translate. The mill turns out twice as many units of plywood as lumber.

Rewording:

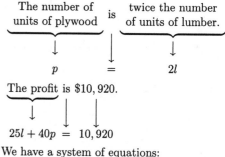

We have a system of equations:

$$p = 2l$$
$$25l + 40p = 10{,}920$$

14. Let x = the number of general interest films rented and y = the number of children's films rented.

$$x + y = 77,$$
$$3x + 1.5y = 213$$

15. *Familiarize*. Let w = the number of wins and t = the number of ties. Then the total number of points received from wins was $2w$ and the total number of points received from ties was t.

***Translate*.**

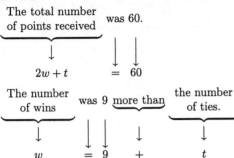

The total number of points received was 60.

$$2w + t = 60$$

The number of wins was 9 more than the number of ties.

$$w = 9 + t$$

We have a system of equations:

$$2w + t = 60,$$
$$w = 9 + t$$

16. Let x = the number of 30-sec commercials and y = the number of 60-sec commercials. Note that 10 min = 10×60 sec = 600 sec.

$$x + y = 12,$$
$$30x + 60y = 600$$

17. *Familiarize*. Let x = the number of ounces of lemon juice and y = the number of ounces of linseed oil to be used.

***Translate*.**

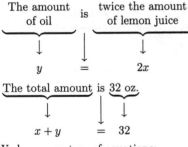

The amount of oil is twice the amount of lemon juice

$$y = 2x$$

The total amount is 32 oz.

$$x + y = 32$$

We have a system of equations:

$$y = 2x,$$
$$x + y = 32$$

18. Let c = the number of coach-class seats and f = the number of first-class seats.

$$c + f = 152,$$
$$c = 5 + 6f$$

19. We use alphabetical order for the variables. We re-

place x by 1 and y by 2.

$$
\begin{array}{c|c}
4x - y = 2 & \\
\hline
4 \cdot 1 - 2 \;?\; 2 & \\
4 - 2 & \\
2 & 2 \quad \text{TRUE}
\end{array}
\qquad
\begin{array}{c|c}
10x - 3y = 4 & \\
\hline
10 \cdot 1 - 3 \cdot 2 \;?\; 4 & \\
10 - 6 & \\
4 & 4 \quad \text{TRUE}
\end{array}
$$

The pair $(1, 2)$ makes both equations true, so it is a solution of the system.

20. Yes

21. We use alphabetical order for the variables. We replace x by 2 and y by 5.

$$
\begin{array}{c|c}
y = 3x - 1 & \\
\hline
5 \;?\; 3 \cdot 2 - 1 & \\
& 6 - 1 \\
5 & 5 \qquad \text{TRUE}
\end{array}
\qquad
\begin{array}{c|c}
2x + y = 4 & \\
\hline
2 \cdot 2 + 5 \;?\; 4 & \\
4 + 5 & \\
9 & 4 \quad \text{FALSE}
\end{array}
$$

The pair $(2, 5)$ is not a solution of $2x + y = 4$. Therefore, it is not a solution of the system of equations.

22. No

23. We replace x by 1 and y by 5.

$$
\begin{array}{c|c}
x + y = 6 & \\
\hline
1 + 5 \;?\; 6 & \\
6 & 6 \quad \text{TRUE}
\end{array}
\qquad
\begin{array}{c|c}
y = 2x + 3 & \\
\hline
5 \;?\; 2 \cdot 1 + 3 & \\
& 2 + 3 \\
5 & 5 \qquad \text{TRUE}
\end{array}
$$

The pair $(1, 5)$ makes both equations true, so it is a solution of the system.

24. Yes

25. We replace x by 3 and y by 1.

$$
\begin{array}{c|c}
3x + 4y = 13 & \\
\hline
3 \cdot 3 + 4 \cdot 1 \;?\; 13 & \\
9 + 4 & \\
13 & 13 \quad \text{TRUE}
\end{array}
$$

$$
\begin{array}{c|c}
5x - 4y = 11 & \\
\hline
5 \cdot 3 - 4 \cdot 1 \;?\; 11 & \\
15 - 4 & \\
11 & 11 \quad \text{TRUE}
\end{array}
$$

The pair $(3, 1)$ makes both equations true, so it is a solution of the system. No

27. Graph both equations.

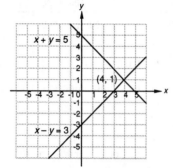

The solution (point of intersection) is apparently $(4, 1)$.

Check:

$x - y = 3$	$x + y = 5$
$4 - 1$? 3	$4 + 1$? 5
$3 \mid 3$ TRUE	$5 \mid 5$ TRUE

The solution is $(4, 1)$.

28. $(3, 1)$

29. Graph the equations.

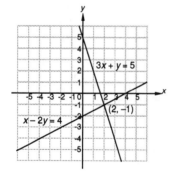

The solution (point of intersection) is apparently $(2, -1)$.

Check:

$3x + y = 5$	$x - 2y = 4$
$3 \cdot 2 + (-1)$? 5	$2 - 2(-1)$? 4
$6 - 1$	$2 + 2$
$5 \mid 5$ TRUE	$4 \mid 4$ TRUE

The solution is $(2, -1)$.

30. $(3, 2)$

31. Graph both equations.

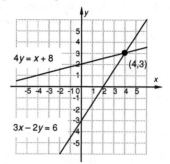

The solution (point of intersection) is apparently $(4, 3)$.

Check:

$4y = x + 8$	$3x - 2y = 6$
$4 \cdot 3$? $4 + 8$	$3 \cdot 4 - 2 \cdot 3$? 6
$12 \mid 12$ TRUE	$12 - 6$
	$6 \mid 6$ TRUE

The solution is $(4, 3)$.

32. $(1, -5)$

33. Graph both equations.

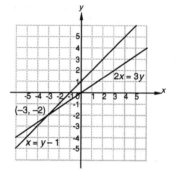

The solution (point of intersection) is apparently $(-3, -2)$.

Check:

$x = y - 1$	$2x = 3y$
-3 ? $-2 - 1$	$2(-3)$? $3(-2)$
$-3 \mid -3$ TRUE	$-6 \mid -6$ TRUE

The solution is $(-3, -2)$.

34. $(2, 1)$

35. Graph both equations.

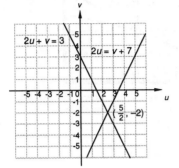

The solution (point of intersection) is apparently $\left(\frac{5}{2}, -2\right)$.

Check:

$2u + v = 3$		$2u = v + 7$	
$2 \cdot \frac{5}{2}$? 3		$2 \cdot \frac{5}{2}$? $-2 + 7$	
$5 - 2$		5 $\mid$ 5	TRUE
3 $\mid$ 3	TRUE		

The solution is $\left(\frac{5}{2}, -2\right)$.

36. $(4, -5)$

37. Graph both equations.

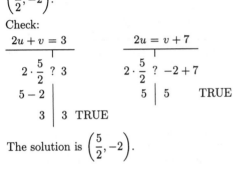

The ordered pair $(-3, 2)$ checks in both equations. It is the solution.

38. $\left(\frac{1}{2}, 3\right)$

39. Enter $y_1 = -5.43x + 10.89$ and $y_2 = 6.29x - 7.04$ on a grapher and use the INTERSECT feature.

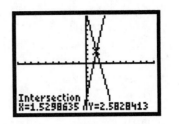

The solution is about $(1.53, 2.58)$.

40. $(-0.26, 57.06)$

41. Graph both equations.

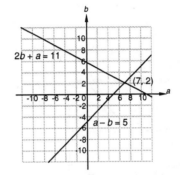

The solution (point of intersection) is apparently $(7, 2)$.

Check:

$2b + a = 11$		$a - b = 5$	
$2 \cdot 2 + 7$? 11		$7 - 2$? 5	
$4 + 7$		5	TRUE
11 $\mid$ 11	TRUE		

The solution is $(7, 2)$.

42. No solution

43. Graph both equations.

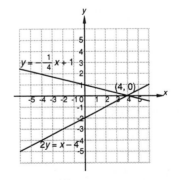

The solution (point of intersection) is apparently $(4, 0)$.

Check:

$$y = -\frac{1}{4}x + 1 \qquad\qquad 2y = x - 4$$

$$0 \;?\; -\frac{1}{4}\cdot 4 + 1 \qquad\qquad 2\cdot 0 \;?\; 4 - 4$$

$$\qquad\qquad -1 + 1 \qquad\qquad\qquad 0 \;\big|\; 0 \quad\text{TRUE}$$

$$0 \;\big|\; 0 \qquad\qquad \text{TRUE}$$

The solution is (4,0).

44. $(3, -2)$

45. Solve each equation for y. We get
$$y = \frac{-2.18x + 13.78}{7.81} \text{ and } y = \frac{-5.79x + 8.94}{-3.45}.$$ Graph
these equations on a grapher and use the INTER-SECT feature.

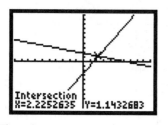

The solution is about $(2.23, 1.14)$.

46. No solution

47. Graph both equations.

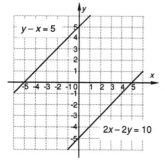

The lines are parallel. The system has no solution.

48. No solution

49. Solve each equation for y. We get $y = \dfrac{45x + 33}{57}$ and
$y = \dfrac{30x + 22}{95}$. Graph these equations on a grapher
and use the INTERSECT feature.

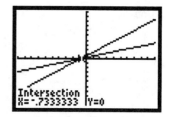

The solution is about $(-0.73, 0)$.

50. $(0.87, -0.32)$

51. Graph both equations.

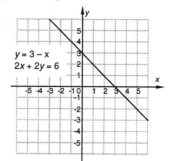

The graphs are the same. Any solution of one equation is a solution of the other. Each equation has infinitely many solutions. The solution set is the set of all pairs (x, y) for which $y = 3 - x$, or $\{(x, y) | y = 3 - x\}$. (In place of $y = 3 - x$ we could have used $2x + 2y = 6$ since the two equations are equivalent.)

52. $(3, -4)$

53. Solve each equation for y. We get $y = \dfrac{1.9x - 1.7}{4.8}$
and $y = \dfrac{12.92x + 23.8}{32.64}$. Graph these equations on a
grapher and use the INTERSECT feature.

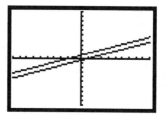

Note that the lines appear to be parallel. This is confirmed by the error message "NO SIGN CHNG" that is returned when we use the INTERSECT feature. The system of equations has no solution.

54. $\{(x, y) | 2x - 3y = 6\}$

55. A system of equations is consistent if it has at least one solution. Of the systems under consideration, only the ones in Exercises 47 and 53 have no solution. Therefore, all except the systems in Exercises 47 and 53 are consistent.

56. All except 42, 46 and 48

57. A system of two equations in two variables is dependent if it has infinitely many solutions. Only the system in Exercise 51 is dependent.

58. 54

59. $3x + 4 = x - 2$

$\quad 2x + 4 = -2$ Adding $-x$ on both sides

$\quad\quad 2x = -6$ Adding -4 on both sides

$\quad\quad\quad x = -3$ Multiplying by $\frac{1}{2}$ on both sides

The solution is -3.

60. -35

61. $4x - 5x = 8x - 9 + 11x$

$\quad\quad -x = 19x - 9$ Collecting like terms

$\quad -20x = -9$ Adding $-19x$ on both sides

$\quad\quad\quad x = \frac{9}{20}$ Multiplying by $-\frac{1}{20}$ on both sides

The solution is $\frac{9}{20}$.

62. $b = a - 4Q$

63. $3x - 21 = 3 \cdot x - 3 \cdot 7 = 3(x - 7)$

64. $a(2 + b - c)$

65. ◈

66. ◈

67. ◈

68. ◈

69. From 1991-1995

70. 1989

71. a) There are many correct answers. One can be found by expressing the sum and difference of the two numbers:

$$x + y = 6,$$
$$x - y = 4$$

b) There are many correct answers. For example, write an equation in two variables. Then write a second equation by multiplying the left side of the first equation by one nonzero constant and multiplying the right side by another nonzero constant.

$$x + y = 1,$$
$$2x + 2y = 3$$

c) There are many correct answers. One can be found by writing an equation in two variables and then writing a nonzero constant multiple of that equation:

$$x + y = 1,$$
$$2x + 2y = 2$$

72. (a) Answers may vary. $(4, -5)$; (b) Infinitely many

73. Substitute 4 for x and -5 for y in the first equation:

$$A(4) - 6(-5) = 13$$
$$4A + 30 = 13$$
$$4A = -17$$
$$A = -\frac{17}{4}$$

Substitute 4 for x and -5 for y in the second equation:

$$4 - B(-5) = -8$$
$$4 + 5B = -8$$
$$5B = -12$$
$$B = -\frac{12}{5}$$

We have $A = -\frac{17}{4}$, $B = -\frac{12}{5}$.

74. Let $x =$ Burl's age now and $y =$ his son's age now.

$$x = 2y,$$
$$x - 10 = 3(y - 10)$$

75. *Familiarize*. Let $x =$ the number of years Lou has taught and $y =$ the number of years Juanita has taught. Two years ago, Lou and Juanita had taught $x - 2$ and $y - 2$ years, respectively.

Translate.

Together, the number of years of service   is 46.

$$\downarrow$$
$$x + y \qquad = 46$$

Two years ago
Lou had taught 2.5 times as many years as Juanita.

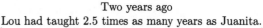

$$x - 2 = 2.5(y - 2)$$

We have a system of equations:
$$x + y = 46,$$
$$x - 2 = 2.5(y - 2)$$

76. Let l = the original length, in inches, and w = the original width, in inches.
$$2l + 2w = 156,$$
$$l = 4(w - 6)$$

77. *Familiarize.* Let b = the number of ounces of baking soda and v = the number of ounces of vinegar to be used. The amount of baking soda in the mixture will be four times the amount of vinegar.

Translate.

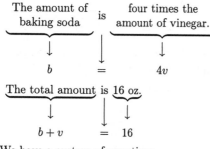

We have a system of equations.
$$b = 4v,$$
$$b + v = 16$$

78. $(3, 3), (-5, 5)$

79. Graph both equations.

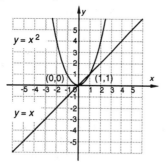

The solutions are apparently $(0, 0)$ and $(1, 1)$. Both pairs check.

80. (d)

81. The equations have the same slope and the same y-intercept. Thus their graphs are the same. Graph (c) matches this system.

82. (a)

83. The equations have the same slope and different y-intercepts. Thus their graphs are parallel lines. Graph (b) matches this system.

Exercise Set 8.2

1. $3x + 5y = 3,$ (1)
   $x = 8 - 4y$ (2)

We substitute $8 - 4y$ for x in the first equation and solve for y.
$$3x + 5y = 3 \qquad (1)$$
$$3(8 - 4y) + 5y = 3 \qquad \text{Substituting}$$
$$24 - 12y + 5y = 3$$
$$24 - 7y = 3$$
$$-7y = -21$$
$$y = 3$$

Next we substitute 3 for y in either equation of the original system and solve for x.
$$x = 8 - 4y \qquad (2)$$
$$x = 8 - 4 \cdot 3 \qquad \text{Substituting}$$
$$x = 8 - 12$$
$$x = -4$$

We check the ordered pair $(-4, 3)$.

$$\begin{array}{c|c} 3x + 5y = 3 \\ \hline 3(-4) + 5 \cdot 3 \ ? \ 3 \\ -12 + 15 \\ \quad 3 \ \big| \ 3 \quad \text{TRUE} \end{array}$$

$$\begin{array}{c|c} x = 8 - 4y \\ \hline -4 \ ? \ 8 - 4 \cdot 3 \\ \quad \big| \ 8 - 12 \\ -4 \ \big| \ -4 \qquad \text{TRUE} \end{array}$$

Since $(-4, 3)$ checks, it is the solution.

2. $(2, -3)$

3. $3x - 6 = y,$ (1)
   $9x - 2y = 3$ (2)

We substitute $3x - 6$ for y in the second equation and solve for x.
$$9x - 2y = 3 \qquad (2)$$
$$9x - 2(3x - 6) = 3 \qquad \text{Substituting}$$
$$9x - 6x + 12 = 3$$
$$3x + 12 = 3$$
$$3x = -9$$
$$x = -3$$

Next we substitute -3 for x in either equation of the original system and solve for y.

$$3x - 6 = y \quad (1)$$
$$3(-3) - 6 = y \quad \text{Substituting}$$
$$-9 - 6 = y$$
$$-15 = y$$

We check the ordered pair $(-3, -15)$.

$$\frac{3x - 6 = y}{3(-3) - 6 \ ? \ -15}$$
$$\begin{array}{c|c} -9 - 6 & \\ -15 & -15 \quad \text{TRUE} \end{array}$$

$$\frac{9x - 2y = 3}{9(-3) - 2(-15) \ ? \ 3}$$
$$\begin{array}{c|c} -27 + 30 & \\ 3 & 3 \quad \text{TRUE} \end{array}$$

Since $(-3, -15)$ checks, it is the solution.

4. $\left(\dfrac{21}{5}, \dfrac{12}{5}\right)$

5. $\quad 4x + y = 1, \quad (1)$
$\qquad x - 2y = 16 \quad (2)$

We solve the second equation for x.

$$x - 2y = 16 \qquad (2)$$
$$x = 2y + 16 \quad (3)$$

We substitute $2y + 16$ for x in the first equation and solve for y.

$$4x + y = 1 \quad (1)$$
$$4(2y + 16) + y = 1 \quad \text{Substituting}$$
$$8y + 64 + y = 1$$
$$9y + 64 = 1$$
$$9y = -63$$
$$y = -7$$

Now we substitute -7 for y in Equation (1), (2), or (3). It is easiest to use Equation (3) since it is already solved for y.

$$x = 2(-7) + 16 = 2$$

We check the ordered pair $(2, -7)$.

$$\frac{4x + y = 1}{4 \cdot 2 + (-7) \ ? \ 1}$$
$$\begin{array}{c|c} 8 - 7 & \\ 1 & 1 \quad \text{TRUE} \end{array}$$

$$\frac{x - 2y = 16}{2 - 2(-7) \ ? \ 16}$$
$$\begin{array}{c|c} 2 + 14 & \\ 16 & 16 \quad \text{TRUE} \end{array}$$

Since $(2, -7)$ checks, it is the solution.

6. $(2, -2)$

7. $\quad -3b + a = 7, \quad (1)$
$\qquad 5a + 6b = 14 \quad (2)$

We solve the first equation for a.

$$-3b + a = 7 \qquad (1)$$
$$a = 3b + 7 \quad (3)$$

Substitute $3b + 7$ for a in the second equation and solve for b.

$$5a + 6b = 14 \quad (2)$$
$$5(3b + 7) + 6b = 14 \quad \text{Substituting}$$
$$15b + 35 + 6b = 14$$
$$21b + 35 = 14$$
$$21b = -21$$
$$b = -1$$

Now substitute -1 for b in Equation (3).

$$a = 3(-1) + 7 = 4$$

We check the ordered pair $(4, -1)$.

$$\frac{-3b + a = 7}{-3(-1) + 4 \ ? \ 7}$$
$$\begin{array}{c|c} 3 + 4 & \\ 7 & 7 \quad \text{TRUE} \end{array}$$

$$\frac{5a + 6b = 14}{5 \cdot 4 + 6(-1) \ ? \ 14}$$
$$\begin{array}{c|c} 20 - 6 & \\ 14 & 14 \quad \text{TRUE} \end{array}$$

Since $(4, -1)$ checks, it is the solution.

8. $(-2, 1)$

9. $\quad 5p + 7q = 1, \quad (1)$
$\qquad 4p - 2q = 16 \quad (2)$

We solve the second equation for q.

$$4p - 2q = 16 \qquad (2)$$
$$-2q = -4p + 16$$
$$q = 2p - 8 \qquad (3)$$

Substitute $2p - 8$ for q in the first equation and solve for p.

$$5p + 7q = 1 \quad (1)$$
$$5p + 7(2p - 8) = 1 \quad \text{Substituting}$$
$$5p + 14p - 56 = 1$$
$$19p - 56 = 1$$
$$19p = 57$$
$$p = 3$$

Now we substitute 3 for p in Equation (3).

$$q = 2 \cdot 3 - 8 = -2$$

We check the ordered pair $(3, -2)$.

$$\begin{array}{c|c}
\underline{5p + 7q = 1} & \\
5 \cdot 3 + 7(-2) \ ? \ 1 & \\
15 - 14 & \\
1 & 1 \quad \text{TRUE}
\end{array}$$

$$\begin{array}{c|c}
\underline{4p - 2q = 16} & \\
4 \cdot 3 - 2(-2) \ ? \ 16 & \\
12 + 4 & \\
16 & 16 \quad \text{TRUE}
\end{array}$$

Since $(3, -2)$ checks, it is the solution.

10. $\left(\dfrac{1}{2}, \dfrac{1}{2}\right)$

$$\begin{array}{c|c}
\underline{3x - y = 1} & \\
3 \cdot \dfrac{1}{2} - \dfrac{1}{2} \ ? \ 1 & \\
\dfrac{3}{2} - \dfrac{1}{2} & \\
1 & 1 \ \text{TRUE}
\end{array}
\qquad
\begin{array}{c|c}
\underline{2x + 2y = 2} & \\
2 \cdot \dfrac{1}{2} + 2 \cdot \dfrac{1}{2} \ ? \ 2 & \\
1 + 1 & \\
2 & 2 \ \text{TRUE}
\end{array}$$

Since $\left(\dfrac{1}{2}, \dfrac{1}{2}\right)$ checks, it is the solution.

11. $5x + 3y = 4, \quad (1)$
$\quad\ \ x - 4y = 3 \qquad (2)$

We solve the second equation for x.

$$x - 4y = 3 \qquad (2)$$
$$x = 4y + 3 \qquad (3)$$

Substitute $4y + 3$ for x in the first equation and solve for y.

$$5x + 3y = 4 \qquad (1)$$
$$5(4y + 3) + 3y = 4 \qquad \text{Substituting}$$
$$20y + 15 + 3y = 4$$
$$23y + 15 = 4$$
$$23y = -11$$
$$y = -\dfrac{11}{23}$$

Now we substitute $-\dfrac{11}{23}$ for y in Equation (3).

$$x = 4\left(-\dfrac{11}{23}\right) + 3 = -\dfrac{44}{23} + 3 = \dfrac{25}{23}$$

The ordered pair $\left(\dfrac{25}{23}, -\dfrac{11}{23}\right)$ checks in both equations. It is the solution.

12. $\left(\dfrac{19}{8}, \dfrac{1}{8}\right)$

13. $y - 2x = 1, \quad (1)$
$\quad\ \ 2x - 3 = y \qquad (2)$

We substitute $2x - 3$ for y in the first equation and solve for x.

$$y - 2x = 1 \quad (1)$$
$$2x - 3 - 2x = 1 \quad \text{Substituting}$$
$$-3 = 1 \quad \text{Collecting like terms}$$

We have a false equation. Therefore, there is no solution.

14. No solution

15. $\quad\ x + 3y = \ 7 \quad (1)$
$\quad \underline{-x + 4y = \ 7} \quad (2)$
$\quad\ \ 0 + 7y = 14 \quad \text{Adding}$
$\qquad\qquad 7y = 14$
$\qquad\qquad\ y = \ 2$

Substitute 2 for y in one of the original equations and solve for x.

$$x + 3y = 7 \quad (1)$$
$$x + 3 \cdot 2 = 7 \quad \text{Substituting}$$
$$x + 6 = 7$$
$$x = 1$$

Check:

$$\begin{array}{c|c}
\underline{x + 3y = 7} & \\
1 + 3 \cdot 2 \ ? \ 7 & \\
1 + 6 & \\
7 & 7 \ \text{TRUE}
\end{array}
\qquad
\begin{array}{c|c}
\underline{-x + 4y = 7} & \\
-1 + 4 \cdot 2 \ ? \ 7 & \\
-1 + 8 & \\
7 & 7 \ \text{TRUE}
\end{array}$$

Since $(1, 2)$ checks, it is the solution.

16. $(2, 7)$

17. $\quad 2x + \ y = 6 \quad (1)$
$\quad\ \underline{\ \ x - \ y = 3} \quad (2)$
$\quad 3x + \ 0 = 9 \quad \text{Adding}$
$\qquad\quad\ 3x = 9$
$\qquad\qquad x = 3$

Substitute 3 for x in one of the original equations and solve for y.

$$2x + y = 6 \quad (1)$$
$$2 \cdot 3 + y = 6 \quad \text{Substituting}$$
$$6 + y = 6$$
$$y = 0$$

We obtain $(3, 0)$. This checks, so it is the solution.

18. $(10, 2)$

19.
$$6x - 3y = 18 \quad (1)$$
$$\underline{6x + 3y = -12 \quad (2)}$$
$$12x + 0 = 6 \quad \text{Adding}$$
$$x = \frac{1}{2}$$

Substitute $\frac{1}{2}$ for x in Equation (2) and solve for y.

$$6x + 3y = -12$$
$$6\left(\frac{1}{2}\right) + 3y = -12 \quad \text{Substituting}$$
$$3 + 3y = -12$$
$$3y = -15$$
$$y = -5$$

We obtain $\left(\frac{1}{2}, -5\right)$. This checks, so it is the solution.

20. $(-1, 2)$

21.
$$3x + 2y = 3, \quad (1)$$
$$9x - 8y = -2 \quad (2)$$

We multiply Equation (1) by 4 to make two terms become opposites.

$$12x + 8y = 12 \quad \text{Multiplying (1) by 4}$$
$$\underline{9x - 8y = -2}$$
$$21x + 0 = 10 \quad \text{Adding}$$
$$x = \frac{10}{21}$$

Substitute $\frac{10}{21}$ for x in Equation (1) and solve for y.

$$3x + 2y = 3$$
$$3\left(\frac{10}{21}\right) + 2y = 3 \quad \text{Substituting}$$
$$\frac{10}{7} + 2y = 3$$
$$2y = \frac{11}{7}$$
$$y = \frac{11}{14}$$

We obtain $\left(\frac{10}{21}, \frac{11}{14}\right)$. This checks, so it is the solution.

22. $\left(\frac{128}{31}, -\frac{17}{31}\right)$

23.
$$5x - 7y = -16, \quad (1)$$
$$2x + 8y = 26 \quad\quad (2)$$

We multiply twice to make two terms become opposites.

From (1): $40x - 56y = -128$ Multiplying by 8

From (2): $14x + 56y = 182$ Multiplying by 7

$$\overline{54x + 0 = 54 \quad \text{Adding}}$$
$$x = 1$$

Substitute 1 for x in Equation (2) and solve for y.

$$2x + 8y = 26$$
$$2 \cdot 1 + 8y = 26 \quad \text{Substituting}$$
$$2 + 8y = 26$$
$$8y = 24$$
$$y = 3$$

We obtain $(1, 3)$. This checks, so it is the solution.

24. $(6, 2)$

25.
$$0.7x - 0.3y = 0.5,$$
$$-0.4x + 0.7y = 1.3$$

We first multiply each equation by 10 to clear decimals.

$$7x - 3y = 5, \quad (1)$$
$$-4x + 7y = 13 \quad (2)$$

We multiply so that the y-terms can be eliminated.

From (1): $49x - 21y = 35$ Multiplying by 7

From (2): $\underline{-12x + 21y = 39}$ Multiplying by 3

$$37x + 0 = 74 \quad \text{Adding}$$
$$x = 2$$

Substitute 2 for x in one of the equations in which the decimals were cleared and solve for y.

$$-4x + 7y = 13 \quad (2)$$
$$-4 \cdot 2 + 7y = 13 \quad \text{Substituting}$$
$$-8 + 7y = 13$$
$$7y = 21$$
$$y = 3$$

We obtain $(2, 3)$. This checks, so it is the solution.

26. $\left(\frac{140}{13}, -\frac{50}{13}\right)$

27. $6x + 7y = 9$,   (1)

$8x + 9y = 11$ (2)

We multiply so that the x-terms can be eliminated.

From (1): $24x + 28y = 36$ Multiplying by 4

From (2): $-24x - 27y = -33$ Multiplying by -3

$\phantom{0 + {}} 0 + y = 3$ Adding

$\phantom{0 + {}} y = 3$

Substitute 3 for y in Equation (1) and solve for x.

$6x + 7y = 9$

$6x + 7 \cdot 3 = 9$ Substituting

$6x + 21 = 9$

$6x = -12$

$x = -2$

We obtain $(-2, 3)$. This checks, so it is the solution.

28. $(3, -1)$

29. $\frac{1}{3}x + \frac{1}{5}y = 7$,   (1)

$\frac{1}{6}x - \frac{2}{5}y = -4$ (2)

First we multiply each equation by the LCM of the denominators to clear the fractions.

$5x + 3y = 105$,   (3)   Multiplying (1) by 15

$5x - 12y = -120$ (4)   Multiplying (2) by 30

Then we multiply Equation (4) by -1 so that the x-terms can be eliminated.

$5x + 3y = 105$ (3)

$-5x + 12y = 120$ Multiplying (4) by -1

$ 0 + 15y = 225$ Adding

$\phantom{0 + {}} y = 15$

Substitute 15 for y in one of the equations in which fractions were cleared and solve for y.

$5x + 3y = 105$ (3)

$5x + 3 \cdot 15 = 105$ Substituting

$5x + 45 = 105$

$5x = 60$

$x = 12$

We obtain $(12, 15)$. This checks, so it is the solution.

30. $\left(\frac{110}{19}, -\frac{12}{19}\right)$

31. $6x + 10y = 14$,   (1)

$3x + 5y = 7$ (2)

We multiply Equation (2) by -2.

$6x + 10y = 14$,

$-6x - 10y = -14$

$ 0 = 0$

We have a true equation. If a pair solves Equation (1), then it will also solve Equation (2). The system is dependent and the solution set is infinite. It can be expressed as $\{(x, y) | 3x + 5y = 7\}$.

32. $\{(x, y) | -4x + 2y = 5\}$

33. $a - 2b = 16$,   (1)

$b + 3 = 3a$ (2)

We will use the substitution method. First solve Equation (1) for a.

$a - 2b = 16$

$a = 2b + 16$ (3)

Now substitute $2b + 16$ for a in Equation (2) and solve for b.

$b + 3 = 3a$ (2)

$b + 3 = 3(2b + 16)$ Substituting

$b + 3 = 6b + 48$

$-45 = 5b$

$-9 = b$

Substitute -9 for b in Equation (3).

$a = 2(-9) + 16 = -2$

We obtain $(-2, -9)$. This checks, so it is the solution.

34. $\left(\frac{1}{2}, -\frac{1}{2}\right)$

35. $10x + y = 306$,   (1)

$10y + x = 90$ (2)

We will use the substitution method. First solve Equation (1) for y.

$10x + y = 306$

$y = -10x + 306$ (3)

Now substitute $-10x + 306$ for y in Equation (2) and solve for y.

$10y + x = 90$ (2)

$10(-10x + 306) + x = 90$ Substituting

$-100x + 3060 + x = 90$

$-99x + 3060 = 90$

$-99x = -2970$

$x = 30$

Substitute 30 for x in Equation (3).

$y = -10 \cdot 30 + 306 = 6$

We obtain $(30, 6)$. This checks, so it is the solution.

36. $\left(-\dfrac{4}{3}, -\dfrac{19}{3}\right)$

37. $3y = x - 2,$ (1)

   $x = 2 + 3y$ (2)

We will use the substitution method. Substitute $2 + 3y$ for x in the first equation and solve for y.

   $3y = x - 2$ (1)

   $3y = 2 + 3y - 2$ Substituting

   $3y = 3y$ Collecting like terms

We get a true equation. The system is dependent and the solution set is infinite. It can be expressed as $\{(x, y) \mid x = 2 + 3y\}$.

38. No solution

39. $2x - 7y = 9,$

   $2x - 7y = -5$

Note that the left sides of the equations are the same, but the right sides are different. This tells us that the system of equations is inconsistent and, thus, has no solution.

40. No solution

41. $0.05x + 0.25y = 22,$ (1)

   $0.15x + 0.05y = 24$ (2)

We first multiply each equation by 100 to clear decimals.

   $5x + 25y = 2200$

   $15x + 5y = 2400$

We multiply by -5 on both sides of the second equation and add.

   $5x + 25y = 2200$

   $\underline{-75x - 25y = -12,000}$ Multiplying (2) by -5

   $-70x = -9800$ Adding

   $x = \dfrac{-9800}{-70}$

   $x = 140$

Substitute 140 for x in one of the equations in which the decimals were cleared and solve for y.

   $5x + 25y = 2200$ (1)

   $5 \cdot 140 + 25y = 2200$ Substituting

   $700 + 25y = 2200$

   $25y = 1500$

   $y = 60$

We obtain $(140, 60)$. This checks, so it is the solution.

42. $(10, 5)$

43. $2x + 3y = 5,$

   $-2x - 3y = -5$

Observe that if we were to add the corresponding sides of the equations we would get $0 = 0$. Thus, the system of equations has infinitely many solutions. We can express them as $\{(x, y) \mid 2x + 3y = 5\}$.

44. $\{(x, y) \mid x - y = 3\}$

45. The point of intersection is $(140, 60)$, so window (d) is the correct answer.

46. (a)

47. The point of intersection is $(30, 6)$, so window (b) is the correct answer.

48. (c)

49. a) Enter the data on a grapher, letting 0, 2, 4, and 6 represent the years. Then use the linear regression feature. We get $a(t) = 12.45x + 113.9$.

   b) $2002 - 1992 = 10$, so we used one of the methods described earlier in the text to find $a(10)$. We find that $a(10) = 238.4$, so we predict that there will be about 238 female athletic directors in 2002.

50. 11%

51. $3x - 14 = x + 2(x - 7)$

   $3x - 14 = x + 2x - 14$

   $3x - 14 = 3x - 14$

   $-14 = -14$ Adding $-3x$ on both sides

We get a true equation, so any real number is a solution. The solution set is the set of all real numbers.

52. $\emptyset$

53.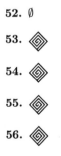

54. ◈

55. ◈

56. ◈

57. First write $f(x) = mx + b$ as $y = mx + b$. Then substitute 1 for x and 2 for y to get one equation and also substitute -3 for x and 4 for y to get a second equation:

   $2 = m \cdot 1 + b$

   $4 = m(-3) + b$

Solve the resulting system of equations.

$$2 = m + b$$
$$4 = -3m + b$$

Multiply the second equation by -1 and add.

$$2 = \ m + b$$
$$\underline{-4 = 3m - b}$$
$$-2 = 4m$$
$$-\frac{1}{2} = \ m$$

Substitute $-\frac{1}{2}$ for m in the first equation and solve for b.

$$2 = -\frac{1}{2} + b$$
$$\frac{5}{2} = b$$

Thus, $m = -\frac{1}{2}$ and $b = \frac{5}{2}$.

58. $p = 2, \ q = -\frac{1}{3}$

59. Substitute -4 for x and -3 for y in both equations and solve for a and b.

$$-4a - 3b = -26, \quad (1)$$
$$-4b + 3a = 7 \qquad\ (2)$$

$$-12a - \ 9b = -78 \quad \text{Multiplying (1) by 3}$$
$$\underline{\ \ 12a - 16b = \ \ 28} \quad \text{Multiplying (2) by 4}$$
$$-25b = -50$$
$$b = \quad 2$$

Substitute 2 for b in Equation (2).

$$-4 \cdot 2 + 3a = 7$$
$$3a = 15$$
$$a = 5$$

Thus, $a = 5$ and $b = 2$.

60. $\left(\dfrac{a + 2b}{7}, \dfrac{a - 5b}{7} \right)$

61. $\dfrac{x + y}{2} - \dfrac{x - y}{5} = 1,$

$\dfrac{x - y}{2} + \dfrac{x + y}{6} = -2$

After clearing fractions we have:

$$3x + 7y = 10, \quad (1)$$
$$4x - 2y = -12 \quad (2)$$

$$6x + 14y = \quad 20 \quad \text{Multiplying (1) by 2}$$
$$\underline{28x - 14y = \ -84} \quad \text{Multiplying (2) by 7}$$
$$34x \qquad\quad = -64$$
$$x = -\frac{32}{17}$$

Substitute $-\dfrac{32}{17}$ for x in Equation (1).

$$3\left(-\frac{32}{17} \right) + 7y = 10$$
$$7y = \frac{266}{17}$$
$$y = \frac{38}{17}$$

The solution is $\left(-\dfrac{32}{17}, \dfrac{38}{17} \right)$.

62. $(23.119, -12.040)$

63. $\dfrac{2}{x} + \dfrac{1}{y} = 0, \qquad\qquad 2 \cdot \dfrac{1}{x} + \dfrac{1}{y} = 0,$

$$\text{or}$$

$\dfrac{5}{x} + \dfrac{2}{y} = -5 \qquad 5 \cdot \dfrac{1}{x} + 2 \cdot \dfrac{1}{y} = -5$

Substitute u for $\dfrac{1}{x}$ and v for $\dfrac{1}{y}$.

$$2u + \ v = 0, \quad (1)$$
$$5u + 2v = -5 \quad (2)$$

$$-4u - 2v = \quad 0 \quad \text{Multiplying (1) by } -2$$
$$\underline{\ \ 5u + 2v = -5} \quad (2)$$
$$u \qquad\quad = -5$$

Substitute -5 for u in Equation (1).

$$2(-5) + v = 0$$
$$-10 + v = 0$$
$$v = 10$$

If $u = -5$, then $\dfrac{1}{x} = -5$. Thus $x = -\dfrac{1}{5}$.

If $v = 10$, then $\dfrac{1}{y} = 10$. Thus $y = \dfrac{1}{10}$.

The solution is $\left(-\dfrac{1}{5}, \dfrac{1}{10} \right)$.

64. $\left(-\dfrac{1}{4}, -\dfrac{1}{2} \right)$

Exercise Set 8.3

1. The Familiarize and Translate steps were done in Exercise 1 of Exercise Set 3.1

Carry out. We solve the system of equations

$$x - y = 11, \quad (1)$$
$$3x + 2y = 123 \quad (2)$$

where $x = $ the larger number and $y = $ the smaller number. We use elimination.

$$
\begin{array}{ll}
2x - 2y = 22 & \text{Multiplying (1) by 2} \\
\underline{3x + 2y = 123} & \\
5x = 145 & \\
x = 29 &
\end{array}
$$

Substitute 29 for x in (1) and solve for y.

$$
\begin{aligned}
29 - y &= 11 \\
-y &= -18 \\
y &= 18
\end{aligned}
$$

Check. The difference between the numbers is $29 - 18$, or 11. Also $2 \cdot 18 + 3 \cdot 29 = 36 + 87 = 123$. The numbers check.

State. The larger number is 29, and the smaller is 18.

2. $5, -47$

3. The Familiarize and Translate steps were done in Exercise 3 of Exercise Set 3.1

Carry out. We solve the system of equations

$$
\begin{array}{ll}
x + y = 45, & (1) \\
850x + 975y = 39,875 & (2)
\end{array}
$$

where $x =$ the number of less expensive brushes sold and $y =$ the number of more expensive brushes sold. We use elimination. Begin by multiplying Equation (1) by -850.

$$
\begin{array}{ll}
-850x - 850y = -38,250 & \text{Multiplying (1)} \\
\underline{850x + 975y = 39,875} & \\
125y = 1625 & \\
y = 13 &
\end{array}
$$

Substitute 13 for y in (1) and solve for x.

$$
\begin{aligned}
x + 13 &= 45 \\
x &= 32
\end{aligned}
$$

Check. The number of brushes sold is $32 + 13$, or 45. The amount taken in was $\$8.50(32) + \$9.75(13) = \$272 + \$126.75 = \$398.75$. The answer checks.

State. 32 of the less expensive brushes were sold, and 13 of the more expensive brushes were sold.

4. 31 solid-color, 9 print

5. The Familiarize and Translate steps were done in Exercise 5 of Exercise Set 3.1

Carry out. We solve the system of equations

$$
\begin{array}{ll}
x + y = 180, & (1) \\
x = 2y - 3 & (2)
\end{array}
$$

where $x =$ the measure of one angle and $y =$ the measure of the other angle. We use substitution.

Substitute $2y - 3$ for x in (1) and solve for y.

$$
\begin{aligned}
2y - 3 + y &= 180 \\
3y - 3 &= 180 \\
3y &= 183 \\
y &= 61
\end{aligned}
$$

Now substitute 61 for y in (2).

$$
x = 2 \cdot 61 - 3 = 122 - 3 = 119
$$

Check. The sum of the angle measures is $119° + 61°$, or $180°$, so the angles are supplementary. Also $2 \cdot 61° - 3° = 122° - 3° = 119°$. The answer checks.

State. The measures of the angles are $119°$ and $61°$.

6. $38°, 52°$

7. The Familiarize and Translate steps were done in Exercise 7 of Exercise Set 3.1

Carry out. We solve the system of equations

$$
\begin{array}{ll}
g + t = 18, & (1) \\
2g + t = 30 & (2)
\end{array}
$$

where $g =$ the number of field goals and $t =$ the number of free throws Amma made. We use elimination.

$$
\begin{array}{ll}
-g - t = -18 & \text{Multiplying (1) by } -1 \\
\underline{2g + t = 30} & \\
g = 12 &
\end{array}
$$

Substitute 12 for g in (1) and solve for t.

$$
\begin{aligned}
12 + t &= 18 \\
t &= 6
\end{aligned}
$$

Check. The total number of scores was $12 + 6$, or 18. The total number of points was $2 \cdot 12 + 6 = 24 + 6 = 30$. The answer checks.

State. Amma made 12 field goals and 6 free throws.

8. 115 children's plates, 135 adult's plates

9. The Familiarize and Translate steps were done in Exercise 9 of Exercise Set 3.1

Carry out. We solve the system of equations

$$
\begin{array}{ll}
h + n = 65, & (1) \\
1575h + 1295n = 95,935 & (2)
\end{array}
$$

where $h =$ the number of vials of Humulin Insulin sold and $n =$ the number of vials of Novolin Insulin sold. We use elimination.

$$
\begin{array}{ll}
-1295h - 1295n = -84,175 & \text{Multiplying (1)} \\
& \text{by } -1295 \\
\underline{1575h + 1295n = 95,935} & \\
280h = 11,760 & \\
h = 42 &
\end{array}
$$

Substitute 42 for h in (1) and solve for n.

$$42 + n = 65$$
$$n = 23$$

Check. A total of $42 + 23$, or 65 vials, was sold. The amount collected was $\$15.75(42) + \$12.95(23) = \$661.50 + \$297.85 = \$959.35$. The answer checks.

State. 42 vials of Humulin Insulin and 23 vials of Novolin Insulin were sold.

10. Length: 94 ft, width: 50 ft

11. The Familiarize and Translate steps were done in Exercise 11 of Exercise Set 3.1

Carry out. We solve the system of equations

$$2l + 2w = 228, \quad (1)$$
$$w = l - 42 \qquad (2)$$

where $l =$ the length, in feet, and $w =$ the width, in feet, of the tennis court. We use substitution.

Substitute $l - 42$ for w in (1) and solve for l.

$$2l + 2(l - 42)w = 228$$
$$2l + 2l - 84 = 228$$
$$4l - 84 = 228$$
$$4l = 312$$
$$l = 78$$

Now substitute 78 for l in (2).

$$w = 78 - 42 = 36$$

Check. The perimeter is $2 \cdot 78$ ft $+ 2 \cdot 36$ ft $= 156$ ft $+ 72$ ft $= 228$ ft. The width, 36 ft, is 42 ft less than the length, 78 ft. The answer checks.

State. The length of the tennis court is 78 ft, and the width is 36 ft.

12. 31 two-point field goals, 9 three-point field goals

13. The Familiarize and Translate steps were done in Exercise 13 of Exercise Set 3.1.

Carry out. We solve the system of equations

$$p = 2l, \qquad\qquad (1)$$
$$25l + 40p = 10,920 \quad (2)$$

where $l =$ the number of units of lumber produced and $p =$ the number of units of plywood produced. We use substitution.

Substitute $2l$ for p in (2) and solve for l.

$$25l + 40 \cdot 2l = 10,920$$
$$25l + 80l = 10,920$$
$$105l = 10,920$$
$$l = 104$$

Substitute 104 for l in (1).

$$p = 2 \cdot 104 = 208$$

Check. The number of units of plywood, 208, is twice the number of units of lumber, 104. The profit is $\$25 \cdot 104 + \$40 \cdot 208 = \$2600 + \$8320 = \$10,920$. The answer checks.

State. 104 units of lumber and 208 units of plywood must be produced.

14. 65 general interest, 12 children's

15. The Familiarize and Translate steps were done in Exercise 15 of Exercise Set 3.1.

Carry out. We solve the system of equations

$$2w + t = 60, \quad (1)$$
$$w = 9 + t \qquad (2)$$

where $w =$ the number of wins and $t =$ the number of ties. We use substitution.

Substitute $9 + t$ for w in (1) and solve for t.

$$2(9 + t) + t = 60$$
$$18 + 2t + t = 60$$
$$18 + 3t = 60$$
$$3t = 42$$
$$t = 14$$

Now substitute 14 for t in (2).

$$w = 9 + 14 = 23$$

Check. The total number of points is $2 \cdot 23 + 14 = 46 + 14 = 60$. The number of wins, 23, is nine more than the number of ties, 14. The answer checks.

State. The Wildcats had 23 wins and 14 ties.

16. 4 30-sec commercials, 8 60-sec commercials

17. The Familiarize and Translate steps were done in Exercise 17 of Exercise Set 3.1.

Carry out. We solve the system of equations

$$y = 2x, \qquad (1)$$
$$x + y = 32 \quad (2)$$

where $x =$ the number of ounces of lemon juice and $y =$ the number of ounces of linseed oil to be used. We use substitution.

Substitute $2x$ for y in (2) and solve for x.

$$x + 2x = 32$$
$$3x = 32$$
$$x = \frac{32}{3}, \text{or} 10\frac{2}{3}$$

Now substitute $\dfrac{32}{3}$ for x in (1).

$$y = 2 \cdot \frac{32}{3} = \frac{64}{3}, \text{ or } 21\frac{1}{3}$$

Check. The amount of oil, $\frac{64}{3}$ oz, is twice the amount of lemon juice, $\frac{32}{3}$ oz. The mixture contains $\frac{32}{3}$ oz $+ \frac{64}{3}$ oz $= \frac{96}{3}$ oz $= 32$ oz. The answer checks.

State. $10\frac{2}{3}$ oz of lemon juice and $21\frac{1}{3}$ oz of linseed oil are needed.

18. 131 coach-class seats, 21 first-class seats

19. Familiarize. Let $x =$ the number of scientific calculators and $y =$ the number of graphing calculators ordered.

Translate. We organize the information in a table.

	Scientific calculators	Graphing calculators	Total order
Number ordered	x	y	45
Price	$9	$58	
Total cost	$9x$	$58y$	1728

We get one equation from the "Numbered ordered" row of the table:

$$x + y = 45$$

The "Total cost" row yields a second equation:

$$9x + 58y = 1728$$

We have translated to a system of equations:

$$x + y = 45, \quad (1)$$
$$9x + 58y = 1728 \quad (2)$$

Carry out. We solve the system of equations using the elimination method.

$$\begin{aligned}
-9x - 9y &= -405 \quad \text{Multiplying (1) by } -9 \\
\underline{9x + 58y} &= \underline{1728} \\
49y &= 1323 \\
y &= 27
\end{aligned}$$

Now substitute 27 for y in (1) and solve for x.

$$x + 27 = 45$$
$$x = 18$$

Check. The total number of calculators ordered was $18 + 27$, or 45. The total cost of the order was $9 \cdot 18 + \$58 \cdot 27 = \$162 + \$1566 = \$1728$. The answer checks.

State. 18 scientific calculators and 27 graphing calculators were ordered.

20. 17 buckets, 11 dinners

21. Familiarize. Let $k =$ the number of pounds of Kenyan French Roast coffee and $s =$ the number of pounds of Sumatran coffee to be used in the mixture. The value of the mixture will be $8.40(20)$, or $168.

Translate. We organize the information in a table.

	Kenyan	Sumatran	Mixture
Number of pounds	k	s	20
Price per pound	$9	$8	$8.40
Value of coffee	$9k$	$8s$	168

The "Number of pounds" row of the table gives us one equation:

$$k + s = 20$$

The "Value of coffee" row yields a second equation:

$$9k + 8s = 168$$

We have translated to a system of equations:

$$k + s = 20, \quad (1)$$
$$9k + 8s = 168 \quad (2)$$

Carry out. We use the elimination method to solve the system of equations.

$$\begin{aligned}
-8k - 8s &= -160 \quad \text{Multiplying (1) by } -8 \\
\underline{9k + 8s} &= \underline{168} \\
k &= 8
\end{aligned}$$

Substitute 8 for k in (1) and solve for s.

$$8 + s = 20$$
$$s = 12$$

Check. The total mixture contains 8 lb + 12 lb, or 20 lb. Its value is $\$9 \cdot 8 + \$8 \cdot 12 = \$72 + \$96 = \$168$. The answer checks.

State. 8 lb of Kenyan French Roast coffee and 12 lb of Sumatran coffee should be used.

22. 20 lb of cashews, 30 lb of Brazil nuts

23. Familiarize. Let $x =$ the number of pounds of Deep Thought Granola and $y =$ the number of pounds of Oat Dream Granola to be used in the mixture. The amount of nuts and dried fruit in the mixture is $19\%(20 \text{ lb})$, or $0.19(20 \text{ lb}) = 3.8$ lb.

Translate. We organize the information in a table.

	Deep Thought	Oat Dream	Mixture
Number of pounds	x	y	20
Percent of nuts and dried fruit	25%	10%	19%
Amount of nuts and dried fruit	$0.25x$	$0.1y$	3.8 lb

We get one equation from the "Number of pounds" row of the table:

$$x + y = 20$$

The last row of the table yields a second equation:

$$0.25x + 0.1y = 3.8$$

After clearing decimals, we have the problem translated to a system of equations:

$$x + y = 20, \quad (1)$$
$$25x + 10y = 380 \quad (2)$$

Carry out. We use the elimination method to solve the system of equations.

$$-10x - 10y = -200 \quad \text{Multiplying (1) by } -10$$
$$\underline{25x + 10y = 380}$$
$$15x = 180$$
$$x = 12$$

Substitute 12 for x in (1) and solve for y.

$$12 + y = 20$$
$$y = 8$$

Check. The amount of the mixture is 12 lb + 8 lb, or 20 lb. The amount of nuts and dried fruit in the mixture is $0.25(12 \text{ lb}) + 0.1(8 \text{ lb}) = 3 \text{ lb} + 0.8 \text{ lb} = 3.8 \text{ lb}$. The answer checks.

State. 12 lb of Deep Thought Granola and 8 lb of Oat Dream Granola should be mixed.

24. 5 lb of each

25. Familiarize. Let x = the number of liters of 25% solution and y = the number of liters of 50% solution to be used. The mixture contains 40%(10 L), or 0.4(10 L) = 4 L of acid.

Translate. We organize the information in a table.

	25% solution	50% solution	Mixture
Number of liters	x	y	10
Percent of acid	25%	50%	40%
Amount of acid	$0.25x$	$0.5y$	4 L

We get one equation from the "Number of liters" row of the table.

$$x + y = 10$$

The last row of the table yields a second equation.

$$0.25x + 0.5y = 4$$

After clearing decimals, we have the problem translated to a system of equations:

$$x + y = 10, \quad (1)$$
$$25x + 50y = 400 \quad (2)$$

Carry out. We use the elimination method to solve the system of equations.

$$-25x - 25y = -250 \quad \text{Multiplying (1) by } -25$$
$$\underline{25x + 50y = 400}$$
$$25y = 150$$
$$y = 6$$

Substitute 6 for y in (1) and solve for x.

$$x + 6 = 10$$
$$x = 4$$

Check. The total amount of the mixture is 4 lb + 6 lb, or 10 lb. The amount of acid in the mixture is $0.25(4 \text{ L}) + 0.5(6 \text{ L}) = 1 \text{ L} + 3 \text{ L} = 4 \text{ L}$. The answer checks.

State. 4 L of the 25% solution and 6 L of the 50% solution should be mixed.

26. 150 lb of soybean meal, 220 lb of corn meal

27. Familiarize. Let x = the amount of the 6% loan and y = the amount of the 9% loan. Recall that the formula for simple interest is

$$\text{Interest} = \text{Principal} \cdot \text{Rate} \cdot \text{Time}.$$

Translate. We organize the information in a table.

	6% loan	9% loan	Total
Principal	x	y	$12,000
Interest Rate	6%	9%	
Time	1 yr	1 yr	
Interest	$0.06x$	$0.09y$	$855

The "Principal" row of the table gives us one equation:

$$x + y = 12,000$$

The last row of the table yields another equation:

$$0.06x + 0.09y = 855$$

After clearing decimals, we have the problem translated to a system of equations:

$$x + y = 12,000 \quad (1)$$
$$6x + 9y = 85,500 \quad (2)$$

Carry out. We use the elimination method to solve the system of equations.

$$-6x - 6y = -72,000 \quad \text{Multiplying (1) by } -6$$
$$\underline{6x + 9y = 85,500}$$
$$3y = 13,500$$
$$y = 4500$$

Substitute 4500 for y in (1) and solve for x.

$$x + 4500 = 12,000$$
$$x = 7500$$

Check. The loans total $7500 + $4500, or $12,000. The total interest is $0.06(\$7500) + 0.09(\$4500) = \$450 + \$405 = \$855$. The answer checks.

State. The 6% loan was for $7500, and the 9% loan was for $4500.

28. $6800 at 9%, $8200 at 10%

29. Familiarize. From the bar graph we see that whole milk is 4% milk fat, milk for cream cheese is 8% milk fat, and cream is 30% milk fat. Let $x =$ the number of pounds of whole milk and $y =$ the number of pounds of cream to be used. The mixture contains 8%(200 lb), or 0.08(200 lb) = 16 lb of milk fat.

Translate. We organize the information in a table.

	Whole milk	Cream	Mixture
Number of pounds	x	y	200
Percent of milk fat	4%	30%	8%
Amount of milk fat	$0.04x$	$0.3y$	16 lb

We get one equation from the " Number of pounds" row of the table:

$$x + y = 200$$

The last row of the table yields a second equation:

$$0.04x + 0.3y = 16$$

After clearing decimals, we have the problem translated to a system of equations:

$$x + y = 200, \quad (1)$$
$$4x + 30y = 1600 \quad (2)$$

Carry out. We use the elimination method to solve the system of equations.

$$-4x - 4y = -800 \quad \text{Multiplying (1) by } -4$$
$$\underline{4x + 30y = 1600}$$
$$26y = 800$$
$$y = \frac{400}{13}, \text{ or } 30\frac{10}{13}$$

Substitute $\frac{400}{13}$ for y in (1) and solve for x.

$$x + \frac{400}{13} = 200$$
$$x = \frac{2200}{13}, \text{ or } 169\frac{3}{13}$$

Check. The total amount of the mixture is $\frac{2200}{13}$ lb $+ \frac{400}{13}$ lb $= \frac{2600}{13}$ lb = 200 lb. The amount of milk fat in the mixture is $0.04\left(\frac{2200}{13} \text{ lb}\right) + 0.3\left(\frac{400}{13} \text{ lb}\right) = \frac{88}{13}$ lb $+ \frac{120}{13}$ lb $= \frac{208}{13}$ lb = 16 lb. The answer checks.

State. $169\frac{3}{13}$ lb of whole milk and $30\frac{10}{13}$ lb of cream should be mixed.

30. 12.5 L of Arctic Antifreeze, 7.5 L of Frost-No-More

31. Familiarize. Let $l =$ the length, in feet, and $w =$ the width, in feet. Recall that the formula for the perimeter P of a rectangle with length l and width w is $P = 2l + 2w$.

Translate.

The perimeter is 860 ft.
$$2l + 2w = 860$$

The length is 100 ft. more than the width.
$$l = 100 + w$$

We have translated to a system of equations:

$$2l + 2w = 860, \quad (1)$$
$$l = 100 + w \quad (2)$$

Carry out. We use the substitution method to solve the system of equations.

Substitute $100 + w$ for l in (1) and solve for w.

$$2(100 + w) + 2w = 860$$
$$200 + 2w + 2w = 860$$
$$200 + 4w = 860$$
$$4w = 660$$
$$w = 165$$

Now substitute 165 for w in (2).

$$l = 100 + 165 = 265$$

Check. The perimeter is $2 \cdot 265$ ft $+ 2 \cdot 165$ ft $= 530$ ft $+ 330$ ft $= 860$ ft. The length, 265 ft, is 100 ft more than the width, 165 ft. The answer checks.

State. The length is 265 ft, and the width is 165 ft.

32. Length: 76 m, width: 19 m

33. Familiarize. Let $x =$ the number of \$5 bills and $y =$ the number of \$1 bills. The total value of the \$5 bills is $5x$, and the total value of the \$1 bills is $1 \cdot y$, or y.

Translate.

The total number of bills is 22.

$$x + y \quad = \quad 22$$

The total value of the bills is \$50.

$$5x + y \quad = \quad 50$$

We have a system of equations:

$$x + y = 22, \quad (1)$$
$$5x + y = 50 \quad (2)$$

Carry out. We use the elimination method.

$$-x - y = -22 \quad \text{Multiplying (1) by } -1$$
$$\underline{5x + y = 50}$$
$$4x = 28$$
$$x = 7$$

$7 + y = 22$ Substituting 7 for x in (1)
$y = 15$

Check. Total number of bills: $7 + 15 = 22$

Total value of bills: $\$5 \cdot 7 + \$1 \cdot 15 = \$35 + \$15 = \$50.$

The numbers check.

State. There are 7 \$5 bills and 15 \$1 bills.

34. 17 quarters, 13 fifty-cent pieces

35. Familiarize. We first make a drawing.

Slow train
d kilometers   75 km/h $(t+2)$ hr

Fast train
d kilometers   125 km/h t hr

From the drawing we see that the distances are the same. Now complete the chart.

	d	$=$	r	$\cdot$	t	
	Distance		Rate		Time	
Slow train	d		75		$t+2$	$\rightarrow d = 75(t+2)$
Fast train	d		125		t	$\rightarrow d = 125t$

Translate. Using $d = rt$ in each row of the table, we get a system of equations:

$$d = 75(t+2),$$
$$d = 125t$$

Carry out. We solve the system of equations.

$$125t = 75(t+2) \quad \text{Using substitution}$$
$$125t = 75t + 150$$
$$50t = 150$$
$$t = 3$$

Then $d = 125t = 125 \cdot 3 = 375$

Check. At 125 km/h, in 3 hr the fast train will travel $125 \cdot 3 = 375$ km. At 75 km/h, in $3 + 2$, or 5 hr the slow train will travel $75 \cdot 5 = 375$ km. The numbers check.

State. The trains will meet 375 km from the station.

36. 3 hr

37. Familiarize. We first make a drawing. Let $d =$ the distance and $r =$ the speed of the canoe in still water. Then when the canoe travels downstream its speed is $r + 6$, and its speed upstream is $r - 6$. From the drawing we see that the distances are the same.

Downstream, 6 mph current

d mi, $r + 6$, 4 hr

Upstream, 6 mph current

d mi, $r - 6$, 10 hr

Organize the information in a table.

	Distance	Rate	Time
With current	d	$r + 6$	4
Against current	d	$r - 6$	10

Translate. Using $d = rt$ in each row of the table, we get a system of equations:

$$d = 4(r+6), \qquad d = 4r + 24,$$
$$\text{or}$$
$$d = 10(r-6) \qquad d = 10r - 60$$

Carry out. Solve the system of equations.

$$4r + 24 = 10r - 60 \quad \text{Using substitution}$$
$$24 = 6r - 60$$
$$84 = 6r$$
$$14 = r$$

Check. When $r = 14$, then $r + 6 = 14 + 6 = 20$, and the distance traveled in 4 hr is $4 \cdot 20 = 80$ km. Also, $r - 6 = 14 - 6 = 8$, and the distance traveled in 10 hr is $8 \cdot 10 = 80$ km. The answer checks.

State. The speed of the canoe in still water is 14 km/h.

38. 24 mph

39. *Familiarize.* We make a drawing. Note that the plane's speed traveling toward London is $360 + 50$, or 410 mph, and the speed traveling toward New York City is $360 - 50$, or 310 mph. Also, when the plane is d mi from New York City, it is $3458 - d$ mi from London.

New York City   London
310 mph t hours t hours   410 mph

$\longleftarrow$————— 3458 mi—————$\longrightarrow$

$\vdash$——— d ———$\vdash$——— 3458 mi $-d$ ———$\dashv$

Organize the information in a table.

	Distance	Rate	Time
Toward NYC	d	310	t
Toward London	$3458 - d$	410	t

Translate. Using $d = rt$ in each row of the table, we get a system of equations:

$$d = 310t, \quad (1)$$
$$3458 - d = 410t \quad (2)$$

Carry out. We solve the system of equations.

$$3458 - 310t = 410t \quad \text{Using substitution}$$
$$3458 = 720t$$
$$4.8028 \approx t$$

Substitute 4.8028 for t in (1).

$$d \approx 310(4.8028) \approx 1489$$

Check. If the plane is 1489 mi from New York City, it can return to New York City, flying at 310 mph, in $1489/310 \approx 4.8$ hr. If the plane is $3458 - 1489$, or 1969 mi from London, it can fly to London, traveling at 410 mph, in $1969/410 \approx 4.8$ hr. Since the times are the same, the answer checks.

State. The point of no return is about 1489 mi from New York City.

40. About 1524 mi

41. a) Enter the years, the percentages of inpatient surgery, and the percentages of outpatient surgery in lists L_1, L_2, and L_3, respectively. Then use the linear regression feature twice to find the desired functions. Note that it will be necessary to specify the lists to be used when finding $u(x)$ since the default when no lists are specified is L_1 and L_2. We get $n(x) = -3.6714x + 84.8571$ and $u(x) = 3.6714x + 15.1429$, where x is the number of years after 1980.

b) Graph the equations in part (a) on a grapher and use the INTERSECT feature.

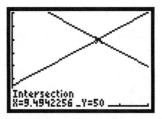

The point of intersection is about $(9.49, 50)$, so we estimate that the number of inpatient surgeries was the same as the number of outpatient surgeries 9 years after 1980, or in 1989.

42. 2112

43. Enter the years, the percentages of women in the work force, and the percentages of men in the work force in lists L_1, L_2, and L_3, respectively. Then use the linear regression feature twice to find the desired functions. Note that it will be necessary to specify the lists to be used when finding the equation giving the percentage of men in the work force since the default when no lists are specified is L_1 and L_2. Let $w(x)$ and $m(x)$ be functions that give the percentage of women and men, respectively, in the work force x years after 1955.

We get $w(x) = 0.6113x + 34.6710$ and $m(x) = -0.2480x + 84.0500$. Now graph the equations and find their point of intersection.

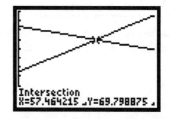

The point of intersection is about $(57, 70)$, so we predict that the percentage of women in the work force will be the same as the percentage of men in the work force about 57 years after 1955, or in 2012.

44. 1995

45. $-3(x-7) - 2[x-(4+3x)]$

$= -3(x-7) - 2[x-4-3x]$ Removing the
                                           inner-most parentheses

$= -3(x-7) - 2(-2x-4)$ Simplifying

$= -3x + 21 + 4x + 8$ Removing parentheses

$= x + 29$ Simplifying

46. $\dfrac{27}{4}$

47. We use the point-slope equation.

$$y - y_1 = m(x - x_1)$$

$$y - (-5) = -\frac{3}{4}(x-2)   \text{ Substituting}$$

$$y + 5 = -\frac{3}{4}x + \frac{3}{2}$$

$$y = -\frac{3}{4}x - \frac{7}{2}$$

48.

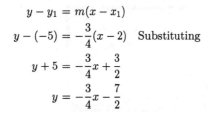

49. Graph $y_1 = 0.45x + 6.82$ and $y_2 = 1.5 - 4.38x$ and find the point of intersection.

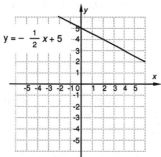

The solution of the given equation is the first coordinate of the point of intersection, or about -1.1014.

50. 10

51.

52. ◈

53. ◈

54. ◈

55. The Familiarize and Translate steps were done in Exercise 74 of Exercise Set 3.1.

Carry out. We solve the system of equations

$$x = 2y, \qquad (1)$$

$$x + 20 = 3y \quad (2)$$

where $x =$ Burl's age now and $y =$ his son's age now.

$$2y + 20 = 3y \quad \text{Substituting } 2y \text{ for } x \text{ in } (2)$$

$$20 = y$$

$$x = 2 \cdot 20 \quad \text{Substituting } 20 \text{ for } y \text{ in } (1)$$

$$x = 40$$

Check. Burl's age now, 40, is twice his son's age now, 20. Ten years ago Burl was 30 and his son was 10, and $30 = 3 \cdot 10$. The numbers check.

State. Now Burl is 40 and his son is 20.

56. Lou: 32 years, Juanita: 14 years

57. The Familiarize and Translate steps were done in Exercise 76 of Exercise Set 3.1.

Carry out. We solve the system of equations

$$2l + 2w = 156, \quad (1)$$

$$l = 4(w-6) \qquad (2)$$

where $l =$ length, in inches, and $w =$ width, in inches.

$$2 \cdot 4(w-6) + 2w = 156 \quad \text{Substituting } 4(w-6)$$
$$\text{for } l \text{ in } (1)$$

$$8w - 48 + 2w = 156$$

$$10w - 48 = 156$$

$$10w = 204$$

$$w = \frac{204}{10}, \text{ or } \frac{102}{5}$$

$$l = 4\left(\frac{102}{5} - 6\right) \quad \text{Substituting } \frac{102}{5} \text{ for } w$$
$$\text{in } (2)$$

$$l = 4\left(\frac{102}{5} - \frac{30}{5}\right)$$

$$l = 4\left(\frac{72}{5}\right)$$

$$l = \frac{288}{5}$$

Check. The perimeter of a rectangle with width $\dfrac{102}{5}$ in. and length $\dfrac{288}{5}$ in. is

$$2\left(\frac{288}{5}\right) + 2\left(\frac{102}{5}\right) = \frac{576}{5} + \frac{204}{5} = \frac{780}{5} = 156 \text{ in.}$$

If 6 in. is cut off the width, the new width is

$$\frac{102}{5} - 6 = \frac{102}{5} - \frac{30}{5} = \frac{72}{5}. \text{ The length, } \frac{288}{5}, \text{ is}$$

$4\left(\dfrac{72}{5}\right)$. The numbers check.

State. The original piece of posterboard had width $\dfrac{102}{5}$ in. and length $\dfrac{288}{5}$ in.

58. $\dfrac{64}{5}$ oz of baking soda, $\dfrac{16}{5}$ oz of vinegar

59. Familiarize. Let x = the amount of the original solution that remains after some of the original solution is drained and replaced with pure antifreeze. Let y = the amount of the original solution that is drained and replaced with pure antifreeze.

Translate. We organize the information in a table. Keep in mind that the table contains information regarding the solution *after* some of the original solution is drained and replaced with pure antifreeze.

	Original Solution	Pure Anti-freeze	New Mixture
Amount of solution	x	y	16 L
Percent of antifreeze	30%	100%	50%
Amount of antifreeze in solution	$0.3x$	$1 \cdot y$, or y	$0.5(16)$, or 8

The "Amount of solution" row gives us one equation:
$x + y = 16$

The last row gives us a second equation:
$0.3x + y = 8$

After clearing the decimal we have the following system of equations:

$$x + y = 16, \qquad (1)$$
$$3x + 10y = 80 \quad (2)$$

Carry out. We use the elimination method.

$$\begin{array}{rl} -3x - 3y = -48 & \text{Multiplying (1) by } -3 \\ \underline{3x + 10y = 80} & \\ 7y = 32 & \\ y = \dfrac{32}{7}, \text{ or } 4\dfrac{4}{7} & \end{array}$$

Although the problem only asks for the amount of pure antifreeze added, we will also find x in order to check.

$$x + 4\dfrac{4}{7} = 16 \qquad \text{Substituting } 4\dfrac{4}{7} \text{ for } y \text{ in (1)}$$
$$x = 11\dfrac{3}{7}$$

Check. Total amount of new mixture: $11\dfrac{3}{7} + 4\dfrac{4}{7} =$ 16 L

Amount of antifreeze in new mixture:
$$0.3\left(11\dfrac{3}{7}\right) + 4\dfrac{4}{7} = \dfrac{3}{10}\cdot\dfrac{80}{7} + \dfrac{32}{7} = \dfrac{56}{7} = 8 \text{ L}$$
The numbers check.

State. Michelle should drain $4\dfrac{4}{7}$ L of the original solution and replace it with pure antifreeze.

60. 4 km

61. Familiarize. Let x = the number of members who ordered one book and y = the number of members who ordered two books. Note that the y members ordered a total of $2y$ books.

Translate.

$$\underbrace{\text{The number of books sold}}_{x + 2y} \underbrace{\text{ was }}_{=} \underbrace{880}_{880}.$$

$$\underbrace{\text{Total sales}}_{12x + 20y} \underbrace{\text{ were }}_{=} \underbrace{\$9840}_{9840}.$$

We have a system of equations.

$$x + 2y = 880, \quad (1)$$
$$12x + 20y = 9840 \quad (2)$$

Carry out. We use the elimination method.

$$\begin{array}{rl} -10x - 20y = -8800 & \text{Multiplying (1) by } -10 \\ \underline{12x + 20y = 9840} & \\ 2x = 1040 & \\ x = 520 & \end{array}$$

Substitute 520 for x in (1) and solve for y.

$$520 + 2y = 880$$
$$2y = 360$$
$$y = 180$$

Check. Total number of books sold: $520 + 2 \cdot 180 = 520 + 360 = 880$

Total sales: $\$12 \cdot 520 + \$20 \cdot 180 = \$6240 + \$3600 = \$9840$

The answer checks.

State. 180 members ordered two books.

62. 82

63. Familiarize. We first make a drawing. Let r_1 = the speed of the first train and r_2 = the speed of the second train. If the first train leaves at 9 A.M. and the second at 10 A.M., we have:

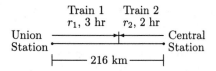

If the second train leaves at 9 A.M. and the first at 10:30 A.M. we have:

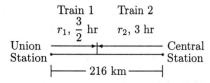

The total distance traveled in each case is 216 km and is equal to the sum of the distances traveled by each train.

Translate. We will use the formula $d = rt$. For each situation we have:

Total distance	is	Train 1's distance	plus	Train 2's distance.
$\downarrow$	$\downarrow$	$\downarrow$	$\downarrow$	$\downarrow$
216	$=$	$3r_1$	$+$	$2r_2$

and $216 = \dfrac{3}{2}r_1 + 3r_2$

Clearing the fraction, we have this system:

$$216 = 3r_1 + 2r_2, \quad (1)$$
$$432 = 3r_1 + 6r_2 \quad (2)$$

Carry out. Solve the system of equations.

$-216 = -3r_1 - 2r_2$ Multiplying (1) by -1

$\underline{432 = 3r_1 + 6r_2}$

$216 = 4r_2$

$54 = r_2$

$216 = 3r_1 + 2(54)$ Substituting 54 for r_2 in (1)

$216 = 3r_1 + 108$

$108 = 3r_1$

$36 = r_1$

Check. If Train 1 travels for 3 hr at 36 km/h and Train 2 travels for 2 hr at 54 km/h, the total distance traveled is $3 \cdot 36 + 2 \cdot 54 = 108 + 108 = 216$ km. If Train 1 travels for $\dfrac{3}{2}$ hr at 36 km/h and Train 2 travels for 3 hr at 54 km/h, then the total distance traveled is $\dfrac{3}{2} \cdot 36 + 3 \cdot 54 = 54 + 162 = 216$ km. The numbers check.

State. The speed of the first train is 36 km/h, and the speed of the second train is 54 km/h.

64. City: 261 mi, highway: 204 mi

65. Familiarize. Let $x =$ the number of gallons of pure brown and $y =$ the number of gallons of neutral stain that should be added to the original 0.5 gal. Note that a total of 1 gal of stain needs to be added to bring the amount of stain up to 1.5 gal. The original 0.5 gal of stain contains 20%(0.5 gal), or $0.2(0.5 \text{ gal}) = 0.1$ gal of brown stain. The final solution contains 60%(1.5 gal), or $0.6(1.5 \text{ gal}) = 0.9$ gal of brown stain. This is composed of the original 0.1 gal and the x gal that are added.

Translate.

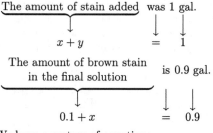

We have a system of equations.

$$x + y = 1, \quad (1)$$
$$0.1 + x = 0.9 \quad (2)$$

Carry out. First we solve (2) for x.

$$0.1 + x = 0.9$$
$$x = 0.8$$

Then substitute 0.8 for x in (1) and solve for y.

$$0.8 + y = 1$$
$$y = 0.2$$

Check. Total amount of stain: $0.5 + 0.8 + 0.2 = 1.5$ gal

Total amount of brown stain: $0.1 + 0.8 = 0.9$ gal

Total amount of neutral stain: $0.8(0.5) + 0.2 = 0.4 + 0.2 = 0.6$ gal $= 0.4(1.5 \text{ gal})$

The answer checks.

State. 0.8 gal of pure brown and 0.2 gal of neutral stain should be added.

66. 4 boys, 3 girls

67. The 1.5 gal mixture contains $0.1 + x$ gal of pure brown stain. (See Exercise 65.). Thus, the function $P(x) = \dfrac{0.1 + x}{1.5}$ gives the percentage of brown in the mixture as a decimal quantity. Using the Table feature, we confirm that when $x = 0.8$, then $P(x) = 0.6$ or 60%.

Exercise Set 8.4

1. Substitute $(2, -1, -2)$ into the three equations, using alphabetical order.

$$\frac{x + y - 2z = 5}{2 + (-1) - 2(-2) \ ? \ 5}$$
$$2 - 1 + 4$$
$$5 \ \Big| \ 5 \quad \text{TRUE}$$

$$\frac{2x - y - z = 7}{2 \cdot 2 - (-1) - (-2) \ ? \ 7}$$
$$4 + 1 + 2$$
$$7 \ \Big| \ 7 \quad \text{TRUE}$$

$$\frac{-x - 2y + 3z = 6}{-2 - 2(-1) + 3(-2) \ ? \ 6}$$
$$-2 + 2 - 6$$
$$-6 \ \Big| \ 6 \quad \text{FALSE}$$

The triple $(2, -1, -2)$ does not make the third equation true, so it is not a solution of the system.

2. Yes

3.　$2x - \ y + \ z = 10, \quad (1)$
$4x + 2y - 3z = 10, \quad (2)$
$x - 3y + 2z = \ 8 \quad (3)$

1., 2.　The equations are already in standard form with no fractions or decimals.

3.　Use Equations (1) and (2) to eliminate y:

$$\frac{4x - 2y + 2z = 20 \quad \text{Multiplying (1) by 2}}{4x + 2y - 3z = 10 \quad (2)}$$
$$8x - \ z = 30 \quad (4)$$

4.　Use a different pair of equations and eliminate y:

$$\frac{-6x + 3y - 3z = -30 \quad \text{Multiplying (1) by } -3}{x - 3y + 2z = \ \ \ 8 \quad (3)}$$
$$-5x - \ z = -22 \quad (5)$$

5.　Now solve the system of Equations (4) and (5).

$$8x - z = 30 \quad (4)$$
$$-5x - z = -22 \quad (5)$$

$$8x - z = 30 \quad (4)$$
$$\frac{5x + z = 22 \quad \text{Multiplying (5) by } -1}{13x = 52}$$
$$x = \ 4$$

$$8 \cdot 4 - z = 30 \quad \text{Substituting in (4)}$$
$$32 - z = 30$$
$$-z = -2$$
$$z = 2$$

6.　Substitute in one of the original equations to find y.

$$2 \cdot 4 - y + 2 = 10 \quad \text{Substituting in (1)}$$
$$10 - y = 10$$
$$-y = 0$$
$$y = 0$$

We obtain $(4, 0, 2)$. This checks, so it is the solution.

4.　$(1, 2, 3)$

5.　$x - \ y + \ z = 6, \quad (1)$
$2x + 3y + 2z = 2, \quad (2)$
$3x + 5y + 4z = \ 4 \quad (3)$

1., 2.　The equations are already in standard form with no fractions or decimals.

3., 4.　We eliminate y from two different pairs of equations.

$$\frac{3x - 3y + 3z = 18 \quad \text{Multiplying (1) by 3}}{2x + 3y + 2z = \ \ 2 \quad (2)}$$
$$5x + 5z = 20 \quad (4)$$

$$\frac{5x - 5y + 5z = 30 \quad \text{Multiplying (1) by 5}}{3x + 5y + 4z = \ \ 4 \quad (3)}$$
$$8x + 9z = 34 \quad (5)$$

5.　Now solve the system of Equations (4) and (5).

$$5x + 5z = 20 \quad (4)$$
$$8x + 9z = 34 \quad (5)$$

$$\frac{45x + 45z = \ \ \ 180 \quad \text{Multiplying (4) by 9}}{-40x - 45z = -170 \quad \text{Multiplying (5) by } -5}$$
$$5x = \ \ \ 10$$
$$x = \ \ \ 2$$

$$5 \cdot 2 + 5z = 20 \quad \text{Substituting in (4)}$$
$$10 + 5z = 20$$
$$5z = 10$$
$$z = 2$$

6.　Substitute in one of the original equations to find y.

$$2 - y + 2 = 6 \quad \text{Substituting in (1)}$$
$$4 - y = 6$$
$$-y = 2$$
$$y = -2$$

We obtain $(2, -2, 2)$. This checks, so it is the solution.

6. $(-1, 5, -2)$

7. $6x - 4y + 5z = 31,$ (1)
$$5x + 2y + 2z = 13,$$ (2)
$$x + y + z = 2$$ (3)

1., 2. The equations are already in standard form with no fractions or decimals.

3., 4. We eliminate y from two different pairs of equations.

$$6x - 4y + 5z = 31 \quad (1)$$
$$\underline{4x + 4y + 4z = 8} \quad \text{Multiplying (3) by 4}$$
$$10x \qquad + 9z = 39 \quad (4)$$

$$5x + 2y + 2z = 13 \quad (2)$$
$$\underline{-2x - 2y - 2z = -4} \quad \text{Multiplying (3) by } -2$$
$$3x \qquad\qquad = 9$$
$$x = 3$$

5. When we used Equations (2) and (3) to eliminate y, we also eliminated z and found that $x = 3$. Substitute 3 for x in Equation (4) to find z.

$$10 \cdot 3 + 9z = 39 \quad \text{Substituting in (4)}$$
$$30 + 9z = 39$$
$$9z = 9$$
$$z = 1$$

6. Substitute in one of the original equations to find y.

$$3 + y + 1 = 2 \quad \text{Substituting in (3)}$$
$$y + 4 = 2$$
$$y = -2$$

We obtain $(3, -2, 1)$. This checks, so it is the solution.

8. $(3, 1, 2)$

9. $x + y + z = 0,$ (1)
$$2x + 3y + 2z = -3,$$ (2)
$$-x + 2y - 3z = -1$$ (3)

1., 2. The equations are already in standard form with no fractions or decimals.

3., 4.

We eliminate x from two different pairs of equations.

$$-2x - 2y - 2z = 0 \quad \text{Multiplying (1) by } -2$$
$$\underline{2x + 3y + 2z = -3} \quad (2)$$
$$y \qquad = -3$$

We eliminated not only x but also z and found that $y = -3$.

5., 6. Substitute -3 for y in two of the original equations to produce a system of two equations in two variables. Then solve this system.

$$x - 3 + z = 0 \quad \text{Substituting in (1)}$$
$$-x + 2(-3) - 3z = -1 \quad \text{Substituting in (3)}$$

Simplifying we have

$$x + z = 3$$
$$\underline{-x - 3z = 5}$$
$$-2z = 8$$
$$z = -4$$

$$x - 3 - 4 = 0 \quad \text{Substituting in (1)}$$
$$x - 7 = 0$$
$$x = 7$$

We obtain $(7, -3, -4)$. This checks, so it is the solution.

10. $(-3, -4, 2)$

11. $2x + y - 3z = -4,$ (1)
$$4x - 2y + z = 9,$$ (2)
$$3x + 5y - 2z = 5$$ (3)

1., 2. The equations are already in standard form with no fractions or decimals.

3., 4. We eliminate z from two different pairs of equations.

$$2x + y - 3z = -4 \quad (1)$$
$$\underline{12x - 6y + 3z = 27} \quad \text{Multiplying (2) by 3}$$
$$14x - 5y \qquad = 23 \quad (4)$$

$$8x - 4y + 2z = 18 \quad \text{Multiplying (2) by 2}$$
$$\underline{3x + 5y - 2z = 5} \quad (3)$$
$$11x + y \qquad = 23 \quad (5)$$

5. Now solve the system of Equations (4) and (5).

$$14x - 5y = 23 \quad (4)$$
$$11x + y = 23 \quad (5)$$

$$14x - 5y = 23 \quad (4)$$
$$\underline{55x + 5y = 115} \quad \text{Multiplying (5) by 5}$$
$$69x \qquad = 138$$
$$x = 2$$

$11 \cdot 2 + y = 23$ Substituting in (5)

$22 + y = 23$

$y = 1$

6. Substitute in one of the original equations to find z.

$4 \cdot 2 - 2 \cdot 1 + z = 9$ Substituting in (2)

$6 + z = 9$

$z = 3$

We obtain $(2, 1, 3)$. This checks, so it is the solution.

12. $(2, 4, 1)$

13. $2x + y + 2z = 11,$ (1)

$3x + 2y + 2z = 8,$ (2)

$x + 4y + 3z = 0$ (3)

1., 2. The equations are already in standard form with no fractions or decimals.

3., 4. We eliminate x from two different pairs of equations.

$2x + y + 2z = 11$ (1)

$\underline{-2x - 8y - 6z = 0}$ Multiplying (3) by -2

$-7y - 4z = 11$ (4)

$3x + 2y + 2z = 8$ (2)

$\underline{-3x - 12y - 9z = 0}$ Multiplying (3) by -3

$-10y - 7z = 8$ (5)

5. Now solve the system of Equations (4) and (5).

$-7y - 4z = 11$ (4)

$-10y - 7z = 8$ (5)

$-49y - 28z = 77$ Multiplying (4) by 7

$\underline{40y + 28z = -32}$ Multiplying (5) by -4

$-9y = 45$

$y = -5$

$-7(-5) - 4z = 11$ Substituting in (4)

$35 - 4z = 11$

$-4z = -24$

$z = 6$

6. Substitute in one of the original equations to find x.

$x + 4(-5) + 3 \cdot 6 = 0$ Substituting in (3)

$x - 2 = 0$

$x = 2$

We obtain $(2, -5, 6)$. This checks, so it is the solution.

14. $(-3, 0, 4)$

15. $-2x + 8y + 2z = 4,$ (1)

$x + 6y + 3z = 4,$ (2)

$3x - 2y + z = 0$ (3)

1., 2. The equations are already in standard form with no fractions or decimals.

3., 4. We eliminate z from two different pairs of equations.

$-2x + 8y + 2z = 4$ (1)

$\underline{-6x + 4y - 2z = 0}$ Multiplying (3) by -2

$-8x + 12y = 4$ (4)

$x + 6y + 3z = 4$ (2)

$\underline{-9x + 6y - 3z = 0}$ Multiplying (3) by -3

$-8x + 12y = 4$ (5)

5. Now solve the system of Equations (4) and (5).

$-8x + 12y = 4$ (4)

$-8x + 12y = 4$ (5)

$-8x + 12y = 4$ (4)

$\underline{8x - 12y = -4}$ Multiplying (5) by -1

$0 = 0$ (6)

Equation (6) indicates that Equations (1), (2), and (3) are dependent. (Note that if Equation (1) is subtracted from Equation (2), the result is Equation (3).) We could also have concluded that the equations are dependent by observing that Equations (4) and (5) are identical.

16. The equations are dependent.

17. $a + 2b + c = 1,$ (1)

$7a + 3b - c = -2,$ (2)

$a + 5b + 3c = 2$ (3)

1., 2. The equations are already in standard form with no fractions or decimals.

3., 4. We eliminate c from two different pairs of equations.

$a + 2b + c = 1$ (1)

$\underline{7a + 3b - c = -2}$ (2)

$8a + 5b = -1$ (4)

$21a + 9b - 3c = -6$ Multiplying (2) by 3

$\underline{a + 5b + 3c = 2}$

$22a + 14b = -4$ (5)

5. Now solve the system of Equations (4) and (5).

$8a + 5b = -1$ (4)

$22a + 14b = -4$ (5)

$$112a + 70b = -14 \quad \text{Multiplying (4) by 14}$$
$$\underline{-110a - 70b = 20} \quad \text{Multiplying (5) by } -5$$
$$2a = 6$$
$$a = 3$$

$$8 \cdot 3 + 5b = -1 \quad \text{Substituting in (4)}$$
$$24 + 5b = -1$$
$$5b = -25$$
$$b = -5$$

6. Substitute in one of the original equations to find c.

$$3 + 2(-5) + c = 1 \quad \text{Substituting in (1)}$$
$$-7 + c = 1$$
$$c = 8$$

We obtain $(3, -5, 8)$. This checks, so it is the solution.

18. $\left(\dfrac{1}{2}, 4, -6\right)$

19.
$$5x + 3y + \frac{1}{2}z = \frac{7}{2},$$
$$0.5x - 0.9y - 0.2z = 0.3,$$
$$3x - 2.4y + 0.4z = -1$$

1. All equations are already in standard form.

2. Multiply the first equation by 2 to clear the fractions. Also, multiply the second and third equations by 10 to clear the decimals.

$$10x + 6y + z = 7, \quad (1)$$
$$5x - 9y - 2z = 3, \quad (2)$$
$$30x - 24y + 4z = -10 \quad (3)$$

3., 4. We eliminate z from two different pairs of equations.

$$20x + 12y + 2z = 14 \quad \text{Multiplying (1) by 2}$$
$$\underline{5x - 9y - 2z = 3} \quad (2)$$
$$25x + 3y = 17 \quad (4)$$

$$10x - 18y - 4z = 6 \quad \text{Multiplying (2) by 2}$$
$$\underline{30x - 24y + 4z = -10} \quad (3)$$
$$40x - 42y = -4 \quad (5)$$

5. Now solve the system of Equations (4) and (5).

$$25x + 3y = 17 \quad (4)$$
$$40x - 42y = -4 \quad (5)$$

$$350x + 42y = 238 \quad \text{Multiplying (4) by 14}$$
$$\underline{40x - 42y = -4} \quad (5)$$
$$390x = 234$$
$$x = \frac{3}{5}$$

$$25\left(\frac{3}{5}\right) + 3y = 17 \quad \text{Substituting in (4)}$$
$$15 + 3y = 17$$
$$3y = 2$$
$$y = \frac{2}{3}$$

6. Substitute in one of the original equations to find z.

$$10\left(\frac{3}{5}\right) + 6\left(\frac{2}{3}\right) + z = 7 \quad \text{Substituting in (1)}$$
$$6 + 4 + z = 7$$
$$10 + z = 7$$
$$z = -3$$

We obtain $\left(\dfrac{3}{5}, \dfrac{2}{3}, -3\right)$. This checks, so it is the solution.

20. $\left(\dfrac{1}{2}, \dfrac{1}{3}, \dfrac{1}{6}\right)$

21.
$$3p + 2r = 11, \quad (1)$$
$$q - 7r = 4, \quad (2)$$
$$p - 6q = 1 \quad (3)$$

1., 2. The equations are already in standard form with no fractions or decimals.

3., 4. Note that there is no q in Equation (1). We will use Equations (2) and (3) to obtain another equation with no q-term.

$$6q - 42r = 24 \quad \text{Multiplying (2) by 6}$$
$$\underline{p - 6q = 1} \quad (3)$$
$$p - 42r = 25 \quad (4)$$

5. Solve the system of Equations (1) and (4).

$$3p + 2r = 11 \quad (1)$$
$$p - 42r = 25 \quad (4)$$

$$3p + 2r = 11 \quad (1)$$
$$\underline{-3p + 126r = -75} \quad \text{Multiplying (4) by } -3$$
$$128r = -64$$
$$r = -\frac{1}{2}$$

$$3p + 2\left(-\frac{1}{2}\right) = 11 \quad \text{Substituting in (1)}$$
$$3p - 1 = 11$$
$$3p = 12$$
$$p = 4$$

6. Substitute in Equation (2) or (3) to find q.

$$q - 7\left(-\frac{1}{2}\right) = 4 \quad \text{Substituting in (2)}$$

$$q + \frac{7}{2} = 4$$

$$q = \frac{1}{2}$$

We obtain $\left(4, \frac{1}{2}, -\frac{1}{2}\right)$. This checks, so it is the solution.

22. $\left(\frac{1}{2}, \frac{2}{3}, -\frac{5}{6}\right)$

23.
$$\begin{aligned} x + y + z &= 105, \quad (1) \\ 10y - z &= 11, \quad (2) \\ 2x - 3y &= 7 \quad (3) \end{aligned}$$

1., 2. The equations are already in standard form with no fractions or decimals.

3., 4. Note that there is no z in Equation (3). We will use Equations (1) and (2) to obtain another equation with no z-term.

$$\begin{aligned} x + y + z &= 105 \quad (1) \\ \underline{10y - z} &= \underline{11} \quad (2) \\ x + 11y &= 116 \quad (4) \end{aligned}$$

5. Now solve the system of Equations (3) and (4).

$$\begin{aligned} 2x - 3y &= 7 \quad (3) \\ x + 11y &= 116 \quad (4) \end{aligned}$$

$$\begin{aligned} 2x - 3y &= 7 \quad (3) \\ \underline{-2x - 22y} &= \underline{-232} \quad \text{Multiplying (4) by } -2 \\ - 25y &= -225 \\ y &= 9 \end{aligned}$$

$$x + 11 \cdot 9 = 116 \quad \text{Substituting in (4)}$$
$$x + 99 = 116$$
$$x = 17$$

6. Substitute in Equation (1) or (2) to find z.
$$17 + 9 + z = 105 \quad \text{Substituting in (1)}$$
$$26 + z = 105$$
$$z = 79$$

We obtain $(17, 9, 79)$. This checks, so it is the solution.

24. $(15, 33, 9)$

25.
$$\begin{aligned} 2a - 3b &= 2, \quad (1) \\ 7a + 4c &= \frac{3}{4}, \quad (2) \\ -3b + 2c &= 1 \quad (3) \end{aligned}$$

1. The equations are already in standard form.

2. Multiply Equation (2) by 4 to clear the fraction. The resulting system is

$$\begin{aligned} 2a - 3b &= 2, \quad (1) \\ 28a + 16c &= 3, \quad (4) \\ -3b + 2c &= 1 \quad (3) \end{aligned}$$

3. Note that there is no b in Equation (2). We will use Equations (1) and (3) to obtain another equation with no b-term.

$$\begin{aligned} 2a - 3b &= 2 \quad (1) \\ \underline{3b - 2c} &= \underline{-1} \quad \text{Multiplying (3) by } -1 \\ 2a - 2c &= 1 \quad (5) \end{aligned}$$

5. Now solve the system of Equations (4) and (5).

$$\begin{aligned} 28a + 16c &= 3 \quad (4) \\ 2a - 2c &= 1 \quad (5) \end{aligned}$$

$$\begin{aligned} 28a + 16c &= 3 \quad (4) \\ \underline{16a - 16c} &= \underline{8} \quad \text{Multiplying (5) by 8} \\ 44a &= 11 \\ a &= \frac{1}{4} \end{aligned}$$

$$2 \cdot \frac{1}{4} - 2c = 1 \quad \text{Substituting } \frac{1}{4} \text{ for } a \text{ in (5)}$$
$$\frac{1}{2} - 2c = 1$$
$$-2c = \frac{1}{2}$$
$$c = -\frac{1}{4}$$

6. Substitute in Equation (1) or (2) to find b.

$$2\left(\frac{1}{4}\right) - 3b = 2 \quad \text{Substituting } \frac{1}{4} \text{ for } a \text{ in (1)}$$
$$\frac{1}{2} - 3b = 2$$
$$-3b = \frac{3}{2}$$
$$b = -\frac{1}{2}$$

We obtain $\left(\frac{1}{4}, -\frac{1}{2}, -\frac{1}{4}\right)$. This checks, so it is the solution.

26. $(3, 4, -1)$

27.
$$\begin{aligned} x + y + z &= 180, \quad (1) \\ y &= 2 + 3x, \quad (2) \\ z &= 80 + x \quad (3) \end{aligned}$$

1. Only Equation (1) is in standard form.
Rewrite the system with all equations in standard form.

$$x + y + z = 180, \quad (1)$$
$$-3x + y \quad\;\; = \quad 2, \quad (4)$$
$$-x \quad\;\; + z = \quad 80 \quad (5)$$

2. There are no fractions or decimals.

3., 4. Note that there is no z in Equation (4). We will use Equations (1) and (5) to obtain another equation with no z-term.

$$x + y + z = \;\; 180 \quad (1)$$
$$\underline{x \quad\quad - z = -80} \quad \text{Multiplying (5) by } -1$$
$$2x + y \quad\quad = \;\; 100 \quad (6)$$

5. Now solve the system of Equations (4) and (6).

$$-3x + y = \quad 2 \quad (4)$$
$$2x + y = 100 \quad (5)$$

$$-3x + y = \quad\;\; 2 \quad (4)$$
$$\underline{-2x - y = -100} \quad \text{Multiplying (6) by } -1$$
$$-5x \quad\quad = -98$$
$$x = \frac{98}{5}$$

$$-3 \cdot \frac{98}{5} + y = 2 \qquad \text{Substituting } \frac{98}{5} \text{ for}$$
$$x \text{ in } (4)$$
$$-\frac{294}{5} + y = 2$$
$$y = \frac{304}{5}$$

6. Substitute in Equation (1) or (5) to find z.

$$-\frac{98}{5} + z = 80 \quad \text{Substituting } \frac{98}{5} \text{ for } x \text{ in (5)}$$
$$z = \frac{498}{5}$$

We obtain $\left(\frac{98}{5}, \frac{304}{5}, \frac{498}{5}\right)$. This checks, so it is the solution.

28. $(2, 5, -3)$

29.
$$x + y \quad\quad = 0, \quad (1)$$
$$x \quad\quad + z = 1, \quad (2)$$
$$2x + y + z = 2 \quad (3)$$

1., 2. The equations are already in standard form with no fractions or decimals.

3., 4. Note that there is no z in Equation (1). We will use Equations (2) and (3) to obtain another equation with no z-term.

$$-x \quad\quad - z = -1 \quad \text{Multiplying (2) by } -1$$
$$\underline{2x + y + z = \;\; 2} \quad (3)$$
$$x + y \quad\quad = \;\; 1 \quad (4)$$

5. Now solve the system of Equations (1) and (4).

$$x + y = 0 \quad (1)$$
$$x + y = 1 \quad (4)$$

$$x + y = \;\; 0 \quad (1)$$
$$\underline{-x - y = -1} \quad \text{Multiplying (4) by } -1$$
$$0 = -1 \quad \text{Adding}$$

We get a false equation. There is no solution.

30. No solution

31.
$$y + \;\; z = 1, \quad (1)$$
$$x + \;\; y + \;\; z = 1, \quad (2)$$
$$x + 2y + 2z = 2 \quad (3)$$

1., 2. The equations are already in standard form with no fractions or decimals.

3., 4. Note that there is no x in Equation (1). We will use Equations (2) and (3) to obtain another equation with no x-term.

$$-x - \;\; y - \;\; z = -1 \quad \text{Multiplying (2)}$$
$$\text{by } -1$$
$$\underline{x + 2y + 2z = \;\; 2} \quad (3)$$
$$y + \;\; z = \;\; 1 \quad (4)$$

Equations (1) and (4) are identical. This means that Equations (1), (2), and (3) are dependent. (We have seen that if Equation (2) is multiplied by -1 and added to Equation (3), the result is Equation (1).)

32. The equations are dependent.

33.
$$f(x) = 2x + 7$$
$$f(a + 1) = 2(a + 1) + 7 = 2a + 2 + 7 = 2a + 9$$

34. $\{x | x$ is a real number and $x \neq 7\}$

35.
$$K = \frac{1}{2}t(a - b)$$
$$\frac{2K}{t} = a - b \qquad \text{Multiplying by } \frac{2}{t}$$
$$\frac{2K}{t} - a = -b$$
$$-\frac{2K}{t} + a = b \qquad \text{Multiplying by } -1$$

This result can also be expressed as $b = \frac{at - 2K}{t}$.

36. $a = \frac{2K}{t} + b$, or $\frac{2K + bt}{t}$

37. ◈

38. ◈

39. ◈

40. ◈

41. $\dfrac{x+2}{3} - \dfrac{y+4}{2} + \dfrac{z+1}{6} = 0,$

$\dfrac{x-4}{3} + \dfrac{y+1}{4} - \dfrac{z-2}{2} = -1,$

$\dfrac{x+1}{2} + \dfrac{y}{2} + \dfrac{z-1}{4} = \dfrac{3}{4}$

1., 2. We clear fractions and write each equation in standard form.

To clear fractions, we multiply both sides of each equation by the LCM of its denominators. The LCM's are 6, 12, and 4, respectively.

$6\left(\dfrac{x+2}{3} - \dfrac{y+4}{2} + \dfrac{z+1}{6}\right) = 6 \cdot 0$

$2(x+2) - 3(y+4) + (z+1) = 0$

$2x + 4 - 3y - 12 + z + 1 = 0$

$2x - 3y + z = 7$

$12\left(\dfrac{x-4}{3} + \dfrac{y+1}{4} - \dfrac{z-2}{2}\right) = 12 \cdot (-1)$

$4(x-4) + 3(y+1) - 6(z-2) = -12$

$4x - 16 + 3y + 3 - 6z + 12 = -12$

$4x + 3y - 6z = -11$

$4\left(\dfrac{x+1}{2} + \dfrac{y}{2} + \dfrac{z-1}{4}\right) = 4 \cdot \dfrac{3}{4}$

$2(x+1) + 2(y) + (z-1) = 3$

$2x + 2 + 2y + z - 1 = 3$

$2x + 2y + z = 2$

The resulting system is

$2x - 3y + z = 7, \quad (1)$

$4x + 3y - 6z = -11, \quad (2)$

$2x + 2y + z = 2 \quad (3)$

3., 4. We eliminate z from two different pairs of equations.

$12x - 18y + 6z = 42 \quad$ Multiplying (1) by 6

$\underline{4x + 3y - 6z = -11} \quad (2)$

$16x - 15y = 31 \quad (4) \quad$ Adding

$2x - 3y + z = 7 \quad (1)$

$\underline{-2x - 2y - z = -2} \quad$ Multiplying (3) by -1

$-5y = 5 \quad (5) \quad$ Adding

5. Solve (5) for y: $\quad -5y = 5$

$y = -1$

Substitute -1 for y in (4):

$16x - 15(-1) = 31$

$16x + 15 = 31$

$16x = 16$

$x = 1$

6. Substitute 1 for x and -1 for y in (1):

$2 \cdot 1 - 3(-1) + z = 7$

$5 + z = 7$

$z = 2$

We obtain $(1, -1, 2)$. This checks, so it is the solution.

42. $(1, -2, 4, -1)$

43. $\quad w + x - y + z = 0, \quad (1)$

$w - 2x - 2y - z = -5, \quad (2)$

$w - 3x - y + z = 4, \quad (3)$

$2w - x - y + 3z = 7 \quad (4)$

The equations are already in standard form with no fractions or decimals.

Start by eliminating z from three different pairs of equations.

$w + x - y + z = 0 \quad (1)$

$\underline{w - 2x - 2y - z = -5} \quad (2)$

$2w - x - 3y = -5 \quad (5) \quad$ Adding

$w - 2x - 2y - z = -5 \quad (2)$

$\underline{w - 3x - y + z = 4} \quad (3)$

$2w - 5x - 3y = -1 \quad (6) \quad$ Adding

$3w - 6x - 6y - 3z = -15 \quad$ Multiplying (2) by 3

$\underline{2w - x - y + 3z = 7} \quad (4)$

$5w - 7x - 7y = -8 \quad (7) \quad$ Adding

Now solve the system of equations (5), (6), and (7).

$2w - x - 3y = -5, \quad (5)$

$2w - 5x - 3y = -1, \quad (6)$

$5w - 7x - 7y = -8. \quad (7)$

$2w - x - 3y = -5 \quad (5)$

$\underline{-2w + 5x + 3y = 1} \quad$ Multiplying (6) by -1

$4x = -4$

$x = -1$

Substituting -1 for x in (5) and (7) and simplifying, we have

$$2w - 3y = -6, \quad (8)$$
$$5w - 7y = -15. \quad (9)$$

Now solve the system of Equations (8) and (9).

$$10w - 15y = -30 \quad \text{Multiplying (8) by 5}$$
$$\underline{-10w + 14y = 30} \quad \text{Multiplying (9) by } -2$$
$$-y = 0$$
$$y = 0$$

Substitute 0 for y in Equation (8) or (9) and solve for w.

$$2w - 3 \cdot 0 = -6 \quad \text{Substituting in (8)}$$
$$2w = -6$$
$$w = -3$$

Substitute in one of the original equations to find z.

$$-3 - 1 - 0 + z = 0 \quad \text{Substituting in (1)}$$
$$-4 + z = 0$$
$$z = 4$$

We obtain $(-3, -1, 0, 4)$. This checks, so it is the solution.

44. $\left(-1, \dfrac{1}{5}, -\dfrac{1}{2}\right)$

45. $\dfrac{2}{x} + \dfrac{2}{y} - \dfrac{3}{z} = 3,$

$ \dfrac{1}{x} - \dfrac{2}{y} - \dfrac{3}{z} = 9,$

$ \dfrac{7}{x} - \dfrac{2}{y} + \dfrac{9}{z} = -39$

Let u represent $\dfrac{1}{x}$, v represent $\dfrac{1}{y}$, and w represent $\dfrac{1}{z}$. Substituting, we have

$$2u + 2v - 3w = 3, \quad (1)$$
$$u - 2v - 3w = 9, \quad (2)$$
$$7u - 2v + 9w = -39 \quad (3)$$

1., 2. The equations in u, v, and w are in standard form with no fractions or decimals.

3., 4. We eliminate v from two different pairs of equations.

$$2u + 2v - 3w = 3 \quad (1)$$
$$\underline{u - 2v - 3w = 9} \quad (2)$$
$$3u - 6w = 12 \quad (4) \text{ Adding}$$

$$2u + 2v - 3w = 3 \quad (1)$$
$$\underline{7u - 2v + 9w = -39} \quad (3)$$
$$9u + 6w = -36 \quad (5) \text{ Adding}$$

5. Now solve the system of Equations (4) and (5).

$$3u - 6w = 12, \quad (4)$$
$$\underline{9u + 6w = -36} \quad (5)$$
$$12u = -24$$
$$u = -2$$

$$3(-2) - 6w = 12 \quad \text{Substituting in (4)}$$
$$-6 - 6w = 12$$
$$-6w = 18$$
$$w = -3$$

6. Substitute in Equation (1), (2), or (3) to find v.

$$2(-2) + 2v - 3(-3) = 3 \quad \text{Substituting in (1)}$$
$$2v + 5 = 3$$
$$2v = -2$$
$$v = -1$$

Solve for x, y, and z. We substitute -2 for u, -1 for v, and -3 for w.

$$u = \dfrac{1}{x} \qquad v = \dfrac{1}{y} \qquad w = \dfrac{1}{z}$$
$$-2 = \dfrac{1}{x} \qquad -1 = \dfrac{1}{y} \qquad -3 = \dfrac{1}{z}$$
$$x = \dfrac{1}{2} \qquad y = -1 \qquad z = -\dfrac{1}{3}$$

We obtain $\left(-\dfrac{1}{2}, -1, -\dfrac{1}{3}\right)$. This checks, so it is the solution.

46. 12

47. $5x - 6y + kz = -5, \quad (1)$

$ x + 3y - 2z = 2, \quad (2)$

$ 2x - y + 4z = -1 \quad (3)$

Eliminate y from two different pairs of equations.

$$5x - 6y + kz = -5 \quad (1)$$
$$\underline{2x + 6y - 4z = 4} \quad \text{Multiplying (2) by 2}$$
$$7x + (k-4)z = -1 \quad (4)$$

$$x + 3y - 2z = 2 \quad (2)$$
$$\underline{6x - 3y + 12z = -3} \quad \text{Multiplying (3) by 3}$$
$$7x + 10z = -1 \quad (5)$$

Solve the system of Equations (4) and (5).

$$7x + (k-4)z = -1 \quad (4)$$
$$7x + 10z = -1 \quad (5)$$

$$-7x - (k-4)z = 1 \quad \text{Multiplying (4) by } -1$$
$$\underline{7x + 10z = -1} \quad (5)$$
$$(-k + 14)z = 0 \quad (6)$$

The system is dependent for the value of k that makes Equation (6) true. This occurs when $-k + 14$ is 0. We solve for k:

$$-k + 14 = 0$$
$$14 = k$$

48. $3x + 4y + 2z = 12$

49. $z = b - mx - ny$

Three solutions are $(1, 1, 2)$, $(3, 2, -6)$, and $\left(\frac{3}{2}, 1, 1\right)$. We substitute for x, y, and z and then solve for b, m, and n.

$$2 = b - m - n,$$
$$-6 = b - 3m - 2n,$$
$$1 = b - \frac{3}{2}m - n$$

1., 2. Write the equations in standard form. Also, clear the fraction in the last equation.

$$b - m - n = 2, \quad (1)$$
$$b - 3m - 2n = -6, \quad (2)$$
$$2b - 3m - 2n = 2 \quad (3)$$

3., 4. Eliminate b from two different pairs of equations.

$$b - m - n = 2 \quad (1)$$
$$\underline{-b + 3m + 2n = 6} \quad \text{Multiplying (2) by } -1$$
$$2m + n = 8 \quad (4) \quad \text{Adding}$$

$$-2b + 2m + 2n = -4 \quad \text{Multiplying (1) by } -2$$
$$\underline{2b - 3m - 2n = 2} \quad (3)$$
$$-m = -2 \quad (5) \quad \text{Adding}$$

5. We solve Equation (5) for m:

$$-m = -2$$
$$m = 2$$

Substitute in Equation (4) and solve for n.

$$2 \cdot 2 + n = 8$$
$$4 + n = 8$$
$$n = 4$$

6. Substitute in one of the original equations to find b.

$$b - 2 - 4 = 2 \quad \text{Substituting 2 for } m$$
$$\qquad\qquad\qquad \text{and 4 for } n \text{ in (1)}$$
$$b - 6 = 2$$
$$b = 8$$

The solution is $(8, 2, 4)$, so the equation is $z = 8 - 2x - 4y$.

Exercise Set 8.5

1. _Familiarize._ Let $x =$ the first number, $y =$ the second number, and $z =$ the third number.

Translate.

The sum of three numbers is 57.

$$x + y + z = 57$$

The second is 3 more than the first.

$$y = 3 + x$$

The third is 6 more than the first.

$$z = 6 + x$$

We now have a system of equations.

$$x + y + z = 57, \quad \text{or} \quad x + y + z = 57,$$
$$y = 3 + x \qquad\qquad -x + y = 3,$$
$$z = 6 + x \qquad\qquad -x + z = 6$$

Carry out. Solving the system we get $(16, 19, 22)$.

Check. The sum of the three numbers is $16 + 19 + 22$, or 57. The second number, 19, is three more than the first number, 16. The third number, 22, is 6 more than the first number, 16. The numbers check.

State. The numbers are 16, 19, and 22.

2. $4, 2, -1$

3. _Familiarize._ Let $x =$ the first number, $y =$ the second number, and $z =$ the third number.

Translate.

The sum of three numbers is 26.

$$x + y + z = 26$$

Twice the first minus the second is the third less 2.

$$2x - y = z - 2$$

The third is the second minus 3 times the first.

$$z = y - 3x$$

We now have a system of equations.

$$x + y + z = 26, \quad \text{or} \quad x + y + z = 26,$$
$$2x - y = z - 2, \qquad\qquad 2x - y - z = -2,$$
$$z = y - 3x \qquad\qquad 3x - y + z = 0$$

Carry out. Solving the system we get $(8, 21, -3)$.

Check. The sum of the numbers is $8 + 21 - 3$, or 26. Twice the first minus the second is $2 \cdot 8 - 21$, or -5, which is 2 less than the third. The second minus three times the first is $21 - 3 \cdot 8$, or -3, which is the third. The numbers check.

State. The numbers are 8, 21, and -3.

4. 17, 9, 79

5. **Familiarize**. We first make a drawing.

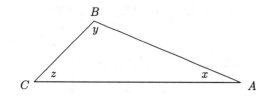

We let x, y, and z represent the measures of angles A, B, and C, respectively. The measures of the angles of a triangle add up to $180°$.

Translate.

The sum of the measures is $180°$.
$$x + y + z = 180$$

The measure of angle B is three times the measure of angle A.
$$y = 3x$$

The measure of angle C is $20°$ more than the measure of angle A.
$$z = x + 20$$

We now have a system of equations.
$$x + y + z = 180,$$
$$y = 3x,$$
$$z = x + 20$$

Carry out. Solving the system we get $(32, 96, 52)$.

Check. The sum of the measures is $32° + 96° + 52°$, or $180°$. Three times the measure of angle A is $3 \cdot 32°$, or $96°$, the measure of angle B. $20°$ more than the measure of angle A is $32° + 20°$, or $52°$, the measure of angle C. The numbers check.

State. The measures of angles A, B, and C are $32°$, $96°$, and $52°$, respectively.

6. $25°$, $50°$, $105°$

7. **Familiarize**. Let $x =$ the cost of automatic transmission, $y =$ the cost of power door locks, and $z =$ the cost of air conditioning. The prices of the options are added to the basic price of \$12,685.

Translate.

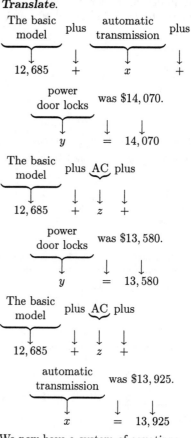

The basic model plus automatic transmission plus power door locks was \$14,070.
$$12{,}685 + x + y = 14{,}070$$

The basic model plus AC plus power door locks was \$13,580.
$$12{,}685 + z + y = 13{,}580$$

The basic model plus AC plus automatic transmission was \$13,925.
$$12{,}685 + z + x = 13{,}925$$

We now have a system of equations.
$$12{,}685 + x + y = 14{,}070,$$
$$12{,}685 + z + y = 13{,}580,$$
$$12{,}685 + z + x = 13{,}925$$

Carry out. Solving the system we get $(865, 520, 375)$.

Check. The basic model with automatic transmission and power door locks costs \$12,685 + \$865 + \$520, or \$14,070. The basic model with AC and power door locks costs \$12,685 + \$375 + \$520, or \$13,580. The basic model with AC and automatic transmission costs \$12,685 + \$375 + \$865, or \$13,925. The numbers check.

State. Automatic transmission costs \$865, power door locks cost \$520, and AC costs \$375.

8. Sven: 220, Tillie: 250, Isaiah: 270

9. **Familiarize**. It helps to organize the information in a table. We let x, y, and z represent the weekly productions of the individual machines.

Machines Working	A	B	C
Weekly Production	x	y	z

Machines Working	A & B	B & C	A, B, & C
Weekly Production	3400	4200	5700

Translate. From the table, we obtain three equations.

$x + y + z = 5700$ (All three machines working)

$x + y \quad = 3400$ (A and B working)

$\quad y + z = 4200$ (B and C working)

Carry out. Solving the system we get $(1500, 1900, 2300)$.

Check. The sum of the weekly productions of machines A, B & C is $1500 + 1900 + 2300$, or 5700. The sum of the weekly productions of machines A and B is $1500 + 1900$, or 3400. The sum of the weekly productions of machines B and C is $1900 + 2300$, or 4200. The numbers check.

State. In a week Machine A can polish 1500 lenses, Machine B can polish 1900 lenses, and Machine C can polish 2300 lenses.

10. Elrod: 20, Dot: 24, Wendy: 30

11. Familiarize. Let $x =$ the number of 10-oz cups, $y =$ the number of 14-oz cups, and $z =$ the number of 20-oz cups that Kyle filled. Note that five 96-oz pots contain $5 \cdot 96$ oz, or 480 oz of coffee. Also, x 10-oz cups contain a total of $10x$ oz of coffee and bring in $\$0.95x$, y 14-oz cups contain $14y$ oz and bring in $\$1.15y$, and z 20-oz cups contain $20z$ oz and bring in $\$1.50z$.

Translate.

The total number of coffees served was 34.

$$x + y + z = 34$$

The total amount of coffee served was 480 oz.

$$10x + 14y + 20z = 480$$

The total amount collected was $39.60.

$$0.95x + 1.15y + 1.50z = 39.60$$

Now we have a system of equations.

$$x + y + z = 34,$$
$$10x + 14y + 20z = 480,$$
$$0.95x + 1.15y + 1.50z = 39.60$$

Carry out. Solving the system we get $(8, 20, 6)$.

Check. The total number of coffees served was $8 + 20 + 6$, or 34, The total amount of coffee served was $10 \cdot 8 + 14 \cdot 20 + 20 \cdot 6 = 80 + 280 + 120 = 480$ oz. The total amount collected was $\$0.95(8) + \$1.15(20) + \$1.50(6) = \$7.60 + \$23.00 + \$9.00 = \$39.60$. The numbers check.

State. Kyle filled 8 10-oz cups, 20 14-oz cups, and 6 20-oz cups.

12. Small: 15, medium: 30, large: 10

13. Familiarize. Let $x =$ the amount invested in the first fund, $y =$ the amount invested in the second fund, and $z =$ the amount invested in the third fund. Then the earnings from the investments were $0.1x$, $0.06y$, and $0.15z$.

Translate.

The total amount invested was $80,000.

$$x + y + z = 80,000$$

The total earnings were $8850.

$$0.1x + 0.06y + 0.15z = 8850$$

The earnings from the first fund were $750 more than the earnings from the third fund.

$$0.1x = 750 + 0.15z$$

Now we have a system of equations.

$$x + y + z = 80,000$$
$$0.1x + 0.06y + 0.15z = 8850,$$
$$0.1x = 750 + 0.15z$$

Carry out. Solving the system we get $(45,000, 10,000, 25,000)$.

Check. The total investment was $\$45,000 + \$10,000 + \$25,000$, or $\$80,000$. The total earnings were $0.1(\$45,000) + 0.06(10,000) + 0.15(25,000) = \$4500 + \$600 + \$3750 = \$8850$. The earnings from the first fund, $\$4500$, were $\$750$ more than the earnings from the second fund, $\$3750$.

State. $\$45,000$ was invested in the first fund, $\$10,000$ in the second fund, and $\$25,000$ in the third fund.

14. Newsaper: \$41.4 billion, television: \$36 billion, radio: \$7.7 billion

15. *Familiarize*. Let r = the number of servings of roast beef, p = the number of baked potatoes, and b = the number of servings of broccoli. Then r servings of roast beef contain $300r$ Calories, $20r$ g of protein, and no vitamin C. In p baked potatoes there are $100p$ Calories, $5p$ g of protein, and $20p$ mg of vitamin C. And b servings of broccoli contain $50b$ Calories, $5b$ g of protein, and $100b$ mg of vitamin C. The patient requires 800 Calories, 55 g of protein, and 220 mg of vitamin C.

Translate. Write equations for the total number of calories, the total amount of protein, and the total amount of vitamin C.

$$300r + 100p + 50b = 800 \quad \text{(Calories)}$$
$$20r + 5p + 5b = 55 \quad \text{(protein)}$$
$$20p + 100b = 220 \quad \text{(vitamin C)}$$

We now have a system of equations.

Carry out. Solving the system we get $(2, 1, 2)$.

Check. Two servings of roast beef provide 600 Calories, 40 g of protein, and no vitamin C. One baked potato provides 100 Calories, 5 g of protein, and 20 mg of vitamin C. And 2 servings of broccoli provide 100 Calories, 10 g of protein, and 200 mg of vitamin C. Together, then, they provide 800 Calories, 55 g of protein, and 220 mg of vitamin C. The values check.

State. The dietician should prepare 2 servings of roast beef, 1 baked potato, and 2 servings of broccoli.

16. Roast beef: $1\frac{1}{8}$, baked potato, $2\frac{3}{4}$, asparagus: $3\frac{3}{4}$

17. *Familiarize*. Let x, y, and z represent the number of fraternal twin births for Asian-Americans, African-Americans, and Caucasians in the U.S., respectively, out of every 15,400 births.

Translate. Out of every 15,400 births, we have the following statistics:

The total number of fraternal twin births is 739.

$$x + y + z = 739$$

The number of fraternal twin births for Asian-Americans is 185 more than the number for African-Americans.

$$x = 185 + y$$

The number of fraternal twin births for Asian-Americans is 231 more than the number for Caucasians.

$$x = 231 + z$$

We have a system of equations.

$$x + y + z = 739,$$
$$x = 185 + y,$$
$$x = 231 + y$$

Carry out. Solving the system we get $(385, 200, 154)$.

Check. The total of the numbers is 739. Also 385 is 185 more than 200, and it is 231 more than 154.

State. Out of every 15,400 births, there are 385 births of fraternal twins for Asian-Americans, 200 for African-Americans, and 154 for Caucasians.

18. Man: 3.6, woman: 18.1, child: 50

19. *Familiarize*. Let x, y, and z represent the number of 2-point field goals, 3-point field goals, and 1-point foul shots made, respectively. The total number of points scored from each of these types of goals is $2x$, $3y$, and z.

Translate.

The total number of points was 92.

$$2x + 3y + z = 92$$

The total number of baskets was 50.

$$x + y + z = 50$$

The number of 2-pointers was 19 more than the number of foul shots.

$$x = 19 + z$$

Now we have a system of equations.

$$2x + 3y + z = 92,$$
$$x + y + z = 50,$$
$$x = 19 + z$$

Carry out. Solving the system we get $(32, 5, 13)$.

Check. The total number of points was $2\cdot 32 + 3 \cdot 5 + 13 = 64 + 15 + 13 = 92$. The number of baskets was $32 + 5 + 13$, or 50. The number of 2-pointers, 32, was 19 more than the number of foul shots, 13. The numbers check.

State. The Knicks made 32 two-point field goals, 5 three-point field goals, and 13 foul shots.

20. 1869

21. $3(5 - x) + 7 = 5(x + 3) - 9$

$15 - 3x + 7 = 5x + 15 - 9$

$-3x + 22 = 5x + 6$

$22 = 8x + 6$

$16 = 8x$

$2 = x$

The solution is 2.

22. 8

23. $\dfrac{(a^2 b^3)^5}{a^7 b^{16}} = \dfrac{a^{10} b^{15}}{a^7 b^{16}} = a^{10-7} b^{15-16} = a^3 b^{-1}$, or $\dfrac{a^3}{b}$

24. $y = -\dfrac{3}{5} x - 7$

25. $g(x) = \dfrac{x - 5}{x + 7}$

We cannot compute $g(x)$ when the denominator is 0. We solve an equation to determine when this occurs.

$x + 7 = 0$

$x = -7$

Thus, the domain of g is $\{x | x$ is a real number and $x \neq -7\}$.

26. 76

27.

28.

29. Familiarize. Let $x =$ the one's digit, $y =$ the ten's digit, and $z =$ the hundred's digit. Then the number is represented by $100z + 10y + x$. When the digits are reversed, the resulting number is represented by $100x + 10y + z$.

Translate.

The sum of the digits is 14.

$\underbrace{}$ $\downarrow$ $\downarrow$

$x + y + z$ $= 14$

The ten's digit is 2 more than the one's digit.

$\downarrow$ $\downarrow$ $\downarrow$ $\underbrace{}$ $\underbrace{}$

y $= 2$ $+$ x

The number is the same as the number with the digits reversed.

$\downarrow$ $\underbrace{}$ $\underbrace{}$

$100z + 10y + x$ $=$ $100x + 10y + z$

Now we have a system of equations.

$x + y + z = 14,$

$y = 2 + x,$

$100z + 10y + x = 100x + 10y + z$

Carry out. Solving the system we get $(4, 6, 4)$.

Check. If the number is 464, then the sum of the digits is $4 + 6 + 4$, or 14. The ten's digit, 6, is 2 more than the one's digit, 4. If the digits are reversed the number is unchanged The result checks.

State. The number is 464.

30. 20

31. Familiarize. Let $x =$ the number of adults, $y =$ the number of students, and $z =$ the number of children in attendance.

Translate. The given information gives rise to two equations.

The total number in attendance was 100.

$\underbrace{}$ $\downarrow$ $\downarrow$

$x + y + z$ $=$ 100

The total amount taken in was \$100.

$\underbrace{}$ $\downarrow$ $\downarrow$

$10x + 3y + 0.5z$ $=$ 100

Now we have a system of equations.

$x + y + z = 100,$

$10x + 3y + 0.5z = 100$

Multiply the second equation by 2 to clear the decimal:

$x + y + z = 100, \quad (1)$

$20x + 6y + z = 200. \quad (2)$

Carry out. We use the elimination method.

$-x - y - z = -100$ Multiplying (1) by -1

$\underline{20x + 6y + z = 200 \quad (2)}$

$19x + 5y = 100 \quad (3)$

In (3), note that 5 is a factor of both $5y$ and 100. Therefore, 5 must also be a factor of $19x$, and hence of x, since 5 is not a factor of 19. Then for some positive integer n, $x = 5n$. (We require $n > 0$, since the number of adults clearly cannot be negative and must also be nonzero since the exercise states that the audience consists of *adults*, students, and children.) We have

$19 \cdot 5n + 5y = 100$, or

$19n + y = 20.$ Dividing by 5 on both sides

Since n and y must both be positive, $n = 1$. Otherwise, $19n+y$ would be greater than 20. Then $x = 5 \cdot 1$, or 5.

$$19 \cdot 5 + 5y = 100 \quad \text{Substituting in (3)}$$
$$95 + 5y = 100$$
$$5y = 5$$
$$y = 1$$
$$5 + 1 + z = 100 \quad \text{Substituting in (1)}$$
$$6 + z = 100$$
$$z = 94$$

Check. The number of people in attendance was $5 + 1 + 94$, or 100. The amount of money taken in was $\$10 \cdot 5 + \$3 \cdot 1 + \$0.50(94) = \$50 + \$3 + \$47 = \$100$. The numbers check.

State. There were 5 adults, 1 student, and 94 children.

32. 35

33. Familiarize. We first make a drawing with additional labels.

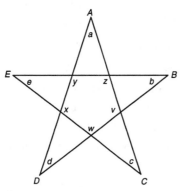

We let a, b, c, d, and e represent the angle measures at the tips of the star. We also label the interior angles of the pentagon v, w, x, y, and z. We recall the following geometric fact:

The sum of the measures of the interior angles of a polygon of n sides is given by $(n-2)180°$.

Using this fact we know:

1. The sum of the angle measures of a triangle is $(3-2)180°$, or $180°$.

2. The sum of the angle measures of a pentagon is $(5-2)180°$, or $3(180°)$.

Translate. Using fact (1) listed above we obtain a system of 5 equations.

$$a + v + d = 180$$
$$b + w + e = 180$$
$$c + x + a = 180$$
$$d + y + b = 180$$
$$e + z + c = 180$$

Carry out. Adding we obtain

$$2a + 2b + 2c + 2d + 2e + v + w + x + y + z = 5(180)$$
$$2(a + b + c + d + e) + (v + w + x + y + z) = 5(180)$$

Using fact (2) listed above we substitute $3(180)$ for $(v + w + x + y + z)$ and solve for $(a + b + c + d + e)$.

$$2(a + b + c + d + e) + 3(180) = 5(180)$$
$$2(a + b + c + d + e) = 2(180)$$
$$a + b + c + d + e = 180$$

Check. We should repeat the above calculations.

State. The sum of the angle measures at the tips of the star is $180°$.

Exercise Set 8.6

1. $5x - 3y = 13,$
$4x + y = 7$

Write a matrix using only the constants.

$$\begin{bmatrix} 5 & -3 & \vdots & 13 \\ 4 & 1 & \vdots & 7 \end{bmatrix}$$

Multiply row 2 by 5 to make the first number in row 2 a multiple of 5.

$$\begin{bmatrix} 5 & -3 & \vdots & 13 \\ 20 & 5 & \vdots & 35 \end{bmatrix} \text{ New Row } 2 = 5(\text{Row } 2)$$

Multiply row 1 by -4 and add it to row 2.

$$\begin{bmatrix} 5 & -3 & \vdots & 13 \\ 0 & 17 & \vdots & -17 \end{bmatrix} \begin{array}{l} \text{New Row } 2 = -4(\text{Row } 1) + \\ \text{Row } 2 \end{array}$$

Reinserting the variables, we have

$$5x - 3y = 13, \quad (1)$$
$$17y = -17. \quad (2)$$

Solve Equation (2) for y.

$$17y = -17$$
$$y = -1$$

Back-substitute -1 for y in Equation (1) and solve for x.

$$5x - 3y = 13$$
$$5x - 3(-1) = 13$$
$$5x + 3 = 13$$
$$5x = 10$$
$$x = 2$$

The solution is $(2, -1)$.

2. $\left(-\dfrac{1}{3}, -4\right)$

3. $x + 4y = 8,$
$3x + 5y = 3$

We first write a matrix using only the constants.

$$\begin{bmatrix} 1 & 4 & \vdots & 8 \\ 3 & 5 & \vdots & 3 \end{bmatrix}$$

Multiply the first row by -3 and add it to the second row.

$$\begin{bmatrix} 1 & 4 & \vdots & 8 \\ 0 & -7 & \vdots & -21 \end{bmatrix} \text{New Row 2} = -3(\text{Row 1}) + \text{Row 2}$$

Reinserting the variables, we have

$$x + 4y = 8, \quad (1)$$
$$-7y = -21. \quad (2)$$

Solve Equation (2) for y.

$$-7y = -21$$
$$y = 3$$

Back-substitute 3 for y in Equation (1) and solve for x.

$$x + 4 \cdot 3 = 8$$
$$x + 12 = 8$$
$$x = -4$$

The solution is $(-4, 3)$.

4. $(-3, 2)$

5. $6x - 2y = 4,$
$7x + y = 13$

Write a matrix using only the constants.

$$\begin{bmatrix} 6 & -2 & \vdots & 4 \\ 7 & 1 & \vdots & 13 \end{bmatrix}$$

Multiply the second row by 6 to make the first number in row 2 a multiple of 6.

$$\begin{bmatrix} 6 & -2 & \vdots & 4 \\ 42 & 6 & \vdots & 78 \end{bmatrix} \text{New Row 2} = 6(\text{Row 2})$$

Now multiply the first row by -7 and add it to the second row.

$$\begin{bmatrix} 6 & -2 & \vdots & 4 \\ 0 & 20 & \vdots & 50 \end{bmatrix} \begin{array}{l} \text{New Row 2} = -7(\text{Row 1}) + \\ \text{Row 2} \end{array}$$

Reinserting the variables, we have

$$6x - 2y = 4, \quad (1)$$
$$20y = 50. \quad (2)$$

Solve Equation (2) for y.

$$20y = 50$$
$$y = \frac{5}{2}$$

Back-substitute $\dfrac{5}{2}$ for y in Equation (1) and solve for x.

$$6x - 2y = 4$$
$$6x - 2\left(\frac{5}{2}\right) = 4$$
$$6x - 5 = 4$$
$$6x = 9$$
$$x = \frac{3}{2}$$

The solution is $\left(\dfrac{3}{2}, \dfrac{5}{2}\right)$.

6. $\left(-1, \dfrac{5}{2}\right)$

7. $4x - y - 3z = 1,$
$8x + y - z = 5,$
$2x + y + 2z = 5$

Write a matrix using only the constants.

$$\begin{bmatrix} 4 & -1 & -3 & \vdots & 1 \\ 8 & 1 & -1 & \vdots & 5 \\ 2 & 1 & 2 & \vdots & 5 \end{bmatrix}$$

First interchange rows 1 and 3 so that each number below the first number in the first row is a multiple of that number.

$$\begin{bmatrix} 2 & 1 & 2 & \vdots & 5 \\ 8 & 1 & -1 & \vdots & 5 \\ 4 & -1 & -3 & \vdots & 1 \end{bmatrix}$$

Multiply row 1 by -4 and add it to row 2.

Multiply row 1 by -2 and add it to row 3.

$$\begin{bmatrix} 2 & 1 & 2 & \vdots & 5 \\ 0 & -3 & -9 & \vdots & -15 \\ 0 & -3 & -7 & \vdots & -9 \end{bmatrix}$$

Multiply row 2 by -1 and add it to row 3.

$$\begin{bmatrix} 2 & 1 & 2 & \vdots & 5 \\ 0 & -3 & -9 & \vdots & -15 \\ 0 & 0 & 2 & \vdots & 6 \end{bmatrix}$$

Reinserting the variables, we have

$$2x + y + 2z = 5, \qquad (1)$$
$$-3y - 9z = -15, \qquad (2)$$
$$2z = 6. \qquad (3)$$

Solve (3) for z.

$$2z = 6$$
$$z = 3$$

Back-substitute 3 for z in (2) and solve for y.

$$-3y - 9z = -15$$
$$-3y - 9(3) = -15$$
$$-3y - 27 = -15$$
$$-3y = 12$$
$$y = -4$$

Back-substitute 3 for z and -4 for y in (1) and solve for x.

$$2x + y + 2z = 5$$
$$2x + (-4) + 2(3) = 5$$
$$2x - 4 + 6 = 5$$
$$2x = 3$$
$$x = \frac{3}{2}$$

The solution is $\left(\frac{3}{2}, -4, 3\right)$.

8. $\left(2, \frac{1}{2}, -2\right)$

9. $p - 2q - 3r = 3,$
$$2p - q - 2r = 4,$$
$$4p + 5q + 6r = 4$$

We first write a matrix using only the constants.

$$\begin{bmatrix} 1 & -2 & -3 & | & 3 \\ 2 & -1 & -2 & | & 4 \\ 4 & 5 & 6 & | & 4 \end{bmatrix}$$

$$\begin{bmatrix} 1 & -2 & -3 & | & 3 \\ 0 & 3 & 4 & | & -2 \\ 0 & 13 & 18 & | & -8 \end{bmatrix}$$ New Row 2 = -2(Row 1) + Row 2
New Row 3 = -4(Row 1) + Row 3

$$\begin{bmatrix} 1 & -2 & -3 & | & 3 \\ 0 & 3 & 4 & | & -2 \\ 0 & 39 & 54 & | & -24 \end{bmatrix}$$ New Row 3 = 3(Row 3)

$$\begin{bmatrix} 1 & -2 & -3 & | & 3 \\ 0 & 3 & 4 & | & -2 \\ 0 & 0 & 2 & | & 2 \end{bmatrix}$$ New Row 3 = -13(Row 2)+ Row 3

Reinstating the variables, we have

$$p - 2q - 3r = 3, \qquad (1)$$
$$3q + 4r = -2, \qquad (2)$$
$$2r = 2 \qquad (3)$$

Solve (3) for r.

$$2r = 2$$
$$r = 1$$

Back-substitute 1 for r in (2) and solve for q.

$$3q + 4 \cdot 1 = -2$$
$$3q + 4 = -2$$
$$3q = -6$$
$$q = -2$$

Back-substitute -2 for q and 1 for r in (1) and solve for p.

$$p - 2(-2) - 3 \cdot 1 = 3$$
$$p + 4 - 3 = 3$$
$$p + 1 = 3$$
$$p = 2$$

The solution is $(2, -2, 1)$.

10. $(-1, 2, -2)$

11. $3p + 2r = 11,$
$$q - 7r = 4,$$
$$p - 6q = 1$$

We first write a matrix using only the constants.

$$\begin{bmatrix} 3 & 0 & 2 & | & 11 \\ 0 & 1 & -7 & | & 4 \\ 1 & -6 & 0 & | & 1 \end{bmatrix}$$

$$\begin{bmatrix} 1 & -6 & 0 & | & 1 \\ 0 & 1 & -7 & | & 4 \\ 3 & 0 & 2 & | & 11 \end{bmatrix}$$ Interchange Row 1 and Row 3

$$\begin{bmatrix} 1 & -6 & 0 & | & 1 \\ 0 & 1 & -7 & | & 4 \\ 0 & 18 & 2 & | & 8 \end{bmatrix}$$ New Row 3 = -3(Row 1) + Row 3

$$\begin{bmatrix} 1 & -6 & 0 & | & 1 \\ 0 & 1 & -7 & | & 4 \\ 0 & 0 & 128 & | & -64 \end{bmatrix}$$ New Row 3 = -18(Row 2) + Row 3

Reinserting the variables, we have

$$p - 6q \qquad\quad = 1, \qquad (1)$$
$$q - \quad 7r = 4, \qquad (2)$$
$$128r = -64. \quad (3)$$

Solve (3) for r.

$$128r = -64$$
$$r = -\frac{1}{2}$$

Back-substitute $-\frac{1}{2}$ for r in (2) and solve for q.

$$q - 7r = 4$$
$$q - 7\left(-\frac{1}{2}\right) = 4$$
$$q + \frac{7}{2} = 4$$
$$q = \frac{1}{2}$$

Back-substitute $\frac{1}{2}$ for q in (1) and solve for p.

$$p - 6 \cdot \frac{1}{2} = 1$$
$$p - 3 = 1$$
$$p = 4$$

The solution is $\left(4, \frac{1}{2}, -\frac{1}{2}\right)$.

12. $\left(\frac{1}{2}, \frac{2}{3}, -\frac{5}{6}\right)$

13.
$$3x + y = 8,$$
$$4x + 5y - 3z = 4,$$
$$7x + 2y - 9z = 1$$

The coefficient matrix is:

$$\begin{bmatrix} 3 & 1 & 0 & 8 \\ 4 & 5 & -3 & 4 \\ 7 & 2 & -9 & 1 \end{bmatrix}$$

We enter this on a grapher and use the "ref (" command to find the row-echelon form of the matrix with the elements expressed in fractional form.

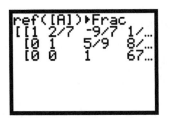

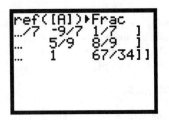

Using this matrix, we reinsert the variables. We have

$$x + \frac{2}{7}y - \frac{9}{7}z = \frac{1}{7}, \qquad (1)$$
$$y + \frac{5}{9}z = \frac{8}{9}, \qquad (2)$$
$$z = \frac{67}{34}. \qquad (3)$$

From equation (3) we see that $z = \frac{67}{34}$. Back-substituting and solving, we have $y = -\frac{7}{34}$, and $x = \frac{93}{34}$. The solution is $\left(\frac{93}{34}, -\frac{7}{34}, \frac{67}{34}\right)$.

14. $\left(\frac{23}{5}, \frac{5}{2}, -2\right)$

15.
$$-0.01x + 0.7y = -0.9,$$
$$0.5x - 0.3y + 0.18z = 0.01,$$
$$50x + 6y - 75z = 12$$

The coefficient matrix is:

$$\begin{bmatrix} -0.01 & 0.7 & 0 & -0.9 \\ 0.5 & -0.3 & 0.18 & 0.01 \\ 50 & 6 & -75 & 12 \end{bmatrix}$$

We enter this on a grapher and use the " ref (" command to find the row-echelon form of the matrix.

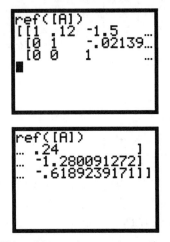

Using this matrix, we reinsert the variables. We have

$$x + 0.12y - 1.5z = 0.24 \qquad (1)$$
$$y - 0.02139z = -1.28009 \quad (2)$$
$$z = -0.61892 \quad (3)$$

From equation (3) we see that $z \approx -0.6189$. Back-substituting and solving, we have $y \approx -1.2933$ and $x \approx -0.5332$. The solution is $(-0.5332, -1.2933, -0.6189)$.

16. $(-2.4559, -3.3382, 3.5)$

17. Rewrite the equations with the variables in alphabetical order.

$$-w + 2x - 3y + z = -8,$$
$$-w + x + y - z = -4,$$
$$w + x + y + z = 22,$$
$$-w + x - y - z = -14$$

Write a matrix using only the constants.

$$\begin{bmatrix} -1 & 2 & -3 & 1 & | & -8 \\ -1 & 1 & 1 & -1 & | & -4 \\ 1 & 1 & 1 & 1 & | & 22 \\ -1 & 1 & -1 & -1 & | & -14 \end{bmatrix}$$

$$\begin{bmatrix} -1 & 2 & -3 & 1 & | & -8 \\ 0 & -1 & 4 & -2 & | & 4 \\ 0 & 3 & -2 & 2 & | & 14 \\ 0 & -1 & 2 & -2 & | & -6 \end{bmatrix}$$

New Row 2 = -1(Row 1) + Row 2
New Row 3 = Row 1 + Row 3
New Row 4 = -1(Row 1) + Row 4

$$\begin{bmatrix} -1 & 2 & -3 & 1 & | & -8 \\ 0 & -1 & 4 & -2 & | & 4 \\ 0 & 0 & 10 & -4 & | & 26 \\ 0 & 0 & -2 & 0 & | & -10 \end{bmatrix}$$

New Row 3 = 3(Row 2) + Row 3
New Row 4 = -1(Row 2) + Row 4

$$\begin{bmatrix} -1 & 2 & -3 & 1 & | & -8 \\ 0 & -1 & 4 & -2 & | & 4 \\ 0 & 0 & 10 & -4 & | & 26 \\ 0 & 0 & -10 & 0 & | & -50 \end{bmatrix}$$

New Row 4 = 5(Row 4)

$$\begin{bmatrix} -1 & 2 & -3 & 1 & | & -8 \\ 0 & -1 & 4 & -2 & | & 4 \\ 0 & 0 & 10 & -4 & | & 26 \\ 0 & 0 & 0 & -4 & | & -24 \end{bmatrix}$$

New Row 4 = Row 3 + Row 4

Reinserting the variables, we have

$$-w + 2x - 3y + z = -8, \quad (1)$$
$$-x + 4y - 2z = 4, \quad (2)$$
$$10y - 4z = 26, \quad (3)$$
$$-4z = -24. \quad (4)$$

Solve (4) for z.

$$-4z = -24$$
$$z = 6$$

Back-substitute 6 for z in (3) and solve for y.

$$10y - 4 \cdot 6 = 26$$
$$10y - 24 = 26$$
$$10y = 50$$
$$y = 5$$

Back-substitute 5 for y and 6 for z in (2) and solve for x.

$$-x + 4 \cdot 5 - 2 \cdot 6 = 4$$
$$-x + 20 - 12 = 4$$
$$-x + 8 = 4$$
$$-x = -4$$
$$x = 4$$

Back-substitute 4 for x, 5 for y, and 6 for z in (1) and solve for w.

$$-w + 2 \cdot 4 - 3 \cdot 5 + 6 = -8$$
$$-w + 8 - 15 + 6 = -8$$
$$-w - 1 = -8$$
$$-w = -7$$
$$w = 7$$

The solution is $(7, 4, 5, 6)$.

18. $(1, -3, -2, -1)$

19. *Familiarize.* Let d = the number of dimes and n = the number of nickels. The value of d dimes is $\$0.10d$, and the value of n nickels is $\$0.05n$.

Translate.

Total number of coins is 34.

$$d + n = 34$$

Total value of coins is $1.90.

$$0.10d + 0.05n = 1.90$$

After clearing decimals, we have this system.

$$d + n = 34,$$
$$10d + 5n = 190$$

Carry out. Solve using matrices.

$$\begin{bmatrix} 1 & 1 & | & 34 \\ 10 & 5 & | & 190 \end{bmatrix}$$

$$\begin{bmatrix} 1 & 1 & | & 34 \\ 0 & -5 & | & -150 \end{bmatrix}$$

New Row 2 = -10(Row 1) + Row 2

Reinserting the variables, we have

$$d + n = \quad 34, \quad (1)$$
$$-5n = -150 \quad (2)$$

Solve (2) for n.

$$-5n = -150$$
$$n = 30$$

$$d + 30 = 34 \quad \text{Back-substituting}$$
$$d = 4$$

Check. The sum of the two numbers is 34. The total value is $\$0.10(4) + \$0.50(30) = \$0.40 + \$1.50 = \$1.90$. The numbers check.

State. There are 4 dimes and 30 nickels.

20. 21 dimes, 22 quarters

21. Familiarize. We let x represent the number of pounds of the $\$4.05$ kind and y represent the number of pounds of the $\$2.70$ kind of granola. We organize the information in a table.

Granola	Number of pounds	Price per pound	Value
$\$4.05$ kind	x	$\$4.05$	$\$4.05x$
$\$2.70$ kind	y	$\$2.70$	$\$2.70y$
Mixture	15	$\$3.15$	$\$3.15 \times 15$ or $\$47.25$

Translate.

Total number of pounds is 15.

$$x + y = 15$$

Total value of mixture is $\$47.25$.

$$4.05x + 2.70y = 47.25$$

After clearing decimals, we have this system:

$$x + \quad y = \quad 15,$$
$$405x + 270y = 4725$$

Carry out. Solve using matrices.

$$\begin{bmatrix} 1 & 1 & \vdots & 15 \\ 405 & 270 & \vdots & 4725 \end{bmatrix}$$

$$\begin{bmatrix} 1 & 1 & \vdots & 15 \\ 0 & -135 & \vdots & -1350 \end{bmatrix} \begin{array}{l} \text{New Row 2} = \\ \quad -405(\text{Row 1}) + \text{Row 2} \end{array}$$

Reinserting the variables, we have

$$x + y = 15, \quad (1)$$
$$-135y = -1350 \quad (2)$$

Solve (2) for y.

$$-135y = -1350$$
$$y = 10$$

Back-substitute 10 for y in (1) and solve for x.

$$x + 10 = 15$$
$$x = 5$$

Check. The sum of the numbers is 15. The total value is $\$4.05(5) + \$2.70(10)$, or $\$20.25 + \$27.00$, or $\$47.25$. The numbers check.

State. 5 pounds of the $\$4.05$ per lb granola and 10 pounds of the $\$2.70$ per lb granola should be used.

22. 14 pounds of nuts, 6 pounds of oats

23. Familiarize. We let x, y, and z represent the amounts invested at 7%, 8%, and 9%, respectively. Recall the formula for simple interest:

$$\text{Interest} = \text{Principal} \times \text{Rate} \times \text{Time}$$

Translate. We organize the imformation in a table.

	First Invest-ment	Second Invest-ment	Third Invest-ment	Total
P	x	y	z	$\$2500$
R	7%	8%	9%	
T	1 yr	1 yr	1 yr	
I	$0.07x$	$0.08y$	$0.09z$	$\$212$

The first row gives us one equation:

$$x + y + z = 2500$$

The last row gives a second equation:

$$0.07x + 0.08y + 0.09z = 212$$

Amount invested at 9% is $\$1100$ more than amount invested at 8%.

$$z = \$1100 + y$$

After clearing decimals, we have this system:

$$x + \quad y + \quad z = \quad 2500,$$
$$7x + \quad 8y + 9z = 21{,}200,$$
$$-y + \quad z = \quad 1100$$

Carry out. Solve using matrices.

$$\begin{bmatrix} 1 & 1 & 1 & \vdots & 2500 \\ 7 & 8 & 9 & \vdots & 21{,}200 \\ 0 & -1 & 1 & \vdots & 1100 \end{bmatrix}$$

$$\begin{bmatrix} 1 & 1 & 1 & \vdots & 2500 \\ 0 & 1 & 2 & \vdots & 3700 \\ 0 & -1 & 1 & \vdots & 1100 \end{bmatrix} \begin{array}{l} \text{New Row 2} = \\ \quad -7(\text{Row 1}) + \text{Row 2} \end{array}$$

$$\begin{bmatrix} 1 & 1 & 1 & | & 2500 \\ 0 & 1 & 2 & | & 3700 \\ 0 & 0 & 3 & | & 4800 \end{bmatrix}$$ New Row 3 =

Row 2 + Row 3

Reinserting the variables, we have

$$\begin{aligned} x + y + z &= 2500, \quad (1) \\ y + 2z &= 3700, \quad (2) \\ 3z &= 4800 \quad (3) \end{aligned}$$

Solve (3) for z.

$$3z = 4800$$

$$z = 1600$$

Back-substitute 1600 for z in (2) and solve for y.

$$y + 2 \cdot 1600 = 3700$$

$$y + 3200 = 3700$$

$$y = 500$$

Back-substitute 500 for y and 1600 for z in (1) and solve for x.

$$x + 500 + 1600 = 2500$$

$$x + 2100 = 2500$$

$$x = 400$$

Check.   The total investment is $400 + $500 + $1600, or $2500. The total interest is 0.07($400) + 0.08($500) + 0.09($1600) = $28 + $40 + $144 = $212. The amount invested at 9%, $1600, is $1100 more than the amount invested at 8%, $500. The numbers check.

State. $400 is invested at 7%, $500 is invested at 8%, and $1600 is invested at 9%.

24. $500 at 8%, $400 at 9%, $2300 at 10%

25. $0.1x - 12 = 3.6x - 2.34 - 4.9x$

$10x - 1200 = 360x - 234 - 490x$ Multiplying
by 100 to clear decimals

$10x - 1200 = -130x - 234$

$140x - 1200 = -234$

$140x = 966$

$$x = \frac{966}{140}, \text{ or } \frac{69}{10}, \text{ or } 6.9$$

The solution is $\dfrac{69}{10}$, or 6.9.

26. -20

27. $4(9 - x) - 6(8 - 3x) = 5(3x + 4)$

$36 - 4x - 48 + 18x = 15x + 20$

$-12 + 14x = 15x + 20$

$-12 = x + 20$

$-32 = x$

The solution is -32.

28. $b = \dfrac{c}{5 + a}$

29.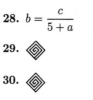

30.

31. **Familiarize**. Let w, x, y, and z represent the thousand's, hundred's, ten's, and one's digits, respectively.

Translate.

The sum of the digits is 10.

$$w + x + y + z = 10$$

Twice the sum of the thousand's and ten's digits is the sum of the hundred's and one's digits less one.

$$2(w + y) = x + z - 1$$

The ten's digit is twice the thousand's digit.

$$y = 2 \cdot w$$

The one's digit equals the sum of the thousand's and hundred's digits.

$$z = w + x$$

We have a system of equations which can be written as

$$\begin{aligned} w + x + y + z &= 10, \\ 2w - x + 2y - z &= -1, \\ -2w + y &= 0, \\ w + x - z &= 0. \end{aligned}$$

Carry out. We can use matrices to solve the system. We get $(1, 3, 2, 4)$.

Check. The sum of the digits is 10. Twice the sum of 1 and 2 is 6. This is one less than the sum of 3 and 4. The ten's digit, 2, is twice the thousand's digit, 1. The one's digit, 4, equals $1 + 3$. The numbers check.

State. The number is 1324.

32. $x = \dfrac{ce - bf}{ae - bd}, \ y = \dfrac{af - cd}{ae - bd}$

Exercise Set 8.7

1. $C(x) = 25x + 270,000 \qquad R(x) = 70x$

a) $P(x) = R(x) - C(x)$

$\quad = 70x - (25x + 270,000)$

$\quad = 70x - 25x - 270,000$

$\quad = 45x - 270,000$

b) To find the break-even point we solve the system

$\quad R(x) = 70x,$

$\quad C(x) = 25x + 270,000.$

Since both $R(x)$ and $C(x)$ are in dollars and they are equal at the break-even point, we can rewrite the system:

$\quad d = 70x, \qquad\qquad (1)$

$\quad d = 25x + 270,000 \quad (2)$

We solve using substitution.

$\quad 70x = 25x + 270,000$ Substituting $65x$ for d in (2)

$\quad 45x = 270,000$

$\quad x = 6000$

Thus, 6000 units must be produced and sold in order to break even.

2. (a) $P(x) = 20x - 300,000$; (b) 15,000 units

3. $C(x) = 10x + 120,000 \qquad R(x) = 60x$

a) $P(x) = R(x) - C(x)$

$\quad = 60x - (10x + 120,000)$

$\quad = 60x - 10x - 120,000$

$\quad = 50x - 120,000$

b) Solve the system

$\quad R(x) = 60x,$

$\quad C(x) = 10x + 120,000.$

Since both $R(x)$ and $C(x)$ are in dollars and they are equal at the break-even point, we can rewrite the system:

$\quad d = 60x, \qquad\qquad (1)$

$\quad d = 10x + 120,000 \quad (2)$

We solve using substitution.

$\quad 60x = 10x + 120,000$ Substituting $60x$ for d in (2)

$\quad 50x = 120,000$

$\quad x = 2400$

Thus, 2400 units must be produced and sold in order to break even.

4. (a) $P(x) = 55x - 49,500$; (b) 900 units

5. $C(x) = 20x + 10,000 \qquad R(x) = 100x$

a) $P(x) = R(x) - C(x)$

$\quad = 100x - (20x + 10,000)$

$\quad = 100x - 20x - 10,000$

$\quad = 80x - 10,000$

b) Solve the system

$\quad R(x) = 100x,$

$\quad C(x) = 20x + 10,000.$

Since both $R(x)$ and $C(x)$ are in dollars and they are equal at the break-even point, we can rewrite the system:

$\quad d = 100x, \qquad\qquad (1)$

$\quad d = 20x + 10,000 \quad (2)$

We solve using substitution.

$\quad 100x = 20x + 10,000$ Substituting $100x$ for d in (2)

$\quad 80x = 10,000$

$\quad x = 125$

Thus, 125 units must be produced and sold in order to break even.

6. (a) $P(x) = 45x - 22,500$; (b) 500 units

7. $C(x) = 22x + 16,000 \qquad R(x) = 40x$

a) $P(x) = R(x) - C(x)$

$\quad = 40x - (22x + 16,000)$

$\quad = 40x - 22x - 16,000$

$\quad = 18x - 16,000$

b) Solve the system

$\quad R(x) = 40x,$

$\quad C(x) = 22x + 16,000.$

Since both $R(x)$ and $C(x)$ are in dollars and they are equal at the break-even point, we can rewrite the system:

$\quad d = 40x, \qquad\qquad (1)$

$\quad d = 22x + 16,000 \quad (2)$

We solve using substitution.

$\quad 40x = 22x + 16,000$ Substituting $40x$ for d in (2)

$\quad 18x = 16,000$

$\quad x \approx 889$ units

Thus, 889 units must be produced and sold in order to break even.

8. (a) $P(x) = 40x - 75,000$; (b) 1875 units

9. $C(x) = 50x + 195,000$ $R(x) = 125x$

a) $P(x) = R(x) - C(x)$

$\qquad = 125x - (50x + 195,000)$

$\qquad = 125x - 50x - 195,000$

$\qquad = 75x - 195,000$

b) Solve the system

$\qquad R(x) = 125x,$

$\qquad C(x) = 50x + 195,000.$

Since $R(x) = C(x)$ at the break-even point, we can rewrite the system:

$\qquad R(x) = 125x, \qquad\quad$ (1)

$\qquad R(x) = 50x + 195,000$ (2)

We solve using substitution.

$\quad 125x = 50x + 195,000$ Substituting $125x$
$\qquad\qquad\qquad\qquad\qquad\quad$ for $R(x)$ in (2)

$\quad\;\; 75x = 195,000$

$\qquad\;\; x = 2600$

To break even 2600 units must be produced and sold.

10. (a) $P(x) = 94x - 928,000$; (b) 9873 units

11. $D(p) = 1000 - 10p,$

$\quad S(p) = 230 + p$

Since both demand and supply are quantities, the system can be rewritten:

$\qquad q = 1000 - 10p,$ (1)

$\qquad q = 230 + p \qquad$ (2)

Substitute $1000 - 10p$ for q in (2) and solve.

$1000 - 10p = 230 + p$

$\qquad\;\; 770 = 11p$

$\qquad\;\;\; 70 = p$

The equilibrium price is \$70 per unit. To find the equilibrium quantity we substitute \$70 into either $D(p)$ or $S(p)$.

$D(70) = 1000 - 10 \cdot 70 = 1000 - 700 = 300$

The equilibrium quantity is 300 units.

The equilibrium point is (\$70, 300).

12. (\$10, 1400)

13. $D(p) = 760 - 13p,$

$\quad S(p) = 430 + 2p$

Rewrite the system:

$\qquad q = 760 - 13p,$ (1)

$\qquad q = 430 + 2p \qquad$ (2)

Substitute $760 - 13p$ for q in (2) and solve.

$760 - 13p = 430 + 2p$

$\qquad\;\; 330 = 15p$

$\qquad\;\;\; 22 = p$

The equilibrium price is \$22 per unit.

To find the equilibrium quantity we substitute \$22 into either $D(p)$ or $S(p)$.

$S(22) = 430 + 2(22) = 430 + 44 = 474$

The equilibrium quantity is 474 units.

The equilibrium point is (\$22, 474).

14. (\$10, 370)

15. $D(p) = 7500 - 25p,$

$\quad S(p) = 6000 + 5p$

Rewrite the system:

$\qquad q = 7500 - 25p,$ (1)

$\qquad q = 6000 + 5p \qquad$ (2)

Substitute $7500 - 25p$ for q in (2) and solve.

$7500 - 25p = 6000 + 5p$

$\qquad\;\; 1500 = 30p$

$\qquad\;\;\; 50 = p$

The equilibrium price is \$50 per unit.

To find the equilibrium quantity we substitute \$50 into either $D(p)$ or $S(p)$.

$D(50) = 7500 - 25(50) = 7500 - 1250 = 6250$

The equilibrium quantity is 6250 units.

The equilibrium point is (\$50, 6250).

16. (\$40, 7600)

17. $D(p) = 1600 - 53p,$

$\quad S(p) = 320 + 75p$

Rewrite the system:

$\qquad q = 1600 - 53p,$ (1)

$\qquad q = 320 + 75p \qquad$ (2)

Substitute $1600 - 53p$ for q in (2) and solve.

$1600 - 53p = 320 + 75p$

$\qquad\;\; 1280 = 128p$

$\qquad\;\;\; 10 = p$

The equilibrium price is \$10 per unit.

To find the equilibrium quantity we substitute \$10 into either $D(p)$ or $S(p)$.

$S(10) = 320 + 75(10) = 320 + 750 = 1070$

The equilibrium quantity is 1070 units.

The equilibrium point is (\$10, 1070).

18. ($36, 4060)

19. a) $C(x)$ = Fixed costs + Variable costs

$C(x) = 22,500 + 40x,$

where x is the number of lamps produced.

b) Each lamp sells for $85. The total revenue is 85 times the number of lamps sold. We assume that all lamps produced are sold.

$R(x) = 85x$

c) $P(x) = R(x) - C(x)$

$P(x) = 85x - (22,500 + 40x)$

$= 85x - 22,500 - 40x$

$= 45x - 22,500$

d) $P(3000) = 45(3000) - 22,500$

$= 135,000 - 22,500$

$= 112,500$

The company will realize a profit of $112,500 when 3000 lamps are produced and sold.

$P(400) = 45(400) - 22,500$

$= 18,000 - 22,500$

$= -4500$

The company will realize a $4500 loss when 400 lamps are produced and sold.

e) Solve the system

$R(x) = 85x,$

$C(x) = 22,500 + 40x.$

Since both $R(x)$ and $C(x)$ are in dollars and they are equal at the break-even point, we can rewrite the system:

$d = 85x,$ (1)

$d = 22,500 + 40x$ (2)

We solve using substitution.

$85x = 22,500 + 40x$ Substituting $85x$ for d

                        in (2)

$45x = 22,500$

$x = 500$

The firm will break even if it produces and sells 500 lamps and takes in a total of $R(500) = 85 \cdot 500 = \$42,500$ in revenue. Thus, the break-even point is (500 lamps, $42,500).

20. (a) $C(x) = 125,100 + 750x$; (b) $R(x) = 1050x$; (c) $P(x) = 300x - 125,100$;(d)$5100 loss, $84,900 profit; (e) (417 computers, $437,850)

21. a) $C(x)$ = Fixed costs + Variable costs

$C(x) = 16,404 + 6x,$

where x is the number of caps produced, in dozens.

b) Each dozen caps sell for $18. The total revenue is 18 times the number of caps sold, in dozens. We assume that all caps produced are sold.

$R(x) = 18x$

c) $P(x) = R(x) - C(x)$

$P(x) = 18x - (16,404 + 6x)$

$= 18x - 16,404 - 6x$

$= 12x - 16,404$

d) $P(3000) = 12(3000) - 16,404$

$= 36,000 - 16,404$

$= 19,596$

The company will realize a profit of $19,596 when 3000 dozen caps are produced and sold.

$P(1000) = 12(1000) - 16,404$

$= 12,000 - 16,404$

$= -4404$

The company will realize a $4404 loss when 1000 dozen caps are produced and sold.

e) Solve the system

$R(x) = 18x,$

$C(x) = 16,404 + 6x.$

Since both $R(x)$ and $C(x)$ are in dollars and they are equal at the break-even point, we can rewrite the system:

$d = 18x,$ (1)

$d = 16,404 + 6x$ (2)

We solve using substitution.

$18x = 16,404 + 6x$ Substituting $18x$ for d

                     in (2)

$12x = 16,404$

$x = 1367$

The firm will break even if it produces and sells 1367 dozen caps and takes in a total of $R(1367) = 18 \cdot 1367 = \$24,606$ in revenue. Thus, the break-even point is (1367 dozen caps, $24,606).

22. (a) $C(x) = 10,000 + 20x$; (b) $R(x) = 100x$; (c) $P(x) = 80x - 10,000$; (d) $150,000 profit, $6000 loss; (e) (125 sport coats, $12,500)

23. a) Use a grapher to find the first coordinate of the point of intersection of $y_1 = -14.97x + 987.35$ and $y_2 = 98.55x - 5.13$, to the nearest hundredth. It is 8.74, so the price per unit that should be charged is \$8.74.

b) Use a grapher to find the first coordinate of the point of intersection of $y_1 = 87,985 + 5.15x$ and $y_2 = 8.74x$. It is about $24,508.4$, so $24,509$ units must be sold in order to break even.

24. (a) (4526 units, \$4,309,156); (b) \$870

25. a) Enter the data and use the linear regression feature to get $S(p) = 15.97p - 1.05$.

b) Enter the data and use the linear regression feature to get $D(p) = -11.26p + 41.16$.

c) Find the point of intersection of the graphs of the functions found in parts (a) and (b).

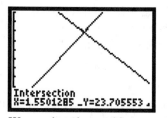

Intersection
X=1.5501285   Y=23.705553

We see that the equilibrium point is (\$1.55, 23.7 million jars).

26. (a) $S(p) = 3.8p - 1.82$; (b) $D(p) = -1.44p + 7.64$; (c) (\$1.81, 5.0 thousand)

27. $y - 3 = \dfrac{2}{5}(x - 1)$

The equation of the line is in point-slope form. We see that the line has slope $\dfrac{2}{5}$ and contains the point $(1, 3)$. Plot $(1, 3)$. Then go up two units and right 5 units to find another point on the line, $(6, 5)$. A third point can be found as a check.

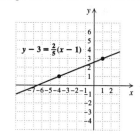

28. 5, 6

29.
$$9x = 5x - \{3(2x - 7) - 4\}$$
$$9x = 5x - \{6x - 21 - 4\}$$
$$9x = 5x - \{6x - 25\}$$
$$9x = 5x - 6x + 25$$
$$9x = -x + 25$$
$$10x = 25$$
$$x = \frac{25}{10}$$
$$x = \frac{5}{2}, \text{ or } 2.5$$

30. $t = \dfrac{rw - v}{-s}$, or $\dfrac{v - rw}{s}$

31.

32.

33. Using the given information we know that $C(x) = 15,400 + 100x$, where x is the number of pairs of speakers produced, and $R(x) = 250x$. Then
$$P(x) = R(x) - C(x)$$
$$= 250x - (15,400 + 100x)$$
$$= 250x - 15,400 - 100x$$
$$= 150x - 15,400$$

The fixed costs of two new facilities are $2 \cdot 15,400$, or \$30,800. We find the value of x for which the profit $P(x)$ is \$30,800:
$$150x - 15,400 = 30,800$$
$$150x = 46,200$$
$$x = 308$$

Thus, 308 pairs of speakers must be produced and sold in order to have enough profit to cover the fixed costs of two new facilities.

34. (\$5, 300)

Chapter 9

Exponents and Radical Functions

1. The square roots of 16 are 4 and -4, because $4^2 = 16$ and $(-4)^2 = 16$.

2. 15, -15

3. The square roots of 144 are 12 and -12, because $12^2 = 144$ and $(-12)^2 = 144$.

4. 3, -3

5. The square roots of 400 are 20 and -20, because $20^2 = 400$ and $(-20)^2 = 400$.

6. 9, -9

7. The square roots of 49 are 7 and -7, because $7^2 = 49$ and $(-7)^2 = 49$.

8. 30, -30

9. $-\sqrt{\dfrac{49}{36}} = -\dfrac{7}{6}$ Since $\sqrt{\dfrac{49}{36}} = \dfrac{7}{6}, -\sqrt{\dfrac{49}{36}} = -\dfrac{7}{6}$.

10. $-\dfrac{19}{3}$

11. $\sqrt{196} = 14$ Remember, $\sqrt{}$ indicates the principle square root.

12. 21

13. $-\sqrt{\dfrac{16}{81}} = -\dfrac{4}{9}$ Since $\sqrt{\dfrac{16}{81}} = \dfrac{4}{9}, -\sqrt{\dfrac{16}{81}} = -\dfrac{4}{9}$.

14. $-\dfrac{3}{4}$

15. $\sqrt{0.09} = 0.3$

16. 0.6

17. $-\sqrt{0.0049} = -0.07$

18. 0.12

19. $5\sqrt{p^2 + 4}$

The radicand is the expression written under the radical sign, $p^2 + 4$.

Since the index is not written, we know it is 2.

20. $y^2 - 8$; 2

21. $x^2 y^2 \sqrt{\dfrac{x}{y+4}}$

The radicand is the expression written under the radical sign, $\dfrac{x}{y+4}$.

The index is 3.

22. $\dfrac{a}{a^2 - b}$; 3

23. $\quad f(y) = \sqrt{5y - 10}$
$\quad f(6) = \sqrt{5 \cdot 6 - 10} = \sqrt{20}$
$\quad f(2) = \sqrt{5 \cdot 2 - 10} = \sqrt{0} = 0$
$\quad f(1) = \sqrt{5 \cdot 1 - 10} = \sqrt{-5}$

Since negative numbers do not have real-number square roots, $f(1)$ does not exist.

$\quad f(-1) = \sqrt{5(-1) - 10} = \sqrt{-15}$

Since negative numbers do not have real-number square roots, $f(-1)$ does not exist.

24. $\sqrt{11}$; does not exist; $\sqrt{11}$; 12

25. $\quad p(z) = \sqrt{2z^2 - 20}$
$\quad p(4) = \sqrt{2 \cdot 4^2 - 20} = \sqrt{12}$
$\quad p(3) = \sqrt{2 \cdot 3^2 - 20} = \sqrt{-2}$;
$\qquad p(3)$ does not exist.
$\quad p(-5) = \sqrt{2(-5)^2 - 20} = \sqrt{30}$
$\quad p(0) = \sqrt{2 \cdot 0^2 - 20} = \sqrt{-20}$;
$\qquad p(0)$ does not exist.

26. -2; -5; -4

27. $\quad g(x) = \sqrt{x^3 + 9}$
$\quad g(-2) = \sqrt{(-2)^3 + 9} = \sqrt{1} = 1$
$\quad g(-3) = \sqrt{(-3)^3 + 9} = \sqrt{-18}$;
$\qquad g(-3)$ does not exist.
$\quad g(3) = \sqrt{3^3 + 9} = \sqrt{36} = 6$

28. Does not exist; $\sqrt{17}$; $\sqrt{54}$

29. $\sqrt{25t^2} = \sqrt{(5t)^2} = |5t| = 5|t|$

Since t might be negative, absolute-value notation is necessary.

30. $4|x|$

31. $\sqrt{(-6b)^2} = |-6b| = |-6| \cdot |b| = 6|b|$

Since b might be negative, absolute-value notation is necessary.

32. $7|c|$

33. $\sqrt{(5-b)^2} = |5-b|$

Since $5-b$ might be negative, absolute-value notation is necessary.

34. $|a+1|$

35. $\sqrt{y^2 + 16y + 64} = \sqrt{(y+8)^2} = |y+8|$

Since $y+8$ might be negative, absolute-value notation is necessary.

36. $|x-2|$

37. $\sqrt{9x^2 - 30x + 25} = \sqrt{(3x-5)^2} = |3x-5|$

Since $3x-5$ might be negative, absolute-value notation is necessary.

38. $|2x+7|$

39. $-\sqrt[4]{256} = -4$ Since $4^4 = 256$

40. 5

41. $-\sqrt[5]{7^5} = -7$

42. -1

43. $\sqrt[5]{-\dfrac{1}{32}} = -\dfrac{1}{2}$ Since $\left(-\dfrac{1}{2}\right)^5 = -\dfrac{1}{32}$

44. $-\dfrac{2}{3}$

45. $\sqrt[8]{y^8} = |y|$

The index is even. Use absolute-value notation since y could have a negative value.

46. $|x|$

47. $\sqrt[4]{(7b)^4} = |7b| = 7|b|$

The index is even. Use absolute-value notation since b could have a negative value.

48. $5|a|$

49. $\sqrt[12]{(-10)^{12}} = |-10| = 10$

50. 6

51. $\sqrt[1976]{(2a+b)^{1976}} = |2a+b|$

The index is even. Use absolute-value notation since $2a+b$ could have a negative value.

52. $|a+b|$

53. $\sqrt{x^{12}} = x^6$ Note that $(x^6)^2 = x^{12}$; x^6 is nonnegative regardless of the value of x.

54. $|a^{11}|$

55. $\sqrt{a^{14}} = |a^7|$ Note that $(a^7)^2 = a^{14}$; a^7 could have a negative value.

56. x^8

57. $\sqrt{25t^2} = \sqrt{(5t)^2} = 5t$ Assuming t is nonnegative

58. $4x$

59. $\sqrt{(7c)^2} = 7c$ Assuming c is nonnegative

60. $6b$

61. $\sqrt{(5+b)^2} = 5+b$ Assuming $5+b$ is nonnegative

62. $a+1$

63. $\sqrt{9x^2 + 36x + 36} = \sqrt{9(x^2 + 4x + 4)} = \sqrt{[3(x+2)]^2} = 3(x+2), \text{ or } 3x+6$

64. $2x+2$

65. $-\sqrt[3]{64} = -4$ $(4^3 = 64)$

66. 3

67. $\sqrt[4]{81x^4} = \sqrt[4]{(3x)^4} = 3x$

68. $2x$

69. $-\sqrt[5]{-100,000} = -(-10) = 10$ $[(-10)^5 = -100,000]$

70. -6

71. $-\sqrt[3]{-64x^3} = -(-4x)$ $[(-4x)^3 = -64x^3]$
$= 4x$

72. $5y$

73. $\sqrt{a^{14}} = \sqrt{(a^7)^2} = a^7$

74. a^{11}

75. $\sqrt{(x+3)^{10}} = \sqrt{[(x+3)^5]^2} = (x+3)^5$

76. $(x-2)^4$

77. $f(x) = \sqrt[3]{x+1}$

$f(7) = \sqrt[3]{7+1} = \sqrt[3]{8} = 2$

$f(26) = \sqrt[3]{26+1} = \sqrt[3]{27} = 3$

$f(-9) = \sqrt[3]{-9+1} = \sqrt[3]{-8} = -2$

$f(-65) = \sqrt[3]{-65+1} = \sqrt[3]{-64} = -4$

78. 1; 5; 3; -5

79. $g(t) = \sqrt[4]{t-3}$

$g(19) = \sqrt[4]{19-3} = \sqrt[4]{16} = 2$

$g(-13) = \sqrt[4]{-13-3} = \sqrt[4]{-16};$

$g(-13)$ does not exist.

$g(1) = \sqrt[4]{1-3} = \sqrt[4]{-2};$

$g(1)$ does not exist.

$g(84) = \sqrt[4]{84-3} = \sqrt[4]{81} = 3$

80. 1; 2; does not exist; 3

81. $f(x) = \sqrt{x-5}$

Since the index is even, the radicand, $x-5$, must be nonnegative. We solve the inequality:

$x - 5 \geq 0$

$x \geq 5$

Domain of $f = \{x | x \geq 5\}$, or $[5, \infty)$

82. $[-8, \infty)$

83. $g(x) = \sqrt[4]{5-x}$

Since the index is even, the radicand, $5-x$, must be nonnegative. We solve the inequality:

$5 - x \geq 0$

$5 \geq x$

Domain of $g = \{x | x \leq 5\}$, or $(-\infty, 5]$

84. $(-\infty, \infty)$

85. $f(t) = \sqrt[5]{2t+9}$

Since the index is odd, the radicand can be any real number.

Domain of $f = \{t | t$ is a real number$\}$, or $(-\infty, \infty)$

86. $\left[-\dfrac{5}{2}, \infty\right)$

87. $h(z) = -\sqrt[6]{5z+3}$

Since the index is even, the radicand, $5z + 3$, must be nonnegative. We solve the inequality:

$5z + 3 \geq 0$

$5z \geq -3$

$z \geq -\dfrac{3}{5}$

Domain of $h = \left\{z \Big| z \geq -\dfrac{3}{5}\right\}$, or $\left[-\dfrac{3}{5}, \infty\right)$

88. $\left[\dfrac{5}{7}, \infty\right)$

89. $f(x) = \sqrt{5-x}$

Find all values of x for which the radicand is non-negative.

$5 - x \geq 0$

$5 \geq x$

The domain is $\{x | x \leq 5\}$, or $(-\infty, 5]$.

We graph the function in the standard window.

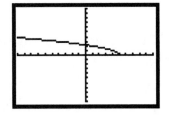

The range appears to be $[0, \infty)$.

90. Domain: $\left[-\dfrac{1}{2}, \infty\right)$; range: $[0, \infty)$

91. $f(x) = 1 - \sqrt{x+1}$

Find all values of x for which the radicand is non-negative.

$x + 1 \geq 0$

$x \geq -1$

The domain is $\{x | x \geq -1\}$, or $[-1, \infty)$.

We graph the function in the window $[-10, 10, -5, 5]$.

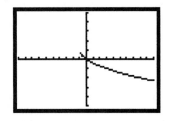

The range appears to be $(-\infty, 1]$.

92. Domain: $\left[\dfrac{5}{3}, \infty\right)$; range: $[2, \infty)$

93. $g(x) = 3 + \sqrt{x^2 + 4}$

Since $x^2 + 4$ is positive for all values of x, the domain is $\{x | x$ is a real number$\}$, or $(-\infty, \infty)$.

We graph the function in the standard window.

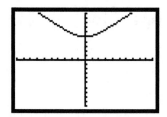

The range appears to be $[5, \infty)$.

94. Domain: $(-\infty, \infty)$; range: $(-\infty, 4]$

95. For $f(x) = \sqrt{x-4}$, the domain is $[4, \infty)$ and all of the function values are nonnegative. Graph (c) corresponds to this function.

96. (a)

97. For $h(x) = \sqrt{x^2 + 4}$, the domain is $(-\infty, \infty)$. Graph (d) corresponds to this function.

98. (b)

99. A scatterplot of the data shows that it could be modeled with a radical function.

100. Yes

101. A scatterplot of the data shows that it cannot be modeled well with a radical function.

102. No

103. $(a^3 b^2 c^5)^3 = a^{3 \cdot 3} b^{2 \cdot 3} c^{5 \cdot 3} = a^9 b^6 c^{15}$

104. $10a^{10}b^9$

105. $(x-3)(x+3) = x^2 - 3^2 = x^2 - 9$

106. $a^2 - b^2 x^2$

107.
$$(2x+1)(x^2 - 3x + 1)$$
$$= 2x^3 - 6x^2 + 2x + x^2 - 3x + 1$$
$$= 2x^3 - 5x^2 - x + 1$$

108. $x^3 - 3x^2 + 7x - 5$

109. ◈

110. ◈

111. ◈

112. ◈

113. $N = 2.5\sqrt{A}$

a) $N = 2.5\sqrt{25} = 2.5(5) = 12.5 \approx 13$

b) $N = 2.5\sqrt{36} = 2.5(6) = 15$

c) $N = 2.5\sqrt{49} = 2.5(7) = 17.5 \approx 18$

d) $N = 2.5\sqrt{64} = 2.5(8) = 20$

114. $[-3, 2)$

115. $g(x) = \dfrac{\sqrt[4]{5-x}}{\sqrt[6]{x+4}}$

The radical expression in the numerator has an even index, so the radicand, $5 - x$, must be nonnegative. We solve the inequality:
$$5 - x \geq 0$$
$$5 \geq x$$

The radical expression in the denominator also has an even index, so the radicand, $x + 4$, must be nonnegative in order for $\sqrt[6]{x+4}$ to exist. In addition, the denominator cannot be zero, so the radicand must be positive. We solve the inequality:
$$x + 4 > 0$$
$$x > -4$$

We have $x \leq 5$ *and* $x > -4$ so

Domain of $g = \{x | -4 < x \leq 5\}$, or $(-4, 5]$.

Exercise Set 9.2

1. $x^{1/4} = \sqrt[4]{x}$

2. $\sqrt[5]{y}$

3. $(16)^{1/2} = \sqrt{16} = 4$

4. 2

5. $81^{1/4} = \sqrt[4]{81} = 3$

6. 2

7. $(xyz)^{1/3} = \sqrt[3]{xyz}$

8. $\sqrt[4]{ab}$

9. $(a^2 b^2)^{1/5} = \sqrt[5]{a^2 b^2}$

10. $\sqrt[4]{x^3 y^3}$

11. $a^{2/3} = \sqrt[3]{a^2}$

12. $\sqrt{b^3}$

13. $16^{3/4} = \sqrt[4]{16^3} = (\sqrt[4]{16})^3 = 2^3 = 8$

14. 128

15. $49^{3/2} = \sqrt{49^3} = (\sqrt{49})^3 = 7^3 = 343$

16. 243

17. $(81x)^{3/4} = \sqrt[4]{(81x)^3} = \sqrt[4]{81^3 x^3}$, or $\sqrt[4]{81^3} \cdot \sqrt[4]{x^3} = (\sqrt[4]{81})^3 \cdot \sqrt[4]{x^3} = 3^3 \sqrt[4]{x^3} = 27\sqrt[4]{x^3}$

18. $25\sqrt[3]{a^2}$

19. $(25x^4)^{3/2} = \sqrt{(25x^4)^3} = \sqrt{25^3 \cdot x^{12}} = \sqrt{25^3} \cdot \sqrt{x^{12}} = (\sqrt{25})^3 x^6 = 5^3 x^6 = 125 x^6$

20. $27y^9$

21. $\sqrt[3]{20} = 20^{1/3}$

22. $19^{1/3}$

23. $\sqrt{17} = 17^{1/2}$

24. $6^{1/2}$

25. $\sqrt{x^3} = x^{3/2}$

26. $a^{5/2}$

27. $\sqrt[5]{m^2} = m^{2/5}$

28. $n^{4/5}$

29. $\sqrt[4]{cd} = (cd)^{1/4}$ Parentheses are required.

30. $(xy)^{1/5}$

31. $\sqrt[5]{xy^2z} = (xy^2z)^{1/5}$

32. $(x^3y^2z^2)^{1/7}$

33. $(\sqrt{3mn})^3 = (3mn)^{3/2}$

34. $(7xy)^{4/3}$

35. $(\sqrt[7]{8x^2y})^5 = (8x^2y)^{5/7}$

36. $(2a^5b)^{7/6}$

37. $\dfrac{2x}{\sqrt[3]{z^2}} = \dfrac{2x}{z^{2/3}}$

38. $\dfrac{3a}{c^{2/5}}$

39. $x^{-1/3} = \dfrac{1}{x^{1/3}}$

40. $\dfrac{1}{y^{1/4}}$

41. $(2rs)^{-3/4} = \dfrac{1}{(2rs)^{3/4}}$

42. $\dfrac{1}{(5xy)^{5/6}}$

43. $\left(\dfrac{1}{10}\right)^{-2/3} = \left(\dfrac{10}{1}\right)^{2/3}$

$= 10^{2/3}$ Finding the reciprocal of the base and changing the sign of the exponent

44. $8^{3/4}$

45. $\dfrac{1}{a^{-5/7}} = a^{5/7}$

46. $a^{3/5}$

47. $2a^{3/4}b^{-1/2}c^{2/3} = 2 \cdot a^{3/4} \cdot \dfrac{1}{b^{1/2}} \cdot c^{2/3} = \dfrac{2a^{3/4}c^{2/3}}{b^{1/2}}$

48. $\dfrac{5y^{4/5}z}{x^{2/3}}$

49. $\left(\dfrac{7x}{8yx}\right)^{-3/5} = \left(\dfrac{8yz}{7x}\right)^{3/5}$ Finding the reciprocal of the base and changing the sign of the exponent

50. $\left(\dfrac{3c}{2ab}\right)^{5/6}$

51. $\dfrac{7x}{\sqrt[3]{z}} = \dfrac{7x}{z^{1/3}}$

52. $\dfrac{6a}{b^{1/4}}$

53. $\dfrac{5a}{3c^{-1/2}} = \dfrac{5a}{3} \cdot c^{1/2} = \dfrac{5ac^{1/2}}{3}$

54. $\dfrac{2x^{1/3}z}{5}$

55. $f(x) = \sqrt[4]{x+7} = (x+7)^{1/4}$

Enter $y = (x+7) \wedge (1/4)$, or $y = (x+7) \wedge 0.25$.

Since the index is even, the domain of the function is the set of all x for which the radicand is nonnegative, or $[-7, \infty)$. One good choice of a viewing window is $[-10, 25, -1, 5]$, Xscl $= 5$.

$$y = (x+7)^{1/4}$$

Xscl = 5

56.

$y = (4 - x)^{1/5}$

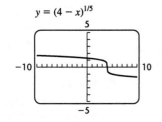

57. $r(x) = \sqrt[7]{3x - 2} = (3x - 2)^{1/7}$

Enter $y = (3x - 2) \wedge (1/7)$. Since the index is odd the domain of the function is $(-\infty, \infty)$. One good choice of a viewing window is $[-10, 10, -5, 5]$.

$y = (3x - 2)^{1/7}$

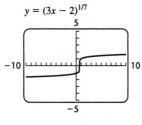

58.

$y = (2x + 3)^{1/6}$

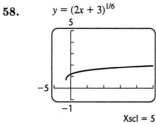

Xscl = 5

59. $f(x) = \sqrt[6]{x^3} = (x^3)^{1/6} = x^{3/6}$

Enter $y = x \wedge (3/6)$. The function is defined only for nonnegative value of x, so the domain is $[0, \infty)$. One good choice of a window is $[-5, 25, -1, 5]$, Xscl = 5.

$y = x^{3/6}$

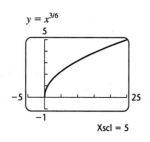

Xscl = 5

60.

$y = x^{2/8}$

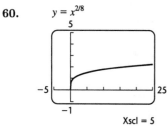

Xscl = 5

61. $\sqrt[5]{9} = 9^{1/5} = 9 \wedge (1/5) \approx 1.552$

62. 1.533

63. $\sqrt[4]{10} = 10^{1/4} = 10 \wedge (1/4) \approx 1.778$

64. -1.998

65. $\sqrt[3]{(-3)^5} = (-3)^{5/3} = (-3) \wedge (5/3) \approx -6.240$

66. 1.275

67. $5^{3/4} \cdot 5^{1/8} = 5^{3/4+1/8} = 5^{6/8+1/8} = 5^{7/8}$

We added exponents after finding a common denominator.

68. $11^{7/6}$

69. $\dfrac{3^{5/8}}{3^{-1/8}} = 3^{5/8-(-1/8)} = 3^{5/8+1/8} = 3^{6/8} = 3^{3/4}$

We subtracted exponents and simplified.

70. $8^{9/11}$

71. $(10^{3/5})^{2/5} = 10^{3/5 \cdot 2/5} = 10^{6/25}$

We multiplied exponents.

72. $5^{15/28}$

73. $a^{2/3} \cdot a^{5/4} = a^{2/3+5/4} = a^{8/12+15/12} = a^{23/12}$

We added exponents after finding a common denominator.

74. $x^{17/12}$

75. $(x^{2/3})^{-3/7} = x^{2/3(-3/7)} = x^{-2/7} = \dfrac{1}{x^{2/7}}$

We multiplied exponents, simplified, and wrote the result without a negative exponent.

76. $\dfrac{1}{a^{1/3}}$

77. $(m^{2/3}n^{-1/4})^{1/2} = m^{2/3 \cdot 1/2}n^{-1/4 \cdot 1/2} = m^{1/3}n^{-1/8} = m^{1/3} \cdot \dfrac{1}{n^{1/8}} = \dfrac{m^{1/3}}{n^{1/8}}$

78. $\dfrac{y^{1/10}}{x^{1/12}}$

79. $\sqrt[6]{a^2} = a^{2/6}$ Converting to exponential notation

$= a^{1/3}$ Simplifying the exponent

$= \sqrt[3]{a}$ Returning to radical notation

80. $\sqrt[3]{t^2}$

81. $\sqrt[3]{x^{15}} = x^{15/3}$ Converting to exponential notation

$= x^5$ Simplifying

82. a^3

83. $(\sqrt[3]{ab})^{15} = (ab)^{15/3}$ Converting to exponential
                                           notation

$\qquad = (ab)^5$ Simplifying the exponent

$\qquad = a^5 b^5$ Using the law of exponents

84. $x^2 y^2$

85. $\sqrt[8]{(3x)^2} = (3x)^{2/8}$ Converting to exponential
                                        notation

$\qquad = (3x)^{1/4}$ Simplifying the exponent

$\qquad = \sqrt[4]{3x}$ Returning to radical notation

86. $\sqrt{7a}$

87. $(\sqrt[10]{3a})^5 = (3a)^{5/10}$ Converting to exponential
                                          notation

$\qquad = (3a)^{1/2}$ Simplifying the exponent

$\qquad = \sqrt{3a}$ Returning to radical
                        notation

88. $\sqrt[4]{8x^3}$

89. $\sqrt[4]{\sqrt{x}} = \sqrt[4]{x^{1/2}}$ Converting to

$\qquad = (x^{1/2})^{1/4}$ exponential notation

$\qquad = x^{1/8}$ Using a law of exponents

$\qquad = \sqrt[8]{x}$ Returning to radical
                        notation

90. $\sqrt[18]{m}$

91. $\sqrt{(ab)^6} = (ab)^{6/2}$ Converting to exponential
                                     notation

$\qquad = (ab)^3$ Using the laws

$\qquad = a^3 b^3$ of exponents

92. $x^3 y^3$

93. $(\sqrt[3]{x^2 y^5})^{12} = (x^2 y^5)^{12/3}$ Converting to
                                                      exponential notation

$\qquad = (x^2 y^5)^4$ Simplifying the
                          exponent

$\qquad = x^8 y^{20}$ Using the laws
                        of exponents

94. $a^6 b^{12}$

95. $\sqrt[3]{\sqrt[4]{xy}} = \sqrt[3]{(xy)^{1/4}}$ Converting to

$\qquad = [(xy)^{1/4}]^{1/3}$ exponential notation

$\qquad = (xy)^{1/12}$ Using a law of exponents

$\qquad = \sqrt[12]{xy}$ Returning to radical notation

96. $\sqrt[10]{2a}$

97. $\qquad x^2 - 1 = 8$

$\qquad x^2 - 9 = 0$

$(x+3)(x-3) = 0$

$x + 3 = 0 \quad or \quad x - 3 = 0$

$\qquad x = -3 \quad or \qquad x = 3$

Both values check. The solutions are -3 and 3.

98. $-\dfrac{11}{2}$

99. $\dfrac{1}{x} + 2 = 5$

$\qquad \dfrac{1}{x} = 3$

$x \cdot \dfrac{1}{x} = x \cdot 3$

$\qquad 1 = 3x$

$\qquad \dfrac{1}{3} = x$

This value checks. The solution is $\dfrac{1}{3}$.

100. $-7, 7$

101. *Familiarize.* Let p = the selling price of the home.

Translate.

$\underbrace{0.5\% \text{ of the selling price}}$ is \$467.50

$\qquad\qquad 0.005p \qquad\qquad = \quad 467.50$

Carry out. We solve the equation.

$\qquad 0.005p = 467.50$

$\qquad p = 93,500$ Dividing by 0.005

Check. 0.5% of \$93,500 is 0.005(\$93,500), or \$467.50. The answer checks.

State. The selling price of the home was \$93,500.

102. $0, 1$

103. ◈

104. ◈

105. ◈

106. ◈

107. $\sqrt[5]{x^2 y \sqrt{xy}} = \sqrt[5]{x^2 y (xy)^{1/2}} = \sqrt[5]{x^2 y x^{1/2} y^{1/2}} =$
$\sqrt[5]{x^{5/2} y^{3/2}} = (x^{5/2} y^{3/2})^{1/5} = x^{5/10} y^{3/10} =$
$(x^5 y^3)^{1/10} = \sqrt[10]{x^5 y^3}$

108. $\sqrt[6]{x^5}$

109. $\sqrt[4]{\sqrt[3]{8x^3y^6}} = \sqrt[4]{(2^3x^3y^6)^{1/3}} = \sqrt[4]{2^{3/3}x^{3/3}y^{6/3}} =$
$\sqrt[4]{2xy^2}$

110. $\sqrt[6]{p+q}$

111. a) $L = \dfrac{(0.000169)60^{2.27}}{1} \approx 1.8$ m

b) $L = \dfrac{(0.000169)75^{2.27}}{0.9906} \approx 3.1$ m

c) $L = \dfrac{(0.000169)80^{2.27}}{2.4} \approx 1.5$ m

d) $L = \dfrac{(0.000169)100^{2.27}}{1.1} \approx 5.3$ m

112. About 7.937×10^{-13} to 1

113. $m = m_0(1 - v^2c^{-2})^{-1/2}$

$m = 8\left[1 - \left(\dfrac{9}{5} \times 10^8\right)^2 (3 \times 10^8)^{-2}\right]^{-1/2}$

$= 8\left[1 - \dfrac{\left(\dfrac{9}{5} \times 10^8\right)^2}{(3 \times 10^8)^2}\right]^{-1/2}$

$= 8\left[1 - \dfrac{\dfrac{81}{25} \times 10^{16}}{9 \times 10^6}\right]^{-1/2}$

$= 8\left[1 - \dfrac{81}{25} \cdot \dfrac{1}{9}\right]^{-1/2}$

$= 8\left[1 - \dfrac{9}{25}\right]^{-1/2}$

$= 8\left(\dfrac{16}{25}\right)^{-1/2} = 8\left(\dfrac{25}{16}\right)^{1/2}$

$= 8 \cdot \dfrac{5}{4}$

$= 10$

The particle's new mass is 10 mg.

114.

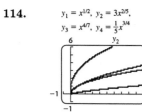

$y_1 = x^{1/2}, \ y_2 = 3x^{2/5},$
$y_3 = x^{4/7}, \ y_4 = \frac{1}{5}x^{3/4}$

Exercise Set 9.3

1. $\sqrt{6}\sqrt{7} = \sqrt{6 \cdot 7} = \sqrt{42}$

2. $\sqrt{35}$

3. $\sqrt[3]{2}\sqrt[3]{5} = \sqrt[3]{2 \cdot 5} = \sqrt[3]{10}$

4. $\sqrt[4]{18}$

5. $\sqrt{5a}\sqrt{3b} = \sqrt{5a \cdot 3b} = \sqrt{15ab}$

6. $\sqrt{26xy}$

7. $\sqrt[5]{9t^2}\sqrt[5]{2t} = \sqrt[5]{9t^2 \cdot 2t} = \sqrt[5]{18t^3}$

8. $\sqrt[5]{80y^4}$

9. $\sqrt{x-a}\sqrt{x+a} = \sqrt{(x-a)(x+a)} = \sqrt{x^2-a^2}$

10. $\sqrt{y^2-b^2}$

11. $\sqrt[3]{0.5x}\sqrt[3]{0.2x} = \sqrt[3]{0.5x \cdot 0.2x} = \sqrt[3]{0.1x^2}$

12. $\sqrt[3]{0.21y^2}$

13. $\sqrt{\dfrac{x}{5}}\sqrt{\dfrac{3}{y}} = \sqrt{\dfrac{x}{5} \cdot \dfrac{3}{y}} = \sqrt{\dfrac{3x}{5y}}$

14. $\sqrt{\dfrac{7s}{11t}}$

15. $\sqrt[7]{\dfrac{x-3}{4}}\sqrt[7]{\dfrac{5}{x+2}} = \sqrt[7]{\dfrac{x-3}{4} \cdot \dfrac{5}{x+2}} = \sqrt[7]{\dfrac{5x-15}{4x+8}}$

16. $\sqrt[6]{\dfrac{3a}{b^2-4}}$

17. $\quad \sqrt[3]{5} \cdot \sqrt{6}$

$= 5^{1/3} \cdot 6^{1/2}$ Converting to exponential nota-tion

$= 5^{2/6} \cdot 6^{3/6}$ Rewriting so that exponents have a common denominator

$= (5^2 \cdot 6^3)^{1/6}$ Using the laws of exponents

$= \sqrt[6]{25 \cdot 216}$ Squaring 5, cubing 6, and returning to radical notation

$= \sqrt[6]{5400}$ Multiplying under the radical

18. $\sqrt[12]{300,125}$

19. $\sqrt{x}\sqrt[3]{7y} = x^{1/2}(7y)^{1/3} = x^{3/6}(7y)^{2/6} =$
$[x^3(7y)^2]^{1/6} = \sqrt[6]{x^3 \cdot 49y^2} = \sqrt[6]{49x^3y^2}$

20. $\sqrt[15]{27y^5z^3}$

21. $\sqrt{x}\sqrt[3]{x-2} = x^{1/2}\cdot(x-2)^{1/3} =$
$x^{3/6}\cdot(x-2)^{2/6} = [x^3(x-2)^2]^{1/6} = \sqrt[6]{x^3(x-2)^2} =$
$\sqrt[6]{x^3(x^2-4x+4)} = \sqrt[6]{x^5-4x^4+4x^3}$

22. $\sqrt[4]{3xy^2+24xy+48x}$

23. $\sqrt[5]{yx^2}\sqrt{xy} = (yx^2)^{1/5}(xy)^{1/2} = y^{1/5}x^{2/5}x^{1/2}y^{1/2} =$
$x^{2/5+1/2}y^{1/5+1/2} = x^{4/10+5/10}y^{2/10+5/10} =$
$x^{9/10}y^{7/10} = (x^9y^7)^{1/10} = \sqrt[10]{x^9y^7}$

24. $\sqrt[10]{4a^9b^9}$

25. $\sqrt[4]{xy^2}\sqrt[3]{x^2y} = (xy^2)^{1/4}(x^2y)^{1/3} =$
$(xy^2)^{3/12}(x^2y)^{4/12} = [(xy^2)^3(x^2y)^4]^{1/12} =$
$\sqrt[12]{x^3y^6\cdot x^8y^4} = \sqrt[12]{x^{11}y^{10}}$

26. $\sqrt[20]{a^{18}b^{17}}$

27. $\sqrt{27}$
$= \sqrt{9\cdot3}$ 9 is the largest perfect square factor of 27.
$= \sqrt{9}\cdot\sqrt{3}$
$= 3\sqrt{3}$

28. $2\sqrt{7}$

29. $\sqrt{12}$
$= \sqrt{4\cdot3}$ 4 is the largest perfect square factor of 12.
$= \sqrt{4}\cdot\sqrt{3}$
$= 2\sqrt{3}$

30. $3\sqrt{5}$

31. $\sqrt{8} = \sqrt{4\cdot2} = \sqrt{4}\cdot\sqrt{2} = 2\sqrt{2}$

32. $3\sqrt{2}$

33. $\sqrt{44} = \sqrt{4\cdot11} = \sqrt{4}\cdot\sqrt{11} = 2\sqrt{11}$

34. $2\sqrt{6}$

35. $\sqrt{36a^4b}$
$= \sqrt{36a^4\cdot b}$ $36a^4$ is a perfect square.
$= \sqrt{36a^4}\cdot\sqrt{b}$ Factoring into two radicals
$= 6a^2\sqrt{b}$ Taking the square root of $36a^4$

36. $5y^4\sqrt{7}$

37. $\sqrt[3]{8x^3y^2}$
$= \sqrt[3]{8x^3\cdot y^2}$ $8x^3$ is a perfect cube.
$= \sqrt[3]{8x^3}\cdot\sqrt[3]{y^2}$ Factoring into two radicals
$= 2x\sqrt[3]{y^2}$ Taking the cube root of $8x^3$

38. $3b^2\sqrt[3]{a}$

39. $\sqrt[3]{-16x^6}$
$= \sqrt[3]{-8x^6\cdot2}$ $-8x^6$ is a perfect cube.
$= \sqrt[3]{-8x^6}\cdot\sqrt[3]{2}$
$= -2x^2\sqrt[3]{2}$ Taking the cube root of $-8x^6$

40. $-2a^2\sqrt[3]{4}$

41. $f(x) = \sqrt[3]{125x^5}$
$= \sqrt[3]{125x^3\cdot x^2}$
$= \sqrt[3]{125x^3}\cdot\sqrt[3]{x^2}$
$= 5x\sqrt[3]{x^2}$

42. $f(x) = 2x^2\sqrt[3]{2}$

43. $f(x) = \sqrt{49(x+5)^2}$ $49(x+5)^2$ is a perfect square.
$= |7(x+5)|$, or $7|x+5|$

44. $f(x) = |9(x-1)|$, or $9|x-1|$

45. $f(x) = \sqrt{5x^2-10x+5}$
$= \sqrt{5(x^2-2x+1)}$
$= \sqrt{5(x-1)^2}$
$= \sqrt{(x-1)^2}\cdot\sqrt{5}$
$= |x-1|\sqrt{5}$

46. $f(x) = |x+2|\sqrt{2}$

47. $\sqrt{a^3b^4}$
$= \sqrt{a^2\cdot a\cdot b^4}$ Identifying the largest even powers of a and b
$= \sqrt{a^2}\sqrt{b^4}\sqrt{a}$ Factoring into several radicals
$= ab^2\sqrt{a}$

48. $x^3y^4\sqrt{y}$

49. $\sqrt[3]{x^5y^6z^{10}}$
$= \sqrt[3]{x^3\cdot x^2\cdot y^6\cdot z^9\cdot z}$ Identifying the largest perfect-cube powers of x, y, and z
$= \sqrt[3]{x^3}\cdot\sqrt[3]{y^6}\cdot\sqrt[3]{z^9}\cdot\sqrt[3]{x^2z}$ Factoring into several radicals
$= xy^2z^3\sqrt[3]{x^2z}$

50. $a^2b^2c^4\sqrt[3]{bc}$

51. $\sqrt[5]{-32a^7b^{11}} = \sqrt[5]{-32 \cdot a^5 \cdot a^2 \cdot b^{10} \cdot b} =$
$\sqrt[5]{-32}\sqrt[5]{a^5}\sqrt[5]{b^{10}}\sqrt[5]{a^2b} = -2ab^2\sqrt[5]{a^2b}$

52. $2xy^2\sqrt[4]{xy^3}$

53. $\sqrt[5]{a^6b^{12}c^7} = \sqrt[5]{a^5 \cdot a \cdot b^{10} \cdot b^2 \cdot c^5 \cdot c^2} =$
$\sqrt[5]{a^5} \cdot \sqrt[5]{b^{10}} \cdot \sqrt[5]{c^5}\sqrt[5]{ab^2c^2} =$
$ab^2c\sqrt[5]{ab^2c^2}$

54. $x^2yz^3\sqrt[5]{x^3y^3z^2}$

55. $\sqrt[4]{810x^9} = \sqrt[4]{81 \cdot 10 \cdot x^8 \cdot x} =$
$\sqrt[4]{81} \cdot \sqrt[4]{x^8} \cdot \sqrt[4]{10x} = 3x^2\sqrt[4]{10x}$

56. $-2a^4\sqrt[3]{10a^2}$

57. $3\sqrt{7} + 2\sqrt{7} = (3+2)\sqrt{7} = 5\sqrt{7}$

58. $17\sqrt{5}$

59. $4\sqrt[3]{y} + 9\sqrt[3]{y} = (4+9)\sqrt[3]{y} = 13\sqrt[3]{y}$

60. $6\sqrt[4]{t}$

61. $8\sqrt{2} - 6\sqrt{2} + 5\sqrt{2} = (8-6+5)\sqrt{2} = 7\sqrt{2}$

62. $7\sqrt{6}$

63. $9\sqrt[3]{7} - \sqrt{3} + 4\sqrt[3]{7} + 2\sqrt{3} =$
$(9+4)\sqrt[3]{7} + (-1+2)\sqrt{3} = 13\sqrt[3]{7} + \sqrt{3}$

64. $6\sqrt{7} + \sqrt[4]{11}$

65. $\qquad 8\sqrt{27} - 3\sqrt{3}$
$= 8\sqrt{9 \cdot 3} - 3\sqrt{3} \qquad$ Factoring the
$= 8\sqrt{9} \cdot \sqrt{3} - 3\sqrt{3} \qquad$ first radical
$= 8 \cdot 3\sqrt{3} - 3\sqrt{3} \qquad$ Taking the square root of 9
$= 24\sqrt{3} - 3\sqrt{3}$
$= 21\sqrt{3} \qquad$ Combining like radicals

66. $41\sqrt{2}$

67. $\qquad 3\sqrt{45} + 7\sqrt{20}$
$= 3\sqrt{9 \cdot 5} + 7\sqrt{4 \cdot 5} \qquad$ Factoring the
$= 3\sqrt{9} \cdot \sqrt{5} + 7\sqrt{4} \cdot \sqrt{5} \qquad$ radicals
$= 3 \cdot 3\sqrt{5} + 7 \cdot 2\sqrt{5} \qquad$ Taking the square roots
$= 9\sqrt{5} + 14\sqrt{5}$
$= 23\sqrt{5} \qquad$ Combining like radicals

68. $58\sqrt{3}$

69. $3\sqrt[3]{16} + \sqrt[3]{54} = 3\sqrt[3]{8 \cdot 2} + \sqrt[3]{27 \cdot 2} =$
$3\sqrt[3]{8} \cdot \sqrt[3]{2} + \sqrt[3]{27} \cdot \sqrt[3]{2} = 3 \cdot 2\sqrt[3]{2} + 3\sqrt[3]{2} =$
$6\sqrt[3]{2} + 3\sqrt[3]{2} = 9\sqrt[3]{2}$

70. -7

71. $\sqrt{5a} + 2\sqrt{45a^3} = \sqrt{5a} + 2\sqrt{9a^2 \cdot 5a} =$
$\sqrt{5a} + 2\sqrt{9a^2} \cdot \sqrt{5a} = \sqrt{5a} + 2 \cdot 3a\sqrt{5a} =$
$\sqrt{5a} + 6a\sqrt{5a} = (1 + 6a)\sqrt{5a}$

72. $4(4x - 2)\sqrt{3x}$

73. $\sqrt[3]{6x^4} + \sqrt[3]{48x} = \sqrt[3]{x^3 \cdot 6x} + \sqrt[3]{8 \cdot 6x} =$
$\sqrt[3]{x^3} \cdot \sqrt[3]{6x} + \sqrt[3]{8} \cdot \sqrt[3]{6x} = x\sqrt[3]{6x} + 2\sqrt[3]{6x} =$
$(x + 2)\sqrt[3]{6x}$

74. $(3 - x)\sqrt[3]{2x}$

75. $\sqrt{4a - 4} + \sqrt{a - 1} = \sqrt{4(a - 4)} + \sqrt{a - 1} =$
$\sqrt{4}\sqrt{a - 1} + \sqrt{a - 1} = 2\sqrt{a - 1} + \sqrt{a - 1} = 3\sqrt{a - 1}$

76. $4\sqrt{y + 3}$

77. $\sqrt{x^3 - x^2} + \sqrt{9x - 9} = \sqrt{x^2(x - 1)} + \sqrt{9(x - 1)} =$
$\sqrt{x^2} \cdot \sqrt{x - 1} + \sqrt{9} \cdot \sqrt{x - 1} =$
$x\sqrt{x - 1} + 3\sqrt{x - 1} = (x + 3)\sqrt{x - 1}$

78. $(2 - x)\sqrt{x - 1}$

79. $f(x) = \sqrt{20x^2 + 4x^3} - 3x\sqrt{45 + 9x} + \sqrt{5x^2 + x^3}$
$= \sqrt{4x^2(5 + x)} - 3x\sqrt{9(5 + x)} + \sqrt{x^2(5 + x)}$
$= \sqrt{4x^2}\sqrt{5 + x} - 3x\sqrt{9}\sqrt{5 + x} + \sqrt{x^2}\sqrt{5 + x}$
$= 2x\sqrt{5 + x} - 3x \cdot 3\sqrt{5 + x} + x\sqrt{5 + x}$
$= 2x\sqrt{5 + x} - 9x\sqrt{5 + x} + x\sqrt{5 + x}$
$= -6x\sqrt{5 + x}$

80. $f(x) = 2x\sqrt{x - 1}$

81. $f(x) = \sqrt[4]{x^5 - x^4} + 3\sqrt[4]{x^9 - x^8}$
$= \sqrt[4]{x^4(x - 1)} + 3\sqrt[4]{x^8(x - 1)}$
$= \sqrt[4]{x^4} \cdot \sqrt[4]{x - 1} + 3\sqrt[4]{x^8}\sqrt[4]{x - 1}$
$= x\sqrt[4]{x - 1} + 3x^2\sqrt[4]{x - 1}$
$= (x + 3x^2)\sqrt[4]{x - 1}$

82. $f(x) = (2x - 2x^2)\sqrt[4]{1 + x}$

83. Familiarize. Let x and y represent the number of 30-sec and 60-sec commercials, respectively. Then the total number of minutes of commercial time during the show is $\dfrac{30x + 60y}{60}$, or $\dfrac{x}{2} + y$. (We divide by 60 to convert seconds to minutes.)

Translate. Rewording when necessary, we write two equations.

$$\underbrace{\text{Total number of commercials}}_{x + y} \underbrace{\text{is}}_{=} \underbrace{\text{12.}}_{12}$$

$$\underbrace{\begin{array}{c}\text{Number of}\\ \text{30-sec}\\ \text{commercials}\end{array}}_{x} \underbrace{\text{is}}_{=} \underbrace{\begin{array}{c}\text{total minutes}\\ \text{of commercial}\\ \text{time}\end{array}}_{\frac{x}{2} + y} \underbrace{\text{less 6.}}_{-\quad 6}$$

Carry out. Solving the system of equations, we get $(4,8)$.

Check. If there are 4 30-sec and 8 60-sec commercials, the total number of commercials is 12. The total amount of commercial time is $4 \cdot 30$ sec $+ 8 \cdot 60$ sec $= 600$ sec, or 10 min. Then the number of 30-sec commercials is 6 less than the total number of minutes of commercial time. The values check.

State. 8 60-sec commercials were used.

84. $5x^3 + 5x^2 - 3x - 16$

85. $\quad (7a^3b^2 + 5a^2b^2 - a^2b) + (2a^3b^2 - 7a^2b + 3ab)$
$= (7+2)a^3b^2 + 5a^2b^2 + (-1-7)a^2b + 3ab$
$= 9a^3b^2 + 5a^2b^2 - 8a^2b + 3ab$

86. $4x^2 - 9$

87. $4x^2 - 49 = (2x)^2 - 7^2 = (2x+7)(2x-7)$

88. $2(x-9)(x-4)$

89. ◈

90. ◈

91. ◈

92. ◈

93. $\quad r(L) = 2\sqrt{5L}$

a) $r(L) = 2\sqrt{5 \cdot 20}$
$= 2\sqrt{100}$
$= 2 \cdot 10 = 20$ mph

b) $r(L) = 2\sqrt{5 \cdot 70}$
$= 2\sqrt{350}$
≈ 37.4 mph   Multiplying and rounding

c) $r(L) = 2\sqrt{5 \cdot 90}$
$= 2\sqrt{450}$
≈ 42.4 mph   Multiplying and rounding

94. (a) $-3.3°$ C; (b) $-16.6°$ C; (c) $-25.5°$ C; (d) $-54.0°$ C

95. $(\sqrt{r^3 t})^7 = \sqrt{(r^3 t)^7} = \sqrt{r^{21} t^7} =$
$\sqrt{r^{20} \cdot r \cdot t^6 \cdot t} = r^{10} t^3 \sqrt{rt}$

96. $25x^5 \sqrt[3]{25x}$

97. $\dfrac{1}{2}\sqrt{36a^5 bc^4} - \dfrac{1}{2}\sqrt[3]{64a^4 bc^6} + \dfrac{1}{6}\sqrt{144a^3 bc^6} =$

$\dfrac{1}{2}\sqrt{36a^4 c^4 \cdot ab} - \dfrac{1}{2}\sqrt[3]{64a^3 c^6 \cdot ab} + \dfrac{1}{6}\sqrt{144a^2 c^6 \cdot ab} =$

$\dfrac{1}{2}(6a^2 c^2)\sqrt{ab} - \dfrac{1}{2}(4ac^2)\sqrt[3]{ab} + \dfrac{1}{6}(12ac^3)\sqrt{ab} =$

$3a^2 c^2 \sqrt{ab} - 2ac^2 \sqrt[3]{ab} + 2ac^3 \sqrt{ab}$

$(3a^2 c^2 + 2ac^3)\sqrt{ab} - 2ac^2 \sqrt[3]{ab}$, or

$ac^2 [(3a + 2c)\sqrt{ab} - 2\sqrt[3]{ab}]$

98. $(7x^2 - 2y^2)\sqrt{x+y}$

99.

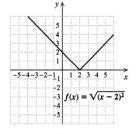

Since $(x-2)^2$ is nonnegative for all values of x, the domain of f is $\{x | x$ is a real number$\}$, or $(-\infty, \infty)$.

100. $(-\infty, \infty)$

Exercise Set 9.4

1. $\sqrt{10}\sqrt{5} = \sqrt{10 \cdot 5} = \sqrt{50} = \sqrt{25 \cdot 2} = 5\sqrt{2}$

2. $3\sqrt{2}$

3. $\sqrt{6}\sqrt{14} = \sqrt{6 \cdot 14} = \sqrt{84} = \sqrt{4 \cdot 21} = 2\sqrt{21}$

4. $3\sqrt{35}$

5. $\sqrt[3]{2}\sqrt[3]{4} = \sqrt[3]{2\cdot 4} = \sqrt[3]{8} = 2$

6. 3

7. $\sqrt[3]{5a^2}\sqrt[3]{2a} = \sqrt[3]{5a^2\cdot 2a} = \sqrt[3]{10a^3} = \sqrt[3]{a^3\cdot 10} = a\sqrt[3]{10}$

8. $x\sqrt[3]{21}$

9. $\sqrt{3x^3}\sqrt{6x^5} = \sqrt{18x^8} = \sqrt{9x^8\cdot 2} = 3x^4\sqrt{2}$

10. $5a^5\sqrt{3}$

11. $\sqrt[3]{s^2t^4}\sqrt[3]{s^4t^6} = \sqrt[3]{s^6t^{10}} = \sqrt[3]{s^6t^9\cdot t} = s^2t^3\sqrt[3]{t}$

12. $xy^3\sqrt[3]{xy}$

13. $\sqrt[3]{(x+5)^2}\sqrt[3]{(x+5)^4} = \sqrt[3]{(x+5)^6} = (x+5)^2$

14. $(a-b)^4$

15. $\sqrt[4]{12a^3b^7}\sqrt[4]{4a^2b^5} = \sqrt[4]{48a^5b^{12}} = \sqrt[4]{16a^4b^{12}\cdot 3a} = 2ab^3\sqrt[4]{3a}$

16. $3x^2y^2\sqrt[4]{xy^3}$

17. $\sqrt[5]{x^3(y+z)^4}\sqrt[5]{x^3(y+z)^6} = \sqrt[5]{x^6(y+z)^{10}} = \sqrt[5]{x^5(y+z)^{10}\cdot x} = x(y+z)^2\sqrt[5]{x}$

18. $a^2(b-c)\sqrt[5]{(b-c)^3}$

19.

$\sqrt{a}\sqrt[4]{a^3}$

$= a^{1/2}\cdot a^{3/4}$ Converting to exponential notation

$= a^{5/4}$ Adding exponents

$= a^{1+1/4}$ Writing 5/4 as a mixed number

$= a\cdot a^{1/4}$ Factoring

$= a\sqrt[4]{a}$ Returning to radical notation

20. $x\sqrt{x}$

21.

$\sqrt[5]{b^2}\sqrt{b^3}$

$= b^{2/5}\cdot b^{3/2}$ Converting to exponential notation

$= b^{19/10}$ Adding exponents

$= b^{1+9/10}$ Writing 19/10 as a mixed number

$= b\cdot b^{9/10}$ Factoring

$= b\sqrt[10]{b^9}$ Returning to radical notation

22. $a\sqrt[12]{a^5}$

23.
$$\begin{aligned}\sqrt{xy^3}\sqrt[3]{x^2y} &= (xy^3)^{1/2}(x^2y)^{1/3}\\ &= (xy^3)^{3/6}(x^2y)^{2/6}\\ &= [(xy^3)^3(x^2y)^2]^{1/6}\\ &= \sqrt[6]{x^3y^9\cdot x^4y^2}\\ &= \sqrt[6]{x^7y^{11}}\\ &= \sqrt[6]{x^6y^6\cdot xy^5}\\ &= xy\sqrt[6]{xy^5}\end{aligned}$$

24. $a\sqrt[10]{ab^7}$

25.
$$\begin{aligned}\sqrt[4]{9ab^3}\sqrt{3a^4b} &= (9ab^3)^{1/4}(3a^4b)^{1/2}\\ &= (9ab^3)^{1/4}(3a^4b)^{2/4}\\ &= [(9ab^3)(3a^4b)^2]^{1/4}\\ &= \sqrt[4]{9ab^3\cdot 9a^8b^2}\\ &= \sqrt[4]{81a^9b^5}\\ &= \sqrt[4]{81a^8b^4\cdot ab}\\ &= 3a^2b\sqrt[4]{ab}\end{aligned}$$

26. $2xy^2\sqrt[6]{2x^5y}$

27.
$$\begin{aligned}\sqrt[3]{xy^2z}\sqrt{x^3yz^2} &= (xy^2z)^{1/3}(x^3yz^2)^{1/2}\\ &= (xy^2z)^{2/6}(x^3yz^2)^{3/6}\\ &= [(xy^2z)^2(x^3yz^2)^3]^{1/6}\\ &= \sqrt[6]{x^2y^4z^2\cdot x^9y^3z^6}\\ &= \sqrt[6]{x^{11}y^7z^8}\\ &= \sqrt[6]{x^6y^6z^6\cdot x^5yz^2}\\ &= xyz\sqrt[6]{x^5yz^2}\end{aligned}$$

28. $a^2b^2c^2\sqrt[6]{a^2bc^2}$

29.
$$\begin{aligned}&\sqrt{27a^5(b+1)}\sqrt[3]{81a(b+1)^4}\\ &= [27a^5(b+1)]^{1/2}[81a(b+1)^4]^{1/3}\\ &= [27a^5(b+1)]^{3/6}[81a(b+1)^4]^{2/6}\\ &= \{[3^3a^5(b+1)]^3[3^4a(b+1)^4]^2\}^{1/6}\\ &= \sqrt[6]{3^9a^{15}(b+1)^3\cdot 3^8a^2(b+1)^8}\\ &= \sqrt[6]{3^{17}a^{17}(b+1)^{11}}\\ &= \sqrt[6]{3^{12}a^{12}(b+1)^6\cdot 3^5a^5(b+1)^5}\\ &= 3^2a^2(b+1)\sqrt[6]{3^5a^5(b+1)^5},\ \text{or}\\ &\quad 9a^2(b+1)\sqrt[6]{243a^5(b+1)^5}\end{aligned}$$

30. $4x(y+z)^3\sqrt[6]{2x(y+z)}$

31. $\sqrt{\dfrac{25}{36}} = \dfrac{\sqrt{25}}{\sqrt{36}} = \dfrac{5}{6}$

32. $\dfrac{10}{9}$

33. $\sqrt[3]{\dfrac{64}{27}} = \dfrac{\sqrt[3]{64}}{\sqrt[3]{27}} = \dfrac{4}{3}$

34. $\dfrac{7}{10}$

35. $\sqrt{\dfrac{49}{y^2}} = \dfrac{\sqrt{49}}{\sqrt{y^2}} = \dfrac{7}{y}$

36. $\dfrac{11}{x}$

37. $\sqrt{\dfrac{25y^3}{x^4}} = \dfrac{\sqrt{25y^3}}{\sqrt{x^4}} = \dfrac{\sqrt{25y^2 \cdot y}}{\sqrt{x^4}} = \dfrac{\sqrt{25y^2}\,\sqrt{y}}{\sqrt{x^4}} = \dfrac{5y\sqrt{y}}{x^2}$

38. $\dfrac{6a^2\sqrt{a}}{b^3}$

39. $\sqrt[3]{\dfrac{27a^4}{8b^3}} = \dfrac{\sqrt[3]{27a^4}}{\sqrt[3]{8b^3}} = \dfrac{\sqrt[3]{27a^3 \cdot a}}{\sqrt[3]{8b^3}} = \dfrac{\sqrt[3]{27a^3}\,\sqrt[3]{a}}{\sqrt[3]{8b^3}} = \dfrac{3a\sqrt[3]{a}}{2b}$

40. $\dfrac{2x^2\sqrt[3]{x}}{3y^2}$

41. $\sqrt[4]{\dfrac{16a^4}{b^4c^8}} = \dfrac{\sqrt[4]{16a^4}}{\sqrt[4]{b^4c^8}} = \dfrac{2a}{bc^2}$

42. $\dfrac{3x}{y^2z}$

43. $\sqrt[4]{\dfrac{a^5b^8}{c^{10}}} = \dfrac{\sqrt[4]{a^5b^8}}{\sqrt[4]{c^{10}}} = \dfrac{\sqrt[4]{a^4b^8 \cdot a}}{\sqrt[4]{c^8 \cdot c^2}} = \dfrac{\sqrt[4]{a^4b^8}\,\sqrt[4]{a}}{\sqrt[4]{c^8}\,\sqrt[4]{c^2}} = \dfrac{ab^2\sqrt[4]{a}}{c^2\sqrt[4]{c^2}}$, or $\dfrac{ab^2}{c^2}\sqrt[4]{\dfrac{a}{c^2}}$

44. $\dfrac{x^2y^3}{z}\sqrt[4]{\dfrac{x}{z^2}}$

45. $\sqrt[5]{\dfrac{32x^6}{y^{11}}} = \dfrac{\sqrt[5]{32x^6}}{\sqrt[5]{y^{11}}} = \dfrac{\sqrt[5]{32x^5 \cdot x}}{\sqrt[5]{y^{10} \cdot y}} = \dfrac{\sqrt[5]{32x^5} \cdot \sqrt[5]{x}}{\sqrt[5]{y^{10}}\,\sqrt[5]{y}} = \dfrac{2x\sqrt[5]{x}}{y^2\sqrt[5]{y}}$, or $\dfrac{2x}{y^2}\sqrt[5]{\dfrac{x}{y}}$

46. $\dfrac{3a}{b^2}\sqrt[5]{\dfrac{a^4}{b^3}}$

47. $\sqrt[6]{\dfrac{x^6y^8}{z^{15}}} = \dfrac{\sqrt[6]{x^6y^8}}{\sqrt[6]{z^{15}}} = \dfrac{\sqrt[6]{x^6y^6 \cdot y^2}}{\sqrt[6]{z^{12} \cdot z^3}} = \dfrac{\sqrt[6]{x^6y^6}\,\sqrt[6]{y^2}}{\sqrt[6]{z^{12}}\,\sqrt[6]{z^3}} = \dfrac{xy\sqrt[6]{y^2}}{z^2\sqrt[6]{z^3}}$, or $\dfrac{xy}{z^2}\sqrt[6]{\dfrac{y^2}{z^3}}$

48. $\dfrac{ab^2}{c^2}\sqrt[6]{\dfrac{a^3}{c}}$

49. $\dfrac{\sqrt{35x}}{\sqrt{7x}} = \sqrt{\dfrac{35x}{7x}} = \sqrt{5}$

50. $\sqrt{7}$

51. $\dfrac{\sqrt[3]{270}}{\sqrt[3]{10}} = \sqrt[3]{\dfrac{270}{10}} = \sqrt[3]{27} = 3$

52. 2

53. $\dfrac{\sqrt{40xy^3}}{\sqrt{8x}} = \sqrt{\dfrac{40xy^3}{8x}} = \sqrt{5y^3} = \sqrt{y^2 \cdot 5y} = \sqrt{y^2}\,\sqrt{5y} = y\sqrt{5y}$

54. $2b\sqrt{2b}$

55. $\dfrac{\sqrt[3]{96a^4b^2}}{\sqrt[3]{12a^2b}} = \sqrt[3]{\dfrac{96a^4b^2}{12a^2b}} = \sqrt[3]{8a^2b} = \sqrt[3]{8}\,\sqrt[3]{a^2b} = 2\sqrt[3]{a^2b}$

56. $3xy\sqrt[3]{y^2}$

57. $\dfrac{\sqrt{100ab}}{5\sqrt{2}} = \dfrac{1}{5}\dfrac{\sqrt{100ab}}{\sqrt{2}} = \dfrac{1}{5}\sqrt{\dfrac{100ab}{2}} = \dfrac{1}{5}\sqrt{50ab} = \dfrac{1}{5}\sqrt{25 \cdot 2ab} = \dfrac{1}{5} \cdot 5\sqrt{2ab} = \sqrt{2ab}$

58. $\dfrac{5}{3}\sqrt{ab}$

59. $\dfrac{\sqrt[4]{48x^9y^{13}}}{\sqrt[4]{3xy^{-2}}} = \sqrt[4]{\dfrac{48x^9y^{13}}{3xy^{-2}}} = \sqrt[4]{16x^8y^{15}} = \sqrt[4]{16x^8y^{12}}\,\sqrt[4]{y^3} = 2x^2y^3\sqrt[4]{y^3}$

60. $2a^2b^6$

61.
$\dfrac{\sqrt[3]{a^2}}{\sqrt[4]{a}}$

$= \dfrac{a^{2/3}}{a^{1/4}}$ Converting to exponential notation

$= a^{2/3 - 1/4}$ Subtracting exponents

$= a^{5/12}$ Converting back

$= \sqrt[12]{a^5}$ to radical notation

62. $\sqrt[15]{x^7}$

63.
$$\frac{\sqrt[4]{x^2y^3}}{\sqrt[3]{xy}}$$

$$= \frac{(x^2y^3)^{1/4}}{(xy)^{1/3}} \qquad \text{Converting to exponential notation}$$

$$= \frac{x^{2/4}y^{3/4}}{x^{1/3}y^{1/3}} \qquad \text{Using the power and product rules}$$

$$= x^{2/4-1/3}y^{3/4-1/3} \qquad \text{Subtracting exponents}$$

$$= x^{2/12}y^{5/12}$$

$$= (x^2y^5)^{1/2} \qquad \text{Converting back to}$$

$$= \sqrt[12]{x^2y^5} \qquad \text{radical notation}$$

64. $\sqrt[15]{\dfrac{a^7}{b^4}}$

65.
$$\frac{\sqrt{ab^3c}}{\sqrt[5]{a^2b^3c^{-1}}} = \frac{(ab^3c)^{1/2}}{(a^2b^3c^{-1})^{1/5}}$$

$$= \frac{a^{1/2}b^{3/2}c^{1/2}}{a^{2/5}b^{3/5}c^{-1/5}}$$

$$= a^{1/10}b^{9/10}c^{7/10} \qquad \text{Subtracting exponents}$$

$$= (ab^9c^7)^{1/10}$$

$$= \sqrt[10]{ab^9c^7}$$

66. $yz\sqrt[10]{xy^8z^3}$

67.
$$\frac{\sqrt[4]{(3x-1)^3}}{\sqrt[5]{(3x-1)^3}}$$

$$= \frac{(3x-1)^{3/4}}{(3x-1)^{3/5}} \qquad \text{Converting to exponential notation}$$

$$= (3x-1)^{3/4-3/5} \qquad \text{Subtracting exponents}$$

$$= (3x-1)^{3/20} \qquad \text{Converting back}$$

$$= \sqrt[20]{(3x-1)^3} \qquad \text{to radical notation}$$

68. $\sqrt[12]{(2+5x)^5}$

69.
$$\frac{12x}{x-4} - \frac{3x^2}{x+4} = \frac{384}{x^2-16}$$

$$\frac{12x}{x-4} - \frac{3x^2}{x+4} = \frac{384}{(x+4)(x-4)},$$

$$\text{LCM is } (x+4)(x-4).$$

Note that $x \neq -4$ and $x \neq 4$.

$$(x+4)(x-4)\left[\frac{12x}{x-4} - \frac{3x^2}{x+4}\right] =$$

$$(x+4)(x-4) \cdot \frac{384}{(x+4)(x-4)}$$

$$12x(x+4) - 3x^2(x-4) = 384$$

$$12x^2 + 48x - 3x^3 + 12x^2 = 384$$

$$-3x^3 + 24x^2 + 48x - 384 = 0$$

$$-3(x^3 - 8x^2 - 16x + 128) = 0$$

$$-3[x^2(x-8) - 16(x-8)] = 0$$

$$-3(x-8)(x^2 - 16) = 0$$

$$-3(x-8)(x+4)(x-4) = 0$$

$$x - 8 = 0 \quad \text{or} \quad x+4 = 0 \quad \text{or} \quad x-4 = 0$$

$$x = 8 \quad \text{or} \quad\quad x = -4 \quad \text{or} \quad\quad x = 4$$

Check: For 8:

$$\frac{12x}{x-4} - \frac{3x^2}{x+4} = \frac{384}{x^2-16}$$

$$\frac{12 \cdot 8}{8-4} - \frac{3 \cdot 8^2}{8+4} \quad \bigg| \quad \frac{384}{8^2-16}$$

$$\frac{96}{4} - \frac{192}{12} \quad \bigg| \quad \frac{384}{48}$$

$$24 - 16 \quad \bigg| \quad 8$$

$$8 \quad \bigg| \quad \text{TRUE}$$

8 is a solution.

For -4:

$$\frac{12x}{x-4} - \frac{3x^2}{x+4} = \frac{384}{x^2-16}$$

$$\frac{12(-4)}{-4-4} - \frac{3(-4)^2}{-4+4} \quad \bigg| \quad \frac{384}{(-4)^2-16}$$

$$\frac{-48}{-8} - \frac{48}{0} \quad \bigg| \quad \frac{384}{16-16} \quad \text{UNDEFINED}$$

-4 is not a solution.

For 4:

$$\frac{12x}{x-4} - \frac{3x^2}{x+4} = \frac{384}{x^2-16}$$

$$\frac{12 \cdot 4}{4-4} - \frac{3 \cdot 4^2}{4+4} \quad \bigg| \quad \frac{384}{4^2-16}$$

$$\frac{48}{0} - \frac{48}{8} \quad \bigg| \quad \frac{384}{16-16} \quad \text{UNDEFINED}$$

4 is not a solution.

The checks confirm that -4 and 4 are not solutions. The solution is 8.

70. $\dfrac{15}{2}$

71. *Familiarize*. Let x and y represent the width and length of the rectangle, respectively.

Translate. We write two equations.

$$\underbrace{\text{The width}}_{\downarrow} \underbrace{\text{is}}_{\downarrow} \underbrace{\text{one-fourth}}_{\downarrow} \underbrace{\text{the length.}}_{\downarrow}$$

$$x \quad = \quad \frac{1}{4}\cdot \quad y$$

$$\underbrace{\text{The area}}_{\downarrow} \underbrace{\text{is}}_{\downarrow} \underbrace{\text{twice}}_{\downarrow} \underbrace{\text{the perimeter.}}_{\downarrow}$$

$$xy \quad = \quad 2\cdot \quad (2x + 2y)$$

Carry out. Solving the system of equations we get $(5,20)$.

Check. The width, 5, is one-fourth the length, 20. The area is $5 \cdot 20$, or 100. The perimeter is $2 \cdot 5 + 2 \cdot 20$, or 50. Since $100 = 2 \cdot 50$, the area is twice the perimeter. The values check.

State. The width is 5, and the length is 20.

72. $-5, 4$

73.
$$A = \frac{m}{a_2 - a_1}$$

$$A(a_2 - a_1) = m \qquad \text{Multiplying by } a_2 - a_1$$

$$Aa_2 - Aa_1 = m$$

$$-Aa_1 = m - Aa_2$$

$$a_1 = \frac{m - Aa_2}{-A}, \text{ or } \frac{Aa_2 - m}{A}, \text{ or}$$

$$a_2 - \frac{m}{A}$$

74. $n = \dfrac{4m - P}{7}$

75. ◈

76. ◈

77. ◈

78. ◈

79. a) $T = 2\pi\sqrt{\dfrac{65}{980}} \approx 1.62$ sec

b) $T = 2\pi\sqrt{\dfrac{98}{980}} \approx 1.99$ sec

c) $T = 2\pi\sqrt{\dfrac{120}{980}} \approx 2.20$ sec

80. a^3bxy^2

81.
$$\frac{(\sqrt[3]{81mn^2})^2}{(\sqrt[3]{mn})^2} = \frac{\sqrt[3]{(81mn^2)^2}}{\sqrt[3]{(mn)^2}}$$

$$= \frac{\sqrt[3]{6561m^2n^4}}{\sqrt[3]{m^2n^2}}$$

$$= \sqrt[3]{\frac{6561m^2n^4}{m^2n^2}}$$

$$= \sqrt[3]{6561n^2}$$

$$= \sqrt[3]{729 \cdot 9n^2}$$

$$= \sqrt[3]{729}\,\sqrt[3]{9n^2}$$

$$= 9\sqrt[3]{9n^2}$$

82. $2yz\sqrt{2z}$

83.
$$\frac{\sqrt{x^5 - 2x^4y} - \sqrt{xy^4 - 2y^5}}{\sqrt{xy^2 - 2y^3} + \sqrt{x^3 - 2x^2y}}$$

$$= \frac{\sqrt{x^4(x - 2y)} - \sqrt{y^4(x - 2y)}}{\sqrt{y^2(x - 2y)} + \sqrt{x^2(x - 2y)}}$$

$$= \frac{x^2\sqrt{x - 2y} - y^2\sqrt{x - 2y}}{y\sqrt{x - 2y} + x\sqrt{x - 2y}}$$

$$= \frac{(x^2 - y^2)\sqrt{x - 2y}}{(y + x)\sqrt{x - 2y}}$$

$$= \frac{(x + y)(x - y)\sqrt{x - 2y}}{(y + x)\sqrt{x - 2y}}$$

$$= (x - y) \cdot \frac{(x + y)\sqrt{x - 2y}}{(y + x)\sqrt{x - 2y}}$$

$$= x - y$$

84. 10

85.
$$\sqrt[5]{4a^{3k+2}}\,\sqrt[5]{8a^{6-k}} = 2a^4$$

$$\sqrt[5]{32a^{2k+8}} = 2a^4$$

$$2\sqrt[5]{a^{2k+8}} = 2a^4$$

$$\sqrt[5]{a^{2k+8}} = a^4$$

$$a^{\frac{2k+8}{5}} = a^4$$

Since the base is the same, the exponents must be equal. We have:

$$\frac{2k + 8}{5} = 4$$

$$2k + 8 = 20$$

$$2k = 12$$

$$k = 6$$

Exercise Set 9.5

1. $\sqrt{7}(3 - \sqrt{7}) = \sqrt{7} \cdot 3 - \sqrt{7} \cdot \sqrt{7} = 3\sqrt{7} - 7$

2. $4\sqrt{3} + 3$

3. $\sqrt{2}(\sqrt{3} - \sqrt{5}) = \sqrt{2} \cdot \sqrt{3} - \sqrt{2} \cdot \sqrt{5} = \sqrt{6} - \sqrt{10}$

4. $5 - \sqrt{10}$

5. $\sqrt{3}(2\sqrt{5} - 3\sqrt{4}) = \sqrt{3}(2\sqrt{5} - 3 \cdot 2) =$
$\sqrt{3} \cdot 2\sqrt{5} - \sqrt{3} \cdot 6 = 2\sqrt{15} - 6\sqrt{3}$

6. $6\sqrt{5} - 4$

7. $\sqrt[3]{2}(\sqrt[3]{4} - 2\sqrt[3]{32}) = \sqrt[3]{2} \cdot \sqrt[3]{4} - \sqrt[3]{2} \cdot 2\sqrt[3]{32} =$
$\sqrt[3]{8} - 2\sqrt[3]{64} = 2 - 2 \cdot 4 = 2 - 8 = -6$

8. $3 - 4\sqrt[3]{63}$

9. $\sqrt[3]{a}(\sqrt[3]{a^2} + \sqrt[3]{24a^2}) = \sqrt[3]{a} \cdot \sqrt[3]{a^2} + \sqrt[3]{a}\sqrt[3]{24a^2} =$
$\sqrt[3]{a^3} + \sqrt[3]{24a^3} = \sqrt[3]{a^3} + \sqrt[3]{8a^3 \cdot 3} =$
$a + 2a\sqrt[3]{3}$

10. $-2x\sqrt[3]{3}$

11. $(5 + \sqrt{6})(5 - \sqrt{6}) = 5^2 - (\sqrt{6})^2 = 25 - 6 = 19$

12. -1

13. $(3 - 2\sqrt{7})(3 + 2\sqrt{7}) = 3^2 - (2\sqrt{7})^2 = 9 - 4 \cdot 7 =$
$9 - 28 = -19$

14. -2

15. $(5 + \sqrt[3]{10})(3 - \sqrt[3]{10})$
$= 15 - 5\sqrt[3]{10} + 3\sqrt[3]{10} - \sqrt[3]{10}\sqrt[3]{10}$ Using FOIL
$= 15 - 5\sqrt[3]{10} + 3\sqrt[3]{10} - \sqrt[3]{100}$ Multiplying radicals
$= 15 - 2\sqrt[3]{10} - \sqrt[3]{100}$ Simplifying

16. $\sqrt[3]{49} + \sqrt[3]{7} - 20$

17. $(2\sqrt{7} - 4\sqrt{2})(3\sqrt{7} + 6\sqrt{2}) =$
$2\sqrt{7} \cdot 3\sqrt{7} + 2\sqrt{7} \cdot 6\sqrt{2} - 4\sqrt{2} \cdot 3\sqrt{7} - 4\sqrt{2} \cdot 6\sqrt{2} =$
$6 \cdot 7 + 12\sqrt{14} - 12\sqrt{14} - 24 \cdot 2 =$
$42 + 12\sqrt{14} - 12\sqrt{14} - 48 = -6$

18. $24 - 7\sqrt{15}$

19. $(2\sqrt[3]{3} - \sqrt[3]{2})(\sqrt[3]{3} + 2\sqrt[3]{2}) =$
$2\sqrt[3]{3} \cdot \sqrt[3]{3} + 2\sqrt[3]{3} \cdot 2\sqrt[3]{2} - \sqrt[3]{2} \cdot \sqrt[3]{3} - \sqrt[3]{2} \cdot 2\sqrt[3]{2} =$
$2\sqrt[3]{9} + 4\sqrt[3]{6} - \sqrt[3]{6} - 2\sqrt[3]{4} = 2\sqrt[3]{9} + 3\sqrt[3]{6} - 2\sqrt[3]{4}$

20. $6\sqrt[4]{63} - 9\sqrt[4]{42} + 2\sqrt[4]{54} - 3\sqrt[4]{36}$

21. $(\sqrt{3x} + \sqrt{y})^2$
$= (\sqrt{3x})^2 + 2 \cdot \sqrt{3x} \cdot \sqrt{y} + (\sqrt{y})^2$ Squaring a binomial
$= 3x + 2\sqrt{3xy} + y$

22. $t - 2\sqrt{2rt} + 2r$

23. $\sqrt[3]{x^2y}(\sqrt{xy} - \sqrt[5]{xy^3})$
$= (x^2y)^{1/3}[(xy)^{1/2} - (xy^3)^{1/5}]$
$= x^{2/3}y^{1/3}(x^{1/2}y^{1/2} - x^{1/5}y^{3/5})$
$= x^{2/3}y^{1/3}x^{1/2}y^{1/2} - x^{2/3}y^{1/3}x^{1/5}y^{3/5}$
$= x^{2/3+1/2}y^{1/3+1/2} - x^{2/3+1/5}y^{1/3+3/5}$
$= x^{7/6}y^{5/6} - x^{13/15}y^{14/15}$
$= x^{1\frac{1}{6}}y^{\frac{5}{6}} - x^{13/15}y^{14/15}$
Writing a mixed numeral
$= x \cdot x^{1/6}y^{5/6} - x^{13/15}y^{14/15}$
$= x(xy^5)^{1/6} - (x^{13}y^{14})^{1/15}$
$= x\sqrt[6]{xy^5} - \sqrt[15]{x^{13}y^{14}}$

24. $a\sqrt[12]{a^2b^7} - \sqrt[20]{a^{18}b^{13}}$

25. $(m + \sqrt[3]{n^2})(2m + \sqrt[4]{n})$
$= (m + n^{2/3})(2m + n^{1/4})$ Converting to exponential notation
$= 2m^2 + mn^{1/4} + 2mn^{2/3} + n^{2/3}n^{1/4}$ Using FOIL
$= 2m^2 + mn^{1/4} + 2mn^{2/3} + n^{2/3+1/4}$ Adding exponents
$= 2m^2 + mn^{1/4} + 2mn^{2/3} + n^{11/12}$
$= 2m^2 + m\sqrt[4]{n} + 2m\sqrt[3]{n^2} + \sqrt[12]{n^{11}}$ Converting back to radical notation

26. $3r^2 - r\sqrt[5]{s} - 3r\sqrt[4]{s^3} + \sqrt[20]{s^{19}}$

27. $f(x) = \sqrt[4]{x}, \; g(x) = \sqrt[4]{2x} - \sqrt[4]{x^{11}}$
$(f \cdot g)(x) = \sqrt[4]{x}(\sqrt[4]{2x} - \sqrt[4]{x^{11}})$
$= \sqrt[4]{2x^2} - \sqrt[4]{x^{12}}$
$= \sqrt[4]{2x^2} - x^3$

28. $x^2 + \sqrt[4]{3x^3}$

29. $f(x) = x + \sqrt{7}, \; g(x) = x - \sqrt{7}$

$$(f \cdot g)(x) = (x + \sqrt{7})(x - \sqrt{7})$$
$$= x^2 - (\sqrt{7})^2$$
$$= x^2 - 7$$

30. $x^2 + x\sqrt{6} - x\sqrt{2} - 2\sqrt{3}$

31. $f(x) = 2 - \sqrt{x}, \; g(x) = 1 - \sqrt{x}$

$$(f \cdot g)(x) = (2 - \sqrt{x})(1 - \sqrt{x})$$
$$= 2 - 2\sqrt{x} - \sqrt{x} + \sqrt{x^2}$$
$$= 2 - 3\sqrt{x} + x$$

32. $x + \sqrt{2x} + \sqrt{3x} + \sqrt{6}$

33. $f(x) = x^2$

$$f(5 - \sqrt{2}) = (5 - \sqrt{2})^2 = 25 - 10\sqrt{2} + (\sqrt{2})^2 =$$
$$25 - 10\sqrt{2} + 2 = 27 - 10\sqrt{2}$$

34. $52 + 14\sqrt{3}$

35. $f(x) = x^2$

$$f(\sqrt{3} + \sqrt{5}) = (\sqrt{3} + \sqrt{5})^2 =$$
$$(\sqrt{3})^2 + 2 \cdot \sqrt{3} \cdot \sqrt{5} + (\sqrt{5})^2 =$$
$$3 + 2\sqrt{15} + 5 = 8 + 2\sqrt{15}$$

36. $9 - 6\sqrt{2}$

37. $f(x) = x^2$

$$f(\sqrt{10} - \sqrt{5}) = (\sqrt{10} - \sqrt{5})^2 =$$
$$(\sqrt{10})^2 - 2 \cdot \sqrt{10} \cdot \sqrt{5} + (\sqrt{5})^2 =$$
$$10 - 2\sqrt{50} + 5 = 15 - 2\sqrt{25 \cdot 2} =$$
$$15 - 2 \cdot 5\sqrt{2} = 15 - 10\sqrt{2}$$

38. $15 + 4\sqrt{14}$

39. $\sqrt{\dfrac{5}{7}} = \sqrt{\dfrac{5}{7} \cdot \dfrac{7}{7}} = \sqrt{\dfrac{35}{49}} = \dfrac{\sqrt{35}}{\sqrt{49}} = \dfrac{\sqrt{35}}{7}$

40. $\dfrac{\sqrt{66}}{6}$

41. $\sqrt{\dfrac{7a}{18}} = \sqrt{\dfrac{7a}{18} \cdot \dfrac{2}{2}} = \sqrt{\dfrac{14a}{36}} = \dfrac{\sqrt{14a}}{\sqrt{36}} = \dfrac{\sqrt{14a}}{6}$

42. $\dfrac{\sqrt{30x}}{10}$

43. $\sqrt{\dfrac{9}{20x^2y}} = \sqrt{\dfrac{9}{20x^2y} \cdot \dfrac{5y}{5y}} = \sqrt{\dfrac{9 \cdot 5y}{100x^2y^2}} =$

$$\dfrac{\sqrt{9 \cdot 5y}}{\sqrt{100x^2y^2}} = \dfrac{3\sqrt{5y}}{10xy}$$

44. $\dfrac{\sqrt{10a}}{8ab}$

45. $\dfrac{5}{7 - \sqrt{2}} = \dfrac{5}{7 - \sqrt{2}} \cdot \dfrac{7 + \sqrt{2}}{7 + \sqrt{2}} = \dfrac{5(7 + \sqrt{2})}{7^2 - (\sqrt{2})^2} =$

$$\dfrac{35 + 5\sqrt{2}}{49 - 2} = \dfrac{35 + 5\sqrt{2}}{47}$$

46. $\dfrac{15 - 3\sqrt{6}}{19}$

47. $\dfrac{\sqrt{x}}{\sqrt{x} + \sqrt{y}} = \dfrac{\sqrt{x}}{\sqrt{x} + \sqrt{y}} \cdot \dfrac{\sqrt{x} - \sqrt{y}}{\sqrt{x} - \sqrt{y}} =$

$$\dfrac{\sqrt{x}(\sqrt{x} - \sqrt{y})}{(\sqrt{x})^2 - (\sqrt{y})^2} = \dfrac{x - \sqrt{xy}}{x - y}$$

48. $\dfrac{\sqrt{ab} + b}{a - b}$

49. $\dfrac{\sqrt{3} + 4\sqrt{5}}{\sqrt{3} - 2\sqrt{6}} = \dfrac{\sqrt{3} + 4\sqrt{5}}{\sqrt{3} - 2\sqrt{6}} \cdot \dfrac{\sqrt{3} + 2\sqrt{6}}{\sqrt{3} + 2\sqrt{6}} =$

$$\dfrac{(\sqrt{3} + 4\sqrt{5})(\sqrt{3} + 2\sqrt{6})}{(\sqrt{3} - 2\sqrt{6})(\sqrt{3} + 2\sqrt{6})} =$$

$$\dfrac{(\sqrt{3})^2 + \sqrt{3} \cdot 2\sqrt{6} + 4\sqrt{5} \cdot \sqrt{3} + 4\sqrt{5} \cdot 2\sqrt{6}}{(\sqrt{3})^2 - (2\sqrt{6})^2} =$$

$$\dfrac{3 + 2\sqrt{18} + 4\sqrt{15} + 8\sqrt{30}}{3 - 4 \cdot 6} =$$

$$\dfrac{3 + 2 \cdot 3\sqrt{2} + 4\sqrt{15} + 8\sqrt{30}}{3 - 24} =$$

$$\dfrac{3 + 6\sqrt{2} + 4\sqrt{15} + 8\sqrt{30}}{-21}$$

50. $\dfrac{5\sqrt{5} - 15\sqrt{3} - \sqrt{15} + 9}{-11}$

51. $\dfrac{5\sqrt{3} - 3\sqrt{2}}{3\sqrt{2} - 2\sqrt{3}} = \dfrac{5\sqrt{3} - 3\sqrt{2}}{3\sqrt{2} - 2\sqrt{3}} \cdot \dfrac{3\sqrt{2} + 2\sqrt{3}}{3\sqrt{2} + 2\sqrt{3}} =$

$$\dfrac{15\sqrt{6} + 10 \cdot 3 - 9 \cdot 2 - 6\sqrt{6}}{9 \cdot 2 - 4 \cdot 3} =$$

$$\dfrac{15\sqrt{6} + 30 - 18 - 6\sqrt{6}}{18 - 12} = \dfrac{9\sqrt{6} + 12}{6} =$$

$$\dfrac{3(3\sqrt{6} + 4)}{3 \cdot 2} = \dfrac{3\sqrt{6} + 4}{2}$$

52. $\dfrac{4\sqrt{6} + 9}{3}$

53. $\dfrac{\sqrt{5}}{\sqrt{7x}} = \dfrac{\sqrt{5}}{\sqrt{7x}} \cdot \dfrac{\sqrt{5}}{\sqrt{5}} = \dfrac{\sqrt{25}}{\sqrt{35x}} = \dfrac{5}{\sqrt{35x}}$

54. $\dfrac{10}{\sqrt{30x}}$

55. $\sqrt{\dfrac{14}{21}} = \sqrt{\dfrac{2}{3}} = \sqrt{\dfrac{2}{3} \cdot \dfrac{2}{2}} = \sqrt{\dfrac{4}{6}} = \dfrac{\sqrt{4}}{\sqrt{6}} = \dfrac{2}{\sqrt{6}}$

56. $\dfrac{2}{\sqrt{5}}$

57. $\sqrt{\dfrac{x^3y}{2}} = \sqrt{\dfrac{x^3y}{2} \cdot \dfrac{xy}{xy}} = \sqrt{\dfrac{x^4y^2}{2xy}} = \dfrac{\sqrt{x^4y^2}}{\sqrt{2xy}} = \dfrac{x^2y}{\sqrt{2xy}}$

58. $\dfrac{ab^3}{\sqrt{3ab}}$

59. $\dfrac{\sqrt{5}+2}{6} = \dfrac{\sqrt{5}+2}{6} \cdot \dfrac{\sqrt{5}-2}{\sqrt{5}-2} = \dfrac{(\sqrt{5})^2 - 2^2}{6(\sqrt{5}-2)} =$

$\dfrac{5-4}{6\sqrt{5}-12} = \dfrac{1}{6\sqrt{5}-12}$

60. $\dfrac{23}{14+2\sqrt{3}}$

61. $\dfrac{\sqrt{3}-5}{\sqrt{2}+5} = \dfrac{\sqrt{3}-5}{\sqrt{2}+5} \cdot \dfrac{\sqrt{3}+5}{\sqrt{3}+5} =$

$\dfrac{3-25}{\sqrt{6}+5\sqrt{2}+5\sqrt{3}+25} = \dfrac{-22}{\sqrt{6}+5\sqrt{2}+5\sqrt{3}+25}$

62. $\dfrac{-3}{3\sqrt{2}+3\sqrt{3}+7\sqrt{6}+21}$

63. $\dfrac{\sqrt{x}+\sqrt{y}}{\sqrt{x}-\sqrt{y}} = \dfrac{\sqrt{x}+\sqrt{y}}{\sqrt{x}-\sqrt{y}} \cdot \dfrac{\sqrt{x}-\sqrt{y}}{\sqrt{x}-\sqrt{y}} =$

$\dfrac{x-y}{x-\sqrt{xy}-\sqrt{xy}+y} = \dfrac{x-y}{x-2\sqrt{xy}+y}$

64. $\dfrac{x-y}{x+2\sqrt{xy}+y}$

65. $\dfrac{1}{2} - \dfrac{1}{3} = \dfrac{1}{t}$, LCD is $6t$

Note that $t \neq 0$.

$$6t\left(\dfrac{1}{2} - \dfrac{1}{3}\right) = 6t\left(\dfrac{1}{t}\right)$$
$$3t - 2t = 6$$
$$t = 6$$

Check:

$$\dfrac{\dfrac{1}{2} - \dfrac{1}{3} = \dfrac{1}{t}}{\begin{array}{c|c} \dfrac{1}{2} - \dfrac{1}{3} & \dfrac{1}{6} \\[2mm] \dfrac{3}{6} - \dfrac{2}{6} & \\[2mm] \dfrac{1}{6} & \text{TRUE} \end{array}}$$

The solution is 6.

66. $-\dfrac{19}{5}$

67. $\dfrac{2x^2 - x - 6}{x^2 + 4x + 3} \div \dfrac{2x^2 + x - 3}{x^2 - 1}$

$= \dfrac{2x^2 - x - 6}{x^2 + 4x + 3} \cdot \dfrac{x^2 - 1}{2x^2 + x - 3}$

$= \dfrac{(2x^2 - x - 6)(x^2 - 1)}{(x^2 + 4x + 3)(2x^2 + x - 3)}$

$= \dfrac{(2x + 3)(x - 2)(x + 1)(x - 1)}{(x + 3)(x + 1)(2x + 3)(x - 1)}$

$= \dfrac{\cancel{(2x+3)}(x - 2)\cancel{(x+1)}\cancel{(x-1)}}{(x + 3)\cancel{(x+1)}\cancel{(2x+3)}\cancel{(x-1)}}$

$= \dfrac{x - 2}{x + 3}$

68. 1

69.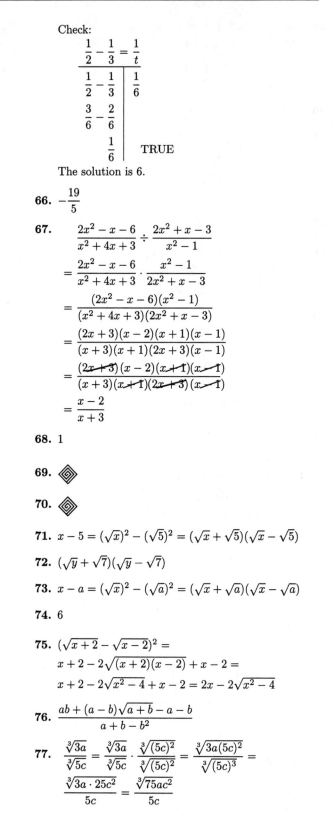

70.

71. $x - 5 = (\sqrt{x})^2 - (\sqrt{5})^2 = (\sqrt{x} + \sqrt{5})(\sqrt{x} - \sqrt{5})$

72. $(\sqrt{y} + \sqrt{7})(\sqrt{y} - \sqrt{7})$

73. $x - a = (\sqrt{x})^2 - (\sqrt{a})^2 = (\sqrt{x} + \sqrt{a})(\sqrt{x} - \sqrt{a})$

74. 6

75. $(\sqrt{x+2} - \sqrt{x-2})^2 =$

$x + 2 - 2\sqrt{(x+2)(x-2)} + x - 2 =$

$x + 2 - 2\sqrt{x^2 - 4} + x - 2 = 2x - 2\sqrt{x^2 - 4}$

76. $\dfrac{ab + (a - b)\sqrt{a+b} - a - b}{a + b - b^2}$

77. $\dfrac{\sqrt[3]{3a}}{\sqrt[3]{5c}} = \dfrac{\sqrt[3]{3a}}{\sqrt[3]{5c}} \cdot \dfrac{\sqrt[3]{(5c)^2}}{\sqrt[3]{(5c)^2}} = \dfrac{\sqrt[3]{3a(5c)^2}}{\sqrt[3]{(5c)^3}} =$

$\dfrac{\sqrt[3]{3a \cdot 25c^2}}{5c} = \dfrac{\sqrt[3]{75ac^2}}{5c}$

78. $\dfrac{y\sqrt[3]{180x^2y}}{6x^2}$

79. $\dfrac{\sqrt{y+18}-\sqrt{y}}{18} = \dfrac{\sqrt{y+18}-\sqrt{y}}{18} \cdot \dfrac{\sqrt{y+18}+\sqrt{y}}{\sqrt{y+18}+\sqrt{y}} =$

$\dfrac{y+18-y}{18(\sqrt{y+18}+\sqrt{y})} = \dfrac{18}{18(\sqrt{y+18}+\sqrt{y})} =$

$\dfrac{1}{\sqrt{y+18}+\sqrt{y}}$

80. $\dfrac{7}{\sqrt[3]{98}}$

81. $\sqrt[3]{\dfrac{2a^5}{5b}} = \dfrac{\sqrt[3]{2a^5}}{\sqrt[3]{5b}} = \dfrac{\sqrt[3]{2a^5}}{\sqrt[3]{5b}} \cdot \dfrac{\sqrt[3]{4a}}{\sqrt[3]{4a}} = \dfrac{\sqrt[3]{8a^6}}{\sqrt[3]{20ab}} =$

$\dfrac{2a^2}{\sqrt[3]{20ab}}$

82. $\dfrac{-3}{\sqrt{a^2-3}}$

83. $5\sqrt{\dfrac{x}{y}}+4\sqrt{\dfrac{y}{x}}-\dfrac{3}{\sqrt{xy}} = \dfrac{5\sqrt{x}}{\sqrt{y}}+\dfrac{4\sqrt{y}}{\sqrt{x}}-\dfrac{3}{\sqrt{xy}} =$

$\dfrac{5\sqrt{x}}{\sqrt{y}} \cdot \dfrac{\sqrt{x}}{\sqrt{x}}+\dfrac{4\sqrt{y}}{\sqrt{x}} \cdot \dfrac{\sqrt{y}}{\sqrt{y}}-\dfrac{3}{\sqrt{xy}} = \dfrac{5x}{\sqrt{xy}}+\dfrac{4y}{\sqrt{xy}}-\dfrac{3}{\sqrt{xy}} =$

$\dfrac{5x+4y-3}{\sqrt{xy}} = \dfrac{5x+4y-3}{\sqrt{xy}} \cdot \dfrac{\sqrt{xy}}{\sqrt{xy}} =$

$\dfrac{(5x+4y-3)\sqrt{xy}}{xy}$

84. $1-\sqrt{w}$

85. $\dfrac{1}{4+\sqrt{3}}+\dfrac{1}{\sqrt{3}}+\dfrac{1}{\sqrt{3}-4} =$

$\dfrac{1}{4+\sqrt{3}} \cdot \dfrac{\sqrt{3}(\sqrt{3}-4)}{\sqrt{3}(\sqrt{3}-4)}+\dfrac{1}{\sqrt{3}} \cdot \dfrac{(4+\sqrt{3})(\sqrt{3}-4)}{(4+\sqrt{3})(\sqrt{3}-4)} +$

$\dfrac{1}{\sqrt{3}-4} \cdot \dfrac{\sqrt{3}(4+\sqrt{3})}{\sqrt{3}(4+\sqrt{3})} =$

$\dfrac{3-4\sqrt{3}-16+3+4\sqrt{3}+3}{\sqrt{3}(4+\sqrt{3})(\sqrt{3}-4)} = \dfrac{-7}{\sqrt{3}(-16+3)} =$

$\dfrac{-7}{-13\sqrt{3}} \cdot \dfrac{\sqrt{3}}{\sqrt{3}} = \dfrac{7\sqrt{3}}{39}$

86. ◈

Exercise Set 9.6

1. $\sqrt{5x+1} = 6$

$(\sqrt{5x+1})^2 = 6^2$ Principle of powers (squaring)

$5x+1 = 36$

$5x = 35$

$x = 7$

Check: $\quad\dfrac{\sqrt{5x+1} = 6}{\sqrt{5\cdot 7+1}\ ?\ 6}$
$\begin{array}{c|c}\sqrt{36} & \\ 6 & 6\end{array}$ TRUE

The solution is 7.

2. 33

3. $\sqrt{3x}+1 = 7$

$\sqrt{3x} = 6$ Adding to isolate the radical

$(\sqrt{3x})^2 = 6^2$ Principle of powers (squaring)

$3x = 36$

$x = 12$

Check: $\quad\dfrac{\sqrt{3x}+1 = 7}{\sqrt{3\cdot 12}+1\ ?\ 7}$
$\begin{array}{c|c}6+1 & \\ 7 & 7\end{array}$ TRUE

The solution is 12.

4. 32

5. $\sqrt{y+1}-5 = 8$

$\sqrt{y+1} = 13$ Adding to isolate the radical

$(\sqrt{y+1})^2 = 13^2$ Principle of powers (squaring)

$y+1 = 169$

$y = 168$

Check: $\quad\dfrac{\sqrt{y+1}-5 = 8}{\sqrt{168+1}-5\ ?\ 8}$
$\begin{array}{c|c}13-5 & \\ 8 & 8\end{array}$ TRUE

The solution is 168.

6. 11

7. $\sqrt[3]{x+5} = 2$

$(\sqrt[3]{x+5})^3 = 2^3$

$x+5 = 8$

$x = 3$

Check: $\dfrac{\sqrt[3]{x+5} = 2}{}$

$\sqrt[3]{3+5}$? 2
$\sqrt[3]{8}$
2 $\Big|$ 2   TRUE

The solution is 3.

8. 29

9. $\sqrt[4]{y-3} = 2$
$(\sqrt[4]{y-3})^4 = 2^4$
$y - 3 = 16$
$y = 19$

Check: $\dfrac{\sqrt[4]{y-3} = 2}{}$

$\sqrt[4]{19-3}$? 2
$\sqrt[4]{16}$
2 $\Big|$ 2   TRUE

The solution is 19.

10. 78

11. $3\sqrt{x} = x$
$(3\sqrt{x})^2 = x^2$
$9x = x^2$
$0 = x^2 - 9x$
$0 = x(x - 9)$
$x = 0$ *or* $x = 9$

Check:
For 0: $\dfrac{3\sqrt{x} = x}{}$

$3\sqrt{0}$? 0
$3 \cdot 0$
0 $\Big|$ 0   TRUE

For 9: $\dfrac{3\sqrt{x} = x}{}$

$3\sqrt{9}$? 9
$3 \cdot 3$
9 $\Big|$ 9   TRUE

The solutions are 0 and 9.

12. 0, 64

13. $2y^{1/2} - 7 = 9$
$2\sqrt{y} - 7 = 9$
$2\sqrt{y} = 16$
$\sqrt{y} = 8$
$(\sqrt{y})^2 = 8^2$
$y = 64$

Check: $\dfrac{2y^{1/2} - 7 = 9}{}$

$2 \cdot 64^{1/2} - 7$? 9
$2 \cdot 8 - 7$
9 $\Big|$ 9   TRUE

The solution is 64.

14. No solution

15. $\sqrt[3]{x} = -3$
$(\sqrt[3]{x})^3 = (-3)^3$
$x = -27$

Check: $\dfrac{\sqrt[3]{x} = -3}{}$

$\sqrt{-27}$? -3
$-3 \Big| -3$ TRUE

The solution is -27.

16. -64

17. $t^{1/3} - 2 = 3$
$t^{1/3} = 5$
$(t^{1/3})^3 = 5^3$ Principle of powers
$t = 125$

Check: $\dfrac{t^{1/3} - 2 = 3}{}$

$125^{1/3} - 2$? 3
$5 - 2$
3 $\Big|$ 3   TRUE

The solution is 125.

18. 81

19. $(x + 2)^{1/2} = -4$
$\sqrt{x+2} = -4$

We might observe that this equation has no real-number solution, since the principal square root of a number is never negative. However, we will go through the solution process.

$(\sqrt{x+2})^2 = (-4)^2$
$x + 2 = 16$
$x = 14$

Check: $\dfrac{(x+2)^{1/2} = -4}{}$

$(14 + 2)^{1/2}$? -4
$16^{1/2}$
4 $\Big| -4$ FALSE

The number 14 does not check. The equation has no solution.

20. No solution

21. $\sqrt[4]{2x+3} - 5 = -2$

$\sqrt[4]{2x+3} = 3$

$(\sqrt[4]{2x+3})^4 = 3^4$

$2x + 3 = 81$

$2x = 78$

$x = 39$

Check:
$$\frac{\sqrt[4]{2x+3} - 5 = -2}{}$$

$\sqrt[4]{2 \cdot 39 + 3} - 5 \ ? \ -2$

$\sqrt[4]{81} - 5$

$3 - 5$

$-2 \ \bigg| \ -2$ TRUE

The solution is 39.

22. $\dfrac{80}{3}$

23. $(y-7)^{1/4} = 3$

$[(y-7)^{1/4}]^4 = 3^4$

$y - 7 = 81$

$y = 88$

Check:
$$\frac{(y-7)^{1/4} = 3}{}$$

$(88 - 7)^{1/4} \ ? \ 3$

$81^{1/4}$

$3 \ \big| \ 3$ TRUE

The solution is 88.

24. 59

25. $\sqrt{2t-7} = \sqrt{3t-12}$

$(\sqrt{2t-7})^2 = (\sqrt{3t-12})^2$

$2t - 7 = 3t - 12$

$-7 = t - 12$

$5 = t$

Check:
$$\frac{\sqrt{2t-7} = \sqrt{3t-12}}{}$$

$\sqrt{2 \cdot 5 - 7} \ ? \ \sqrt{3 \cdot 5 - 12}$

$\sqrt{3} \ \big| \ \sqrt{3}$ TRUE

The solution is 5.

26. 1

27. $2(1-x)^{1/3} = 4^{1/3}$

$[2(1-x)^{1/3}]^3 = (4^{1/3})^3$

$8(1-x) = 4$

$8 - 8x = 4$

$-8x = -4$

$x = \dfrac{1}{2}$

The number $\dfrac{1}{2}$ checks and is the solution.

28. $\dfrac{106}{27}$

29. $x = \sqrt{x-1} + 3$

$x - 3 = \sqrt{x-1}$

$(x-3)^2 = (\sqrt{x-1})^2$

$x^2 - 6x + 9 = x - 1$

$x^2 - 7x + 10 = 0$

$(x-2)(x-5) = 0$

$x = 2 \ \ or \ \ x = 5$

Check:

For 2:
$$\frac{x = \sqrt{x-1} + 3}{}$$

$2 \ ? \ \sqrt{2-1} + 3$

$\sqrt{1} + 3$

$1 + 3$

$2 \ \big| \ 4$ FALSE

For 5:
$$\frac{x = \sqrt{x-1} + 3}{}$$

$5 \ ? \ \sqrt{5-1} + 3$

$\sqrt{4} + 3$

$2 + 3$

$5 \ \big| \ 5$ TRUE

Since 5 checks but 2 does not, the solution is 5.

30. 4

31. $3 + \sqrt{z-6} = \sqrt{z+9}$ One radical is already isolated.

$(3 + \sqrt{z-6})^2 = (\sqrt{z+9})^2$ Squaring both sides

$9 + 6\sqrt{z-6} + z - 6 = z + 9$

$6\sqrt{z-6} = 6$

$\sqrt{z-6} = 1$ Multiplying by $\dfrac{1}{6}$

$(\sqrt{z-6})^2 = 1^2$

$z - 6 = 1$

$z = 7$

The number 7 checks and is the solution.

32. 3, 7

33. $\sqrt{20-x}+8 = \sqrt{9-x}+11$

$\sqrt{20-x} = \sqrt{9-x}+3$ Isolating one radical

$(\sqrt{20-x})^2 = (\sqrt{9-x}+3)^2$ Squaring both sides

$20-x = 9-x+6\sqrt{9-x}+9$

$2 = 6\sqrt{9-x}$ Isolating the remaining radical

$1 = 3\sqrt{9-x}$ Multiplying by $\frac{1}{2}$

$1^2 = (3\sqrt{9-x})^2$ Squaring both sides

$1 = 9(9-x)$

$1 = 81-9x$

$-80 = -9x$

$\frac{80}{9} = x$

The number $\frac{80}{9}$ checks and is the solution.

34. $\frac{15}{4}$

35. $\sqrt{x+2}+\sqrt{3x+4} = 2$

$\sqrt{x+2} = 2-\sqrt{3x+4}$ Isolating one radical

$(\sqrt{x+2})^2 = (2-\sqrt{3x+4})^2$

$x+2 = 4-4\sqrt{3x+4}+3x+4$

$-2x-6 = -4\sqrt{3x+4}$ Isolating the remaining radical

$x+3 = 2\sqrt{3x+4}$ Multiplying by $-\frac{1}{2}$

$(x+3)^2 = (2\sqrt{3x+4})^2$

$x^2+6x+9 = 4(3x+4)$

$x^2+6x+9 = 12x+16$

$x^2-6x-7 = 0$

$(x-7)(x+1) = 0$

$x-7=0 \ \text{ or } \ x+1=0$

$x=7 \ \text{ or } \ x=-1$

Check:

For 7:

$$\frac{\sqrt{x+2}+\sqrt{3x+4} = 2}{\sqrt{7+2}+\sqrt{3\cdot 7+4} \ ? \ 2}$$
$$\sqrt{9}+\sqrt{25} \ \Big| $$
$$8 \ \Big| \ 2 \quad \text{FALSE}$$

For -1:

$$\frac{\sqrt{x+2}+\sqrt{3x+4} = 2}{\sqrt{-1+2}+\sqrt{3\cdot(-1)+4} \ ? \ 2}$$
$$\sqrt{1}+\sqrt{1} \ \Big| $$
$$2 \ \Big| \ 2 \quad \text{TRUE}$$

Since -1 checks but 7 does not, the solution is -1.

36. $-1, \frac{1}{3}$

37. We must have $f(a)=7$, or $\sqrt{a-7}=7$.

$\sqrt{a-7} = 7$

$(\sqrt{a-7})^2 = 7^2$

$a-7 = 49$

$a = 56$

The number 56 checks, so $f(a)=7$ when $a=56$.

38. -3

39. We must have $f(a)=5$ or $\sqrt[3]{6a+9}+8=5$.

$\sqrt[3]{6a+9}+8 = 5$

$\sqrt[3]{6a+9} = -3$

$(\sqrt[3]{6a+9})^3 = (-3)^3$

$6a+9 = -27$

$6a = -36$

$a = -6$

The number -6 checks, so $f(a)=5$ when $a=-6$.

40. $-\frac{5}{3}$

41. We must have $f(x)=2$, or $\sqrt{x}+\sqrt{x-9}=1$.

$\sqrt{x}+\sqrt{x-9} = 1$

$\sqrt{x-9} = 1-\sqrt{x}$ Isolating one radical term

$(\sqrt{x-9})^2 = (1-\sqrt{x})^2$

$x-9 = 1-2\sqrt{x}+x$

$-10 = -2\sqrt{x}$ Isolating the remaining radical term

$5 = \sqrt{x}$

$25 = x$

This value does not check. There is no solution, so there is no value of x for which $f(x)=1$.

42. 9

43. We must have $g(a)=-1$, or $\sqrt{2a+7}-\sqrt{a+15}=-1$.

$$\sqrt{2a+7} - \sqrt{a+15} = -1$$
$$\sqrt{2a+7} = \sqrt{a+15} - 1 \quad \text{Isolating}$$
$$\text{one radical term}$$
$$(\sqrt{2a+7})^2 = (\sqrt{a+15} - 1)^2$$
$$2a+7 = a+15 - 2\sqrt{a+15} + 1$$
$$a - 9 = -2\sqrt{a+15} \quad \text{Isolating the}$$
$$\text{remaining radical}$$
$$(a-9)^2 = (-2\sqrt{a+15})^2$$
$$a^2 - 18a + 81 = 4(a+15)$$
$$a^2 - 18a + 81 = 4a + 60$$
$$a^2 - 22a + 21 = 0$$
$$(a-1)(a-21) = 0$$
$$a = 1 \quad or \quad a = 21$$

Since 1 checks but 21 does not, we have $g(a) = -1$ when $a = 1$.

44. 2, 6

45. We must have $\sqrt{2x-3} = \sqrt{x+7} - 2$.
$$\sqrt{2x-3} = \sqrt{x+7} - 2$$
$$(\sqrt{2x-3})^2 = (\sqrt{x+7} - 2)^2$$
$$2x - 3 = x + 7 - 4\sqrt{x+7} + 4$$
$$x - 14 = -4\sqrt{x+7}$$
$$(x-14)^2 = (-4\sqrt{x+7})^2$$
$$x^2 - 28x + 196 = 16(x+7)$$
$$x^2 - 28x + 196 = 16x + 112$$
$$x^2 - 44x + 84 = 0$$
$$(x-2)(x-42) = 0$$
$$x = 2 \quad or \quad x = 42$$

Since 2 checks but 42 does not, we have $f(x) = g(x)$ when $x = 2$.

46. 10

47. We must have $4 - \sqrt{a-3} = (a+5)^{1/2}$.
$$4 - \sqrt{a-3} = (a+5)^{1/2}$$
$$(4 - \sqrt{a-3})^2 = [(a+5)^{1/2}]^2$$
$$16 - 8\sqrt{a-3} + a - 3 = a + 5$$
$$-8\sqrt{a-3} = -8$$
$$\sqrt{a-3} = 1$$
$$(\sqrt{a-3})^2 = 1^2$$
$$a - 3 = 1$$
$$a = 4$$

The number 4 checks, so we have $f(a) = g(a)$ when $a = 4$.

48. 15

49.
$$\frac{3}{2x} + \frac{1}{x} = \frac{2x+3.5}{3x} \quad \text{LCD is } 6x$$

Note that $x \neq 0$.
$$6x\left(\frac{3}{2x} + \frac{1}{x}\right) = 6x\left(\frac{2x+3.5}{3x}\right)$$
$$9 + 6 = 4x + 7$$
$$8 = 4x$$
$$2 = x$$

The number 2 checks and is the solution.

50. Height: 7 in., base: 9 in.

51. Graph: $f(x) = \frac{2}{5}x - 7$

The y-intercept is $(0, -7)$, and the slope is $\frac{2}{5}$. From the y-intercept we go up 2 units and to the right 5 units to the point $(5, -5)$. Knowing two points, we can draw the graph.

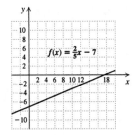

$f(x) = \frac{2}{5}x - 7$

52.

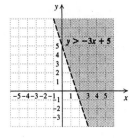

$y > -3x + 5$

53.

54. ◈

55. ◈

56. ◈

57.
$$v = \sqrt{2gr}\sqrt{\frac{h}{r+h}}$$

$$v^2 = 2gr \cdot \frac{h}{r+h} \qquad \text{Squaring both sides}$$

$$v^2(r+h) = 2grh \qquad \text{Multiplying by } r+h$$

$$v^2 r + v^2 h = 2grh$$

$$v^2 r = 2grh - v^2 h$$

$$v^2 r = h(2gr - v^2)$$

$$\frac{v^2 r}{2gr - v^2} = h$$

58. $r = \dfrac{v^2 h}{2gh - v^2}$

59.
$$D(h) = 1.2\sqrt{h}$$
$$180 = 1.2\sqrt{h}$$
$$(180)^2 = (1.2\sqrt{h})^2$$
$$32,400 = 1.44h$$
$$22,500 = h$$

The pilot must fly 22,500 ft above sea level.

60. 72.25 ft

61.
$$\frac{x + \sqrt{x+1}}{x - \sqrt{x+1}} = \frac{5}{11}$$

$$11(x + \sqrt{x+1}) = 5(x - \sqrt{x+1})$$

$$11x + 11\sqrt{x+1} = 5x - 5\sqrt{x+1}$$

$$16\sqrt{x+1} = -6x$$

$$8\sqrt{x+1} = -3x$$

$$(8\sqrt{x+1})^2 = (-3x)^2$$

$$64(x+1) = 9x^2$$

$$64x + 64 = 9x^2$$

$$0 = 9x^2 - 64x - 64$$

$$0 = (9x+8)(x-8)$$

$$9x + 8 = 0 \quad \text{or} \quad x - 8 = 0$$
$$9x = -8 \quad \text{or} \quad x = 8$$
$$x = -\frac{8}{9} \quad \text{or} \quad x = 8$$

Since $-\dfrac{8}{9}$ checks but 8 does not, the solution is $-\dfrac{8}{9}$.

62. 20.032, 19.968

63.
$$(z^2 + 17)^{3/4} = 27$$
$$[(z^2 + 17)^{3/4}]^{4/3} = (3^3)^{4/3}$$
$$z^2 + 17 = 3^4$$
$$z^2 + 17 = 81$$
$$z^2 - 64 = 0$$
$$(z+8)(z-8) = 0$$
$$z = -8 \quad \text{or} \quad z = 8$$

Both -8 and 8 check. They are the solutions.

64. 0

65.
$$x^2 - 5x - \sqrt{x^2 - 5x - 2} = 4$$
$$x^2 - 5x - \sqrt{x^2 - 5x - 2} = 2 + 2$$
$$x^2 - 5x - 2 - \sqrt{x^2 - 5x - 2} - 2 = 0$$

Let $u = \sqrt{x^2 - 5x - 2}$.
$$u^2 - u - 2 = 0$$
$$(u+1)(u-2) = 0$$
$$u = -1 \quad \text{or} \quad u = 2$$

Now we replace u with $\sqrt{x^2 - 5x - 2}$.

$$\sqrt{x^2 - 5x - 2} = -1 \;\text{or}\; \sqrt{x^2 - 5x - 2} = 2$$
$$\text{No solution} \qquad (\sqrt{x^2 - 5x - 2})^2 = 2^2$$
$$x^2 - 5x - 2 = 4$$
$$x^2 - 5x - 6 = 0$$
$$(x-6)(x+1) = 0$$
$$x = 6 \quad \text{or} \quad x = -1$$

Both 6 and -1 check. They are the solutions.

66. 1, 8

67. We find the values of x for which $f(x) = 0$.
$$\sqrt{x-2} - \sqrt{x+2} + 2 = 0$$
$$\sqrt{x-2} + 2 = \sqrt{x+2}$$
$$(\sqrt{x-2} + 2)^2 = (\sqrt{x+2})^2$$
$$x - 2 + 4\sqrt{x-2} + 4 = x + 2$$
$$4\sqrt{x-2} = 0$$
$$\sqrt{x-2} = 0$$
$$(\sqrt{x-2})^2 = 0^2$$
$$x - 2 = 0$$
$$x = 2$$

The number 2 checks. The x-intercept is $(2, 0)$.

68. $\left(\dfrac{1}{36}, 0\right)$, $(36, 0)$

69. We find the values of x for which $f(x) = 0$.

$$(x^2 + 30x)^{1/2} - x - (5x)^{1/2} = 0$$
$$\sqrt{x^2 + 30x} - x - \sqrt{5x} = 0$$
$$\sqrt{x^2 + 30x} - x = \sqrt{5x}$$
$$(\sqrt{x^2 + 30x} - x)^2 = (\sqrt{5x})^2$$
$$x^2 + 30x - 2x\sqrt{x^2 + 30x} + x^2 = 5x$$
$$2x^2 + 25x = 2x\sqrt{x^2 + 30x}$$
$$(2x^2 + 25x)^2 = (2x\sqrt{x^2 + 30x})^2$$
$$4x^4 + 100x^3 + 625x^2 = 4x^2(x^2 + 30x)$$
$$4x^4 + 100x^3 + 625x^2 = 4x^4 + 120x^3$$
$$-20x^3 + 625x^2 = 0$$
$$-5x^2(4x - 125) = 0$$

$$x = 0 \text{ or } x = \frac{125}{4}$$

Both 0 and $\dfrac{125}{4}$ check. The x-intercepts are $(0, 0)$ and $\left(\dfrac{125}{4}, 0\right)$.

Exercise Set 9.7

1. $a = 5, \quad b = 3$

Find c.
$$c^2 = a^2 + b^2 \quad \text{Pythagorean equation}$$
$$c^2 = 5^2 + 3^2 \quad \text{Substituting}$$
$$c^2 = 25 + 9$$
$$c^2 = 34$$
$$c = \sqrt{34} \quad \text{Exact answer}$$
$$c \approx 5.831 \quad \text{Approximation}$$

2. $\sqrt{164}$, 12.806

3. $a = 7, \quad b = 7$

Find c.
$$c^2 = a^2 + b^2 \quad \text{Pythagorean equation}$$
$$c^2 = 7^2 + 7^2 \quad \text{Substituting}$$
$$c^2 = 49 + 49$$
$$c^2 = 98$$
$$c = \sqrt{98} \quad \text{Exact answer}$$
$$c \approx 9.899 \quad \text{Approximation}$$

4. $\sqrt{200}$, 14.142

5. $b = 12, \quad c = 13$

Find a.
$$a^2 + b^2 = c^2 \quad \text{Pythagorean equation}$$
$$a^2 + 12^2 = 13^2 \quad \text{Substituting}$$
$$a^2 + 144 = 169$$
$$a^2 = 25$$
$$a = 5$$

6. $\sqrt{119}$, 10.909

7. $c = 6, \quad a = \sqrt{5}$

Find b.
$$c^2 = a^2 + b^2$$
$$(\sqrt{5})^2 + b^2 = 6^2$$
$$5 + b^2 = 36$$
$$b^2 = 31$$
$$b = \sqrt{31} \quad \text{Exact answer}$$
$$b \approx 5.568 \quad \text{Approximation}$$

8. 4

9. $b = 1, \quad c = \sqrt{13}$

Find a.
$$a^2 + b^2 = c^2 \quad \text{Pythagorean equation}$$
$$a^2 + 1^2 = (\sqrt{13})^2 \quad \text{Substituting}$$
$$a^2 + 1 = 13$$
$$a^2 = 12$$
$$a = \sqrt{12} \quad \text{Exact answer}$$
$$a \approx 3.464 \quad \text{Approximation}$$

10. $\sqrt{19}$, 4.359

11. $a = 1, \quad c = \sqrt{n}$

Find b.
$$a^2 + b^2 = c^2$$
$$1^2 + b^2 = (\sqrt{n})^2$$
$$1 + b^2 = n$$
$$b^2 = n - 1$$
$$b = \sqrt{n - 1}$$

12. $\sqrt{4 - n}$

13. We make a drawing and let $d = $ the length of the guy wire.

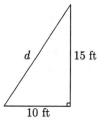

We use the Pythagorean equation to find d.

$d^2 = 10^2 + 15^2$

$d^2 = 100 + 225$

$d^2 = 325$

$d = \sqrt{325}$

$d \approx 18.028$

The wire is $\sqrt{325}$, or about 18.028 ft long.

14. $\sqrt{8450}$ ft, 91.924 ft

15. We first make a drawing and let $d =$ the distance, in feet, to second base. A right triangle is formed in which the length of the leg from second base to third base is 90 ft. The length of the leg from third base to where the catcher fields the ball is $90 - 10$, or 80 ft.

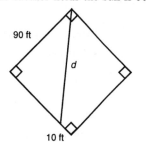

We substitute these values into the Pythagorean equation to find d.

$d^2 = 90^2 + 80^2$

$d^2 = 8100 + 6400$

$d^2 = 14,500$

$d = \sqrt{14,500}$

Exact answer: $d = \sqrt{14,500}$ ft

Approximation: $d \approx 120.416$ ft

16. 12 in.

17. We make a drawing.

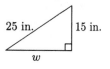

We use the Pythagorean equation to find w.

$w^2 + 15^2 = 25^2$

$w^2 + 225 = 625$

$w^2 = 400$

$w = 20$

The width is 20 in.

18. $\sqrt{340} + 8$ ft, 26.439 ft

19.

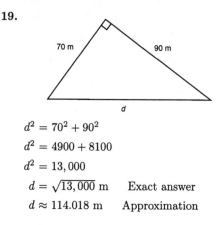

$d^2 = 70^2 + 90^2$

$d^2 = 4900 + 8100$

$d^2 = 13,000$

$d = \sqrt{13,000}$ m   Exact answer

$d \approx 114.018$ m   Approximation

20. 50 ft

21. Since one acute angle is 45°, this is an isosceles right triangle with $b = 5$. Then $a = 5$ also. We substitute to find c.

$c = a\sqrt{2}$

$c = 5\sqrt{2}$

Exact answer: $a = 5$, $c = 5\sqrt{2}$

Approximation: $c \approx 7.071$

22. $a = 14$, $c = 14\sqrt{2} \approx 19.799$.

23. This is a 30-60-90 right triangle with $c = 14$. We substitute to find a and b.

$c = 2a$

$14 = 2a$

$7 = a$

$b = a\sqrt{3}$

$b = 7\sqrt{3}$

Exact answer: $a = 7$, $b = 7\sqrt{3}$

Approximation: $b \approx 12.124$

24. $a = 9$, $b = 9\sqrt{3} \approx 15.588$

25. This is a 30-60-90 right triangle with $b = 15$. We substitute to find a and c.

$$b = a\sqrt{3}$$
$$15 = a\sqrt{3}$$
$$\frac{15}{\sqrt{3}} = a$$
$$\frac{15\sqrt{3}}{3} = a \quad \text{Rationalizing the denominator}$$
$$5\sqrt{3} = a \quad \text{Simplifying}$$
$$c = 2a$$
$$c = 2 \cdot 5\sqrt{3}$$
$$c = 10\sqrt{3}$$

Exact answer: $a = 5\sqrt{3}$, $c = 10\sqrt{3}$

Approximations: $a \approx 8.660$, $c \approx 17.321$

26. $a = 4\sqrt{2} \approx 5.657$ $b = 4\sqrt{2} \approx 5.657$

27. This is an isosceles right triangle with $c = 13$. We substitute to find a.
$$a = \frac{c\sqrt{2}}{2}$$
$$a = \frac{13\sqrt{2}}{2}$$

Since $a = b$, we have $b = \dfrac{13\sqrt{2}}{2}$ also.

Exact answer: $a = \dfrac{13\sqrt{2}}{2}$, $b = \dfrac{13\sqrt{2}}{2}$

Approximations: $a \approx 9.192$, $b \approx 9.192$

28. $a = \dfrac{7\sqrt{3}}{3} \approx 4.041$, $c = \dfrac{14\sqrt{3}}{3} \approx 8.083$

29. This is a 30-60-90 triangle with $a = 14$. We substitute to find b and c.
$$b = a\sqrt{3} \qquad c = 2a$$
$$b = 14\sqrt{3} \qquad c = 2 \cdot 14$$
$$c = 28$$

Exact answer: $b = 14\sqrt{3}$, $c = 28$

Approximation: $b \approx 24.249$

30. $b = 9\sqrt{3} \approx 15.588$, $c = 18$

31.

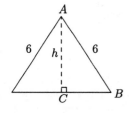

This is an equilateral triangle, so all the angles are 60°. The altitude bisects one angle and one side. Then triangle ABC is a 30-60-90 right triangle with the shorter leg of length 6/2, or 3, and hypotenuse of length 6. We substitute to find the length of the other leg.
$$b = a\sqrt{3}$$
$$h = 3\sqrt{3} \quad \text{Substituting } h \text{ for } b \text{ and 3 for } a$$

Exact answer: $h = 3\sqrt{3}$

Approximation: $h \approx 5.196$

32. $5\sqrt{3} \approx 8.660$

33.

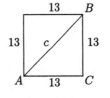

Triangle ABC is an isosceles right triangle with $a = 13$. We substitute to find c.
$$c = a\sqrt{2}$$
$$c = 13\sqrt{2}$$

Exact answer: $c = 13\sqrt{2}$

Approximation: $c \approx 18.385$

34. $7\sqrt{2} \approx 9.899$

35.

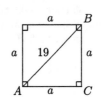

Triangle ABC is an isosceles right triangle with $c = 19$. We substitute to find a.
$$a = \frac{c\sqrt{2}}{2}$$
$$a = \frac{19\sqrt{2}}{2}$$

Exact answer: $a = \dfrac{19\sqrt{2}}{2}$

Approximation: $a \approx 13.435$

36. $\dfrac{15\sqrt{2}}{2} \approx 10.607$

37. We will express all distances in feet. Recall that 1 mi = 5280 ft.

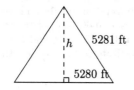

We use the Pythagorean equation to find h.

$$h^2 + (5280)^2 = (5281)^2$$
$$h^2 + 27,878,400 = 27,888,961$$
$$h^2 = 10,561$$
$$h = \sqrt{10,561}$$
$$h \approx 102.767$$

The height of the bulge is $\sqrt{10,561}$ ft, or about 102.767 ft.

38. Neither; they have the same area, 300 ft^2

39.

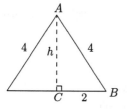

The entrance is an equilateral triangle, so all the angles are 60°. The altitude bisects one angle and one side. Then triangle ABC is a 30-60-90 right triangle with the shorter leg of length 4/2, or 2, and hypotenuse of length 4. We substitute to find h, the height of the tent.

$$b = a\sqrt{3}$$

$$h = 2\sqrt{3} \qquad \text{Substituting } h \text{ for } b \text{ and 2 for } a$$

Exact answer: $h = 2\sqrt{3}$ ft

Approximation: $h \approx 3.464$ ft

40. $d = s + s\sqrt{2}$

41.

Triangle ABC is an isosceles right triangle with $c = 8\sqrt{2}$. We substitute to find a.

$$a = \frac{c\sqrt{2}}{2} = \frac{8\sqrt{2} \cdot \sqrt{2}}{2} = \frac{8 \cdot 2}{2} = 8$$

The length of a side of the square is 8 ft.

42. $\sqrt{181}$ cm, 13.454 cm

43.

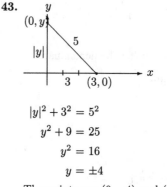

$$|y|^2 + 3^2 = 5^2$$
$$y^2 + 9 = 25$$
$$y^2 = 16$$
$$y = \pm 4$$

The points are $(0, -4)$ and $(0, 4)$.

44. $(3, 0)$, $(-3, 0)$

45.
$$d = \sqrt{(x_2 - x_1)^2 + (y_2 + y_1)^2} \quad \text{Distance formula}$$
$$= \sqrt{(6 - 2)^2 + (10 - 7)^2} \qquad \text{Substituting}$$
$$= \sqrt{4^2 + 3^2}$$
$$= \sqrt{25} = 5$$

46. 10

47.
$$d = \sqrt{(x_2 - x_1)^2 + (y_2 - y_1)^2} \quad \text{Distance formula}$$
$$= \sqrt{(3 - 0)^2 + [-4 - (-7)]^2} \quad \text{Substituting}$$
$$= \sqrt{3^2 + 3^2}$$
$$= \sqrt{18} \approx 4.243 \quad \text{Simplifying and approximating}$$

48. 10

(Since these points are on a vertical line, we could have found the distance between them by computing $|-8 - 2|$.)

49.
$$d = \sqrt{(x_2 - x_1)^2 + (y_2 - y_1)^2}$$
$$= \sqrt{[5 - (-5)]^2 + (-5 - 5)^2}$$
$$= \sqrt{200} \approx 14.142$$

50. $\sqrt{464}$, 21.541

51.
$$d = \sqrt{(x_2 - x_1)^2 + (y_2 - y_1)^2}$$
$$= \sqrt{(-9.2 - 8.6)^2 + [-3.4 - (-3.4)]^2}$$
$$= \sqrt{(-17.8)^2 + 0^2}$$
$$= \sqrt{316.84} = 17.8$$

(Since these points are on a horizontal line, we could have found the distance between them by finding $|x_2 - x_1| = |-9.2 - 8.6| = |-17.8| = 17.8$.)

52. $\sqrt{98.93}$, 9.946

53. $d = \sqrt{(x_2 - x_1)^2 + (y_2 - y_1)^2}$

$d = \sqrt{(\sqrt{6} - 0)^2 + (0 - \sqrt{7})^2}$

$= \sqrt{(\sqrt{6})^2 + (-\sqrt{7})^2}$

$= \sqrt{6 + 7}$

$= \sqrt{13} \approx 3.606$

54. $\sqrt{8}$, 2.828

55. $d = \sqrt{(x_2 - x_1)^2 + (y_2 - y_1)^2}$

$d = \sqrt{(s - 0)^2 + (t - 0)^2}$

$= \sqrt{s^2 + t^2}$

56. $\sqrt{p^2 + q^2}$

57. $(x - 2)^2 + (y - 5)^2 = 10^2$

The equation is in standard form. The center is $(2, 5)$ and the radius is 10.

58. $(0, 1)$; 5

59. $(x + 2)^2 + y^2 = 64$

We write the equation in standard form.

$[x - (-2)]^2 + (y - 0)^2 = 8^2$

The center is $(-2, 0)$ and the radius is 8.

60. $(7, -1)$; 1

61. $(x - 3)^2 + (y + 4)^2 = 7$

We write the equation in standard form.

$(x - 3)^2 + [y - (-4)]^2 = (\sqrt{7})^2$

The center is $(3, -4)$ and the radius is $\sqrt{7}$.

62. $(-1, 1)$; $\sqrt{13}$

63. $(x - h)^2 + (y - k)^2 = r^2$ Standard form

$(x - 0)^2 + (y - 3)^2 = 6^2$, or

$x^2 + (y - 3)^2 = 36$

64. $(x - 2)^2 + (y - 1)^2 = 16$

65. $(x - h)^2 + (y - k)^2 = r^2$ Standard form

$(x - (-5))^2 + (y - (-7))^2 = 1^2$, or

$(x + 5)^2 + (y + 7)^2 = 1$

66. $(x + 4)^2 + y^2 = 9$

67. $(x - h)^2 + (y - k)^2 = r^2$ Standard form

$(x - 5)^2 + (y - 7)^2 = (\sqrt{3})^2$, or

$(x - 5)^2 + (y - 7)^2 = 3$

68. $(x + 10)^2 + (y + 10)^2 = 5$

69. $x^2 - 11x + 24 = 0$

$(x - 8)(x - 3) = 0$

$x - 8 = 0$ or $x - 3 = 0$

$x = 8$ or $x = 3$

The solutions are 8 and 3.

70. $-7, \dfrac{3}{2}$

71. $|3x - 5| = 7$

$3x - 5 = 7$ or $3x - 5 = -7$

$3x = 12$ or $3x = -2$

$x = 4$ or $x = -\dfrac{2}{3}$

The solution set is $\left\{ 4, -\dfrac{2}{3} \right\}$.

72. $\left\{ 10, -\dfrac{4}{3} \right\}$

73. ◈

74. ◈

75.

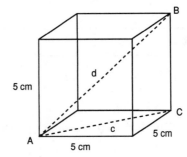

First find the length of a diagonal of the base of the cube. It is the hypotenuse of an isosceles right triangle with $a = 5$ cm. Then $c = a\sqrt{2} = 5\sqrt{2}$ cm.

Triangle ABC is a right triangle with legs of $5\sqrt{2}$ cm and 5 cm and hypotenuse d. Use the Pythagorean equation to find d, the length of the diagonal that connects two opposite corners of the cube.

$d^2 = (5\sqrt{2})^2 + 5^2$

$d^2 = 25 \cdot 2 + 25$

$d^2 = 50 + 25$

$d^2 = 75$

$d = \sqrt{75}$

Exact answer: $d = \sqrt{75}$ cm

76. 9

77.

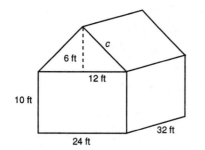

The area to be painted consists of two 10 ft by 24 ft rectangles, two 10 ft by 32 ft rectangles, and two triangles with height 6 ft and base 24 ft. The area of the two 10 ft by 24 ft rectangle is $2 \cdot 10 \text{ ft} \cdot 24 \text{ ft} = 480 \text{ ft}^2$. The area of the two 10 ft by 32 ft rectangles is $2 \cdot 10 \text{ ft} \cdot 32 \text{ ft} = 640 \text{ ft}^2$. The area of the two triangles is $2 \cdot \dfrac{1}{2} \cdot 24 \text{ ft} \cdot 6 \text{ ft} = 144 \text{ ft}^2$. Thus, the total area to be painted is $480 \text{ ft}^2 + 640 \text{ ft}^2 + 144 \text{ ft}^2 = 1264 \text{ ft}^2$.

One gallon of paint covers 275 ft^2, so we divide to determine how many gallons of paint are required: $\dfrac{1264}{275} \approx 4.6$. Thus, 4 gallons of paint should be bought to paint the house. This answer assumes that the total area of the doors and windows is at least 164 ft^2 $(4 \cdot 275 = 1100 \text{ and } 1264 = 1100 + 164)$.

Exercise Set 9.8

1. $\sqrt{-25} = \sqrt{-1 \cdot 25} = \sqrt{-1} \cdot \sqrt{25} = i \cdot 5 = 5i$

2. $6i$

3. $\sqrt{-13} = \sqrt{-1 \cdot 13} = \sqrt{-1} \cdot \sqrt{13} = i\sqrt{13}$, or $\sqrt{13}i$

4. $i\sqrt{19}$, or $\sqrt{19}i$

5. $\sqrt{-18} = \sqrt{-1} \cdot \sqrt{9} \cdot \sqrt{2} = i \cdot 3 \cdot \sqrt{2} = 3i\sqrt{2}$, or $3\sqrt{2}i$

6. $7i\sqrt{2}$, or $7\sqrt{2}i$

7. $\sqrt{-3} = \sqrt{-1 \cdot 3} = \sqrt{-1} \cdot \sqrt{3} = i\sqrt{3}$, or $\sqrt{3}i$

8. $2i$

9. $\sqrt{-81} = \sqrt{-1 \cdot 81} = \sqrt{-1} \cdot \sqrt{81} = i \cdot 9 = 9i$

10. $3i\sqrt{3}$, or $3\sqrt{3}i$

11. $\sqrt{-300} = \sqrt{-1} \cdot \sqrt{100} \cdot \sqrt{3} = i \cdot 10 \cdot \sqrt{3} = 10i\sqrt{3}$, or $10\sqrt{3}i$

12. $-5i\sqrt{3}$, or $-5\sqrt{3}i$

13. $-\sqrt{-49} = -\sqrt{-1 \cdot 49} = -\sqrt{-1} \cdot \sqrt{49} = -i \cdot 7 = -7i$

14. $-5i\sqrt{5}$, or $-5\sqrt{5}i$

15. $4 - \sqrt{-60} = 4 - \sqrt{-1 \cdot 60} = 4 - \sqrt{-1} \cdot \sqrt{60} = 4 - i \cdot 2\sqrt{15} = 4 - 2\sqrt{15}i$, or $4 - 2i\sqrt{15}$

16. $6 - 2i\sqrt{21}$, or $6 - 2\sqrt{21}i$

17. $\sqrt{-4} + \sqrt{-12} = \sqrt{-1 \cdot 4} + \sqrt{-1 \cdot 12} = \sqrt{-1} \cdot \sqrt{4} + \sqrt{-1} \cdot \sqrt{12} = i \cdot 2 + i \cdot 2\sqrt{3} = (2 + 2\sqrt{3})i$

18. $(-2\sqrt{19} + 5\sqrt{5})i$

19. $\quad (4 + 7i) + (5 - 2i)$
$\quad = (4 + 5) + (7 - 2)i \qquad$ Combining the real and the imaginary parts
$\quad = 9 + 5i$

20. $12 + i$

21. $\quad (-2 + 8i) + (5 + 3i)$
$\quad = (-2 + 5) + (8 + 3)i \qquad$ Combining the real and the imaginary parts
$\quad = 3 + 11i$

22. $7 + 4i$

23. $(9 + 8i) - (5 + 3i) = (9 - 5) + (8 - 3)i$
$\qquad\qquad\qquad\qquad = 4 + 5i$

24. $7 + 3i$

25. $(8 - 3i) - (9 + 2i) = (8 - 9) + (-3 - 2)i$
$\qquad\qquad\qquad\qquad = -1 - 5i$

26. $2 - i$

27. $(-2 + 6i) - (-7 + i) = -2 - (-7) + (6 - 1)i$
$\qquad\qquad\qquad\qquad = 5 + 5i$

28. $-12 - 5i$

29. $6i \cdot 5i = 30 \cdot i^2$
$\qquad\quad = 30 \cdot (-1) \qquad\qquad i^2 = -1$
$\qquad\quad = -30$

30. -42

31. $7i \cdot (-9i) = -63 \cdot i^2$
$\qquad\qquad = -63 \cdot (-1) \qquad\qquad i^2 = -1$
$\qquad\qquad = 63$

32. -24

33. $\sqrt{-49}\sqrt{-25} = \sqrt{-1} \cdot \sqrt{49} \cdot \sqrt{-1} \cdot \sqrt{25}$
$$= i \cdot 7 \cdot i \cdot 5$$
$$= i^2 \cdot 35$$
$$= -1 \cdot 35$$
$$= -35$$

34. -18

35. $\sqrt{-6}\sqrt{-7} = \sqrt{-1} \cdot \sqrt{6} \cdot \sqrt{-1} \cdot \sqrt{7}$
$$= i \cdot \sqrt{6} \cdot i \cdot \sqrt{7}$$
$$= i^2 \cdot \sqrt{42}$$
$$= -1 \cdot \sqrt{42}$$
$$= -\sqrt{42}$$

36. $-\sqrt{10}$

37. $\sqrt{-15}\sqrt{-10} = \sqrt{-1} \cdot \sqrt{15} \cdot \sqrt{-1} \cdot \sqrt{10}$
$$= i \cdot \sqrt{15} \cdot i \cdot \sqrt{10}$$
$$= i^2 \cdot \sqrt{150}$$
$$= -\sqrt{25 \cdot 6}$$
$$= -5\sqrt{6}$$

38. $-3\sqrt{14}$

39. $2i(7 + 3i)$
$$= 2i \cdot 7 + 2i \cdot 3i \quad \text{Using the distributive law}$$
$$= 14i + 6i^2$$
$$= 14i - 6 \qquad i^2 = -1$$
$$= -6 + 14i$$

40. $-30 + 10i$

41. $-4i(6 - 5i) = -4i \cdot 6 - 4i(-5i)$
$$= -24i + 20i^2$$
$$= -24i - 20$$
$$= -20 - 24i$$

42. $-28 - 21i$

43. $(2 + 5i)(4 + 3i)$
$$= 8 + 6i + 20i + 15i^2 \quad \text{Using FOIL}$$
$$= 8 + 6i + 20i - 15 \quad i^2 = -1$$
$$= -7 + 26i$$

44. $1 + 5i$

45. $(5 - 6i)(2 + 5i) = 10 + 25i - 12i - 30i^2$
$$= 10 + 25i - 12i + 30$$
$$= 40 + 13i$$

46. $38 + 9i$

47. $(-4 + 5i)(3 - 4i) = -12 + 16i + 15i - 20i^2$
$$= -12 + 16i + 15i + 20$$
$$= 8 + 31i$$

48. $2 - 46i$

49. $(7 - 3i)(4 - 7i) = 28 - 49i - 12i + 21i^2 =$
$28 - 49i - 12i - 21 = 7 - 61i$

50. $5 - 37i$

51. $(-3 + 6i)(-3 + 4i) = 9 - 12i - 18i + 24i^2 =$
$9 - 12i - 18i - 24 = -15 - 30i$

52. $-11 - 16i$

53. $(2 + 9i)(-3 - 5i) = -6 - 10i - 27i - 45i^2 =$
$-6 - 10i - 27i + 45 = 39 - 37i$

54. $13 - 47i$

55. $(5 - 2i)^2$
$$= 5^2 - 2 \cdot 5 \cdot 2i + (2i)^2 \quad \text{Squaring a binomial}$$
$$= 25 - 20i + 4i^2$$
$$= 25 - 20i - 4 \qquad i^2 = -1$$
$$= 21 - 20i$$

56. $5 - 12i$

57. $(4 + 2i)^2$
$$= 4^2 + 2 \cdot 4 \cdot 2i + (2i)^2 \quad \text{Squaring a binomial}$$
$$= 16 + 16i + 4i^2$$
$$= 16 + 16i - 4 \qquad i^2 = -1$$
$$= 12 + 16i$$

58. $-5 + 12i$

59. $(-5 - 2i)^2 = 25 + 20i + 4i^2 = 25 + 20i - 4 =$
$21 + 20i$

60. $-5 - 12i$

61. $\dfrac{7}{2 - i}$
$$= \dfrac{7}{2 - i} \cdot \dfrac{2 + i}{2 + i} \quad \text{Multiplying by 1, using the conjugate}$$
$$= \dfrac{14 + 7i}{4 - i^2} \quad \text{Multiplying}$$
$$= \dfrac{14 + 7i}{4 - (-1)} \qquad i^2 = -1$$
$$= \dfrac{14 + 7i}{5}$$
$$= \dfrac{14}{5} + \dfrac{7}{5}i$$

62. $\dfrac{6}{5} - \dfrac{2}{5}i$

63.

$$\dfrac{3i}{5 + 2i}$$

$$= \dfrac{3i}{5 + 2i} \cdot \dfrac{5 - 2i}{5 - 2i} \quad \text{Multiplying by 1,} \\ \text{using the conjugate}$$

$$= \dfrac{15i - 6i^2}{25 - 4i^2} \quad \text{Multiplying}$$

$$= \dfrac{15i + 6}{25 + 4}$$

$$= \dfrac{15i + 6}{29}$$

$$= \dfrac{6}{29} + \dfrac{15}{29}i$$

64. $-\dfrac{6}{17} + \dfrac{10}{17}i$

65. $\dfrac{8}{9i} = \dfrac{8}{9i} \cdot \dfrac{-9i}{-9i} = \dfrac{-72i}{-81i^2} = \dfrac{-72i}{81} = -\dfrac{8}{9}i$

66. $-\dfrac{5}{8}i$

67. $\dfrac{7 - 2i}{6i} = \dfrac{7 - 2i}{6i} \cdot \dfrac{-6i}{-6i} = \dfrac{-42i + 12i^2}{-36i^2} =$

$\dfrac{-42i - 12}{36} = -\dfrac{12}{36} - \dfrac{42}{36}i = -\dfrac{1}{3} - \dfrac{7}{6}i$

68. $\dfrac{8}{9} - \dfrac{1}{3}i$

69. $\dfrac{4 + 5i}{3 - 7i} = \dfrac{4 + 5i}{3 - 7i} \cdot \dfrac{3 + 7i}{3 + 7i} = \dfrac{12 + 28i + 15i + 35i^2}{9 - 49i^2} =$

$\dfrac{12 + 28i + 15i - 35}{9 + 49} = \dfrac{-23 + 43i}{58} = -\dfrac{23}{58} + \dfrac{43}{58}i$

70. $\dfrac{23}{65} + \dfrac{41}{65}i$

71. $\dfrac{3 - 2i}{4 + 3i} = \dfrac{3 - 2i}{4 + 3i} \cdot \dfrac{4 - 3i}{4 - 3i} = \dfrac{12 - 9i - 8i + 6i^2}{16 - 9i^2} =$

$\dfrac{12 - 9i - 8i - 6}{16 + 9} = \dfrac{6 - 17i}{25} = \dfrac{6}{25} - \dfrac{17}{25}i$

72. $\dfrac{1}{15} - \dfrac{4}{5}i$

73. $i^7 = i^6 \cdot i = (i^2)^3 \cdot i = (-1)^3 \cdot i = -1 \cdot i = -i$

74. $-i$

75. $i^{24} = (i^2)^{12} = (-1)^{12} = 1$

76. $-i$

77. $i^{42} = (i^2)^{21} = (-1)^{21} = -1$

78. 1

79. $i^9 = (i^2)^4 \cdot i = (-1)^4 \cdot i = 1 \cdot i = i$

80. i

81. $i^6 = (i^2)^3 = (-1)^3 = -1$

82. 1

83. $(5i)^3 = 5^3 \cdot i^3 = 125 \cdot i^2 \cdot i = 125(-1)(i) = -125i$

84. $-243i$

85. $i^2 + i^4 = -1 + (i^2)^2 = -1 + (-1)^2 = -1 + 1 = 0$

86. i

87. $i^5 + i^7 = i^4 \cdot i + i^6 \cdot i = (i^2)^2 \cdot i + (i^2)^3 \cdot i =$
$(-1)^2 \cdot i + (-1)^3 \cdot i = 1 \cdot i + (-1)i = i - i = 0$

88. 0

89. $\dfrac{x + 2}{x} + \dfrac{1}{x + 2} = \dfrac{4}{x^2 + 2x}$

Note: $x^2 + 2x = x(x + 2)$.

The LCD $= x(x + 2)$.

Note that $x \neq 0$ and $x \neq -2$.

$$x(x + 2)\left(\dfrac{x + 2}{x} + \dfrac{1}{x + 2} \right) =$$

$$x(x + 2) \cdot \dfrac{4}{x^2 + 2x}$$

$$(x + 2)(x + 2) + x \cdot 1 = 4$$

$$x^2 + 4x + 4 + x = 4$$

$$x^2 + 5x + 4 = 4$$

$$x^2 + 5x = 0$$

$$x(x + 5) = 0$$

$$x = 0 \quad or \quad x + 5 = 0$$
$$x = 0 \quad or \qquad x = -5$$

As noted above, 0 cannot be a solution. The number -5 checks. It is the solution.

90. $\dfrac{70}{29}$

91. $28 = 3x^2 - 17x$

$$0 = 3x^2 - 17x - 28$$

$$0 = (3x + 4)(x - 7)$$

$$3x + 4 = 0 \quad \text{or} \quad x - 7 = 0$$
$$3x = -4 \quad \text{or} \qquad x = 7$$
$$x = -\frac{4}{3} \quad \text{or} \qquad x = 7$$

Both values check. The solutions are $-\dfrac{4}{3}$ and 7.

92. $\left\{ x \,\middle|\, -\dfrac{29}{3} < x < 5 \right\}$, or $\left(-\dfrac{29}{3}, 5 \right)$

93. ◈

94. ◈

95. ◈

96. ◈

97. $g(2i) = \dfrac{(2i)^4 - (2i)^2}{2i - 1} = \dfrac{16i^4 - 4i^2}{-1 + 2i} = \dfrac{20}{-1 + 2i} =$

$\dfrac{20}{-1 + 2i} \cdot \dfrac{-1 - 2i}{-1 - 2i} = \dfrac{-20 - 40i}{5} = -4 - 8i;$

$g(i + 1) = \dfrac{(i + 1)^4 - (i + 1)^2}{(i + 1) - 1} =$

$\dfrac{(i + 1)^2[(i + 1)^2 - 1]}{i} = \dfrac{2i(2i - 1)}{i} = 2(2i - 1) =$

$-2 + 4i;$

$g(2i - 1) = \dfrac{(2i - 1)^4 - (2i - 1)^2}{(2i - 1) - 1} =$

$\dfrac{(2i - 1)^2[(2i - 1)^2 - 1]}{2i - 2} = \dfrac{(-3 - 4i)(-4 - 4i)}{-2 + 2i} =$

$\dfrac{(-3 - 4i)(-2 - 2i)}{-1 + i} = \dfrac{-2 + 14i}{-1 + i} =$

$\dfrac{-2 + 14i}{-1 + i} \cdot \dfrac{-1 - i}{-1 - i} = \dfrac{16 - 12i}{2} = 8 - 6i$

98. $\dfrac{250}{41} + \dfrac{200}{41}i$

99. $\dfrac{i^5 + i^6 + i^7 + i^8}{(1 - i)^4} =$

$\dfrac{(i^2)^2 \cdot i + (i^2)^3 + (i^2)^3 \cdot i + (i^2)^4}{(1 - i)^2(1 - i)^2} =$

$\dfrac{(-1)^2 \cdot i + (-1)^3 + (-1)^3 \cdot i + (-1)^4}{-2i(-2i)} =$

$\dfrac{i - 1 - i + 1}{-4} = 0$

100. 8

101. $\dfrac{5 - \sqrt{5}i}{\sqrt{5}i} = \dfrac{5 - \sqrt{5}i}{\sqrt{5}i} \cdot \dfrac{-\sqrt{5}i}{-\sqrt{5}i} = \dfrac{-5\sqrt{5}i - 5}{5} =$

$-\dfrac{5}{5} - \dfrac{5\sqrt{5}}{5}i = -1 - \sqrt{5}i$

102. $\dfrac{3}{5} + \dfrac{9}{5}i$

103. $\left(\dfrac{1}{2} - \dfrac{1}{3}i\right)^2 - \left(\dfrac{1}{2} + \dfrac{1}{3}i\right)^2 =$

$\dfrac{1}{4} - \dfrac{1}{3}i - \dfrac{1}{9} - \left(\dfrac{1}{4} + \dfrac{1}{3}i - \dfrac{1}{9}\right) =$

$\dfrac{1}{4} - \dfrac{1}{3}i - \dfrac{1}{9} - \dfrac{1}{4} - \dfrac{1}{3}i + \dfrac{1}{9} = -\dfrac{2}{3}i$

104. 1

Chapter 10

Quadratic Functions and Equations

Exercise Set 10.1

1. There are 2 x-intercepts, so there are 2 real-number solutions.

2. 0

3. There is 1 x-intercept, so there is 1 real-number solution.

4. 2

5. There are no x-intercepts, so there are no real-number solutions.

6. 1

7.
$$5x^2 = 15$$
$$x^2 = 3 \qquad \text{Multiplying by } \frac{1}{5}$$
$$x = \sqrt{3} \text{ or } x = -\sqrt{3} \qquad \text{Using the principle of square roots}$$
The solutions are $\sqrt{3}$ and $-\sqrt{3}$, or $\pm\sqrt{3}$.

8. $\pm\sqrt{5}$

9.
$$25x^2 + 4 = 0$$
$$x^2 = -\frac{4}{25} \qquad \text{Isolating } x^2$$
$$x = \sqrt{-\frac{4}{25}} \text{ or } x = -\sqrt{-\frac{4}{25}} \qquad \text{Principle of square roots}$$
$$x = \sqrt{\frac{4}{25}}\sqrt{-1} \text{ or } x = -\sqrt{\frac{4}{25}}\sqrt{-1}$$
$$x = \frac{2}{5}i \text{ or } x = -\frac{2}{5}i$$
The solutions are $\frac{2}{5}i$ and $-\frac{2}{5}i$, or $\pm\frac{2}{5}i$.

10. $\pm\frac{4}{3}i$

11.
$$2x^2 - 3 = 0$$
$$x^2 = \frac{3}{2}$$
$$x = \sqrt{\frac{3}{2}} \text{ or } x = -\sqrt{\frac{3}{2}} \qquad \text{Principle of square roots}$$
$$x = \sqrt{\frac{3}{2}\cdot\frac{2}{2}} \text{ or } x = -\sqrt{\frac{3}{2}\cdot\frac{2}{2}} \qquad \text{Rationalizing denominators}$$
$$x = \frac{\sqrt{6}}{2} \text{ or } x = -\frac{\sqrt{6}}{2}$$
The solutions are $\sqrt{\frac{3}{2}}$ and $-\sqrt{\frac{3}{2}}$. This can also be written as $\pm\sqrt{\frac{3}{2}}$ or, if we rationalize the denominator, $\pm\frac{\sqrt{6}}{2}$.

12. $\pm\frac{\sqrt{21}}{3}$

13.
$$(x + 2)^2 = 49$$
$$x + 2 = 7 \text{ or } x + 2 = -7 \qquad \text{Principle of square roots}$$
$$x = 5 \text{ or } x = -9$$
The solutions are 5 and -9.

14. $1 \pm \sqrt{6}$

15.
$$(a + 5)^2 = 8$$
$$a + 5 = \sqrt{8} \text{ or } a + 5 = -\sqrt{8} \qquad \text{Principle of square roots}$$
$$a + 5 = 2\sqrt{2} \text{ or } a + 5 = -2\sqrt{2} \qquad (\sqrt{8} = \sqrt{4\cdot2} = 2\sqrt{2})$$
$$a = -5 + 2\sqrt{2} \text{ or } a = -5 - 2\sqrt{2}$$
The solutions are $-5 + 2\sqrt{2}$ and $-5 - 2\sqrt{2}$, or $-5 \pm 2\sqrt{2}$.

16. 5, 21

17.
$$(x - 7)^2 = -4$$
$$x - 7 = \sqrt{-4} \quad \text{or} \quad x - 7 = -\sqrt{-4}$$
$$x - 7 = 2i \quad \text{or} \quad x - 7 = -2i$$
$$x = 7 + 2i \quad \text{or} \quad x = 7 - 2i$$
The solutions are $7 + 2i$ and $7 - 2i$, or $7 \pm 2i$.

18. $-1 \pm 3i$

19. $\left(x + \dfrac{3}{2}\right)^2 = \dfrac{7}{2}$

$$x + \dfrac{3}{2} = \sqrt{\dfrac{7}{2}} \ or \ x + \dfrac{3}{2} = -\sqrt{\dfrac{7}{2}}$$

$$x + \dfrac{3}{2} = \sqrt{\dfrac{7}{2} \cdot \dfrac{2}{2}} \ or \ x + \dfrac{3}{2} = -\sqrt{\dfrac{7}{2} \cdot \dfrac{2}{2}}$$

$$x + \dfrac{3}{2} = \dfrac{\sqrt{14}}{2} \ or \ x + \dfrac{3}{2} = -\dfrac{\sqrt{14}}{2}$$

$$x = -\dfrac{3}{2} + \dfrac{\sqrt{14}}{2} \ or \ x = -\dfrac{3}{2} - \dfrac{\sqrt{14}}{2}$$

$$x = \dfrac{-3 + \sqrt{14}}{2} \ or \ x = \dfrac{-3 - \sqrt{14}}{2}$$

The solutions are $\dfrac{-3 + \sqrt{14}}{2}$ and $\dfrac{-3 - \sqrt{14}}{2}$, or $\dfrac{-3 + \sqrt{14}}{2}$.

20. $\dfrac{-3 \pm \sqrt{17}}{4}$

21. $x^2 - 6x + 9 = 100$

$$(x - 3)^2 = 100$$
$$x - 3 = 10 \ or \ x - 3 = -10$$
$$x = 13 \ or \ x = -7$$

The solutions are 13 and −7.

22. −3, 13

23. $f(x) = 16$

$$(x - 7)^2 = 16 \qquad \text{Substituting}$$
$$x - 7 = 4 \ or \ x - 7 = -4$$
$$x = 11 \ \ or \ \ x = 3$$

The solutions are 11 and 3.

24. −3, 7

25. $F(x) = 13$

$$(x - 3)^2 = 13 \quad \text{Substituting}$$
$$x - 3 = \sqrt{13} \qquad or \ x - 3 = -\sqrt{13}$$
$$x = 3 + \sqrt{13} \ or \qquad x = 3 - \sqrt{13}$$

The solutions are $3 + \sqrt{13}$ and $3 - \sqrt{13}$, or $3 \pm \sqrt{13}$.

26. $-3 \pm \sqrt{17}$

27. $g(x) = 36$

$$x^2 + 14x + 49 = 36 \quad \text{Substituting}$$
$$(x + 7)^2 = 36$$
$$x + 7 = 6 \quad or \ x + 7 = -6$$
$$x = -1 \ or \qquad x = -13$$

The solutions are −1 and −13.

28. −7, −1

29. $x^2 + 10x$

We take half the coefficient of x and square it:
Half of 10 is 5, and $5^2 = 25$. We add 25.
$x^2 + 10x + 25$, $(x + 5)^2$

30. $x^2 + 16x + 64$, $(x + 8)^2$

31. $x^2 - 6x$

We take half the coefficient of x and square it:
Half of −6 is −3, and $(-3)^2 = 9$. We add 9.
$x^2 - 6x + 9$, $(x - 3)^2$

32. $x^2 - 8x + 16$, $(x - 4)^2$

33. $x^2 + 9x$

$\dfrac{1}{2} \cdot 9 = \dfrac{9}{2}$, and $\left(\dfrac{9}{2}\right)^2 = \dfrac{81}{4}$. We add $\dfrac{81}{4}$.

$x^2 + 9x + \dfrac{81}{4}$, $\left(x + \dfrac{9}{2}\right)^2$

34. $x^2 + 3x + \dfrac{9}{4}$, $\left(x + \dfrac{3}{2}\right)^2$

35. $x^2 - 3x$

We take half the coefficient of x and square it:

$\dfrac{1}{2}(-3) = -\dfrac{3}{2}$ and $\left(-\dfrac{3}{2}\right)^2 = \dfrac{9}{4}$. We add $\dfrac{9}{4}$.

$x^2 - 3x + \dfrac{9}{4}$, $\left(x - \dfrac{3}{2}\right)^2$

36. $x^2 - 7x + \dfrac{49}{4}$, $\left(x - \dfrac{7}{2}\right)^2$

37. $x^2 + \dfrac{2}{3}x$

$\dfrac{1}{2} \cdot \dfrac{2}{3} = \dfrac{1}{3}$, and $\left(\dfrac{1}{3}\right)^2 = \dfrac{1}{9}$. We add $\dfrac{1}{9}$.

$x^2 + \dfrac{2}{3}x + \dfrac{1}{9}$, $\left(x + \dfrac{1}{3}\right)^2$

38. $x^2 + \dfrac{2}{5}x + \dfrac{1}{25}$, $\left(x + \dfrac{1}{5}\right)^2$

39. $x^2 - \dfrac{5}{6}x$

$\dfrac{1}{2}\left(-\dfrac{5}{6}\right) = -\dfrac{5}{12}$, and $\left(-\dfrac{5}{12}\right)^2 = \dfrac{25}{144}$. We add $\dfrac{25}{144}$.

$x^2 - \dfrac{5}{6}x + \dfrac{25}{144}$, $\left(x - \dfrac{5}{12}\right)^2$

40. $x^2 - \dfrac{5}{3}x + \dfrac{25}{36}, \ \left(x - \dfrac{5}{6}\right)^2$

41.
$$x^2 + 6x = 7$$
$$x^2 + 6x + 9 = 7 + 9 \qquad \text{Adding 9 on both sides to complete the square}$$
$$(x + 3)^2 = 16 \qquad \text{Factoring}$$
$$x + 3 = \pm 4 \qquad \text{Principle of square roots}$$
$$x = -3 \pm 4$$
$$x = -3 + 4 \ \ or \ \ x = -3 - 4$$
$$x = 1 \qquad or \ \ x = -7$$
The solutions are 1 and -7.

42. $-3, \ -2$

43.
$$x^2 + 6x + 5 = 0$$
$$x^2 + 6x = -5 \qquad \text{Adding } -5 \text{ on both sides}$$
$$x^2 + 6x + 9 = -5 + 9 \quad \text{Completing the square}$$
$$(x + 3)^2 = 4$$
$$x + 3 = \pm 2$$
$$x = -3 \pm 2$$
$$x = -3 - 2 \ \ or \ \ x = -3 + 2$$
$$x = -5 \qquad or \ \ x = -1$$
The solutions are -5 and -1.

44. $-9, \ -1$

45.
$$x^2 - 10x + 21 = 0$$
$$x^2 - 10x = -21$$
$$x^2 - 10x + 25 = -21 + 25$$
$$(x - 5)^2 = 4$$
$$x - 5 = \pm 2$$
$$x = 5 \pm 2$$
$$x = 5 - 2 \ \ or \ \ x = 5 + 2$$
$$x = 3 \qquad or \ \ x = 7$$
The solutions are 3 and 7.

46. $4, \ 6$

47.
$$x^2 + 4x + 1 = 0$$
$$x^2 + 4x = -1$$
$$x^2 + 4x + 4 = -1 + 4$$
$$(x + 2)^2 = 3$$
$$x + 2 = \pm\sqrt{3}$$
$$x = -2 \pm \sqrt{3}$$
The solutions are $-2 \pm \sqrt{3}$.

48. $-3 \pm \sqrt{2}$

49.
$$x^2 + 6x + 13 = 0$$
$$x^2 + 6x = -13$$
$$x^2 + 6x + 9 = -13 + 9$$
$$(x + 3)^2 = -4$$
$$x + 3 = \pm 2i$$
$$x = -3 \pm 2i$$
The solutions are $-3 \pm 2i$.

50. $-4 \pm 3i$

51.
$$2x^2 - 5x - 3 = 0$$
$$2x^2 - 5x = 3$$
$$x^2 - \dfrac{5}{2}x = \dfrac{3}{2} \qquad \text{Dividing by 2 on both sides}$$
$$x^2 - \dfrac{5}{2}x + \dfrac{25}{16} = \dfrac{3}{2} + \dfrac{25}{16}$$
$$\left(x - \dfrac{5}{4}\right)^2 = \dfrac{49}{16}$$
$$x - \dfrac{5}{4} = \pm\dfrac{7}{4}$$
$$x = \dfrac{5}{4} \pm \dfrac{7}{4}$$
$$x = \dfrac{5}{4} - \dfrac{7}{4} \ \ or \ \ x = \dfrac{5}{4} + \dfrac{7}{4}$$
$$x = -\dfrac{1}{2} \qquad or \ \ x = 3$$
The solutions are $-\dfrac{1}{2}$ and 3.

52. $-\dfrac{5}{6} \pm \dfrac{7}{6}$

53.
$$4x^2 + 8x + 3 = 0$$
$$4x^2 + 8x = -3$$
$$x^2 + 2x = -\dfrac{3}{4}$$
$$x^2 + 2x + 1 = -\dfrac{3}{4} + 1$$
$$(x + 1)^2 = \dfrac{1}{4}$$
$$x + 1 = \pm\dfrac{1}{2}$$
$$x = -1 \pm \dfrac{1}{2}$$
$$x = -1 - \dfrac{1}{2} \ \ or \ \ x = -1 + \dfrac{1}{2}$$
$$x = -\dfrac{3}{2} \qquad or \ \ x = -\dfrac{1}{2}$$
The solutions are $-\dfrac{3}{2}$ and $-\dfrac{1}{2}$.

54. $-\dfrac{4}{3}, \ -\dfrac{2}{3}$

55.
$$6x^2 - x = 15$$
$$x^2 - \frac{1}{6}x = \frac{5}{2}$$
$$x^2 - \frac{1}{6}x + \frac{1}{144} = \frac{5}{2} + \frac{1}{144}$$
$$\left(x - \frac{1}{12}\right)^2 = \frac{361}{144}$$
$$x - \frac{1}{12} = \pm\frac{19}{12}$$
$$x = \frac{1}{12} \pm \frac{19}{12}$$
$$x = \frac{1}{12} + \frac{19}{12} \ \ or \ \ x = \frac{1}{12} - \frac{19}{12}$$
$$x = \frac{20}{12} \qquad or \qquad x = -\frac{18}{12}$$
$$x = \frac{5}{3} \qquad or \qquad x = -\frac{3}{2}$$

The solutions are $\frac{5}{3}$ and $-\frac{3}{2}$.

56. $-\frac{1}{2}, \frac{2}{3}$

57.
$$2x^2 + 4x + 1 = 0$$
$$2x^2 + 4x = -1$$
$$x^2 + 2x = -\frac{1}{2}$$
$$x^2 + 2x + 1 = -\frac{1}{2} + 1$$
$$(x + 1)^2 = \frac{1}{2}$$
$$x + 1 = \pm\sqrt{\frac{1}{2}}$$
$$x + 1 = \pm\frac{\sqrt{2}}{2} \qquad \text{Rationalizing the denominator}$$
$$x = -1 \pm \frac{\sqrt{2}}{2}$$

The solutions are $-1 \pm \frac{\sqrt{2}}{2}$, or $\frac{-2 \pm \sqrt{2}}{2}$.

58. $-2, \ -\frac{1}{2}$

59. Familiarize. We are already familiar with the compound-interest formula.

Translate. We substitute into the formula.
$$A = P(1 + r)^t$$
$$2420 = 2000(1 + r)^2$$

Carry out. We solve for r.

$$2420 = 2000(1 + r)^2$$
$$\frac{2420}{2000} = (1 + r)^2$$
$$\frac{121}{100} = (1 + r)^2$$
$$\pm\sqrt{\frac{121}{100}} = 1 + r$$
$$\pm\frac{11}{10} = 1 + r$$
$$-\frac{10}{10} + \frac{11}{10} = r$$
$$\frac{1}{10} = r \ or \ -\frac{21}{10} = r$$

Check. Since the interest rate cannot be negative, we need only check $\frac{1}{10}$, or 10%. If $2000 were invested at 10% interest, compounded annually, then in 2 years it would grow to $2000(1.1)^2$, or $2420. The number 10% checks.

State. The interest rate is 10%.

60. 6.25%

61. Familiarize. We are already familiar with the compound-interest formula.

Translate. We substitute into the formula.
$$A = P(1 + r)^t$$
$$1805 = 1280(1 + r)^2$$

Carry out. We solve for r.

$$1805 = 1280(1 + r)^2$$
$$\frac{1805}{1280} = (1 + r)^2$$
$$\frac{361}{256} = (1 + r)^2$$
$$\pm\frac{19}{16} = 1 + r$$
$$-\frac{16}{16} \pm \frac{19}{16} = r$$
$$\frac{3}{16} = r \ or \ -\frac{35}{16} = r$$

Check. Since the interest rate cannot be negative, we need only check $\frac{3}{16}$ or 18.75%. If $1280 were invested at 18.75% interest, compounded annually, then in 2 years it would grow to $1280(1.1875)^2$, or $1805. The number 18.75% checks.

State. The interest rate is 18.75%.

62. 20%

63. Familiarize. We are already familiar with the compound-interest formula.

Translate. We substitute into the formula.

$$A = P(1+r)^t$$
$$6760 = 6250(1+r)^2$$

Carry out. We solve for r.

$$\frac{6760}{6250} = (1+r)^2$$

$$\frac{676}{625} = (1+r)^2$$

$$\pm\frac{26}{25} = 1+r$$

$$-\frac{25}{25} \pm \frac{26}{25} = r$$

$$\frac{1}{25} = r \ or \ -\frac{51}{25} = r$$

Check. Since the interest rate cannot be negative, we need only check $\frac{1}{25}$, or 4%. If \$6250 were invested at 4% interest, compounded annually, then in 2 years it would grow to \$6250(1.04)², or \$6760. The number 4% checks.

State. The interest rate is 4%.

64. 8%

65. Familiarize. We will use the formula $s = 16t^2$.

Translate. We substitute into the formula.

$$s = 16t^2$$
$$1815 = 16t^2$$

Carry out. We solve for t.

$$1815 = 16t^2$$

$$\frac{1815}{16} = t^2$$

$$\sqrt{\frac{1815}{16}} = t \qquad \text{Principle of square roots;} \\ \text{rejecting the negative} \\ \text{square root}$$

$$10.7 \approx t$$

Check. Since $16(10.7)^2 = 1831.84 \approx 1815$, our answer checks.

State. It would take an object about 10.7 sec to fall freely from the top of the CN Tower.

66. About 6.8 sec

67. Familiarize. We will use the formula $s = 16t^2$.

Translate. We substitute into the formula.

$$s = 16t^2$$
$$640 = 16t^2$$

Carry out. We solve for t.

$$640 = 16t^2$$
$$40 = t^2$$
$$\sqrt{40} = t \qquad \text{Principle of square roots;} \\ \text{rejecting the negative square} \\ \text{root}$$
$$6.3 \approx t$$

Check. Since $16(6.3)^2 = 635.04 \approx 640$, our answer checks.

State. It would take an object about 6.3 sec to fall freely from the top of the Gateway Arch.

68. About 9.5 sec

69. Graph: $f(x) = 5 - 2x$

Select some x-values and find the corresponding values of $f(x)$. Then plot these ordered pairs and draw the graph.

x	$f(x)$, or y
-1	7
0	5
2	1
4	-3

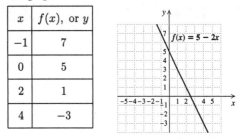

70.

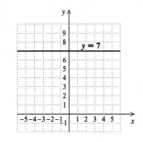

71. $\sqrt[3]{270} = \sqrt[3]{27 \cdot 10} = \sqrt[3]{27}\sqrt[3]{10} = 3\sqrt[3]{10}$

72. $4\sqrt{5}$

73. $f(x) = \sqrt{3x - 5}$
$f(10) = \sqrt{3 \cdot 10 - 5} = \sqrt{30 - 5} = \sqrt{25} = 5$

74. 7

75. ◈

76. ◈

77. ◈

78. ◈

79.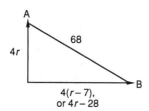

80. ± 14

81. $x(2x^2 - 9x - 56)(x^2 - 5) = 0$

$x(2x + 7)(x - 8)(x^2 - 5) = 0$

$x=0$ or $2x+7=0$ or $x-8=0$ or $x^2-5=0$

$x=0$ or $2x=-7$ or $x=8$ or $x^2=5$

$x=0$ or $x=-\dfrac{7}{2}$ or $x=8$ or $x=\pm\sqrt{5}$

The solutions are 0, $-\dfrac{7}{2}$, 8, $\sqrt{5}$, and $-\sqrt{5}$.

82. $-\dfrac{1}{2}$, $\dfrac{1}{3}$, $\dfrac{1}{2}$

83. *Familiarize*. It is helpful to list information in a chart and make a drawing. Let r represent the speed of the fishing boat. Then $r - 7$ represents the speed of the barge.

Boat	r	t	d
Fishing	r	4	$4r$
Barge	$r - 7$	4	$4(r - 7)$

Translate. We use the Pythagorean equation:

$a^2 + b^2 = c^2$

$(4r - 28)^2 + (4r)^2 = 68^2$

Carry out.

$(4r - 28)^2 + (4r)^2 = 68^2$

$16r^2 - 224r + 784 + 16r^2 = 4624$

$32r^2 - 224r - 3840 = 0$

$r^2 - 7r - 120 = 0$

$(r + 8)(r - 15) = 0$

$r + 8 = 0$ or $r - 15 = 0$

$r = -8$ or $r = 15$

Check. We check only 15 since the speeds of the boats cannot be negative. If the speed of the fishing boat is 15 km/h, then the speed of the barge is $15 - 7$, or 8 km/h, and the distances they travel are $4 \cdot 15$ (or 60) and $4 \cdot 8$ (or 32).

$60^2 + 32^2 = 3600 + 1024 = 4624 = 68^2$

The values check.

State. The speed of the fishing boat is 15 km/h, and the speed of the barge is 8 km/h.

84. 5, 6, 7

Exercise Set 10.2

---

1. $x^2 + 7x + 4 = 0$

$a = 1$, $b = 7$, $c = 4$

$x = \dfrac{-b \pm \sqrt{b^2 - 4ac}}{2a}$

$x = \dfrac{-7 \pm \sqrt{7^2 - 4 \cdot 1 \cdot 4}}{2 \cdot 1} = \dfrac{-7 \pm \sqrt{49 - 16}}{2}$

$x = \dfrac{-7 \pm \sqrt{33}}{2}$

The solutions are $\dfrac{-7 + \sqrt{33}}{2}$ and $\dfrac{-7 - \sqrt{33}}{2}$.

2. $\dfrac{7 \pm \sqrt{61}}{2}$

3. $3p^2 = -8p - 5$

$3p^2 + 8p + 5 = 0$

$(3p + 5)(p + 1) = 0$

$3p + 5 = 0$ or $p + 1 = 0$

$p = -\dfrac{5}{3}$ or $p = -1$

The solutions are $-\dfrac{5}{3}$ and -1.

4. $3 \pm \sqrt{7}$

5. $x^2 - x + 2 = 0$

$a = 1$, $b = -1$, $c = 2$

$x = \dfrac{-(-1) \pm \sqrt{(-1)^2 - 4 \cdot 1 \cdot 2}}{2 \cdot 1} = \dfrac{1 \pm \sqrt{1 - 8}}{2}$

$x = \dfrac{1 \pm \sqrt{-7}}{2} = \dfrac{1 \pm i\sqrt{7}}{2}$

The solutions are $\dfrac{1 + i\sqrt{7}}{2}$ and $\dfrac{1 - i\sqrt{7}}{2}$.

6. $\dfrac{1 \pm i\sqrt{3}}{2}$

7. $x^2 + 13 = 6x$

$x^2 - 6x + 13 = 0$

$a = 1$, $b = -6$, $c = 13$

$x = \dfrac{-(-6) \pm \sqrt{(-6)^2 - 4 \cdot 1 \cdot 13}}{2 \cdot 1} = \dfrac{6 \pm \sqrt{36 - 52}}{2}$

$x = \dfrac{6 \pm \sqrt{-16}}{2} = \dfrac{6 \pm 4i}{2} = 3 \pm 2i$

The solutions are $3 + 2i$ and $3 - 2i$.

8. $2 \pm 3i$

9.
$$h^2 + 4 = 6h$$
$$h^2 - 6h + 4 = 0$$
$$a = 1,\ b = -6,\ c = 4$$
$$x = \frac{-(-6) \pm \sqrt{(-6)^2 - 4 \cdot 1 \cdot 4}}{2 \cdot 1} = \frac{6 \pm \sqrt{36 - 16}}{2}$$
$$x = \frac{6 \pm \sqrt{20}}{2} = \frac{6 \pm \sqrt{4 \cdot 5}}{2} = \frac{6 \pm 2\sqrt{5}}{2}$$
$$x = 3 \pm \sqrt{5}$$
The solutions are $3 + \sqrt{5}$ and $3 - \sqrt{5}$.

10. $\dfrac{-3 \pm \sqrt{41}}{2}$

11.
$$3 + \frac{8}{x} = \frac{1}{x^2}, \text{ LCD is } x^2$$
$$x^2\left(3 + \frac{8}{x}\right) = x^2 \cdot \frac{1}{x^2}$$
$$3x^2 + 8x = 1$$
$$3x^2 + 8x - 1 = 0$$
$$a = 3,\ b = 8,\ c = -1$$
$$x = \frac{-8 \pm \sqrt{8^2 - 4 \cdot 3 \cdot (-1)}}{2 \cdot 3} = \frac{-8 \pm \sqrt{64 + 12}}{6}$$
$$x = \frac{-8 \pm \sqrt{76}}{6} = \frac{-8 \pm \sqrt{4 \cdot 19}}{6} = \frac{-8 \pm 2\sqrt{19}}{6}$$
$$x = \frac{-4 \pm \sqrt{19}}{3}$$
The solutions are $\dfrac{-4 + \sqrt{19}}{3}$ and $\dfrac{-4 - \sqrt{19}}{3}$.

12. $\dfrac{9 \pm \sqrt{41}}{4}$

13.
$$3x + x(x - 2) = 0$$
$$3x + x^2 - 2x = 0$$
$$x^2 + x = 0$$
$$x(x + 1) = 0$$
$$x = 0 \ \text{ or } \ x + 1 = 0$$
$$x = 0 \ \text{ or } \ \quad x = -1$$
The solutions are 0 and -1.

14. $-1,\ 0$

15.
$$14x^2 + 9x = 0$$
$$x(14x + 9) = 0$$
$$x = 0 \ \text{ or } \ 14x + 9 = 0$$
$$x = 0 \ \text{ or } \quad 14x = -9$$
$$x = 0 \ \text{ or } \quad x = -\frac{9}{14}$$
The solutions are 0 and $-\dfrac{9}{14}$.

16. $-\dfrac{8}{19},\ 0$

17.
$$25x^2 - 20x + 4 = 0$$
$$(5x - 2)(5x - 2) = 0$$
$$5x - 2 = 0 \ \text{ or } \ 5x - 2 = 0$$
$$5x = 2 \ \text{ or } \quad 5x = 2$$
$$x = \frac{2}{5} \ \text{ or } \quad x = \frac{2}{5}$$
The solution is $\dfrac{2}{5}$.

18. $-\dfrac{7}{6}$

19.
$$7x(x + 2) + 6 = 3x(x + 1)$$
$$7x^2 + 14x + 6 = 3x^2 + 3x \quad \text{Removing}$$
$$\text{parentheses}$$
$$4x^2 + 11x + 6 = 0$$
$$(4x + 3)(x + 2) = 0$$
$$4x + 3 = 0 \ \text{ or } \ x + 2 = 0$$
$$4x = -3 \ \text{ or } \quad x = -2$$
$$x = -\frac{3}{4} \ \text{ or } \quad x = -2$$
The solutions are $-\dfrac{3}{4}$ and -2.

20. $-2,\ -1$

21.
$$14(x - 4) - (x + 2) = (x + 2)(x - 4)$$
$$14x - 56 - x - 2 = x^2 - 2x - 8 \quad \text{Removing}$$
$$\text{parentheses}$$
$$13x - 58 = x^2 - 2x - 8$$
$$0 = x^2 - 15x + 50$$
$$0 = (x - 10)(x - 5)$$
$$x - 10 = 0 \ \text{ or } \ x - 5 = 0$$
$$x = 10 \ \text{ or } \quad x = 5$$
The solutions are 10 and 5.

22. $1,\ 15$

23.
$$5x^2 = 13x + 17$$
$$5x^2 - 13x - 17 = 0$$
$$a = 5,\ b = -13,\ c = -17$$
$$x = \frac{-(-13) \pm \sqrt{(-13)^2 - 4(5)(-17)}}{2 \cdot 5}$$
$$x = \frac{13 \pm \sqrt{169 + 340}}{10} = \frac{13 \pm \sqrt{509}}{10}$$
The solutions are $\dfrac{13 + \sqrt{509}}{10}$ and $\dfrac{13 - \sqrt{509}}{10}$.

24. $\dfrac{4}{3},\ 7$

25.
$$x^2 + 9 = 4x$$
$$x^2 - 4x + 9 = 0$$
$$a = 1, b = -4, c = 9$$
$$x = \frac{-(-4) \pm \sqrt{(-4)^2 - 4 \cdot 1 \cdot 9}}{2 \cdot 1} = \frac{4 \pm \sqrt{16 - 36}}{2}$$
$$x = \frac{4 \pm \sqrt{-20}}{2} = \frac{4 \pm \sqrt{-4 \cdot 5}}{2}$$
$$x = \frac{4 \pm 2i\sqrt{5}}{2} = 2 \pm i\sqrt{5}$$
The solutions are $2 + i\sqrt{5}$ and $2 - i\sqrt{5}$.

26. $\dfrac{3 \pm i\sqrt{19}}{2}$

27.
$$x + \frac{1}{x} = \frac{13}{6}, \text{ LCD is } 6x$$
$$6x\left(x + \frac{1}{x}\right) = 6x \cdot \frac{13}{6}$$
$$6x^2 + 6 = 13x$$
$$6x^2 - 13x + 6 = 0$$
$$(2x - 3)(3x - 2) = 0$$
$$2x - 3 = 0 \quad or \quad 3x - 2 = 0$$
$$2x = 3 \quad or \qquad 3x = 2$$
$$x = \frac{3}{2} \quad or \qquad x = \frac{2}{3}$$
The solutions are $\dfrac{3}{2}$ and $\dfrac{2}{3}$.

28. $\dfrac{3}{2}, 6$

29.
$$f(x) = 0$$
$$3x^2 - 5x - 1 = 0 \qquad \text{Substituting}$$
$$a = 3, b = -5, c = -1$$
$$x = \frac{-(-5) \pm \sqrt{(-5)^2 - 4 \cdot 3 \cdot (-1)}}{2 \cdot 3}$$
$$x = \frac{5 \pm \sqrt{25 + 12}}{6} = \frac{5 \pm \sqrt{37}}{6}$$
The solutions are $\dfrac{5 + \sqrt{37}}{6}$ and $\dfrac{5 - \sqrt{37}}{6}$.

30. $\dfrac{1 \pm \sqrt{13}}{4}$

31.
$$f(x) = 1$$
$$\frac{7}{x} + \frac{7}{x + 4} = 1 \qquad \text{Substituting}$$
$$x(x + 4)\left(\frac{7}{x} + \frac{7}{x + 4}\right) = x(x + 4) \cdot 1$$
$$\qquad\qquad\qquad\qquad \text{Multiplying by the LCD}$$
$$7(x + 4) + 7x = x^2 + 4x$$
$$7x + 28 + 7x = x^2 + 4x$$
$$14x + 28 = x^2 + 4x$$
$$0 = x^2 - 10x - 28$$
$$a = 1, b = -10, c = -28$$
$$x = \frac{-(-10) \pm \sqrt{(-10)^2 - 4 \cdot 1 \cdot (-28)}}{2 \cdot 1}$$
$$x = \frac{10 \pm \sqrt{100 + 112}}{2} = \frac{10 \pm \sqrt{212}}{2}$$
$$x = \frac{10 \pm \sqrt{4 \cdot 53}}{2} = \frac{10 \pm 2\sqrt{53}}{2}$$
$$x = 5 \pm \sqrt{53}$$
The solutions are $5 + \sqrt{53}$ and $5 - \sqrt{53}$.

32. $-2, 3$

33.
$$F(x) = G(x)$$
$$\frac{x + 3}{x} = \frac{x - 4}{3} \qquad \text{Substituting}$$
$$3x\left(\frac{x + 3}{x}\right) = 3x\left(\frac{x - 4}{3}\right) \quad \begin{array}{l}\text{Multiplying}\\\text{by the LCD}\end{array}$$
$$3x + 9 = x^2 - 4x$$
$$0 = x^2 - 7x - 9$$
$$a = 1, b = -7, c = -9$$
$$x = \frac{-(-7) \pm \sqrt{(-7)^2 - 4 \cdot 1 \cdot (-9)}}{2 \cdot 1}$$
$$x = \frac{7 \pm \sqrt{49 + 36}}{2} = \frac{7 \pm \sqrt{85}}{2}$$
The solutions are $\dfrac{7 + \sqrt{85}}{2}$ and $\dfrac{7 - \sqrt{85}}{2}$.

34. $\pm 2\sqrt{7}$

35. There are no x-intercepts, so the equation has no real-number solutions. This tells us that the discriminant is negative.

36. Positive

37. There is 1 x-intercept, so the equation has 1 real-number solution. This tells us that the discriminant is 0.

38. Negative

39. $x^2 - 4x + 3 = 0$

$a = 1,\ b = -4,\ c = 3$

We substitute and compute the discriminant.

$b^2 - 4ac = (-4)^2 - 4 \cdot 1 \cdot 3$

$\qquad = 16 - 12$

$\qquad = 4$

Since the discriminant is positive and a perfect square, there are two rational solutions.

40. Two rational

41. $x^2 + 5 = 0$

$a = 1,\ b = 0,\ c = 5$

We substitute and compute the discriminant.

$b^2 - 4ac = 0^2 - 4 \cdot 1 \cdot 5$

$\qquad = -20$

Since the discriminant is negative, there are two imaginary-number solutions.

42. Two imaginary

43. $x^2 - 2 = 0$

$a = 1,\ b = 0,\ c = -2$

We substitute and compute the discriminant.

$b^2 - 4ac = 0^2 - 4 \cdot 1 \cdot (-2)$

$\qquad = 8$

Since the discriminant is a positive number that is not a perfect square, there are two irrational solutions.

44. Two irrational

45. $4x^2 - 12x + 9 = 0$

$a = 4,\ b = -12,\ c = 9$

We substitute and compute the discriminant.

$b^2 - 4ac = (-12)^2 - 4 \cdot 4 \cdot 9$

$\qquad = 144 - 144$

$\qquad = 0$

Since the discriminant is 0, there is just one solution, and it is a rational number.

46. Two rational

47. $x^2 - 2x + 4 = 0$

$a = 1,\ b = -2,\ c = 4$

We substitute and compute the discriminant.

$b^2 - 4ac = (-2)^2 - 4 \cdot 1 \cdot 4$

$\qquad = 4 - 16$

$\qquad = -12$

Since the discriminant is negative, there are two imaginary-number solutions.

48. Two imaginary

49. $a^2 + 11a + 28 = 0$

$a = 1,\ b = 11,\ c = 28$

We substitute and compute the discriminant.

$b^2 - 4ac = 11^2 - 4 \cdot 1 \cdot 28$

$\qquad = 121 - 112 = 9$

Since the discriminant is a positive number and a perfect square, there are two rational solutions.

50. One rational

51. $6x^2 + 5x - 4 = 0$

$a = 6,\ b = 5,\ c = -4$

We substitute and compute the discriminant.

$b^2 - 4ac = 5^2 - 4 \cdot 6 \cdot (-4)$

$\qquad = 25 + 96 = 121$

Since the discriminant is a positive number and a perfect square, there are two rational solutions.

52. Two rational

53. $9t^2 - 3t = 0$

$a = 9,\ b = -3,\ c = 0$

We substitute and compute the discriminant.

$b^2 - 4ac = (-3)^2 - 4 \cdot 9 \cdot 0$

$\qquad = 9 - 0$

$\qquad = 9$

Since the discriminant is a positive number and a perfect square, there are two rational solutions.

54. Two rational

55. $x^2 + 5x = 7$

$x^2 + 5x - 7 = 0$ Standard form

$a = 1,\ b = 5,\ c = -7$

We substitute and compute the discriminant.

$b^2 - 4ac = 5^2 - 4 \cdot 1 \cdot (-7)$

$\qquad = 25 + 28 = 53$

Since the discriminant is a positive number that is not a perfect square, there are two irrational solutions.

56. Two irrational

57. $\qquad 2a^2 - 3a = -5$

$2a^2 - 3a + 5 = 0$ Standard form

$a = 2,\ b = -3,\ c = 5$

We substitute and compute the discriminant.

$$b^2 - 4ac = (-3)^2 - 4 \cdot 2 \cdot 5$$
$$= 9 - 40$$
$$= -31$$

Since the discriminant is negative, there are two imaginary-number solutions.

58. Two imaginary

59.
$$y^2 + \frac{9}{4} = 4y$$
$$y^2 - 4y + \frac{9}{4} = 0 \quad \text{Standard form}$$
$$a = 1,\, b = -4,\, c = \frac{9}{4}$$

We substitute and compute the discriminant.
$$b^2 - 4ac = (-4)^2 - 4 \cdot 1 \cdot \frac{9}{4}$$
$$= 16 - 9$$
$$= 7$$

The discriminant is a positive number that is not a perfect square. There are two irrational solutions.

60. Two imaginary

61. **Familiarize.** Let x = the number of pounds of Kenyan coffee and y = the number of pounds of Peruvian coffee in the mixture. We organize the information in a table.

Type of Coffee	Kenyan	Peruvian	Mixture
Price per pound	$6.75	$11.25	$8.55
Number of pounds	x	y	50
Total cost	$6.75x$	$11.25y$	8.55×50, or $427.50

Translate. From the last two rows of the table we get a system of equations.
$$x + y = 50,$$
$$6.75x + 11.25y = 427.50$$

Solve. Solving the system of equations, we get $(30, 20)$.

Check. The total number of pounds in the mixture is $30 + 20$, or 50. The total cost of the mixture is $6.75(30) + 11.25(20) = 427.50$. The values check.

State. The mixture should consist of 30 lb of Kenyan coffee and 20 lb of Peruvian coffee.

62.

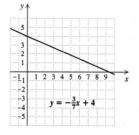

$y = -\frac{3}{7}x + 4$

63. Graph: $f(x) = -x - 3$.

Select some x-values and find the corresponding values of $f(x)$. Then plot these ordered pairs and draw the graph.

x	$f(x)$
-5	2
0	-3
3	-6

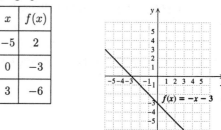

$f(x) = -x - 3$

64.

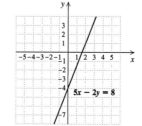

$5x - 2y = 8$

65.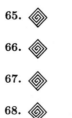

66. ◈

67. ◈

68. ◈

69. Consider a quadratic equation in standard form, $ax^2 + bx + c = 0$. The solutions are
$$\frac{-b \pm \sqrt{b^2 - 4ac}}{2a}.$$
The product of the solutions is
$$\left(\frac{-b + \sqrt{b^2 - 4ac}}{2a}\right)\left(\frac{-b - \sqrt{b^2 - 4ac}}{2a}\right) =$$
$$\frac{(-b)^2 - (\sqrt{b^2 - 4ac})^2}{(2a)^2} = \frac{b^2 - (b^2 - 4ac)}{4a^2} =$$
$$\frac{4ac}{4a^2} = \frac{c}{a}.$$

70. (a) $-\dfrac{3}{5}$; (b) $-\dfrac{1}{3}$

71. a) $x^2 - kx + 2 = 0$; one solution is $1 + i$

We first find k by substituting $1 + i$ for x.
$$x^2 - kx + 2 = 0$$
$$(1+i)^2 - k(1+i) + 2 = 0$$
$$1 + 2i - 1 - k - ki + 2 = 0$$
$$2i + 2 = k + ki$$
$$2i + 2 = k(1+i)$$
$$\frac{2(i+1)}{1+i} = k$$
$$2 = k$$

b) Now substitute 2 for k in the original equation.
$$x^2 - 2x + 2 = 0$$
$$x = \frac{2 \pm \sqrt{4-8}}{2} = \frac{2 \pm 2i}{2}$$
$$x = 1 \pm i$$

The other solution is $1 - i$.

72. $\dfrac{-b + \sqrt{b^2 - 4ac}}{2a} + \dfrac{-b - \sqrt{b^2 - 4ac}}{2a} =$

$\dfrac{-2b}{2a} = -\dfrac{b}{a}$

73. From Exercise 69 we know that the product of the solutions is c/a. Then
$$\frac{2k-1}{k} = 3$$
$$2k - 1 = 3k$$
$$-1 = k.$$

74. $h = -36$, $k = 15$

75. ◈

76. $(-5 - \sqrt{37}, 0)$, $(-5 + \sqrt{37}, 0)$

77. $f(x) = \dfrac{x^2}{x-2} + 1$

To find the x-coordinates of the x-intercepts of the graph of f, we solve $f(x) = 0$.
$$\frac{x^2}{x-2} + 1 = 0, \text{ LCD is } x - 2$$
$$(x-2)\left(\frac{x^2}{x-2} + 1\right) = (x-2) \cdot 0$$
$$x^2 + x - 2 = 0$$
$$(x+2)(x-1) = 0$$
$$x = -2 \quad or \quad x = 1$$

The x-intercepts are $(-2, 0)$ and $(1, 0)$.

78. $4 \pm 2\sqrt{2}$

79. $x^2 - 0.75x - 0.5 = 0$
$$x = \frac{-(-0.75) \pm \sqrt{(-0.75)^2 - 4 \cdot 1 \cdot (-0.5)}}{2 \cdot 1}$$
$$x = \frac{0.75 \pm \sqrt{2.5625}}{2}$$
$$x = \frac{0.75 + \sqrt{2.5625}}{2} \approx 1.17539053$$
$$x = \frac{0.75 - \sqrt{2.5625}}{2} \approx -0.42539053$$

80. 0.3392101158, -1.179210116

81. $\sqrt{2}x^2 + 5x + \sqrt{2} = 0$
$$x = \frac{-5 \pm \sqrt{5^2 - 4 \cdot \sqrt{2} \cdot \sqrt{2}}}{2\sqrt{2}} = \frac{-5 \pm \sqrt{17}}{2\sqrt{2}}, \text{ or}$$
$$x = \frac{-5 \pm \sqrt{17}}{2\sqrt{2}} \cdot \frac{\sqrt{2}}{\sqrt{2}} = \frac{-5\sqrt{2} \pm \sqrt{34}}{4}$$

82. $\dfrac{3 + \sqrt{3}}{1 + \sqrt{3}}$, $\dfrac{\sqrt{3}}{1 + \sqrt{3}}$

83. $ix^2 - 2x + 1 = 0$
$$x = \frac{-(-2) \pm \sqrt{(-2)^2 - 4 \cdot i \cdot 1}}{2i} = \frac{2 \pm \sqrt{4 - 4i}}{2i}$$
$$x = \frac{2 \pm 2\sqrt{1-i}}{2i} = \frac{1 \pm \sqrt{1-i}}{i}, \text{ or}$$
$$x = \frac{1 \pm \sqrt{1-i}}{i} \cdot \frac{-i}{-i} = -i \pm i\sqrt{1-i}$$

84. ◈

Exercise Set 10.3

1. *Familiarize*. We first make a drawing, labeling it with the known and unknown information. We can also organize the information in a table. We let r represent the speed and t the time for the first part of the trip.

r mph	t hr		$r - 10$ mph	$4 - t$ hr
	120 mi	•		100 mi

Trip	Distance	Speed	Time
1st part	120	r	t
2nd part	100	$r - 10$	$4 - t$

Translate. Using $r = \dfrac{d}{t}$, we get two equations from the table, $r = \dfrac{120}{t}$ and $r - 10 = \dfrac{100}{4-t}$.

Carry out. We substitute $\dfrac{120}{t}$ for r in the second equation and solve for t.

$$\frac{120}{t} - 10 = \frac{100}{4-t}, \text{ LCD is } t(4-t)$$

$$t(4-t)\left(\frac{120}{t} - 10\right) = t(4-t) \cdot \frac{100}{4-t}$$

$$120(4-t) - 10t(4-t) = 100t$$

$$480 - 120t - 40t + 10t^2 = 100t$$

$$10t^2 - 260t + 480 = 0 \quad \text{Standard form}$$

$$t^2 - 26t + 48 = 0 \quad \text{Multiplying by } \frac{1}{10}$$

$$(t-2)(t-24) = 0$$

$$t = 2 \ \text{ or } \ t = 24$$

Check. Since the time cannot be negative (If $t = 24$, $4 - t = -20$.), we check only 2 hr. If $t = 2$, then $4 - t = 2$. The speed of the first part is $\frac{120}{2}$, or 60 mph. The speed of the second part is $\frac{100}{2}$, or 50 mph. The speed of the second part is 10 mph slower than the first part. The value checks.

State. The speed of the first part was 60 mph, and the speed of the second part was 50 mph.

2. First part: 12 km/h, second part: 8 km/h

3. Familiarize. We first make a drawing. We also organize the information in a table. We let $r =$ the speed and $t =$ the time of the slower trip.

200 mi	r mph	t hr
200 mi	$r + 10$ mph	$t - 1$ hr

Trip	Distance	Speed	Time
Slower	200	r	t
Faster	200	$r + 10$	$t - 1$

Translate. Using $t = d/r$, we get two equations from the table:

$$t = \frac{200}{r} \text{ and } t - 1 = \frac{200}{r + 10}$$

Carry out. We substitute $\frac{200}{r}$ for t in the second equation and solve for r.

$$\frac{200}{r} - 1 = \frac{200}{r + 10}, \text{ LCD is } r(r + 10)$$

$$r(r + 10)\left(\frac{200}{r} - 1\right) = r(r + 10) \cdot \frac{200}{r + 10}$$

$$200(r + 10) - r(r + 10) = 200r$$

$$200r + 2000 - r^2 - 10r = 200r$$

$$0 = r^2 + 10r - 2000$$

$$0 = (r + 50)(r - 40)$$

$r = -50 \ \text{ or } \ r = 40$

Check. Since negative speed has no meaning in this problem, we check only 40. If $r = 40$, then the time for the slower trip is $\frac{200}{40}$, or 5 hours. If $r = 40$, then $r + 10 = 50$ and the time for the faster trip is $\frac{200}{50}$, or 4 hours. This is 1 hour less time than the slower trip took, so we have an answer to the problem.

State. The speed is 40 mph.

4. 35 mph

5. Familiarize. We make a drawing and then organize the information in a table. We let $r =$ the speed and $t =$ the time of the Cessna.

600 mi	r mph	t hr
1000 mi	$r + 50$ mph	$t + 1$ hr

Plane	Distance	Speed	Time
Cessna	600	r	t
Beechcraft	1000	$r + 50$	$t + 1$

Translate. Using $t = d/r$, we get two equations from the table:

$$t = \frac{600}{r} \text{ and } t + 1 = \frac{1000}{r + 50}$$

Carry out. We substitute $\frac{600}{r}$ for t in the second equation and solve for r.

$$\frac{600}{r} + 1 = \frac{1000}{r + 50},$$

$$\text{LCD is } r(r + 50)$$

$$r(r + 50)\left(\frac{600}{r} + 1\right) = r(r + 50) \cdot \frac{1000}{r + 50}$$

$$600(r + 50) + r(r + 50) = 1000r$$

$$600r + 30,000 + r^2 + 50r = 1000r$$

$$r^2 - 350r + 30,000 = 0$$

$$(r - 150)(r - 200) = 0$$

$r = 150 \ \text{ or } r = 200$

Check. If $r = 150$, then the Cessna's time is $\frac{600}{150}$, or 4 hr and the Beechcraft's time is $\frac{1000}{150 + 50}$, or $\frac{1000}{200}$, or 5 hr. If $r = 200$, then the Cessna's time is $\frac{600}{200}$, or 3 hr and the Beechcraft's time is $\frac{1000}{200 + 50}$, or $\frac{1000}{250}$, or 4 hr. Since the Beechcraft's time is 1 hr longer in each case, both values check. There are two solutions.

State. The speed of the Cessna is 150 mph and the speed of the Beechcraft is 200 mph; or the speed of the Cessna is 200 mph and the speed of the Beechcraft is 250 mph.

6. Super-prop: 350 mph, turbo-jet: 400 mph

7. *Familiarize*. We make a drawing and then organize the information in a table. We let r represent the speed and t the time of the trip to Hillsboro.

Hillsboro

40 mi r mph t hr

40 mi $r - 6$ mph $14 - t$ hr

Trip	Distance	Speed	Time
To Hillsboro	40	r	t
Return	40	$r - 6$	$14 - t$

Translate. Using $t = \dfrac{d}{r}$, we get two equations from the table,

$$t = \frac{40}{r} \text{ and } 14 - t = \frac{40}{r - 6}.$$

Carry out. We substitute $\dfrac{40}{r}$ for t in the second equation and solve for r.

$$14 - \frac{40}{r} = \frac{40}{r - 6},$$

$$\text{LCD is } r(r - 6)$$

$$r(r - 6)\left(14 - \frac{40}{r}\right) = r(r - 6) \cdot \frac{40}{r - 6}$$

$$14r(r - 6) - 40(r - 6) = 40r$$

$$14r^2 - 84r - 40r + 240 = 40r$$

$$14r^2 - 164r + 240 = 0$$

$$7r^2 - 82r + 120 = 0$$

$$(7r - 12)(r - 10) = 0$$

$$r = \frac{12}{7} \quad or \quad r = 10$$

Check. Since negative speed has no meaning in this problem (If $r = \dfrac{12}{7}$, then $r - 6 = -\dfrac{30}{7}$.), we check only 10 mph. If $r = 10$, then the time of the trip to Hillsboro is $\dfrac{40}{10}$, or 4 hr. The speed of the return trip is $10 - 6$, or 4 mph, and the time is $\dfrac{40}{4}$, or 10 hr. The total time for the round trip is 4 hr + 10 hr, or 14 hr. The value checks.

State. Naoki's speed on the trip to Hillsboro was 10 mph and it was 4 mph on the return trip.

8. To Richmond: 60 mph, return trip: 50 mph

9. *Familiarize*. We make a drawing and organize the information in a table. Let r represent the speed of the barge in still water, and let t represent the time of the trip upriver.

24 mi $r - 4$ mph t hr
→ Upriver

Downriver ←   24 mi $r + 4$ mph $5 - t$ hr

Trip	Distance	Speed	Time
Upriver	24	$r - 4$	t
Downriver	24	$r + 4$	$5 - t$

Translate. Using $t = \dfrac{d}{r}$, we get two equations from the table,

$$t = \frac{24}{r - 4} \text{ and } 5 - t = \frac{24}{r + 4}.$$

Carry out. We substitute $\dfrac{24}{r - 4}$ for t in the second equation and solve for r.

$$5 - \frac{24}{r - 4} = \frac{24}{r + 4},$$

$$\text{LCD is } (r-4)(r+4)$$

$$(r - 4)(r + 4)\left(5 - \frac{24}{r - 4}\right) = (r - 4)(r + 4) \cdot \frac{24}{r + 4}$$

$$5(r - 4)(r + 4) - 24(r + 4) = 24(r - 4)$$

$$5r^2 - 80 - 24r - 96 = 24r - 96$$

$$5r^2 - 48r - 80 = 0$$

We use the quadratic formula.

$$r = \frac{-(-48) \pm \sqrt{(-48)^2 - 4 \cdot 5 \cdot (-80)}}{2 \cdot 5}$$

$$r = \frac{48 \pm \sqrt{3904}}{10}$$

$$r \approx 11 \quad or \quad r \approx -1.5$$

Check. Since negative speed has no meaning in this problem, we check only 11 mph. If $r \approx 11$, then the speed upriver is about $11 - 4$, or 7 mph, and the time is about $\dfrac{24}{7}$, or 3.4 hr. The speed downriver is about $11 + 4$, or 15 mph, and the time is about $\dfrac{24}{15}$, or 1.6 hr. The total time of the round trip is $3.4 + 1.6$, or 5 hr. The value checks.

State. The barge must be able to travel about 11 mph in still water.

10. About 14 mph

11. *Familiarize*. Let x represent the time it takes the smaller hose to fill the pool. Then $x - 6$ represents the time it takes the larger hose to fill the pool. It takes them 4 hr to fill the pool when both hoses are working together, so they can fill $\frac{1}{4}$ of the pool in 1 hr. The smaller hose will fill $\frac{1}{x}$ of the pool in 1 hr, and the larger hose will fill $\frac{1}{x-6}$ of the pool in 1 hr.

Translate. We have an equation.

$$\frac{1}{x} + \frac{1}{x-6} = \frac{1}{4}$$

Carry out. We solve the equation.

We multiply by the LCD, $4x(x-6)$.

$$4x(x-6)\left(\frac{1}{x} + \frac{1}{x-6}\right) = 4x(x-6) \cdot \frac{1}{4}$$
$$4(x-6) + 4x = x(x-6)$$
$$4x - 24 + 4x = x^2 - 6x$$
$$0 = x^2 - 14x + 24$$
$$0 = (x-2)(x-12)$$

$x = 2$ *or* $x = 12$

Check. Since negative time has no meaning in this problem, 2 is not a solution ($2 - 6 = -4$). We check only 12 hr. This is the time it would take the smaller hose working alone. Then the larger hose would take $12 - 6$, or 6 hr working alone. The larger hose would fill $4\left(\frac{1}{6}\right)$, or $\frac{2}{3}$, of the pool in 4 hr, and the smaller hose would fill $4\left(\frac{1}{12}\right)$, or $\frac{1}{3}$, of the pool in 4 hr. Thus in 4 hr they would fill $\frac{2}{3} + \frac{1}{3}$ of the pool. This is all of it, so the numbers check.

State. It takes the smaller hose, working alone, 12 hr to fill the pool.

12. 6 hr

13. Familiarize. We make a drawing and then organize the information in a table. We let r represent Dan's speed in still water. Then $r-5$ is the speed upstream and $r+5$ is the speed downstream. Using $t = \frac{d}{r}$, we let $\frac{10}{r-5}$ represent the time upstream and $\frac{10}{r+5}$ represent the time downstream.

```
  10 km            r - 5 km/h
●─────────────────────────────▶  Upstream
              10 km        r + 5 km/h
Downstream ◀─────────────────────────────
```

Trip	Distance	Speed	Time
Upstream	10	$r-5$	$\frac{10}{r-5}$
Downstream	10	$r+5$	$\frac{10}{r+5}$

Translate. The time for the round trip is 3 hours. We now have an equation.

$$\frac{10}{r-5} + \frac{10}{r+5} = 3$$

Carry out. We solve the equation. We multiply by the LCD, $(r-5)(r+5)$.

$$(r-5)(r+5)\left(\frac{10}{r-5} + \frac{10}{r+5}\right) = (r-5)(r+5) \cdot 3$$
$$10(r+5) + 10(r-5) = 3(r^2 - 25)$$
$$10r + 50 + 10r - 50 = 3r^2 - 75$$
$$0 = 3r^2 - 20r - 75$$

We use the quadratic formula

$$r = \frac{-(-20) \pm \sqrt{(-20)^2 - 4 \cdot 3 \cdot (-75)}}{2 \cdot 3}$$
$$r = \frac{20 \pm \sqrt{400 + 900}}{6} = \frac{20 \pm \sqrt{1300}}{6}$$
$$r \approx 9.34 \quad or \quad r \approx -2.68$$

Check. Since negative speed has no meaning in this problem, we check only 9.34. If $r \approx 9.34$, then $r-5 \approx 4.34$ and $r+5 \approx 14.34$. The time it takes to travel upstream is approximately $\frac{10}{4.34}$, or 2.3 hr, and the time it takes to travel downstream is approximately $\frac{10}{14.34}$, or 0.7 hr. The total time is approximately $2.3 + 0.7$ or approximately 3 hr. The value checks.

State. Dan's speed in still water is approximately 9.34 km/h.

14. About 3.24 mph

15. $A = 4\pi r^2$

$$\frac{A}{4\pi} = r^2 \qquad \text{Dividing by } 4\pi$$

$$\frac{1}{2}\sqrt{\frac{A}{\pi}} = r \qquad \text{Taking the positive square root}$$

16. $s = \sqrt{\dfrac{A}{6}}$

17. $A = 2\pi r^2 + 2\pi rh$

$$0 = 2\pi r^2 + 2\pi rh - A \qquad \text{Standard form}$$
$$a = 2\pi, \ b = 2\pi h, \ c = -A$$
$$r = \frac{-2\pi h \pm \sqrt{(2\pi h)^2 - 4 \cdot 2\pi \cdot (-A)}}{2 \cdot 2\pi} \qquad \begin{array}{l}\text{Using the}\\ \text{quadratic formula}\end{array}$$
$$r = \frac{-2\pi h \pm \sqrt{4\pi^2 h^2 + 8\pi A}}{4\pi}$$
$$r = \frac{-2\pi h \pm 2\sqrt{\pi^2 h^2 + 2\pi A}}{4\pi}$$
$$r = \frac{-\pi h \pm \sqrt{\pi^2 h^2 + 2\pi A}}{2\pi}$$

Since taking the negative square root would result in a negative answer, we take the positive one.

$$r = \frac{-\pi h + \sqrt{\pi^2 h^2 + 2\pi A}}{2\pi}$$

$$t = \frac{-v_0 + \sqrt{v_0^2 + 2gs}}{g}$$

18. $r = \sqrt{\dfrac{Gm_1 m_2}{F}}$

26. $r = \dfrac{-\pi s + \sqrt{\pi^2 s^2 + 4\pi A}}{2\pi}$

19.
$$N = \frac{kQ_1 Q_2}{s^2}$$

$Ns^2 = kQ_1 Q_2$ Multiplying by s^2

$s^2 = \dfrac{kQ_1 Q_2}{N}$ Dividing by N

$s = \sqrt{\dfrac{kQ_1 Q_2}{N}}$ Taking the positive square root

20. $r = \sqrt{\dfrac{A}{\pi}}$

21.
$$T = 2\pi \sqrt{\frac{l}{g}}$$

$\dfrac{T}{2\pi} = \sqrt{\dfrac{l}{g}}$ Multiplying by $\dfrac{1}{2\pi}$

$\dfrac{T^2}{4\pi^2} = \dfrac{l}{g}$ Squaring

$gT^2 = 4\pi^2 l$ Multiplying by $4\pi^2 g$

$g = \dfrac{4\pi^2 l}{T^2}$ Multiplying by $\dfrac{1}{T^2}$

22. $b = \sqrt{c^2 - a^2}$

23. $a^2 + b^2 + c^2 = d^2$

     $c^2 = d^2 - a^2 - b^2$ Subtracting a^2 and b^2

     $c = \sqrt{d^2 - a^2 - b^2}$ Taking the positive square root

24. $k = \dfrac{3 + \sqrt{9 + 8N}}{2}$

25. $s = v_0 t + \dfrac{gt^2}{2}$

$0 = \dfrac{gt^2}{2} + v_0 t - s$ Standard form

$a = \dfrac{g}{2},\ b = v_0,\ c = -s$

$t = \dfrac{-v_0 \pm \sqrt{v_0^2 - 4\left(\frac{g}{2}\right)(-s)}}{2\left(\frac{g}{2}\right)}$

$t = \dfrac{-v_0 \pm \sqrt{v_0^2 + 2gs}}{g}$

Since taking the negative square root would result in a negative answer, we take the positive one.

27. $N = \dfrac{1}{2}(n^2 - n)$

$N = \dfrac{1}{2}n^2 - \dfrac{1}{2}n$

$0 = \dfrac{1}{2}n^2 - \dfrac{1}{2}n - N$

$a = \dfrac{1}{2},\ b = -\dfrac{1}{2},\ c = -N$

$$n = \frac{-\left(-\frac{1}{2}\right) \pm \sqrt{\left(-\frac{1}{2}\right)^2 - 4 \cdot \frac{1}{2} \cdot (-N)}}{2\left(\frac{1}{2}\right)}$$

$n = \dfrac{1}{2} \pm \sqrt{\dfrac{1}{4} + 2N}$

$n = \dfrac{1}{2} \pm \sqrt{\dfrac{1 + 8N}{4}}$

$n = \dfrac{1}{2} \pm \dfrac{1}{2}\sqrt{1 + 8N}$

Since taking the negative square root would result in a negative answer, we take the positive one.

$n = \dfrac{1}{2} + \dfrac{1}{2}\sqrt{1 + 8N}$, or $\dfrac{1 + \sqrt{1 + 8N}}{2}$

28. $r = 1 - \sqrt{\dfrac{A}{A_0}}$

29.
$$V = 3.5\sqrt{h}$$

$V = 12.25h$ Squaring

$\dfrac{V^2}{12.25} = h$

30. $L = \dfrac{1}{W^2 C}$

31. $A = P_1(1 + r)^2 + P_2(1 + r)$

$0 = P_1(1 + r)^2 + P_2(1 + r) - A$

Let $u = 1 + r$.

$0 = P_1 u^2 + P_2 u - A$ Substituting

$u = \dfrac{-P_2 \pm \sqrt{P_2^2 - 4(P_1)(-A)}}{2P_1}$

$u = \dfrac{-P_2 + \sqrt{P_2^2 + 4AP_1}}{2P_1}$ Simplifying and taking the positive square root

$1 + r = \dfrac{-P_2 + \sqrt{P_2^2 + 4AP_1}}{2P_1}$ Substituting $1 + r$ for u

$r = -1 + \dfrac{-P_2 + \sqrt{P_2^2 + 4AP_1}}{2P_1}$

32. $r = -2 + \dfrac{-P_2 + \sqrt{P_2^2 + 4AP_1}}{P_1}$

33. a) *Familiarize and Translate*. From Example 4, we know
$$t = \frac{-v_0 + \sqrt{v_0{}^2 + 19.6s}}{9.8}.$$

Carry out. Substituting 500 for s and 0 for v_0, we have
$$t = \frac{0 + \sqrt{0^2 + 19.6(500)}}{9.8}$$
$$t \approx 10.1$$

Check. Substitute 10.1 for t and 0 for v_0 in the original formula. (See Example 4.)
$$s = 4.9t^2 + v_0 t = 4.9(10.1)^2 + 0 \cdot (10.1)^2$$
$$\approx 500$$
The answer checks.

State. It takes about 10.1 sec to reach the ground.

b) *Familiarize and Translate*. From Example 4, we know
$$t = \frac{-v_0 + \sqrt{v_0^2 + 19.6s}}{9.8}.$$

Carry out. Substitute 500 for s and 30 for v_0.
$$t = \frac{-30 + \sqrt{30^2 + 19.6(500)}}{9.8}$$
$$t \approx 7.49$$

Check. Substitute 30 for v_0 and 7.49 for t in the original formula. (See Example 4.)
$$s = 4.9t^2 + v_0 t = 4.9(7.49)^2 + (30)(7.49)$$
$$\approx 500$$
The answer checks.

State. It takes about 7.49 sec to reach the ground.

c) *Familiarize and Translate*. We will use the formula in Example 4, $s = 4.9t^2 + v_0 t$.

Carry out. Substitute 5 for t and 30 for v_0.
$$s = 4.9(5)^2 + 30(5) = 272.5$$

Check. We can substitute 30 for v_0 and 272.5 for s in the form of the formula we used in part (b).
$$t = \frac{-v_0 + \sqrt{v_0^2 + 19.6s}}{9.8}$$
$$= \frac{-30 + \sqrt{(30)^2 + 19.6(272.5)}}{9.8} = 5$$
The answer checks.

State. The object will fall 272.5 m.

34. (a) 3.9 sec; (b) 1.9 sec; (c) 79.6 m

35. *Familiarize and Translate*. From Example 4, we know
$$t = \frac{-v_0 + \sqrt{v_0^2 + 19.6s}}{9.8}.$$

Carry out. Substituting 40 for s and 0 for v_0 we have
$$t = \frac{0 + \sqrt{0^2 + 19.6(40)}}{9.8}$$
$$t \approx 2.9$$

Check. Substitute 2.9 for t and 0 for v_0 in the original formula. (See Example 4.)
$$s = 4.9t^2 + v_0 t = 4.9(2.9)^2 + 0(2.9)$$
$$\approx 40$$
The answer checks.

State. He will be falling for about 2.9 sec.

36. 30.625 m

37. *Familiarize and Translate*. From Example 3, we know
$$T = \frac{\sqrt{3V}}{12}.$$

Carry out. Substituting 36 for V, we have
$$T = \frac{\sqrt{3 \cdot 36}}{12}$$
$$T \approx 0.87$$

Check. Substitute 0.87 for T in the original formula. (See Example 3.)
$$48T^2 = V$$
$$48(0.87)^2 = V$$
$$36 \approx V$$

The answer checks.

State. Anfernee Hardaway's hang time is about 0.87 sec.

38. 12

39. *Familiarize and Translate*. We will use the formula in Example 4, $s = 4.9t^2 + v_0 t$.

Carry out. Solve the formula for v_0.
$$s - 4.9t^2 = v_0 t$$
$$\frac{s - 4.9t^2}{t} = v_0$$

Now substitute 51.6 for s and 3 for t.
$$\frac{51.6 - 4.9(3)^2}{3} = v_0$$
$$2.5 = v_0$$

Check. Substitute 3 for t and 2.5 for v_0 in the original formula.

$$s = 4.9(3)^2 + 2.5(3) = 51.6$$

The solution checks.

State. The initial velocity is 2.5 m/sec.

40. 3.2 m/sec

41. **Familiarize and Translate**. From Exercise 31 we know that

$$r = -1 + \frac{-P_2 + \sqrt{P_2^2 + 4P_1 A}}{2P_1},$$

where A is the total amount in the account after two years, P_1 is the amount of the original deposit, P_2 is deposited at the beginning of the second year, and r is the annual interest rate.

Carry out. Substitute 3000 for P_1, 1700 for P_2, and 5253.70 for A.

$$r = -1 + \frac{-1700 + \sqrt{(1700)^2 + 4(3000)(5253.70)}}{2(3000)}$$

Using a calculator, we have $r = 0.07$.

Check. Substitute in the original formula in Exercise 31.

$$P_1(1 + r)^2 + P_2(1 + r) = A$$
$$3000(1.07)^2 + 1700(1.07) = A$$
$$5253.70 = A$$

The answer checks.

State. The annual interest rate is 0.07, or 7%.

42. 8.5%

43.
$$\sqrt{3x + 1} = \sqrt{2x - 1} + 1$$
$$3x + 1 = 2x - 1 + 2\sqrt{2x + 1} + 1$$
$$\text{Squaring both sides}$$
$$x + 1 = 2\sqrt{2x - 1}$$
$$x^2 + 2x + 1 = 4(2x - 1) \quad \text{Squaring both sides}$$
$$\text{again}$$
$$x^2 + 2x + 1 = 8x - 4$$
$$x^2 - 6x + 5 = 0$$
$$(x - 1)(x - 5) = 0$$
$$x = 1 \quad \text{or} \quad x = 5$$

Both numbers check. The solutions are 1 and 5.

44. $\dfrac{1}{x - 2}$

45. $\sqrt[3]{18y^3} \ \sqrt[3]{4x^2} = \sqrt[3]{72x^2y^3} = \sqrt[3]{8y^3 \cdot 9x^2} = 2y\sqrt[3]{9x^2}$

46. $\dfrac{1}{7}$

47. ◈

48. ◈

49. ◈

50. $\pm\sqrt{2}$

51. **Familiarize**. Let $x =$ the number of beach towels purchased for \$250.

Then $\dfrac{250}{x} = $ cost per towel,

$\dfrac{250}{x} + 3.50 = $ amount received per towel,

$x - 15 = $ number of towels sold,

$\left(\dfrac{250}{x} + 3.50\right)(x - 15) = $ total amount received from the sale of $x - 15$ towels,

$2x + 4 = $ number of towels in new purchase,

and $\dfrac{250}{x}(2x + 4) = $ total amount spent on new purchase.

Translate. The total amount received from the sale of $x - 15$ towels is the same as the total amount spent on the new purchase. We now have an equation.

$$\left(\frac{250}{x} + 3.50\right)(x - 15) = \frac{250}{x}(2x + 4)$$

Carry out. After multiplying and simplifying we have:

$$7x^2 - 605x - 9500 = 0$$
$$(7x + 95)(x - 100) = 0$$
$$x = -\frac{95}{7} \quad \text{or} \quad x = 100$$

Check. Since the cost per towel cannot be negative, we check only 100. When 100 towels are purchased for \$250, the cost per towel is \$250/100, or \$2.50. The amount received per towel is \$2.50 + \$3.50, or \$6. When all but 15 towels, or $100 - 15$, or 85, towels are sold, the total amount received is $\$6 \cdot 85$, or \$510. If 4 more than twice as many towels as before were purchased, then $2 \cdot 100 + 4$, or 204 towels would be purchased. At \$2.50 per towel, this would cost \$510. Since this is the same as the amount received from the sale of the original towels, the answer checks.

State. The cost per towel was $\dfrac{\$250}{100}$, or \$2.50.

52. $n = \pm\sqrt{\dfrac{r^2 \pm \sqrt{r^4 + 4m^4r^2p - 4mp}}{2m}}$

53.
$$\frac{w}{l} = \frac{l}{w+l}$$
$$l(w+l)\cdot\frac{w}{l} = l(w+l)\cdot\frac{l}{w+l}$$
$$w(w+l) = l^2$$
$$w^2 + lw = l^2$$
$$0 = l^2 - lw - w^2$$

Use the quadratic formula with $a = 1$, $b = -w$, and $c = -w^2$.
$$l = \frac{-(-w)\pm\sqrt{(-w)^2 - 4\cdot 1\cdot(-w^2)}}{2\cdot 1}$$
$$l = \frac{w\pm\sqrt{w^2 + 4w^2}}{2} = \frac{w\pm\sqrt{5w^2}}{2}$$
$$l = \frac{w\pm w\sqrt{5}}{2}$$

Since $\dfrac{w - w\sqrt{5}}{2}$ is negative we use the positive square root:
$$l = \frac{w + w\sqrt{5}}{2}$$

54. $L(A) = \sqrt{\dfrac{A}{2}}$

55.
$$m = \frac{m_0}{\sqrt{1 - \dfrac{v^2}{c^2}}}$$
$$m\sqrt{1 - \frac{v^2}{c^2}} = m_0$$
$$\sqrt{1 - \frac{v^2}{c^2}} = \frac{m_0}{m}$$
$$1 - \frac{v^2}{c^2} = \frac{m_0^2}{m^2} \quad \text{Squaring}$$
$$c^2m^2 - m^2v^2 = c^2m_0^2 \quad \text{Multiplying by } c^2m^2$$
$$c^2m^2 - c^2m_0^2 = m^2v^2$$
$$c^2(m^2 - m_0^2) = m^2v^2$$
$$c^2 = \frac{m^2v^2}{m^2 - m_0^2}$$
$$c = \frac{mv}{\sqrt{m^2 - m_0^2}} \quad \text{Taking the positive square root}$$

56. $d = \dfrac{-\pi h + \sqrt{\pi^2 h^2 + 2\pi A}}{\pi}$

57. Let s represent a length of a side of the cube, let S represent the surface area of the cube, and let A represent the surface area of the sphere. Then the diameter of the sphere is s, so the radius r is $s/2$. From Exercise 15, we know, $A = 4\pi r^2$, so when $r = s/2$ we have $A = 4\pi\left(\dfrac{s}{2}\right)^2 = 4\pi\cdot\dfrac{s^2}{4} = \pi s^2$. From the formula for the surface area of a cube (See Exercise 16.) we know that $S = 6s^2$, so $\dfrac{S}{6} = s^2$ and then $A = \pi\cdot\dfrac{S}{6}$, or $A(S) = \dfrac{\pi S}{6}$.

Exercise Set 10.4

1. $x^4 - 5x^2 + 4 = 0$

Let $u = x^2$ and think of x^4 as $(x^2)^2$.
$$u^2 - 5u + 4 = 0 \quad \text{Substituting } u \text{ for } x^2$$
$$(u - 1)(u - 4) = 0$$
$$u - 1 = 0 \quad\text{or}\quad u - 4 = 0$$
$$u = 1 \quad\text{or}\quad u = 4$$

Now replace u with x^2 and solve these equations:
$$x^2 = 1 \quad\text{or}\quad x^2 = 4$$
$$x = \pm 1 \quad\text{or}\quad x = \pm 2$$
The numbers 1, -1, 2, and -2 check. They are the solutions.

2. ± 1, ± 3

3. $x^4 - 12x^2 + 27 = 0$

Let $u = x^2$.
$$u^2 - 12u + 27 = 0 \quad \text{Substituting } u \text{ for } x^2$$
$$(u - 9)(u - 3) = 0$$
$$u = 9 \quad\text{or}\quad u = 3$$

Now replace u with x^2 and solve these equations:
$$x^2 = 9 \quad\text{or}\quad x^2 = 3$$
$$x = \pm 3 \quad\text{or}\quad x = \pm\sqrt{3}$$
The numbers 3, -3, $\sqrt{3}$, and $-\sqrt{3}$ check. They are the solutions.

4. ± 2, $\pm\sqrt{5}$

5. $4x^4 - 19x^2 + 12 = 0$

Let $u = x^2$.
$$4u^2 - 19u + 12 = 0 \quad \text{Substituting } u \text{ for } x^2$$
$$(4u - 3)(u - 4) = 0$$
$$4u - 3 = 0 \quad\text{or}\quad u - 4 = 0$$
$$u = \frac{3}{4} \quad\text{or}\quad u = 4$$

Now replace u with x^2 and solve these equations:
$$x^2 = \frac{3}{4} \quad\text{or}\quad x^2 = 4$$
$$x = \pm\frac{\sqrt{3}}{2} \quad\text{or}\quad x = \pm 2$$
The numbers $\dfrac{\sqrt{3}}{2}$, $-\dfrac{\sqrt{3}}{2}$, 2, and -2 check. They are the solutions.

6. $\pm\dfrac{\sqrt{5}}{3}$, ± 1

7. $x - 4\sqrt{x} - 1 = 0$

Let $u = \sqrt{x}$ and view x as $(\sqrt{x})^2$.

$$u^2 - 4u - 1 = 0 \qquad \text{Substituting } u \text{ for } \sqrt{x}$$

$$u = \frac{-(-4) \pm \sqrt{(-4)^2 - 4 \cdot 1 \cdot (-1)}}{2 \cdot 1}$$

$$u = \frac{4 \pm \sqrt{20}}{2} = \frac{2 \cdot 2 \pm 2\sqrt{5}}{2}$$

$$u = 2 \pm \sqrt{5}$$

$u = 2 + \sqrt{5}$ or $u = 2 - \sqrt{5}$

Replace u with $\sqrt{x}$ and solve these equations.

$\sqrt{x} = 2 + \sqrt{5}$ or $\sqrt{x} = 2 - \sqrt{5}$

$(\sqrt{x})^2 = (2 + \sqrt{5})^2$ No solution: $2 - \sqrt{5}$ is negative

$x = 4 + 4\sqrt{5} + 5$

$x = 9 + 4\sqrt{5}$

The number $9 + 4\sqrt{5}$ checks. It is the solution.

8. $8 + 2\sqrt{7}$

9. $(x^2 - 7)^2 - 3(x^2 - 7) + 2 = 0$

Let $u = x^2 - 7$.

$$u^2 - 3u + 2 = 0 \quad \text{Substituting } u \text{ for } x^2 - 7$$

$$(u - 1)(u - 2) = 0$$

$u = 1$ or $u = 2$

$x^2 - 7 = 1$ or $x^2 - 7 = 2$ Replacing u with $x^2 - 7$

$x^2 = 8$ or $x^2 = 9$

$x = \pm\sqrt{8}$ or $x = \pm 3$

$x = \pm 2\sqrt{2}$ or $x = \pm 3$

The numbers $2\sqrt{2}$, $-2\sqrt{3}$, 3, and -3 check. They are the solutions.

10. $\pm\sqrt{3}$, ± 2

11. $(3 + \sqrt{x})^2 + 3(3 + \sqrt{x}) - 10 = 0$

Let $u = 3 + \sqrt{x}$.

$$u^2 + 3u - 10 = 0 \quad \text{Substituting } u \text{ for } 3 + \sqrt{x}$$

$$(u + 5)(u - 2) = 0$$

$u = -5$ or $u = 2$

$3 + \sqrt{x} = -5$ or $3 + \sqrt{x} = 2$ Replacing u with $3 + \sqrt{x}$

$\sqrt{x} = -8$ or $\sqrt{x} = -1$

Since the principal square root cannot be negative, this equation has no solution.

12. No solution

13. $x^{-2} - x^{-1} - 6 = 0$

Let $u = x^{-1}$ and think of x^{-2} as $(x^{-1})^2$.

$$u^2 - u - 6 = 0 \quad \text{Substituting } u \text{ for } x^{-1}$$

$$(u - 3)(u + 2) = 0$$

$u = 3$ or $u = -2$

Now we replace u with x^{-1} and solve these equations:

$x^{-1} = 3$ or $x^{-1} = -2$

$\dfrac{1}{x} = 3$ or $\dfrac{1}{x} = -2$

$\dfrac{1}{3} = x$ or $-\dfrac{1}{2} = x$

Both $\dfrac{1}{3}$ and $-\dfrac{1}{2}$ check. They are the solutions.

14. -2, 1

15. $4x^{-2} + x^{-1} - 5 = 0$

Let $u = x^{-1}$.

$$4u^2 + u - 5 = 0 \quad \text{Substituting } u \text{ for } x^{-1}$$

$$(4u + 5)(u - 1) = 0$$

$$u = -\frac{5}{4} \text{ or } u = 1$$

Now we replace u with x^{-1} and solve these equations:

$x^{-1} = -\dfrac{5}{4}$ or $x^{-1} = 1$

$\dfrac{1}{x} = -\dfrac{5}{4}$ or $\dfrac{1}{x} = 1$

$4 = -5x$ or $1 = x$

$-\dfrac{4}{5} = x$ or $1 = x$

The numbers $-\dfrac{4}{5}$ and 1 check. They are the solutions.

16. $-\dfrac{1}{10}$, 1

17. $t^{2/3} + t^{1/3} - 6 = 0$

Let $u = t^{1/3}$ and think of $t^{2/3}$ as $(t^{1/3})^2$.

$$u^2 + u - 6 = 0 \quad \text{Substituting } u \text{ for } t^{1/3}$$

$$(u + 3)(u - 2) = 0$$

$u = -3$ or $u = 2$

Now we replace u with $t^{1/3}$ and solve these equations:

$t^{1/3} = -3$ or $t^{1/3} = 2$

$t = (-3)^3$ or $t = 2^3$ Raising to the third power

$t = -27$ or $t = 8$

Both -27 and 8 check. They are the solutions.

18. -8, 64

19. $y^{1/3} - y^{1/6} - 6 = 0$

Let $u = y^{1/6}$.

$\quad u^2 - u - 6 = 0$ Substituting u for $y^{1/6}$

$(u - 3)(u + 2) = 0$

$u = 3$ or $u = -2$

Now we replace u with $y^{1/6}$ and solve these equations:

$\quad y^{1/6} = 3 \quad or \quad y^{1/6} = -2$

$\quad \sqrt[6]{y} = 3 \quad or \quad \sqrt[6]{y} = -2$

$\quad y = 3^6 \qquad$ This equation has no

$\quad y = 729 \qquad$ solution since principal

$\qquad\qquad\qquad$ sixth roots are never negative.

The number 729 checks and is the solution.

20. No solution

21. $\qquad t^{1/3} + 2t^{1/6} = 3$

$\quad t^{1/3} + 2t^{1/6} - 3 = 0$

Let $u = t^{1/6}$.

$\quad u^2 + 2u - 3 = 0$ Substituting u for $t^{1/6}$

$(u + 3)(u - 1) = 0$

$\quad u = -3 \quad or \quad u = 1$

$t^{1/6} = -3 \ or \ t^{1/6} = 1$ Substituting $t^{1/6}$ for u

No solution $\qquad t = 1$

The number 1 checks and is the solution.

22. 16, 81

23. $(3 - \sqrt{x})^2 - 10(3 - \sqrt{x}) + 23 = 0$

Let $u = 3 - \sqrt{x}$.

$\quad u^2 - 10u + 23 = 0 \qquad$ Substituting u for $3 - \sqrt{x}$

$$u = \frac{-(-10) \pm \sqrt{(-10)^2 - 4 \cdot 1 \cdot 23}}{2 \cdot 1}$$

$$u = \frac{10 \pm \sqrt{8}}{2} = \frac{2 \cdot 5 \pm 2\sqrt{2}}{2}$$

$$u = 5 \pm \sqrt{2}$$

$u = 5 + \sqrt{2}$ or $u = 5 - \sqrt{2}$

Now we replace u with $3 - \sqrt{x}$ and solve these equations:

$3 - \sqrt{x} = 5 + \sqrt{2} \quad or \quad 3 - \sqrt{x} = 5 - \sqrt{2}$

$\quad -\sqrt{x} = 2 + \sqrt{2} \quad or \quad -\sqrt{x} = 2 - \sqrt{2}$

$\quad \sqrt{x} = -2 - \sqrt{2} \ or \quad \sqrt{x} = -2 + \sqrt{2}$

Since both $-2 - \sqrt{2}$ and $-2 + \sqrt{2}$ are negative and principal square roots are never negative, the equation has no solution.

24. $4 + 2\sqrt{3}$

25. $16\left(\dfrac{x-1}{x-8}\right)^2 + 8\left(\dfrac{x-1}{x-8}\right) + 1 = 0$

Let $u = \dfrac{x-1}{x-8}$.

$\quad 16u^2 + 8u + 1 = 0$ Substituting u for $\dfrac{x-1}{x-8}$

$(4u + 1)(4u + 1) = 0$

$\quad u = -\dfrac{1}{4}$

Now we replace u with $\dfrac{x-1}{x-8}$ and solve this equation:

$\dfrac{x-1}{x-8} = -\dfrac{1}{4}$

$4x - 4 = -x + 8$ Multiplying by $4(x - 8)$

$\quad 5x = 12$

$\quad x = \dfrac{12}{5}$

The number $\dfrac{12}{5}$ checks and is the solution.

26. $-\dfrac{3}{2}$

27. The x-intercepts occur where $f(x) = 0$. Thus, we must have $5x + 13\sqrt{x} - 6 = 0$.

Let $u = \sqrt{x}$.

$\quad 5u^2 + 13u - 6 = 0$ Substituting

$(5u - 2)(u + 3) = 0$

$u = \dfrac{2}{5}$ or $u = -3$

Now replace u with $\sqrt{x}$ and solve these equations:

$\quad \sqrt{x} = \dfrac{2}{5} \quad or \quad \sqrt{x} = -3$

$\quad x = \dfrac{4}{25} \qquad$ No solution

The number $\dfrac{4}{25}$ checks. Thus, the x-intercept is $\left(\dfrac{4}{25}, 0\right)$.

28. $\left(\dfrac{4}{9}, 0\right)$

29. The x-intercepts occur where $f(x) = 0$. Thus, we must have $(x^2 - 3x)^2 - 10(x^2 - 3x) + 24 = 0$.

Let $u = x^2 - 3x$.

$\quad u^2 - 10u + 24 = 0$ Substituting

$(u - 6)(u - 4) = 0$

$u = 6$ or $u = 4$

Now replace u with $x^2 - 3x$ and solve these equations:

$\quad x^2 - 3x = 6 \quad or \quad x^2 - 3x = 4$

$x^2 - 3x - 6 = 0 \ or \ x^2 - 3x - 4 = 0$

$$x = \frac{-(-3) \pm \sqrt{(-3)^2 - 4(1)(-6)}}{2 \cdot 1} \quad or$$

$$(x - 4)(x + 1) = 0$$

$$x = \frac{3 \pm \sqrt{33}}{2} \quad or \quad x = 4 \ or \ x = -1$$

All four numbers check. Thus, the x-intercepts are $\left(\frac{3 + \sqrt{33}}{2}, 0\right)$, $\left(\frac{3 - \sqrt{33}}{2}, 0\right)$, $(4, 0)$, and $(-1, 0)$.

30. $(7, 0)$, $(-1, 0)$, $(5, 0)$, $(1, 0)$

31. The x-intercepts occur where $f(x) = 0$. Thus, we must have $x^{2/5} + x^{1/5} - 6 = 0$.

Let $u = x^{1/5}$.

$$u^2 + u - 6 = 0 \quad \text{Substituting } u \text{ for } x^{1/5}$$

$$(u + 3)(u - 2) = 0$$

$$u = -3 \quad or \quad u = 2$$

$$x^{1/5} = -3 \quad or \quad x^{1/5} = 2 \quad \text{Replacing } u \text{ with } x^{1/5}$$

$$x = -243 \ or \quad x = 32 \quad \text{Raising to the fifth power}$$

Both -243 and 32 check. Thus, the x-intercepts are $(-243, 0)$ and $(32, 0)$.

32. $(81, 0)$

33. The x-intercepts occur where $f(x) = 0$. Thus, we must have $\left(\frac{x^2 - 2}{x}\right)^2 - 7\left(\frac{x^2 - 2}{x}\right) - 18 = 0$.

Let $u = \frac{x^2 - 2}{x}$.

$$u^2 - 7u - 18 = 0 \quad \text{Substituting}$$

$$(u - 9)(u + 2) = 0$$

$$u = 9 \quad or \quad u = -2$$

$$\frac{x^2 - 2}{x} = 9 \quad or \quad \frac{x^2 - 2}{x} = -2$$

$$\text{Replacing } u \text{ with } \frac{x^2 - 2}{x}$$

$$x^2 - 2 = 9x \quad or \quad x^2 - 2 = -2x$$

$$x^2 - 9x - 2 = 0 \quad or \quad x^2 + 2x - 2 = 0$$

$$x = \frac{-(-9) \pm \sqrt{(-9)^2 - 4 \cdot 1 \cdot (-2)}}{2 \cdot 1} \quad or$$

$$x = \frac{-2 \pm \sqrt{2^2 - 4 \cdot 1 \cdot (-2)}}{2 \cdot 1}$$

$$x = \frac{9 \pm \sqrt{89}}{2} \quad or \quad x = \frac{-2 \pm \sqrt{12}}{2}$$

$$x = \frac{9 \pm \sqrt{89}}{2} \quad or \quad x = \frac{-2 \pm 2\sqrt{3}}{2}$$

$$x = \frac{9 \pm \sqrt{89}}{2} \quad or \quad x = -1 \pm \sqrt{3}$$

All four numbers check. Thus, the x-intercepts are

$\left(\frac{9 + \sqrt{89}}{2}, 0\right)$, $\left(\frac{9 - \sqrt{89}}{2}, 0\right)$, $(-1 + \sqrt{3}, 0)$, and $(-1 - \sqrt{3}, 0)$.

34. $(3 + \sqrt{10}, 0)$, $(3 - \sqrt{10}, 0)$, $(-1 + \sqrt{2}, 0)$, $(-1 - \sqrt{2}, 0)$

35. The solutions are -7 and 3.

$$x = -7 \quad or \quad x = 3$$

$$x + 7 = 0 \quad or \quad x - 3 = 0$$

$$(x + 7)(x - 3) = 0 \quad \text{Principle of zero products}$$

$$x^2 + 4x - 21 = 0 \quad \text{FOIL}$$

36. $x^2 + 2x - 24 = 0$

37. The only solution is 3. It must be a repeated solution.

$$x = 3 \quad or \quad x = 3$$

$$x - 3 = 0 \quad or \quad x - 3 = 0$$

$$(x - 3)(x - 3) = 0 \quad \text{Principle of zero products}$$

$$x^2 - 6x + 9 = 0 \quad \text{FOIL}$$

38. $x^2 + 10x + 25 = 0$

39. The solutions are 4 and $\frac{2}{3}$.

$$x = 4 \quad or \quad x = \frac{2}{3}$$

$$x - 4 = 0 \quad or \quad x - \frac{2}{3} = 0$$

$$(x - 4)\left(x - \frac{2}{3}\right) = 0$$

$$x^2 - \frac{2}{3}x - 4x + \frac{8}{3} = 0$$

$$x^2 - \frac{14}{3}x + \frac{8}{3} = 0$$

$$3x^2 - 14x + 8 = 0 \quad \text{Multiplying by 3}$$

40. $4x^2 - 23x + 15 = 0$

41. The solutions are $\frac{1}{2}$ and $\frac{1}{3}$.

$$x = \frac{1}{2} \quad or \quad x = \frac{1}{3}$$

$$x - \frac{1}{2} = 0 \quad or \quad x - \frac{1}{3} = 0$$

$$\left(x - \frac{1}{2}\right)\left(x - \frac{1}{3}\right) = 0$$

$$x^2 - \frac{1}{3}x - \frac{1}{2}x + \frac{1}{6} = 0$$

$$x^2 - \frac{5}{6}x + \frac{1}{6} = 0$$

$$6x^2 - 5x + 1 = 0 \quad \text{Multiplying by 6}$$

42. $8x^2 + 6x + 1 = 0$

43. The solutions are -0.6 and 1.4.
$$x = -0.6 \quad or \quad x = 1.4$$
$$x + 0.6 = 0 \quad or \quad x - 1.4 = 0$$
$$(x + 0.6)(x - 1.4) = 0$$
$$x^2 - 1.4x + 0.6x - 0.84 = 0$$
$$x^2 - 0.8x - 0.84 = 0$$

44. $x^2 - 2.1x - 1 = 0$

45. The solutions are $-\sqrt{7}$ and $\sqrt{7}$.
$$x = -\sqrt{7} \quad or \quad x = \sqrt{7}$$
$$x + \sqrt{7} = 0 \quad or \quad x - \sqrt{7} = 0$$
$$(x + \sqrt{7})(x - \sqrt{7}) = 0$$
$$x^2 - 7 = 0$$

46. $x^2 - 3 = 0$

47. The solutions are $3\sqrt{2}$ and $-3\sqrt{2}$.
$$x = 3\sqrt{2} \quad or \quad x = -3\sqrt{2}$$
$$x - 3\sqrt{2} = 0 \quad or \quad x + 3\sqrt{2} = 0$$
$$(x - 3\sqrt{2})(x + 3\sqrt{2}) = 0$$
$$x^2 - (3\sqrt{2})^2 = 0$$
$$x^2 - 9 \cdot 2 = 0$$
$$x^2 - 18 = 0$$

48. $x^2 - 20 = 0$

49. The solutions are $3i$ and $-3i$.
$$x = 3i \quad or \quad x = -3i$$
$$x - 3i = 0 \quad or \quad x + 3i = 0$$
$$(x - 3i)(x + 3i) = 0$$
$$\cdot \; x^2 - (3i)^2 = 0$$
$$x^2 + 9 = 0$$

50. $x^2 + 16 = 0$

51. The solutions are $5 - 2i$ and $5 + 2i$.
$$x = 5 - 2i \quad or \quad x = 5 + 2i$$
$$x - 5 + 2i = 0 \quad or \quad x - 5 - 2i = 0$$
$$[x + (-5 + 2i)][x + (-5 - 2i)] = 0$$
$$x^2 + x(-5 - 2i) + x(-5 + 2i) + (-5 + 2i)(-5 - 2i) = 0$$
$$x^2 - 5x - 2xi - 5x + 2xi + 25 - 4i^2 = 0$$
$$x^2 - 10x + 29 = 0$$
$$(i^2 = -1)$$

52. $x^2 - 4x + 53 = 0$

53. The solutions are $2 - \sqrt{10}$ and $2 + \sqrt{10}$.
$$x = 2 - \sqrt{10} \quad or \quad x = 2 + \sqrt{10}$$
$$x - (2 - \sqrt{10}) = 0 \quad or \quad x - (2 + \sqrt{10}) = 0$$
$$[x - (2 - \sqrt{10})][x - (2 + \sqrt{10})] = 0$$
$$x^2 - x(2 + \sqrt{10}) - x(2 - \sqrt{10}) + (2 - \sqrt{10})(2 + \sqrt{10}) = 0$$
$$x^2 - 2x - x\sqrt{10} - 2x + x\sqrt{10} + 4 - 10 = 0$$
$$x^2 - 4x - 6 = 0$$

54. $x^2 - 6x - 5 = 0$

55. The solutions are -3, 0, and 4.
$$x = -3 \quad or \quad x = 0 \quad or \quad x = 4$$
$$x + 3 = 0 \quad or \quad x = 0 \quad or \quad x - 4 = 0$$
$$(x + 3)(x)(x - 4) = 0$$
$$(x^2 + 3x)(x - 4) = 0$$
$$x^3 - 4x^2 + 3x^2 - 12x = 0$$
$$x^3 - x^2 - 12x = 0$$

56. $x^3 + 3x^2 - 10x = 0$

57. The solutions are -1, 1, and 2.
$$x = -1 \quad or \quad x = 1 \quad or \quad x = 2$$
$$x + 1 = 0 \quad or \quad x - 1 = 0 \quad or \quad x - 2 = 0$$
$$(x + 1)(x - 1)(x - 2) = 0$$
$$(x^2 - 1)(x - 2) = 0$$
$$x^3 - 2x^2 - x + 2 = 0$$

58. $x^3 - 3x^2 - 4x + 12 = 0$

59. $\sqrt{3x^2}\sqrt{3x^3} = \sqrt{3x^2 \cdot 3x^3} = \sqrt{9x^5} = \sqrt{9x^4 \cdot x} = 3x^2\sqrt{x}$

60. 4 L of A, 8 L of B

61. a) Enter the data and use the linear regression feature. We get $n(t) = 12.5308690523x - 11.61122034342$.

b) Graph $y_1 = n(t)$ and $y_2 = 100$ and use the Intersect feature to find the first coordinate of the point of intersection. It is approximately 9, so there were 100 insect species resistant to pesticide 9 years after 1948, or in 1957.

62. $a^2 + a$

63.

64.

65.

66. $\pm\sqrt{\dfrac{-5\pm\sqrt{37}}{6}}$

67. $5x^4 - 7x^2 + 1 = 0$

Let $u = x^2$.

$5u^2 - 7u + 1 = 0$

$$u = \frac{-(-7) \pm \sqrt{(-7)^2 - 4\cdot 5\cdot 1}}{2\cdot 5}$$

$$u = \frac{7 \pm \sqrt{29}}{10}$$

$$x^2 = \frac{7 \pm \sqrt{29}}{10}$$

$$x = \pm\sqrt{\frac{7 \pm \sqrt{29}}{10}}$$

All four numbers check and are the solutions.

68. $-2, -1, 6, 7$

69. $(x^2 - 4x - 2)^2 - 13(x^2 - 4x - 2) + 30 = 0$

Let $u = x^2 - 4x - 2$.

$u^2 - 13u + 30 = 0$

$(u - 3)(u - 10) = 0$

$\qquad\qquad u = 3 \;\; or \qquad\qquad u = 10$

$x^2 - 4x - 2 = 3 \;\; or \quad x^2 - 4x - 2 = 10$

$\; x^2 - 4x - 5 = 0 \;\; or \quad x^2 - 4x - 12 = 0$

$(x - 5)(x + 1) = 0 \;\; or \;\; (x - 6)(x + 2) = 0$

$x = 5 \; or \; x = -1 \; or \; x = 6 \; or \; x = -2$

The numbers 5, -1, 6, and -2 check and are the solutions.

70. $\dfrac{100}{99}$

71. $\left(\sqrt{\dfrac{x}{x-3}}\right)^2 - 24 = 10\sqrt{\dfrac{x}{x-3}}$

Let $u = \sqrt{\dfrac{x}{x-3}}$, substitute, and write in standard form.

$u^2 - 10u - 24 = 0$

$(u - 12)(u + 2) = 0$

$\qquad u = 12 \qquad\qquad or \qquad\qquad u = -2$

$\sqrt{\dfrac{x}{x-3}} = 12 \qquad or \quad \sqrt{\dfrac{x}{x-3}} = -2$

$\dfrac{x}{x-3} = 144 \qquad or \qquad$ No solution

$\qquad x = 144x - 432$

$\qquad 432 = 143x$

$\qquad \dfrac{432}{143} = x$

The number $\dfrac{432}{143}$ checks. It is the solution.

72. $0, 5, -5, 2, -2, 3, -3$

73. $a^3 - 26a^{3/2} - 27 = 0$

Let $u = a^{3/2}$.

$u^2 - 26u - 27 = 0$ Substituting

$(u - 27)(u + 1) = 0$

$\quad u = 27 \qquad or \quad u = -1$

$a^{3/2} = 27 \qquad or\; a^{3/2} = -1$ Replacing u with $a^{3/2}$

$\quad a = 27^{2/3} \qquad$ No solution

$\quad a = (3^3)^{2/3}$

$\quad a = 9$

The number 9 checks. It is the solution.

74. $1, 3$

75. $x^6 + 7x^3 - 8 = 0$

Let $u = x^3$.

$u^2 + 7u - 8 = 0$

$(u + 8)(u - 1) = 0$

$u = -8 \; or \;\; u = 1$

$x^3 = -8 \; or \; x^3 = 1$

$x = -2 \; or \;\; x = 1$

Both -2 and 1 check. They are the solutions.

76. $-3, -1, 1, 4$

77. We substitute $(-3, 0)$, $\left(\dfrac{1}{2}, 0\right)$, and $(0, -12)$ in $f(x) = ax^2 + bx + c$ and get three equations.

$0 = 9a - 3b + c,$

$0 = \dfrac{1}{4}a + \dfrac{1}{2}b + c,$

$-12 = c$

The solution of this system of equations is $a = 8$, $b = 20$, $c = -12$.

78. $x^4 - 14x^3 + 70x^2 - 126x + 29 = 0$

79. $[x - (1-\sqrt{5})][x - (1+\sqrt{5})][x - (3-2i)][x - (3+2i)] = 0$

$\qquad (x^2 - 2x - 4)(x^2 - 6x + 13) = 0$

$\qquad\qquad x^4 - 8x^3 + 21x^2 - 2x - 52 = 0$

80. $x^4 - 5x^2 + 6 = 0$

81. The graph includes the points $(-3, 0)$, $(0, -3)$, and $(1, 0)$. Substituting in $y = ax^2 + bx + c$, we have three equations.

$$0 = 9a - 3b + c,$$
$$-3 = \qquad\quad c,$$
$$0 = a + b + c$$

The solution of this system of equations is $a = 1$, $b = 2$, $c = -3$.

Exercise Set 10.5

1. $y = kx$

$28 = k \cdot 7$ Substituting

$4 = k$

The variation constant is 4.
The equation of variation is $y = 4x$.

2. $k = \dfrac{5}{12}$; $y = \dfrac{5}{12}x$

3. $y = kx$

$3.4 = k \cdot 2$ Substituting

$1.7 = k$

The variation constant is 1.7.
The equation of variation is $y = 1.7x$.

4. $k = \dfrac{2}{5}$; $y = \dfrac{2}{5}x$

5. $y = kx$

$30 = k \cdot 8$ Substituting

$\dfrac{30}{8} = k$

$\dfrac{15}{4} = k$

The variation constant is $\dfrac{15}{4}$.
The equation of variation is $y = \dfrac{15}{4}x$.

6. $k = 3$; $y = 3x$

7. $y = kx$

$0.8 = k(0.5)$ Substituting

$8 = k \cdot 5$ Clearing decimals

$\dfrac{8}{5} = k$

$1.6 = k$

The variation constant is 1.6.
The equation of variation is $y = 1.6x$.

8. $k = 1.5$; $y = 1.5x$

9. *Familiarize.* Because of the phrase "I ... varies directly as ... V," we express the current as a function of the voltage. Thus we have $I(V) = kV$. We know that $I(15) = 5$.

Translate. We find the variation constant and then find the equation of variation.

$$I(V) = kV$$
$$I(15) = k \cdot 15 \quad \text{Replacing } V \text{ with } 15$$
$$5 = k \cdot 15 \quad \text{Replacing } I(15) \text{ with } 5$$
$$\frac{5}{15} = k$$
$$\frac{1}{3} = k \qquad \text{Variation constant}$$

The equation of variation is $I(V) = \dfrac{1}{3}V$.

Carry out. We compute $I(18)$.

$$I(V) = \frac{1}{3}V$$
$$I(18) = \frac{1}{3} \cdot 18 \quad \text{Replacing } V \text{ with } 18$$
$$= 6$$

Check. Reexamine the calculations. Note that the answer seems reasonable since $15/5 = 18/6$.

State. The current is 6 amperes when 18 volts is applied.

10. $33\dfrac{1}{3}$ cm

11. *Familiarize.* Because N varies directly as the number of people P using the cans, we write N as a function of P: $N(P) = kP$. We know that $N(250) = 60,000$.

Translate.
$$N(P) = kP$$
$$N(250) = k \cdot 250 \quad \text{Replacing } P \text{ with } 250$$
$$60,000 = k \cdot 250 \quad \text{Replacing } N(250) \text{ with } 60{,}000$$
$$\frac{60,000}{250} = k$$
$$240 = k \qquad \text{Variation constant}$$
$$N(P) = 240P \quad \text{Equation of variation}$$

Carry out. Find $N(1,008,000)$.
$$N(P) = 240P$$
$$N(1,008,000) = 240 \cdot 1,008,000$$
$$= 241,920,000$$

Check. Reexamine the calculation.

State. 241,920,000 aluminum cans are used each year in Dallas.

12. $4.29

13. Familiarize. The amount A of lead released varies directly as the population P. We write A as a function of P: $A(P) = kP$. We know that $A(12,500) = 385$.

Translate.

$$A(P) = kP$$

$$A(12,500) = k \cdot 12,500 \quad \text{Replacing } P \text{ with } 12{,}500$$

$$385 = k \cdot 12,500 \quad \text{Replacing } A(12,500) \text{ with } 385$$

$$0.0308 = k \quad \text{Variation constant}$$

$$A(P) = 0.0308P \quad \text{Equation of variation}$$

Carry out. Find $A(250,000,000)$.

$$A(P) = 0.0308P$$

$$A(250,000,000) = 0.0308(250,000,000)$$

$$= 7,700,000$$

Check. Reexamine the calculations.

State. 7,700,000 tons of lead were released nationally.

14. 3.36

15. $y = \dfrac{k}{x}$

$$6 = \dfrac{k}{10} \quad \text{Substituting}$$

$$60 = k$$

The variation constant is 60.

The equation of variation is $y = \dfrac{60}{x}$.

16. $k = 64$; $y = \dfrac{64}{x}$

17. $y = \dfrac{k}{x}$

$$4 = \dfrac{k}{3} \quad \text{Substituting}$$

$$12 = k$$

The variation constant is 12.

The equation of variation is $y = \dfrac{12}{x}$.

18. $k = 36$; $y = \dfrac{36}{x}$

19. $y = \dfrac{k}{x}$

$$12 = \dfrac{k}{3} \quad \text{Substituting}$$

$$36 = k$$

The variation constant is 36.

The equation of variation is $y = \dfrac{36}{x}$.

20. $k = 45$; $y = \dfrac{45}{x}$

21. $y = \dfrac{k}{x}$

$$27 = \dfrac{k}{\frac{1}{3}} \quad \text{Substituting}$$

$$9 = k$$

The variation constant is 9.

The equation of variation is $y = \dfrac{9}{x}$.

22. $k = 9$; $y = \dfrac{9}{x}$

23. Familiarize. Because t varies inversely as r, we express t as a function of r. Thus we write $t(r) = k/r$. We know that $t(600) = 45$.

Translate.

$$t(r) = \dfrac{k}{r}$$

$$t(600) = \dfrac{k}{600} \quad \text{Replacing } r \text{ with } 600$$

$$45 = \dfrac{k}{600} \quad \text{Replacing } t(600) \text{ with } 45$$

$$27,000 = k \quad \text{Variation constant}$$

$$t(r) = \dfrac{27,000}{r} \quad \text{Equation of variation}$$

Carry out. Find $t(1000)$.

$$t(1000) = \dfrac{27,000}{1000}$$

$$= 27$$

Check. Reexamine the calculation. Note that, as expected, when the rate increases the time decreases.

State. It will take the pump 27 min to empty the tank at the rate of 1000 kL/min.

24. $\dfrac{2}{9}$ ampere

25. Familiarize. Because V varies inversely as P, we write $V(P) = k/P$. We know that $V(32) = 200$.

Translate.

$$V(P) = \frac{k}{P}$$

$$V(32) = \frac{k}{32} \qquad \text{Replacing } P \text{ with } 32$$

$$200 = \frac{k}{32} \qquad \text{Replacing } V(32) \text{ with } 200$$

$$6400 = k \qquad \text{Variation constant}$$

$$V(P) = \frac{6400}{P} \qquad \text{Equation of variation}$$

Carry out. Find $V(40)$.

$$V(40) = \frac{6400}{40}$$

$$= 160$$

Check. Reexamine the calculations.

State. The volume will be 160 cm^3.

26. $5\dfrac{5}{7}$ hr

27. As the mass increases, the amount of water increases and the points fall approximately on a straight line. Thus, the graph appears to represent direct variation.

28. Inverse

29. As time increases, the height first increases and then decreases. No equation of the form $y = kx$ or $y = \dfrac{k}{x}$ can model this data. Thus, neither direct nor inverse variation is represented.

30. Direct

31. As the frequency increases the corresponding wavelength decreases and a curve drawn through the points would look like the graph of $y = \dfrac{k}{x}$. Thus, the graph appears to represent inverse variation.

32. Neither

33. $y = kx^2$

$$6 = k \cdot 3^2 \qquad \text{Substituting}$$

$$6 = 9k$$

$$\frac{6}{9} = k$$

$$\frac{2}{3} = k \qquad \text{Variation constant}$$

The equation of variation is $y = \dfrac{2}{3}x^2$.

34. $y = 15x^2$

35. $y = \dfrac{k}{x^2}$

$$6 = \frac{k}{3^2} \qquad \text{Substituting}$$

$$6 = \frac{k}{9}$$

$$6 \cdot 9 = k$$

$$54 = k \qquad \text{Variation constant}$$

The equation of variation is $y = \dfrac{54}{x^2}$.

36. $y = \dfrac{0.0015}{x^2}$

37. $y = kxz$

$$56 = k \cdot 14 \cdot 8 \qquad \text{Substituting 56 for } y, \text{ 14 for } x, \text{ and 8 for } z$$

$$56 = 112k$$

$$0.5 = k \qquad \text{Variation constant}$$

The equation of variation is $y = 0.5xz$.

38. $y = \dfrac{5x}{z}$

39. $y = kxz^2$

$$105 = k \cdot 14 \cdot 5^2 \qquad \text{Substituting 105 for } y, \text{ 14 for } x, \text{ and 5 for } z$$

$$105 = 350k$$

$$\frac{105}{350} = k$$

$$0.3 = k$$

The equation of variation is $y = 0.3xz^2$.

40. $y = \dfrac{xz}{w}$

41. $y = k \cdot \dfrac{wx^2}{z}$

$$49 = k \cdot \frac{3 \cdot 7^2}{12} \qquad \text{Substituting}$$

$$4 = k \qquad \text{Variation constant}$$

The equation of variation is $y = \dfrac{4wx^2}{z}$.

42. $y = \dfrac{6x}{wz^2}$

43. *Familiarize.* Because d varies directly as the square of r, we write $d = kr^2$. We know that $d = 200$ when $r = 60$.

Translate.

$$d = kr^2$$

$$200 = k(60)^2$$

$$\frac{1}{18} = k$$

$$d = \frac{1}{18}r^2 \quad \text{Equation of variation}$$

Carry out. Substitute 72 for d and solve for r.

$$72 = \frac{1}{18}r^2$$

$$1296 = r^2$$

$$36 = r$$

Check. Recheck the calculations and perhaps make an estimate to see if the answer seems reasonable.

State. The car can go 36 mph.

44. 220 cm^3

45. *Familiarize.* I varies inversely as d^2, so we write $I = k/d^2$. We know that $I = 90$ when $d = 5$.

Translate. Find k.

$$I = \frac{k}{d^2}$$

$$90 = \frac{k}{5^2}$$

$$2250 = k$$

$$I = \frac{2250}{d^2} \quad \text{Equation of variation}$$

Carry out. Substitute 40 for I and solve for d.

$$40 = \frac{2250}{d^2}$$

$$d^2 = \frac{2250}{40}$$

$$d = 7.5$$

We subtract to find how much farther this is:

$$7.5 - 5 = 2.5$$

Check. Reexamine the calculations.

State. It would be 2.5 m farther.

46. 6.25 km

47. *Familiarize.* W varies inversely as d^2, so we write $W = k/d^2$. We know that $W = 100$ when $d = 6400$.

Translate. Find k.

$$W = \frac{k}{d^2}$$

$$100 = \frac{k}{(6400)^2}$$

$$4,096,000,000 = k$$

$$W = \frac{4,096,000,000}{d^2} \quad \text{Equation of variation}$$

Carry out. Substitute 64 for w and solve for d.

$$64 = \frac{4,096,000,000}{d^2}$$

$$d^2 = \frac{4,096,000,000}{64}$$

$$d = 8000$$

Note that a distance of 8000 km from the center of the earth is $8000 - 6400$, or 1600 km, above the earth.

Check. Recheck the calculations.

State. The astronaut must be 1600 km above the earth in order to weigh 64 lb.

48. 2 mm

49. *Familiarize.* The drag D varies jointly as the surface area A and velocity v, so we write $D = kAv$. We know that $D = 222$ when $A = 37.8$ and $v = 40$.

Translate. Find k.

$$D = kAv$$

$$222 = k(37.8)(40)$$

$$\frac{222}{37.8(40)} = k$$

$$\frac{37}{252} = k$$

$$D = \frac{37}{252}Av \quad \text{Equation of variation}$$

Carry out. Substitute 51 for A and 430 for D and solve for v.

$$430 = \frac{37}{252} \cdot 51 \cdot v$$

$$57.42 \text{ mph} \approx v$$

(If we had used the rounded value 0.1468 for k, the resulting speed would have been approximately 57.43 mph.)

Check. Reexamine the calculations.

State. The car must travel about 57.42 mph.

50. About 8.2 mph

51. Use the slope-interest form, $y = mx + b$, where m is the slope and b is the y-intercept.

$$y = -\frac{2}{3}x - 5$$

52. $y - 7 = -\frac{2}{7}(x - 4)$

53. $\dfrac{\dfrac{1}{ab} - \dfrac{2}{bc}}{\dfrac{3}{ab} + \dfrac{4}{bc}} = \dfrac{\left(\dfrac{1}{ab} - \dfrac{2}{bc}\right)abc}{\left(\dfrac{3}{ab} + \dfrac{4}{bc}\right)abc}$

$$= \frac{c - 2a}{3c + 4a}$$

54. $\dfrac{18}{-x - 10}$

55. $f(x) = x^3 - 2x^2$

$f(3) = 3^3 - 2 \cdot 3^2 = 27 - 18 = 9$

56. $9x^2 - 12xy + 4y^2$

57. ◈

58. ◈

59. ◈

60. ◈

61. Write y as a function of x, and then substitute $0.5x$ for x.

$$y(x) = \frac{k}{x^3}$$

$$y(0.5x) = \frac{k}{(0.5x)^3} = \frac{k}{0.125x^3} = \frac{1}{0.125} \cdot \frac{k}{x^3}$$

$$= 8 \cdot y(x)$$

y is multiplied by 8.

62. Q varies directly as the square of p and inversely as the cube of q.

63. $W = \dfrac{km_1 M_1}{d^2}$

W varies jointly as m_1 and M_1 and inversely as the square of d.

64. About 1.697 m

65. a) ***Familiarize.*** We write $N = \dfrac{kP_1P_2}{d^2}$. We let P_1 = the population of Indianapolis and P_2 = the population of Cincinnati. We know that $N = 11,153$ when $P_1 = 752,279$, $P_2 = 358,170$, and $d = 174$.

Translate. We substitute.

$$11,153 = \frac{k(752,279)(358,170)}{(174)^2}$$

Carry out. We solve for k.

$$11,153 = \frac{k(752,279)(358,170)}{(174)^2}$$

$$11,153 = \frac{k(752,279)(358,170)}{30,276}$$

$$337,668,228 = k(752,279)(358,170)$$

$$0.001 \approx k$$

Check. Reexamine the calculations.

State. The value of k is approximately 0.001. The equation of variation is $N = \dfrac{0.001P_1P_2}{d^2}$.

b) ***Familiarize.*** We will use the equation of variation found in part (a): $N = \dfrac{0.001P_1P_2}{d^2}$. We let P_1 = the population of Indianapolis and P_2 = the population of New York. We know that $N = 4270$ when $P_1 = 752,279$ and $P_2 = 7,333,153$.

Translate. We substitute.

$$4270 = \frac{0.001(752,279)(7,333,153)}{d^2}$$

Carry out. We solve for d.

$$4270 = \frac{0.001(752,279)(7,333,153)}{d^2}$$

$$d^2 = \frac{0.001(752,279)(7,333,153)}{4270}$$

$$d^2 \approx 1,291,938$$

$$d \approx 1137$$

Check. Reexamine the calculations.

State. The distance between Indianapolis and New York is approximately 1137 km.

66. $7.20

67. *Familiarize*. Because d varies inversely as s, we write $d(s) = k/s$. We know that $d(0.56) = 50$.

Translate.

$$d(s) = \frac{k}{s}$$

$$d(0.56) = \frac{k}{0.56} \quad \text{Replacing } s \text{ with } 0.56$$

$$50 = \frac{k}{0.56} \quad \text{Replacing } d(0.56) \text{ with } 50$$

$$28 = k$$

$$d(s) = \frac{28}{s} \quad \text{Equation of variation}$$

Carry out. Find $d(0.40)$.

$$d(0.40) = \frac{28}{0.40}$$

$$= 70$$

Check. Reexamine the calculations. Also observe that, as expected, when d decreases, then s increases.

State. The distance is 70 yd.

Exercise Set 10.6

---

1. a) The parabola opens upward, so a is positive.

b) The vertex is $(3, 1)$.

c) The axis of symmetry is $x = 3$.

d) The range is $[1, \infty)$.

2. (a) Negative; (b) $(-1, 2)$; (c) $x = -1$:(d) $(-\infty, 2]$

3. a) The parabola opens downward, so a is negative.

b) The vertex is $(-2, -3)$.

c) The axis of symmetry is $x = -2$.

d) The range is $(-\infty, -3]$.

4. (a) Positive; (b) $(2, 0)$; (c) $x = 2$;(d) $[0, \infty)$

5. a) The parabola opens upward, so a is positive.

b) The vertex is $(-3, 0)$.

c) The axis of symmetry is $x = -3$.

d) The range is $[0, \infty)$.

6. (a) Negative; (b) $(1, -2)$; (c) $x = 1$; (d) $(-\infty, -2]$

7. $a = 3$ and $3 > 0$, so the graph opens up; the vertex is $(0, 0)$. Graph (f) matches this function.

8. (c)

9. $a = -1$ and $-1 < 0$, so the graph opens down; the vertex is $(2, 0)$. Graph (e) matches this function.

10. (b)

11. $a = \frac{2}{3}$ and $\frac{2}{3} > 0$, so the graph opens up; the vertex is $(-3, 1)$. Graph (d) matches this function.

12. (a)

13. $f(x) = x^2$

See Example 1 in the text.

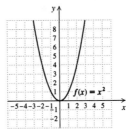

14.

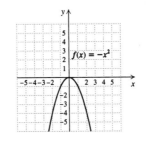

15. $f(x) = -2x^2$

We choose some numbers for x and compute $f(x)$ for each one. Then we plot the ordered pairs $(x, f(x))$ and connect them with a smooth curve.

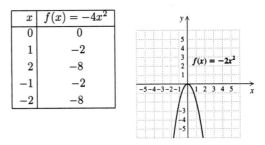

x	$f(x) = -4x^2$
0	0
1	-2
2	-8
-1	-2
-2	-8

16.

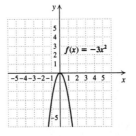

17. $g(x) = \frac{1}{4}x^2$

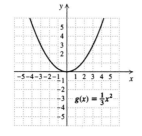

x	$g(x) = \frac{1}{4}x^2$
0	0
1	$\frac{1}{4}$
2	1
3	$\frac{9}{4}$
-1	$\frac{1}{4}$
-2	1
-3	$\frac{9}{4}$

18.

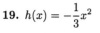

19. $h(x) = -\frac{1}{3}x^2$

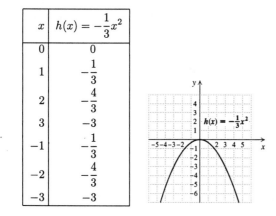

x	$h(x) = -\frac{1}{3}x^2$
0	0
1	$-\frac{1}{3}$
2	$-\frac{4}{3}$
3	-3
-1	$-\frac{1}{3}$
-2	$-\frac{4}{3}$
-3	-3

20.

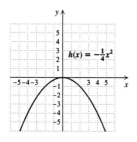

21. $f(x) = \frac{3}{2}x^2$

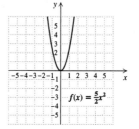

x	$f(x) = \frac{3}{2}x^2$
0	0
1	$\frac{3}{2}$
2	6
-1	$\frac{3}{2}$
-2	6

22.

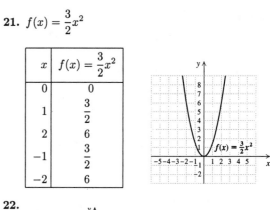

23. $g(x) = (x+1)^2 = [x - (-1)]^2$

We know that the graph of $g(x) = (x+1)^2$ looks like the graph of $f(x) = x^2$ (see Exercise 13) but moved to the left 1 unit.

Vertex: $(-1, 0)$, axis of symmetry: $x = -1$

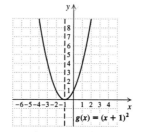

24. Vertex: $(-4, 0)$, axis of symmetry: $x = -4$

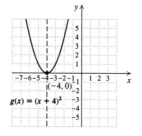

25. $f(x) = (x-2)^2$

The graph of $f(x) = (x-2)^2$ looks like the graph of $f(x) = x^2$ (see Exercise 13) but moved to the right 2 units.

Vertex: $(2, 0)$, axis of symmetry: $x = 2$

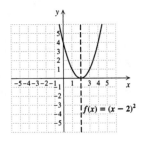

26. Vertex: $(1, 0)$, axis of symmetry: $x = 1$

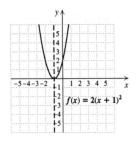

30. Vertex: $(-4, 0)$, axis of symmetry: $x = -4$

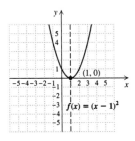

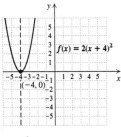

27. $f(x) = -(x + 4)^2 = -[x - (-4)]^2$

The graph of $f(x) = -(x + 4)^2$ looks like the graph of $f(x) = x^2$ (see Exercise 13) but moved to the left 4 units. It will also open downward because of the negative coefficient, -1.

Vertex: $(-4, 0)$, axis of symmetry: $x = -4$

31. $h(x) = -\dfrac{1}{2}(x - 3)^2$

The graph of $h(x) = -\dfrac{1}{2}(x - 3)^2$ looks like the graph of $g(x) = \dfrac{1}{2}x^2$ (see graph following Example 1) but moved to the right 3 units. It will also open downward because of the negative coefficient, $-\dfrac{1}{2}$.

Vertex: $(3, 0)$, axis of symmetry: $x = 3$

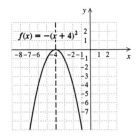

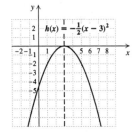

28. Vertex: $(2, 0)$, axis of symmetry: $x = 2$

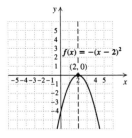

32. Vertex: $(2, 0)$, axis of symmetry: $x = 2$

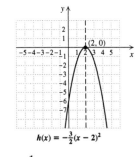

29. $f(x) = 2(x + 1)^2$

The graph of $f(x) = 2(x + 1)^2$ looks like the graph of $h(x) = 2x^2$ (see graph following Example 1) but moved to the left 1 unit.

Vertex: $(-1, 0)$, axis of symmetry: $x = -1$

33. $f(x) = \dfrac{1}{2}(x - 1)^2$

The graph of $f(x) = \dfrac{1}{2}(x - 1)^2$ looks like the graph of $g(x) = \dfrac{1}{2}x^2$ (see graph following Example 1) but moved to the right 1 unit.

Vertex: $(1, 0)$, axis of symmetry: $x = 1$

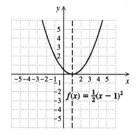

34. Vertex: $(-2, 0)$, axis of symmetry: $x = -2$

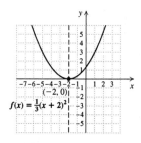

35. $f(x) = (x - 5)^2 + 1$

We know that the graph looks like the graph of $f(x) = x^2$ (see Example 1) but moved to the right 5 units and up 1 unit. The vertex is $(5, 1)$, and the axis of symmetry is $x = 5$. Since the coefficient of $(x-5)^2$ is positive $(1 > 0)$, there is a minimum function value, 1.

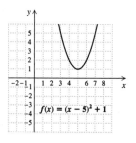

36. Vertex: $(-3, -2)$, axis of symmetry: $x = -3$

Minimum: -2

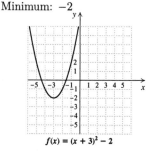

37. $f(x) = (x + 1)^2 - 2$

We know that the graph looks like the graph of $f(x) = x^2$ (see Example 1) but moved to the left 1 unit and down 2 units. The vertex is $(-1, -2)$, and the axis of symmetry is $x = -1$. Since the coefficient of $(x + 1)^2$ is positive $(1 > 0)$, there is a minimum function value, -2.

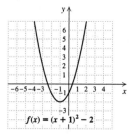

38. Vertex: $(2, -4)$, axis of symmetry: $x = 2$

Maximum: -4

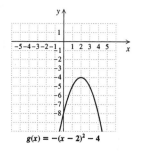

39. $h(x) = -2(x - 1)^2 - 3$

We know that the graph looks like the graph of $h(x) = 2x^2$ (see graph following Example 1) but moved to the right 1 unit and down 3 units and turned upside down. The vertex is $(1, -3)$, and the axis of symmetry is $x = 1$. The maximum function value is -3.

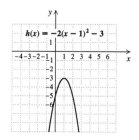

40. Vertex: $(-1, 4)$, axis of symmetry: $x = -1$

Maximum: 4

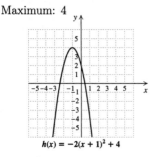

$h(x) = -2(x+1)^2 + 4$

41. $f(x) = 2(x+4)^2 + 1$

We know that the graph looks like the graph of $f(x) = 2x^2$ (see graph following Example 1) but moved to the left 4 units and up 1 unit. The vertex is $(-4, 1)$, the axis of symmetry is $x = -4$, and the minimum function value is 1.

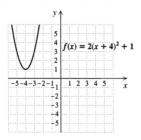

$f(x) = 2(x+4)^2 + 1$

42. Vertex: $(5, -3)$, axis of symmetry: $x = 5$

Minimum: -3

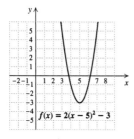

$f(x) = 2(x-5)^2 - 3$

43. $g(x) = -\dfrac{3}{2}(x-1)^2 + 2$

We know that the graph looks like the graph of $f(x) = \dfrac{3}{2}x^2$ (see Exercise 21) but moved to the right 1 unit and up 2 units and turned upside down. The vertex is $(1, 2)$, the axis of symmetry is $x = 1$, and the maximum function value is 2.

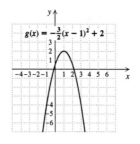

$g(x) = -\dfrac{3}{2}(x-1)^2 + 2$

44. Vertex: $(-2, -1)$, axis of symmetry: $x = -2$

Minimum: -1

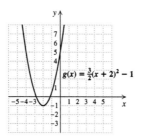

$g(x) = \dfrac{3}{2}(x+2)^2 - 1$

45. $f(x) = 8(x-9)^2 + 5$

This function is of the form $f(x) = a(x-h)^2 + k$ with $a = 8$, $h = 9$, and $k = 5$. The vertex is (h, k), or $(9, 5)$. The axis of symmetry is $x = h$, or $x = 9$. Since $a > 0$, then k, or 5, is the minimum function value. The range is $[5, \infty)$.

46. Vertex: $(-5, -8)$

Axis of symmetry: $x = -5$

Minimum: -8

Range: $[-8, \infty)$

47. $h(x) = -\dfrac{2}{7}(x+6)^2 + 11$

This function is of the form $f(x) = a(x-h)^2 + k$ with $a = -\dfrac{2}{7}$, $h = -6$, and $k = 11$. The vertex is (h, k), or $(-6, 11)$. The axis of symmetry is $x = h$, or $x = -6$. Since $a < 0$, then k, or 11, is the maximum function value. The range is $(-\infty, 11]$.

48. Vertex: $(7, -9)$

Axis of symmetry: $x = 7$

Maximum: -9

Range: $(-\infty, -9]$

49. $f(x) = 5\left(x + \dfrac{1}{4}\right)^2 - 13$

This function is of the form $f(x) = a(x-h)^2 + k$ with $a = 5$, $h = -\dfrac{1}{4}$, and $k = -13$. The vertex is (h, k), or $\left(-\dfrac{1}{4}, -13\right)$. The axis of symmetry is

$x = h$, or $x = -\frac{1}{4}$. Since $a > 0$, then k, or -13, is the minimum function value. The range is $[-13, \infty)$.

50. Vertex: $\left(\frac{1}{4}, 19\right)$

Axis of symmetry: $x = \frac{1}{4}$

Minimum: 19

Range: $[19, \infty)$

51. $f(x) = \sqrt{2}(x + 4.58)^2 + 65\pi$

This function is of the form $f(x) = a(x - h)^2 + k$ with $a = \sqrt{2}$, $h = -4.58$, and $k = 65\pi$. The vertex is (h, k), or $(-4.58, 65\pi)$. The axis of symmetry is $x = h$, or $x = -4.58$. Since $a > 0$, then k, or 65π, is the minimum function value. The range is $[65\pi, \infty)$.

52. Vertex: $(38.2, -\sqrt{34})$

Axis of symmetry: $x = 38.2$

Minimum: $-\sqrt{34}$

Range: $[-\sqrt{34}, \infty)$

53. $3x + 4y = -19,$ (1)

       $7x - 6y = -29$ (2)

Multiply Equation (1) by 3 and multiply Equation (2) by 2. Then add the equations to eliminate the y-term.

$$\begin{array}{r} 9x + 12y = -57 \\ 14x - 12y = -58 \\ \hline 23x = -115 \\ x = -5 \end{array}$$

Now substitute -5 for x in one of the original equations and solve for y. We use Equation (1).

$$3(-5) + 4y = -19$$
$$-15 + 4y = -19$$
$$4y = -4$$
$$y = -1$$

The pair $(-5, -1)$ checks and it is the solution.

54. $(-1, 2)$

55. $x^2 + 5x$

We take half the coefficient of x and square it.

$$\frac{1}{2} \cdot 5 = \frac{5}{2}, \; \left(\frac{5}{2}\right)^2 = \frac{25}{4}$$

Then we have $x^2 + 5x + \frac{25}{4}$.

56. $x^2 - 9x + \frac{81}{4}$

57.

58.

59.

60.

61. Since there is a minimum at $(5, 0)$, the parabola will have the same shape as $f(x) = 2x^2$. It will be of the form $f(x) = 2(x - h)^2 + k$ with $h = 5$ and $k = 0$: $f(x) = 2(x - 5)^2$

62. $f(x) = 2(x - 2)^2$

63. Since there is a maximum at $(-4, 0)$, the parabola will have the same shape as $f(x) = -2x^2$. It will be of the form $f(x) = -2(x - h)^2 + k$ with $h = -4$ and $k = 0$: $g(x) = -2[x - (-4)]^2$, or $f(x) = -2(x + 4)^2$

64. $g(x) = -2x^2 + 3$

65. Since there is a maximum at $(3, 8)$, the parabola will have the same shape as $f(x) = -2x^2$. It will be of the form $f(x) = -2(x - h)^2 + k$ with $h = 3$ and $k = 8$: $g(x) = -2(x - 3)^2 + 8$

66. $f(x) = 2(x + 2)^2 + 3$

67. The maximum value of $g(x)$ occurs at the point $(5, 1)$, so for $F(x)$ we have $h = 5$ and $k = 1$. $F(x)$ has the same shape as $f(x)$ and has a minimum, so $a = 3$. Thus, $F(x) = 3(x - 5)^2 + 1$.

68. $F(x) = -\frac{1}{3}(x + 4)^2 - 6$

69. The minimum value of $g(x)$ occurs at the point $(-3, -4)$, so for $F(x)$ we have $h = -3$ and $k = -4$. $F(x)$ has the same shape as $f(x)$ and has a maximum, so $a = -\frac{1}{2}$. Thus, $F(x) = -\frac{1}{2}(x + 3) - 4$.

70. $F(x) = 5\left(x + \frac{1}{2}\right)^2 + \frac{2}{3}$

71. The graph of $y = f(x - 1)$ looks like the graph of $y = f(x)$ moved horizontally 1 unit to the right.

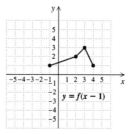

72.

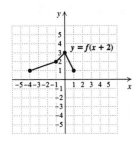

73. The graph of $y = f(x) + 2$ looks like the graph of $y = f(x)$ moved up 2 units.

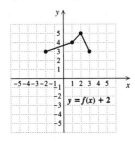

74.

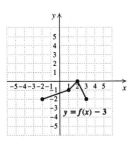

75. The graph of $y = f(x+3) - 2$ looks like the graph of $y = f(x)$ moved horizontally 3 units to the left and also moved down 2 units.

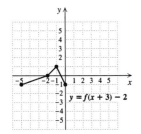

76.

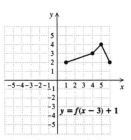

Exercise Set 10.7

1. a) $f(x) = x^2 - 4x + 5$
$$= (x^2 - 4x + 4 - 4) + 5 \quad \text{Adding } 4 - 4$$
$$= (x^2 - 4x + 4) - 4 + 5 \quad \text{Regrouping}$$
$$= (x - 2)^2 + 1$$

b) The vertex is $(2, 1)$; the axis of symmetry is $x = 2$.

2. a) $f(x) = (x + 3)^2 + 4$;

b) Vertex: $(-3, 4)$; line of symmetry: $x = -3$

3. a) $f(x) = -x^2 + 3x - 10$
$$= -(x^2 - 3x) - 10$$
$$= -\left(x^2 - 3x + \frac{9}{4} - \frac{9}{4}\right) - 10$$
$$= -\left(x^2 - 3x + \frac{9}{4}\right) + \left[-\left(-\frac{9}{4}\right)\right] - 10$$
$$= -\left(x - \frac{3}{2}\right)^2 + \frac{9}{4} - 10$$
$$= -\left(x - \frac{3}{2}\right)^2 - \frac{31}{4}$$

b) The vertex is $\left(\frac{3}{2}, -\frac{31}{4}\right)$; the axis of symmetry is $x = \frac{3}{2}$.

4. a) $f(x) = \left(x + \frac{5}{2}\right)^2 - \frac{9}{4}$;

b) Vertex: $\left(-\frac{5}{2}, -\frac{9}{4}\right)$; axis of symmetry: $x = -\frac{5}{2}$

5. a) $f(x) = 2x^2 - 7x + 1$
$$= 2\left(x^2 - \frac{7}{2}x\right) + 1$$
$$= 2\left(x^2 - \frac{7}{2}x + \frac{49}{16} - \frac{49}{16}\right) + 1$$
$$= 2\left(x^2 - \frac{7}{2}x + \frac{49}{16}\right) + 2\left(-\frac{49}{16}\right) + 1$$
$$= 2\left(x - \frac{7}{4}\right)^2 - \frac{49}{8} + 1$$
$$= 2\left(x - \frac{7}{4}\right)^2 - \frac{41}{8}$$

b) Vertex: $\left(\frac{7}{4}, -\frac{41}{8}\right)$; axis of symmetry: $x = \frac{7}{4}$

6. a) $f(x) = -2\left(x - \dfrac{5}{4}\right)^2 + \dfrac{17}{8}$;

b) Vertex: $\left(\dfrac{5}{4}, \dfrac{17}{8}\right)$; axis of symmetry: $x = \dfrac{5}{4}$

7. $f(x) = x^2 + 2x - 5$
$= (x^2 + 2x + 1 - 1) - 5 \quad$ Adding $1 - 1$
$= (x^2 + 2x + 1) - 1 - 5 \quad$ Regrouping
$= (x + 1)^2 - 6$

The vertex is $(-1, -6)$, the axis of symmetry is $x = -1$, and the graph opens upward since the coefficient 1 is positive. We plot a few points on either side of the vertex and draw the curve.

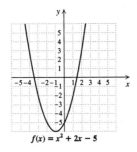

$f(x) = x^2 + 2x - 5$

8. Vertex: $(-2, 1)$, axis of symmetry: $x = -2$

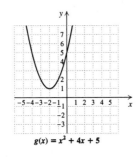

$g(x) = x^2 + 4x + 5$

9. $f(x) = x^2 + 8x + 20$
$= (x^2 + 8x + 16 - 16) + 20 \quad$ Adding $16 - 16$
$= (x^2 + 8x + 16) - 16 + 20 \quad$ Regrouping
$= (x + 4)^2 + 4$

The vertex is $(-4, 4)$, the axis of symmetry is $x = -4$, and the graph opens upward since the coefficient 1 is positive.

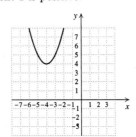

10. Vertex: $(5, -4)$, axis of symmetry: $x = 5$

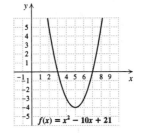

$f(x) = x^2 - 10x + 21$

11. $h(x) = 2x^2 + 16x + 25$
$= 2(x^2 + 8x) + 25 \quad$ Factoring 2 from the first two terms
$= 2(x^2 + 8x + 16 - 16) + 25 \quad$ Adding $16 - 16$ inside the parentheses
$= 2(x^2 + 8x + 16) + 2(-16) + 25$
$\quad$ Distributing to obtain a trinomial square
$= 2(x + 4)^2 - 7$

The vertex is $(-4, -7)$, the axis of symmetry is $x = -4$, and the graph opens upward since the coefficient 2 is positive.

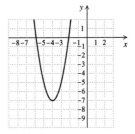

12. Vertex: $(4, -9)$, axis of symmetry: $x = 4$

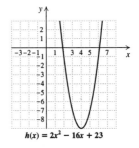

$h(x) = 2x^2 - 16x + 23$

13. $f(x) = -x^2 + 2x + 5$
$= -(x^2 - 2x) + 5 \quad$ Factoring -1 from the first two terms
$= -(x^2 - 2x + 1 - 1) + 5$
$\quad$ Adding $1 - 1$ inside the parentheses
$= -(x^2 - 2x + 1) - (-1) + 5$
$= -(x - 1)^2 + 6$

The vertex is $(1, 6)$, the axis of symmetry is $x = 1$,

and the graph opens downward since the coefficient -1 is negative.

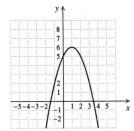

14. Vertex: $(-1, 8)$, axis of symmetry: $x = -1$

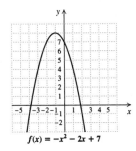

$f(x) = -x^2 - 2x + 7$

15. $g(x) = x^2 + 7x - 1$

$$= \left(x^2 + 7x + \frac{49}{4} - \frac{49}{4}\right) - 1$$

$$= \left(x^2 + 7x + \frac{49}{4}\right) - \frac{49}{4} - 1$$

$$= \left(x + \frac{7}{2}\right)^2 - \frac{53}{4}$$

The vertex is $\left(-\frac{7}{2}, -\frac{53}{4}\right)$, the axis of symmetry is $x = -\frac{7}{2}$, and the graph opens upward since the coefficient 1 is positive.

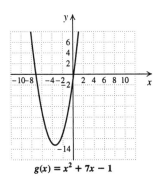

$g(x) = x^2 + 7x - 1$

16. Vertex: $\left(-\frac{3}{2}, \frac{11}{4}\right)$, axis of symmetry: $x = -\frac{3}{2}$

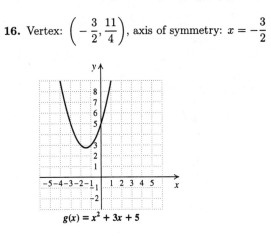

$g(x) = x^2 + 3x + 5$

17. $h(x) = x^2 - 9x$

$$= \left(x^2 - 9x + \frac{81}{4}\right) - \frac{81}{4}$$

$$= \left(x - \frac{9}{2}\right)^2 - \frac{81}{4}$$

The vertex is $\left(\frac{9}{2}, -\frac{81}{4}\right)$, the axis of symmetry is $x = \frac{9}{2}$, and the graph opens upward since the coefficient 1 is positive.

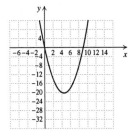

18. Vertex: $\left(-\frac{1}{2}, -\frac{1}{4}\right)$, axis of symmetry: $x = -\frac{1}{2}$

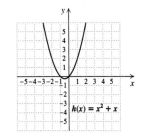

$h(x) = x^2 + x$

19. $f(x) = -2x^2 - 6 = -2(x - 0)^2 - 6$

The vertex is $(0, -6)$, the axis of symmetry is $x = 0$, and the graph opens downward since the coefficient -2 is negative.

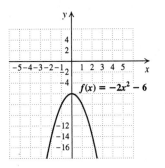

20. Vertex: $(0, 2)$, axis of symmetry: $x = 0$

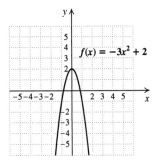

21. $f(x) = -3x^2 + 5x - 2$

$$= -3\left(x^2 - \frac{5}{3}x\right) - 2 \qquad \text{Factoring}$$

$$= -3\left(x^2 - \frac{5}{3}x + \frac{25}{36} - \frac{25}{36}\right) - 2$$

$$\text{Adding } \frac{25}{36} - \frac{25}{36} \text{ inside}$$
$$\text{the parentheses}$$

$$= -3\left(x^2 - \frac{5}{3}x + \frac{25}{36}\right) - 3\left(-\frac{25}{36}\right) - 2$$

$$= -3\left(x - \frac{5}{6}\right)^2 + \frac{1}{12}$$

The vertex is $\left(\frac{5}{6}, \frac{1}{12}\right)$, the axis of symmetry is $x = \frac{5}{6}$, and the graph opens downward since the co-efficient -3 is negative.

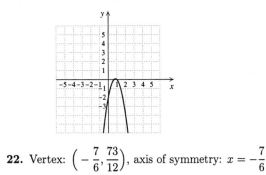

22. Vertex: $\left(-\frac{7}{6}, \frac{73}{12}\right)$, axis of symmetry: $x = -\frac{7}{6}$

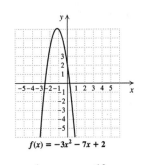

23. $h(x) = \frac{1}{2}x^2 + 4x + \frac{19}{3}$

$$= \frac{1}{2}(x^2 + 8x) + \frac{19}{3} \qquad \text{Factoring}$$

$$= \frac{1}{2}(x^2 + 8x + 16 - 16) + \frac{19}{3}$$

$$\text{Adding } 16 - 16 \text{ inside}$$
$$\text{the parentheses}$$

$$= \frac{1}{2}(x^2 + 8x + 16) + \frac{1}{2}(-16) + \frac{19}{3}$$

$$= \frac{1}{2}(x + 4)^2 - \frac{5}{3}$$

The vertex is $\left(-4, -\frac{5}{3}\right)$, the axis of symmetry is $x = -4$, and the graph opens upward since the coef-ficient $\frac{1}{2}$ is positive.

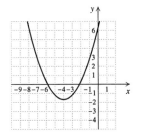

24. Vertex: $\left(3, -\frac{5}{2}\right)$, axis of symmetry: $x = 3$

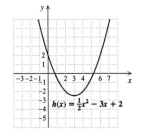

25. $f(x) = x^2 + x - 6$

The coefficient of x^2 is positive so the graph opens upward and the function has a minimum value. Graph the function in a window that shows the ver-tex. The standard window is one good choice. Then use the Minimum feature from the CALC menu to find that the vertex is $(-0.5, -6.25)$.

26. $(-1, -6)$

27. $f(x) = 5x^2 - x + 1$

The coefficient of x^2 is positive so the graph opens upward and the function has a minimum value. Graph the function in a window that shows the vertex. The standard window is one good choice. Then use the Minimum feature from the CALC menu to find that the vertex is $(0.1, 0.95)$.

28. $(-0.375, 7.5625)$

29. $f(x) = -0.2x^2 + 1.4x - 6.7$

The coefficient of x^2 is negative so the graph opens downward and the function has a maximum value. Graph the function in a window that shows the vertex. The standard window is one good choice. Then use the Maximum feature from the CALC menu to find that the vertex is $(3.5, -4.25)$.

30. $(-2.4, 0.32)$

31. $f(x) = x^2 - 6x + 3$

To find the x-intercepts, solve the equation $0 = x^2 - 6x + 3$. Use the quadratic formula.

$$x = \frac{-(-6) \pm \sqrt{(-6)^2 - 4 \cdot 1 \cdot 3}}{2 \cdot 1}$$

$$x = \frac{6 \pm \sqrt{24}}{2} = \frac{6 \pm 2\sqrt{6}}{2} = 3 \pm \sqrt{6}$$

The x-intercepts are $(3 - \sqrt{6}, 0)$ and $(3 + \sqrt{6}, 0)$.

The y-intercept is $(0, f(0))$, or $(0, 3)$.

32. $\left(\frac{-5 - \sqrt{17}}{2}, 0\right)$, $\left(\frac{-5 + \sqrt{17}}{2}, 0\right)$; $(0, 2)$

33. $g(x) = -x^2 + 2x + 3$

To find the x-intercepts, solve the equation $0 = -x^2 + 2x + 3$. We factor.

$0 = -x^2 + 2x + 3$

$0 = x^2 - 2x - 3$ Multiplying by -1

$0 = (x - 3)(x + 1)$

$x = 3$ or $x = -1$

The x-intercepts are $(-1, 0)$ and $(3, 0)$.

The y-intercept is $(0, g(0))$, or $(0, 3)$.

34. $(3, 0)$; $(0, 9)$

35. $f(x) = x^2 - 3x + 4$

To find the x-intercepts, solve the equation $0 = x^2 - 3x + 4$. We use the quadratic formula.

$$x = \frac{-(-3) \pm \sqrt{(-3)^2 - 4 \cdot 1 \cdot 4}}{2 \cdot 1}$$

$$x = \frac{3 \pm \sqrt{-7}}{2} = \frac{3 \pm i\sqrt{7}}{2}$$

The equation has no real solutions, so there is no x-intercept.

The y-intercept is $(0, f(0))$, or $(0, 4)$.

36. $\left(\frac{7 - \sqrt{57}}{2}, 0\right)$, $\left(\frac{7 + \sqrt{57}}{2}, 0\right)$; $(0, -2)$

37. $h(x) = -x^2 + 4x - 4$

To find the x-intercepts, solve the equation $0 = -x^2 + 4x - 4$. We factor.

$0 = -x^2 + 4x - 4$

$0 = x^2 - 4x + 4$ Multiplying by -1

$0 = (x - 2)(x - 2)$

$x = 2$ or $x = 2$

The x-intercept is $(2, 0)$.

The y-intercept is $(0, h(0))$, or $(0, -4)$.

38. No x-intercepts; $(0, 6)$

39. $f(x) = 4x^2 - 12x + 3$

To find the x-intercepts, solve the equation $0 = 4x^2 - 12x + 3$. We use the quadratic formula.

$$x = \frac{-(-12) \pm \sqrt{(-12)^2 - 4 \cdot 4 \cdot 3}}{2 \cdot 4}$$

$$x = \frac{12 \pm \sqrt{96}}{8} = \frac{12 \pm 4\sqrt{6}}{8} = \frac{3 \pm \sqrt{6}}{2}$$

The x-intercepts are $\left(\frac{3 - \sqrt{6}}{2}, 0\right)$ and $\left(\frac{3 + \sqrt{6}}{2}, 0\right)$.

The y-intercept is $(0, f(0))$, or $(0, 3)$.

40. No x-intercepts; $(0, 2)$

41. $f(x) = 2.31x^2 - 3.135x - 5.89$

a) The coefficient of x^2 is positive so the graph opens upward and the function has a minimum value. Graph the function in a window that shows the vertex. The standard window is one good choice. Then use the Minimum feature from the CALC menu to find that the minimum value is about -6.95.

b) To find the first coordinates of the x-intercepts we use the Zero feature from the CALC menu to find the zeros of the function. They are about -1.06 and 2.41, so the x-intercepts are $(-1.06, 0)$ and $(2.41, 0)$.

The y-intercept is $(0, f(0))$, or $(0, -5.89)$.

42. (a) Maximum: 7.01; (b) $(-0.40, 0)$, $(0.82, 0)$; $(0, 6.18)$

43. $g(x) = -1.25x^2 + 3.42x - 2.79$

a) The coefficient of x^2 is negative so the graph opens downward and the function has a maximum value. Graph the function in a window that shows the vertex. The standard window is one good choice. Then use the Maximum feature from the CALC menu to find that the maximum value is about -0.45.

b) The graph has no x-intercepts. The y-intercept is $(0, f(0))$, or $(0, -2.79)$.

44. (a) Minimum: 11.28; (b) no x-intercepts; $(0, 12.92)$

45.
$$\sqrt{4x - 4} = \sqrt{x + 4} + 1$$
$$4x - 4 = x + 4 + 2\sqrt{x + 4} + 1$$
Squaring both sides
$$3x - 9 = 2\sqrt{x + 4}$$
$$9x^2 - 54x + 81 = 4(x + 4) \quad \text{Squaring both sides again}$$
$$9x^2 - 54x + 81 = 4x + 16$$
$$9x^2 - 58x + 65 = 0$$
$$(9x - 13)(x - 5) = 0$$
$$x = \frac{13}{9} \quad \text{or} \quad x = 5$$

Check: For $x = \dfrac{13}{9}$:

$$\frac{\sqrt{4x - 4} = \sqrt{x + 4} + 1}{\sqrt{4\left(\frac{13}{9}\right) - 4} \; ? \; \sqrt{\frac{13}{9} + 4} + 1}$$

$$\begin{array}{c|c} \sqrt{\dfrac{16}{9}} & \sqrt{\dfrac{49}{9}} + 1 \\[2mm] \dfrac{4}{3} & \dfrac{7}{3} + 1 \\[2mm] \dfrac{4}{3} & \dfrac{10}{3} \quad \text{FALSE} \end{array}$$

For $x = 5$:

$$\frac{\sqrt{4x - 4} = \sqrt{x + 4} + 1}{\sqrt{4 \cdot 5 - 4} \; ? \; \sqrt{5 + 4} + 1}$$

$$\begin{array}{c|c} \sqrt{16} & \sqrt{9} + 1 \\ 4 & 3 + 1 \\ 4 & 4 \quad \text{TRUE} \end{array}$$

5 checks, but $\dfrac{13}{9}$ does not. The solution is 5.

46. 4

47.
$$A = \frac{3Q + nT}{n}$$
$$An = 3Q + nT \quad \text{Multiplying by } n$$
$$An - nT = 3Q \quad \text{Adding } -nT$$
$$n(A - T) = 3Q \quad \text{Factoring}$$
$$n = \frac{3Q}{A - T} \quad \text{Dividing by } A - T$$

48. $\dfrac{x^2 - 2x - 3}{5}$

49. ◈

50. ◈

51. ◈

52. (a) -2.4, 3.4; (b) -1.3, 2.3

53. $f(x) = \dfrac{x^2}{8} + \dfrac{x}{4} - \dfrac{3}{8}$

a) The solutions of $\dfrac{x^2}{8} + \dfrac{x}{4} - \dfrac{3}{8} = 0$ are the first coordinates of the x-intercepts of the graph of $f(x) = \dfrac{x^2}{8} + \dfrac{x}{4} - \dfrac{3}{8}$. From the graph we see that the solutions are -3 and 1.

b) The solutions of $\dfrac{x^2}{8} + \dfrac{x}{4} - \dfrac{3}{8} = 1$ are the first coordinates of the points of intersection of the graph of $f(x) = \dfrac{x^2}{8} + \dfrac{x}{4} - \dfrac{3}{8}$ and $y = 1$. From the graph we see that they are approximately -4.5 and 2.5.

c) The solutions of $\dfrac{x^2}{8} + \dfrac{x}{4} - \dfrac{3}{8} = 2$ are the first coordinates of the points of intersection of the graphs of $f(x) = \dfrac{x^2}{8} + \dfrac{x}{4} - \dfrac{3}{8}$ and $y = 2$. From the graph we see that they are approximately -5.5 and 3.5.

54. $f(x) = m\left(x - \dfrac{n}{2m}\right)^2 + \dfrac{-n^2 + 4mp}{4m}$, or

$$m\left(x - \frac{n}{2m}\right)^2 + \frac{4mp - n^2}{4m}$$

55. $f(x) = 3x^2 + mx + m^2$

$$= 3\left(x^2 + \frac{m}{3}x\right) + m^2$$

$$= 3\left(x^2 + \frac{m}{3}x + \frac{m^2}{36} - \frac{m^2}{36}\right) + m^2$$

$$= 3\left(x + \frac{m}{6}\right)^2 - \frac{m^2}{12} + m^2$$

$$= 3\left[x - \left(-\frac{m}{6}\right)\right]^2 + \frac{11m^2}{12}$$

56. $f(x) = \frac{5}{16}x^2 - \frac{15}{8}x - \frac{35}{16}$

57. The horizontal distance from $(4, 0)$ to $(-1, 7)$ is $|-1 - 4|$, or 5, so by symmetry the other x-intercept is $(-1 - 5, 0)$, or $(-6, 0)$. Substituting the three ordered pairs $(4, 0)$, $(-1, 7)$, and $(-6, 0)$ in the equation $f(x) = ax^2 + bx + c$ yields a system of equations:

$$0 = a \cdot 4^2 + b \cdot 4 + c,$$
$$7 = a(-1)^2 + b(-1) + c,$$
$$0 = a(-6)^2 + b(-6) + c$$

or

$$0 = 16a + 4b + c,$$
$$7 = a - b + c,$$
$$0 = 36a - 6b + c$$

The solution of this system of equations is $(-0.28, -0.56, 6.72)$, so $f(x) = -0.28x^2 - 0.56x + 6.72$.

58.

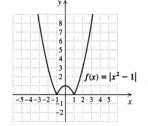

59. $f(x) = |x^2 - 3x - 4|$

We plot some points and draw the curve. Note that it will lie entirely on or above the x-axis since absolute value is never negative.

x	$f(x)$
-4	24
-3	14
-2	6
-1	0
0	4
1	6
2	6
3	4
4	0
5	6
6	14

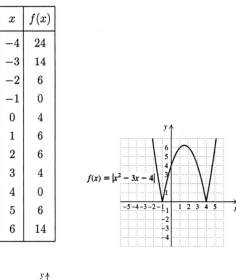

60.

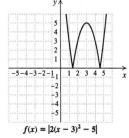

$$f(x) = |2(x - 3)^2 - 5|$$

Exercise Set 10.8

1. Familiarize. We make a drawing and label it.

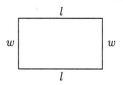

Perimeter: $2l + 2w = 56$ ft

Area: $A = l \cdot w$

Translate. We have a system of equations.

$$2l + 2w = 56$$
$$A = lw$$

Carry out. Solving the first equation for l, we get $l = 28 - w$. Substituting for l in the second equation we get a quadratic function A:

$$A = (28 - w)w$$
$$A = -w^2 + 28w$$

Completing the square, we get

$$A = -(w - 14)^2 + 196.$$

The maximum function value is 196. It occurs when w is 14. When $w = 14$, $l = 28 - 14$, or 14.

Check. We check a function value for w less than 14 and for w greater than 14.
$$A(13) = -(13)^2 + 28 \cdot 13 = 195$$
$$A(15) = -(15)^2 + 28 \cdot 15 = 195$$
Since 196 is greater than these numbers, it looks as though we have a maximum.

State. The maximum area of 196 ft^2 occurs when the dimensions are 14 ft by 14 ft.

2. 21 in. by 21 in.

3. Familiarize. We let x and y represent the two numbers, and we let P represent their product.

Translate. We have two equations.
$$x - y = 6,$$
$$P = xy$$

Carry out. Solve the first equation for x.
$$x = 6 + y$$
Substitute for x in the second equation.
$$P = (6 + y)y$$
$$P = y^2 + 6y$$
Completing the square, we get
$$P = (y + 3)^2 - 9.$$
The minimum function value is -9. It occurs when $y = -3$. When $y = -3$, $x = 6 + (-3)$, or 3.

Check. Check a function value for y less than -3 and for y greater than -3.
$$P(-4) = (-4)^2 + 6(-4) = -8$$
$$P(-2) = (-2)^2 + 6(-2) = -8$$
Since -9 is less than these numbers, it looks as though we have a minimum.

State. The minimum product of -9 occurs for the numbers 3 and -3.

4. 81; 9 and 9

5. Familiarize. We let x and y represent the two numbers, and we let P represent their product.

Translate. We have two equations.
$$x + y = -12,$$
$$P = xy$$

Carry out. Solve the first equation for y.
$$y = -12 - x$$
Substitute for y in the second equation.
$$P = x(-12 - x)$$
$$P = -x^2 - 12x$$

Completing the square, we get
$$P = -(x + 6)^2 + 36$$
The maximum function value is 36. It occurs when $x = -6$. When $x = -6$, $y = -12 - (-6)$, or -6.

Check. Check a function value for x less than -6 and for x greater than -6.
$$P(-7) = -(-7)^2 - 12(-7) = 35$$
$$P(-5) = -(-5)^2 - 12(-5) = 35$$
Since 36 is greater than these numbers, it looks as though we have a maximum.

State. The maximum product of 36 occurs for the numbers -6 and -6.

6. $-\dfrac{81}{4}$; $\dfrac{9}{2}$ and $-\dfrac{9}{2}$

7. Familiarize. We make a drawing and label it.

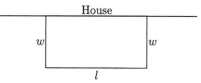

Translate. We have two equations.
$$l + 2w = 60,$$
$$A = lw$$

Carry out. Solve the first equation for l.
$$l = 60 - 2w$$
Substitute for l in the second equation.
$$A = (60 - 2w)w$$
$$A = -2w^2 + 60w$$
Completing the square, we get
$$A = -2(w - 15)^2 + 450.$$
The maximum function value of 450 occurs when $w = 15$. When $w = 15$, $l = 60 - 2 \cdot 15 = 30$.

Check. Check a function value for w less than 15 and for w greater than 15.
$$A(14) = -2 \cdot 14^2 + 60 \cdot 14 = 448$$
$$A(16) = -2 \cdot 16^2 + 60 \cdot 16 = 448$$
Since 450 is greater than these numbers, it looks as though we have a maximum.

State. The maximum area of 450 ft^2 will occur when the dimensions are 15 ft by 30 ft.

8. 200 ft^2; 10 ft by 20 ft

9. Familiarize. Let x represent the height of the file and y represent the width. We make a drawing.

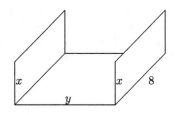

Translate. We have two equations.

$2x + y = 14$

$V = 8xy$

Carry out. Solve the first equation for y.

$y = 14 - 2x$

Substitute for y in the second equation.

$V = 8x(14 - 2x)$

$V = -16x^2 + 112x$

Completing the square, we get

$$V = -16\left(x - \frac{7}{2}\right)^2 + 196.$$

The maximum function value of 196 occurs when $x = \frac{7}{2}$. When $x = \frac{7}{2}$, $y = 14 - 2 \cdot \frac{7}{2} = 7$.

Check. Check a function value for x less than $\frac{7}{2}$ and for x greater than $\frac{7}{2}$.

$$V(3) = -16 \cdot 3^2 + 112 \cdot 3 = 192$$
$$V(4) = -16 \cdot 4^2 + 112 \cdot 4 = 192$$

Since 196 is greater than these numbers, it looks as though we have a maximum.

State. The file should be $\frac{7}{2}$ in., or 3.5 in., tall.

10. 4 ft by 4 ft

11. Familiarize and Translate. We want to find the value of x for which $C(x) = 0.1x^2 - 0.7x + 2.425$ is a minimum.

Carry out. We complete the square.

$C(x) = 0.1(x^2 - 7x + 12.25) + 2.425 - 1.225$

$C(x) = 0.1(x - 3.5)^2 + 1.2$

The minimum function value of 1.2 occurs when $x = 3.5$.

Check. Check a function value for x less than 3.5 and for x greater than 3.5.

$C(3) = 0.1(3)^2 - 0.7(3) + 2.425 = 1.225$

$C(4) = 0.1(4)^2 - 0.7(4) + 2.425 = 1.225$

Since 1.2 is less than these numbers, it looks as though we have a minimum.

State. The shop should build 3.5 hundred, or 350 bicycles.

12. 2700 yd^2

13. Find the total profit:

$$P(x) = R(x) - C(x)$$
$$P(x) = (1000x - x^2) - (3000 + 20x)$$
$$P(x) = -x^2 + 980x - 3000$$

To find the maximum value of the total profit and the value of x at which it occurs we complete the square:

$$P(x) = -(x^2 - 980x) - 3000$$
$$= -(x^2 - 980x + 240,100 - 240,100) - 3000$$
$$= -(x^2 - 980x + 240,100) - (-240,100) - 3000$$
$$= -(x - 490)^2 + 237,100$$

The maximum profit of \$237,100 occurs at $x = 490$.

14. $P(x) = -x^2 + 192x - 5000$; \$4216 at $x = 96$

15. The data points fall and then rise, resembling a parabola that opens upward. A quadratic model might be appropriate.

16. Linear

17. The data points rise, then fall, then rise again, then fall again. Neither a linear nor a quadratic model is appropriate.

18. Quadratic

19. The data points rise and then fall, resembling a parabola that opens downward. A quadratic model might be appropriate.

20. Quadratic or linear

21. We look for a function of the form $f(x) = ax^2 + bx + c$. Substituting the data points, we get

$$4 = a(1)^2 + b(1) + c,$$
$$-2 = a(-1)^2 + b(-1) + c,$$
$$13 = a(2)^2 + b(2) + c,$$

or

$$4 = a + b + c,$$
$$-2 = a - b + c,$$
$$13 = 4a + 2b + c.$$

Solving this system, we get

$$a = 2, b = 3, \text{ and } c = -1.$$

Therefore the function we are looking for is

$$f(x) = 2x^2 + 3x - 1.$$

22. $f(x) = 3x^2 - x + 2$

23. We look for a function of the form $f(x) = ax^2 + bx + c$. Substituting the data points, we get

$$0 = a(2)^2 + b(2) + c,$$
$$3 = a(4)^2 + b(4) + c,$$
$$-5 = a(12)^2 + b(12) + c,$$

or

$$0 = 4a + 2b + c,$$
$$3 = 16a + 4b + c,$$
$$-5 = 144a + 12b + c.$$

Solving this system, we get

$$a = -\frac{1}{4},\ b = 3,\ c = -5.$$

Therefore the function we are looking for is

$$f(x) = -\frac{1}{4}x^2 + 3x - 5.$$

24. $f(x) = -\dfrac{1}{3}x^2 + 5x - 12$

25. a) **Familiarize.** We look for a function of the form $A(s) = as^2 + bs + c$, where $A(s)$ represents the number of nighttime accidents (for every 200 million km) and s represents the travel speed (in km/h).

Translate. We substitute the given values of s and $A(s)$.

$$400 = a(60)^2 + b(60) + c,$$
$$250 = a(80)^2 + b(80) + c,$$
$$250 = a(100)^2 + b(100) + c,$$

or

$$400 = 3600a + 60b + c,$$
$$250 = 6400a + 80b + c,$$
$$250 = 10{,}000a + 100b + c.$$

Carry out. Solving the system of equations, we get

$$a = \frac{3}{16},\ b = -\frac{135}{4},\ c = 1750.$$

Check. Recheck the calculations.

State. The function

$$A(s) = \frac{3}{16}s^2 - \frac{135}{4}s + 1750 \text{ fits the data.}$$

b) Find $A(50)$.

$$A(50) = \frac{3}{16}(50)^2 - \frac{135}{4}(50) + 1750 = 531.25$$

About 531 accidents occur at 50 km/h.

26. (a) $A(s) = 0.05x^2 - 5.5x + 250$; (b) 100

27. **Familiarize.** Think of a coordinate system placed on the drawing in the text with the origin at the point where the arrow is released. Then three points

on the arrow's parabolic path are $(0, 0)$, $(63, 27)$, and $(126, 0)$. We look for a function of the form $h(d) = ad^2 + bd + c$, where $h(d)$ represents the arrow's height and d represents the distance the arrow has traveled horizontally.

Translate. We substitute the values given above for d and $h(d)$.

$$0 = a \cdot 0^2 + b \cdot 0 + c,$$
$$27 = a \cdot 63^2 + b \cdot 63 + c,$$
$$0 = a \cdot 126^2 + b \cdot 126 + c$$

or

$$0 = c,$$
$$27 = 3969a + 63b + c,$$
$$0 = 15{,}876a + 126b + c$$

Carry out. Solving the system of equations, we get $a \approx -0.0068$, $b \approx 0.8571$, and $c = 0$.

Check. Recheck the calculations.

State. The function $h(d) = -0.0068d^2 + 0.8571d$ expresses the arrow's height as a function of the distance it has traveled horizontally.

28. (a) $f(x) = 65.6x^2 - 143.1x + 131.5$; (b) \$608.7 million

29. a) We look for a function of the form $f(x) = ax^2 + bx + c$. The data points we will use are $(0, 35)$, $(3, 325)$, and $(7, 35)$. Substituting, we get

$$35 = a \cdot 0^2 + b \cdot 0 + c,$$
$$325 = a \cdot 3^2 + b \cdot 3 + c,$$
$$35 = a \cdot 7^2 + b \cdot 7 + c,$$

or

$$35 = c,$$
$$325 = 9a + 3b + c,$$
$$35 = 49a + 7b + c.$$

Solving this system, we get

$$a = -\frac{145}{6},\ b = \frac{1015}{6},\ c = 35.$$

Thus, $f(x) = -\dfrac{145}{6}x^2 + \dfrac{1015}{6}x + 35$.

b) September corresponds to $x = 5$.

$f(5) \approx 277$, so in September we estimate that about 277 metric tons of particulates are retained.

c) The estimate in Example 4 is larger than that in part (b). The former is probably more accurate since more data points were used to find the model that produced it.

30. (a) $f(x) = -\dfrac{79}{3}x^2 + \dfrac{532}{3}x + 84$; (b) 312 metric tons; (c) The regression function gives a closer prediction.

31. a) Enter the data and use the quadratic regression feature. We get $b(x) = 0.1142857143x^2 - 0.4851428571x + 1.522571429$.

b) $1996 - 1990 = 6$, so we find $b(6)$.

$b(6) = 2.726$, so we estimate that the bumping rate in 1996 was 2.726 per 10,000 passengers.

32. $w(x) = 5.660714286x^2 - 2.275x + 5.964285714$

33. Enter the data and use the quadratic regression feature. We get $f(x) = -3.820651428x^2 + 53.15961719x + 499.7568332$.

34. $f(x) = -52.36512912x^2 + 4533.45938x - 49,405.13732$

35.
$$\frac{x}{x^2 + 17x + 72} - \frac{8}{x^2 + 15x + 56}$$
$$= \frac{x}{(x+8)(x+9)} - \frac{8}{(x+8)(x+7)}$$
$$= \frac{x}{(x+8)(x+9)} \cdot \frac{x+7}{x+7} - \frac{8}{(x+8)(x+7)} \cdot \frac{x+9}{x+9}$$
$$= \frac{x(x+7) - 8(x+9)}{(x+8)(x+9)(x+7)}$$
$$= \frac{x^2 + 7x - 8x - 72}{(x+8)(x+9)(x+7)}$$
$$= \frac{x^2 - x - 72}{(x+8)(x+9)(x+7)} = \frac{(x-9)(x+8)}{(x+8)(x+9)(x+7)}$$
$$= \frac{x-9}{(x+9)(x+7)}$$

36. $\dfrac{(x-3)(x+1)}{(x-7)(x+3)}$

37. ◈

38. ◈

39. *Familiarize.* We add labels to the drawing in the text.

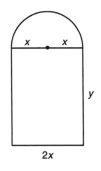

The perimeter of the semicircular portion of the window is $\frac{1}{2} \cdot 2\pi x$, or πx. The perimeter of the rectangular portion is $y + 2x + y$, or $2x + 2y$. The area of

the semicircular portion of the window is $\frac{1}{2} \cdot \pi x^2$, or $\frac{\pi}{2}x^2$. The area of the rectangular portion is $2xy$.

Translate. We have two equations, one giving the perimeter of the window and the other giving the area.
$$\pi x + 2x + 2y = 24,$$
$$A = \frac{\pi}{2}x^2 + 2xy$$

Carry out. Solve the first equation for y.
$$\pi x + 2x + 2y = 24$$
$$2y = 24 - \pi x - 2x$$
$$y = 12 - \frac{\pi x}{2} - x$$

Substitute for y in the second equation.
$$A = \frac{\pi}{2}x^2 + 2x\left(12 - \frac{\pi x}{2} - x\right)$$
$$A = \frac{\pi}{2}x^2 + 24x - \pi x^2 - 2x^2$$
$$A = -2x^2 - \frac{\pi}{2}x^2 + 24x$$
$$A = -\left(2x + \frac{\pi}{2}\right)x^2 + 24x$$

Completing the square, we get
$$A = -\left(2 + \frac{\pi}{2}\right)\left(x^2 + \frac{24}{-\left(2 + \frac{\pi}{2}\right)}x\right)$$
$$A = -\left(2 + \frac{\pi}{2}\right)\left(x^2 - \frac{48}{4 + \pi}x\right)$$
$$A = -\left(2 + \frac{\pi}{2}\right)\left(x - \frac{24}{4 + \pi}\right)^2 + \left(\frac{24}{4 + \pi}\right)^2$$

The maximum function value occurs when $x = \dfrac{24}{4 + \pi}$. When $x = \dfrac{24}{4 + \pi}$,
$$y = 12 - \frac{\pi}{2}\left(\frac{24}{4 + \pi}\right) - \frac{24}{4 + \pi} =$$
$$\frac{48 + 12\pi}{4 + \pi} - \frac{12\pi}{4 + \pi} - \frac{24}{4 + \pi} = \frac{24}{4 + \pi}.$$

Check. Recheck the calculations.

State. The radius of the circular portion of the window and the height of the rectangular portion should each be $\dfrac{24}{4 + \pi}$ ft, or approximately 3.36 ft.

40. Length of the piece used to form the circle: $\dfrac{36\pi}{4 + \pi}$ in., or approximately 15.836 in.; length of the piece used to form the square: $\dfrac{144}{4 + \pi}$ in, or approximately 20.164 in.

41. _Familiarize_. Let x represent the number of trees added to an acre. Then $20 + x$ represents the total number of trees per acre and $40 - x$ represents the corresponding yield per tree. Let T represent the total yield per acre.

Translate. Since total yield is number of trees times yield per tree we have the following function for total yield per acre.

$$T(x) = (20 + x)(40 - x)$$
$$T(x) = -x^2 + 20x + 800$$

Carry out. Completing the square, we get

$$T(x) = -(x - 10)^2 + 900.$$

The maximum function value of 900 occurs when $x = 10$. When $x = 10$, the number of trees per acre is $20 + 10$, or 30.

Check. We check a function value for x less than 10 and for x greater than 10.

$$T(9) = (20 + 9)(40 - 9) = 899$$
$$T(11) = (20 + 11)(40 - 11) = 899$$

Since 900 is greater than these numbers, it looks as though we have a maximum.

State. The grower should plant 30 trees per acre.

42. $15

43. _Familiarize_. We want to find the maximum value of a function of the form $h(t) = at^2 + bt + c$ that fits the following data.

Time (sec)	Height (ft)
0	0
3	0
3 + 2, or 5	-64

Translate. Substitute the given values for t and $h(t)$.

$$0 = a(0)^2 + b(0) + c,$$
$$0 = a(3)^2 + b(3) + c,$$
$$-64 = a(5)^2 + b(5) + c,$$

or

$$0 = c,$$
$$0 = 9a + 3b + c,$$
$$-64 = 25a + 5b + c.$$

Carry out. Solving the system of equations, we get $a = -6.4$, $b = 19.2$, $c = 0$. The function $h(t) = -6.4t^2 + 19.2t$ fits the data.

Completing the square, we get

$$h(t) = -6.4(t - 1.5)^2 + 14.4.$$

The maximum function value of 14.4 occurs at $t = 1.5$.

Check. Recheck the calculations. Also check a function value for t less than 1.5 and for t greater than 1.5.

$$h(1) = -6.4(1)^2 + 19.2(1) = 12.8$$
$$h(2) = -6.4(2)^2 + 19.2(2) = 12.8$$

Since 14.4 is greater than these numbers, it looks as though we have a maximum.

State. The maximum height above the cliff is 14.4 ft. The maximum height above sea level is $64 + 14.4$, or 78.4 ft.

44. 158 ft

Exercise Set 10.9

1. We see that $p(x) = 0$ when $x = -4$ or $x = \frac{3}{2}$, and $p(x) < 0$ between -4 and $\frac{3}{2}$. The solution set of the inequality is $\left[-4, \frac{3}{2} \right]$.

2. $\left(-4, -\frac{2}{3} \right)$

3.
$$x^4 + 12x > 3x^3 + 4x^2$$
$$x^4 - 3x^3 - 4x^2 + 12x > 0$$

From the graph we see that $p(x) > 0$ on $(-\infty, -2) \cup (0, 2) \cup (3, \infty)$. This is the solution set of the inequality.

4. $(-\infty, -3] \cup \{0\} \cup [2, \infty)$

5.
$$\frac{x - 1}{x + 2} < 3$$
$$\frac{x - 1}{x + 2} - 3 < 0$$

We see that $r(x) < 0$ on $\left(-\infty, -\frac{7}{2} \right) \cup (-2, \infty)$. This is the solution set of the inequality.

6. $(-\infty, -4] \cup (5, \infty)$

7. $(x + 4)(x - 3) > 0$

We solve the related equation.

$$(x + 4)(x - 3) = 0$$
$$x + 4 = 0 \quad or \quad x - 3 = 0$$
$$x = -4 \quad or \quad x = 3$$

The numbers -4 and 3 divide the number line into 3 intervals.

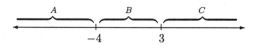

We graph $p(x) = (x + 4)(x - 3)$ in the window $[-10, 10, -15, 5]$ and determine the sign of the function in each interval.

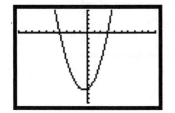

We see that $p(x) > 0$ in intervals A and C, or in $(-\infty, -4)$ and $(3, \infty)$. Thus, the solution set of the inequality is $(-\infty, -4) \cup (3, \infty)$.

8. $(-\infty, -2) \cup (5, \infty)$

9. $(x + 7)(x - 2) \leq 0$

The solutions of $(x + 7)(x - 2) = 0$ are -7 and 2. They divide the number line into three intervals as shown:

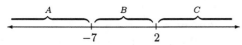

We graph $p(x) = (x + 7)(x - 2)$ in the window $[-10, 10, -25, 5]$, Yscl $= 5$.

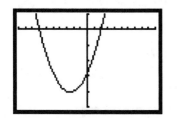

We see that $p(x) < 0$ in interval B, or in $(-7, 2)$. We also know that $p(-7) = 0$ and $p(2) = 0$. Thus, the solution set of the inequality is $[-7, 2]$.

10. $[-4, 1]$

11. $x^2 - x - 2 < 0$

$(x + 1)(x - 2) < 0$ Factoring

The solutions of $(x + 1)(x - 2) = 0$ are -1 and 2. They divide the number line into three intervals as shown:

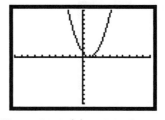

We enter $p(x) = x^2 - x - 2$ on a grapher and try a test number in each interval. We choose -2 from interval A, 0 from B, and 3 from C.

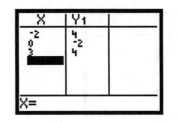

We see that $p(x) < 0$ in interval B, so the solution set is $(-1, 2)$.

12. $(-2, 1)$

13. $9 - x^2 \leq 0$

$(3 - x)(3 + x) \leq 0$

The solutions of $(3 - x)(3 + x) = 0$ are 3 and -3. Graph $p(x) = 9 - x^2$ in the standard window.

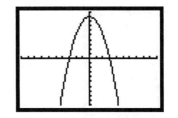

We see that $p(x) < 0$ in $(-\infty, -3)$ and $(3, \infty)$; also $p(-3) = 0$ and $p(3) = 0$. The solution set is $(-\infty, -3] \cup [3, \infty)$.

14. $[-2, 2]$

15. $x^2 - 2x + 1 \geq 0$

$(x - 1)^2 \geq 0$

The solution of $(x - 1)^2 = 0$ is 1. Graph $p(x) = x^2 - 2x + 1$ in the standard window.

We see that $p(x) > 0$ in the intervals $(-\infty, 1)$ and $(1, \infty)$; also $p(1) = 0$. Thus $p(x) \geq 0$ for $(-\infty, 1) \cup \{1\} \cup (1, \infty)$, or $(-\infty, \infty)$.

16. $\emptyset$

17. $x^2 - 4x < 12$

$x^2 - 4x - 12 < 0$

$(x - 6)(x + 2) < 0$

The solutions of $(x - 6)(x + 2) = 0$ are 6 and -2. Graph $p(x) = x^2 - 4x - 12$ in the window $[-10, 10, -20, 5]$, Yscl $= 5$.

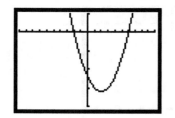

We see that $p(x) < 0$ in the interval $(-2, 6)$. This is the solution set of the inequality.

18. $(-\infty, -4) \cup (-2, \infty)$

19. $3x(x+2)(x-2) < 0$

The solutions of $3x(x+2)(x-2) = 0$ are 0, -2, and 2. Graph $p(x) = 3x(x+2)(x-2)$ in the window $[-5, 5, -10, 10]$.

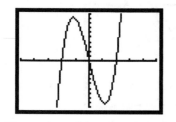

We see that $p(x) < 0$ on $(-\infty, -2) \cup (0, 2)$. This is the solution set of the inequality.

20. $(-1, 0) \cup (1, \infty)$

21. $(x+3)(x-2)(x+1) > 0$

The solutions of $(x+3)(x-2)(x+1) = 0$ are -3, 2, and -1. Graph $p(x) = (x+3)(x-2)(x-1)$ in the window $[-5, 5, -10, 10]$.

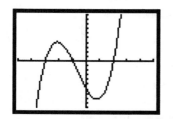

We see that $p(x) > 0$ on $(-3, -1) \cup (2, \infty)$. This is the solution set of the inequality.

22. $(-\infty, -2) \cup (1, 4)$

23. $(x+3)(x+2)(x-1) < 0$

The solutions of $(x+3)(x+2)(x-1) = 0$ are -3, -2, and 1. Graph $p(x) = (x+3)(x+2)(x-1)$ in the window $[-5, 5, -10, 10]$.

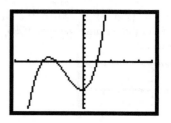

We see that $p(x) < 0$ in $(-\infty, -3) \cup (-2, 1)$. This is the solution set of the inequality.

24. $(-\infty, -1) \cup (2, 3)$

25. $4.32x^2 - 3.54x - 5.34 \le 0$

Graph $p(x) = 4.32x^2 - 3.54x - 5.34$ in the window $[-5, 5, -10, 10]$.

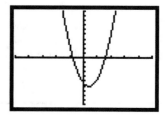

Using the Zero feature we find that $p(x) = 0$ when $x \approx -0.78$ and when $x \approx 1.59$. Also observe that $p(x) < 0$ on the interval $(-0.78, 1.59)$. Thus, the solution set of the inequality is $[-0.78, 1.59]$.

26. $(-\infty, -0.21] \cup [2.47, \infty)$

27. $x^3 - 2x^2 - 5x + 6 < 0$

Graph $p(x) = x^3 - 2x^2 - 5x + 6$ in the window $[-5, 5, -10, 10]$.

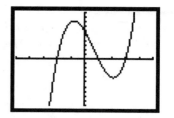

Using the Zero feature we find that $p(x) = 0$ when $x = -2$, when $x = 1$, and when $x = 3$. Then we see that $p(x) < 0$ on $(-\infty, -2) \cup (1, 3)$. This is the solution set of the inequality.

28. $(-2, 1) \cup (1, \infty)$

29. $\dfrac{1}{x+7} < 0$

We write the related equation by changing the $<$ symbol to $=$:

$$\frac{1}{x+7} = 0$$

We solve the related equation.

$$(x + 7) \cdot \frac{1}{x + 7} = (x + 7) \cdot 0$$
$$1 = 0$$

The related equation has no solution.

Next we find the values that make the denominator 0 by setting the denominate equal to 0 and solving:

$$x + 7 = 0$$
$$x = -7$$

We use -7 to divide the number line into two intervals as shown:

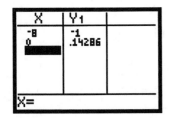

We try a test number in each interval. Enter $y = \frac{1}{x + 7}$ on a grapher and use the Table feature set in ASK mode. We try -8 in interval A and 0 in B.

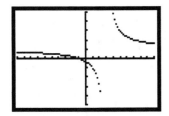

We see that $y < 0$ in interval A, so the solution set of the inequality is $(-\infty, -7)$.

30. $(-4, \infty)$

31. $\dfrac{x + 1}{x - 3} \geq 0$

Graph $r(x) = \dfrac{x + 1}{x - 3}$ using DOT mode in the window $[-10, 10, -5, 5]$.

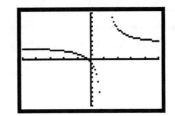

Using the Zero feature we find that $r(x) = 0$ when $x = -1$. Also observe that $r(x) > 0$ on the intervals $(-\infty, -1)$ and $(3, \infty)$. Thus, the solution set of the inequality is $(-\infty, -1] \cup (3, \infty)$.

32. $(-5, 2]$

33. $\dfrac{3x + 2}{x - 3} \leq 0$

Graph $r(x) = \dfrac{3x + 2}{x - 3}$ using DOT mode in the window $[-15, 15, -10, 10]$, Xscl $= 3$.

Using the Zero feature we find that $r(x) = 0$ when $x = -0.\overline{6}$, or $-\dfrac{2}{3}$. Also observe that $r(x) < 0$ on $\left(-\dfrac{2}{3}, 3\right)$. Thus, the solution set is $\left[-\dfrac{2}{3}, 3\right)$.

34. $\left(-\infty, -\dfrac{3}{4}\right) \cup \left[\dfrac{5}{2}, \infty\right)$

35. $\dfrac{x + 1}{2x - 3} > 1$

$$\frac{x + 1}{2x - 3} - 1 > 0$$

If $r(x) = \dfrac{x + 1}{2x - 3} - 1$, the solution set of the inequality is all values of x for which $r(x) > 0$.

First we solve $r(x) = 0$.

$$\frac{x + 1}{2x - 3} - 1 = 0$$
$$(2x - 3)\left(\frac{x + 1}{2x - 3} - 1\right) = (2x - 3) \cdot 0$$
$$(2x - 3)\left(\frac{x + 1}{2x - 3}\right) - (2x - 3) \cdot 1 = 0$$
$$x + 1 - 2x + 3 = 0$$
$$-x + 4 = 0$$
$$4 = x$$

Find the values that make the denominator 0.

$$2x - 3 = 0$$
$$2x = 3$$
$$x = \frac{3}{2}$$

Use $\dfrac{3}{2}$ and 4 to divide the number line into intervals.

Enter $y = r(x)$ on a grapher and evaluate a test number in each interval. We test 0, 2, and 5.

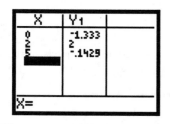

We see that $r(x) > 0$ in interval B. The solution set is $\left(\dfrac{3}{2}, 4\right)$.

36. $(-\infty, 2)$

37. $\dfrac{(x-2)(x+1)}{x-5} \le 0$

Solve the related equation.

$$\dfrac{(x-2)(x+1)}{x-5} = 0$$

$$(x-2)(x+1) = 0$$

$$x = 2 \ or \ x = -1$$

Find the values that make the denominator 0.

$$x - 5 = 0$$

$$x = 5$$

Use the numbers 2, -1, and 5 to divide the number line into intervals as shown:

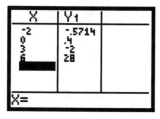

Enter $r(x) = \dfrac{(x-2)(x+1)}{x-5}$ and evaluate a test number in each interval. We test -2, 0, 3, and 6.

We see that $r(x) < 0$ in intervals A and C. From above we also know that $r(x) = 0$ when $x = 2$ or $x = -1$. Thus, the solution set is $(-\infty, -1] \cup [2, 5)$.

38. $[-4, -3) \cup [1, \infty)$

39. $\dfrac{x}{x+3} \ge 0$

Graph $r(x) = \dfrac{x}{x+3}$ using DOT mode in the window $[-10, 10, -5, 5]$.

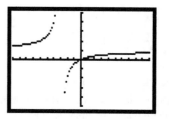

Using the Zero feature we find that $r(x) = 0$ when $x = 0$. Also observe that $r(x) > 0$ in the interval $(-\infty, -3)$ and in $(0, \infty)$. Then the solution set is $(-\infty, -3) \cup [0, \infty)$.

40. $(0, 2]$

41. $\dfrac{x-5}{x} < 1$

$$\dfrac{x-5}{x} - 1 < 0$$

Let $r(x) = \dfrac{x-5}{x} - 1$ and solve $r(x) = 0$.

$$\dfrac{x-5}{x} - 1 = 0$$

$$x\left(\dfrac{x-5}{x} - 1\right) = x \cdot 0$$

$$x\left(\dfrac{x-5}{x}\right) - x \cdot 1 = 0$$

$$x - 5 - x = 0$$

$$-5 = 0$$

This equation has no solution.

Find the values that make the denominator 0.

$$x = 0$$

Use the number 0 to divide the number line into two intervals as shown.

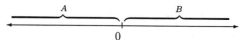

Enter $y = r(x)$ in a grapher and evaluate a test number in each interval. We test -1 and 1.

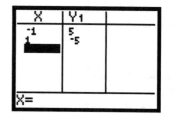

We see that $r(x) < 0$ in interval B. Thus, the solution set is $(0, \infty)$.

42. $(1, 2)$

43. $\dfrac{x-1}{(x-3)(x+4)} \le 0$

Solve the related equation.

$$\dfrac{x-1}{(x-3)(x+4)} = 0$$

$$x - 1 = 0$$

$$x = 1$$

Find the values that make the denominator 0.

$$(x-3)(x+4) = 0$$

$$x = 3 \ or \ x = -4$$

Use the numbers 1, 3, and -4 to divide the number line into intervals as shown:

Enter $r(x) = \dfrac{x-1}{(x-3)(x+4)}$ in a grapher and evaluate a test point in each interval. We test -5, 0, 2, and 4.

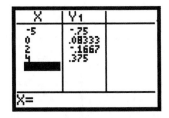

We see that $r(x) < 0$ in intervals A and C. From above we also know that $r(x) = 0$ when $x = 1$. Thus, the solution set is $(-\infty, -4) \cup [1, 3)$.

44. $(-7, -2] \cup (2, \infty)$

45. $4 < \dfrac{1}{x}$

$$4 - \dfrac{1}{x} < 0$$

Graph $r(x) = 4 - \dfrac{1}{x}$ in the window $[-10, 10, -5, 10]$.

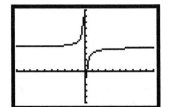

Using the Zero feature we find that $r(x) = 0$ when $x = 0.25$. Observe that $r(x) < 0$ on $(0, 0.25)$, or $\left(0, \dfrac{1}{4}\right)$. This is the solution set of the inequality.

46. $(-\infty, 0) \cup \left[\dfrac{1}{5}, \infty\right)$

47. $\sqrt[5]{a^2 b}\,\sqrt[3]{ab^2} = (a^2 b)^{1/5}(ab^2)^{1/3}$ Converting to
                                           exponential notation

$$= a^{2/5}b^{1/5}a^{1/3}b^{2/3}$$

$$= a^{2/5+1/3}b^{1/5+2/3}$$

$$= a^{11/15}b^{13/15}$$

$$= (a^{11}b^{13})^{1/15}$$

$$= \sqrt[15]{a^{11}b^{13}}$$ Converting back
                          to radical notation

48. 6

49. ◈

50. ◈

51. $x^2 + 2x > 4$

$$x^2 + 2x - 4 > 0$$

Using the quadratic formula, we find that the solutions of the related equation are $x = -1 \pm \sqrt{5}$. Graph $p(x) = x^2 + 2x - 4$ in the standard window. Observe that $p(x) > 0$ on $(-\infty, -1-\sqrt{5}) \cup (-1+\sqrt{5}, \infty)$. This is the solution set of the inequality. This can also be expressed as $(-\infty, -3.24) \cup (1.24, \infty)$.

52. $(-\infty, \infty)$

53. $x^4 + 3x^2 \le 0$

$$x^2(x^2 + 3) \le 0$$

$x^2 = 0$ for $x = 0$, $x^2 > 0$ for $x \ne 0$, $x^2 + 3 > 0$ for all x

The solution set is $\{0\}$.

54. $(-\infty, 0.25] \cup [2.5, \infty)$

55. a) $-3x^2 + 630x - 6000 > 0$

$$x^2 - 210x + 2000 < 0 \quad \text{Multiplying by } -\dfrac{1}{3}$$

$$(x - 200)(x - 10) < 0$$

The solutions of $f(x) = (x - 200)(x - 10) = 0$ are 200 and 10. They divide the number line as shown:

Enter $p(x) = x^2 - 210x + 2000$ in a grapher and evaluate a test point in each interval. We test 9, 11, and 201.

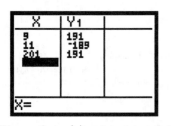

We see that $p(x) < 0$ in interval B, so the company makes a profit for values of x such that $10 < x < 200$, or for values of x in the interval $(10, 200)$.

b) See part (a). Keep in mind that x must be nonnegative since negative numbers have no meaning in this application.

The company loses money for values of x such that $0 \leq x < 10$ or $x > 200$, or for values of x in the interval $[0, 10) \cup (200, \infty)$.

56. a) $\{t | 0 \text{ sec } < t < 2 \text{ sec}\}$

b) $\{t | t > 10 \text{ sec}\}$

57. We find values of n such that $N \geq 66$ and $N \leq 300$.

For $N \geq 66$:
$$\frac{n(n-1)}{2} \geq 66$$
$$n(n-1) \geq 132$$
$$n^2 - n - 132 \geq 0$$
$$(n-12)(n+11) \geq 0$$

The solutions of $f(n) = (n-12)(n+11) = 0$ are 12 and -11. They divide the number line as shown:

However, only positive values of n have meaning in this exercise so we need only consider the intervals shown below:

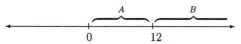

Enter $p(x) = x^2 - x - 132$ in a grapher and evaluate a test point in each interval. We test 1 and 13.

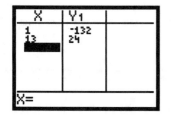

We see that $p(x) > 0$ in interval B. From above we also know that $p(12) = 0$, so the solution set for this inequality is $[12, \infty)$.

For $N \leq 300$:
$$\frac{n(n-1)}{2} \leq 300$$
$$n(n-1) \leq 600$$
$$n^2 - n - 600 \leq 0$$
$$(n-25)(n+24) \leq 0$$

The solutions of $f(n) = (n-25)(n+24) = 0$ are 25 and -24. They divide the number line as shown:

However, only positive values of n have meaning in this exercise so we need only consider the intervals shown below:

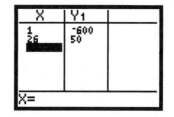

Enter $p(x) = x^2 - x - 600$ in a grapher and evaluate a test point in each interval. We test 1 and 26.

We see that $p(x) < 0$ in interval A. From above we also know that $p(25) = 0$, so the solution set for this inequality is $(0, 25]$. Then $66 \leq N \leq 300$ for $[12, \infty) \cap (0, 25]$, or on $[12, 25]$.

58. $\{n | 9 \leq n \leq 23\}$

59. From the graph we determine the following:

$f(x)$ has no zeros.

The solutions $f(x) < 0$ are $(-\infty, 0)$.

The solutions of $f(x) \geq 0$ are $(0, \infty)$.

60. $f(x) = 0$ for $x = 0$ or $x = 1$;

$f(x) < 0$ for $(0, 1)$;

$f(x) \geq 0$ for $[1, \infty) \cup \{0\}$.

61. From the graph we determine the following:

The solutions of $f(x) = 0$ are -2, 1, 2, and 3.

The solutions of $f(x) < 0$ are $(-2, 1) \cup (2, 3)$.

The solutions of $f(x) \geq 0$ are $(-\infty, -2] \cup [1, 2] \cup [3, -\infty)$.

62. $f(x) = 0$ for $x = -2$, $x = 0$, or $x = 1$;

$f(x) < 0$ for
$(-\infty, -3) \cup (-2, 0) \cup (1, 2)$;

$f(x) > 0$ for
$(-3, -2] \cup [0, 1] \cup (2, \infty)$.

63. a) Enter the data and use the quadratic regression feature. We get $p(x) = 34.04540449x^2 - 1242.727373x + 22,659.5843$.

b) Graph $y_1 = p(x)$ and $y_2 = 20,000$. We use the window $[-3, 40, 10,000, 25,000]$, Xscl = 5, Yscl = 2500.

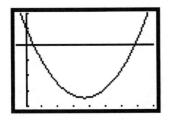

Use Intersect to find the points of intersection. The first coordinates are about 2 and 34. Observe that $y_1 > y_2$ to the left of the left-hand point of intersection and to the right of the right-hand point of intersection. Then the population is greater than 20,000 less than 2 years from 1970 and more than 34 years from 1970 or for $\{x | x \leq 1972 \text{ or } x \geq 2004\}$.

Chapter 11

Exponential and Logarithmic Functions

Exercise Set 11.1

1. The function values increase as x increases, so $a > 1$.

2. $0 < a < 1$

3. The function values decrease as x increases, so $0 < a < 1$.

4. $a > 1$

5. Graph: $y = 2^x$

We compute some function values, thinking of y as $f(x)$, and keep the results in a table.

$f(0) = 2^0 = 1$

$f(1) = 2^1 = 2$

$f(2) = 2^2 = 4$

$f(-1) = 2^{-1} = \dfrac{1}{2^1} = \dfrac{1}{2}$

$f(-2) = 2^{-2} = \dfrac{1}{2^2} = \dfrac{1}{4}$

x	y, or $f(x)$
0	1
1	2
2	4
-1	$\dfrac{1}{2}$
-2	$\dfrac{1}{4}$

Next we plot these points and connect them with a smooth curve.

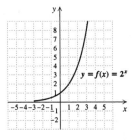

6.

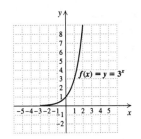

7. Graph: $y = 5^x$

We compute some function values, thinking of y as $f(x)$, and keep the results in a table.

$f(0) = 5^0 = 1$

$f(1) = 5^1 = 5$

$f(2) = 5^2 = 25$

$f(-1) = 5^{-1} = \dfrac{1}{5^1} = \dfrac{1}{5}$

$f(-2) = 5^{-2} = \dfrac{1}{5^2} = \dfrac{1}{25}$

x	y, or $f(x)$
0	1
1	5
2	25
-1	$\dfrac{1}{5}$
-2	$\dfrac{1}{25}$

Next we plot these points and connect them with a smooth curve.

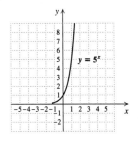

8.

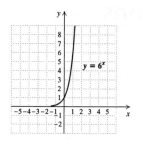

10.

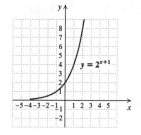

9. Graph: $y = 2^{x-1}$

We compute some function values, thinking of y as $f(x)$, and keep the results in a table.

$f(0) = 2^{0-1} = 2^{-1} = \dfrac{1}{2}$

$f(-1) = 2^{-1-1} = 2^{-2} = \dfrac{1}{2^2} = \dfrac{1}{4}$

$f(-2) = 2^{-2-1} = 2^{-3} = \dfrac{1}{2^3} = \dfrac{1}{8}$

$f(1) = 2^{1-1} = 2^0 = 1$

$f(2) = 2^{2-1} = 2^1 = 2$

$f(3) = 2^{3-1} = 2^2 = 4$

$f(4) = 2^{4-1} = 2^3 = 8$

x	y, or $f(x)$
0	$\dfrac{1}{2}$
-1	$\dfrac{1}{4}$
-2	$\dfrac{1}{8}$
1	1
2	2
3	4
4	8

Next we plot these points and connect them with a smooth curve.

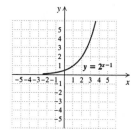

11. Graph: $y = 3^{x+2}$

We compute some function values, thinking of y as $f(x)$, and keep the results in a table.

$f(0) = 3^{0+2} = 3^2 = 9$

$f(1) = 3^{1+2} = 3^3 = 27$

$f(-1) = 3^{-1+2} = 3^1 = 3$

$f(-2) = 3^{-2+2} = 3^0 = 1$

$f(-3) = 3^{-3+2} = 3^{-1} = \dfrac{1}{3^1} = \dfrac{1}{3}$

$f(-4) = 3^{-4+2} = 3^{-2} = \dfrac{1}{3^2} = \dfrac{1}{9}$

$f(-5) = 3^{-5+2} = 3^{-3} = \dfrac{1}{3^3} = \dfrac{1}{27}$

x	y, or $f(x)$
0	9
1	27
-1	3
-2	1
-3	$\dfrac{1}{3}$
-4	$\dfrac{1}{9}$
-5	$\dfrac{1}{27}$

Next we plot these points and connect them with a smooth curve.

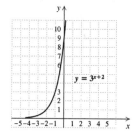

12.

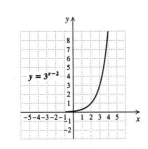

13. Graph: $y = 2^x - 1$

We construct a table of values, thinking of y as $f(x)$. Then we plot the points and connect them with a smooth curve.

$f(0) = 2^0 - 1 = 1 - 1 = 0$

$f(1) = 2^1 - 1 = 2 - 1 = 1$

$f(2) = 2^2 - 1 = 4 - 1 = 3$

$f(3) = 2^3 - 1 = 8 - 1 = 7$

$f(-1) = 2^{-1} - 1 = \dfrac{1}{2} - 1 = -\dfrac{1}{2}$

$f(-2) = 2^{-2} - 1 = \dfrac{1}{4} - 1 = -\dfrac{3}{4}$

$f(-4) = 2^{-4} - 1 = \dfrac{1}{16} - 1 = -\dfrac{15}{16}$

x	y, or $f(x)$
0	0
1	1
2	3
3	7
-1	$-\dfrac{1}{2}$
-2	$-\dfrac{3}{4}$
-4	$-\dfrac{15}{16}$

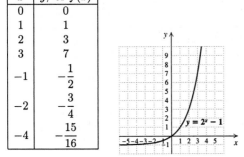

14.

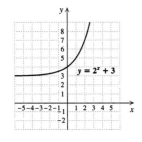

15. Graph: $y = 1.7^x$

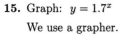
We use a grapher.

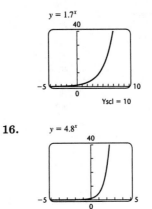

16.

$y = 4.8^x$

17. Graph: $y = \left(\dfrac{1}{2}\right)^x$

We construct a table of values, thinking of y as $f(x)$. Then we plot the points and connect them with a smooth curve.

$f(0) = \left(\dfrac{1}{2}\right)^0 = 1$

$f(1) = \left(\dfrac{1}{2}\right)^1 = \dfrac{1}{2}$

$f(2) = \left(\dfrac{1}{2}\right)^2 = \dfrac{1}{4}$

$f(3) = \left(\dfrac{1}{2}\right)^3 = \dfrac{1}{8}$

$f(-1) = \left(\dfrac{1}{2}\right)^{-1} = \dfrac{1}{\left(\dfrac{1}{2}\right)^1} = \dfrac{1}{\dfrac{1}{2}} = 2$

$f(-2) = \left(\dfrac{1}{2}\right)^{-2} = \dfrac{1}{\left(\dfrac{1}{2}\right)^2} = \dfrac{1}{\dfrac{1}{4}} = 4$

$f(-3) = \left(\dfrac{1}{2}\right)^{-3} = \dfrac{1}{\left(\dfrac{1}{2}\right)^3} = \dfrac{1}{\dfrac{1}{8}} = 8$

x	y, or $f(x)$
0	1
1	$\dfrac{1}{2}$
2	$\dfrac{1}{4}$
3	$\dfrac{1}{8}$
-1	2
-2	4
-3	8

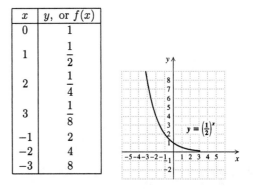

18.

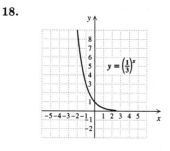

19. Graph: $y = \left(\dfrac{1}{5}\right)^x$

We construct a table of values, thinking of y as $f(x)$. Then we plot the points and connect them with a smooth curve.

$$f(0) = \left(\frac{1}{5}\right)^0 = 1$$

$$f(1) = \left(\frac{1}{5}\right)^1 = \frac{1}{5}$$

$$f(2) = \left(\frac{1}{5}\right)^2 = \frac{1}{25}$$

$$f(-1) = \left(\frac{1}{5}\right)^{-1} = \frac{1}{\frac{1}{5}} = 5$$

$$f(-2) = \left(\frac{1}{5}\right)^{-2} = \frac{1}{\frac{1}{25}} = 25$$

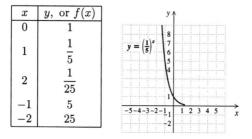

x	y, or $f(x)$
0	1
1	$\dfrac{1}{5}$
2	$\dfrac{1}{25}$
-1	5
-2	25

20.

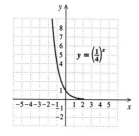

21. Graph: $y = 0.15^x$

We use a grapher.

$y = 0.15^x$

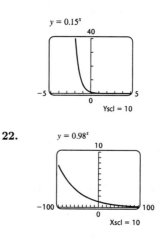
Yscl = 10

22.

$y = 0.98^x$

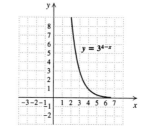
Xscl = 10

23. Graph: $y = 2^{2x-1}$

We construct a table of values, thinking of y as $f(x)$. Then we plot the points and connect them with a smooth curve.

$$f(0) = 2^{2\cdot0-1} = 2^{-1} = \frac{1}{2}$$

$$f(1) = 2^{2\cdot1-1} = 2^1 = 2$$

$$f(2) = 2^{2\cdot2-1} = 2^3 = 8$$

$$f(-1) = 2^{2(-1)-1} = 2^{-3} = \frac{1}{8}$$

$$f(-2) = 2^{2(-2)-1} = 2^{-5} = \frac{1}{32}$$

x	y, or $f(x)$
0	$\dfrac{1}{2}$
1	2
2	8
-1	$\dfrac{1}{8}$
-2	$\dfrac{1}{32}$

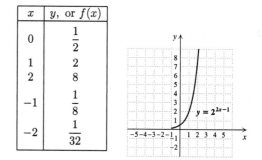

24.

25. Graph: $x = 3^y$

We can find ordered pairs by choosing values for y and then computing values for x.

For $y = 0$, $x = 3^0 = 1$.

For $y = 1$, $x = 3^1 = 3$.

For $y = 2$, $x = 3^2 = 9$.

For $y = 3$, $x = 3^3 = 27$.

For $y = -1$, $x = 3^{-1} = \dfrac{1}{3^1} = \dfrac{1}{3}$.

For $y = -2$, $x = 3^{-2} = \dfrac{1}{3^2} = \dfrac{1}{9}$.

For $y = -3$, $x = 3^{-3} = \dfrac{1}{3^3} = \dfrac{1}{27}$.

x	y
1	0
3	1
9	2
27	3
$\dfrac{1}{3}$	-1
$\dfrac{1}{9}$	-2
$\dfrac{1}{27}$	-3

   (1) Choose values for y.

   (2) Compute values for x.

We plot the points and connect them with a smooth curve.

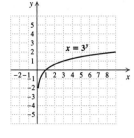

26.

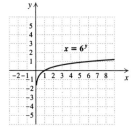

27. Graph: $x = \left(\dfrac{1}{2}\right)^y$

We can find ordered pairs by choosing values for y and then computing values for x. Then we plot these points and connect them with a smooth curve.

For $y = 0$, $x = \left(\dfrac{1}{2}\right)^0 = 1$.

For $y = 1$, $x = \left(\dfrac{1}{2}\right)^1 = \dfrac{1}{2}$.

For $y = 2$, $x = \left(\dfrac{1}{2}\right)^2 = \dfrac{1}{4}$.

For $y = 3$, $x = \left(\dfrac{1}{2}\right)^3 = \dfrac{1}{8}$.

For $y = -1$, $x = \left(\dfrac{1}{2}\right)^{-1} = \dfrac{1}{\dfrac{1}{2}} = 2$.

For $y = -2$, $x = \left(\dfrac{1}{2}\right)^{-2} = \dfrac{1}{\dfrac{1}{4}} = 4$.

For $y = -3$, $x = \left(\dfrac{1}{2}\right)^{-3} = \dfrac{1}{\dfrac{1}{8}} = 8$.

x	y
1	0
$\dfrac{1}{2}$	1
$\dfrac{1}{4}$	2
$\dfrac{1}{8}$	3
2	-1
4	-2
8	-3

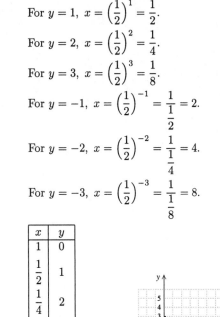

28.

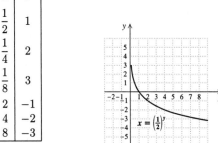

29. Graph: $x = 5^y$

We can find ordered pairs by choosing values for y and then computing values for x. Then we plot these points and connect them with a smooth curve.

For $y = 0$, $x = 5^0 = 1$.

For $y = 1$, $x = 5^1 = 5$.

For $y = 2$, $x = 5^2 = 25$.

For $y = -1$, $x = 5^{-1} = \dfrac{1}{5}$.

For $y = -2$, $x = 5^{-2} = \dfrac{1}{25}$.

x	y
1	0
5	1
25	2
$\dfrac{1}{5}$	-1
$\dfrac{1}{25}$	-2

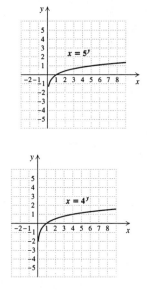

30.

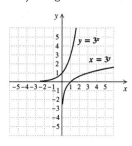

31. Graph $y = 3^x$ (see Exercise 6) and $x = 3^y$ (see Exercise 25) using the same set of axes.

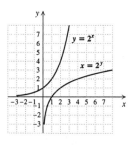

32.

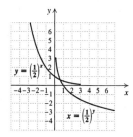

33. Graph $y = \left(\frac{1}{2}\right)^x$ (see Exercise 17) and $x = \left(\frac{1}{2}\right)^y$ (see Exercise 27) using the same set of axes.

34.

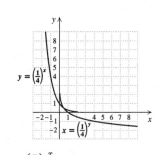

35. $y = \left(\frac{5}{2}\right)^x$ is an exponential function of the form $y = a^x$ with $a > 1$, so y-values will increase as x-values increase. Also, observe that when $x = 0$, $y = 1$. Thus, graph (d) corresponds to this equation.

36. (e)

37. For $x = \left(\frac{2}{5}\right)^y$, when $y = 0$, $x = 1$. The only graph that contains the point $(1, 0)$ is (f). This graph corresponds to the given equation.

38. (a)

39. $y = \left(\frac{2}{5}\right)^{x-2}$ is an exponential function of the form $y = a^x$ with $0 < a < 1$, so y-values will decrease as x-values increase. Also, observe that when $x = 2$, $y = 1$. Thus, graph (c) corresponds to the given equation.

40. (b)

41. Keep in mind that t represents the number of years after 1989 and that N is in thousands.

a) For 1993, $t = 1993 - 1989$, or 4:
$$N(4) = 100(1.4)^4$$
$$= 384.16$$

Thus, 384.16 thousand, or 384,160 Americans had been infected as of 1993.

b) For 1998, $t = 1998 - 1989$, or 9:
$$N(9) = 100(1.4)^9$$
$$\approx 2,066.105$$

Then about 2066.105 thousand, or about 2,066,105 Americans will have been infected as of 1998.

c) We use the function values computed in parts (a) and (b), and others if we wish, to draw the graph. Note that the axes are scaled differently because of the large numbers.

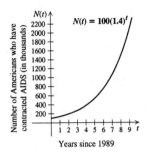

We could also use a graphing calculator to graph the function.

42. a) 4243; 6000; 8485; 12,000; 24,000;

b)

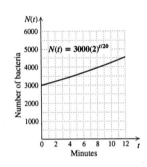

43. a) Substitute for t.

$$N(0) = 250,000\left(\frac{2}{3}\right)^0 = 250,000 \cdot 1 = 250,000;$$

$$N(1) = 250,000\left(\frac{2}{3}\right)^1 = 250,000 \cdot \frac{2}{3} = 166,667;$$

$$N(4) = 250,000\left(\frac{2}{3}\right)^4 = 250,000 \cdot \frac{16}{81} \approx 49,383;$$

$$N(10) = 250,000\left(\frac{2}{3}\right)^{10} = 250,000 \cdot \frac{1024}{59,049} \approx 4335$$

b) We use the function values computed in part (a) to draw the graph of the function. Note that the axes are scaled differently because of the large function values.

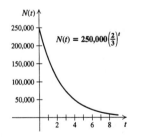

We could also use a graphing calculator to graph the function.

44. a) \$5200; \$4160; \$3328; \$1703.94; \$558.35;

b)

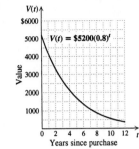

45. a) Substitute for t.

$N(0) = 62(1.018)^0 = 62 \cdot 1 = 62$ billion cubic feet;

$N(1) = 62(1.018)^1 = 62(1.018) \approx 63.1$ billion cubic feet

b) The year 2000 corresponds to $t = 3$ and 2010 corresponds to $t = 13$. We use a table to find $N(3)$ and $N(13)$.

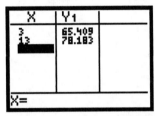

We see that $N(3) \approx 65.4$ billion cubic feet and $N(13) \approx 78.2$ billion cubic feet.

c) We use a graphing calculator.

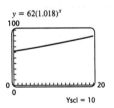

46. a) 19 wpm; 66 wpm; 110 wpm;

b)

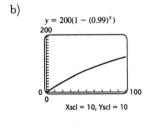

47. $x^{-5} \cdot x^3 = x^{-5+3} = x^{-2}$, or $\dfrac{1}{x^2}$

48. x^{-12}, or $\dfrac{1}{x^{12}}$

49. $\dfrac{x^{-3}}{x^4} = x^{-3-4} = x^{-7}$, or $\dfrac{1}{x^7}$

50. 1

51.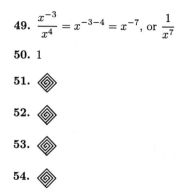

52. ◈

53. ◈

54. ◈

55. Since the bases are the same, the one with the larger exponent is the larger number. Thus $\pi^{2.4}$ is larger.

56. $8^{\sqrt{3}}$

57. Graph: $y = 2^x + 2^{-x}$

Construct a table of values, thinking of y as $f(x)$. Then plot these points and connect them with a curve.

$f(0) = 2^0 + 2^{-0} = 1 + 1 = 2$

$f(1) = 2^1 + 2^{-1} = 2 + \dfrac{1}{2} = 2\dfrac{1}{2}$

$f(2) = 2^2 + 2^{-2} = 4 + \dfrac{1}{4} = 4\dfrac{1}{4}$

$f(3) = 2^3 + 2^{-3} = 8 + \dfrac{1}{8} = 8\dfrac{1}{8}$

$f(-1) = 2^{-1} + 2^{-(-1)} = \dfrac{1}{2} + 2 = 2\dfrac{1}{2}$

$f(-2) = 2^{-2} + 2^{-(-2)} = \dfrac{1}{4} + 4 = 4\dfrac{1}{4}$

$f(-3) = 2^{-3} + 2^{-(-3)} = \dfrac{1}{8} + 8 = 8\dfrac{1}{8}$

x	y, or $f(x)$
0	2
1	$2\dfrac{1}{2}$
2	$4\dfrac{1}{4}$
3	$8\dfrac{1}{8}$
-1	$2\dfrac{1}{2}$
-2	$4\dfrac{1}{4}$
-3	$8\dfrac{1}{8}$

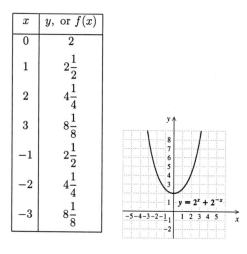

58.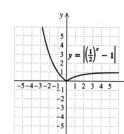

59. Graph: $y = |2^x - 2|$

We construct a table of values, thinking of y as $f(x)$. Then plot these points and connect them with a curve.

$f(0) = |2^0 - 2| = |1 - 2| = |-1| = 1$

$f(1) = |2^1 - 2| = |2 - 2| = |0| = 0$

$f(2) = |2^2 - 2| = |4 - 2| = |2| = 2$

$f(3) = |2^3 - 2| = |8 - 2| = |6| = 6$

$f(-1) = |2^{-1} - 2| = \left|\dfrac{1}{2} - 2\right| = \left|-\dfrac{3}{2}\right| = \dfrac{3}{2}$

$f(-3) = |2^{-3} - 2| = \left|\dfrac{1}{8} - 2\right| = \left|-\dfrac{15}{8}\right| = \dfrac{15}{8}$

$f(-5) = |2^{-5} - 2| = \left|\dfrac{1}{32} - 2\right| = \left|-\dfrac{63}{32}\right| = \dfrac{63}{32}$

x	y, or $f(x)$
0	1
1	0
2	2
3	6
-1	$\dfrac{3}{2}$
-3	$\dfrac{15}{8}$
-5	$\dfrac{63}{32}$

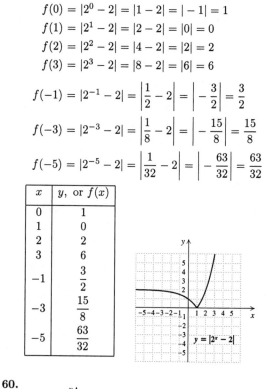

60.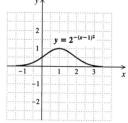

61. Graph: $y = |2x^2 - 1|$

We construct a table of values, thinking of y as $f(x)$. Then we plot these points and connect them with a curve.

$$f(0) = |2^{0^2} - 1| = |1 - 1| = 0$$
$$f(1) = |2^{1^2} - 1| = |2 - 1| = 1$$
$$f(2) = |2^{2^2} - 1| = |16 - 1| = 15$$
$$f(-1) = |2^{(-1)^2} - 1| = |2 - 1| = 1$$
$$f(-2) = |2^{(-2)^2} - 1| = |16 - 1| = 15$$

x	y, or $f(x)$
0	0
1	1
2	15
-1	1
-2	15

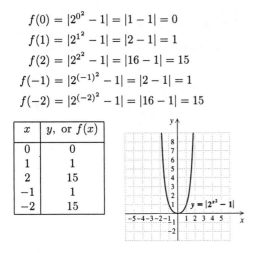

62.

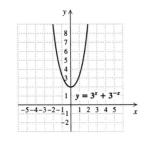

63. $y = 3^{-(x-1)}$ $x = 3^{-(y-1)}$

x	y
0	3
1	1
2	$\frac{1}{3}$
3	$\frac{1}{9}$
-1	9

x	y
3	0
1	1
$\frac{1}{3}$	2
$\frac{1}{9}$	3
9	-1

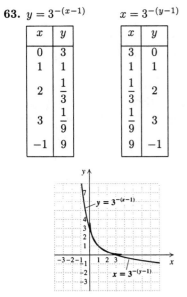

64.

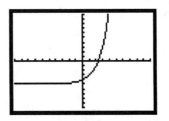

65. We graph $f(x) = 2^x - 5$ in the standard window.

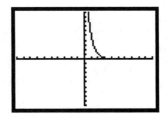

The range appears to be $(-5, \infty)$.

66. $(0, \infty)$

67. We graph $g(x) = 5^{2-x}$ in the standard window.

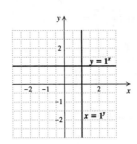

The range appears to be $(0, \infty)$.

68. $(3, \infty)$

Exercise Set 11.2

1. $f \circ g(x) = f(g(x)) = f(2x + 3) =$
$$3(2x + 3)^2 - 1 =$$
$$3(4x^2 + 12x + 9) - 1 =$$
$$12x^2 + 36x + 27 - 1 =$$
$$12x^2 + 36x + 26$$

$g \circ f(x) = g(f(x)) = g(3x^2 - 1) =$
$$2(3x^2 - 1) + 3 = 6x^2 - 2 + 3 =$$
$$6x^2 + 1$$

2. $f \circ g(x) = 8x^2 - 17$; $g \circ f(x) = 32x^2 + 48x + 13$

3. $f \circ g(x) = f(g(x)) = f\left(\dfrac{2}{x}\right) =$

$$4\left(\dfrac{2}{x}\right)^2 - 1 =$$

$$4\left(\dfrac{4}{x^2}\right) - 1 = \dfrac{16}{x^2} - 1$$

$$g \circ f(x) = g(f(x)) = g(4x^2 - 1) = \dfrac{2}{4x^2 - 1}$$

4. $f \circ g(x) = \dfrac{3}{2x^2 + 3}; \; g \circ f(x) = \dfrac{18}{x^2} + 3$

5. $f \circ g(x) = f(g(x)) = f(x^2 + 1) = (x^2 + 1)^2 - 3 =$
$$x^4 + 2x^2 + 1 - 3 = x^4 + 2x^2 - 2$$

$g \circ f(x) = g(f(x)) = g(x^2 - 3) = (x^2 - 3)^2 + 1 =$
$$x^4 - 6x^2 + 9 + 1 = x^4 - 6x^2 + 10$$

6. $f \circ g(x) = \dfrac{1}{x^2 + 4x + 4}; \; g \circ f(x) = \dfrac{1}{x^2} + 2$

7. $h(x) = (7 - 5x)^2$

This is $7 - 5x$ raised to the second power, so the two most obvious functions are $f(x) = x^2$ and $g(x) = 7 - 5x$.

8. $f(x) = 4x^2 + 9; \; g(x) = 3x - 1$

9. $h(x) = (3x^2 - 7)^5$

This is $3x^2 - 7$ to the fifth power, so the two most obvious functions are $f(x) = x^5$ and $g(x) = 3x^2 - 7$.

10. $f(x) = \sqrt{x}; \; g(x) = 5x + 2$

11. $h(x) = \dfrac{2}{x - 3}$

This is 2 divided by $x - 3$, so two functions that can be used are $f(x) = \dfrac{2}{x}$ and $g(x) = x - 3$.

12. $f(x) = x + 4; \; g(x) = \dfrac{3}{x}$

13. $h(x) = \dfrac{1}{\sqrt{7x + 2}}$

This is the reciprocal of the square root of $7x + 2$. Two functions that can be used are $f(x) = \dfrac{1}{\sqrt{x}}$ and $g(x) = 7x + 2$.

14. $f(x) = \sqrt{x} - 3; \; g(x) = x - 7$

15. $h(x) = \dfrac{x^3 + 1}{x^3 - 1}$

Two functions that can be used are $f(x) = \dfrac{x + 1}{x - 1}$ and $g(x) = x^3$.

16. $f(x) = x^4; \; g(x) = \sqrt{x} + 5$

17. The graph of $f(x) = x - 5$ is shown below.

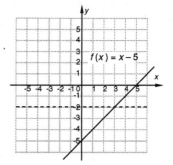

Since there is no horizontal line that crosses the graph more than once, the function is one-to-one.

18. Yes

19. The graph of $f(x) = x^2 + 1$ is shown below.

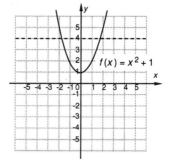

There are many horizontal lines that cross the graph more than once. In particular, the line $y = 4$ crosses the graph more than once. The function is not one-to-one.

20. No

21. The graph of $g(x) = 3^x$ is shown below.

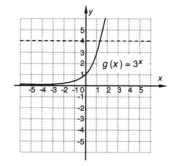

Since no horizontal line crosses the graph more than once, the function is one-to-one.

22. Yes

23. The graph of $g(x) = |x|$ is shown below.

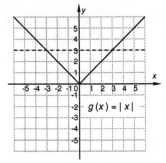

There are many horizontal lines that cross the graph more than once. In particular, the line $y = 3$ crosses the graph more than once. The function is not one-to-one.

24. No

25. a) The function $f(x) = x + 6$ is a linear function that is not constant, so it passes the horizontal-line test. Thus, f is one-to-one.

b) Replace $f(x)$ by y: $y = x + 6$

Interchange x and y: $x = y + 6$

Solve for y: $x - 6 = y$

Replace y by $f^{-1}(x)$: $f^{-1}(x) = x - 6$

26. (a) Yes; (b) $f^{-1}(x) = x - 7$

27. a) The function $f(x) = 3 - x$ is a linear function that is not constant, so it passes the horizontal-line test. Thus, f is one-to-one.

b) Replace $f(x)$ by y: $y = 3 - x$

Interchange x and y: $x = 3 - y$

Solve for y: $y = 3 - x$

Replace y by $f^{-1}(x)$: $f^{-1}(x) = 3 - x$

28. (a) Yes; (b) $f^{-1}(x) = 9 - x$

29. a) The function $g(x) = x - 5$ is a linear function that is not constant, so it passes the horizontal-line test. Thus, g is one-to-one.

b) Replace $g(x)$ by y: $y = x - 5$

Interchange x and y: $x = y - 5$

Solve for y: $x + 5 = y$

Replace y by $g^{-1}(x)$: $g^{-1}(x) = x + 5$

30. (a) Yes; (b) $g^{-1}(x) = x + 8$

31. a) The function $f(x) = 4x$ is a linear function that is not constant, so it passes the horizontal-line test. Thus, f is one-to-one.

b) Replace $f(x)$ by y: $y = 4x$

Interchange x and y: $x = 4y$

Solve for y: $\dfrac{x}{4} = y$

Replace y by $f^{-1}(x)$: $f^{-1}(x) = \dfrac{x}{4}$

32. (a) Yes; (b) $f^{-1}(x) = \dfrac{x}{7}$

33. a) The function $g(x) = 4x + 3$ is a linear function that is not constant, so it passes the horizontal-line test. Thus, g is one-to-one.

b) Replace $g(x)$ by y: $y = 4x + 3$

Interchange variables: $x = 4y + 3$

Solve for y: $x - 3 = 4y$

$$\dfrac{x-3}{4} = y$$

Replace y by $g^{-1}(x)$: $g^{-1}(x) = \dfrac{x-3}{4}$

34. (a) Yes; (b) $g^{-1}(x) = \dfrac{x-7}{4}$

35. a) The graph of $h(x) = 5$ is shown below. The horizontal line $y = 5$ crosses the graph more than once, so the function is not one-to-one.

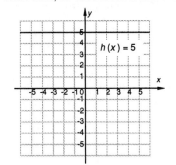

36. (a) No

37. a) The graph of $f(x) = \dfrac{1}{x}$ is shown below. It passes the horizontal-line test, so the function is one-to-one.

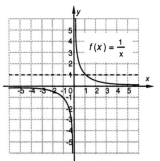

b) Replace $f(x)$ by y: $y = \dfrac{1}{x}$

Interchange x and y: $x = \dfrac{1}{y}$

Solve for y: $xy = 1$

$$y = \dfrac{1}{x}$$

Replace y by $f^{-1}(x)$: $f^{-1}(x) = \dfrac{1}{x}$

38. (a) Yes; (b) $f^{-1}(x) = \dfrac{3}{x}$

39. a) The function $f(x) = \dfrac{2x+1}{3} = \dfrac{2}{3}x + \dfrac{1}{3}$ is a linear function that is not constant, so it passes the horizontal-line test. Thus, f is one-to-one.

b) Replace $f(x)$ by y: $y = \dfrac{2x+1}{3}$

Interchange x and y: $x = \dfrac{2y+1}{3}$

Solve for y: $3x = 2y + 1$

$$3x - 1 = 2y$$

$$\dfrac{3x-1}{2} = y$$

Replace y by $f^{-1}(x)$: $f^{-1}(x) = \dfrac{3x-1}{2}$

40. (a) Yes; (b) $f^{-1}(x) = \dfrac{5x-2}{3}$

41. a) The graph of $f(x) = x^3 - 5$ is shown below. It passes the horizontal-line test, so the function is one-to-one.

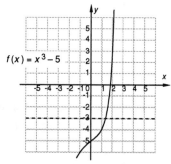

b) Replace $f(x)$ by y: $y = x^3 - 5$

Interchange x and y: $x = y^3 - 5$

Solve for y: $x + 5 = y^3$

$$\sqrt[3]{x+5} = y$$

Replace y by $f^{-1}(x)$: $f^{-1}(x) = \sqrt[3]{x+5}$

42. (a) Yes; (b) $f^{-1}(x) = \sqrt[3]{x-2}$

43. a) The graph of $g(x) = (x-2)^3$ is shown below. It passes the horizontal-line test, so the function is one-to-one.

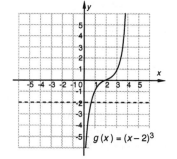

b) Replace $g(x)$ by y: $y = (x-2)^3$

Interchange x and y: $x = (y-2)^3$

Solve for y: $\sqrt[3]{x} = y - 2$

$$\sqrt[3]{x} + 2 = y$$

Replace y by $g^{-1}(x)$: $g^{-1}(x) = \sqrt[3]{x} + 2$

44. (a) Yes; (b) $g^{-1}(x) = \sqrt[3]{x} - 7$

45. a) The graph of $f(x) = \sqrt{x}$ is shown below. It passes the horizontal-line test, so the function is one-to-one.

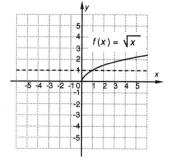

b) Replace $f(x)$ by y: $y = \sqrt{x}$ (Note that $f(x) \geq 0$.)

Interchange x and y: $x = \sqrt{y}$

Solve for y: $x^2 = y$

Replace y by $f^{-1}(x)$: $f^{-1}(x) = x^2,\ x \geq 0$

46. (a) Yes; (b) $f^{-1}(x) = x^2 + 1,\ x \geq 0$

47. a) The graph of $f(x) = 2x^2 + 1$, $x \geq 0$, is shown below. It passes the horizontal-line test, so the function is one-to-one.

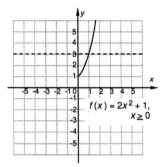

b) Replace $f(x)$ by y: $y = 2x^2 + 1$

Interchange x and y: $x = 2y^2 + 1$

Solve for y: $x - 1 = 2y^2$

$$\frac{x-1}{2} = y^2$$

$$\sqrt{\frac{x-1}{2}} = y$$

(We take the principal square root since $y \geq 0$.)

Replace y by $f^{-1}(x)$: $f^{-1}(x) = \sqrt{\frac{x-1}{2}}$

48. (a) Yes; (b) $f^{-1}(x) = \sqrt{\frac{x+2}{3}}$

49. First graph $f(x) = \frac{1}{3}x - 2$. Then graph the inverse function by reflecting the graph of $f(x) = \frac{1}{3}x - 2$ across the line $y = x$. The graph of the inverse function can also be found by first finding a formula for the inverse, substituting to find function values, and then plotting points.

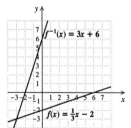

50.

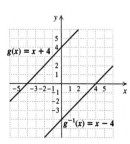

51. Follow the procedure described in Exercise 49 to graph the function and its inverse.

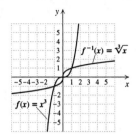

52.

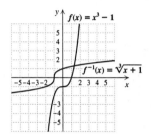

53. Use the procedure described in Exercise 49 to graph the function and its inverse.

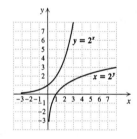

54.

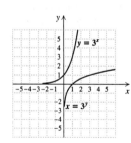

55. Use the procedure described in Exercise 49 to graph the function and its inverse.

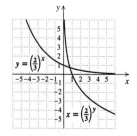

56.

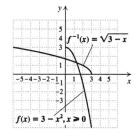

57. Use the procedure described in Exercise 49 to graph the function and its inverse.

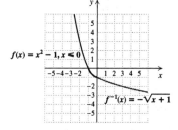

58.

59. Let $y_1 = f(x)$, $y_2 = g(x)$, $y_3 = y_1(y_2)$, and $y_4 = y_2(y_1)$. A table of values shows that $y_3 \neq x$ nor is $y_4 = x$, so $f(x)$ and $g(x)$ are not inverses of each other.

60. Yes

61. Let $y_1 = f(x)$, $y_2 = g(x)$, $y_3 = y_1(y_2)$, and $y_4 = y_2(y_1)$. A table of values shows that $y_3 = x$ and $y_4 = x$ for any value of x, so $f(x)$ and $g(x)$ are inverses of each other.

62. No

63. (1) C; (2) D; (3) B; (4) A

64. (1) D; (2) C; (3) B; (4) A

65. We check to see that $f^{-1} \circ f(x) = x$ and $f \circ f^{-1}(x) = x$.

a) $f^{-1} \circ f(x) = f^{-1}(f(x)) = f^{-1}\left(\frac{4}{5}x\right) =$

$\frac{5}{4} \cdot \frac{4}{5}x = x$

b) $f \circ f^{-1}(x) = f(f^{-1}(x)) = f\left(\frac{5}{4}x\right) =$

$\frac{4}{5} \cdot \frac{5}{4}x = x$

66. a) $f^{-1} \circ f(x) = 3\left(\frac{x+7}{3}\right) - 7 = x + 7 - 7 = x$

b) $f \circ f^{-1}(x) = \frac{(3x - 7) + 7}{3} = \frac{3x}{3} = x$

67. We check to see that $f^{-1} \circ f(x) = x$ and $f \circ f^{-1}(x) = x$.

a) $f^{-1} \circ f(x) = f^{-1}(f(x)) = f^{-1}\left(\frac{1-x}{x}\right) =$

$\frac{1}{\frac{1-x}{x} + 1} = \frac{1}{\frac{1-x}{x} + 1} \cdot \frac{x}{x} = \frac{x}{1-x+x} =$

$\frac{x}{1} = x$

b) $f \circ f^{-1}(x) = f(f^{-1}(x)) = f\left(\frac{1}{x+1}\right) =$

$\frac{1 - \frac{1}{x+1}}{\frac{1}{x+1}} = \frac{1 - \frac{1}{x+1}}{\frac{1}{x+1}} \cdot \frac{x+1}{x+1} =$

$\frac{x+1-1}{1} = \frac{x}{1} = x$

68. a) $f^{-1} \circ f(x) = \sqrt[3]{x^3 - 5 + 5} = \sqrt[3]{x^3} = x$

b) $f \circ f^{-1}(x) = (\sqrt[3]{x+5})^3 - 5 = x + 5 - 5 = x$

69. a) $f(8) = 8 + 32 = 40$

Size 40 in France corresponds to size 8 in the U.S.

$f(10) = 10 + 32 = 42$

Size 42 in France corresponds to size 10 in the U.S.

$f(14) = 14 + 32 = 46$

Size 46 in France corresponds to size 14 in the U.S.

$f(18) = 18 + 32 = 50$

Size 50 in France corresponds to size 18 in the U.S.

b) The function $f(x) = x + 32$ is a linear function that is not constant, so it passes the horizontal-line test. Thus, f is one-to-one and, hence, has an inverse that is a function. We now find a formula for the inverse.

Replace $f(x)$ by y: $y = x + 32$

Interchange x and y: $x = y + 32$

Solve for y: $x - 32 = y$

Replace y by $f^{-1}(x)$: $f^{-1}(x) = x - 32$

c) $f^{-1}(40) = 40 - 32 = 8$

Size 8 in the U.S. corresponds to size 40 in France.

$f^{-1}(42) = 42 - 32 = 10$

Size 10 in the U.S. corresponds to size 42 in France.

$f^{-1}(46) = 46 - 32 = 14$

Size 14 in the U.S. corresponds to size 46 in France.

$f^{-1}(50) = 50 - 32 = 18$

Size 18 in the U.S. corresponds to size 50 in France.

70. a) 40, 44, 52, 60;

    b) $f^{-1}(x) = \dfrac{x - 24}{2}$, or $\dfrac{x}{2} - 12$;

    c) 8, 10, 14, 18

71. $y = kx$

    $7.2 = k(0.8)$ Substituting

    $9 = k$ Variation constant

    $y = 9x$ Equation of variation

72. $y = \dfrac{21.35}{x}$

73. $(a^3 b^2)^5 (a^2 b^7) = (a^{3 \cdot 5} b^{2 \cdot 5})(a^2 b^7) =$
$a^{15} b^{10} a^2 b^7 = a^{15+2} b^{10+7} = a^{17} b^{17}$

74. $x^{11} y^6 z^8$

75. ◈

76. ◈

77. ◈

78. ◈

79. From Exercise 70(b), we know that a function that converts dress sizes in Italy to those in the United States is $g(x) = \dfrac{x - 24}{2}$. From Exercise 63, we know that a function that converts dress sizes in the United States to those in France is $f(x) = x + 32$. Then a function that converts dress sizes in Italy to those in France is

$h(x) = f \circ g(x)$

$h(x) = f\left(\dfrac{x - 24}{2}\right)$

$h(x) = \dfrac{x - 24}{2} + 32$

$h(x) = \dfrac{x}{2} - 12 + 32$

$h(x) = \dfrac{x}{2} + 20.$

80. ◈

81. a) Graph $f(x) = 2^x$ in the standard window and then draw its inverse.

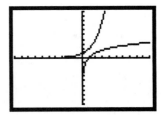

Domain of f: $(-\infty, \infty)$; range of f: $(0, \infty)$

Domain of f^{-1}: $(0, \infty)$; range of f^{-1}: $(-\infty, \infty)$

b) Graph $g(x) = \sqrt{x + 1}$ in the standard window and then draw its inverse.

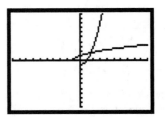

Domain of g: $[-1\infty)$; range of g: $[0, \infty)$

Domain of g^{-1}: $[0, \infty)$; range of g^{-1}: $[-1, \infty)$

c) Graph $h(x) = \dfrac{1}{x - 2}$ in the standard window and then draw its inverse.

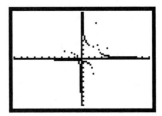

Domain of h: $(-\infty, 2) \cup (2, \infty)$; range of h: $(-\infty, 0) \cup (0\infty)$

Domain of h^{-1}: $(-\infty, 0) \cup (0, \infty)$; range of h^{-1}: $(-\infty, 2) \cup (2, \infty)$

The domain of the function is the range of its inverse, and the range of the function is the domain of the inverse.

Exercise Set 11.3

1. Graph: $y = \log_2 x$

The equation $y = \log_2 x$ is equivalent to $2^y = x$. We can find ordered pairs by choosing values for y and computing the corresponding x-values.

For $y = 0$, $x = 2^0 = 1$.

For $y = 1$, $x = 2^1 = 2$.

For $y = 2$, $x = 2^2 = 4$.

For $y = 3$, $x = 2^3 = 8$.

For $y = -1$, $x = 2^{-1} = \dfrac{1}{2}$.

For $y = -2$, $x = 2^{-2} = \dfrac{1}{4}$.

x, or 2^y	y
1	0
2	1
4	2
8	3
$\dfrac{1}{2}$	-1
$\dfrac{1}{4}$	-2

        (1) Select y.

        (2) Compute x.

We plot the set of ordered pairs and connect the points with a smooth curve.

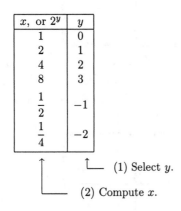

2.

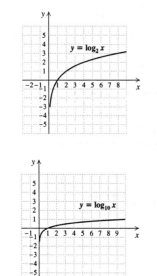

3. Graph: $y = \log_7 x$

The equation $y = \log_7 x$ is equivalent to $7^y = x$. We can find ordered pairs by choosing values for y and computing the corresponding x-values.

For $y = 0$, $x = 7^0 = 1$.

For $y = 1$, $x = 7^1 = 7$.

For $y = 2$, $x = 7^2 = 49$.

For $y = -1$, $x = 7^{-1} = \dfrac{1}{7}$.

For $y = -2$, $x = 7^{-2} = \dfrac{1}{49}$.

x, or 7^y	y
1	0
7	1
49	2
$\dfrac{1}{7}$	-1
$\dfrac{1}{49}$	-2

We plot the set of ordered pairs and connect the points with a smooth curve.

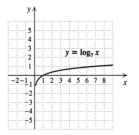

4.

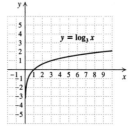

5. Graph: $f(x) = \log_4 x$

Think of $f(x)$ as y. Then $y = \log_4 x$ is equivalent to $4^y = x$. We find ordered pairs by choosing values for y and computing the corresponding x-values. Then we plot the points and connect them with a smooth curve.

For $y = 0$, $x = 4^0 = 1$.

For $y = 1$, $x = 4^1 = 4$.

For $y = 2$, $x = 4^2 = 16$.

For $y = -1$, $x = 4^{-1} = \dfrac{1}{4}$.

For $y = -2$, $x = 4^{-2} = \dfrac{1}{16}$.

x, or 4^y	y
1	0
4	1
16	2
$\dfrac{1}{4}$	-1
$\dfrac{1}{16}$	-2

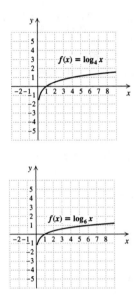

6.

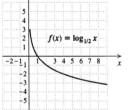

7. Graph: $f(x) = \log_{1/2} x$

Think of $f(x)$ as y. Then $y = \log_{1/2} x$ is equivalent to $\left(\dfrac{1}{2}\right)^y = x$. We construct a table of values, plot these points and connect them with a smooth curve.

For $y = 0$, $x = \left(\dfrac{1}{2}\right)^0 = 1$.

For $y = 1$, $x = \left(\dfrac{1}{2}\right)^1 = \dfrac{1}{2}$.

For $y = 2$, $x = \left(\dfrac{1}{2}\right)^2 = \dfrac{1}{4}$.

For $y = -1$, $x = \left(\dfrac{1}{2}\right)^{-1} = 2$.

For $y = -2$, $x = \left(\dfrac{1}{2}\right)^{-2} = 4$.

For $y = -3$, $x = \left(\dfrac{1}{2}\right)^{-3} = 8$.

x, or $\left(\dfrac{1}{2}\right)^y$	y
1	0
$\dfrac{1}{2}$	1
$\dfrac{1}{4}$	2
2	−1
4	−2
8	−3

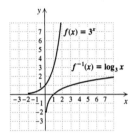

8.

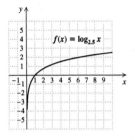

9. Graph $f(x) = 3^x$ (see Exercise Set 9.1, Exercise 2) and $f^{-1}(x) = \log_3 x$ (see Exercise 4 above) on the same set of axes.

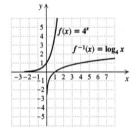

10.

11. $\log 4 \approx 0.6021$; $10^{0.6021} \approx 4$

12. 0.6990

13. $\log 13{,}400 \approx 4.1271$; $10^{4.1271} \approx 13{,}400$

14. 4.9689

15. $\log 0.527 \approx -0.2782$; $10^{-0.2782} \approx 0.527$

16. -0.3072

17. $10^{2.3} \approx 199.5262$; $\log 199.5262 \approx 2.3$

18. 1.4894

19. $10^{-2.9523} \approx 0.0011$; $\log 0.0011 \approx -2.9523$

20. $79{,}104.2833$

21. $10^{0.0012} \approx 1.0028$; $\log 1.0028 \approx 0.0012$

22. 0.0001

23.

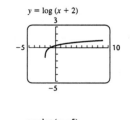

$y = \log (x + 2)$

24.

$y = \log (x - 5)$

25.

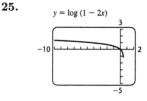

$y = \log (1 - 2x)$

26.

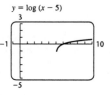

$y = \log (3x + 2.7)$

27.

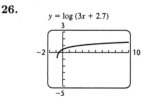

$y = \log (x^2)$

28.

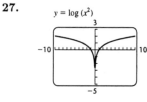

$y = \log (x^2 + 1)$

29.

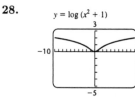

The exponent is the logarithm.

$$10^4 = 10,000 \Rightarrow 4 = \log_{10} 10,000$$

The base remains the same.

30. $2 = \log_{10} 100$

31.

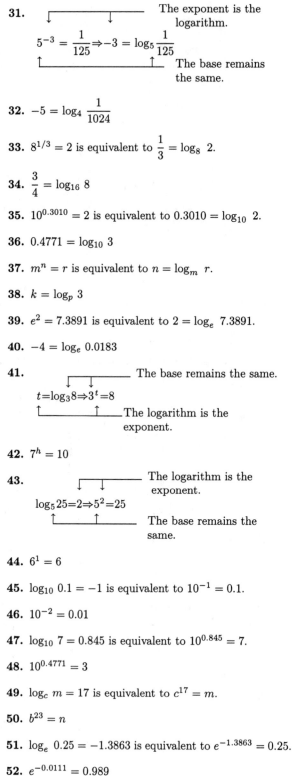

The exponent is the logarithm.

$$5^{-3} = \frac{1}{125} \Rightarrow -3 = \log_5 \frac{1}{125}$$

The base remains the same.

32. $-5 = \log_4 \dfrac{1}{1024}$

33. $8^{1/3} = 2$ is equivalent to $\dfrac{1}{3} = \log_8 2$.

34. $\dfrac{3}{4} = \log_{16} 8$

35. $10^{0.3010} = 2$ is equivalent to $0.3010 = \log_{10} 2$.

36. $0.4771 = \log_{10} 3$

37. $m^n = r$ is equivalent to $n = \log_m r$.

38. $k = \log_p 3$

39. $e^2 = 7.3891$ is equivalent to $2 = \log_e 7.3891$.

40. $-4 = \log_e 0.0183$

41.

The base remains the same.

$$t = \log_3 8 \Rightarrow 3^t = 8$$

The logarithm is the exponent.

42. $7^h = 10$

43.

The logarithm is the exponent.

$$\log_5 25 = 2 \Rightarrow 5^2 = 25$$

The base remains the same.

44. $6^1 = 6$

45. $\log_{10} 0.1 = -1$ is equivalent to $10^{-1} = 0.1$.

46. $10^{-2} = 0.01$

47. $\log_{10} 7 = 0.845$ is equivalent to $10^{0.845} = 7$.

48. $10^{0.4771} = 3$

49. $\log_c m = 17$ is equivalent to $c^{17} = m$.

50. $b^{23} = n$

51. $\log_e 0.25 = -1.3863$ is equivalent to $e^{-1.3863} = 0.25$.

52. $e^{-0.0111} = 0.989$

53. $\log_r T = -x$ is equivalent to $r^{-x} = T$.

54. $c^{-w} = M$

55. $\log_3 x = 4$
$3^4 = x$ Converting to an exponential equation
$81 = x$ Computing 3^4

56. 16

57. $\log_x 125 = 3$
$x^3 = 125$ Converting to an exponential equation
$x = 5$ Taking cube roots

58. 4

59. $\log_2 16 = x$
$2^x = 16$ Converting to an exponential equation
$2^x = 2^4$
$x = 4$ The exponents must be the same.

60. 2

61. $\log_3 27 = x$
$3^x = 27$ Converting to an exponential equation
$3^x = 3^3$
$x = 3$ The exponents must be the same.

62. 2

63. $\log_x 8 = 1$
$x^1 = 8$ Converting to an exponential equation
$x = 8$ Simplifying x^1

64. 7

65. $\log_6 x = 0$
$6^0 = x$ Converting to an exponential equation
$1 = x$ Computing 6^0

66. 9

67. $\log_2 x = -1$
$2^{-1} = x$ Converting to an exponential equation
$\frac{1}{2} = x$ Simplifying

68. $\frac{1}{9}$

69. $\log_8 x = \frac{2}{3}$
$8^{2/3} = x$
$(2^3)^{2/3} = x$
$2^2 = x$
$4 = x$

70. 4

71. Let $\log_{10} 10,000 = x$. Then
$10^x = 10,000$
$10^x = 10^4$
$x = 4.$
Thus, $\log_{10} 10,000 = 4$.

72. 5

73. Let $\log_{10} 1 = x$. Then
$10^x = 1$
$10^x = 10^0$ $(10^0 = 1)$
$x = 0.$
Thus, $\log_{10} 1 = 0$.

74. 1

75. Let $\log_5 625 = x$. Then
$5^x = 625$
$5^x = 5^4$
$x = 4.$
Thus, $\log_5 625 = 4$.

76. 0

77. Let $\log_5 \frac{1}{25} = x$. Then
$5^x = \frac{1}{25}$
$5^x = 5^{-2}$
$x = -2.$
Thus, $\log_5 \frac{1}{25} = -2$.

78. 3

79. Let $\log_3 3 = x$. Then
$3^x = 3$
$3^x = 3^1$
$x = 1.$
Thus, $\log_3 3 = 1$.

80. -4

81. Let $\log_7 1 = x$. Then

$7^x = 1$

$7^x = 7^0 \qquad (7^0 = 1)$

$x = 0.$

Thus, $\log_7 1 = 0.$

82. 1

83. Let $\log_6 15 = x$. Then

$6^x = 15$

$6^{\log_6 15} = 15. \qquad (x = \log_6 \ 15)$

Thus, $6^{\log_6 15} = 15.$

84. 23

85. Let $\log_{27} 9 = x$. Then

$27^x = 9$

$(3^3)^x = 3^2$

$3^{3x} = 3^2$

$3x = 2$

$x = \dfrac{2}{3}.$

Thus, $\log_{27} 9 = \dfrac{2}{3}.$

86. $\dfrac{1}{3}$

87. Let $\log_b \ b^7 = x$. Then

$b^x = b^7$

$x = 7.$

Thus, $\log_b \ b^7 = 7.$

88. 8

89. $\dfrac{\dfrac{3}{x} - \dfrac{2}{xy}}{\dfrac{2}{x^2} + \dfrac{1}{xy}}$

The LCD of all the denominators is x^2y. We multiply numerator and denominator by the LCD.

$$\frac{\dfrac{3}{x} - \dfrac{2}{xy}}{\dfrac{2}{x^2} + \dfrac{1}{xy}} \cdot \frac{x^2y}{x^2y} = \frac{\left(\dfrac{3}{x} - \dfrac{2}{xy}\right)x^2y}{\left(\dfrac{2}{x^2} + \dfrac{1}{xy}\right)x^2y}$$

$$= \frac{\dfrac{3}{x} \cdot x^2y - \dfrac{2}{xy} \cdot x^2y}{\dfrac{2}{x^2} \cdot x^2y + \dfrac{1}{xy} \cdot x^2y}$$

$$= \frac{3xy - 2x}{2y + x}, \text{ or}$$

$$\frac{x(3y - 2)}{2y + x}$$

90. $\dfrac{x + 2}{x + 1}$

91. $8^{-4} = \dfrac{1}{8^4}$, or $\dfrac{1}{4096}$

92. $\sqrt[5]{x}$

93. $t^{-1/3} = \dfrac{1}{t^{1/3}} = \dfrac{1}{\sqrt[3]{t}}$

94. 5

95.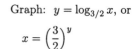

96.

97.

98.

99. Graph: $y = \left(\dfrac{3}{2}\right)^x$ $\qquad$ Graph: $y = \log_{3/2} x$, or

$$x = \left(\dfrac{3}{2}\right)^y$$

x	y, or $\left(\dfrac{3}{2}\right)^x$	x, or $\left(\dfrac{3}{2}\right)^y$	y
0	1	1	0
1	$\dfrac{3}{2}$	$\dfrac{3}{2}$	1
2	$\dfrac{9}{4}$	$\dfrac{9}{4}$	2
3	$\dfrac{27}{8}$	$\dfrac{27}{8}$	3
-1	$\dfrac{2}{3}$	$\dfrac{2}{3}$	-1
-2	$\dfrac{4}{9}$	$\dfrac{4}{9}$	-2

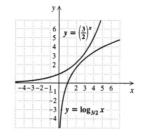

100.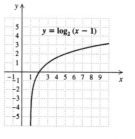

101. Graph: $y = \log_3 |x + 1|$

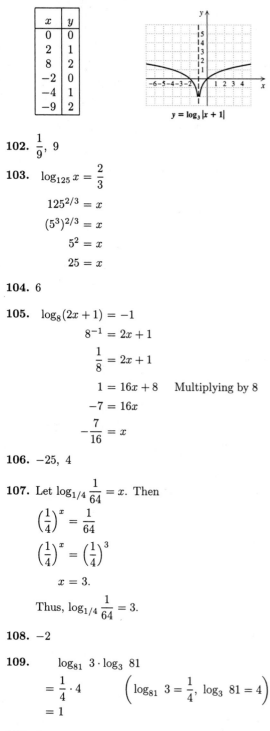

x	y
0	0
2	1
8	2
-2	0
-4	1
-9	2

$y = \log_3 |x + 1|$

102. $\dfrac{1}{9}$, 9

103. $\log_{125} x = \dfrac{2}{3}$

$125^{2/3} = x$

$(5^3)^{2/3} = x$

$5^2 = x$

$25 = x$

104. 6

105. $\log_8(2x + 1) = -1$

$8^{-1} = 2x + 1$

$\dfrac{1}{8} = 2x + 1$

$1 = 16x + 8$ Multiplying by 8

$-7 = 16x$

$-\dfrac{7}{16} = x$

106. -25, 4

107. Let $\log_{1/4} \dfrac{1}{64} = x$. Then

$\left(\dfrac{1}{4}\right)^x = \dfrac{1}{64}$

$\left(\dfrac{1}{4}\right)^x = \left(\dfrac{1}{4}\right)^3$

$x = 3$.

Thus, $\log_{1/4} \dfrac{1}{64} = 3$.

108. -2

109. $\log_{81} 3 \cdot \log_3 81$

$= \dfrac{1}{4} \cdot 4$ $\left(\log_{81} 3 = \dfrac{1}{4}, \ \log_3 81 = 4\right)$

$= 1$

110. 0

111. $\log_2(\log_2(\log_4 256))$

$= \log_2(\log_2 4)$ $(\log_4 256 = 4)$

$= \log_2 2$ $(\log_2 4 = 2)$

$= 1$

112. Let $b = 0$, $x = 1$, and $y = 2$. Then $0^1 = 0^2$, but $1 \neq 2$. Let $b = 1$, $x = 1$, and $y = 2$. Then $1^1 = 1^2$, but $1 \neq 2$. Let $b = -1$, $x = 1$, and $y = 3$. Then $(-1)^1 = (-1)^3$, but $1 \neq 3$.

Exercise Set 11.4

1. $\log_3 (81 \cdot 27) = \log_3 81 + \log_3 27$ Using the product rule

2. $\log_2 16 + \log_2 32$

3. $\log_4 (64 \cdot 16) = \log_4 64 + \log_4 16$ Using the product rule

4. $\log_5 25 + \log_5 125$

5. $\log_c xyz$

$= \log_c x + \log_c y + \log_c z$ Using the product rule

6. $\log_t 3 + \log_t a + \log_t b$

7. $\log_a 5 + \log_a 14 = \log_a (5 \cdot 14)$ Using the product rule

The result can also be expressed as $\log_a 70$.

8. $\log_b (65 \cdot 2)$, or $\log_b 130$

9. $\log_c t + \log_c y = \log_c (t \cdot y)$ Using the product rule

10. $\log_t HM$

11. $\log_a t^7 = 7 \log_a t$ Using the power rule

12. $7 \log_{10} y$

13. $\log_b C^{-3} = -3 \log_b C$ Using the power rule

14. $-5 \log_c M$

15. $\log_2 \dfrac{64}{16} = \log_2 64 - \log_2 16$ Using the quotient rule

16. $\log_3 27 - \log_3 9$

17. $\log_b \dfrac{m}{n} = \log_b m - \log_b n$ Using the quotient rule

18. $\log_a y - \log_a x$

19. $\log_a 15 - \log_a 7 = \log_a \dfrac{15}{7}$ Using the quotient rule

20. $\log_b \dfrac{42}{7}$, or $\log_b 6$

21. $\log_a x^2 y^3 z$

$= \log_a x^2 + \log_a y^3 + \log_a z$ Using the product rule

$= 2 \log_a x + 3 \log_a y + \log_a z$ Using the power rule

22. $\log_a x + 4 \log_a y + 3 \log_a z$

23. $\log_b \dfrac{xy^2}{z^3}$

$= \log_b xy^2 - \log_b z^3$ Using the quotient rule

$= \log_b x + \log_b y^2 - \log_b z^3$ Using the product rule

$= \log_b x + 2 \log_b y - 3 \log_b z$ Using the power rule

24. $2 \log_b x + 5 \log_b y - 4 \log_b w - 7 \log_b z$

25. $\log_b \dfrac{xy^2}{wz^3}$

$= \log_b xy^2 - \log_b wz^3$ Using the quotient rule

$= \log_b x + \log_b y^2 - (\log_b w + \log_b z^3)$ Using the product rule

$= \log_b x + \log_b y^2 - \log_b w - \log_b z^3$ Removing parentheses

$= \log_b x + 2\log_b y - \log_b w - 3\log_b z$ Using the power rule

26. $2 \log_b w + \log_b x - 3 \log_b y - \log_b z$

27. $\log_a \sqrt{\dfrac{x^6}{y^5 z^8}}$

$= \log_a \left(\dfrac{x^6}{y^5 z^8}\right)^{1/2}$

$= \dfrac{1}{2} \log_a \dfrac{x^6}{y^5 z^8}$ Using the power rule

$= \dfrac{1}{2}(\log_a x^6 - \log_a y^5 z^8)$ Using the quotient rule

$= \dfrac{1}{2}\left[\log_a x^6 - (\log_a y^5 + \log_a z^8)\right]$ Using the product rule

$= \dfrac{1}{2}(\log_a x^6 - \log_a y^5 - \log_a z^8)$ Removing parentheses

$= \dfrac{1}{2}(6 \log_a x - 5 \log_a y - 8 \log_a z)$ Using the power rule

28. $\dfrac{1}{3}(4 \log_c x - 3 \log_c y - 2 \log_c z)$

29. $\log_a \sqrt[3]{\dfrac{x^6 y^3}{a^2 z^7}}$

$= \log_a \left(\dfrac{x^6 y^3}{a^2 z^7}\right)^{1/3}$

$= \dfrac{1}{3} \log_a \dfrac{x^6 y^3}{a^2 z^7}$ Using the power rule

$= \dfrac{1}{3}(\log_a x^6 y^3 - \log_a a^2 z^7)$ Using the quotient rule

$= \dfrac{1}{3}[\log_a x^6 + \log_a y^3 - (\log_a a^2 + \log_a z^7)]$ Using the product rule

$= \dfrac{1}{3}(\log_a x^6 + \log_a y^3 - \log_a a^2 - \log_a z^7)$ Removing parentheses

$= \dfrac{1}{3}(\log_a x^6 + \log_a y^3 - 2 - \log_a z^7)$ 2 is the number to which we raise a to get a^2.

$= \dfrac{1}{3}(6 \log_a x + 3 \log_a y - 2 - 7 \log_a z)$ Using the power rule

30. $\dfrac{1}{4}(8 \log_a x + 12 \log_a y - 3 - 5 \log_a z)$

31. $4 \log_a x + 3 \log_a y$

$= \log_a x^4 + \log_a y^3$ Using the power rule

$= \log_a x^4 y^3$ Using the product rule

32. $\log_b m^2 n^{1/2}$, or $\log_b m^2 \sqrt{n}$

33. $\log_a x^2 - 2 \log_a \sqrt{x}$

$= \log_a x^2 - \log_a (\sqrt{x})^2$ Using the power rule

$= \log_a x^2 - \log_a x$ $(\sqrt{x})^2 = x$

$= \log_a \dfrac{x^2}{x}$ Using the quotient rule

$= \log_a x$ Simplifying

34. $\log_a \dfrac{\sqrt{a}}{x}$

35. $\dfrac{1}{2} \log_a x + 3 \log_a y - 2 \log_a x$

$= \log_a x^{1/2} + \log_a y^3 - \log_a x^2$ Using the power rule

$= \log_a x^{1/2} y^3 - \log_a x^2$ Using the product rule

$= \log_a \dfrac{x^{1/2} y^3}{x^2}$ Using the quotient rule

The result can also be expressed as $\log_a \dfrac{\sqrt{x} y^3}{x^2}$ or as $\log_a \dfrac{y^3}{x^{3/2}}$.

36. $\log_a \dfrac{2x^4}{y^3}$

37.
$$\log_a(x^2 - 4) - \log_a(x - 2)$$
$$= \log_a \frac{x^2 - 4}{x - 2} \qquad \text{Using the quotient rule}$$
$$= \log_a \frac{(x + 2)(x - 2)}{x - 2}$$
$$= \log_a \frac{(x + 2)(\cancel{x - 2})}{\cancel{x - 2}} \qquad \text{Simplifying}$$
$$= \log_a(x + 2)$$

38. $\log_a \dfrac{2}{x - 5}$

39.
$$\log_b 15 = \log_b (3 \cdot 5)$$
$$= \log_b 3 + \log_b 5 \qquad \text{Using the product rule}$$
$$= 1.099 + 1.609$$
$$= 2.708$$

40. 0.51

41.
$$\log_b \frac{3}{5} = \log_b 3 - \log_b 5 \qquad \text{Using the quotient rule}$$
$$= 1.099 - 1.609$$
$$= -0.51$$

42. -1.099

43.
$$\log_b \frac{1}{5} = \log_b 1 - \log_b 5 \qquad \text{Using the quotient rule}$$
$$= 0 - 1.609 \qquad (\log_b 1 = 0)$$
$$= -1.609$$

44. $\dfrac{1}{2}$

45. $\log_b \sqrt{b^3} = \log_b b^{3/2} = \dfrac{3}{2}$ $3/2$ is the number to which we raise b to get $b^{3/2}$.

46. 2.099

47. $\log_b 6$

Since 6 cannot be expressed using the numbers 1, 3, and 5, we cannot find $\log_b 6$ using the given information.

48. 3.807

49.
$$\log_b 75$$
$$= \log_b(3 \cdot 5^2)$$
$$= \log_b 3 + \log_b 5^2 \quad \text{Using the product rule}$$
$$= \log_b 3 + 2\log_b 5 \quad \text{Using the power rule}$$
$$= 1.099 + 2(1.609)$$
$$= 4.317$$

50. Cannot be found

51. $\log_t t^9 = 9$ 9 is the number to which we raise t to get t^9.

52. 4

53. $\log_e e^m = m$

54. -2

55. $\log_5 125 = 3$ and $\log_5 625 = 4$, so $\log_5 (125 \cdot 625) = 3 + 4 = 7$.

56. 6

57. $\log_2 128 = 7$ and $\log_2 16 = 4$, so
$$\log_2 \left(\frac{128}{16} \right) = 7 - 4 = 3.$$

58. 2

59. $i^{29} = i^{28} \cdot i = (i^4)^7 \cdot i = 1^7 \cdot i = 1 \cdot i = i$, or $0 + i$

60. $3 + 4i$

61. $5i(2 - i) = 10i - 5i^2 = 10i - 5(-1) = 10i + 5$, or $5 + 10i$

62. -1

63. $(5 - 3i)^2 = 25 - 30i + 9i^2 = 25 - 30i + 9(-1) = 25 - 30i - 9 = 16 - 30i$

64. $-7 - 28i$

65. ◈

66. ◈

67. ◈

68. $\log_a (x^6 - x^4y^2 + x^2y^4 - y^6)$

69. $\log_a (x + y) + \log_a (x^2 - xy + y^2) = \log_a (x + y)(x^2 - xy + y^2) = \log_a (x^3 + y^3)$

70. $\dfrac{1}{2} \log_a (1 - s) + \dfrac{1}{2} \log_a (1 + s)$

71. $\log_a \dfrac{c - d}{\sqrt{c^2 - d^2}}$
$$= \log_a (c - d) - \frac{1}{2} \log_a (c + d)(c - d)$$
$$= \log_a (c - d) - \frac{1}{2} \log_a (c + d) - \frac{1}{2} \log_a (c - d)$$
$$= \frac{1}{2} \log_a (c - d) - \frac{1}{2} \log_a (c + d)$$

72. $\dfrac{10}{3}$

73. $\log_a \left(\dfrac{1}{x}\right) = \log_a x^{-1} = -1 \cdot \log_a x = -1 \cdot 2 = -2$

74. -2

75. False. Let $a = 10$, $P = 100$, $Q = 10$, and $x = 2$.

Then $\log_{10} \left(\dfrac{100}{10}\right)^2 = \log_{10} 10^2 = 2\log_{10} 10 = 2 \cdot 1 = 2$, but $2\log_{10} 100 - \log_{10} 10 = 2 \cdot 2 - 1 = 3$.

76. True

77.

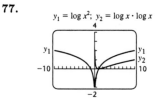

$y_1 = \log x^2; \; y_2 = \log x \cdot \log x$

The graphs do not coincide, so $\log x^2 \neq \log x \cdot \log x$.

Exercise Set 11.5

1. 1.6094

2. 0.6931

3. 4.1271

4. 3.4012

5. 8.3814

6. 6.8037

7. -5.0832

8. -7.2225

9. 15.0293

10. 21.3276

11. 0.0305

12. 0.0714

13. 1 (Any nonzero number raised to the 0 power is 1.)

14. 0

15. 1 (The power to which we raise e to get e is 1.)

16. 6

17. -3.5 (The power to which we raise e to get $e^{-3.5}$, is -3.5.)

18. -4

19. We will use common logarithms for the conversion. Let $a = 10$, $b = 6$, and $M = 100$ and substitute in the change-of-base formula.
$$\log_b M = \frac{\log_a M}{\log_a b}$$
$$\log_6 100 = \frac{\log_{10} 100}{\log_{10} 6}$$
$$\approx \frac{2}{0.7782}$$
$$\approx 2.5702$$

20. 4.1918

21. We will use common logarithms for the conversion. Let $a = 10$, $b = 2$, and $M = 100$ and substitute in the change-of-base formula.
$$\log_2 100 = \frac{\log_{10} 100}{\log_{10} 2}$$
$$\approx \frac{2}{0.3010}$$
$$\approx 6.6439$$

22. 2.3666

23. We will use natural logarithms for the conversion. Let $a = e$, $b = 7$, and $M = 65$ and substitute in the change-of-base formula.
$$\log_7 65 = \frac{\ln 65}{\ln 7}$$
$$\approx \frac{4.1744}{1.9459}$$
$$\approx 2.1452$$

24. 2.3223

25. We will use natural logarithms for the conversion. Let $a = e$, $b = 0.5$, and $M = 5$ and substitute in the change-of-base formula.
$$\log_{0.5} 5 = \frac{\ln 5}{\ln 0.5}$$
$$\approx \frac{1.6094}{-0.6931}$$
$$\approx -2.3219$$

26. -0.4771

27. We will use common logarithms for the conversion. Let $a = 10$, $b = 2$, and $M = 0.2$ and substitute in the change-of-base formula.

$$\log_2 0.2 = \frac{\log_{10} 0.2}{\log_{10} 2}$$
$$\approx \frac{-0.6990}{0.3010}$$
$$\approx -2.3219$$

28. -3.6439

29. We will use natural logarithms for the conversion. Let $a = e$, $b = \pi$, and $M = 58$ and substitute in the change-of-base formula.

$$\log_\pi 58 = \frac{\ln 58}{\ln \pi}$$
$$\approx \frac{4.0604}{1.1447}$$
$$\approx 3.5471$$

30. 4.6284

31. Graph: $f(x) = e^x$

We find some function values with a calculator. We use these values to plot points and draw the graph.

x	e^x
0	1
1	2.7
2	7.4
3	20.1
-1	0.4
-2	0.1

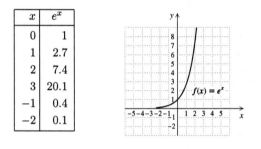

32.

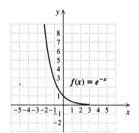

33. Graph: $f(x) = e^{-5x}$

We find some function values with a calculator. We use these values to plot points and draw the graph.

x	e^{-5x}
0	1
0.5	0.082
1	-0.007
-0.5	12.2
-1	148.4

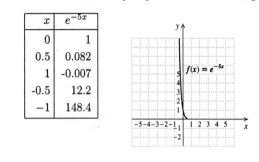

34.

35. Graph: $f(x) = e^{x-1}$

We find some function values, plot points, and draw the graph.

x	e^{x-1}
0	0.4
1	1
2	2.7
3	7.4
4	20.1
-1	0.1
-2	0.05

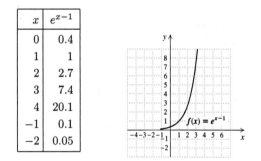

36.

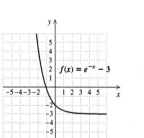

37. Graph: $f(x) = e^x + 3$

We find some function values, plot points, and draw the graph.

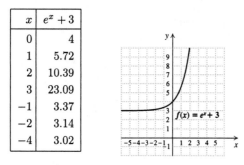

x	$e^x + 3$
0	4
1	5.72
2	10.39
3	23.09
−1	3.37
−2	3.14
−4	3.02

38.

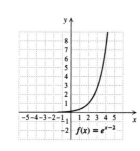

39. Graph: $f(x) = 2e^{-0.5x}$

We find some function values, plot points, and draw the graph.

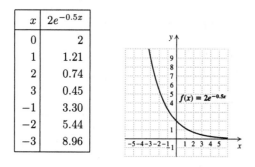

x	$2e^{-0.5x}$
0	2
1	1.21
2	0.74
3	0.45
−1	3.30
−2	5.44
−3	8.96

40.

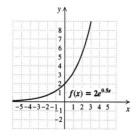

41. Graph: $f(x) = \ln(x + 1)$

We find some function values, plot points, and draw the graph.

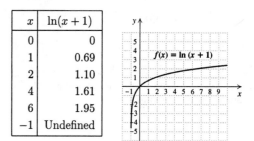

x	$\ln(x + 1)$
0	0
1	0.69
2	1.10
4	1.61
6	1.95
−1	Undefined

42.

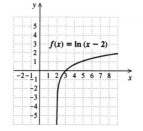

43. Graph: $f(x) = 2 \ln x$

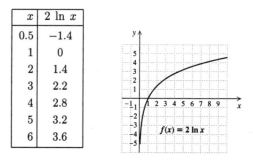

x	$2 \ln x$
0.5	−1.4
1	0
2	1.4
3	2.2
4	2.8
5	3.2
6	3.6

44.

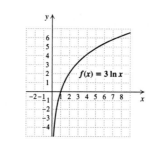

45. Graph: $f(x) = \ln x + 2$

x	$\ln x + 2$
0.01	-2.6
0.25	0.6
0.5	1.3
1	2
2	2.7
4	3.4
6	3.8

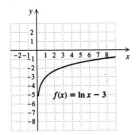

46.

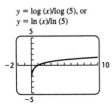

47. We use the change of base formula:
$$f(x) = \frac{\log x}{\log 5} \text{ or } f(x) = \frac{\ln x}{\ln 5}$$

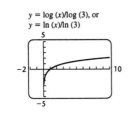

y = log (x)/log (5), or
y = ln (x)/ln (5)

48.

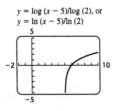

y = log (x)/log (3), or
y = ln (x)/ln (3)

49. We use the change of base formula.
$$f(x) = \frac{\log(x-5)}{\log 2} \text{ or } f(x) = \frac{\ln(x-5)}{\ln 2}$$

y = log (x − 5)/log (2), or
y = ln (x − 5)/ln (2)

50.

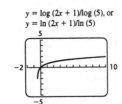

y = log (2x + 1)/log (5), or
y = ln (2x + 1)/ln (5)

51. We use the change of base formula.
$$f(x) = \frac{\log x}{\log 3} + x \text{ or } f(x) = \frac{\ln x}{\ln 3} + x$$

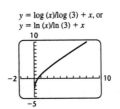

y = log (x)/log (3) + x, or
y = ln (x)/ln (3) + x

52.

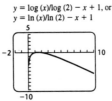

y = log (x)/log (2) − x + 1, or
y = ln (x)/ln (2) − x + 1

53.
$$4x^2 - 25 = 0$$
$$(2x + 5)(2x - 5) = 0$$
$$2x + 5 = 0 \quad \text{or} \quad 2x - 5 = 0$$
$$2x = -5 \quad \text{or} \quad 2x = 5$$
$$x = -\frac{5}{2} \quad \text{or} \quad x = \frac{5}{2}$$

The solutions are $-\frac{5}{2}$ and $\frac{5}{2}$.

54. $0, \dfrac{7}{5}$

55.
$$17x - 15 = 0$$
$$17x = 15$$
$$x = \frac{15}{17}$$

The solution is $\dfrac{15}{17}$.

56. $\dfrac{9}{13}$

57. $x^{1/2} - 6x^{1/4} + 8 = 0$

Let $u = x^{1/4}$.
$$u^2 - 6u + 8 = 0 \qquad \text{Substituting}$$
$$(u - 4)(u - 2) = 0$$

$$u = 4 \quad or \quad u = 2$$
$$x^{1/4} = 4 \quad or \quad x^{1/4} = 2$$
$$x = 256 \quad or \quad x = 16 \quad \text{Raising both sides to the fourth power}$$

Both numbers check. The solutions are 256 and 16.

58. $\frac{1}{4}$, 9

Both numbers check.

59. ◈

60. ◈

61. ◈

62. ◈

63. Use the change-of-base formula with $a = 10$ and $b = e$. We obtain
$$\ln M = \frac{\log M}{\log e}.$$

64. $\log M = \dfrac{\ln M}{\ln 10}$

65.
$$\log(275x^2) = 38$$
$$10^{38} = 275x^2$$
$$\frac{10^{38}}{275} = x^2$$
$$\pm\sqrt{\frac{10^{38}}{275}} = x$$
$$\pm 6.0302 \times 10^{17} \approx x$$

66. 1086.5129

67.
$$\frac{3.01}{\ln x} = \frac{28}{4.31}$$
$$4.31(3.01) = 28\ln x \quad \text{Multiplying by } 4.31\ln x$$
$$\frac{4.31(3.01)}{28} = \ln x$$
$$0.463325 = \ln x$$
$$1.5893 \approx x$$

68. 4.9855

69. (a) $(0, \infty)$;

(b) $[-2, 5, -50, 100]$, Yscl = 10; answers may vary

(c)
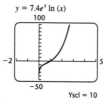

70. (a) $(0, \infty)$;

(b) $[-1, 5, -10, 5]$; answers may vary;

(c)
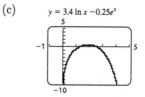

71. (a) $(2.1, \infty)$;

(b) $[-1, 10, -20, 20]$, Yscl = 5; answers may vary;

(c)
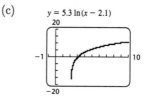

72. (a) $(0, \infty)$;

(b) $[-1, 5, -1, 10]$; answers may vary;

(c)
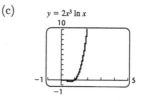

Exercise Set 11.6

1. $3^x = 81$
$$3^x = 3^4$$
$$x = 4 \quad \text{The exponents must be the same.}$$

The solution is 4.

2. 3

3. $4^x = 256$
$$4^x = 4^4$$
$$x = 4 \quad \text{The exponents must be the same.}$$
The solution is 4.

4. 3

5. $2^{x+3} = 32$
$$2^{x+3} = 2^5$$
$$x + 3 = 5$$
$$x = 2$$
The solution is 2.

6. 1

7. $5^{3x} = 625$

$5^{3x} = 5^4$

$3x = 4$

$x = \dfrac{4}{3}$

The solution is $\dfrac{4}{3}$.

8. 2

9. $4^{2x-1} = 64$

$4^{2x-1} = 4^3$

$2x - 1 = 3$

$2x = 4$

$x = 2$

The solution is 2.

10. $\dfrac{5}{2}$

11. $3^{2x^2} \cdot 3^{5x} = 27$

$3^{2x^2+5x} = 3^3$

$2x^2 + 5x = 3$

$2x^2 + 5x - 3 = 0$

$(2x - 1)(x + 3) = 0$

$x = \dfrac{1}{2}$ or $x = -3$

The solutions are $\dfrac{1}{2}$ and -3.

12. $-3, -1$

13. $2^x = 13$

$\log 2^x = \log 13$

$x \log 2 = \log 13$

$x = \dfrac{\log 13}{\log 2}$

$x \approx 3.700$

The solution is $\log 13 / \log 2$, or approximately 3.700.

14. $\dfrac{\log 19}{\log 2} \approx 4.248$

15. $4^x = 7$

$\log 4^x = \log 7$

$x \log 4 = \log 7$

$x = \dfrac{\log 7}{\log 4}$

$x \approx 1.404$

The solution is $\log 7 / \log 4$, or approximately 1.404.

16. $\dfrac{1}{\log 8} \approx 1.107$

17. $e^t = 100$

$\ln e^t = \ln 100$ Taking ln on both sides

$t = \ln 100$ Finding the logarithm of the base to a power

$t \approx 4.605$ Using a calculator

18. $\ln 1000 \approx 6.908$

19. $e^{-0.07t} = 0.08$

$\ln e^{-0.07t} = \ln 0.08$ Taking ln on both sides

$-0.07t = \ln 0.08$ Finding the logarithm of the base to a power

$t = \dfrac{\ln 0.08}{-0.07}$

$t \approx 36.082$

20. $\dfrac{\ln 5}{0.03} \approx 53.648$

21. $2^x = 3^{x-1}$

$\log 2^x = \log 3^{x-1}$

$x \log 2 = (x - 1) \log 3$

$x \log 2 = x \log 3 - \log 3$

$\log 3 = x \log 3 - x \log 2$

$\log 3 = x(\log 3 - \log 2)$

$\dfrac{\log 3}{\log 3 - \log 2} = x$

$2.710 \approx x$

22. $\dfrac{\log 3}{\log 5 - \log 3} \approx 2.151$

23. $e^{0.5x} - 7 = 2x + 6$

Graph $y_1 = e^{0.5x} - 7$ and $y_2 = 2x + 6$ in a window that shows the points of intersection of the graphs. One good choice is $[-10, 10, -10, 25]$, Yscl $= 5$. Use Intersect to find the first coordinates of the points of intersection. They are the solutions of the given equation. They are about -6.480 and 6.519.

24. -1.873

25. $20 - (1.7)^x = 0$

$20 = (1.7)^x$

$\log 20 = \log (1.7)^x$

$\log 20 = x \log 1.7$

$\dfrac{\log 20}{\log 1.7} = x$

$5.646 \approx x$

26. $\dfrac{\log 125}{\log 4.5} \approx 3.210$

27. $\log_5 x = 4$

$\qquad x = 5^4$ Writing an equivalent exponential equation

$\qquad x = 625$

28. 27

29. $\log x = 3$ The base is 10.

$\qquad x = 10^3$

$\qquad x = 1000$

30. 10

31. $2\log x = -6$

$\qquad \log x = -3$ The base is 10.

$\qquad x = 10^{-3}$

$\qquad x = \dfrac{1}{1000}$, or 0.001

32. $\dfrac{1}{100}$, or 0.01

33. $\ln x = 1$

$\qquad x = e \approx 2.718$

34. $e^2 \approx 7.389$

35. $5\ln x = -15$

$\qquad \ln x = -3$

$\qquad x = e^{-3} \approx 0.050$

36. $e^{-1} \approx 0.368$

37. $\log_2(8 - 6x) = 5$

$\qquad 8 - 6x = 2^5$

$\qquad 8 - 6x = 32$

$\qquad -6x = 24$

$\qquad x = -4$

The answer checks. The solution is -4.

38. 66

39. $\log(x + 9) + \log x = 1$ The base is 10.

$\qquad \log_{10}[(x + 9)(x)] = 1$ Using the product rule

$\qquad x(x + 9) = 10^1$

$\qquad x^2 + 9x = 10$

$\qquad x^2 + 9x - 10 = 0$

$\qquad (x - 1)(x + 10) = 0$

$\qquad x = 1 \text{ or } x = -10$

Check: For 1:

$$\log(x + 9) + \log x = 1$$

$\log(1 + 9) + \log 1$? 1

$\qquad \log 10 + \log 1 \,\big|$

$\qquad\qquad 1 + 0 \,\big|$

$\qquad\qquad\quad 1 \,\big|\, 1$ TRUE

For -10:

$$\log(x + 9) + \log x = 1$$

$\log(-10 + 9) + \log(-10)$? 1   FALSE

The number -10 does not check, because negative numbers do not have logarithms. The solution is 1.

40. 10

41. $\log x - \log(x + 7) = 1$ The base is 10.

$\qquad \log_{10}\dfrac{x}{x + 7} = 1$ Using the quotient rule

$\qquad \dfrac{x}{x + 7} = 10^1$

$\qquad x = 10(x + 7)$

$\qquad x = 10x + 70$

$\qquad -9x = 70$

$\qquad x = -\dfrac{70}{9}$

The number $-\dfrac{70}{9}$ does not check. The equation has no solution.

42. $\dfrac{1}{3}$

43. $\log_4(x + 3) - \log_4(x - 5) = 2$

$\qquad \log_4\dfrac{x + 3}{x - 5} = 2$ Using the quotient rule

$\qquad \dfrac{x + 3}{x - 5} = 4^2$

$\qquad \dfrac{x + 3}{x - 5} = 16$

$\qquad x + 3 = 16(x - 5)$

$\qquad x + 3 = 16x - 80$

$\qquad 83 = 15x$

$\qquad \dfrac{83}{15} = x$

The number $\dfrac{83}{15}$ checks. It is the solution.

44. 5

45. $\log_7(x+2) + \log_7(x+1) = \log_7 6$

$\log_7[(x+2)(x+1)] = \log_7 6$ Using the product rule

$\log_7(x^2+3x+2) = \log_7 6$

$x^2 + 3x + 2 = 6$ Using the property of logarithmic equality

$x^2 + 3x - 4 = 0$

$(x+4)(x-1) = 0$

$x = -4 \quad or \quad x = 1$

The number 1 checks, but -4 does not. The solution is 1.

46. 2

47. $\log_5(x+4) + \log_5(x-4) = 2$

$\log_5[(x+4)(x-4)] = 2$

$(x+4)(x-4) = 5^2$

$x^2 - 16 = 25$

$x^2 = 41$

$x = \pm\sqrt{41}$

The number $\sqrt{41}$ checks, but $-\sqrt{41}$ does not. The solution is $\sqrt{41}$.

48. 4

49. $\log_2(x-2) + \log_2 x = 3$

$\log_2[(x-2)(x)] = 3$

$x(x-2) = 2^3$

$x^2 - 2x = 8$

$x^2 - 2x - 8 = 0$

$(x-4)(x+2) = 0$

$x = 4 \quad or \quad x = -2$

The number 4 checks, but -2 does not. The solution is 4.

50. $\dfrac{2}{5}$

51. $\ln 3x = 3x - 8$

Graph $y_1 = \ln 3x$ and $y_2 = 3x - 8$ in a window that shows the points of intersection of the graphs. One good choice is $[-5, 5, -15, 5]$. When we use Intersect in this window we can find only the coordinates of the right-hand point of intersection. They are about $(3.445, 2.336)$, so one solution of the equation is about 3.445. To find the coordinates of the left-hand point of intersection we make the window smaller. One window that is appropriate is $[-1, 1, -15, 5]$. Using Intersect again we find that the other solution of the equation is about 0.0001. (The answer approximated to the nearest thousandth is 0.000, so we express it to the nearest ten-thousandth.)

52. $-0.753, 0.753$

53. Solve $\ln x = \log x$.

Graph $y_1 = \ln x$ and $y_2 = \log x$ in a window that shows the point of intersection of the graphs. One good choice is $[-5, 5, 5, 5]$. Use Intersect to find the first coordinate of the point of intersection. It is the solution of the given equation. It is 1.

54. 1, 100

55. $\log_{125} 5 = \dfrac{1}{3}$ and $\log_5 125 = 3$, so $x = \left(\dfrac{1}{3}\right)^3$, or 3^{-3}, and thus $\log_3 x = -3$.

56. 7

57. $\log x^{\log x} = \log x \cdot \log x = (\log x)^2$

If $(\log x)^2 = 25$, then $\log x = -5$ or $\log x = 5$ and $x = 10^{-5}$, or 0.00001, or $x = 10^5$, or $100,000$.

58. $-625, 625$

59. $(125x^7 y^{-2} z^6)^{-2/3} =$

$(5^3)^{-2/3}(x^7)^{-2/3}(y^{-2})^{-2/3}(z^6)^{-2/3} =$

$5^{-2} x^{-14/3} y^{4/3} z^{-4} = \dfrac{1}{25} x^{-14/3} y^{4/3} z^{-4}$, or

$\dfrac{y^{4/3}}{25 x^{14/3} z^4}$

60. $-i$

61. $(3+5i)^2 = 9 + 30i + 25i^2 = 9 + 30i - 25 = -16 + 30i$

62. $c = \sqrt{\dfrac{E}{m}}$

63. $x^4 + 400 = 104x^2$

$x^4 - 104x^2 + 400 = 0$

Let $u = x^2$.

$u^2 - 104u + 400 = 0$

$(u - 100)(u - 4) = 0$

$u = 100 \quad or \quad u = 4$

$x^2 = 100 \quad or \quad x^2 = 4$ Replacing u with x^2

$x = \pm 10 \quad or \quad x = \pm 2$

The solutions are ± 10 and ± 2.

64. $\dfrac{3 \pm \sqrt{29}}{2}$

65. ◈

66. ◈

67. ◈

68. ◈

69. $27^x = 81^{2x-3}$

$$(3^3)^x = (3^4)^{2x-3}$$

$$3^{3x} = 3^{8x-12}$$

$$3x = 8x - 12$$

$$12 = 5x$$

$$\frac{12}{5} = x$$

The solution is $\frac{12}{5}$.

70. -4

71. $\log_x (\log_3 27) = 3$

$$\log_3 27 = x^3$$

$$3 = x^3 \qquad (\log_3 27 = 3)$$

$$\sqrt[3]{3} = x$$

The solution is $\sqrt[3]{3}$.

72. 2

73. $x \cdot \log \frac{1}{8} = \log 8$

$$x \cdot \log 8^{-1} = \log 8$$

$$x(-\log 8) = \log 8 \quad \text{Using the power rule}$$

$$x = -1$$

The solution is -1.

74. $\pm\sqrt{34}$

75. $2^{x^2+4x} = \frac{1}{8}$

$$2^{x^2+4x} = \frac{1}{2^3}$$

$$2^{x^2+4x} = 2^{-3}$$

$$x^2 + 4x = -3$$

$$x^2 + 4x + 3 = 0$$

$$(x+3)(x+1) = 0$$

$$x = -3 \text{ or } x = -1$$

The solutions are -3 and -1.

76. $10^{100,000}$

77. $\log \sqrt{2x} = \sqrt{\log 2x}$

$$\log (2x)^{1/2} = \sqrt{\log 2x}$$

$$\frac{1}{2} \log 2x = \sqrt{\log 2x}$$

$$\frac{1}{4} (\log 2x)^2 = \log 2x \quad \text{Squaring both sides}$$

$$\frac{1}{4}(\log 2x)^2 - \log 2x = 0$$

Let $u = \log 2x$.

$$\frac{1}{4}u^2 - u = 0$$

$$u\left(\frac{1}{4}u - 1\right) = 0$$

$$u = 0 \quad or \quad \frac{1}{4}u - 1 = 0$$

$$u = 0 \quad or \quad \frac{1}{4}u = 1$$

$$u = 0 \quad or \quad u = 4$$

$$\log 2x = 0 \quad or \quad \log 2x = 4 \qquad \begin{array}{l}\text{Replacing } u \\ \text{with } \log 2x\end{array}$$

$$2x = 10^0 \quad or \quad 2x = 10^4$$

$$2x = 1 \quad or \quad 2x = 10,000$$

$$x = \frac{1}{2} \quad or \quad x = 5000$$

Both numbers check. The solutions are $\frac{1}{2}$ and 5000.

78. $1, \dfrac{\log 5}{\log 3} \approx 1.465$

79. $(81^{x-2})(27^{x+1}) = 9^{2x-3}$

$$[(3^4)^{x-2}][(3^3)^{x+1}] = (3^2)^{2x-3}$$

$$(3^{4x-8})(3^{3x+3}) = 3^{4x-6}$$

$$3^{7x-5} = 3^{4x-6}$$

$$7x - 5 = 4x - 6$$

$$3x = -1$$

$$x = -\frac{1}{3}$$

The solution is $-\frac{1}{3}$.

80. $\dfrac{3}{2}$

Exercise Set 11.7

1. a) 2000 is 10 years after 1990, so we find $S(10)$.

$$S(10) = 52.4(1.16)^{10} \approx 231.16$$

We estimate that Thanksgiving to Christmas credit card spending in 2000 will be about \$231.16 billion.

b) \$1 trillion = \$1000 billion, so we replace $S(t)$ with 1000 and solve for t.

$$1000 = 52.4(1.16)^t$$
$$19.084 \approx 1.16^t$$
$$\log 19.084 \approx \log(1.16^t)$$
$$\log 19.084 \approx t \log 1.16$$
$$\frac{\log 19.084}{\log 1.16} \approx t$$
$$19.9 \approx t$$

Spending will be \$1 trillion about 19.9 years after 1990 or in 2009. (If we round t to 20, the answer would be 2010.)

c) The spending in 1990 was $S(0) = 52.4(1.16)^0 = 52.4$. Twice this amount is $2(52.4)$, or 104.8. We substitute 104.8 for $S(t)$ and solve for t.

$$104.8 = 52.4(1.16)t$$
$$2 = 1.16^t$$
$$\log 2 = \log(1.16^t)$$
$$\log 2 = t \log 1.16$$
$$\frac{\log 2}{\log 1.16} = t$$
$$4.67 \approx t$$

The doubling time is about 4.67 years.

2. (a) \$14,793; (b) 2011; (c) 11.9 years

3. a) Replace $A(t)$ with 40,000 and solve for t.

$$A(t) = 29,000(1.08)^t$$
$$40,000 = 29,000(1.08)^t$$
$$1.379 \approx (1.08)^t$$
$$\log 1.379 \approx \log(1.08)^t$$
$$\log 1.379 \approx t \log 1.08$$
$$\frac{\log 1.379}{\log 1.08} \approx t$$
$$4.2 \approx t$$

The amount due will reach \$40,000 after about 4.2 years.

b) Replace $A(t)$ with $2(29,000)$, or 58,000, and solve for t.

$$58,000 = 29,000(1.08)^t$$
$$2 = (1.08)^t$$
$$\log 2 = \log(1.08)^t$$
$$\log 2 = t \log 1.08$$
$$\frac{\log 2}{\log 1.08} = t$$
$$9.0 \approx t$$

The doubling time is about 9.0 years.

4. (a) 3.6 days; (b) 0.6 days

5. a) We replace $N(t)$ with 60,000 and solve for t:

$$60,000 = 250,000\left(\frac{2}{3}\right)^t$$
$$\frac{60,000}{250,000} = \left(\frac{2}{3}\right)^t$$
$$0.24 = \log\left(\frac{2}{3}\right)^t$$
$$\log 0.24 = \log\left(\frac{2}{3}\right)^t$$
$$\log 0.24 = t \log \frac{2}{3}$$
$$t = \frac{\log 0.24}{\log \frac{2}{3}} \approx \frac{-0.61979}{-0.17609} \approx 3.5$$

After about 3.5 years 60,000 cans will still be in use.

b) We replace $N(t)$ with 1000 and solve for t.

$$1000 = 250,000\left(\frac{2}{3}\right)^t$$
$$\frac{1000}{250,000} = \left(\frac{2}{3}\right)^t$$
$$0.004 = \log\left(\frac{2}{3}\right)^t$$
$$\log 0.004 = \log\left(\frac{2}{3}\right)^t$$
$$\log 0.004 = t \log \frac{2}{3}$$
$$t = \frac{\log 0.004}{\log \frac{2}{3}} \approx \frac{-2.39794}{-0.17609} \approx 13.6$$

After about 13.6 years 1000 cans will still be in use.

6. (a) 6.6 yr; (b) 3.1 yr

7.
$$\text{pH} = -\log[H^+]$$
$$= -\log[1.3 \times 10^{-5}]$$
$$\approx -(-4.886057) \quad \text{Using a calculator}$$
$$\approx 4.9$$

The pH of fresh-brewed coffee is about 4.9.

8. 6.8

9.
$$\text{pH} = -\log[H^+]$$
$$7.0 = -\log[H^+]$$
$$-7.0 = \log[H^+]$$
$$10^{-7.0} = [H^+] \quad \text{Converting to an} \atop \text{exponential equation}$$

The hydrogen ion concentration is 10^{-7} moles per liter.

10. 1.58×10^{-8} moles per liter

11. $L = 10 \cdot \log \dfrac{I}{I_0}$

$= 10 \cdot \log \dfrac{3.2 \times 10^{-6}}{10^{-12}}$

$= 10 \cdot \log(3.2 \times 10^6)$

$\approx 10(6.5)$

≈ 65

The intensity of sound in normal conversation is about 65 decibels.

12. 95 dB

13.

$L = 10 \cdot \log \dfrac{I}{I_0}$

$105 = 10 \cdot \log \dfrac{I}{10^{-12}}$

$10.5 = \log \dfrac{I}{10^{-12}}$

$10.5 = \log I - \log 10^{-12}$ Using the
                                                                    quotient rule

$10.5 = \log I - (-12)$ $(\log 10^a = a)$

$10.5 = \log I + 12$

$-1.5 = \log I$

$10^{-1.5} = I$ Converting to an
                                  exponential equation

$3.2 \times 10^{-2} \approx I$

The intensity of the sound is $10^{-1.5}$ W/m^2, or about 3.2×10^{-2} W/m^2.

14. $10^{-9.2}$ W/m^2, or 6.3×10^{-10} W/m^2

15. a) Substitute 0.06 for k:

$P(t) = P_0 \, e^{0.06t}$

b) To find the balance after one year, replace P_0 with 5000 and t with 1. We find $P(1)$:

$P(1) = 5000 \, e^{0.06(1)} = 5000 \, e^{0.06} \approx$

$5000(1.061836547) \approx \$5309.18$

To find the balance after 2 years, replace P_0 with 5000 and t with 2. We find $P(2)$:

$P(2) = 5000 \, e^{0.06(2)} = 5000 \, e^{0.12} \approx$

$5000(1.127496852) \approx \$5637.48$

c) To find the doubling time, replace P_0 with 5000 and $P(t)$ with 10,000 and solve for t.

$10,000 = 5000 \, e^{0.06t}$

$2 = e^{0.06t}$

$\ln 2 = \ln e^{0.06t}$ Taking the natural loga-
                                              rithm on both sides

$\ln 2 = 0.06t$ Finding the logarithm of
                                  the base to a power

$\dfrac{\ln 2}{0.06} = t$

$11.6 \approx t$

The investment will double in about 11.6 years.

16. (a) $P(t) = P_0 e^{0.05t}$; (b) \$1051.27, \$1105.17; (c) 13.9 years

17. a) $P(t) = 29.1e^{0.008t}$, where $P(t)$ is in millions and t is the number of years after 1997.

b) $2010 - 1997 = 13$, so we find $P(13)$.

$P(13) = 2.91e^{0.008(13)}$

$= 2.91e^{0.104}$

≈ 32.3

We predict that the population of Canada in 2010 will be about 32.3 million.

c) Replace $P(t)$ with 33 and solve for t.

$33 = 29.1e^{0.008t}$

$1.134 \approx e^{0.008t}$

$\ln 1.134 \approx \ln e^{0.008t}$

$\ln 1.134 \approx 0.008t$

$\dfrac{\ln 1.134}{0.008} \approx t$

$16 \approx t$

We predict that the population will reach 33 million about 16 years after 1997, or in 2013.

18. (a) $P(t) = 20.1e^{0.034t}$, where $P(t)$ is in millions and t is the number of years after 1997; (b) about 31.3 million; (c) 2017

19. a) Replace a with 1 and compute $N(1)$.

$N(a) = 2000 + 500 \log a$

$N(1) = 2000 + 500 \log 1$

$N(1) = 2000 + 500 \cdot 0$

$N(1) = 2000$

2000 units were sold after \$1000 was spent.

b) Find $N(8)$.

$N(8) = 2000 + 500 \log 8$

$N(8) \approx 2451.5$

About 2452 units were sold after \$8000 was spent.

c) Using the values we computed in parts (a) and (b) and any others we wish to calculate, we sketch the graph:

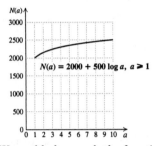

$N(a) = 2000 + 500 \log a, \; a \geq 1$

We could also graph the function using a grapher.

d) Replace $N(a)$ with 5000 and solve for a.

$$5000 = 2000 + 500 \log a$$
$$3000 = 500 \log a$$
$$6 = \log a$$
$$a = 10^6 = 1,000,000$$

$1,000,000$ thousand, or $1,000,000,000$ would have to be spent.

20. a) 68%;

b) 54% ; 40%

c)

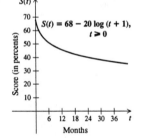

$S(t) = 68 - 20 \log (t + 1),$
$t \geq 0$

Score (in percents)

Months

d) 6.9 months

21. a) We use the growth equation $N(t) = N_0 e^{kt}$, where t is the number of years since 1995. In 1995, at $t = 0$, 17 people were infected. We substitute 17 for N_0:

$$N(t) = 17 e^{kt}.$$

To find the exponential growth rate k, observe that 1 year later 29 people were infected.

$$N(1) = 17 e^{k \cdot 1} \quad \text{Substituting 1 for } t$$
$$29 = 17 e^{k} \quad \text{Substituting 29 for } N(1)$$
$$1.706 \approx e^{k}$$
$$\ln 1.706 \approx \ln e^{k}$$
$$\ln 1.706 \approx k$$
$$0.534 \approx k$$

The exponential function is $N(t) = 17 e^{0.534t}$, where t is the number of years since 1995.

b) In 2001, $t = 2001 - 1995$, or 6. Find $N(6)$.

$$N(6) = 17 e^{0.534(6)}$$
$$= 17 e^{3.204}$$
$$\approx 418.7$$

Approximately 419 people will be infected in 2001.

22. (a) $N(t) = e^{0.363t}$, where t is the number of years after 1967; (b) 329,391

23. We start with the exponential growth equation
$$D(t) = D_0 e^{kt}, \text{ where } t \text{ is the number of}$$
years after 1999.

Substitute $2 D_0$ for $D(t)$ and 0.018 for t and solve for t.

$$2 D_0 = D_0 e^{0.018t}$$
$$2 = e^{0.018t}$$
$$\ln 2 = \ln e^{0.018t}$$
$$\ln 2 = 0.018t$$
$$\frac{\ln 2}{0.018} = t$$
$$39 \approx t$$

The demand will be double that of 1999 about 39 years after 1999, or in 2038.

24. In 2005

25. a) We use the decay equation $S(t) = S_0 e^{-kt}$, where t is the number of years since 1983 and $S(t)$ is in millions. In 1983, at $t = 0$, 205 million records were sold. We substitute 205 for S_0.

$$S(t) = 205 e^{-kt}.$$

To find the exponential decay rate k, observe that 10 years later, in 1993, 1.2 million records were sold.

$$1.2 = 205 e^{-k \cdot 10} \quad \text{Substituting}$$
$$0.00585 \approx e^{10k}$$
$$\ln 0.00585 \approx \ln e^{-10k}$$
$$-5.14 \approx -10k$$
$$0.514 \approx k$$

Then $k \approx 0.514$ and the exponential function is $S(t) = 205 e^{-0.514t}$, where $S(t)$ in millions and t is the number of years since 1983.

b) In 2001, $t = 2001 - 1983$, or 18.
$$S(18) = 205e^{-0.514(18)}$$
$$= 205e^{-9.252}$$
$$\approx 0.019664$$

In 2001, about 0.019664 million, or 19,664 records will be sold.

c) 1 is equivalent to 0.000001 million.
$$0.000001 = 205e^{-0.514t}$$
$$4.89 \times 10^{-9} = e^{-0.514t}$$
$$\ln(4.89 \times 10^{-9}) = \ln e^{-0.514t}$$
$$-19.1 \approx -0.514t$$
$$37.2 \approx t$$

Only one record will be sold in 1983+38, or 2021.

26. (a) $k \approx 0.016$, $C(t) = 80e^{-0.016t}$, where t is the number of years after 1985; (b) 62 lb; (c) 2072

27. We will use the function derived in Example 7:
$$P(t) = P_0 e^{-0.00012t}$$

If the scrolls had lost 22.3% of their carbon-14 from an initial amount P_0, then $77.7\%(P_0)$ is the amount present. To find the age t of the scrolls, we substitute $77.7\%(P_0)$, or $0.777P_0$, for $P(t)$ in the function above and solve for t.
$$0.777P_0 = P_0 e^{-0.00012t}$$
$$0.777 = e^{-0.00012t}$$
$$\ln 0.777 = \ln e^{-0.00012t}$$
$$-0.2523 \approx -0.00012t$$
$$t \approx \frac{-0.2523}{-0.00012} \approx 2103$$

The scrolls are about 2103 years old.

28. About 1654 yr

29. The function $P(t) = P_0 e^{-kt}$, $k > 0$, can be used to model decay. For iodine-131, $k = 9.6\%$, or 0.096. To find the half-life we substitute 0.096 for k and $\frac{1}{2} P_0$ for $P(t)$, and solve for t.
$$\frac{1}{2} P_0 = P_0 e^{-0.096t}, \text{ or } \frac{1}{2} = e^{-0.096t}$$
$$\ln \frac{1}{2} = \ln e^{-0.096t} = -0.096t$$
$$t = \frac{\ln 0.5}{-0.096} \approx \frac{-0.6931}{-0.096} \approx 7.2 \text{ days}$$

30. About 11 yr

31. The function $P(t) = P_0 e^{-kt}$, $k > 0$, can be used to model decay. We substitute $\frac{1}{2} P_0$ for $P(t)$ and 1 for t and solve for the decay rate k.
$$\frac{1}{2} P_0 = P_0 e^{-k \cdot 1}$$
$$\frac{1}{2} = e^{-k}$$
$$\ln \frac{1}{2} = \ln e^{-k}$$
$$-0.693 \approx -k$$
$$0.693 \approx k$$

The decay rate is 0.693, or 69.3% per year.

32. 3.15% per year

33. a) We start with the exponential growth equation
$$V(t) = V_0 e^{kt}, \text{ where } t \text{ is the number of years after 1991.}$$

Substituting 451,000 for V_0, we have
$$V(t) = 451,000 e^{kt}.$$

To find the exponential growth rate k, observe that the card sold for $640,500 in 1996, or 5 years after 1991. We substitute and solve for k.
$$V(5) = 451,000 e^{k \cdot 5}$$
$$640,500 = 451,000 e^{5k}$$
$$1.42 = e^{5k}$$
$$\ln 1.42 = \ln e^{5k}$$
$$\ln 1.42 = 5k$$
$$\frac{\ln 1.42}{5} = k$$
$$0.07 \approx k$$

Thus the exponential growth function is $V(t) = 451,000 e^{0.07t}$, where t is the number of years after 1991.

b) In 2002, $t = 2002 - 1991$, or 11.
$$V(11) = 451,000 e^{0.07(11)} \approx 974,055$$

The card's value in 2002 will be about $974,055.

c) Substitute $902,000 for $V(t)$ and solve for t.
$$902,000 = 451,000 e^{0.07t}$$
$$2 = e^{0.07t}$$
$$\ln 2 = \ln e^{0.07t}$$
$$\ln 2 = 0.07t$$
$$\frac{\ln 2}{0.07} = t$$
$$9.9 \approx t$$

The doubling time is about 9.9 years.

d) Substitute $1,000,000 for $V(t)$ and solve for t.

$$1,000,000 = 451,000\,e^{0.07t}$$

$$2.217 \approx e^{0.07t}$$

$$\ln 2.217 \approx \ln e^{0.07t}$$

$$\ln 2.217 \approx 0.07t$$

$$\frac{\ln 2.217}{0.07} \approx t$$

$$11.4 \approx t$$

The value of the card will be $1,000,000 in 1991 + 12, or 2003.

34. (a) $k \approx 0.16$, $V(t) = 84e^{0.16t}$, where $V(t)$ is in thousands of dollars and t is the number of years after 1947; (b) $1,455,437 thousand, or $1,455,437,000;(c) 4.3 yr; (d) 58.7 yr

35. Motor vehicle efficiency increased from 1990 to 1995. The amount of increase was fairly steady, however, so it does not appear that an exponential function would fit the data.

36. Yes

37. The payment decreases as the time of the loan increases and the amount of decrease gets smaller as the time increases. It appears that an exponential function would fit the data.

38. No

39. a) Enter the data and use the exponential regression feature. We get $f(x) = 1.809071941(2.316985337)^x$, where $f(x)$ is in millions.

b) Since $\ln 2.316985337 \approx 0.84$, we have $e^{0.84} \approx 2.316985337$ and we can write the function as $f(x) = 1.809071941e^{0.84x}$. We see that the exponential growth rate is 0.84, or 84%.

c) $2004 - 1993 = 11$, so we find $f(11)$.

$f(11) \approx 18,690$ so we predict that 18,690 million ink-jet printers will be sold in 2004.

40. (a) $f(x) = 2037.539502(0.9746321868)^x$; (b) 2.57%; (c) $1071.83

41. a) Enter the data. Be sure to enter the number of subscribers in millions. That is, enter 340,123 as 0.340123, enter 1,230,855 as 1.230855, and so on. Then use the exponential regression feature. We get $P(t) = 0.4728252114(1.542506387)^t$. Since $\ln 1.542506387 \approx 0.4334086175$, we can write the function as $P(t) = 0.4728252114e^{0.4334086175}$.

(Answers may vary slightly due to rounding differences.)

b) $P(20) \approx 2749$ million, or 2,749,000,000

42. (a) $P(t) = 0.838265956e^{0.009494879t}$; (b) 8.7 billion

43. a) Enter the data and use the exponential regression feature. We get $f(x) = 647.6297124(0.5602992676)^x$.

b) Since $\ln 0.5602992676 \approx -0.579$, we can write the function as $f(x) = 647.6297124e^{-0.579x}$. We see that the exponential decay rate is 0.579, or 57.9%.

c) $f(2.5) \approx 152$, so we estimate that there are 152 decayed, missing, or filled teeth per 100 patients if the fluoride count of the water is 2.5 ppm.

44. (a) $f(x) = 9047.179795(1.393338213)^x$; (b) 33.17%; (c) about 6,881,000

45.

$$\dfrac{\dfrac{x-5}{x+3}}{\dfrac{x}{x-3} + \dfrac{2}{x+3}}$$

$$= \dfrac{\dfrac{x-5}{x+3}}{\dfrac{x}{x-3} \cdot \dfrac{x+3}{x+3} + \dfrac{2}{x+3} \cdot \dfrac{x-3}{x-3}}$$

Finding the LCD and adding in the denominator

$$= \dfrac{\dfrac{x-5}{x+3}}{\dfrac{x^2 + 3x + 2x - 6}{(x-3)(x+3)}}$$

$$= \dfrac{\dfrac{x-5}{x+3}}{\dfrac{x^2 + 5x - 6}{(x-3)(x+3)}}$$

$$= \dfrac{x-5}{x+3} \cdot \dfrac{(x-3)(x+3)}{x^2 + 5x - 6}$$

Multiplying by the reciprocal of the denominator

$$= \dfrac{(x-5)(x-3)(x+3)}{(x+3)\,(x+6)(x-1)}$$

Factoring $x^2 + 5x - 6$ and multiplying

$$= \dfrac{(x-5)(x-3)(x\!\!\!\!\diagup\!\!\!+\!3)}{(x\!\!\!\!\diagup\!\!\!+\!3)\,(x+6)(x-1)}$$

$$= \dfrac{(x-5)(x-3)}{(x+6)(x-1)}, \text{ or } \dfrac{(x-5)(x-3)}{x^2 + 5x - 6}$$

46. $\dfrac{3ab^2 + 5a^2b}{2b^2 - 4a^2}$

47. $\dfrac{6a^3b^{-7}}{8a^{-5}b^{-10}} = \dfrac{3a^{3-(-5)}b^{-7-(-10)}}{4} = \dfrac{3a^8b^3}{4}$

48. $\dfrac{ab^2 + a^2}{b^2 - a^2b}$

49. ◈

50. ◈

51. ◈

52. ◈

53. a)

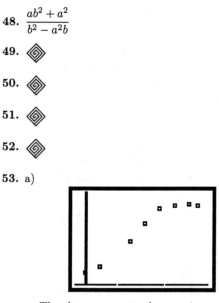

The data appear to be growing exponentially, particularly through 1980.

b) We substitute. First we use the point $(0, 35.0)$.
$$35.0 = ab^0$$
$$35.0 = a$$

Next we use the function $f(x) = 35b^x$ and the point $(50, 90.5)$.
$$90.5 = 35b^{50}$$
$$2.5857 \approx b^{50}$$
$$\log 2.5857 \approx \log b^{50}$$
$$\log 2.5857 \approx 50 \log b$$
$$\frac{\log 2.5857}{50} \approx \log b$$
$$0.0083 \approx \log b$$
$$b \approx 10^{0.0083}$$
$$b \approx 1.0192$$

We have $f(x) = 35.0(1.0192)^x$.

c) $f(90) = 35.0(1.0192)^{90} \approx 194\%$

This estimate does not make sense, since it predicts that more than 100% of U.S. households will have telephones in 2010.

d) $f(x) = \dfrac{102.8706542}{1 + 2.261365043e^{-0.0479171592x}}$

e) $f(90) \approx 99.8\%$

This estimate makes sense.

54. a) $f(x) = \dfrac{19.11252764}{1 + 4.175198683e^{-0.2798470918x}}$;

b) \$18.82 billion

55. Set $S(x) = D(x)$, and solve for x.
$$e^x = 162,755\, e^{-x}$$
$$e^{2x} = 162,755 \qquad \text{Multiplying by } e^x \text{ on both sides}$$
$$\ln\ e^{2x} = \ln\ 162,755$$
$$2x = \ln\ 162,755$$
$$x = \frac{\ln\ 162,755}{2}$$
$$x \approx 6$$

To find the second coordinate of the equilibrium point, find $S(6)$ or $D(6)$. We will find $S(6)$.
$$S(6) = e^6 \approx 403$$

The equilibrium point is $(6, \$403)$.

Chapter 12

Sequences, Series, and the Binomial Theorem

1. $a_n = 5n - 3$

$a_1 = 5 \cdot 1 - 3 = 2$,

$a_2 = 5 \cdot 2 - 3 = 7$,

$a_3 = 5 \cdot 3 - 3 = 12$,

$a_4 = 5 \cdot 4 - 3 = 17$;

$a_{10} = 5 \cdot 10 - 3 = 47$;

$a_{15} = 5 \cdot 15 - 3 = 72$

$u(n) = 5n - 3$

2. 7, 9, 11, 13; 25; 35

$u(n) = 2n + 5$

3. $a_n = \dfrac{n}{n + 2}$

$a_1 = \dfrac{1}{1 + 2} = \dfrac{1}{3}$,

$a_2 = \dfrac{2}{2 + 2} = \dfrac{2}{4} = \dfrac{1}{2}$,

$a_3 = \dfrac{3}{3 + 2} = \dfrac{3}{5}$,

$a_4 = \dfrac{4}{4 + 2} = \dfrac{4}{6} = \dfrac{2}{3}$;

$a_{10} = \dfrac{10}{10 + 2} = \dfrac{10}{12} = \dfrac{5}{6}$;

$a_{15} = \dfrac{15}{15 + 2} = \dfrac{15}{17}$

$u(n) = n/(n + 2)$

4. 2, 5, 10, 17; 101; 226

$u(n) = n^2 + 1$

5. $a_n = n^2 - 2n$

$a_1 = 1^2 - 2 \cdot 1 = -1$,

$a_2 = 2^2 - 2 \cdot 2 = 0$,

$a_3 = 3^2 - 2 \cdot 3 = 3$,

$a_4 = 4^2 - 2 \cdot 4 = 8$;

$a_{10} = 10^2 - 2 \cdot 10 = 80$;

$a_{15} = 15^2 - 2 \cdot 15 = 195$

$u(n) = n^2 - 2n$

6. $0, \dfrac{3}{5}, \dfrac{4}{5}, \dfrac{15}{17}; \dfrac{99}{101}; \dfrac{112}{113}$

$u(n) = (n^2 - 1)/(n^2 + 1)$

7. $a_n = n + \dfrac{1}{n}$

$a_1 = 1 + \dfrac{1}{1} = 2,$

$a_2 = 2 + \dfrac{1}{2} = 2\dfrac{1}{2},$

$a_3 = 3 + \dfrac{1}{3} = 3\dfrac{1}{3},$

$a_4 = 4 + \dfrac{1}{4} = 4\dfrac{1}{4};$

$a_{10} = 10 + \dfrac{1}{10} = 10\dfrac{1}{10};$

$a_{15} = 15 + \dfrac{1}{15} = 15\dfrac{1}{15}$

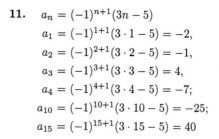

8. $1, -\dfrac{1}{2}, \dfrac{1}{4}, -\dfrac{1}{8}; -\dfrac{1}{512}; \dfrac{1}{16,384}$

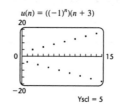

9. $a_n = (-1)^n n^2$

$a_1 = (-1)^1 1^2 = -1,$

$a_2 = (-1)^2 2^2 = 4,$

$a_3 = (-1)^3 3^2 = -9,$

$a_4 = (-1)^4 4^2 = 16;$

$a_{10} = (-1)^{10} 10^2 = 100;$

$a_{15} = (-1)^{15} 15^2 = -225$

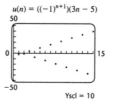

10. $-4, 5, -6, 7; 13; -18$

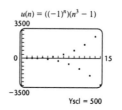

11. $a_n = (-1)^{n+1}(3n - 5)$

$a_1 = (-1)^{1+1}(3 \cdot 1 - 5) = -2,$

$a_2 = (-1)^{2+1}(3 \cdot 2 - 5) = -1,$

$a_3 = (-1)^{3+1}(3 \cdot 3 - 5) = 4,$

$a_4 = (-1)^{4+1}(3 \cdot 4 - 5) = -7;$

$a_{10} = (-1)^{10+1}(3 \cdot 10 - 5) = -25;$

$a_{15} = (-1)^{15+1}(3 \cdot 15 - 5) = 40$

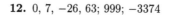

12. $0, 7, -26, 63; 999; -3374$

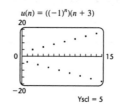

13. $a_n = (3n + 4)(2n - 5)$

$a_9 = (3 \cdot 9 + 4)(2 \cdot 9 - 5) = 31 \cdot 13 = 403$

14. 400

15. $a_n = (-1)^{n-1}(3.4n - 17.3)$

$a_{12} = (-1)^{12-1}[3.4(12) - 17.3] = -23.5$

16. $-37,916,508.16$

17. $a_n = \log 10^n$

$a_{43} = \log 10^{43} = 43$

18. 67

19. $1, 3, 5, 7, 9, \ldots$

These are odd integers, so the general term could be $2n - 1$.

20. 3^n

21. $-2, 6, -18, 54, \ldots$

We can see a pattern if we write the sequence as

$-1 \cdot 2 \cdot 1, 1 \cdot 2 \cdot 3, -1 \cdot 2 \cdot 9, 1 \cdot 2 \cdot 27, \ldots$

The general term could be $(-1)^n 2(3)^{n-1}$.

22. $5n - 7$

23. $\dfrac{1}{2}, \dfrac{2}{3}, \dfrac{3}{4}, \dfrac{4}{5}, \dfrac{5}{6}, \ldots$

These are fractions in which the denominator is 1 greater than the numerator. Also, each numerator is 1 greater than the preceding numerator. The general term could be $\dfrac{n}{n+1}$.

24. $\sqrt{2n - 1}$

25. $\sqrt{3}, 3, 3\sqrt{3}, 9, 9\sqrt{3}, \ldots$

These are powers of $\sqrt{3}$. The general term could be $(\sqrt{3})^n$, or $3^{n/2}$.t

26. $n(n + 1)$

27. $-1, -4, -7, -10, -13, \ldots$

Each term is 3 less than the preceding term. The general term may be $-1 - 3(n - 1)$. After removing parentheses and simplifying, we can express the general term as $-3n + 2$, or $-(3n - 2)$.

28. $\log 10^{n-1}$, or $n - 1$

29. $1, -2, 3, -4, 5, -6, \ldots$

$S_7 = 1 - 2 + 3 - 4 + 5 - 6 + 7 = 4$

30. -8

31. $2, 4, 6, 8, \ldots$

$S_5 = 2 + 4 + 6 + 8 + 10 = 30$

32. $\dfrac{5269}{3600}$

33. $\displaystyle\sum_{k=1}^{5} \dfrac{1}{2k} = \dfrac{1}{2 \cdot 1} + \dfrac{1}{2 \cdot 2} + \dfrac{1}{2 \cdot 3} + \dfrac{1}{2 \cdot 4} + \dfrac{1}{2 \cdot 5}$

$= \dfrac{1}{2} + \dfrac{1}{4} + \dfrac{1}{6} + \dfrac{1}{8} + \dfrac{1}{10}$

$= \dfrac{60}{120} + \dfrac{30}{120} + \dfrac{20}{120} + \dfrac{15}{120} + \dfrac{12}{120}$

$= \dfrac{137}{120}$

34. $1 + \dfrac{1}{3} + \dfrac{1}{5} + \dfrac{1}{7} + \dfrac{1}{9} + \dfrac{1}{11} = \dfrac{6508}{3465}$

35. $\displaystyle\sum_{k=0}^{4} 3^k = 3^0 + 3^1 + 3^2 + 3^3 + 3^4$

$= 1 + 3 + 9 + 27 + 81$

$= 121$

36. $\sqrt{9} + \sqrt{11} + \sqrt{13} + \sqrt{15} \approx 13.7952$

37. $\displaystyle\sum_{k=1}^{8} \dfrac{k}{k+1} = \dfrac{1}{1+1} + \dfrac{2}{2+1} + \dfrac{3}{3+1} + \dfrac{4}{4+1} +$

$\dfrac{5}{5+1} + \dfrac{6}{6+1} + \dfrac{7}{7+1} + \dfrac{8}{8+1}$

$= \dfrac{1}{2} + \dfrac{2}{3} + \dfrac{3}{4} + \dfrac{4}{5} + \dfrac{5}{6} + \dfrac{6}{7} + \dfrac{7}{8} + \dfrac{8}{9}$

$= \dfrac{15,551}{2520}$

38. $-\dfrac{1}{4} + 0 + \dfrac{1}{6} + \dfrac{2}{7} = \dfrac{17}{84}$

39. $\displaystyle\sum_{k=1}^{5} (-1)^k$

$= (-1)^1 + (-1)^2 + (-1)^3 + (-1)^4 + (-1)^5$

$= -1 + 1 - 1 + 1 - 1$

$= -1$

40. $1 - 1 + 1 - 1 + 1 = 1$

41. $\displaystyle\sum_{k=1}^{8} (-1)^{k+1} 2^k = (-1)^2 2^1 + (-1)^3 2^2 + (-1)^4 2^3 +$

$(-1)^5 2^4 + (-1)^6 2^5 + (-1)^7 2^6 +$

$(-1)^8 2^7 + (-1)^9 2^8$

$= 2 - 4 + 8 - 16 + 32 - 64 +$

$128 - 256$

$= -170$

42. $-4^2 + 4^3 - 4^4 + 4^5 - 4^6 + 4^7 - 4^8 = -52,432$

43. $\displaystyle\sum_{k=0}^{5} (k^2 - 2k + 3)$

$= (0^2 - 2 \cdot 0 + 3) + (1^2 - 2 \cdot 1 + 3) +$

$(2^2 - 2 \cdot 2 + 3) + (3^2 - 2 \cdot 3 + 3) +$

$(4^2 - 2 \cdot 4 + 3) + (5^2 - 2 \cdot 5 + 3)$

$= 3 + 2 + 3 + 6 + 11 + 18$

$= 43$

44. $4 + 2 + 2 + 4 + 8 + 14 = 34$

45. $\dfrac{2}{3} + \dfrac{3}{4} + \dfrac{4}{5} + \dfrac{5}{6} + \dfrac{6}{7}$

This is a sum of fractions in which the denominator is one greater than the numerator. Also, each numerator is 1 greater than the preceding numerator. Sigma notation is

$$\sum_{k=1}^{5} \dfrac{k+1}{k+2}.$$

46. $\displaystyle\sum_{k=1}^{5} 3k$

47. $1 + 4 + 9 + 16 + 25 + 36$

This is the sum of the squares of the first six natural numbers. Sigma notation is

$$\sum_{k=1}^{6} k^2.$$

48. $\displaystyle\sum_{k=1}^{5} \frac{1}{k^2}$

49. $4 - 9 + 16 - 25 + \ldots + (-1)^n n^2$

This is a sum of terms of the form $(-1)^k k^2$, beginning with $k = 2$ and continuing through $k = n$. Sigma notation is

$$\sum_{k=2}^{n} (-1)^k k^2.$$

50. $\displaystyle\sum_{k=3}^{n} (-1)^{k+1} k^2$

51. $5 + 10 + 15 + 20 + 25 + \ldots$

This is a sum of multiples of 5, and it is an infinite series. Sigma notation is

$$\sum_{k=1}^{\infty} 5k.$$

52. $\displaystyle\sum_{k=1}^{\infty} 7k$

53. $\dfrac{1}{1 \cdot 2} + \dfrac{1}{2 \cdot 3} + \dfrac{1}{3 \cdot 4} + \dfrac{1}{4 \cdot 5} + \ldots$

This is a sum of fractions in which the numerator is 1 and the denominator is a product of two consecutive integers. The larger integer in each product is the smaller integer in the succeeding product. It is an infinite series. Sigma notation is

$$\sum_{k=1}^{\infty} \frac{1}{k(k+1)}.$$

54. $\displaystyle\sum_{k=1}^{\infty} \frac{1}{k(k+1)^2}$

55. Note that $\log_6 29$ is the power to which 6 is raised to get 29. Then

$$6^{\log_6 29} = 29.$$

56. 43

57. $\log_3 3 = 1$

1 is the power to which you raise 3 to get 3.

58. 0

59. $\log_3 3^7 = 7$

7 is the power to which you raise 3 to get 3^7.

60. 1

61. ◈

62. ◈

63. ◈

64. 1, 3, 13, 63, 313, 1563

65. $a_1 = 0,\ a_{n+1} = a_n^2 + 3$

$a_1 = 0$

$a_2 = 0^2 + 3 = 3$

$a_3 = 3^2 + 3 = 12$

$a_4 = 12^2 + 3 = 147$

$a_5 = 147^2 + 3 = 21{,}612$

$a_6 = 21{,}612^2 + 3 = 467{,}078{,}547$

66. 1, 2, 4, 8, 16, 32, 64, 128, 256, 512, 1024,

2048, 4096, 8192, 16,384, 32,768, 65,536

67. Find each term by multiplying the preceding term by 0.75:

$5200, $3900, $2925, $2193.75, $1645.31,

$1233.98, $925.49, $694.12, $520.59, $390.44

68. $8.20, $8.60, $9.00, $9.40, $9.80, $10.20, $10.60,

$11.00, $11.40, $11.80

69. $a_n = \dfrac{1}{2^n} \log 1000^n$

$a_1 = \dfrac{1}{2^1} \log 1000^1 = \dfrac{1}{2} \log 10^3 = \dfrac{1}{2} \cdot 3 = \dfrac{3}{2}$

$a_2 = \dfrac{1}{2^2} \log 1000^2 = \dfrac{1}{4} \log (10^3)^2 = \dfrac{1}{4} \log 10^6 =$

$\dfrac{1}{4} \cdot 6 = \dfrac{3}{2}$

$a_3 = \dfrac{1}{2^3} \log 1000^3 = \dfrac{1}{8} \log (10^3)^3 = \dfrac{1}{8} \log 10^9 =$

$\dfrac{1}{8} \cdot 9 = \dfrac{9}{8}$

$a_4 = \dfrac{1}{2^4} \log 1000^4 = \dfrac{1}{16} \log (10^3)^4 =$

$\dfrac{1}{16} \log 10^{12} = \dfrac{1}{16} \cdot 12 = \dfrac{3}{4}$

$$a_5 = \frac{1}{2^5} \log \ 1000^5 = \frac{1}{32} \log \ (10^3)^5 =$$

$$\frac{1}{32} \log \ 10^{15} = \frac{1}{32} \cdot 15 = \frac{15}{32}$$

$$S_5 = \frac{3}{2} + \frac{3}{2} + \frac{9}{8} + \frac{3}{4} + \frac{15}{32} = \frac{171}{32}$$

70. $i, \ -1, \ -i, \ 1, \ i; \ i$

71. $\displaystyle\sum_{k=1}^{x} i^k = -1$

Note that $i + i^2 + i^3 = i - 1 - i = -1$. Also $i^4 + i^5 + i^6 + i^7 = 1 + i - 1 - i = 0$, $i^8 + i^9 + i^{10} + i^{11} = 1 + i - 1 - i = 0$, and so on.

Thus, the sum is -1 when $x = 3, \ 7, \ 11, \cdots$, or for $\{x | x = 4n - 1, \text{ where n is a natural number}\}$.

72. 11th term

73. We get the recursion formula $a_2 = 1$, $a_n = a_{n-1} + n - 1$. Enter $u_n = u(n-1) + n - 1$ and use the table, set in ASK mode, to find that $u_{50} = 1225$. Thus, 1225 handshakes will occur if a group of 50 people shake hands with one another.

Exercise Set 12.2

1. $3, \ 8, \ 13, \ 18, \ . . .$

$a_1 = 3$

$d = 5 \quad (8 - 3 = 5, \ 13 - 8 = 5, \ 18 - 13 = 5)$

2. $a_1 = 1.06, \ d = 0.06$

3. $6, \ 2, \ -2, \ -6, \ . . .$

$a_1 = 6$

$d = -4 \quad (2 - 6 = -4, \ -2 - 2 = -4,$
$\qquad\qquad\quad -6 - (-2) = -4)$

4. $a_1 = -9, \ d = 3$

5. $\dfrac{3}{2}, \ \dfrac{9}{4}, \ 3, \ \dfrac{15}{4}, \ . . .$

$a_1 = \dfrac{3}{2}$

$d = \dfrac{3}{4} \quad \left(\dfrac{9}{4} - \dfrac{3}{2} = \dfrac{3}{4}, \ 3 - \dfrac{9}{4} = \dfrac{3}{4}\right)$

6. $a_1 = \dfrac{3}{5}, \ d = -\dfrac{1}{2}$

7. $\$2.12, \ \$2.24, \ \$2.36, \ \$2.48, \ . . .$

$a_1 = \$2.12$

$d = \$0.12 \quad (\$2.24 - \$2.12 = \$0.12, \ \$2.36 - \$2.24 = \$0.12, \ \$2.48 - \$2.36 = \$0.12)$

8. $a_1 = \$214, \ d = -\$3$

9. $3, \ 7, \ 11, \ . . .$

$a_1 = 3, \ d = 4, \text{ and } n = 12$

$a_n = a_1 + (n - 1)d$

$a_{12} = 3 + (12 - 1)4 = 3 + 11 \cdot 4 = 3 + 44 = 47$

10. 0.57

11. $7, \ 4, \ 1, \ . . .$

$a_1 = 7, \ d = -3, \text{ and } n = 17$

$a_n = a_1 + (n - 1)d$

$a_{17} = 7 + (17 - 1)(-3) = 7 + 16(-3) =$
$\qquad 7 - 48 = -41$

12. $-\dfrac{17}{3}$

13. $\$1200, \ \$964.32, \ \$728.64, \ . . .$

$a_1 = \$1200, \ d = \$964.32 - \$1200 = -\$235.68,$
$\qquad \text{and } n = 13$

$a_n = a_1 + (n - 1)d$

$a_{13} = \$1200 + (13 - 1)(-\$235.68) =$
$\qquad \$1200 + 12(-\$235.68) = \$1200 - \$2828.16 =$
$\qquad -\$1628.16$

14. $\$7941.62$

15. $a_1 = 3, \ d = 4$

$a_n = a_1 + (n - 1)d$

Let $a_n = 107$, and solve for n.

$107 = 3 + (n - 1)(4)$

$107 = 3 + 4n - 4$

$107 = 4n - 1$

$108 = 4n$

$27 = n$

The 27th term is 107.

16. 33rd

17. $a_1 = 7, \ d = -3$

$a_n = a_1 + (n - 1)d$

$-296 = 7 + (n - 1)(-3)$

$-296 = 7 - 3n + 3$

$-306 = -3n$

$102 = n$

The 102nd term is -296.

18. 46th

19. $a_n = a_1 + (n-1)d$

$a_{17} = 2 + (17-1)5$ Substituting 17 for n,
                       2 for a_1, and 5 for d

$= 2 + 16 \cdot 5$

$= 2 + 80$

$= 82$

20. -43

21. $a_n = a_1 + (n-1)d$

$33 = a_1 + (8-1)4$ Substituting 33 for a_8,
                  8 for n, and 4 for d

$33 = a_1 + 28$

$5 = a_1$

(Note that this procedure is equivalent to subtracting d from a_8 seven times to get a_1: $33-7(4) = 33-28 = 5$)

22. -54

23. $a_n = a_1 + (n-1)d$

$-76 = 5 + (n-1)(-3)$ Substituting -76 for
                     a_n, 5 for a_1, and -3 for d

$-76 = 5 - 3n + 3$

$-76 = 8 - 3n$

$-84 = -3n$

$28 = n$

24. 39

25. We know that $a_{17} = -40$ and $a_{28} = -73$. We would have to add d eleven times to get from a_{17} to a_{28}. That is,

$-40 + 11d = -73$

$11d = -33$

$d = -3.$

Since $a_{17} = -40$, we subtract d sixteen times to get to a_1.

$a_1 = -40 - 16(-3) = -40 + 48 = 8$

We write the first five terms of the sequence:

$8, 5, 2, -1, -4$

26. $a_1 = \frac{1}{3}$; $d = \frac{1}{2}$; $\frac{1}{3}, \frac{5}{6}, \frac{4}{3}, \frac{11}{6}, \frac{7}{3}$

27. $1 + 5 + 9 + 13 + \ldots$

Note that $a_1 = 1$, $d = 4$, and $n = 20$. Before using the formula for S_n, we find a_{20}:

$a_{20} = 1 + (20-1)4$ Substituting into the formula for a_n

$= 1 + 19 \cdot 4$

$= 77$

Then

$S_{20} = \frac{20}{2}(1+77)$ Using the formula for S_n

$= 10(78)$

$= 780.$

28. -210

29. The sum is $1 + 2 + 3 + \ldots + 299 + 300$. This is the sum of the arithmetic sequence for which $a_1 = 1$, $a_n = 300$, and $n = 300$. We use the formula for S_n.

$S_n = \frac{n}{2}(a_1 + a_n)$

$S_{300} = \frac{300}{2}(1+300) = 150(301) = 45,150$

30. 80,200

31. The sum is $2 + 4 + 6 + \ldots + 98 + 100$. This is the sum of the arithmetic sequence for which $a_1 = 2$, $a_n = 100$, and $n = 50$. We use the formula for S_n.

$S_n = \frac{n}{2}(a_1 + a_n)$

$S_{50} = \frac{50}{2}(2+100) = 25(102) = 2550$

32. 2500

33. The sum is $6 + 12 + 18 + \ldots + 96 + 102$. This is the sum of the arithmetic sequence for which $a_1 = 6$, $a_n = 102$, and $n = 17$. We use the formula for S_n.

$S_n = \frac{n}{2}(a_1 + a_n)$

$S_{17} = \frac{17}{2}(6+102) = \frac{17}{2}(108) = 918$

34. 34,036

35. Before using the formula for S_n, we find a_{20}:

$a_{20} = 2 + (20-1)5$ Substituting into the formula for a_n

$= 2 + 19 \cdot 5 = 97$

Then

$S_{20} = \frac{20}{2}(2+97)$ Using the formula for S_n

$= 10(99) = 990.$

36. -1264

37. *Familiarize.* We want to find the fifteenth term and the sum of an arithmetic sequence with $a_1 = 14$, $d = 2$, and $n = 15$. We will first use the formula for a_n to find a_{15}. This result is the number of marchers in the last row. Then we will use the formula for S_n to find S_{15}. This is the total number of marchers.

Translate. Substituting into the formula for a_n, we have

$a_{15} = 14 + (15 - 1)2$.

Carry out. We first find a_{15}.

$a_{15} = 14 + 14 \cdot 2 = 42$

Then use the formula for S_n to find S_{15}.

$$S_{15} = \frac{15}{2}(14 + 42) = \frac{15}{2}(56) = 420$$

Check. We can do the calculations again. We can also do the entire addition.

$14 + 16 + 18 + \cdots + 42$.

State. There are 42 marchers in the last row, and there are 420 marchers altogether.

38. 3; 210

39. Familiarize. We go from 50 poles in a row, down to six poles in the top row, so there must be 45 rows. We want the sum $50 + 49 + 48 + \ldots + 6$. Thus we want the sum of an arithmetic sequence. We will use the formula $S_n = \frac{n}{2}(a_1 + a_n)$.

Translate. We want to find the sum of the first 45 terms of an arithmetic sequence with $a_1 = 50$ and $a_{45} = 6$.

Carry out. Substituting into the formula for S_n, we have

$$S_{45} = \frac{45}{2}(50 + 6)$$

$$= \frac{45}{2} \cdot 56 = 1260$$

Check. We can do the calculation again, or we can do the entire addition:

$50 + 49 + 48 + \ldots + 6$.

State. There will be 1260 poles in the pile.

40. $49.60

41. Familiarize. We want to find the sum of an arithmetic sequence with $a_1 = \$600$, $d = \$100$, and $n = 20$. We will use the formula for a_n to find a_{20}, and then we will use the formula for S_n to find S_{20}.

Translate. Substituting into the formula for a_n, we have

$$a_{20} = 600 + (20 - 1)(100).$$

Carry out. We first find a_{20}.

$a_{20} = 600 + 19 \cdot 100 = 600 + 1900 = 2500$

Then we use the formula for S_n to find S_{20}.

$$S_{20} = \frac{20}{2}(600 + 2500) = 10(3100) = 31,000$$

Check. We can do the calculation again.

State. They save $31,000 (disregarding interest).

42. $10,230

43. Familiarize. We want to find the sum of an arithmetic sequence with $a_1 = 20$, $d = 2$, and $n = 19$. We will use the formula for a_n to find a_{19}, and then we will use the formula for S_n to find S_{19}.

Translate. Substituting into the formula for a_n, we have

$$a_{19} = 20 + (19 - 1)(2).$$

Carry out. We find a_{19}.

$a_{19} = 20 + 18 \cdot 2 = 56$

Then we use the formula for S_n to find S_{19}.

$$S_{19} = \frac{19}{2}(20 + 56) = 722$$

Check. We can do the calculation again.

State. There are 722 seats.

44. $462,500

45.

$$\log_a P = k \qquad a^k = P$$

The logarithm is the exponent.

The base does not change.

46. $e^a = t$

47. $e^t = 0.1579$

The exponent is the logarithm. The base remains the same.

$e^t = 0.1579$ is equivalent to $t = \log_e 0.1579$, or $t = \ln 0.1579$.

48. $\log_2 64 = 6$

49. ◈

50. ◈

51. $a_1 = 1$, $d = 2$, $n = n$

$a_n = 1 + (n - 1)2 = 1 + 2n - 2 = 2n - 1$

$S_n = \frac{n}{2}[1 + (2n - 1)] = \frac{n}{2} \cdot 2n = n^2$

Thus, the formula $S_n = n^2$ can be used to find the sum of the first n consecutive odd numbers starting with 1.

52. 3, 5, 7

53. $a_1 = \$8760$

$a_2 = \$8760 + (-\$798.23) = \$7961.77$

$a_3 = \$8760 + 2(-\$798.23) = \$7163.54$

$a_4 = \$8760 + 3(-\$798.23) = \$6365.31$

$a_5 = \$8760 + 4(-\$798.23) = \$5567.08$

$a_6 = \$8760 + 5(-\$798.23) = \$4768.85$

$a_7 = \$8760 + 6(-\$798.23) = \$3970.62$

$$a_8 = \$8760 + 7(-\$798.23) = \$3172.39$$
$$a_9 = \$8760 + 8(-\$798.23) = \$2374.16$$
$$a_{10} = \$8760 + 9(-\$798.23) = \$1575.93$$

54. $51,679.65

55. See the answer section in the text.

56. Yes; $a_n = 150 - 0.75(n-1)$, where $n = 1$ corresponds to age 20, $n = 2$ corresponds to age 21, and so on.

57. We graph the data points, where the first coordinate 1 represents 1993, 2 represents 1994, and so on.

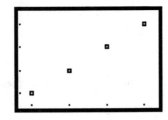

The points appear to lie on a straight line, so this could be the graph of an arithmetic sequence. The general term is

$$a_n = 23 + (n - 1),$$

where $n = 1$ corresponds to 1993, $n = 2$ corresponds to 1994, and so on.

58. No

59. We graph the data points, where the first coordinate 1 represents 1991, 2 represents 1992, and so on.

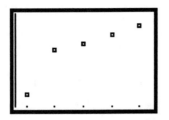

The points do not lie on a straight line, so this is not the graph of an arithmetic sequence.

60. (a) $a_t = \$5200 - \$512.50t$; (b) $5200, $4687.50, $4175, $3662.50, $3150, $1612.50, $1100; (c) $a_0 = \$5200$, $a_t = a_{t-1} - \$512.50$

Exercise Set 12.3

1. 5, 10, 20, 40, ...
$$\frac{10}{5} = 2, \quad \frac{20}{10} = 2, \quad \frac{40}{20} = 2$$
$$r = 2$$

2. 3

3. 5, −5, 5, −5, ...
$$\frac{-5}{5} = -1, \quad \frac{5}{-5} = -1, \quad \frac{-5}{5} = -1$$
$$r = -1$$

4. 0.1

5. $\dfrac{1}{2}, -\dfrac{1}{4}, \dfrac{1}{8}, -\dfrac{1}{16}, \ldots$
$$\frac{-\frac{1}{4}}{\frac{1}{2}} = -\frac{1}{4} \cdot \frac{2}{1} = -\frac{2}{4} = -\frac{1}{2}$$
$$\frac{\frac{1}{8}}{-\frac{1}{4}} = \frac{1}{8} \cdot \left(-\frac{4}{1}\right) = -\frac{4}{8} = -\frac{1}{2}$$
$$\frac{-\frac{1}{16}}{\frac{1}{8}} = -\frac{1}{16} \cdot \frac{8}{1} = -\frac{8}{16} = -\frac{1}{2}$$
$$r = -\frac{1}{2}$$

6. −2

7. 75, 15, 3, $\dfrac{3}{5}$, ...
$$\frac{15}{75} = \frac{1}{5}, \quad \frac{3}{15} = \frac{1}{5}, \quad \frac{\frac{3}{5}}{3} = \frac{3}{5} \cdot \frac{1}{3} = \frac{1}{5}$$
$$r = \frac{1}{5}$$

8. $-\dfrac{1}{3}$

9. $\dfrac{1}{m}, \dfrac{3}{m^2}, \dfrac{9}{m^3}, \dfrac{27}{m^4}, \ldots$
$$\frac{\frac{3}{m^2}}{\frac{1}{m}} = \frac{3}{m^2} \cdot \frac{m}{1} = \frac{3}{m}$$
$$\frac{\frac{9}{m^3}}{\frac{3}{m^2}} = \frac{9}{m^3} \cdot \frac{m^2}{3} = \frac{3}{m}$$
$$\frac{\frac{27}{m^4}}{\frac{9}{m^3}} = \frac{27}{m^4} \cdot \frac{m^3}{9} = \frac{3}{m}$$
$$r = \frac{3}{m}$$

10. $\dfrac{m}{5}$

11. 5, 10, 20, . . .

$a_1 = 5$, $n = 7$, and $r = \dfrac{10}{5} = 2$

We use the formula $a_n = a_1 r^{n-1}$.

$a_7 = 5 \cdot 2^{7-1} = 5 \cdot 2^6 = 5 \cdot 64 = 320$

12. 131,072

13. 3, $3\sqrt{2}$, 6, . . .

$a_1 = 3$, $n = 9$, and $r = \dfrac{3\sqrt{2}}{3} = \sqrt{2}$

$a_n = a_1 r^{n-1}$

$a_9 = 3(\sqrt{2})^{9-1} = 3(\sqrt{2})^8 = 3 \cdot 16 = 48$

14. $108\sqrt{3}$

15. $-\dfrac{8}{243}$, $\dfrac{8}{81}$, $-\dfrac{8}{27}$, . . .

$a_1 = -\dfrac{8}{243}$, $n = 10$, and $r = \dfrac{\frac{8}{81}}{-\frac{8}{243}} =$

$\dfrac{8}{81}\left(-\dfrac{243}{8}\right) = -3$

$a_n = a_1 r^{n-1}$

$a_{10} = -\dfrac{8}{243}(-3)^{10-1} = -\dfrac{8}{243}(-3)^9 =$

$-\dfrac{8}{243}(-19,683) = 648$

16. 2,734,375

17. $1000, $1080, $1166.40, . . .

$a_1 = \$1000$, $n = 12$, and $r = \dfrac{\$1080}{\$1000} = 1.08$

$a_n = a_1 r^{n-1}$

$a_{12} = \$1000(1.08)^{12-1} \approx \$1000(2.331638997) \approx$
$\$2331.64$

18. $1967.15

19. 1, 3, 9, . . .

$a_1 = 1$ and $r = \dfrac{3}{1}$, or 3

$a_n = a_1 r^{n-1}$

$a_n = 1(3)^{n-1} = 3^{n-1}$

20. 5^{3-n}

21. 1, -1, 1, -1, . . .

$a_1 = 1$ and $r = \dfrac{-1}{1} = -1$

$a_n = a_1 r^{n-1}$

$a_n = 1(-1)^{n-1} = (-1)^{n-1}$

22. 2^n

23. $\dfrac{1}{x}$, $\dfrac{1}{x^2}$, $\dfrac{1}{x^2}$, . . .

$a_1 = \dfrac{1}{x}$ and $r = \dfrac{\frac{1}{x^2}}{\frac{1}{x}} = \dfrac{1}{x^2} \cdot \dfrac{x}{1} = \dfrac{1}{x}$

$a_n = a_1 r^{n-1}$

$a_n = \dfrac{1}{x}\left(\dfrac{1}{x}\right)^{n-1} = \dfrac{1}{x} \cdot \dfrac{1}{x^{n-1}} = \dfrac{1}{x^{1+n-1}} = \dfrac{1}{x^n}$

24. $a_n = 5\left(\dfrac{m}{2}\right)^{n-1}$

25. $7 + 14 + 28 + . . .$

$a_1 = 7$, $n = 7$, and $r = \dfrac{14}{7} = 2$

$S_n = \dfrac{a_1(1 - r^n)}{1 - r}$

$S_7 = \dfrac{7(1 - 2^7)}{1 - 2} = \dfrac{7(1 - 128)}{-1} = \dfrac{7(-127)}{-1} = 889$

26. 10.5

27. $\dfrac{1}{18} - \dfrac{1}{6} + \dfrac{1}{2} - . . .$

$a_1 = \dfrac{1}{18}$, $n = 7$, and $r = \dfrac{-\frac{1}{6}}{\frac{1}{18}} = -\dfrac{1}{6} \cdot \dfrac{18}{1} = -3$

$S_n = \dfrac{a_1(1 - r^n)}{1 - r}$

$S_7 = \dfrac{\frac{1}{18}\left[1 - (-3)^7\right]}{1 - (-3)} = \dfrac{\frac{1}{18}(1 + 2187)}{4} = \dfrac{\frac{1}{18}(2188)}{4} =$

$\dfrac{1}{18}(2188)\left(\dfrac{1}{4}\right) = \dfrac{547}{18}$

28. 6.6666

29. $1 + x + x^2 + x^3 + . . .$

$a_1 = 1$, $n = 8$, and $r = \dfrac{x}{1}$, or x

$S_n = \dfrac{a_1(1 - r^n)}{1 - r}$

$S_8 = \dfrac{1(x - x^8)}{1 - x} = \dfrac{(1 + x^4)(1 - x^4)}{1 - x} =$

$\dfrac{(1 + x^4)(1 + x^2)(1 - x^2)}{1 - x} =$

$\dfrac{(1 + x^4)(1 + x^2)(1 + x)(1 - x)}{1 - x} =$

$(1 + x^4)(1 + x^2)(1 + x)$

30. $\dfrac{1 - x^{20}}{1 - x^2}$

31. $200, $200(1.06), $200(1.06)^2, \ldots$

$$a_1 = \$200, \ n = 16, \ \text{and} \ r = \frac{\$200(1.06)}{\$200} = 1.06$$

$$S_n = \frac{a_1(1 - r^n)}{1 - r}$$

$$S_{16} = \frac{\$200[1 - (1.06)^{16}]}{1 - 1.06} \approx$$

$$\frac{\$200(1 - 2.540351685)}{-0.06} \approx \$5134.51$$

32. $60,893.30

33. $9 + 3 + 1 + \ldots$

$\left|r\right| = \left|\dfrac{3}{9}\right| = \left|\dfrac{1}{3}\right| = \dfrac{1}{3}$, and since $|r| < 1$, the series does have a sum.

$$S_\infty = \frac{a_1}{1 - r} = \frac{9}{1 - \dfrac{1}{3}} = \frac{9}{\dfrac{2}{3}} = 9 \cdot \frac{3}{2} = \frac{27}{2}$$

34. 16

35. $7 + 3 + \dfrac{9}{7} + \ldots$

$\left|r\right| = \left|\dfrac{3}{7}\right| = \dfrac{3}{7}$, and since $|r| < 1$, the series does have a sum.

$$S_\infty = \frac{a_1}{1 - r} = \frac{7}{1 - \dfrac{3}{7}} = \frac{7}{\dfrac{4}{7}} = 7 \cdot \frac{7}{4} = \frac{49}{4}$$

36. 48

37. $3 + 15 + 75 + \ldots$

$\left|r\right| = \left|\dfrac{15}{3}\right| = |5| = 5$, and since $|r| \not< 1$ the series does not have a sum.

38. No

39. $4 - 6 + 9 - \dfrac{27}{2} + \ldots$

$\left|r\right| = \left|\dfrac{-6}{4}\right| = \left|-\dfrac{3}{2}\right| = \dfrac{3}{2}$, and since $|r| \not< 1$ the series does not have a sum.

40. -4

41. $0.43 + 0.0043 + 0.000043 + \ldots$

$\left|r\right| = \left|\dfrac{0.0043}{0.43}\right| = |0.01| = 0.01$, and since $|r| < 1$, the series does have a sum.

$$S_\infty = \frac{a_1}{1 - r} = \frac{0.43}{1 - 0.01} = \frac{0.43}{0.99} = \frac{43}{99}$$

42. $\dfrac{37}{99}$

43. $\$500(1.02)^{-1} + \$500(1.02)^{-2} + \$500(1.02)^{-3} + \ldots$

$\left|r\right| = \left|\dfrac{\$500(1.02)^{-2}}{\$500(1.02)^{-1}}\right| = |(1.02)^{-1}| = (1.02)^{-1}$, or

$\dfrac{1}{1.02}$, and since $|r| < 1$, the series does have a sum.

$$S_\infty = \frac{a_1}{1 - r} = \frac{\$500(1.02)^{-1}}{1 - \left(\dfrac{1}{1.02}\right)} = \frac{\dfrac{\$500}{1.02}}{\dfrac{0.02}{1.02}} =$$

$$\frac{\$500}{1.02} \cdot \frac{1.02}{0.02} = \$25,000$$

44. $12,500

45. $0.7777\ldots = 0.7 + 0.07 + 0.007 + 0.0007 + \ldots$

This is an infinite geometric series with $a_1 = 0.7$.

$\left|r\right| = \left|\dfrac{0.07}{0.7}\right| = |0.1| = 0.1 < 1$, so the series has a sum.

$$S_\infty = \frac{a_1}{1 - r} = \frac{0.7}{1 - 0.1} = \frac{0.7}{0.9} = \frac{7}{9}$$

Fractional notation for $0.7777\ldots$ is $\dfrac{7}{9}$.

46. $\dfrac{2}{9}$

47. $8.3838\ldots = 8.3 + 0.083 + 0.00083 + \ldots$

This is an infinite geometric series with $a_1 = 8.3$.

$\left|r\right| = \left|\dfrac{0.083}{8.3}\right| = |0.01| = 0.01 < 1$, so the series has a sum.

$$S_\infty = \frac{a_1}{1 - r} = \frac{8.3}{1 - 0.01} = \frac{8.3}{0.99} = \frac{830}{99}$$

Fractional notation for $8.3838\ldots$ is $\dfrac{830}{99}$.

48. $\dfrac{740}{99}$

49. $0.15151515\ldots = 0.15 + 0.0015 + 0.000015 + \ldots$

This is an infinite geometric series with $a_1 = 0.15$.

$\left|r\right| = \left|\dfrac{0.0015}{0.15}\right| = |0.01| = 0.01 < 1$, so the series has a sum.

$$S_\infty = \frac{a_1}{1 - r} = \frac{0.15}{1 - 0.01} = \frac{0.15}{0.99} = \frac{15}{99} = \frac{5}{33}$$

Fractional notation for $0.15151515\ldots$ is $\dfrac{5}{33}$.

50. $\dfrac{4}{33}$

51. Familiarize. The rebound distances form a geometric sequence:

$$\frac{1}{4} \times 20, \quad \left(\frac{1}{4}\right)^2 \times 20, \quad \left(\frac{1}{4}\right)^3 \times 20, \ldots,$$

or $5, \quad \frac{1}{4} \times 5, \quad \left(\frac{1}{4}\right)^2 \times 5, \ldots$

The height of the 6th rebound is the 6th term of the sequence.

Translate. We will use the formula $a_n = a_1 r^{n-1}$, with $a_1 = 5$, $r = \frac{1}{4}$, and $n = 6$:

$$a_6 = 5\left(\frac{1}{4}\right)^{6-1}$$

Carry out. We calculate to obtain $a_6 = \frac{5}{1024}$.

Check. We can do the calculation again.

State. It rebounds $\frac{5}{1024}$ ft the 6th time.

52. $6\frac{2}{3}$ ft

53. Familiarize. In one year, the population will be $100,000 + 0.03(100,000)$, or $(1.03)100,000$. In two years, the population will be $(1.03)100,000 + 0.03(1.03)100,000$, or $(1.03)^2 100,000$. Thus the populations form a geometric sequence:

$100,000, \quad (1.03)100,000, \quad (1.03)^2 100,000, \ldots$

The population in 15 years will be the 16th term of the sequence.

Translate. We will use the formula $a_n = a_1 r^{n-1}$ with $a_1 = 100,000$, $r = 1.03$, and $n = 16$:

$$a_{16} = 100,000(1.03)^{16-1}$$

Carry out. We calculate to obtain $a_{16} \approx 155,797$.

Check. We can do the calculation again.

State. In 15 years the population will be about 155,797.

54. About 24 years

55. Familiarize. The amounts owed at the beginning of successive years form a geometric sequence:

$\$15,000, \quad (1.085)\$15,000, \quad (1.085)^2\$15,000,$
$(1.085)^3\$15,000, \ldots$

The amount to be repaid at the end of 13 years is the amount owed at the beginning of the 14th year.

Translate. We use the formula $a_n = a_1 r^{n-1}$ with $a_1 = 15,000$, $r = 1.085$, and $n = 14$:

$$a_{14} = 15,000(1.085)^{14-1}$$

Carry out. We calculate to obtain $a_{14} \approx 43,318.94$.

Check. We can do the calculation again.

State. At the end of 13 years, $\$43,318.94$ will be repaid.

56. 2710

57. We have a geometric sequence

$5000, \ 5000(0.96), \ 5000(0.96)^2, \ldots$

where the general term $5000(0.96)^n$ represents the number of fruit flies remaining alive after n minutes. We find the value of n for which the general term is 1800.

$$1800 = 5000(0.96)^n$$
$$0.36 = (0.96)^n$$
$$\log 0.36 = \log(0.96)^n$$
$$\log 0.36 = n \log 0.96$$
$$\frac{\log 0.36}{\log 0.96} = n$$
$$25 \approx n$$

It will take about 25 minutes for only 1800 fruit flies to remain alive.

58. $\$213,609.57$

59. Familiarize. The lengths of the falls form a geometric sequence:

$$556, \quad \left(\frac{3}{4}\right)556, \quad \left(\frac{3}{4}\right)^2 556, \quad \left(\frac{3}{4}\right)^3 556, \ldots$$

The total length of the first 6 falls is the sum of the first six terms of this sequence. The heights of the rebounds also form a geometric sequence:

$$\left(\frac{3}{4}\right)556, \quad \left(\frac{3}{4}\right)^2 556, \quad \left(\frac{3}{4}\right)^3 556, \ldots, \quad \text{or}$$

$$417, \quad \left(\frac{3}{4}\right)417, \quad \left(\frac{3}{4}\right)^2 417, \ldots$$

When the ball hits the ground for the 6th time, it will have rebounded 5 times. Thus the total length of the rebounds is the sum of the first five terms of this sequence.

Translate. We use the formula $S_n = \dfrac{a_1(1 - r^n)}{1 - r}$ twice, once with $a_1 = 556$, $r = \frac{3}{4}$, and $n = 6$ and a second time with $a_1 = 417$, $r = \frac{3}{4}$, and $n = 5$.

$D = $ Length of falls + length of rebounds

$$= \frac{556\left[1 - \left(\frac{3}{4}\right)^6\right]}{1 - \frac{3}{4}} + \frac{417\left[1 - \left(\frac{3}{4}\right)^5\right]}{1 - \frac{3}{4}}.$$

Carry out. We use a calculator to obtain $D \approx 3100.35$.

Check. We can do the calculations again.

State. The ball will have traveled about 3100.35 ft.

60. 3892 ft

61. *Familiarize*. The heights of the stack form a geometric sequence:

$0.02, 0.02(2), 0.02(2^2), \ldots$

The height of the stack after it is doubled 10 times is given by the 11th term of this sequence.

Translate. We have a geometric sequence with $a_1 = 0.02$, $r = 2$, and $n = 11$. We use the formula

$$a_n = a_1 r^{n-1}.$$

Carry out. We substitute and calculate.

$$a_{11} = 0.02(2^{11-1})$$

$$a_{11} = 0.02(1024) = 20.48$$

Check. We can do the calculation again.

State. The final stack will be 20.48 in. high.

62. $2,684,354.55

63. The points lie on a straight line, so this is the graph of an arithmetic sequence.

64. Geometric

65. The points lie on the graph of an exponential function, so this is the graph of a geometric series.

66. Arithmetic

67. The points lie on the graph of an exponential function, so this is the graph of a geometric series.

68. Arithmetic

69. $5x - 2y = -3, \quad (1)$

$ 2x + 5y = -24 \quad (2)$

Multiply Eq. (1) by 5 and Eq. (2) by 2 and add.

$$\begin{aligned} 25x - 10y &= -15 \\ 4x + 10y &= -48 \\ \hline 29x &= -63 \end{aligned}$$

$$x = -\frac{63}{29}$$

Substitute $-\dfrac{63}{29}$ for x in the second equation and solve for y.

$$2\left(-\frac{63}{29}\right) + 5y = -24$$

$$-\frac{126}{29} + 5y = -24$$

$$5y = -\frac{570}{29}$$

$$y = -\frac{114}{29}$$

The solution is $\left(-\dfrac{63}{29}, -\dfrac{114}{29}\right)$.

70. $(-1, 2, 3)$

71.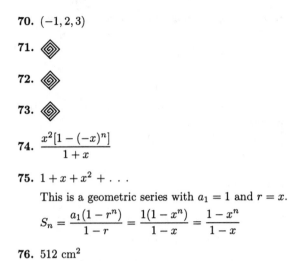

72.

73.

74. $\dfrac{x^2[1 - (-x)^n]}{1 + x}$

75. $1 + x + x^2 + \ldots$

This is a geometric series with $a_1 = 1$ and $r = x$.

$$S_n = \frac{a_1(1 - r^n)}{1 - r} = \frac{1(1 - x^n)}{1 - x} = \frac{1 - x^n}{1 - x}$$

76. 512 cm^2

Exercise Set 12.4

1. $8! = 8 \cdot 7 \cdot 6 \cdot 5 \cdot 4 \cdot 3 \cdot 2 \cdot 1 = 40,320$

2. $362,880$

3. $10! = 10 \cdot 9 \cdot 8 \cdot 7 \cdot 6 \cdot 5 \cdot 4 \cdot 3 \cdot 2 \cdot 1 = 3,628,800$

4. $39,916,800$

5. $\dfrac{7!}{4!} = \dfrac{7 \cdot 6 \cdot 5 \cdot 4!}{4!} = 7 \cdot 6 \cdot 5 = 210$

6. 56

7. $\dfrac{10!}{7!} = \dfrac{10 \cdot 9 \cdot 8 \cdot 7!}{7!} = 10 \cdot 9 \cdot 8 = 720$

8. 3024

9. $\dbinom{8}{2} = \dfrac{8!}{(8-2)!2!} = \dfrac{8!}{6!2!} = \dfrac{8 \cdot 7 \cdot 6!}{6! \cdot 2 \cdot 1} = \dfrac{8 \cdot 7}{2} = 4 \cdot 7 = 28$

10. 35

11. $\dbinom{10}{6} = \dfrac{10!}{(10-6)!6!} = \dfrac{10!}{4!6!} = \dfrac{10 \cdot 9 \cdot 8 \cdot 7 \cdot 6!}{4 \cdot 3 \cdot 2 \cdot 6!} =$

$\dfrac{10 \cdot 9 \cdot 8 \cdot 7}{4 \cdot 3 \cdot 2} = 10 \cdot 3 \cdot 7 = 210$

12. 126

13. $\dbinom{20}{18} = \dfrac{20!}{(20-18)!18!} = \dfrac{20!}{2!18!} = \dfrac{20 \cdot 19 \cdot 18!}{2 \cdot 1 \cdot 18!} =$

$\dfrac{20 \cdot 19}{2} = 10 \cdot 19 = 190$

14. 4060

15. $\dbinom{35}{2} = \dfrac{35!}{(35-2)!2!} = \dfrac{35!}{33!2!} = \dfrac{35 \cdot 34 \cdot 33!}{33! \cdot 2 \cdot 1} =$

$\dfrac{35 \cdot 34}{2} = 35 \cdot 17 = 595$

16. 780

17. Expand $(m+n)^5$.

Form 1: The expansion of $(m+n)^5$ has $5+1$, or 6 terms. The sum of the exponents in each term is 5. The exponents of m start with 5 and decrease to 0. The last term has no factor of m. The first term has no factor of n. The exponents of n start in the second term with 1 and increase to 5. We get the coefficients from the 6th row of Pascal's triangle.

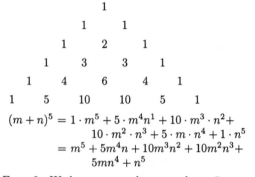

$(m+n)^5 = 1 \cdot m^5 + 5 \cdot m^4 n^1 + 10 \cdot m^3 \cdot n^2 +$
$\qquad 10 \cdot m^2 \cdot n^3 + 5 \cdot m \cdot n^4 + 1 \cdot n^5$
$\qquad = m^5 + 5m^4 n + 10m^3 n^2 + 10m^2 n^3 +$
$\qquad\qquad 5mn^4 + n^5$

Form 2: We have $a = m$, $b = n$, and $n = 5$.

$(m+n)^5 = \dbinom{5}{0} m^5 + \dbinom{5}{1} m^4 n + \dbinom{5}{2} m^3 n^2 +$
$\qquad \dbinom{5}{3} m^2 n^3 + \dbinom{5}{4} mn^4 + \dbinom{5}{5} n^5$
$\qquad = \dfrac{5!}{5!0!} m^5 + \dfrac{5!}{4!1!} m^4 n + \dfrac{5!}{3!2!} m^3 n^2 +$
$\qquad \dfrac{5!}{2!3!} m^2 n^3 + \dfrac{5!}{1!4!} mn^4 + \dfrac{5!}{0!5!} m^5$
$\qquad = m^5 + 5m^4 n + 10m^3 n^2 + 10m^2 n^3 +$
$\qquad\qquad 5mn^4 + n^5$

18. $a^4 - 4a^3 b + 6a^2 b^2 - 4ab^3 + b^4$

19. Expand $(x-y)^6$.

Form 1: The expansion of $(x-y)^6$ has $6+1$, or 7 terms. The sum of the exponents in each term is 6. The exponents of x start with 6 and decrease to 0. The last term has no factor of x. The first term has no factor of $-y$. The exponents of $-y$ start in the second term with 1 and increase to 6. We get the coefficients from the 7th row of Pascal's triangle.

$$
\begin{array}{ccccccccccccc}
 & & & & & & 1 & & & & & & \\
 & & & & & 1 & & 1 & & & & & \\
 & & & & 1 & & 2 & & 1 & & & & \\
 & & & 1 & & 3 & & 3 & & 1 & & & \\
 & & 1 & & 4 & & 6 & & 4 & & 1 & & \\
 & 1 & & 5 & & 10 & & 10 & & 5 & & 1 & \\
1 & & 6 & & 15 & & 20 & & 15 & & 6 & & 1
\end{array}
$$

$(x-y)^6 = 1 \cdot x^6 + 6 \cdot x^5 \cdot (-y) + 15 \cdot x^4 \cdot (-y)^2 +$
$\qquad 20 \cdot x^3 \cdot (-y)^3 + 15 \cdot x^2 \cdot (-y)^4 +$
$\qquad 6 \cdot x \cdot (-y)^5 + 1 \cdot (-y)^6$
$\qquad = x^6 - 6x^5 y + 15x^4 y^2 - 20x^3 y^3 +$
$\qquad\qquad 15x^2 y^4 - 6xy^5 + y^6$

Form 2: We have $a = x$, $b = -y$, and $n = 6$.

$(x-y)^6 = \dbinom{6}{0} x^6 + \dbinom{6}{1} x^5 (-y) + \dbinom{6}{2} x^4 (-y)^2 +$
$\qquad \dbinom{6}{3} x^3 (-y)^3 + \dbinom{6}{4} x^2 (-y)^4 +$
$\qquad \dbinom{6}{5} x(-y)^5 + \dbinom{6}{6} (-y)^6$
$\qquad = \dfrac{6!}{6!0!} x^6 + \dfrac{6!}{5!1!} x^5 (-y) + \dfrac{6!}{4!2!} x^4 y^2 +$
$\qquad \dfrac{6!}{3!3!} x^3 (-y^3) + \dfrac{6!}{2!4!} x^2 y^4 + \dfrac{6!}{1!5!} x(-y^5) +$
$\qquad \dfrac{6!}{0!6!} y^6$
$\qquad = x^6 - 6x^5 y + 15x^4 y^2 - 20x^3 y^3 +$
$\qquad\qquad 15x^2 y^4 - 6xy^5 + y^6$

20. $p^7 + 7p^6 q + 21p^5 q^2 + 35p^4 q^3 + 35p^3 q^4 + 21p^2 q^5 + 7pq^6 + q^7$

21. Expand $(x^2 - 3y)^5$.

We have $a = x^2$, $b = -3y$, and $n = 5$.

Form 1: We get the coefficients from the 6th row of Pascal's triangle. From Exercise 17 we know that the coefficients are

$\qquad 1 \quad 5 \quad 10 \quad 10 \quad 5 \quad 1.$

$(x^2 - 3y)^5 = 1 \cdot (x^2)^5 + 5 \cdot (x^2)^4 \cdot (-3y) +$
$\qquad 10 \cdot (x^2)^3 \cdot (-3y)^2 + 10 \cdot (x^2)^2 \cdot (-3y)^3 +$
$\qquad 5 \cdot (x^2) \cdot (-3y)^4 + 1 \cdot (-3y)^5$
$\qquad = x^{10} - 15x^8 y + 90x^6 y^2 - 270x^4 y^3 +$
$\qquad\qquad 405x^2 y^4 - 243y^5$

Form 2:

$$(x^2+3y)^5 = \binom{5}{0}(x^2)^5 + \binom{5}{1}(x^2)^4(-3y)+$$

$$\binom{5}{2}(x^2)^3(-3y)^2+\binom{5}{3}(x^2)^2(-3y)^3+$$

$$\binom{5}{4}x^2(-3y)^4 + \binom{5}{5}(-3y)^5$$

$$= \frac{5!}{5!0!}x^{10} + \frac{5!}{4!1!}x^8(-3y) + \frac{5!}{3!2!}x^6(9y^2)+$$

$$\frac{5!}{2!3!}x^4(-27y^3) + \frac{5!}{1!4!}x^2(81y^4)+$$

$$\frac{5!}{0!5!}(-243y^5)$$

$$= x^{10} - 15x^8y + 90x^6y^2 - 270x^4y^3+$$

$$405x^2y^4 - 243y^5$$

22. $2187c^7 - 5103c^6d + 5103c^5d^2 - 2835c^4d^3 + 945c^3d^4 - 189c^2d^5 + 21cd^6 - d^7$

23. Expand $(3c - d)^6$.

We have $a = 3c$, $b = -d$, and $n = 6$.

Form 1: We get the coefficients from the 7th row of Pascal's triangle. From Exercise 19 we know that the coefficients are

$$1 \quad 6 \quad 15 \quad 20 \quad 15 \quad 6 \quad 1.$$

$$(3c - d)^6 = 1 \cdot (3c)^6 + 6 \cdot (3c)^5 \cdot (-d)+$$

$$15 \cdot (3c)^4 \cdot (-d)^2 + 20 \cdot (3c)^3 \cdot (-d)^3+$$

$$15 \cdot (3c)^2 \cdot (-d)^4 + 6 \cdot (3c) \cdot (-d)^5+$$

$$1 \cdot (-d)^6$$

$$= 3^6c^6 - 6 \cdot 3^5c^5d + 15 \cdot 3^4c^4d^2-$$

$$20 \cdot 3^3c^3d^3 + 15 \cdot 3^2c^2d^4 - 6 \cdot 3cd^5 + d^6$$

$$= 729c^6 - 6 \cdot 243c^5d + 15 \cdot 81c^4d^2-$$

$$20 \cdot 27c^3d^3 + 15 \cdot 9c^2d^4 - 6 \cdot 3cd^5 + d^6$$

$$= 729c^6 - 1458c^5d + 1215c^4d^2 - 540c^3d^3+$$

$$135c^2d^4 - 18cd^5 + d^6$$

Form 2:

$$(3c - d)^6 = \binom{6}{0}(3c)^6 + \binom{6}{1}(3c)^5(-d)+$$

$$\binom{6}{2}(3c)^4(-d)^2+\binom{6}{3}(3c)^3(-d)^3+$$

$$\binom{6}{4}(3c)^2(-d)^4 + \binom{6}{5}(3c)(-d)^5+$$

$$\binom{6}{6}(-d)^6$$

$$= \frac{6!}{6!0!}(729c^6) + \frac{6!}{5!1!}(243c^5)(-d)+$$

$$\frac{6!}{4!2!}(81c^4)(d^2) + \frac{6!}{3!3!}(27c^3)(-d^3)+$$

$$\frac{6!}{2!4!}(9c^2)(d^4) + \frac{6!}{1!5!}(3c)(-d^5)+$$

$$\frac{6!}{0!6!}d^6$$

$$= 729c^6 - 1458c^5d + 1215c^4d^2 - 540c^3d^3+$$

$$135c^2d^4 - 18cd^5 + d^6$$

24. $t^{-12} + 12t^{-10} + 60t^{-8} + 160t^{-6} + 240t^{-4} + 192t^{-2} + 64$

25. Expand $(x - y)^3$.

We have $a = x$, $b = -y$, and $n = 3$.

Form 1: We get the coefficients from the 4th row of Pascal's triangle.

$$1$$
$$1 \quad 1$$
$$1 \quad 2 \quad 1$$
$$1 \quad 3 \quad 3 \quad 1$$

$$(x - y)^3$$

$$= 1 \cdot x^3 + 3x^2(-y) + 3x(-y)^2 + 1 \cdot (-y)^3$$

$$= x^3 - 3x^2y + 3xy^2 - y^3$$

Form 2:

$$(x - y)^3$$

$$= \binom{3}{0}x^3 + \binom{3}{1}x^2(-y) + \binom{3}{2}x(-y)^2+$$

$$\binom{3}{3}(-y)^3$$

$$= \frac{3!}{3!0!}x^3 + \frac{3!}{2!1!}x^2(-y) + \frac{3!}{1!2!}xy^2+$$

$$\frac{3!}{0!3!}(-y^3)$$

$$= x^3 - 3x^2y + 3xy^2 - y^3$$

26. $x^5 - 5x^4y + 10x^3y^2 - 10x^2y^3 + 5xy^4 - y^5$

27. Expand $\left(x + \dfrac{2}{y}\right)^9$.

We have $a = x$, $b = \dfrac{2}{y}$, and $n = 9$.

Form 1: We get the coefficients from the 10th row of Pascal's triangle.

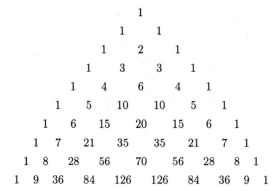

$$\left(x+\frac{2}{y}\right)^9 = 1\cdot x^9 + 9x^8\left(\frac{2}{y}\right) + 36x^7\left(\frac{2}{y}\right)^2 +$$
$$84x^6\left(\frac{2}{y}\right)^3 + 126x^5\left(\frac{2}{y}\right)^4 +$$
$$126x^4\left(\frac{2}{y}\right)^5 + 84x^3\left(\frac{2}{y}\right)^6 +$$
$$36x^2\left(\frac{2}{y}\right)^7 + 9x\left(\frac{2}{y}\right)^8 + 1\cdot\left(\frac{2}{y}\right)^9$$
$$= x^9 + \frac{18x^8}{y} + \frac{144x^7}{y^2} + \frac{672x^6}{y^3} +$$
$$\frac{2016x^5}{y^4} + \frac{4032x^4}{y^5} + \frac{5376x^3}{y^6} +$$
$$\frac{4608x^2}{y^7} + \frac{2304x}{y^8} + \frac{512}{y^9}$$

Form 2:
$$\left(x-\frac{2}{y}\right)^9$$
$$= \binom{9}{0}x^9 + \binom{9}{1}x^8\left(\frac{2}{y}\right) + \binom{9}{2}x^7\left(\frac{2}{y}\right)^2 +$$
$$\binom{9}{3}x^6\left(\frac{2}{y}\right)^3 + \binom{9}{4}x^5\left(\frac{2}{y}\right)^4 +$$
$$\binom{9}{5}x^4\left(\frac{2}{y}\right)^5 + \binom{9}{6}x^3\left(\frac{2}{y}\right)^6 +$$
$$\binom{9}{7}x^2\left(\frac{2}{y}\right)^7 + \binom{9}{8}x\left(\frac{2}{y}\right)^8 +$$
$$\binom{9}{9}\left(\frac{2}{y}\right)^9$$
$$= \frac{9!}{9!0!}x^9 + \frac{9!}{8!1!}x^8\left(\frac{2}{y}\right) + \frac{9!}{7!2!}x^7\left(\frac{4}{y^2}\right) +$$
$$\frac{9!}{6!3!}x^6\left(\frac{8}{y^3}\right) + \frac{9!}{5!4!}x^5\left(\frac{16}{y^4}\right) +$$
$$\frac{9!}{4!5!}x^4\left(\frac{32}{y^5}\right) + \frac{9!}{3!6!}x^3\left(\frac{64}{y^6}\right) +$$
$$\frac{9!}{2!7!}x^2\left(\frac{128}{y^7}\right) + \frac{9!}{1!8!}x\left(\frac{256}{y^8}\right) +$$
$$\frac{9!}{0!9!}\left(\frac{512}{y^9}\right)$$

$$= x^9 + 9x^8\left(\frac{2}{y}\right) + 36x^7\left(\frac{4}{y^2}\right) + 84x^6\left(\frac{8}{y^3}\right) +$$
$$126x^5\left(\frac{16}{y^4}\right) + 126x^4\left(\frac{32}{y^5}\right) + 84x^3\left(\frac{64}{y^6}\right) +$$
$$36x^2\left(\frac{128}{y^7}\right) + 9x\left(\frac{256}{y^8}\right) + \frac{512}{y^9}$$
$$= x^9 + \frac{18x^8}{y} + \frac{144x^7}{y^2} + \frac{672x^6}{y^3} +$$
$$\frac{2016x^5}{y^4} + \frac{4032x^4}{y^5} + \frac{5376x^3}{y^6} +$$
$$\frac{4608x^2}{y^7} + \frac{2304x}{y^8} + \frac{512}{y^9}$$

28. $19,683s^9 + \dfrac{59,049s^8}{t} + \dfrac{78,732s^7}{t^2} + \dfrac{61,236s^6}{t^3} +$
$$\frac{30,618s^5}{t^4} + \frac{10,206s^4}{t^5} + \frac{2268s^3}{t^6} + \frac{324s^2}{t^7} +$$
$$\frac{27s}{t^8} + \frac{1}{t^9}$$

29. Expand $(a^2 - b^3)^5$.

We have $a = a^2$, $b = -b^3$, and $n = 5$.

Form 1: We get the coefficient from the 6th row of Pascal's triangle. From Exercise 17 we know that the coefficients are

   1   5   10   10   5   1.

$$(a^2 - b^3)^5$$
$$= 1\cdot(a^2)^5 + 5(a^2)^4(-b^3) + 10(a^2)^3(-b^3)^2 +$$
$$10(a^2)^2(-b^3)^3 + 5(a^2)(-b^3)^4 + 1\cdot(-b^3)^5$$
$$= a^{10} - 5a^8b^3 + 10a^6b^6 - 10a^4b^9 +$$
$$5a^2b^{12} - b^{15}$$

Form 2:
$$(a^2 - b^3)^5$$
$$= \binom{5}{0}(a^2)^5 + \binom{5}{1}(a^2)^4(-b^3) +$$
$$\binom{5}{2}(a^2)^3(-b^3)^2 + \binom{5}{3}(a^2)^2(-b^3)^3 +$$
$$\binom{5}{4}(a^2)(-b^3)^4 + \binom{5}{5}(-b^3)^5$$
$$= \frac{5!}{5!0!}a^{10} + \frac{5!}{4!1!}a^8(-b^3) + \frac{5!}{3!2!}a^6(b^6) +$$
$$\frac{5!}{2!3!}a^4(-b^9) + \frac{5!}{1!4!}a^2(b^{12}) + \frac{5!}{0!5!}(-b^{15})$$
$$= a^{10} - 5a^8b^3 + 10a^6b^6 - 10a^4b^9 +$$
$$5a^2b^{12} - b^{15}$$

30. $x^{15} - 10x^{12}y + 40x^9y^2 - 80x^6y^3 + 80x^3y^4 - 32y^5$

31. Expand $(\sqrt{3} - t)^4$.

We have $a = \sqrt{3}$, $b = -t$, and $n = 4$.

Form 1: We get the coefficients from the 5th row of Pascal's triangle.

$$1$$
$$1 \quad 1$$
$$1 \quad 2 \quad 1$$
$$1 \quad 3 \quad 3 \quad 1$$
$$1 \quad 4 \quad 6 \quad 4 \quad 1$$

$(\sqrt{3} - t)^4 = 1 \cdot (\sqrt{3})^4 + 4(\sqrt{3})^3(-t) +$
$$6(\sqrt{3})^2(-t)^2 + 4(\sqrt{3})(-t)^3 + 1 \cdot (-t)^4$$
$$= 9 - 12\sqrt{3}t + 18t^2 - 4\sqrt{3}t^3 + t^4$$

Form 2:

$(\sqrt{3} - t)^4 = \binom{4}{0}(\sqrt{3})^4 + \binom{4}{1}(\sqrt{3})^3(-t) +$
$$\binom{4}{2}(\sqrt{3})^2(-t)^2 + \binom{4}{3}(\sqrt{3})(-t)^3 +$$
$$\binom{4}{4}(-t)^4$$
$$= \frac{4!}{4!0!}(9) + \frac{4!}{3!1!}(3\sqrt{3})(-t) +$$
$$\frac{4!}{2!2!}(3)(t^2) + \frac{4!}{1!3!}(\sqrt{3})(-t^3) +$$
$$\frac{4!}{0!4!}(t^4)$$
$$= 9 - 12\sqrt{3}t + 18t^2 - 4\sqrt{3}t^3 + t^4$$

32. $125 + 150\sqrt{5}\,t + 375t^2 + 100\sqrt{5}\,t^3 + 75t^4 + 6\sqrt{5}\,t^5 + t^6$

33. Expand $(x^{-2} + x^2)^4$.

We have $a = x^{-2}$, $b = x^2$, and $n = 4$.

Form 1: We get the coefficients from the fifth row of Pascal's triangle. From Exercise 31 we know that the coefficients are

$$1 \quad 4 \quad 6 \quad 4 \quad 1.$$
$(x^{-2} + x^2)^4$
$$= 1 \cdot (x^{-2})^4 + 4(x^{-2})^3(x^2) + 6(x^{-2})^2(x^2)^2 +$$
$$4(x^{-2})(x^2)^3 + 1 \cdot (x^2)^4$$
$$= x^{-8} + 4x^{-4} + 6 + 4x^4 + x^8$$

Form 2:
$$(x^{-2} + x^2)^4$$
$$= \binom{4}{0}(x^{-2})^4 + \binom{4}{1}(x^{-2})^3(x^2) +$$
$$\binom{4}{2}(x^{-2})^2(x^2)^2 + \binom{4}{3}(x^{-2})(x^2)^3 +$$
$$\binom{4}{4}(x^2)^4$$
$$= \frac{4!}{4!0!}(x^{-8}) + \frac{4!}{3!1!}(x^{-6})(x^2) + \frac{4!}{2!2!}(x^{-4})(x^4) +$$
$$\frac{4!}{1!3!}(x^{-2})(x^6) + \frac{4!}{0!4!}(x^8)$$
$$= x^{-8} + 4x^{-4} + 6 + 4x^4 + x^8$$

34. $x^{-3} - 6x^{-2} + 15x^{-1} - 20 + 15x - 6x^2 + x^3$

Form 2:
$$\left(\frac{1}{\sqrt{x}} - \sqrt{x}\right)^6$$
$$= \binom{6}{0}\left(\frac{1}{\sqrt{x}}\right)^6 + \binom{6}{1}\left(\frac{1}{\sqrt{x}}\right)^5(-\sqrt{x}) +$$
$$\binom{6}{2}\left(\frac{1}{\sqrt{x}}\right)^4(-\sqrt{x})^2 + \binom{6}{3}\left(\frac{1}{\sqrt{x}}\right)^3(-\sqrt{x})^3 +$$
$$\binom{6}{4}\left(\frac{1}{\sqrt{x}}\right)^2(-\sqrt{x})^4 + \binom{6}{5}\left(\frac{1}{\sqrt{x}}\right)(-\sqrt{x})^5 +$$
$$\binom{6}{6}(-\sqrt{x})^6$$
$$= x^{-3} - 6x^{-2} + 15x^{-1} - 20 + 15x - 6x^2 + x^3$$

35. Find the 3rd term of $(a + b)^6$.

First, we note that $3 = 2 + 1$, $a = a$, $b = b$, and $n = 6$. Then the 3rd term of the expansion of $(a + b)^6$ is

$$\binom{6}{2}a^{6-2}b^2, \text{ or } \frac{6!}{4!2!}a^4b^2, \text{ or } 15a^4b^2.$$

36. $21x^2y^5$

37. Find the 12th term of $(a - 3)^{14}$.

First, we note that $12 = 11 + 1$, $a = a$, $b = -3$, and $n = 14$. Then the 12th term of the expansion of $(a - 3)^{14}$ is

$$\binom{14}{11}a^{14-11} \cdot (-3)^{11} = \frac{14!}{3!11!}a^3(-177,147)$$
$$= 364a^3(-177,147)$$
$$= -64,481,508a^3$$

38. $67,584x^2$

39. Find the 5th term of $(2x^3 - \sqrt{y})^8$.

First, we note that $5 = 4 + 1$, $a = 2x^3$, $b = -\sqrt{y}$, and $n = 8$. Then the 5th term of the expansion of $(2x^3 - \sqrt{y})^8$ is

$$\binom{8}{4}(2x^3)^{8-4}(-\sqrt{y})^4$$

$$= \frac{8!}{4!4!}(2x^3)^4(-\sqrt{y})^4$$

$$= 70(16x^{12})(y^2)$$

$$= 1120x^{12}y^2$$

40. $\dfrac{35c^3}{b^8}$

41. The expansion of $(2u - 3v^2)^{10}$ has 11 terms so the 6th term is the middle term. Note that $6 = 5 + 1$, $a = 2u$, $b = -3v^2$, and $n = 10$. Then the 6th term of the expansion of $(2u - 3v^2)^{10}$ is

$$\binom{10}{5}(2u)^{10-5}(-3v^2)^5$$

$$= \frac{10!}{5!5!}(2u)^5(-3v^2)^5$$

$$= 252(32u^5)(-243v^{10})$$

$$= -1,959,552u^5v^{10}$$

42. $30x\sqrt{x}$, $30x\sqrt{3}$

43. $\log_2 x + \log_2(x-2) = 3$
$$\log_2 x(x-2) = 3$$
$$x(x-2) = 2^3$$
$$x^2 - 2x = 8$$
$$x^2 - 2x - 8 = 0$$
$$(x-4)(x+2) = 0$$
$x = 4 \ or \ x = -2$

Only 4 checks.

44. $\dfrac{5}{2}$

45. $e^t = 280$
$$\ln e^t = \ln 280$$
$$t = \ln 280$$
$$t \approx 5.6348$$

46. ± 5

47. ◈

48. Consider a set of 5 elements, $\{A, B, C, D, E\}$. List all the subsets of size 3:

$\{A, B, C\}$, $\{A, B, D\}$, $\{A, B, E\}$, $\{A, C, D\}$,
$\{A, C, E\}$, $\{A, D, E\}$, $\{B, C, D\}$, $\{B, C, E\}$,
$\{B, D, E\}$, $\{C, D, E\}$.

There are exactly 10 subsets of size 3 and $\binom{5}{3} = 10$,

so there are exactly $\binom{5}{3}$ ways of forming a subset of size 3 from a set of 5 elements.

49. Find the third term of $(0.313 + 0.687)^5$:

$$\binom{5}{2}(0.313)^{5-2}(0.687)^2 = \frac{5!}{3!2!}(0.313)^3(0.687)^2 \approx$$

0.145

50. $\binom{8}{5}(0.15)^3(0.85)^5 \approx 0.084$

51. Find and add the 3rd through 6th terms of $(0.313 + 0.687)^5$:

$$\binom{5}{2}(0.313)^3(0.687)^2 + \binom{5}{3}(0.313)^2(0.687)^3 +$$

$$\binom{5}{4}(0.313)(0.687)^4 + \binom{5}{5}(0.687)^5 \approx 0.964$$

52. $\binom{8}{6}(0.15)^2(0.85)^6 + \binom{8}{7}(0.15)(0.85)^7 +$

$$\binom{8}{8}(0.85)^8 \approx 0.89$$

53. See the answer section in the text.

54. $\dfrac{55}{144}$

55. The expansion of $(x^2 - 6y^{3/2})^6$ has 7 terms, so the 4th term is the middle term.
$$\binom{6}{3}(x^2)^3(-6y^{3/2})^3 = \frac{6!}{3!3!}(x^6)(-216y^{9/2}) =$$
$$-4320x^6y^{9/2}$$

56. $-\dfrac{\sqrt[3]{q}}{2p}$

57. The $(r+1)$st term of $\left(\sqrt[3]{x} - \dfrac{1}{\sqrt{x}}\right)^7$ is

$\binom{7}{r}(\sqrt[3]{x})^{7-r}\left(-\dfrac{1}{\sqrt{x}}\right)^r$. The term containing $\dfrac{1}{x^{1/6}}$ is the term in which the sum of the exponents is $-1/6$. That is,

$$\left(\frac{1}{3}\right)(7-r) + \left(-\frac{1}{2}\right)(r) = -\frac{1}{6}$$

$$\frac{7}{3} - \frac{r}{3} - \frac{r}{2} = -\frac{1}{6}$$

$$-\frac{5r}{6} = -\frac{15}{6}$$

$$r = 3$$

Find the $(3+1)$st, or 4th term.

$$\binom{7}{3}(\sqrt[3]{x})^4\left(-\frac{1}{\sqrt{x}}\right)^3 = \frac{7!}{4!3!}(x^{4/3})(-x^{-3/2}) =$$
$$-35x^{-1/6}, \text{ or } -\frac{35}{x^{1/6}}.$$

58. 8

Exercise Set 12.5

1. Since there are 52 cards and each is as likely to be selected as any other, there are 52 equally likely outcomes.

2. $\frac{1}{13}$

3. Since there are 52 equally likely outcomes and there are 13 ways to obtain a heart, by the Primary Principle of Probability we have
$$P(\text{drawing a heart}) = \frac{13}{52}, \text{ or } \frac{1}{4}.$$

4. $\frac{1}{2}$

5. Since there are 52 equally likely outcomes and there are 26 ways to obtain a red card (13 hearts and 13 diamonds), by the Primary Principle of Probability we have
$$P(\text{drawing a red card}) = \frac{26}{52}, \text{ or } \frac{1}{2}.$$

6. $\frac{2}{13}$

7. Since there are 52 equally likely outcomes and there are 2 ways to obtain a black ace (the ace of spades and the ace of clubs), by the Primary Principle of Probability we have
$$P(\text{drawing a black ace}) = \frac{2}{52}, \text{ or } \frac{1}{26}.$$

8. $\frac{2}{7}$

9. Since there are 14 equally likely ways of selecting a marble from a bag containing 4 red marbles and 10 green marbles, by the Primary Principle of Probability we have
$$P(\text{selecting a green marble}) = \frac{10}{14} = \frac{5}{7}.$$

10. 0

11. There are 14 equally likely ways of selecting any marble from a bag containing 4 red marbles and 10 green marbles. Since the bag does not contain any white marbles, there are 0 ways of selecting a white marble. By the Primary Principle of Probability, we have
$$P(\text{selecting a white marble}) = \frac{0}{14} = 0.$$

12. $\frac{9}{19}$

13. The roulette wheel contains 38 equally likely slots. Eighteen are red and eighteen are black, so $18 + 18$, or 36, are either red or black. Thus, by the Primary Principle of Probability,
$$P(\text{the ball falls in a red or black slot}) = \frac{36}{38} = \frac{18}{19}.$$

14. $\frac{1}{38}$

15. The roulette wheel contains 38 equally likely slots. One is the 00 slot and one is the 0 slot. Thus, by the Primary Principle of Probability,
$$P(\text{the ball falls in the 00 or 0 slot}) = \frac{2}{38} = \frac{1}{19}.$$

16. $\frac{5}{12}$

17. The yellow region occupies $\frac{1}{3}$ of one side of the dartboard or $\frac{1}{3} \cdot \frac{1}{2}$ or $\frac{1}{6}$ of the board. Thus,
$$P(\text{yellow}) = \frac{1}{6}.$$

18. $\frac{7}{12}$

19. The one red region on the left-hand side of the dartboard occupies $\frac{1}{3}$ of that side or $\frac{1}{3} \cdot \frac{1}{2}$, or $\frac{1}{6}$ of the dartboard. The two red regions on the right-hand side of the dartboard each occupy $\frac{1}{4}$ of that side, so together they occupy $2 \cdot \frac{1}{4} \cdot \frac{1}{2}$, or $\frac{1}{4}$ of the dartboard. Then all of the red regions together occupy $\frac{1}{6} + \frac{1}{4}$, or $\frac{5}{12}$ of the dartboard. The blue regions occupy the same amount of space as the red regions, or $\frac{5}{12}$ of the dartboard. Thus,
$$P(\text{red or blue}) = \frac{5}{12} + \frac{5}{12} = \frac{10}{12} = \frac{5}{6}.$$

20. 1

21. There is no green region on the dartboard. Thus, $P(\text{green}) = 0.$

22. $\frac{11}{4165}$

23. The number of ways of drawing 4 cards from a deck of 52 cards is $_{52}C_4$. Now 13 of the 52 cards are hearts, so the number of ways of drawing 4 hearts is $_{13}C_4$. Thus,

$$P(\text{getting 4 hearts}) = \frac{_{13}C_4}{_{52}C_4}, \text{ or } \frac{11}{4165}.$$

24. $\dfrac{30}{323}$

25. The number of ways to select 4 people from a group of $8 + 7$, or 15, is $_{15}C_4$. Two men can be chosen in $_8C_2$ ways and two women in $_7C_2$ ways. By the fundamental counting principle, the number of ways to select 2 men and 2 women is $_8C_2 \cdot _7C_2$. Thus,

$$P(\text{2 men and 2 women}) = \frac{_8C_2 \cdot _7 C_2}{_{15}C_4}, \text{ or } \frac{28}{65}.$$

26. $\dfrac{5}{36}$

27. On each die there are 6 possible outcomes. The outcomes are paired so there are $6 \cdot 6$, or 36 possible ways in which the two can fall. Only the pair $(1, 1)$ totals 2. The probability is $\dfrac{1}{36}$.

28. $\dfrac{1}{6}$

29. On each die there are 6 possible outcomes. The outcomes are paired so there are $6 \cdot 6$, or 36 possible ways in which the two can fall. There are 6 possible doubles: $(1,1)$, $(2,2)$, $(3,3)$, $(4,4)$, $(5,5)$, and $(6,6)$, so the probability of rolling doubles is $\dfrac{6}{36}$, or $\dfrac{1}{6}$. Then the probability of rolling doubles three times in a row is $\dfrac{1}{6} \cdot \dfrac{1}{6} \cdot \dfrac{1}{6}$, or $\dfrac{1}{216}$.

30. $\dfrac{5}{12}$

31. The bottle contains $7 \cdot 4$, or 28 vitamins. The number of ways of selecting 4 vitamins from a group of 28 is $_{28}C_4$. The number of ways of selecting 1 vitamin A tablet from a group of 7 is $_7C_1$. The same is true for selecting 1 vitamin C, E, or B-12 tablet from a group of 7 each. Thus

$$P(\text{selecting 1 each of vitamins A, C, E, and B-12}) =$$
$$\frac{_7C_1 \cdot _7 C_1 \cdot _7 C_1 \cdot _7 C_1}{_{28}C_4}, \text{ or } \frac{343}{2925}.$$

32. $\dfrac{24}{253}$

33. $2x + 5y = 7,$ (1)
   $3x + 2y = 16$ (2)

Multiply Equation (1) by 2, multiply Equation (2) by -5, and add.

$$\begin{aligned} 4x + 10y &= 14 \\ -15x - 10y &= -80 \\ \hline -11x &= -66 \\ x &= 6 \end{aligned}$$

Substitute 6 for x in Equation (2) and solve for y.

$$\begin{aligned} 3 \cdot 6 + 2y &= 16 \\ 18 + 2y &= 16 \\ 2y &= -2 \\ y &= -1 \end{aligned}$$

The solution is $(6, -1)$.

34. -1

35.
$$\log_a \frac{x^2 y}{z^3}$$
$$= \log_a x^2 y - \log_a z^3 \qquad \text{Quotient rule}$$
$$= \log_a x^2 + \log_a y - \log_a z^3 \qquad \text{Product rule}$$
$$= 2\log_a x + \log_a y - 3\log_a z \qquad \text{Power rule}$$

36. $x^2 + (y+3)^2 = 12$

37. $3^4 = x$

38. $\log_4 10 = y$

39.

40.

41.

42.

43. $_{52}C_5 = \dfrac{52!}{47!5!} = \dfrac{52 \cdot 51 \cdot 50 \cdot 49 \cdot 48 \cdot 47!}{47! \cdot 5 \cdot 4 \cdot 3 \cdot 2 \cdot 1}$
$$= 26 \cdot 17 \cdot 10 \cdot 49 \cdot 12$$
$$= 2,598,960$$

44. (a) 4; **(b)** $\dfrac{4}{_{52}C_5} \approx 0.0000015$

45. Consider a suit

A K Q J 10 9 8 7 6 5 4 3 2

A straight flush can be any of the following combinations in the same suit.

K   Q   J   10   9
Q   J   10   9   8
J   10   9   8   7
10   9   8   7   6
9   8   7   6   5
8   7   6   5   4
7   6   5   4   3
6   5   4   3   2
5   4   3   2   A

Remember a straight flush does not include A K Q J 10 which is a royal flush.

a) Since there are 9 straight flushes per suit, there are $9 \cdot 4$, or 36 straight flushes in all 4 suits.

b) Since 2,598,960, or $_{52}C_5$, poker hands can be dealt from a standard 52-card deck and 36 of those hands are straight flushes, the probability of getting a straight flush is $\dfrac{36}{2,598,960}$, or 0.0000139.

46. (a) $13 \cdot 48 = 624$; **(b)** $\dfrac{624}{_{52}C_5} \approx 0.00024$

47. a) There are 13 ways to select a denomination. Then from that denomination there are $_4C_3$ ways to pick 3 of the 4 cards in that denomination. Now there are 12 ways to select any one of the remaining 12 denominations and $_4C_2$ ways to pick 2 cards from the 4 cards in that denomination. Thus the number of full houses is $(13 \cdot _4C_3) \cdot (12 \cdot _4C_2)$ or 3744.

b) $\dfrac{3744}{_{52}C_5} = \dfrac{3744}{2,598,960} \approx 0.00144$

48. (a) $13 \cdot \dbinom{4}{2}\dbinom{12}{3}\dbinom{4}{1}\dbinom{4}{1}\dbinom{4}{1} = 1,098,240$;

(b) $\dfrac{1,098,240}{_{52}C_5} \approx 0.423$

49. a) There are 13 ways to select a denomination and then $\dbinom{4}{3}$ ways to choose 3 of the 4 cards in that denomination. Now there are $\dbinom{48}{2}$ ways to choose 2 cards from the 12 remaining denominations ($4 \cdot 12$, or 48 cards). But these combinations include the 3744 hands in a full house like Q-Q-Q-4-4 (Exercise 53), so these must be subtracted. Thus the number of three of a kind hands is $13 \cdot \dbinom{4}{3} \cdot \dbinom{48}{2} - 3744$, or 54,912.

b) $\dfrac{54,912}{_{52}C_5} = \dfrac{54,912}{2,598,960} \approx 0.0211$

50. (a) $4 \cdot \dbinom{13}{5} - 4 - 36 = 5108$; **(b)** $\dfrac{5108}{_{52}C_5} \approx 0.00197$

51. a) There are $\dbinom{13}{2}$ ways to select 2 denominations from the 13 denominations. Then in each denomination there are $\dbinom{4}{2}$ ways to choose 2 of the 4 cards. Finally there are $\dbinom{44}{1}$ ways to choose the fifth card from the 11 remaining denominations ($4 \cdot 11$, or 44 cards). Thus the number of two pairs hands is
$$\dbinom{13}{2} \cdot \dbinom{4}{2} \cdot \dbinom{4}{2} \cdot \dbinom{44}{1}, \text{ or } 123{,}552.$$
b) $\dfrac{123,552}{_{52}C_5} = \dfrac{123,552}{2,598,960} \approx 0.0475$

52. (a) $10 \cdot 4 \cdot 4 \cdot 4 \cdot 4 \cdot 4 - 4 - 36 = 10,200$;

(b) $\dfrac{10,200}{_{52}C_5} \approx 0.00392$